The Practitioner's Handbook of Project Performance

Practitioners operate in a necessary reality. We work in a space where project performance is above theory or methodology. In the best environments, delivery and an affirmative culture are what matter most. In the worst, it is politics and survival. In any environment, we are challenged to adopt best practices and adapt our style to the environment in which the project is occurring. This is a book about those best practices and practitioner experiences. It is a must-have reference and guidebook for project managers, general managers, business leaders and project management researchers.

This book is the result of the hard work and dedication of more than 35 authors from more than 15 countries across four continents. It brings a diversity of experience, professional and personal. It includes practitioners, leading academics, renowned theorists and many who straddle those roles. The chapters cover experiences in software, large-scale infrastructure projects, finance and health care, to name a few. The chapters themselves take many forms. Check out the Table of Contents to get a deeper sense of the topics included. All provide real-world guidance on delivering high-performing projects and show you how to build, lead and manage high-performing teams.

The Practitioner's Handbook of Project Performance is complete in itself. It can also be an enticing start to an ongoing dialogue with the authors and a pleasurable path to get deeper into the subject of project performance. Find your favorite place to begin learning from these chapters, to begin taking notes and taking away nuggets to use in your everyday. But don't stop there. Contact information and further resources for this diverse team of experts are found throughout. *The Practitioner's Handbook* is a modern guide to the leading edge of project performance management and a path to the future of project delivery.

Mark Phillips is an accomplished business leader and innovator through a range of business cycles. His experiences include start-ups, cutting-edge defense projects and senior leadership in the automotive sector. The author of *Reinventing Communication*, he has presented to thousands of people globally on project performance.

The Practitioner's Handbook of Project Performance

Agile, Waterfall and Beyond

Edited by Mark Phillips

Routledge
Taylor & Francis Group

LONDON AND NEW YORK

First published in paperback 2024

First published 2020
by Routledge
4 Park Square, Milton Park, Abingdon, Oxon OX14 4RN

and by Routledge
605 Third Avenue, New York, NY 10158

Routledge is an imprint of the Taylor & Francis Group, an informa business

Publisher's Note
The publisher has gone to great lengths to ensure the quality of this reprint but points out that some imperfections in the original copies may be apparent.

British Library Cataloguing-in-Publication Data
A catalogue record for this book is available from the British Library

Library of Congress Cataloging-in-Publication Data
Names: Phillips, Mark, 1960- editor.
Title: The practitioner's handbook of project performance: agile, waterfall and beyond/edited by Mark Phillips.
Description: 1. Edition. | New York: Routledge, 2019. | Includes bibliographical references and index. |
Identifiers: LCCN 2019026302 (print) | LCCN 2019026303 (ebook) |
ISBN 9781138288225 (hardback) | ISBN 9781315268040 (ebook)
Subjects: LCSH: Project management. | Leadership.
Classification: LCC HD69.P75 P6578 2019 (print) | LCC HD69.P75 (ebook) |
DDC 658.4/04–dc23
LC record available at https://lccn.loc.gov/2019026302
LC ebook record available at https://lccn.loc.gov/2019026303

ISBN: 978-1-138-28822-5 (hbk)
ISBN: 978-1-03-283882-3 (pbk)
ISBN: 978-1-315-26804-0 (ebk)

DOI: 10.4324/9781315268040

Typeset in Bembo
by Deanta Global Publishing Services, Chennai, India

For our children.
With all our love.
—Mom and Dad

Contents

List of figures   x
List of tables   xii
Introduction by Mark Phillips   xiv

SECTION I
Individuals and interactions   I

1   Chasing mercury: the emotional and social pillars of high-performing teams   3
    A. GEOFFERY CRANE

2   Values as the basis for successful teams: a Scrum perspective and primer   17
    STEVE BERCZUK

3   The power of empowering others: coaching as a leadership model for
    high-performing teams   33
    SUSANNE MADSEN

4   Coping with the unexpected: flexibility, resilience and culture   47
    ANDREAS G.M. NACHBAGAUER AND IRIS SCHIRL-BOECK

5   Leading without authority   63
    ANDREW KALLMAN, JEFF KISSINGER AND TED KALLMAN

SECTION II
Processes, tools and techniques   79

6   Performance: a combined project and portfolio perspective   81
    JAMAL MOUSTAFAEV

7   Communications shape reality   100
    ANN PILKINGTON

8   Knowledge management shapes culture   113
     STEPHEN DUFFIELD

9   Risk management principles   125
     GLEN B. ALLEMAN, TOM COONCE AND RICK PRICE

10   Risk management practices   144
     GLEN B. ALLEMAN, TOM COONCE AND RICK PRICE

11   Act fast and think fast: Agile schedule performance   170
     ROBERT VAN DE VELDE

12   Monitoring and controlling: understanding your project's status   191
     KRISTINE A. HAYES MUNSON

     The Project Management Office (PMO)   205
     EMMA-RUTH ARNAZ-PEMBERTON

13   Managing change: from adoption to completion   210
     JIM YOUNG

14   Securing benefits   220
     JIM YOUNG

15   Beyond the triple constraints: creating conditions for optimal performance   232
     MARISA SILVA

SECTION III
Experience   241

16   Critical success and failure factors in large-scale complex projects   243
     AZADEH REZVANI AND POURIA KHOSRAVI

17   Performance and measurement: an interdisciplinary study of public sector projects 255
     MAUDE BRUNET, JEAN-SÉBASTIEN MARCHAND AND MYLAINE BRETON

18   Creating value in infrastructure projects: the Public Value Chain   268
     LEONIE KOOPS, MARIAN BOSCH-REKVELDT, HANS BAKKER AND MARCEL HERTOGH

19   Evaluating project performance: a comprehensive approach studying
     EU structural programs   286
     GÖRAN BRULIN AND LENNART SVENSSON

20   Project performance in the financial sector   296
     TIAGO CARDOSO

SECTION IV
Responding to change

317

21 Matching theory to practice in a complex world: a philosophical approach   319
LOUIS KLEIN

22 The future of global program leadership: a sci-fi narrative   336
ALEJANDRO ARROYO WELBERS AND THOMAS GRISHAM

23 Mindfulness: achieving performance in an accelerating technology landscape   360
ANTHONY PHILLIPS

24 Continuous Digital and #NoProjects   374
ALLAN KELLY

Afterword: what the heck are we studying? Projects, performance, and laws
*   by Mark Phillips*   393
References and further reading   398
Author profiles and resources   435
Index   445

Figures

1.1	Trait model of emotional intelligence	4
1.2	Mediating model of project manager EI and project success	11
1.3	Emotional skills-performance relationship in a team context	13
1.4	Emotional skills-performance relationship in a team context	14
1.5	Behavioural change stairway model	15
3.1	Three levels of success	35
3.2	Diminisher vs. multiplier	37
3.3	The GROW model	42
4.1	Project types	49
5.1	The Unified Vision Framework and the importance of vision	64
5.2	Foundations of the Unified Vision Framework	65
5.3	Foundations: The Four Ds	67
5.4	Identifying anti-Flow with the Team Issue Diagnostic Chart	69
7.1	RADAR model of communication planning by Dr Kevin Ruck	101
7.2	Myers-Briggs Type Indicator (MBTI), contrasting communication preferences	111
8.1	The Systemic Lessons Learned Knowledge model	120
8.2	Wiring an organisation with knowledge and lessons learned	122
9.1	Root causes reducing probability of success on complex programs	126
10.1	Data and processes to increase probability of success	146
10.2	Modeling non-traditional risk relationships	147
10.3	Design structure matrix connecting risk drivers to task risks	147
10.4	Modeling loops not captured in traditional risk models	148
10.5	Risk modeling using a design structure matrix (DSM)	154
10.6	Risk interactions modeled as a network	156
10.7	Monte Carlo and schedule margin on Wright Brothers schedule	160
10.8	Monte Carlo schedule risk assessment	164
10.9	Monte Carlo showing 94% probability of completing on time	164
11.1	Earned schedule definition	174
11.2	Baseline earned schedule burndown	178
11.3	Earned schedule burndown	178
11.4	Earned schedule burndown and performance efficiency	179
11.5	Earned schedule burndown, performance efficiency, estimated dates	180

11.6	Point burndown convergence with plan	187
11.7	Earned schedule burndown divergence from plan	187
12.1	Deming's PDCA cycle	203
13.1	Project and change management integration	212
13.2	Impact of change	218
14.1	Benefits realisation process	222
14.2	Example benefits map	226
14.3	Benefits realisation process	227
14.4	Product lifecycle	228
16.1	Publication per year	246
16.2	Projects per country	247
16.3	Research methods	247
18.1	Different interfaces in project organizations	269
18.2	Porters Value Chain and the Public Value Chain	271
18.3	Public–private interface becomes an internal interface	274
18.4	Interface public parent – public project delivery organization	275
18.5	Overview of expert meeting setup	278
18.6	Interface public parent – public project delivery	282
21.1	Scott's laws of observation	322
21.2	Social complexity	323
21.3	Stakeholder multicausality	324
21.4	Stakeholder interdependence	324
21.5	Stakeholder polycentricity	325
21.6	Rabbit-duck	329
21.7	Tai Chi of change	332
21.8	Systemic perspective on good governance	334
21.9	Captainship	335
22.1	Collaborative program enterprise (CPE)	344
22.2	Time line for CPE sessions	347
24.1	Raspberry Pi 3B+ computer	375
24.2	Classic project manager's iron triangle	376
24.3	Time-value profile over time	380
24.4	Minimally viable team model of organic growth	385

Tables

6.1	Overview of project management	83
6.2	Sample project portfolio scoring model	84
6.3	Project performance over the years	86
6.4	Successful vs troubled vs failed projects	90
6.5	Root causes of project failure	91
6.6	Recovery decision matrix	96
7.1	Denning's Narrative Patterns	109
9.1	For complex projects, Root Causes (Condition, Action, Outcome) have been shown to reduce the Probability of Project Success	127
9.2	Framing assumptions for Principles of Project Success	129
9.3	Nine programmatic risk areas to program success	132
10.1	Risks to inputs of increased probability of success	148
10.2	Risks to processes of increased probability of success	149
10.3	Risks to outputs of processes for increased probability of success	150
10.4	Wright Brothers metrics to increase probability of success	159
10.5	Defining acceptable alternative points of integration	163
10.6	Questions for managing risk	168
10.7	Processes supporting five principles of success	168
10.8	Conditions and outcomes for the 10 practices	159
11.1	Sample threshold values for schedule efficiency	179
11.2	Sample threshold values for EACt	181
11.3	SPIt and EACt divergence from plan	187
12.1	Monitor processes	194
12.2	Control processes	195
12.3	Monitor and control process	196
12.4	Validate scope	196
12.5	Integrated change control	196
14.1	Project products, outcomes and benefits	224
14.2	Benefit variance	225
14.3	Example benefits	227
14.4	Benefits planning template	230
16.1	Academic journals and number of publications	248

16.2	Success factors	249
16.3	Failure factors	251
17.1	Recommendations to improve public sector projects	265
18.1	Activities at different levels	274
18.2	Connecting CPO and public parent organization	275
18.3	Activities in CPO and processes linking activities to parent organizations	277
18.4	Public Value Chain of a combined project organization	279

Introduction

Mark Phillips

Practitioners operate in a necessary reality. We work in a space where project performance is above doctrine implementation of theory or methodology. In the best environments, shipping and an affirmative culture are what matter most. In the worst, it is politics and survival. In any environment practitioners are challenged to adopt best practices and adapt their style to the environment in which the project is occurring. This is a book about those best practices.

Best practices and the manifestation of practitioners' adaptations can be observed in a range of vectors. Rituals, artifacts, tools, techniques, discussions, lessons learned all populate these vectors. This volume encompasses most of them. It does so by inviting a broad spectrum of contributors. The rallying call for this volume was the value of a diverse range of voices, speaking authentically, within and without the confines of their disciplines, to create a lasting dialogue with readers on the realities of a practitioners' world.

It is, in my opinion, a rousing success. However, you, the reader, are the most important decider. This book is the result of the hard work and dedication of more than 35 authors from more than 15 countries across four continents. It brings a diversity of experience, professional and personal. It includes practitioners, leading academics, renowned theorists and many who straddle those roles. The chapters cover experiences in software, finance, large scale infrastructure projects and health care, to name a few.

The overarching theme is project performance with an overarching tenant of reflecting the diversity of environments we operate in and the broad range of ways we can talk about the challenges we face. Some chapters approach the conversation using the form of academic research. Others use the form of a how-to article or musings on our well-being or the contexts we use to think about problem solving. And still others take the form of science fiction narratives, finding a novel way to engage with readers and advance the conversations. Not every form may appeal to every reader. But it is my hope that every reader will find many appealing, thought-provoking and useful chapters in the book.

Organizing a work with this wide approach required an organic grouping process, without a planned, initial outline into which chapters and topics fell. I provided rough prompts, approached specific authors, gratefully received contributions from authors then organized the volume. The approach put people and their individual contributions first, then sequenced them into a work with an organizing principle to help make reading and way-finding within the book easier and more clear.

The Agile Manifesto seemed to offer the base for the most sensible organizing principle, with further sense making provided by the APM (Association of Project Management) and PMI's (Project Management Institute) definition of project management.

The Agile Manifesto states:

Through this work we have come to value:

Individuals and interactions over processes and tools
Working software over comprehensive documentation
Customer collaboration over contract negotiation
Responding to change over following a plan

That is, while there is value in the items on
the right, we value the items on the left more.

APM defines project management:

Project management is the application of processes, methods, knowledge, skills and experience to achieve the project objectives.

PMI defines project management:

Project management, then, is the application of knowledge, skills, tools and techniques to project activities to meet the project requirements.

This volume is thus organized along these spectrums. The book opens with a section titled "Individuals and Interactions." It includes tools and techniques focused on people, interactions and culture. This is followed by a section dedicated to and titled "Processes, Tools and Techniques." It includes models of our project realities including artifacts such as schedules and risk. It also includes less obvious models such as our communication objects and knowledge created through lessons learned. There is a noticeable crossover between some of these less obvious models and items in people, interactions and culture. Perhaps this is due to the interplay between people and artifacts. That is, the way people create value through project models is often connected to the impact these models have on people, interactions and culture.

This interplay lingers in the next section, "Experience," which follows "Processes, Tools and Techniques." Though, the "Experience" section most prominently provides deep focus on lessons learned across some of the largest and most complex projects in the world, as well as the world of finance. The book closes with a section titled "Responding to Change." This section challenges many of the fundamental ways we think about projects and offers responses, and guidance, to the stresses and complexity of the evolving world in which we operate.

The book can be read straight through, with an overarching narrative flow, or you can select specific chapters which provide the most value. References and sources for further reading are grouped in the back, by chapter, to assist in the former. Abstracts are included to aid the latter. Notes about the authors can be found in the back, with many including links to publicly available information about the authors, their work and ways to connect with them.

The book may sound a bit lofty for a practitioner's handbook. And it may be for those looking for a simple how-to. But the truth is, as practitioners, we live in the world of the subtle, nuanced and anything but simple. This is reflected in the incredible depth of many of the chapters included in this book.

That being said, were one to look for a single, simple guiding principle for managing projects it would be to focus on people. People deliver projects. People decide the value of projects and people are impacted by the projects we all do. People come from many different backgrounds. Each of us is an individual. And it is this beautiful, classically messy mix of individuals which creates high-performing projects and the world we live in. (As an aside, for those operating in more homogeneous environments interested in widening their perspective on, and emotional connection to, the diverse range of people in our world I recommend The Moth podcast. It is a podcast of often raw, incredibly personal, eye-opening stories told by everyday people.)

Understanding and working with people is key to project performance. To paraphrase Einstein, "Project management without tools is blind. Project management without understanding people is lamed." Or to quote the Maori proverb Jim Young brings up in his chapter on managing change, "What is the most important thing in the world?

It is the people, it is the people, it is the people."

This book is a connection to some great people in project performance. My hope is that it is the start of a conversation, a treasured beginning or re-meeting with the wonderful writers included here. It can be part of the continual flow of the changing project environment and our approaches to it which practitioners face every day. We hope it becomes incorporated as part of your reality and helps you deliver better and higher-performing projects.

Thank you to all the authors who helped make this volume possible. Those whose work I was able to include and those whose work I wasn't. I am deeply grateful for your enthusiasm for this project and belief in it. To my wife and children, there are never sufficient opportunities to tell you how much I love you and thank you.

Section I

Individuals and interactions

Chapter 1

Chasing mercury

The emotional and social pillars of high-performing teams

A. Geoffery Crane

"The strength of the team is each individual member", wrote basketball great Phil Jackson, and "the strength of each member is the team". These words resonate with people across all walks of life, in every industry where people must work together. They imply that a high-performing team is more than just the sum of the individuals who make it up, and because of that, teams can perform great things together. Looking back over history, every human endeavour that ever meant anything came to be because people were able to come together as one unit and pour all of their best qualities into the creation of something wonderful. It should come as no surprise that the magic of a high-performing team is something that many would like to see bottled and made available for others to copy.

Unfortunately, one must first understand what makes a team successful before they can replicate its formula. In this regard, managers across the globe struggle every day to find the magic ingredient. Organizations like the Project Management Institute provide a vast library of technical and analytical tools to aid practitioners in creating effective teams. But these instruments often fail to capture the X factor necessary to breathe life into a dynamic system. The fact is that not every team can fare as well as others and leaders who enjoy tremendous interpersonal success on one project can never guarantee that next project with a new batch of people will work as well. A high-performing team is a challenging thing to create. This chapter will attempt to identify several important factors that could help. In particular, it will examine project teams from a non-technical perspective, looking at "softer" interplays between team members, their leadership, the nature of project work and important challenges project resources must face. It appears that many of these factors are emotional and social in nature, leading many organizations to search for clues in this domain.

Emotional intelligence

In 1995, Daniel Goleman published his popular book, *Emotional Intelligence*, capturing the world's attention. The business community was especially interested in Goleman's work, fascinated by its implications for hiring, training and business improvements. Indeed, *Time Magazine* hailed Goleman's tome as one of the twenty-five most influential business management books of all time. As public interest in emotional intelligence (EI) grew, so too did the volume of serious literature intent on exploring its value in predicting occupational success, from a variety of perspectives. Researchers who study high-performing teams were especially interested in the value of EI. How does this construct help a team function? What skills do teams need to thrive? Most importantly, how can we harness the emotional and social structure of the top-performing teams so that we can replicate them?

What is EI?

The idea of emotional intelligence is not new and has deep roots in academic literature. Well over a century ago, Charles Darwin (1872) spoke of the *adaptive utility of emotions*, drawing connections between evolution and emotional expression. Fifty years later, Edward Thorndike (1920) would describe the concept of *social intelligence* as "the ability to understand and manage men and women … to act wisely in human relations". More recently, Howard Gardner (1983) proposed his *theory of multiple intelligences*, which included self-awareness and interpersonal skills not traditionally associated with cognitive intelligence.

While scientists generally recognize that humans possess mental abilities that traditional measures of intelligence (like IQ) can't touch, quantifying these skills has proven difficult. Many researchers have risen to the challenge, however, and one model in particular has emerged that enjoys wide consensus in the industry. EI, it suggests, is a constellation of skills and abilities that represents a cross-section of social, emotional and motivational attributes. Arguably the most popular representation of this model is the *Bar-On Emotional Quotient Inventory* (1997). This assessment decomposes EI into four different dimensions. They are intrapersonal abilities, interpersonal abilities, adaptability and stress management. Each one of these skill groups overlaps with the others as per the diagram in Figure 1.1.

For a variety of genetic and environmental reasons, each person possesses different levels of each of these skills and will use them for different reasons and in different ways. Because these dimensions exist in a personality-like space, measurement of this EI model results in unique profiles for each individual. However, groups of people can

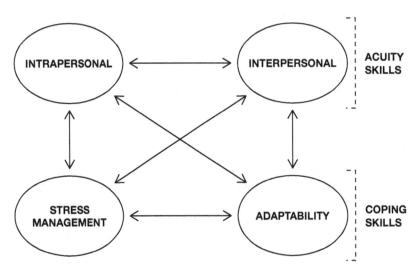

Figure 1.1 Trait model of emotional intelligence. Adapted from Bar-On (1997).

share certain traits. Project managers, for example, tend to have similar experiences around planning, negotiation, management of scarce resources and more that help give shape to their overall EI. What follows is a breakdown of the above four dimensions presented in a project management context.

Interpersonal Skills

As the name suggests, this cluster of abilities involves activities associated with the emotions of other people. Project professionals would leverage these skills during negotiations with vendors, managing team members and working with stakeholders. Individuals high in interpersonal functioning would be able to easily sell ideas and get buy-in from those around them. Adept at finding common ground and developing non-zero-sum solutions where everybody wins, those with strong interpersonal skills would present empathy at the right times and find the easiest path through emotional challenges with others.

Adaptability Skills

These talents have to do with a project professional's ability to process and tolerate change. Essentially the cognitive side of coping, individuals high in this area would be excellent decision makers, be able to think laterally and have a firm grasp of reality even under pressure. Adaptable project managers would rarely let strong emotions overcome their ability to think rationally—others would look to their leadership during times of crisis.

Stress Management Skills

This group of abilities represents the physiological side of coping. Central here are bodily regulation of stress and management of impulses. Project professionals who score highly in this area would be able to control inappropriate urges and not make rash decisions without first thinking them through. These individuals will place a priority on taking good physical care of themselves so that they have the resources to deal with the effects that their stressful careers have on their bodies.

Intrapersonal Skills

Finally, this cluster of skills catalogues an individual's potential for self-awareness and the ability to look inward. Project workers with high intrapersonal scores would have no problem setting boundaries for themselves or for their projects. Indeed, when stakeholders attempt to push the limits of their authority, project managers with strong intrapersonal skills would respectfully but firmly maintain scope control. Highly self-reflective, these individuals would understand the consequences of their actions and promptly recognize red flags that suggest their project is in jeopardy.

It is unlikely that even the most skilled project manager will excel in all of the above areas. Everyone has areas for improvement. However, just as analytical skills improve with exposure to project work, so too do the skills we associate with EI. Simply working in the project space can help build your sense of perceived competence and mastery of discipline-specific emotional and social skills. It might, however, sometimes be a bumpy ride.

What EI is not

As buzzwords enter popular consciousness, their definitions often get twisted around as people try to interpret them outside of their original context. EI is no exception to this phenomenon and frequent public discourse around the topic has resulted in misconceptions regarding its definition. The following are some common EI myths debunked:

EI is not about "being nice". Indeed, there are many times in our lives when we have to "park our empathy" to deal with a particular situation. One would not, for example, say "that's okay" to an employee who has defied a supervisor, or stop to make sure nobody's feelings are hurt during a fire alarm. An emotionally intelligent individual would be able to recognize occasions where an empathetic response would be inappropriate and would instead use emotional information to guide their decision-making process.

EI is not about giving free rein to emotions. Regardless of circumstance, it is not always appropriate to express our feelings, and some situations even call for disingenuousness. A funeral director, for example, would be ill-advised to laugh or tell jokes at work even if they found something funny. A trading floor manager, however, might need to leverage humour to help his or her staff maintain perspective during a crisis. Those with high levels of EI would immediately recognize the time and place for certain emotional expressions and comport themselves accordingly.

EI is not fixed. Because of the similarity in names, many people confuse cognitive intelligence, which remains fairly stable over a person's life, with EI. This, however, is a misnomer. EI tends to improve with every challenge we survive. "That which doesn't kill you makes you stronger" is an old adage that reflects this process. Each time we overcome difficult situations, we develop emotional and social strategies to deal with that situation the next time it occurs. This is the essence of emotional maturity and it never stops improving. You will be your most emotionally intelligent on your deathbed!

Why EI matters in the workplace

Possibly because of its many cross-discipline commercial applications, leadership has become an important target for many EI researchers. Teams led by scientists such as Janet Kellett (Virginia Commonwealth University), Thomas Sy (University of California Riverside), Joyce Bono (University of Florida) and Stéphane Côte (Rotman School of Management) each studied the role of EI in leadership emergence, an important precursor to workplace success. In each case, researchers consistently found that leadership was more likely to manifest when an individual possessed higher levels of EI. In a 360-degree study of 38 senior managers in a large manufacturing organization, Ulster University's Robert Kerr interviewed the managers' subordinates to gauge the leadership effectiveness of the subjects in question. Researchers then offered the managers themselves an EI self-report measure. Kerr and colleagues discovered a very powerful relationship between leadership effectiveness and how well the managers perceived emotions and how well the managers used emotions. This finding suggests not only that EI and leadership are well connected, but that, at least for leaders, higher levels of EI also favourably influence others' perceptions of how well they do at their job.

Of course, not everyone needs to find success for themselves through a position of leadership. For those with humbler ambitions, EI may still be an important factor in their ability to perform well at work. According to Ernest O'Boyle at Indiana University, emotional labour is a feature of work in which employees need to change their outward emotional expression in order to effectively do their job. A funeral director, for example, would be ill-advised to tell jokes while at work; lawyers need to appear trustworthy. In fact, many occupations require the ability to effectively modulate emotions and behaviours during the routine execution of duties. As one might expect, research shows higher levels of EI predict better job performance in sales, hospitality, law enforcement and finance positions.

It appears that EI may even play a role in predicting individuals' occupational happiness. Offering high school English teachers a series of self-report questionnaires, Konstantinos Kafetsios and his team at the University of Crete found a strong positive relationship between EI and job satisfaction. Nahid Anari of Islamic Azad University found similar results in a duplicate study. However, recognizing that job satisfaction represents an internal disposition, Anari took his research a step further, also comparing EI to external influences. He noted significant relationships between EI and organizational commitment and between job satisfaction and organizational commitment, suggesting an important three-way relationship between EI and both internal and external motivators.

The importance of EI for project resources

From a project manager's perspective, then, the foregoing suggests that EI should be an important tool in the pursuit of project delivery. After all, many publications suggest that 80% of a project manager's job is spent in some form of interpersonal communication. Much of this communication is arguably associated with helping the project team cope with the emotional and social aspects of project change and stress. Above and beyond the obvious applications for EI within the project space, however, are certain aspects that cannot be overcome without a working command of one's own emotions. This is not to say that other professions don't experience these challenges; just that project workers tend to experience them more. What follows is a list of three important vulnerability factors that can influence a project manager's ability to perform their work and maintain a certain level of mental health.

Insufficient Stress Reduction. Project work is stressful, and opportunities for stress management can change from one project to the next depending on the nature of higher-order organizational relationships. Client companies, for example, don't need to provide any stress management opportunities to project workers who are not their direct employees. Professional service firms are in a position to offer loose commitments to those staff whom they contract out; however, these commitments tend to be ephemeral since the employee performs their duties elsewhere. Self-employed professionals have no such shelter.

Organizational commitment to the employee should not be underestimated. Beyond straight compensation (e.g., benefits, salary, etc.), companies traditionally offer their permanent employees psychological protections not always available along the project management pathway. Vacation time, for example, is a feature built-in to most full-time employment that allows employees to recuperate after periods of intense work. Contract and professional service workers often neglect these rest periods either because their organization measures them on billable uptime, or because they need to focus on finding their next project. Indeed, many project professionals recognize the lack of suitable recuperation as a major source of stress.

Identity Reconstruction. Exhaustion is not the only source of stress to a project worker. Incumbents also need to have a sense of who they are within an occupational context. As workers move from one job to the next, they have no opportunity to develop a stable identity within their company. To make matters worse, the transitory nature of their work often forces individuals to rebuild their identity in a manner that is consistent with their new community—every time they shift jobs. The consequences of continuous reconfiguration of one's identity can be harmful. According to Beech (2011), contract workers often get treated like outsiders in the workplace. As a result, many project professionals find themselves making repeated, frustrated attempts to fit in. The longer these attempts remain unsuccessful, the more likely these individuals will be to develop negative dispositions towards their colleagues, company and ultimately, themselves.

Disengagement. As a worker's sense of self deteriorates, it is easy to imagine that their decision-making abilities may become compromised. In 2014, Reevy and Deason recognized that university faculty who worked in contract positions might feel isolated from their tenured counterparts. Not surprisingly, their respondents overwhelmingly identified the precariousness of their employment as the single greatest stressor in their professional experience. The team noted that their results were consistent with earlier research suggesting that contract work is itself a source of stress. Most importantly, they noted that 50% of their sample was especially at risk for negative health outcomes. A review of their regression matrix showed that this finding may be a direct consequence of outlook: in general, the longer participants worked in a temporary capacity, the more likely they were to adopt disengagement coping mechanisms as a way to deal with their predicament. This cluster of strategies includes denial, occupational disengagement ("giving up") and substance abuse.

The complex nature of project work may also influence the decision-making paradigms of its practitioners. London School of Economics' Richard Sennett argues that "character corrosion" is becoming an important hallmark of project-based work. He contends that the flexibility a project environment demands often separates the people who work within it. Workers who are more adaptable tend to form more secure relationships with their colleagues than those who have trouble with new ideas. As a result, professionals with a more rigid outlook towards their project may find themselves increasingly vulnerable to the vagaries of their position. Further, project-based work is susceptible to the legal dilemma known as "the moral hazard". This occurs when those paying for a project (or paying the salary of a worker on that project) have objectives that do not align with the objectives of the project itself. This phenomenon can place undue pressure on workers to behave in unethical ways so as to placate those controlling their income.

While the above risks in no way account for the breadth of potential derailments to a project professional's career, one can infer that, in combination, they comprise an important threat to success. To be effective, then, project workers should be able to: (1) manage the stress inherent in a job devoid of the usual securities, (2) adapt to the vagaries of a career spent in transition and (3) retain their moral compass in the face of multiple, conflicting stakeholder demands. For purposes of discussion, we will label this collection of attributes as "resilience". According to the foregoing, one would expect project managers with poor resilience to struggle. Those with poor adaptability, for example, may find themselves unable to let go of old ways of working (which new employers may find undesirable). Workers unable to cope with stress, or who find themselves making poor decisions under pressure, may develop poor reputations. Since project professionals often shift jobs even while working for the same employer, cues to deficiencies in resilience may appear in the frequency and duration of these transitions. In other words, professionals with high resilience should move from project to project with a minimum of disruption while workers with poor resilience should struggle through each break, with longer and more frequent gaps than highly resilient professionals.

The role of EI in a larger project management competency framework

The aforementioned challenges offer a unique insight into why project teams may run into trouble. After all, they represent the emotional context within which individual team members must function if they are to survive. However, project leadership bears a substantial amount of responsibility for the team's success. Ralf Müller of the Umeå School of Business and Rodney Turner of the Lille School of Management worked together in 2010 to understand the importance of specific leadership competencies that could facilitate successful delivery. From their perspective, EI was likely very important to the delivery of successful projects; however, they recognized that other, more tangible skill sets must somehow come into play. Surely cognitive skills must be important to project success, as should be managerial skills—after all, these are the competencies upon which many hiring managers build their recruitment strategies. To plan this study out, Müller and Turner first needed to settle on the skill sets that they would measure. Ultimately, they chose the following collection of leadership competencies first proposed by Dulewicz and Higgs in 2005.

Intellectual Competencies (IQ). This cluster of skills focused on skills that pertained to a project manager's cognitive abilities. The team identified three specific skills in this area including *critical analysis and judgement* (the ability to make informed decisions based on objective and thorough evaluation), *vision and imagination* (the ability to formulate and communicate the shape of a long-range end-state) and *strategic perspective* (the ability to make ongoing choices that lead to the end-state in question).

Managerial Competencies (MQ). The researchers also evaluated a collection of practical managerial skills that represented important project-based competencies. These included *engaging communication* (the ability to initiate and retain the interest of others), *managing resources* (the ability to direct the flow of work and delegate), *empowering* (the ability to allow others to be accountable for their own work), *developing* (the ability to guide and teach others) and *achieving* (the ability to make good on commitments).

Emotional Competencies (EQ). Here, Müller and Turner identified a variety of emotion-based skills that spanned the gamut of categories identified above. The **intrapersonal** skills that appeared on their list included *self-awareness* (the ability to understand one's own feelings, thoughts and decision-making rationale) and *intuitiveness* (the ability to leverage experience to infer connections). **Interpersonal** skills were also important, including *sensitivity* (which includes the art of tact as well as empathy) and *influence* (the ability to encourage others to follow a prescribed path). **Adaptability** constructs included *motivation* (the ability to drive oneself towards a goal) and *conscientiousness* (the ability to be responsible and diligent). Finally, *emotional resilience* (the ability to roll with the punches in the face of adversity) rounded out the **stress management** skills on their list.

Once the researchers identified the competencies they would measure, they set up an online portal containing a battery of assessments designed to measure the skills in question, as well as a self-report questionnaire that asked participants to describe their last project. In particular, Müller and Turner wanted to understand: (1) the project's application area (organizational change, IT and telecoms, engineering/construction), (2) the project's complexity (high, medium, low), (3) the strategic importance of the project to the organization (mandatory, repositioning, renewal) and finally (4) the contract type (fixed price, remeasurement, alliance). The scientists expected that different kinds of projects would ultimately demand different kinds of skills from the project manager in order to be successful. In total, 400 participants from organizations all over the world participated in the study.

Overwhelmingly, the pair discovered that high levels of emotional competencies were present in the profiles of managers of all successful projects, regardless of type, complexity or importance. Specifically, those who enjoyed the most success were adept at *influencing* others to achieve a specific objective, they had high levels of *motivation* to get things done and were very *conscientious* about maintaining a strong work ethic. However, *critical thinking*, which the team identified as a predominantly cognitive skill, also appeared to be strongly associated with successful project managers. At a minimum, these results suggest that project managers will find more success if they can somehow leverage and improve these core skills.

It is worth noting, however, this profile was not the only one that resulted in a top-performing project. IT projects rated in this study, for example, demanded high levels of almost all of the IQ, MQ and EQ skills on the list, with the exception of vision and intuitiveness. Given the levels of uncertainty in these types of projects, this should not be surprising. Fixed bid projects demanded high levels of all skills but intuitiveness, suggesting that the nuances of buy-sell relationships require a broader set of competencies. Finally, high complexity projects demanded high levels of every one of the fifteen skills on the list, validating the common-sense belief that well-seasoned project managers are best recruited for roles of this nature.

Important mediating factors

At least on the surface, Müller and Turner acknowledged the importance of EI in project success in their results. They also suspected, however, that there might be more to this story than met the eye. Project managers must establish and maintain a relationship with their project teams and their study did not explore the mechanisms behind this connection in any depth. In their paper, they put out a call for further research into this area to try and understand the nature of the connection between a project manager and his or her project team. This is a call that Azadeh Rezvani at the University of Queensland answered. Not satisfied that EI was the panacea to occupational success that some research might have us believe, she chose to understand what factors might cause a project manager's levels of EI to affect their project's outcome.

To begin, Rezvani and her team turned to a 2006 study by National University of Singapore's Pheng and Chuan which suggested that a project manager's job satisfaction has a direct bearing on his or her job performance, and that this influence increases with project complexity. Second, Rezvani's crew examined work done by an array of researchers suggesting that the trust a project manager places in his or her project team reliably predicts the performance and effectiveness of a project as well as creativity on the team, fluidity and transparency of information sharing, stakeholder satisfaction and ultimately, project success. According to this background literature, she recognized that the dynamics of a high-performing team appear to be predicated on specific abilities connected to the project manager.

Buoyed by these findings, Rezvani assembled a model that she believed would shed some light on the complex relationship between a project team and its leadership. As the previous literature suggested, she continued to expect to find that a project manager's EI would be positively related to project success. However, she also anticipated positive relationships between the project manager's EI and both job satisfaction and the trust that they had in their team. If these relationships held up under scrutiny, she then wanted to find out if a project manager's high EI would cause a project to be successful, or if project success was a function of these other two variables. In other words, Rezvani's team wanted to find out whether or not job satisfaction and trust mediate the relationship between EI and a project's outcome. The diagram in Figure 1.2 illustrates her theory.

With her mediation model clearly established, Rezvani then prepared a self-assessment questionnaire that consisted of measures of EI, job satisfaction and trust. She also collected information that pertained to participants' perception of project success based on four factors: level of intra-team communication, amount of troubleshooting necessary, mission clarity and executive support. The survey was completed by 373 project managers from a broad cross-section of industry. Rezvani's team then performed structural equation modelling on the finished responses to validate the diagram.

Results showed very strong, very significant relationships between each of the factors in her model. A project manager's EI is an important factor in the success of a project. However, high levels of EI by themselves are insufficient to cause a project to perform well. Job satisfaction and trust need to be in place for a project manager's EI to have relevance. While project managers can clearly benefit from understanding this model, there are important implications here for the performance of a project team as a whole.

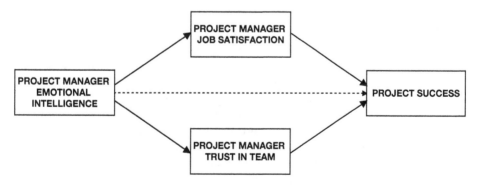

Figure 1.2 Mediating model of project manager EI and project success. Adapted from Rezvani et al. (2016).

It appears that projects are less likely to enjoy success if the team is hampered by a project manager who neither trusts them nor enjoys his or her job. In other words, a high-performing team is one whose leader is happy at work, encourages trust and positive work attitudes and also (incidentally) possesses high levels of EI.

Essential project features

Of course, a project team's leadership is not the only variable that can impact collective team performance. In 2006, Druskat and Druskat examined the nature of project work and determined that team-level EI was essential to be able to deliver a finished product within the allotted constraints. In particular, the pair recognized four important attributes of projects that demanded skilled emotional responses on the part of all practitioners.

Attribute 1: Projects are temporary. The lifespan of a project is very time-limited and opportunities to redo work are few. Project practitioners (both project managers and team members) must therefore be adept at selling ideas efficiently and with a minimum of conflict. Sullied first impressions can be extremely costly, since a stakeholder's short-term loss of confidence in a project resource can result in the team spending their precious time undoing any damage that was done before they can properly get to work on more tangible deliverables.

Attribute 2: Projects are unique. This implies a constant level of risk for which project practitioners must be prepared. While there are many analytical tools available from a variety of outlets specifically designed to deal with project risk, they require a certain level of sensitivity to deliver effectively. Project resources who fail to communicate project risks in a way that stakeholders can appreciate and understand will find themselves struggling to put appropriate strategies in place to manage risk events when they arise.

Attribute 3: Projects are progressively elaborated. This means that regardless of best intentions, a project's definition will likely change considerably between inception and completion. Along the way, the project team will have to adapt work in progress to keep up with new learning. To do so requires a mental flexibility that can easily respond and incorporate changes to expectations and ongoing work. Resources who are intransigent or who possess a rigid outlook and unwillingness to adapt can hurt a project's chances of success every bit as much as resources who are unprepared for this change.

Attribute 4: Project stakeholders are diverse. Stakeholders can come from all corners of an organization and may bring different views and even cultural considerations to the table. As a result, project teams will have to contend with many, sometimes competing, definitions of project success that must be consolidated prior to delivering work. Further, stakeholders may lack the vocabulary to effectively articulate their desires for the project and team members must be able to efficiently and sensitively extract relevant information in order to contribute towards the project's vision.

It is important to note that the emotional labour associated with the above features is episodic. This means that project team members will not be leveraging any one emotional skill continuously, but rather that they must adapt from moment to moment, choosing to express a particular skill in response to unfolding situations. While more skilled individuals may have an easier time "going with the flow" in this manner, they will still likely find their abilities tested as the pace and complexity of a project increases. For this reason, project team members need to be able to rely on each other to weather the inevitable stresses of high change environments. In particular, team members must be able to draw upon their teammates' strengths and compensate for their teammates' weaknesses.

Team-based skills: Emotional management and awareness

This interplay between team members' emotional and social skills is an essential feature of high-performing teams. Indeed, it seems that environments in which all team members present high levels of EI offer the highest levels of work performance. In 2012, Griffith University researcher Ashlea Troth attempted to tease apart the multiple soft skills that seemed most involved in the performance of project team task performance. Using Druskat and Druskat's work as a guide, she and her team recognized that both emotional awareness and emotional management of self and others held important implications for the ability to improve communication within the team and ultimately improve performance. Importantly, Troth recognized that these emotional skills needed to work at both the individual and team levels. Working through the different possible combinations of each of these abilities, she developed the model in Figure 1.3.

Troth's research team anticipated that increases in both individual team member's emotional awareness and emotional management would show similar increases in their ability to communicate within their team and task performance overall. However, her team also expected to find a similar pattern when looking at the team as a whole—that is, increases to the overall emotional awareness and management skills of the entire team should show improvements to individual team members' communication and task performance.

To test this theory, Troth recruited a pool of 244 undergraduate students and split them into 57 teams. Each team was deliberately composed entirely of strangers (i.e.,

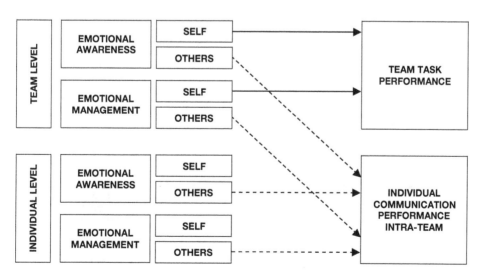

Figure 1.3 Emotional skills-performance relationship in a team context. Adapted from Troth et al. (2012).

none of the members previously knew one another). Together, they had to work together under pressure in order to deliver a presentation to be evaluated by a subject matter expert in the topic. If Troth's hypothesis held true, then a team composed entirely of high-EI members should receive a top rating on their assignment. As per the theory, each team member should be able to effectively manage their own strong evaluation-related feelings of stage fright and anxiety while outwardly displaying audience engagement and humour. However, they should also be able to "pick up the slack" and provide ongoing emotional support and strength to help their teammates do the same. In combination, even teams inexperienced in their topic of presentation should present a confident, united front that should impress the judges.

Her findings were illuminating. Contrary to expectations, individual EI had very little to do with either team task performance or individual communication performance within the team. This is surprising because on the surface, the literature suggests that higher EI predicts better results at work. As with Azadeh Rezvani's research cited above, the picture seems to be a little more complicated than we might expect. Powerful effects start to appear, however, when the emotional awareness and emotional management scores of every member on a team are grouped together. As expected, when everyone in the group demonstrated high awareness of their own emotions and high awareness of their teammates' emotions, their presentation performance significantly improved. The same was true when everyone in the group demonstrated high emotional management of their teammates' emotions. Interestingly, group self-management did not seem to matter. Finally, team level emotional management of others improved the ratings that team members received from one another in terms of their individual communication effectiveness. The diagram in Figure 1.4 demonstrates Troth's modified model after analysis.

These results suggest that a high-performing team is one in which all team members are aware of their own emotions as well as the emotions of each other. Most important,

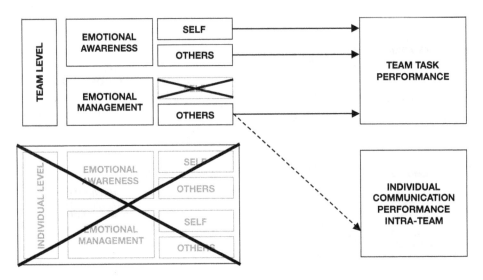

Figure 1.4 Emotional skills-performance relationship in a team context. Adapted from Troth et al. (2012).

however, is the finding that emotional management of others at the team level predicts improved performance on a stressful task. The implication here is that team members need to look out for one another in order for work to get done effectively. As negative emotions such as fear, anxiety, frustration and anger appear in a work environment, teammates who work together to quell and resolve those strong feelings as a group will be much more likely to overcome challenges than groups with less supportive members. Similarly, teammates who provide strength and encouragement to one another when things are going well will be more likely to build momentum in their work than teams with members who pay less attention to such cues.

How can team members develop their own EI?

The foregoing demonstrates that there are many factors that influence whether or not a team will function well. Further, it seems that EI alone is not the only variable that will influence the success of a project. However, it does seem that the greater proportion of team members (including their leadership) possess high levels of EI, the more likely a project will perform well. For that reason it would behove an organization to encourage its team members to develop their emotional and social skills as much as possible. Fortunately, as mentioned earlier, EI is highly malleable. With attention and work, anyone can set themselves up for success with significant improvements to their emotional and social. The following are just a few tips to help build confidence and performance in each of the four EI domains.

Interpersonal Improvements. Empathy is central to so many tasks that a project manager needs to perform. Negotiation, selling ideas, influence without authority and more—they all begin with the ability to empathize and understand the position of another. The Federal Bureau of Investigation (FBI) has long recognized the importance of empathy in driving behaviour changes of people who find themselves on the brink of committing dangerous behaviours. In fact, their Behaviour Change Stairway Model (see Figure 1.5) works just as well for hostage negotiators as it does for project managers seeking to drive specific interpersonal outcomes. According to the model, deliberate attention to active listening offers a path to empathy. From there, a rapport develops, which can lead to the influence required to effect specific changes in others' behaviour. When used effectively, project professionals can substantially improve their interpersonal skills.

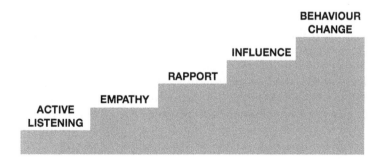

Figure 1.5 Behavioural change stairway model. Adapted from Vecchi et al. (2005).

Adaptability Improvements. When you know that a particular upcoming event is likely to be stressful (e.g., terminating a team member, placating an angry stakeholder), you can improve your performance by planning the event out ahead of time. Think through possible emotions that could emerge during such situations and make decisions about how you will handle them if they arise. How should you best respond, for example, to a display of anger? Sadness? Contempt? Should your behaviour change depending on your seniority against the person making the display? Your answers to these questions should address more than just your own feelings. We often think through immediate consequences of our actions and decisions but seldom think two, three or four steps beyond them. In the face of someone's hostility, tears or bitterness, what is likely to happen if you take a firm position? What would happen after that? And after that?

Stress Management Improvements. As our world becomes more and more connected it becomes increasingly difficult to disengage from it. This, however, is precisely what we need to be able to develop personal resilience. We can no longer expect to just switch off personal electronic devices during scheduled downtimes and find relaxation. Last-minute communications can create stress long after the distracting technology has been put away. Successful disengagement from stressful stimuli requires planning out a schedule. This schedule should include "winding down" periods that allow you to mentally prepare to relax. Unwinding is a crucial step in the process of disconnection and provides the opportunity to put stressors in their proper perspective. Maintaining a healthy lifestyle and making time for technology-free social activities can help prevent stress from becoming chronic.

Intrapersonal Improvements. Self-awareness is perhaps the most challenging of the emotional and social skill families to improve because it requires a substantial amount of introspection. In general, it is good practice to spend at least a part of each day thinking over your most recent experiences and trying to articulate how you feel about them. One technique that has withstood the test of time is journaling. Keep a diary handy and document your day before you go to bed. Pay particular attention to the feelings you had toward your colleagues, your work and the decisions you made over the course of the day. Did you wish you had handled something differently? How might you do it next time? If you find it challenging to think about what to write, you may find it helpful to plan out a series of journaling prompts to start your thoughts flowing. Busy millennials have found that "bullet journals" (BuJo) make for an easy variation on this technique—the Internet abounds with BuJo templates that make this experience easy and fun.

Of course, the above techniques only scratch the surface of EI development. The categories of emotional and social skills identified above are excellent catch-alls with which to divide the spectrum of human emotion. As we have seen, above, however, these skills are varied, complex and require much practice to perform effectively. That being said, awareness of these skills is the first step towards long term mastery. All project team members would find tremendous success for themselves if they recognize that emotional and social skills play a crucial role in their ability to do their work, integrate with their team and find the joy that comes from working in a high-performing unit. If you are at the start of this journey, I wish you all the best of success.

Chapter 2

Values as the basis for successful teams
A Scrum perspective and primer

Steve Berczuk

Introduction

As an engineer by training, I like building things. Over time I've realized that while technical skill is essential, it's not sufficient to build a non-trivial system. The hardest part of building complex software systems with a team of people is creating an environment where *the team* works together towards a common goal. Fostering this kind of collaboration in a way that creates minimal overhead is, for me, a major goal of project management.

Getting a group of people to work together to build something *useful* in an *efficient enough* way, takes a combination of technical skill – including a good engineering process that coordinates the technical work – good people management to help the team form effectively and be resilient, and a good project management process to ensure that the team is creating business value. Getting all these elements working together can be hard, but it's easier if you have a process framework that establishes some values that allow for this synergy.

My view of this is heavily influenced by my interest and experience within Agile Software Development, Patterns, and Software Configuration Management. For me "process" and "engineering" are deeply related. A "perfect" development process won't work well at all without engineering practices to support it. And without a good project management framework, the team will either build the wrong thing, or take longer to build it.

Unfortunately, too many engineers and project managers alike have had experiences where the two domains were seemingly at odds. Engineers sometimes have no sense of how the "process" helped them get work done, and the "managers" (people and project) didn't have a clear sense of how all of the work engineers did fit into the project plan. This is unfortunate, though it explains why many engineers eye glaze over at the work "process."

Value

Good process is what helps teams focus on the important thing: building things that add value. The line between process and engineering practice can, and should, be fuzzy. *Software Configuration Management Patterns* – the book Brad Appleton and I wrote in 2001 – is about how to use version control effectively, and is as much about technical practices as it is about software development processes. *Code lines* and *branching strategy* define the software development process and have a huge impact on how teams write code together, and in turn can be influenced by practices around testing and design.

Agile Software Development in general, and Scrum in particular, further blur the lines between process and development on a software team, emphasizing what needs to get done to deliver a product, and de-emphasizing roles, and in many cases saying nothing about technical practices other than "the development team figures out what best to do."

The best way to align technical skill, people, and process to deliver software effectively is to make sure that everyone is aware of and understands the values that underlie your chosen process. You then need to continuously validate whether the engineering, people management and project management processes are consistent with those values. This is easy to say, and hard to do. But worth the effort, as with the right foundation, make delivering software appear easy.

The project

For the purposed of this discussion, I consider a project to be a *group of people working together to accomplish something*, such as building a software product or an internal service, or remodeling a house. You can even think of the collection of daily chores as a project of sorts, and some project management techniques are as much at home in a family setting (Agile Family Book) as a project. All of these sorts of projects have some things in common:

- A goal. At the end of the project we want to have something valuable done, be it an application, a new kitchen, or a clear conscience that we've done all of the important things we need to do.
- A need to collaborate to get the work done. Any significant undertaking will be worked on by more than one person and whenever the team is larger than one, communication and collaboration are important.
- A changeable environment, and a need to adapt. While we may have some idea of what we want, and how a plan to build these things will progress, things are likely to change for any number of reasons.

My experience is primarily in applying Agile development methods, in particular Scrum, to software *product* projects with small- to medium-size teams.

Agile methods

As much as some teams proudly proclaim a lack of process, all projects follow some sort of process, though in the limit the process can be described as *chaos*. And in some cases *intentional chaos* may well be the right approach. But *accidental chaos* almost never is. Successful projects are intentional in their choices and revisit decisions periodically.

While Scrum or other Agile methods may not be the right approach for every project, I've found that Scrum can work quite well for projects that deal with uncertainty, or which fit into the "complex" quadrant in the Cynefin Framework. In my experience, this is most projects, as there is always some uncertainty, even seemingly (though not actually) trivial ones.

Uncertainty in projects can be in the business requirements, the technology choice, the schedule, the staff, or any number of other things. And while we can attempt to plan for certain contingencies, there always seem to be "unknown unknowns" that frustrate any attempt to plan. Because of this, it's hard to know in advance when most software projects are "done." In some cases, there are always enhancements or improvements to do, and a need to deliver periodically. In others, you may discover that the system is "good enough" early in the process.

While each project has unique elements, complex projects involve people working together to *deliver value incrementally and frequently.* And a robust project management approach has a framework to allow teams to manage the risks associated with the unknowns.

Project performance defined

One measure of performance is whether a project is delivering incremental "value" – functionality with quality – on a regular basis. This sounds simple, but teams often fall short in how they approach the idea of increment and value, as value can be subjective, and it's not always clear who decides what value is. If we're talking about delivering value, we need to define what value is. The challenge for all projects is to clearly state what value is, and who sees that value. Gerald Weinberg once defined quality as "Value to some person," and with that definition, and the definition of value, knowing who decides what is "valuable" is the first step.

Even when the value is quantitative, it can be hard to measure. "Value" can sometimes be identified immediately, but sometimes only in retrospect. And what is valuable can change over time as the business environment changes. The best we can often do is to start with a definition, work with it and then periodically evaluate it.

Who decides value

One challenge all projects face is understanding what to build. It's a rare project that knows *exactly* what to build at the start. Usually there is someone who defines the scope of the project. This person can be a *customer* (the person paying for the development), a *user* (the person using the system once it's delivered), or even some other *stakeholder.* Ideally, members of these three groups can align their interests and priorities. Often they don't, making it difficult for teams to feel like *they* are doing valuable work. More importantly, not understanding the intended value of a task makes it more difficult to make appropriate engineering decisions that can help deliver value at a potentially lower cost.

Scrum addresses this problem by having a single person – *The Product Owner* – responsible for making decisions about scope and priority. In a high functioning team, the *Product Owner* role can be a formality, as the team has a good shared understanding about what to do. But this is not common. A clear sense of vision and priorities make it easier for the team to make decisions that align with the product vision.

Increments

Often project sponsors want a master plan at the start of a project and measure performance in terms of compliance with the plan. In practice it's hard to plan over a long term with any reliability, as the business and technical landscape changes over time. While having a vision and some idea of how the project will go is useful, the master plan approach ignores the uncertainty in most projects and also requires a lot of upfront effort to plan work that may not be done. The challenge is often simply *acknowledging* the uncertainty in a project.

Agile methods manage uncertainty by delivering in increments. One important criterion for a performing project is to make incremental progress visible so that the business can make adjustments, and perhaps decide that enough work has already been done.

An aside: Because the future is uncertain, spending too much effort on planning for things that may not happen is wasteful. Acknowledging uncertainty and doing lower fidelity planning is not the same as having a long-term plan. Successful projects still need roadmaps, and longer term (anticipated) plans, but the further in the future an item is, the less effort you invest in planning activities such as detailed specifications or estimation. This make sense because *you don't know that you'll do the work.* And while planning and forecasting are helpful, they do not, by themselves, deliver value, and can be somewhat *wasteful.* So concentrating planning effort on the near term is a way to minimize waste. One example is a user story, which starts out as a simple statement, and, as it gets closer to implementation, becomes more detailed.

Progress

For an Agile project, performance means delivering increments of value consistently. What is in the increment can vary from team to team, but the important thing is that the person who decides value – The Product Owner in Scrum, for example – is happy with the results.

Performance indicators

High performance

A high-performing project is continually delivering value, and demonstrates adaptability to changes to business without devolving into chaos. This includes being able to deliver in increments, and have the technical skill to build adaptable code that allows the project to change direction relatively easily. *Refactoring* and *testing* are part of the engineering culture, as well as *automation* and a goal of *frequent integration of code* and *frequent delivery.* Much of this is less about the deliverables – which are being implemented effectively – than about the team.

A high-performing team is also always reviewing and improving how they work. Things that slow down the project management or engineering process are viewed as challenges. High-performing projects are built on teams that have a culture of trust, so that people can freely identify problems and fix them without fear of retribution. High-performing teams often laugh together, and you'll likely observe that there are not sharp lines between team building/social times and "work" times.

High-performing teams will usually have a collaborative dynamic, where the emphasis is less on individual stars – though people's strengths are acknowledged and celebrated – and more on the team. Work boundaries are treated with skepticism and pragmatism in favor of acknowledged "domains of expertise" – too much deep knowledge in one person can become a problem. The people who work on successful projects often embrace the idea of "T-Shaped" team members, where everyone strives to have basic competence in most skills, even while having a few areas where they are deeply skilled.

The ethic of collaboration and trust also extends to interactions between the business (which defines what) and the team (which implements). A healthy degree of skepticism is OK as long as it is in service of building something useful soon.

At the center of all of this are often shared, and well understood, values, that inform how people work together.

Low performance

High-performing teams have a lot in common. They collaborate, resolve problems quickly, and get things done. A low-performing team project may be easy to identify, but it can be harder to define.

Superficially, lower-performing teams don't deliver the value reliably or quickly. If you look more deeply, you may find a team that doesn't seem collaborative, and not open to taking initiative, to improve the product or the process.

There are many ways that this can manifest itself, but some warning signs are a low level of engagement when discussing features, design, or planning. User stories may be taken at face value, and specification problems are consistently not identified until well into implementation.

Often underlying this lack of engagement is a lack of trust between team members, or between management (people or product) and the team members. A common observation in low-performing teams is a lack of "congruent action" – where actual behavior conflicts with stated values.

Measuring and predicting project performance?

Many of the measures of "value" I've discussed are subjective. Having data, though, is essential to making progress towards any goal, and project performance is no exception. The challenge is finding meaningful, efficient metrics that help you to understand what you need. Often measures that are easy to collect are often of limited value, and once we have a measure we are often tempted to extrapolate beyond its validity, and the measurement skews behavior. This is not to say that you always need precise, high fidelity measures to understand a project. You just need to understand the gaps in your measurements and use them appropriately, and be willing to adapt.

Start by understanding the things people *really* care about. Some examples are:

- Are we building the right thing? Does it provide the value you want? Does it give you what you need?
- Are we delivering with quality?
- Are we delivering with appropriate speed and meeting expectations?
- Are we spending too much money on the project?

Once you know what's important, pick some things to measure, and periodically evaluate whether these measurements correlate with something that matters to your business and keep your eyes open for additional measures. Some, such as financial metrics, are easier to understand – if you are over budget, you need to understand why, but you know that there is a problem. Other metrics, such as "velocity" (the forecast number of story points an Agile team is using), can be deceptive, and not as precise as they sound.

Some value propositions can be aligned with quantitative measures. For example, if the vision for a product is "to reduce the cost of a business process by 30%," we can calculate the costs before and after the update and have our answer.

Often the measure of value is vaguer, and the best that you can do is to pick a measurement criterion and continually re-evaluate it. For example, in Scrum, the success of a sprint can be based on feedback from the Product Owner at the Sprint Review, where the Product Owner can see working software that reflects the work done in a sprint.

When measuring performance, it's important to be wary of measures that appear more quantitative than they are. For example, if your team is estimating using story points, it's tempting to use measures of the number of story points completed as a measure of performance. Since Agile estimation is intentionally imprecise, it's important to understand that these numbers are most useful as a guideline for identifying whether the team is making reasonable commitments, rather than as a measure of absolute work. For example, if a team is meeting its commitments *and* delivering software that meets the Product Owner's expectations, that indicates good performance, regardless of the number of points completed.

It's also worth considering that measures of project performance should not be limited to work on the backlog but also include coordination with metrics collected after work is completed. For example, a plan executed precisely and on time is not as valuable if it results in more customer complaints. And since the key to performance is the team being mindful of things like team happiness, measures that incorporate this area can be helpful.

Achieving performance

Many of us have had an experience of working with a team where things *just seemed to work*. Sometime this dynamic is the result of good fortune, but most of the time this dynamic comes from a period of trial and error where the members of the team learn to work together. These teams often have shared values, a well-understood sense of why the team exists, and a strong desire to always evaluate the current state of the team (and project) and improve.

While some groups achieve this high-performing state on their own, there are things people and project managers can do to facilitate the process. A simple place to start is setting up a baseline of values that will support an effective team, and establishing some basic practices that reinforce those values.

Values and practice

A common question is whether it is *values* or *practices* are more important to success, and which to start with. While it's easy to state values, it's hard to *understand* them without seeing them in action. Practices, on the other hand, are easy to explain, though unless informed by the appropriate values, a new practice may just be seen as some sort of bureaucratic policy, and may not change the dynamic of the team as you expect.

This is further complicated by the Agile ethic of "adaptability," which some misinterpret as "doing whatever feels right."

In my experience, while values are what make for a great team, establishing good basic practices help teams realize the benefits of a new way of looking at a process. And while each team is different enough that their Scrum process may vary between them, starting with some "textbook" practices, and making time to evaluate them after a while, often works well to change team dynamics, which encourages the right values.

For example, I was introducing Extreme Programming to my team, and wanted to encourage more unit testing and test driven development (TTD). I was met with some reluctance by one team member, but I insisted that he give TDD a try for a couple of days. The next day he realized that the practice was increasing his productivity, and he stopped seeing writing unit tests as a distraction from his work. Establishing a trial run of a practice that supported the value of continuous inspection – and allowing for slightly slower delivery at the start – worked far better than any amount of discussion of the value.

Improving the performance of a team isn't going to be instant, but it can be straightforward. Introduce values that will lead to a more collaborative team, with tighter feedback loops, and then introduce new practices that demonstrate those values, and review the results.

I'll get more concrete about how to do this with Scrum.

A recipe for project success

Many families have a story along the lines of there being someone – usually a grandparent – who prepares traditional recipes to the joy of everyone. As the person ages, someone decides to learn (and document) their recipe. Often this person repeats all the steps *exactly* to surprisingly mediocre results. What we realize is that the grandparent did a bunch of improvisation and *adaptation* to achieve the result that everyone enjoyed. The transcribed recipe is sound, but the new preparer neglected to adapt the recipe to the specifics of the environment, and the quality of the actual ingredients in use. The traditional cook *follows a framework, and inspects and adapts.*

Recipes for project success are like this. Take one successful project and follow the exact same steps in another context, and it won't work quite as well. The team is different, with different skills and values. The organization is different, and the project is different. This does not mean that all is lost. There are things that are likely to work, and simply trying something different may help the team change dynamics that were getting in the way of effectiveness. Quite often overcoming resistance to change is the hardest, and most important, step in process improvement.

You can make reasonable guesses about what to try given some context. What makes the difference between success, mediocrity, and even failure, is that successful teams start with something concrete, internalize the values of the new approach, inspect how they are working periodically, and adapt the process based on the values and what they have learned. Less successful teams don't fully embrace the idea of change, and follow a new process with the principles and values of the old one in mind.

"Inspect and adapt" is central to the Scrum process framework. Scrum has a few rules. The Scrum Guide is a handful of pages, and it defines three roles, five events, and three classes of artifacts. More precisely, *the process that evolves from applying the Scrum Framework, with a reasonable starting point, and adapting it in the context of Scrum Values* can work well.

But even though the rules sound simple, the difference between a success or failure in adopting Scrum is often the difference between the team members simply "following" the process, vs "embracing" and "internalizing" the process. To do this successfully, you need to understand the *Pillars* of Scrum, as well as the *Scrum Values*, and ensure that your project management and technical processes work in harmony with them.

Since complex systems need a certain amount of autonomy to work well, and since you can't micromanage every interaction, you need some framework to help people understand how to work together well, and make decisions that will help move the project forward. The Pillars and Values of Scrum do this.

An overview of Scrum

To set the stage for this discussion, here is a brief overview of the Scrum Framework. For more details consult the Scrum Guide. For more details on Scrum in practice, see one of the many excellent books on Scrum (Mike Cohn, Ken Rubin).

The Scrum Guide describes Scrum as "a framework for developing, delivering, and sustaining complex products" and the definition of Scrum consists of Scrum's *roles*, *events*, *artifacts*, and the *rules* that bind them together.

Scrum Roles

The Defined Roles are:

- Product Owner: The person "responsible for maximizing the value of the product resulting from work of the Development Team."
- Development Team: "professionals who do the work of delivering a potentially releasable Increment of 'Done' product at the end of each Sprint."
- Scrum Master: The person "responsible for promoting and supporting Scrum as defined in the Scrum Guide."

In some cases one person can assume more than one of these roles, but the roles should all exist. Scrum does not define other roles or titles within the team, and encourages the team to work across disciplines to get work done. In particular, the entire team is accountable for getting the work done. In practice this means that, if you have a database (DB) specialist on the team, but there is other work to do, the DB specialist should help with that rather than being idle or working on something else. Not all teams reach this state of having a team composed of truly cross-functional (or "T-Shaped") people, but having that as a goal is important to success.

Scrum Events

The Scrum Events are:

- The sprint, where the work gets done.
- Sprint Planning, where the team figures out what can get done, and how to get it done.

- The Daily Scrum, where the team collaborates and identifies roadblocks and inspects progress.
- The Sprint Review, where the Product Owner reviews the work done during the sprint, and views it in context with the project plan.
- The Sprint Retrospective, where the team discusses and reviews how they worked together.

These events or meetings are meant to be useful, and quick, and reduce other meetings that distract from getting work done. There are other times team members meet, if they need to. But the Scrum Events are intended to establish a framework for collaboration between the team members, and between team members at the business. When some see this list, they complain that Scrum has "too many meetings." If you head that meeting, you should consider if the meetings can improve and be more constructive and collaborative.

Scrum artifacts

The Scrum artifacts are:

- The Product Backlog: "an ordered list of everything that is known to be needed in the product."
- The Sprint Backlog: "the set of Product Backlog items selected for the Sprint, plus a plan for delivering the product Increment and realizing the Sprint Goal."
- Increment: "the sum of all the Product Backlog items completed during a Sprint and the value of the increments of all previous Sprints." Usually this means working software.

These artifacts are the work products of the Scrum team, with the backlogs reflecting the planning process, and the "increment" is the one that demonstrates value at the end of a sprint. There are many ways to construct these artifacts using a variety of tools and techniques, though the more lightweight the process, the better, as more complex processes distract the team from their work.

Scrum Pillars and Values

In addition to the physical things in Scrum – roles, events, and artifacts – the *Scrum Guide* explains that Scrum is built on three Pillars, and that these Pillars are supported by five Values. These Pillars, and the supporting Values, are what make Scrum work, and the key to an effective Scrum process is helping the team keep these in mind as they work. It's possible to have a process where you have all of these artifacts, roles, and events, and you are still not doing Scrum, or at least not realizing the value of Scrum. There are details to how the events are executed, the roles fulfilled, and the artifacts represented that makes the difference between something that looks like Scrum, and something that is Scrum. The Pillars and Values of Scrum are what make the difference.

The Pillars are:

- Transparency: Significant aspects of the process must be visible to those responsible for the outcome.
- Inspection: Frequent inspection of Scrum artifacts and progress towards the Sprint Goal.
- Adaptation: Making adjustments, either in the work to be done, or how the work is done, to facilitate better results.

The Values (with definitions adapted from the Scrum Guide) are:

- Commitment: Team members personally commit to the Sprint Goal.
- Courage: Team members have the courage to do the right things to solve tough problems.
- Focus: Everyone focuses on the work to be done for the sprint.
- Openness: The Scrum Team and its stakeholders agree to be open about all the work and the challenges with performing the work.
- Respect: Team members respect each other to be capable, independent people.

The Values support the Pillars, and without a coherent connection between the Pillars and Values, you can be going through the motions of Scrum yet not realize the benefits.

Pillars in practice

Let's get concrete and give some examples of what the Pillars of Scrum mean on a day-to-day basis, as well as how the Values help us implement the process.

Scrum is different from how teams often work, and the values are sometimes at odds with the actual (if not stated) values of some organizations – even organizations that *want* to adapt Scrum. In some cases the differences are structural: HR and purchasing processes might not have been built with self-organizing teams in mind, for example. In other cases they might be cultural: the idea of a plan evolving as we see what's delivered in each sprint might be uncomfortable for those used to developing detailed plans (even if the detailed plans were not realistic).

In some cases the resistance to implementing Scrum may come from team members who are uncomfortable with the idea of autonomy. To help a team adopt Scrum and be productive you need to set up an environment where they can change successfully, and often successful change means being tolerant of failure. In particular, you need to make sure that the actions of the team and the organization are congruent with the values of Scrum.

Planning

Planning is a Scrum Event that can easily be done in a way that conflicts with Scrum Values. You can have a sprint backlog that is more work than the team can reasonably do, and interject numerous support items into the sprint without acknowledging that it may change what the team can deliver. In this case you may have a Scrum artifact (the backlog) but the values of commitment and focus are missing, and the Pillars of transparency, inspection, and adaptation aren't being supported.

The Sprint Review

The Sprint Review is a Scrum that is meant for collaboration. Unfortunately, sometimes the review meeting is seen as a "demo" where the team shows off its work. A Sprint Review that is more aligned with the Pillars of Scrum is seen as an opportunity to discuss the current state of the project, and identify changes, either based on incorrect work or new discoveries. While a review that only shows the work supports *Inspection*, a review that facilitates open conversation, and discussions about what to do next, also supports *Adaptation* and *Transparency*.

I once facilitated a Sprint Review which led to two sets of stakeholders discovering that they had some common needs from a feature. More remarkably, these two groups were physically located next to each other, while the development team was in a different city. While identifying these needs sooner would have been ideal, the process acknowledges that communication is not perfect, and creating opportunities to collaborate at fixed points is essential.

Sprint Retrospectives

Another obvious *Adaptation* event is the Sprint Retrospective. As the Sprint Review is an opportunity to review the *Increment* (the work), the Retrospective is a chance for the team to review the process. Some teams use the Retrospective time as a chance to identify problems and vent (both about each other, and external forces). This is an example of *Inspection* and *Transparency*, but without actionable findings, it does not allow for *Adaptation*. Good Sprint Retrospectives allow the team to discover problems, celebrate successes, and identify core reasons behind each, resulting in things to try so that subsequent sprints can be better.

There are many good books written about Retrospective techniques, and I suggest consulting one to figure out how to make Retrospectives better. A good Sprint Retrospective – where people feel safe to raise issues – is the best indicator of a team that can improve.

The Daily Scrum

The Daily Scrum is both the most well-known Scrum Event (also often referred to as a "Stand Up") and one of the more misunderstood ones. The Daily Scrum is a forum where the team meets daily to share progress and identify backlogs with *each other*. One of the common mistakes teams make is treating this event as a status meeting, where people are *reporting* rather than collaborating. Sometimes the team will treat the Scrum Master as someone to report to.

When I've been in the Scrum Master role, I've tried to break the team of the habit of reporting to me by walking away from the Scrum for a second. This sometimes infuriated my management, but the team – once I explained what I was doing – took it as a reminder of the values of Scrum and a sign of my trust in the team.

As the most frequent, and eponymous Scrum Event, it is important that the way that it is executed reflects the right values.

Execution

Scrum says nothing about technical execution, but many teams often use a common set of practices that support the Pillars. For example, Automated Testing and Continuous Delivery and Deployment support *Transparency* and allow for *Inspection*, for example. And Automated Testing supports *Adaptation* by making code changes less risky.

Self-organizing teams

Self-organization is the one aspect of Scrum that most challenges organizations. Self-organization means that given a problem and group that is committed to solving it, the group will organize itself in a way that works best. This works because the team knows more about the situation than someone external to the team, such as a manager. The group can react more quickly on their own than if they have to wait for instructions..

Self-organization – which is Adaptation at the team level – can work very well, though not every choice the team makes will be ideal. But a team won't become self-organizing unless they have autonomy and the ability to make mistakes without consequences. Management can facilitate autonomy by giving the team clear boundaries, even if the boundaries are not as open as the team would prefer, and freedom to move without those boundaries. Nothing slows down initiative more than the second-guessing that happens when people hit "invisible fences."

Self-organization, even with well-defined limits, is both one of the most powerful elements of an Agile process, and one of the ones that often meets the greatest organizational resistance.

Inspecting and adapting – The right way

A common problem for teams new to Scrum is when someone latches on to the idea that Scrum is a Process Framework, and mean to be adapted, and they adapt techniques whenever things fall outside of their comfort zone. While *Adaptation* is a Pillar of Scrum, and a central part of any Agile process, it's essential to adapt it only after understanding your current situation and how the change will support your desired process change. If a change doesn't align with the Pillars and Values, consider whether the change is motivated by a real need, or reluctance to change some basic dynamic in your organization.

The best way I have found to overcome this tendency for teams to "adapt back to their old style" is to following a process "by the book" for a time and change slowly. The Scrum Guide may not be enough, but Scrum.org and the Scrum Alliance have many articles that can guide you. Or find a good book (Cohn, Rubin).

What you end up with may be very different than what you first thought of as Scrum, but if it aligns with the values, and you see benefits, you've done the right thing.

Summary of the recipe

Scrum is a process framework that defines a few events, artifacts, and roles, and how those concrete things work are informed by the values the Scrum Guide defines. This lack of detail and the adaptability, which is a hallmark of Agile methods, can lead some teams astray. Resist the temptation to think that "Scrum can be anything that works."

Scrum is built on a set of Pillars that are supported by the Values. There is a fair amount of flexibility consistent with those Values, but it is too easy to follow the motions of a Scrum-Like Process and not realize the value of Scrum.

Start with a series of practices that seem more traditional before adapting, and then inspect and adapt, taking time to discuss how they work. You may slow down initially, though it is likely that what you will build will be more aligned with customer needs. But you are likely to be more successful in the end.

Pitfalls and challenges

Change is hard. Even in organizations which assert that they want to change there is often resistance, either explicit or implicit. And even if the change process starts, it can slow down as the team can lose energy for improvement.

This is true for any change, but it's especially difficult when moving to an Agile approach, as doing Agile well requires significant cultural changes. Trust and delegation are essential. This can be a challenge both from the side of management – which may be used to "command and control," and from the side of the team, which may be expecting more concrete guidance.

The answer sounds simple, but is challenging: setting a goal, and trusting the team to deliver is very different from the way many organizations operate.

Change can also be slow, even if the end result will be a more performant team. It's useful to set the expectations for the whole process, and while planning sprints, quickly get to a point where you can deliver on commitments. By demonstrating that your team can meet its commitments, you can short circuit that process, especially as the business realizes that they get their most important work done.

Explicit resistance can come from people in the organization who might feel threatened by a dynamic that delegates authority to the team. The reasons for this can range from fear of losing organizational value or authority, to a lack of congruence between someone's role and the new approach. Or the process may contradict what people know to have worked in the past. A lot of this sort of behavior is driven by fear. Jerry Weinberg refers to "survival rules" which are not bad things, but which may no longer be valid in a new context. (Weinberg Survival rules)

Assuming that the resistance isn't deeply embedded in the organization, in these cases you can attempt to have conversations directly with those serving as roadblocks. Linda Rising and Mary Lynn Manns also have some excellent advice for overcoming resistance in their book *More Fearless Change*.

Preventing backsliding

Addressing active resistance to change is relatively easy. While you may not be able to overcome it, it's easy to identify and you quickly become aware that you need to react to it.

Complacency following small successes is harder. In some cases review processes become less effective and the engine that is driving the success of the team will fail. Or, more insidiously, if things are working well, the team can become complacent, working through the process steps and not engaging as fully as they could.

Once a team is doing well, you can't simply rely on inertia for continual success. Even if a team is doing well, things can change. Business situations, team composition, or other external forces can cause a high-performing team to change. Perhaps something in the company causes morale to change, or the business problem become less compelling to the team members. Even if everything is status quo, it's possible for teams to fall into habits that reduce their resilience.

A common situation for Scrum teams is having the Scrum Events become so routine that people become disengaged. Perhaps people stop mentioning challenges at the Daily Scrum. Or Retrospectives become formulaic and routine, and people stop believing that they can result in significant changes. Or gaps in the product are not given as much emphasis during the Sprint Review.

The Scrum Master, as the process shepherd in Scrum, can play a key role in identifying and perhaps avoiding these situations. The main forum for improvement is the Sprint Retrospective, and the Scrum Master as facilitator can keep the events fresh by introducing new exercises to keep the activities fresh.

Sprint Retrospectives can focus on certain aspects of the process so as to give the team a chance to stay on top of things before complacency sets in. Gathering data about how the team feels using surveys and adding the results as data to a Retrospective can be useful as well. After a period of time it is also appropriate to have a Retrospective that focuses on a different time frame, such as the past quarter, or the project to date.

It's also important to keep the team engaged in the Retrospective by making sure that each one ends with actions that the team can (and does) accomplish.

The difference between healthy teams and less healthy ones is that healthy teams identify issues more rapidly, and have the tools to adjust, and they are willing to use them.

Benefits

It's a basic premise of human nature that people will embrace their ideas more fully than others, and the approach of Scrum to encourage teams to self-organize and commit to work has the advantage that, once people accept the process, they are likely to begin to embrace it, because they *own* it.

Similarly, the ethics of continuous improvement means that the process should be self-correcting. The challenge is for management to not send mixed messages.

When the team owns the process, or at least has the ability to influence it, and has pride of ownership, things happen more easily. Product Managers and Managers still have a hard job of establishing a clear vision and creating spaces for good communication, but this is still more productive than micromanaging the team.

Autonomy and Trust, combined with a clear vision, can create a situation where things happen that are better than you expected.

As idyllic as this sounds, it may not always work.

In the end, some teams, and some projects, will have a more difficult time adopting Agile methods than others. For these teams, patience is one approach. Barring that, staff changes might be appropriate. If you can trade the people who are uncomfortable with Agile with people who are, you can build a successful team, and thus generate comfort with the approach in the larger organization.

But not every approach will work in every team. The best you can do is to introduce the process *and* its foundational values, and be responsible to concerns.

Is Scrum right for me?

As I mentioned at the start of this chapter, Agile development techniques do tend to work well for a certain class of problem that is common in many software projects. For Agile to be successful, however, the organization needs to support the Principles of Agile – the Pillars and Values of Scrum, for example. The project space fit is easy to identify. The organization fit is more challenging.

Any project that is complex, with changing requirements, and unknown unknowns, with team members who are highly skilled can benefit from this project. The challenge is for the organization to realize the complexity and see the risks in *not* changing a process. It's too common to believe that there is risk in *doing* something, while maintaining the *status quo* is not risky. In the context of a changing environment, this intuition is often backwards.

Sometimes the bias is so deep that it's less about practices than names. I recall once working on a project with a government contractor where we were very much doing "iterative" development (which at the time was *new*). During a presentation, the Lead Engineer described our process as "modified Waterfall," to which I thought "modified to the point that it is no longer a Waterfall."

If the sponsors of your work see value in the new approach, changing locally and managing the external interfaces may be a good incremental step. Ultimately, you need to consider your problem and business environment. Are things changing? They usually are, and Agile makes sense.

The organizational issues are harder to figure out, but if you have a runway where you can make a change, then you should have success.

Odds and ends

In as much as a process change is a *big* thing, what makes a transition to an Agile process work are details on the person level. What makes a team "Agile" is the people on it and how they interact with each other and other organizations. Something at a larger scale can change the team dynamic, but the problem will be visible, and can be rectified on the team level, if at all.

Central to the values of Agility and Scrum is the idea that "Agile Leaders" are "Servant Leaders," which is to say that the job of leaders is to help the team remove obstacles, not to control or direct. The role of a leader is to facilitate, and help create good environments. In some cases doing nothing is both the hardest and most important thing a leader can do.

Also, it's important to always remember that change is hard and can be slow. Any successful change process needs room to fail – in acceptable ways. To be successful, address each risk, be it in process technology, or organization, by experiments which you can afford to be unsuccessful, and which you can learn something from. For example, teams often address technical risk by doing "Spikes" – time boxed end to end experiments – thereby limiting the cost of a failure to the time invested. Likewise, by developing from an ordered backlog in small increments, any undone work will be the items at the bottom of the list.

Conclusion

Picking a process is only the first step in improving your delivery. Even if the team's chosen process matches the problem space you need to solve, teams exist in a context of the organization, and the history of the team and its members.

While it's tempting to suggest that there is a set of process steps that can help every team be successful, software development is a human endeavor, and the team is what makes a good process a successful process.

Successful Scrum is about values and people. As someone who is trying to help a team improve, the success of the change is less about what you do, as what opportunities to help the team to see and do.

Technology, Process, and Management all need to work together. And remember, the reason that you are considering a new approach is that the old one is not working. Take care not to morph the new approach to fit your old mold. That is likely to be less effective than your old way of working. The key to a successful process is a successful culture, one based on clear values that drive the actions of everyone on the team.

Chapter 3

The power of empowering others
Coaching as a leadership model
for high-performing teams

Susanne Madsen

Introduction

I still remember the first time I was coached. I was working long hours on a large, complex project in financial services with demanding clients and tight deadlines. I was stressed and overworked and I wasn't leading my team or myself in the best way. I spent a lot of my time tracking tasks and dealing with urgent issues. There wasn't much time left for thinking ahead or spending quality time with team members and stakeholders. I was under a lot of pressure and I didn't feel I had anyone to delegate to. But more importantly, I wasn't enjoying myself and the project wasn't performing as well as it could have.

My first coaching session had a profound effect on me. It took place during a five-day leadership course, which I was invited to attend. During the course we examined our predominant leadership styles and how we could expand on them. To support the process everyone was assigned a personal coach who would help us work through any personal issues and queries. The topic I chose for my first session was the extremely long hours I put into running my project. I felt that everything depended on me and that I personally had to oversee every aspect of the project. Needless to say that I felt exhausted and that my approach wasn't the most effective.

The coaching session opened my eyes. I still remember the AHA moment I had when I realised exactly how much I could influence my circumstances and my behaviour in challenging situations. I began to examine myself as a project manager and the values that were driving my work. I realised that in order to increase my project's performance and my wellbeing, I had to change the way I was leading my team and myself. All of these thoughts were put in motion because someone took the time to coach me through a very challenging time and ask me a set of insightful questions that made me reflect on my situation.

Coaching has tremendous potential to increase the performance of the managers who lead projects, the people who help execute them and ultimately, on the project itself. By making use of coaching it's possible to empower a person to overcome an issue that's been holding them back for months. It's interesting how it works. It's as if the person who is coaching is holding up a large mirror in front of the other person where all their habits, fears, excuses, ambitions and talents are being reflected back so that they see their situation in a much clearer light.

I'm pleased that more and more project managers contact me because they would like to get better at coaching their team members. I'm thrilled about this interest as it's likely that coaching will make them better people and leaders in the process. That's because when we coach, we learn to engage others and to be more present during a conversation. We are better able to listen and empathise and to understand what's important to the person we're speaking with. In this way, coaching is a life skill and a necessity for project leaders. It helps us take responsibility and build better relationships at work and in life in general.

Coaching in a project environment

In this chapter I will explore how coaching can help project managers make the most of the team's valuable resources by building a fire within. I'm choosing this particular topic because I consider people to be the underlying engine that drives project performance. It's people who deliver projects and it's when people feel safe, appreciated, rewarded, listened to, challenged and understood that high performance can occur. This is when they begin to open up and contribute with all of their strengths towards the project's outcomes.

The skills I will share apply to all projects where there is a team of people who needs to coordinate a delivery aligned to a common goal. This encompasses large and small-scale projects as well as projects that use different types of methodologies. Coaching is a way to empower people to take responsibility for their work and it's equally effective on Agile and Waterfall projects and across industries. I have personally used coaching in industries as wide-ranging as manufacturing, construction, information technology, software, financial services, professional services, education, publishing, retail and architectural engineering.

The type of coaching I am considering in this chapter is primarily where the project manager learns to use coaching as a leadership style. When this happens the project manager becomes skilled at empowering people to think for themselves and thereby shifts responsibility onto the team. They do that by asking insightful questions that encourage the team to come forward and fill in the blanks.

The second type of coaching I'm considering is where someone external to the organisation coaches the project manager. Working with a professional coach will help the project manager develop better relationships with stakeholders, communicate more effectively and improve the way they lead the team. It will also help them learn about coaching with a view to using these skills within their project.

These two different applications of coaching in a project environment complement each other and can happen simultaneously.

The impact of coaching on project performance

When we evaluate the effect of coaching on project performance I suggest that there are three levels of success we need to consider: Project Management Success, Business Case Success and Project Team Success. Coaching has the potential to impact all three (Figure 3.1).

Project management success

The first aspect is the most basic and the traditional way of measuring whether a project is successful or not. This is where we use the triple constraints of time, cost and quality to measure project performance. If the project is delivered on time, within budget and to the expected level of quality, we usually say that it's successful in project management terms.

Figure 3.1 Three levels of success.

Business case success

The second aspect of project performance is whether the business case has been met and the extent to which the project is adding value to its clients, sponsors and end users. We can measure this through the three dimensions of impact, relevance and sustainability. Impact measures the effect the project has on the organisation's strategic objectives. Relevance is the extent to which the project's output is relevant to the users, and sustainability measures whether the project's solution and outputs are durable, maintainable and produced in a sustainable manner. These criteria are an indication of the project's success on a long-term basis and are more strategic than the dimensions of time, cost and quality.

Project team success

The last dimension of project performance is how well the team worked together in the process of delivering the project's outputs. This dimension is somewhat less measurable. I suggest we ask the following questions to ascertain if the project performed well at a team level: Did the team agree on a common set of behavioural ground rules and did they abide by them? Was the team able to effectively solve problems and overcome conflict? Were the team members and stakeholders able to communicate effectively? Did everyone contribute in line with agreed roles and responsibilities? Did people feel empowered to contribute with all of their strengths and ideas? This dimension of Project Team Success is about internal efficiency of the project team. It relates to how the project was executed, not just what was achieved.

Project performance comprises all three levels of success. Of these three levels, Project Team Success is the most fundamental because it's people who deliver projects. If the team isn't able to work well together, communicate effectively and make sound and timely decisions it will most certainly affect its ability to deliver the project within the triple constraints of time, cost and quality and to produce valuable long-term benefits.

Coaching as a leadership style has a direct effect on Project Team Success, as it's a way to optimise human potential. Therefore, coaching also has an effect on Project Management Success and to some extent on Business Case Success.

The psychology of successful teams

At a psychological level a project team can only be successful if its members feel safe and are encouraged to contribute with all of their ideas and talents. It is when people thrive and trust each other that their best thinking is unleashed.

Studies from the Massachusetts Institute of Technology (MIT) and Google show that in teams where performance is high everybody on the team is actively communicating with each other and team members speak and contribute in roughly the same amount. On projects where a few members are allowed to dominate discussions or where the project leader is too controlling or judging, many members don't come forward with their views out of fear of being disregarded. This kind of open and equal communication only happens when team members feel psychologically safe enough to contribute.

In high-performing environments, the project manager is comfortable taking the role of a facilitator and coach. He moderates the team's discussions in such a way that there is space for everyone to come forward and give input into discussions and decisions. When psychological safety is present, people feel free to share what's on their mind – whether it's a bright new idea or a tough personal challenge. They are able to talk about their doubts and worries and to have difficult conversations with colleagues who have different opinions. A really important aspect is that the team is able to resolve conflict and have unfiltered, passionate debate about things that matter. This kind of environment, where people create space for each other, is based on trust and openness, which is one of the building blocks of high performance.

Moderating a conversation and making people feel safe can happen when the project manager is able to fully listen, empathise and draw people into the debate with the right kind of questions and words of encouragement. In other words, the project manager needs to have a good level of emotional intelligence – something which coaching can help us bring forth. EQ or emotional intelligence encompasses the ability to recognise and manage our own and other people's emotions. That's vital for a project team that wants to create space for each member in order that high performance can occur.

But the project manager also needs to hold team members to account in order for high performance to happen. A successful team is one that is equally supported and challenged to stretch and meet the project's objectives. The project manager as a coach isn't someone who blindly trusts that the team is sufficiently resourceful to autonomously run with things. Nor is it a person who only nurtures and supports people. A successful project manager plays an active role in empowering and challenging team members to come up with ideas and solutions and will hold them to account in delivering what they said they would.

Diminishers and multipliers

When inclusion and psychological safety aren't present on the project, we get dysfunctional teams that struggle to deliver the project's objectives and meet the success criteria. Communication and trust between team members is lacking and the team struggles to work towards a centrally coordinated goal. Misunderstandings and conflict arise and individuals don't buy-in to the work they do. I'm guessing we have all been part of a dysfunctional team at some point in our careers. They are characterised by underlying tension, discontented team members and inattention to results.

Another way to spot a dysfunctional team is by observing the person leading it. Some projects are led by a project manager who is directive and controlling and who struggles to delegate and trust the team. Whilst thinking they are doing the right thing, such managers have an adverse effect on the team's performance. In her book, *Multipliers*, Liz Wiseman calls such a leader a Diminisher. She writes that Diminishers tell people how to do their jobs and they test people's knowledge to see if they are doing it right. Diminishers consider themselves thought leaders but rarely share their knowledge in a way that invites contribution. They tend to sell their ideas rather than learning what others know. They ask questions to make a point rather than generating insight or collective learning. Rather than shifting responsibility onto other people, Diminishers stay in charge and tell others how to do their jobs.

Instead of psychological safety, this directive and commanding leadership style fosters fear and poor performance. It creates a diminished team that lacks creativity and autonomous thinking. Many Diminishers think that they are doing the organisation and their team a favour by firmly driving the project forward but don't realise the restrictive impact they have on others.

The opposite of being an overly directive and diminishing leader is a Multiplier. A Multiplier is somebody who is skilled at making people flourish by coaching and mentoring them to high performance. Liz Wiseman writes that Multipliers help team members become smarter and more capable by liberating them to think, speak and act with reason. They amplify the smarts and capabilities of the people around them and they create an environment where the best ideas surface. Multipliers get people to step into a challenge by shifting the burden of the thinking onto others. They do that by asking the hard questions and by inviting the team to fill in the blanks. When a manager initially presents a challenge to the team, she will carry the burden of thinking, but will quickly empower the team to step up and carry it forward (Figure 3.2).

Diminisher – The Directive Manager	*Multiplier* – The Coaching Manager
Drives results through their personal involvement	Gives other people the ownership of results and invests in their success
Believes they are the smartest person in the room with all the great ideas	Coaches and teaches in order to unleash the team's best thinking
Doesn't leave enough space for people to think through challenges themselves	Creates a safe environment for team members to contribute
Gives directives that showcases how much they personally know	Defines an opportunity that causes people to stretch
Creates a tense environment that suppresses people's thinking capability	Creates an intense environment that requires people's best thinking and work

Figure 3.2 Diminisher vs. multiplier.

When Multipliers lead they make use of a coaching approach. They create an environment where people can flourish and where team members are challenged to stretch and grow. Rather than telling people what to do, they involve them in decisions and empower them to find their own answers.

Coaching as a leadership style

As we will explore in more detail, asking the right questions is at the heart of how a coaching-leader achieves results. Being a good project leader isn't about having the right answers. It's about unleashing people's genius rather than displaying our own. That can only happen when the leader asks insightful questions that enable people to come forward and weigh in. It's when team members weigh in that we gain their buy-in and commitment. If I'm being told to deliver a task by a certain date by the project manager, it will be easy for me to blame him if I can't make it. But if I have been involved, supported and challenged to produce my own plan, I'll feel much more responsible to deliver it.

One of the most fundamental mind-set shifts project managers need to make when they begin to use coaching as a leadership style is to accept that their role isn't to give advice and to come up with solutions. On the contrary, their role is to surface understanding and insight in the team member and to help them move forward without directly telling them what to do. Coaching is built on the belief that people can generate their own answers and solutions.

As managers we often think that being directive is the right way. Many project managers with a technical background are experts in their field and tend to give advice more than they coach. When we give advice we go into problem-solving mode and come up with instructions and ideas for how the other person should move forward. It makes us feel great to pass on our knowledge and to help someone progress a task in an effective way. But when we give advice we don't empower people to grow and to find their own answers. We are effectively imposing our solution to their problem, which isn't an effective way to get others to take ownership.

Leading from the front and telling team members what to do is great in situations where the team needs direction, for instance when there is a crisis that quickly needs to be resolved. But it can be detrimental to project performance if it's used extensively throughout the project. If a team member is looking for guidance on how to approach a problem, contact a stakeholder, resolve a conflict or conduct a meeting, it's often more appropriate to coach them through it.

Mentoring is different from coaching

Many people use mentoring and coaching synonymously, but although there are many overlaps between the two disciplines, there are also differences. A mentor is typically someone who has significantly more experience than the person they are mentoring. It's someone who has been there, done it and who is giving advice based on their own experiences. A mentor can be of great help to junior team members who wish to learn more about the business or advance a specific skill. A project manager could, for instance, take a junior project administrator under their wing and teach them the tricks of the trade.

But as the project administrator grows in confidence and competence, mentoring will cease to be effective.

Whereas mentors are good at teaching team members specific skills, coaches are great at helping them find their own solutions. A coaching approach is particularly helpful when there is a need to assist people in developing the 'softer' side of the job, e.g. how to collaborate, communicate, build trust, resolve conflict and lead. In these situations it is not appropriate to simply advise someone. When team members see for themselves how they need to change their behaviour and what the first steps are, the impact is more powerful. The coaching manager is simply the facilitator who helps surface the insight. There are many situations on a project that lend themselves to a coaching approach because team members need help with the softer side of the job.

A good coach listens and asks open questions

We have already mentioned that coaching isn't about giving advice. It's about helping a person to see a given situation in a clearer light so that they feel empowered to take the next steps. This means that the team member gains a better understanding of what the real problem is, what the options are for solving the problem and what action they can take to overcome it. The way in which the manager helps a team member gain this insight is primarily by asking open questions, such as:

What do you feel the problem is?
Can you explain the situation in more detail?
What's the real challenge for you here?
What would you like to achieve?
What have you already tried?
What else?
What worked? What didn't work?
What steps can we take to change this?
Which option would be the fastest/easiest?
What will you do right now?
What help do you need?

What's happening is that the coaching project manager effectively switches mode from telling to asking and listening. The listening part is important and is one of the big building blocks of coaching. Fully listen to what the team member has to say without interrupting or impatiently wanting to butt in enables the manager to really grasp the situation and see it from the team member's point of view.

In contrast to hearing, which is an automatic reflex, active listening takes effort and requires that we put our own internal mind–chatter aside and concentrate on the person who is speaking. To practice listening at the highest level, it's important to fully focus on the team member instead of considering what to say next. In this state of heightened awareness it will become much clearer what the team member is really trying to say. The project manager can further maintain their focus on the other person by repeating and paraphrasing their words, e.g. what I hear you're saying is that the client isn't able to articulate clearly what they need. Is that right?

There are three levels of listening: Internal listening, focused listening and global listening.

Level I – Internal listening

Listening at level I is the level that people listen at most of the time. This is when we are primarily focused on our own inner voice, thoughts, feelings and opinions whilst the other person is speaking. As the team member is talking, our internal dialogue is trying to figure out what to say next or we are thinking about all the things we still need to get done today. In other words, we're not paying full attention to the person speaking. Needless to say that it's difficult to coach or lead someone effectively when we only listen at this level.

Level II – Focused listening

Level II is a higher level of listening. This is when we are focused on the other person and are paying attention to their words and expressions. We are not thinking about what we want to say next but are present with the team member, paying them our full attention. Focused listening is a step up from internal listening.

Level III – Global listening

When we listen at level III not only do we listen with our ears but we also listen with our body. As we are fully present with the other person we use our intuition and are able to detect their mood and if there is any incongruence between what they say and what the rest of their body is communicating. This level of listening is the highest possible level. It's incredibly powerful because other people will feel fully understood when we listen to them with all of our senses. To listen at this level we need to consciously empty our mind before we engage with the other person.

It may take some time for project managers to learn to listen at level III as many of us are focused on our own internal dialogue as we work. To practice global listening, we can begin to observe people when they speak. It's about being fully present and trying to hear beyond the words, noticing people's body language and emotions and what they are really trying to say.

People who have a tendency to interrupt others can try to put their tongue on pause. This happens when we draw our tongue backwards so that it neither touches the upper part nor the lower part of our mouth. The tongue is effectively pulled backwards and is floating in the middle of the mouth. In that way, we're less likely to speak as the tongue is in a neutral position.

Identifying opportunities to coach the team

Coaching isn't just a tool to be used for the big conversations where the team members are at a crossroad. It's a way of life and a leadership style which can be used in a variety of project situations. When a team member asks for advice about how to approach a situation, the project manager should see it as a coaching opportunity and resist the temptation of telling them what to do. They need to give the team member their full attention.

Listen at the highest possible level and ask lots of open questions that begin with what, how and who. It's important to avoid asking why. Why often makes people feel defensive, which defeats the purpose of a coaching conversation. If a team member asks how to structure a client meeting, for instance, the project manager could ask these questions that shed light on the topic.

- What is the purpose of the meeting?
- What would you like the outcome to be?
- How do you want people to feel as a result of the meeting?
- Who will be attending?
- What was discussed at the last meeting?
- What are your thoughts about how you might structure the meeting?
- What are the advantages and disadvantages of these options?
- What else?
- What do you feel is the best way forward?
- What's the first step?
- What support do you need?
- What else do you need to consider?

The conversation may last a bit longer than had the project manager simply given the team member instructions, but the outcome is likely to be far more rewarding and effective for everyone involved. When people identify the solution for themselves they will feel more empowered and motivated to take ownership of their part of the project.

I recently had a conversation with John, a senior project manager, who had been assigned a new big project. John told me that he had visited the new client on site and that he had brought along a junior project administrator, Gemma. He had never worked with Gemma before but hoped that she was the right support person for the project. Gemma had been invited along to the client meeting so that she could get introduced to the client and take minutes. John was busy and had enough problems to deal with. He assumed that Gemma was a capable project administrator and trusted that she would produce a decent set of meeting minutes. When he asked her if she was okay doing so she agreed.

Gemma didn't say much during the client meeting, which disappointed John a bit. He told me that she'd probably felt intimidated by his seniority. But he didn't bring it up with her. After the meeting he patiently waited for her to distribute the minutes. But it didn't happen. After five days he called her and reminded her. She said she'd do it but still nothing happened. One more week passed without a word from Gemma. Finally, John reflected on his approach and what he could have done differently. He realised that he hadn't taken the time to get to know her, let alone brief her, and that he'd made incorrect assumptions about her abilities.

If John had acted more like a Multiplier and made use of a coaching approach, he would have asked Gemma some engaging questions instead of giving her orders. He could have asked her: How do you feel about this client meeting? What questions do you have before we go? He could have also taken the time to find out about her background and listen to her story. Which other projects have you supported and what was your role? What information do you need on this project to be effective? How would you like us to work together? Has your boss freed you up to work on this project? What concerns do you have? Throughout this conversation John should have listened at level

III and tried to see the situation from Gemma's point of view. He could have also created a safe space for her by expressing his appreciation for her involvement and efforts.

The GROW model as a framework

As some people learn best from having a model or framework as a guide, we will spend some time examining the GROW model. The GROW model is one of the most common frameworks for structuring a coaching conversation and can be used in most situations. GROW stands for Goal, Reality, Options and Way Forward (Figure 3.3).

Goal – Establish a goal for the conversation

The idea of the GROW model is that we start the conversation by establishing what the problem, issue or goal is. So before the project manager launches into the conversation, they essentially try to frame it by understanding what the topic is. There is little point talking about solutions to a problem if they are unsure they are talking about the same thing. The project manager might ask:

What's on your mind?
Tell me about the issue or what you feel is wrong.
What would you like to achieve?
How do you imagine the situation when it is resolved?
How can you make that more specific?
By when do you want to have achieved this goal/resolved this issue?
What will achieving this goal mean for you/us?
Which aspect is the most important for you to focus on right now?
Where would you say you are today in resolving this issue?

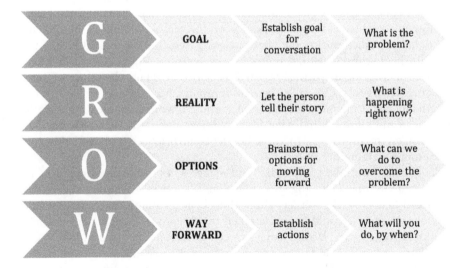

Figure 3.3 The GROW model.

Reality – Let the person tell their story

When the project manager has clarity over the goal they begin to explore the reality of the situation. This is where they let the team member tell their story and explain what is going on for them right now. This part of the GROW model is important because it helps the project manager empathise with the team member and understand how they are experiencing the situation. When we are trying to help someone move forward we often make assumptions that are incorrect. Asking open and exploratory questions help us avoid that. It's reasonable to expect that the majority of the conversation may take place in this second step of the model.

Tell me what is going on at the moment.
What is happening right now?
How do you know there is an issue?
Can you describe that in more detail?
What's the real challenge here for you?
What are the different elements you need to consider when tackling this?
What have you done so far to improve things?
What have you already tried?
What worked? What did not work?
What obstacles are in your way?

Options – Brainstorm options for moving forward

When the project manager has explored the current situation in enough depth, they move to the third step of the GROW model – options. This is where they explore how the problem could be resold. Together with the team member they brainstorm options for moving forward and look at what the team member could do to overcome the problem. It's important to give the team member enough time to consider how they can overcome their obstacle. If they get stuck the project manager can chip in with ideas, but it's important not to generate all the options for them.

Let's brainstorm all ideas and options for resolving this problem.
What can you do to overcome this obstacle?
What steps can you take towards this goal?
What have you seen work in similar situations?
If you could devote all your time to this one thing, what would you do?
What else could you do?
Which option would be the fastest/easiest/preferred?
What are the pros and cons of each option?

Way forward – Establish actions

The last part of the GROW model is to develop commitment to a plan of action. Coaching as a leadership style isn't just a nice conversation that supports the team member. It's very much a way to encourage them and challenge them to take responsibility for their situation and their contributions. This part of the model establishes what specific action the team member will take to move forward and by when.

What are you ready to do to resolve this issue?
What are your next steps?
By when will you take this action?
What are the benefits of choosing these options?
When are you going to start and complete each action?
Where are you recording these actions?
What might stop you from carrying them out?
What additional support do you need? Who can help you?
What else do you need to consider?
How are you going to reward yourself when you achieve this?

In a project situation I doubt that the project manager will follow the GROW model to a tee as that may make the conversation rigid and unnatural. Keeping the GROW model in mind, however, as they experiment with the coaching style will provide structure to the conversations.

How to apply coaching

There are a few different ways in which coaching can be applied in a project management environment. One of the quickest ways to improve project performance is to give each project manager access to a dedicated coach, someone who is professionally trained and who can help the project manager to better lead their projects. The coach would typically help the project manager to develop better relationships with team members and stakeholders, communicate more effectively and improve their emotional intelligence. But the external coach shouldn't be restricted to only working with the project manager. They could also conduct team sessions, for instance during project kick-off, to help the team set ground rules and assist them with unresolved conflict.

An external coach can also be of great help if the project gets off track and the team stops performing. It can be hard for the project manager to take a step back in that situation and assess what isn't working whilst simultaneously trying to move the project forward in light of tight schedules. In that situation an external pair of eyes from a coach who is skilled at observing human behaviour, asking the right questions and navigating conflict can be a huge help in getting the team and the project back on track. The coach would help the team to discuss and resolve their issues in a constructive way and would also look at the team dynamic and how to improve collaboration.

Another option, which can be combined with the previous one, is to teach project managers how to coach their team in a way that's empowering and motivating. That means showing them and helping them to apply the methods from this chapter. The way to do that would be to enroll the project managers into a training programme where they learn to use coaching as a leadership style.

A third option is one where the organisation pairs up their project managers so that they can coach each other across projects. This is an extremely powerful and sustainable option that not only helps the individual project manager to better manage their projects, but it also builds long-lasting friendships and a support network. Being a project manager can be a lonely job, not least for project managers who are working on a client's site. With peer-to-peer coaching, each person is given a safe space to share and discuss the most difficult situations on their project. They benefit from the insights of another experienced project manager and they get to practice their coaching skills.

These different applications of coaching complement each other and can happen simultaneously. But organisations certainly shouldn't expect their project managers to be able to coach their teams without providing them with the necessary training. It takes time and effort to learn to relate differently to people – asking insightful questions, listening and creating a safe space.

Potential pitfalls

Asking project managers to coach without training them first is definitely a pitfall to look out for. But there are others. When project managers begin to coach they must be careful to not overuse the coaching style without using other leadership approaches. Although the coaching style is one of the most powerful for improving project performance, some situations call for the application of other leadership styles.

When the project is in the start-up phase, for instance, it can be very powerful to coach the team to define how they would like to work together. But team members also need clear directions from the project manager and a vision to work towards. They need to know what the project is all about. What is expected of them and what will they personally gain from being involved? In this situation it may be most appropriate for the project manager to lead from the front, being visionary and setting the example. As they lead from the front, the project manager will identify and communicate the strategic goals and allow team members to figure out the best way to accomplish them. As the team begins to find its own two feet, the project manager can slowly begin to take a step back and coach from behind.

There will also be situations where the project manager needs to make use of a directive leadership style. As we have already discussed, a command and control style can have a diminishing effect on a project team, but that doesn't mean that it should never be used. A highly directive style works well in crisis situations and in times when the stakes are high. Under those circumstances it's important that orders are followed so that the issue can be resolved in an effective manner. If the building is burning, get out!

There may also be situations where the project manager needs to lead from the front by demonstrating how something is done. This may be the case when the team's standard is not up to scratch or when the team is very inexperienced. Imagine a situation where a team member is new in their role and genuinely doesn't know how to do something. The new team member may need the project manager to handhold them and perhaps mentor them before they start using a coaching approach.

One of the biggest mistakes I personally made when I first qualified as a coach and wanted to use the skills on my team was that I became overly supportive. I distanced myself too much from the directive leadership style that I had previously used. At a subconscious level I was probably trying to make amends by being overly empathic and supportive. Offering our support and encouragement is great, but team members also need to be challenged and held to account. An effective project manager will do that by using the GROW model: First, by encouraging the team member to come up with possible options to resolve the problem (what could you do to resolve this?) and second, by asking them what action they will take (what will you do to resolve this and by when?). If the project manager is only supportive, they will end up owning the actions along with the responsibly for implementing them. This is not an empowering approach and it won't lead to a high-performing team where all members contribute.

Conclusion

When project managers begin to use coaching as a leadership style, we can expect it to have a direct positive effect on project performance. That's because the project managers will understand how to better unleash and utilise human potential on the project team. They will learn how to engage and involve people by listening, asking questions, empathising and challenging the team to take ownership for solutions and actions. Their leadership and emotional intelligence skills will improve and they will be better able to support the team by leading from behind. In this way they will create a safe and stimulating space for team members to come forward and contribute. I would say that coaching is a life skill and a necessity for project leaders.

Chapter 4

Coping with the unexpected

Flexibility, resilience and culture

Andreas G.M. Nachbagauer and Iris Schirl-Boeck

Introduction

Despite undoubted improvements in knowledge, methods and practice in project management, performance, especially of unique, large and complex projects, is still not satisfactory. While much has been written both by academics and practitioners on risk management and dealing with uncertainty in the last decade, we believe that considering the impact of the unexpected allows for better project results and robust efficacy. Challenged by potential disruptions characterized by growing volatility, uncertainty and ambiguity, we must calculate for the increasing importance of surprising incidents. Projects and project management need to adapt quickly to environmental and internal changes while still targeting the aim of the project – and we cannot get rid of this challenge.

To be sure, the unexpected was always an issue in projects. Alas, undeterred by the expeditionary character, project management for a long time stuck to the idea of controlling outcomes and steering the project in a rational and predictable manner, neglecting the effects of the unexpected on time, budget and scope. Modern approaches to project management attempt to get a grip on uncertainties by anticipating and preparing for changes as early as possible. Recent methodologies of organizing such as Agile and lean project management, design thinking or the open-source movement are proposing other ways of coordination to deal with uncertainty as a central feature of projects. They believe a high degree of freedom for the parties involved allowing for quicker decisions and self-determined choice to be promising in uncertain situations.

We argue that learnings from adjacent fields can improve and stabilize the performance of projects. Especially, we focus on practices in high-risk and safety-critical environments that are usually named when exemplifying dealing with the unexpected in an urgent manner: Managing in these settings cannot afford ignoring the unexpected, as the consequences of one mistake can lead to major losses of life and value. In organization theory, capabilities to deal with abrupt changes in the environment have been investigated from various theoretical viewpoints, particularly high-reliability organizations and organizational resilience.

The unexpected

The unexpected is that event, that one does not expect – that sounds trivial. The expected and the unexpected are not entities in themselves but are 'produced' by and from the perspective of an observer, either an organization, an employee or a team (Dorniok & Mohe 2011, Weick 1993). Thus, the unexpected can only be understood in relation to an observer. Observations are not deliberate, however; they are based on individual and shared expectations, and within organizations on strategy, structure and culture.

Taking a closer look, we can differentiate between events that occur totally surprising, and 'outcomes or events that actors have identified as possibly existing, but do not know whether they will take place or not' (Geraldi et. al 2010: 553). This spectrum of growing uncertainty is frequently known by the labels of known knowns, known unknowns, unknown knowns and unknown unknowns (De Meyer et al. 2002, Cléden 2009, Winch 2010). Unknown knowns are events where we lack data necessary to assign objective probabilities but can ground expectations in historical practices, known unknowns are incidents that are possible in principle, but we do not know when, where and how they will occur (Sanderson 2012, Winch & Maytorena 2012). Ultimately, unknown unknowns demark the passage from uncertainty to the unexpected. The conceptualization of the 'unknown unknowns' reflects 'the actuality of projects as social processes requiring ongoing construction of the appearance of certainty and clarity in the midst of complex uncertainty and ambiguity' (Atkinson et al. 2006: 696).

For unexpected situations that long for a long-term reaction only, organizations will have enough time to search for additional information, calculate by sophisticated analysis methods and plan in-depth. The proper time of the organization allows for an uncoupling from the external pressures of expectation, groups can 'muddle through' or wait for the next decision-making opportunity ('garbage can') and individuals will sense when the time for decisions (regarding their own interests) has come. However, issues become more complicated when they are urgent. Even though there can be degrees of urgency and different understandings thereof, the value of delivering the work to be done is agreed to be greater than the likely extra cost. Urgent unexpected situations always mean working faster than normal and this usually involves increased costs, for example, for unplanned temporary use of additional resources, or quality reduction (Wearne & White-Hunt 2014). Thus, we will concentrate on the unexpected that urges short-term reaction.

Projects and project performance

Project types, risk and uncertainty

For our purpose, we will differentiate projects according to their level of complexity and their level of uniqueness in a 2 × 2 matrix (Figure 4.1).

In simple contexts, predictions seem to be feasible: Cause-and-effect relationships are stable and known, patterns are repetitive, information needed to predict and control is available. In complicated contexts, many thousand components might exist, nevertheless, coherence is comprehensible and effects between elements can be separated from each other. There is a correct interpretation of the functioning of the system, but as it is not obvious, analysis requires time and expertise (Snowden & Boone 2007). In the spectrum of growing uncertainty, these states are domains of the 'known knowns' and the 'known unknowns'.

For simple and complicated projects, risk management is sufficient. Risk is, at least in principle, calculable, and predictions can be expressed by a statistically or mathematically

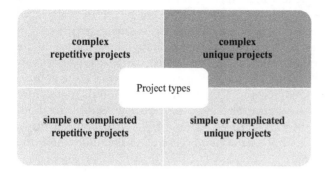

Figure 4.1 Project types.

determined probability. Risk can be seen as an a priori probability where the decision maker is able to either assign objective probabilities to a known range of future events on the basis of mathematically 'known chances', or to assign objective probabilities on the basis of empirical/statistical data about such events in the past (Sanderson 2012). Uncertainty demarks events in the future that are unknown, and/or their consequences cannot be estimated. In this case, we do not possess an appropriate simple method to 'calculate' probabilities or we do not have enough information to feed our algorithm, or both. Still, conventional management in uncertain environments is feasible. Going beyond traditional risk management, advanced project risk and planning methods based on stochastics and learning will do for this type of project. Quite a lot of recent advances in project management center round complicated repetitive projects: Decision support and expert system, neuronal networks, big data and data mining, Monte-Carlo algorithms and simulations, to name a few.

Complexity is defined as a state where more linkages exist than we (normally) can describe or analyze – again, we refer to an observer (Luhmann 2000). Furthermore, the system comprises a high number and variety of elements to be coordinated, behavior is not (fully) depending on the past. System boundaries change over time with unstable input-output relationships (Checkland 1999, Stacey 2011). This holds true for large, long-lasting projects with a variety of strong and interdependent stakeholders. Given there is no ultimate level or rule of decision-making, different observers will end up with different explanations and dissenting forecasts for the same observations. Individuals and organizations are increasingly overwhelmed to describe and process complexity. With long-term outcomes being partly emergent and partly intentional, interventions could be planned, but the outcome could not be predicted by running the system once.

Yet, the system behavior in complex projects is not chaotic or random. Even though the chance to interpret mutually influencing, recursive or simultaneous effects is limited within the linear perspective, and we might find non-determined tipping points, we still have the chance to understand some basic mechanics of the system, when we have time to learn from previous experiences in a trial-and-error approach. Cause and effect can be deduced in retrospect, and we find emergent instructive patterns that we can use to make assumptions about the future behavior of the system (Senge 1990, Snowden & Boone 2007).

While processes of risk management are supposed to make it possible to transfer threats and opportunities into – calculable and therefore decidable – risks, advanced methods respect uncertainty. Alas, they are grounded in learning and experience from similar projects and environments. With repetitive projects, individuals, the teams and organizations can learn from previous events, and based on that, can manage even complex projects. While single loop learning, i.e. correcting individual error, is the domain of simple and complicated projects, complex projects are the application field of double loop learning, i.e. understanding the systems behavior to develop new working methods or optimize prevailing work routines (Argyris & Schön 1978). With non-repetitive, unique projects that cannot rely on well-established processes, chances for single and even double loop learning shrink up.

We doubt that, these conceptions, even advanced ones, are capable of handling the unexpected, at least when we capitalize beyond complicated, repetitive projects. While simple and complicated projects allow for ordered processes and repetition for learnings, our article will mainly focus on complex projects that previously have not existed in a comparable way.

Project performance as project resilience

The project's reason to exist is to deliver (defined) values to the customer or project sponsor. Within this framework, the maxim of project management is to ensure conformance to time, budget and scope constraints. We do not question these assumptions. But achieving these goals is challenged by growing instability and complexity in non-repetitive projects. We define high-performing projects as projects where the unexpected is dealt with effectively. We believe that these endeavors can be best met by incorporating ideas of resilient organizing into project management and managing the project-oriented organization.

'Resilio' (Latin) means to rebound, thus suggesting a material that can absorb high pressure and quickly bounce back without breaking or a relatively quick response to a crisis (Bodin & Wiman 2004, Norris et al. 2008). Originating from psychology and thus focusing on the individual, the notion of resilience connects to the ability to sense and correct maladaptive tendencies and to cope positively with unexpected situations (Bandura 1998).

Individual resilience is the psychological capacity that allows individuals to withstand stress, to cope with adverse situations and even grow in the face of crisis (Masten 2007, Ong et al. 2009, Wright et al. 2013). Factors normally connected to resilience can be grouped into four categories: personality traits, problem-solving skills, social competences and emotions. Furthermore, literature describes personal characteristics to be important for resilience in the work context: confidence (positive emotions and optimism), purposefulness (self-control and conscientiousness), adaptability (intelligence and problem solving, ability to improvise) and social support (self-awareness and sociability) (Rees et al. 2015, Cooper et al. 2013). While older research treated resilience as a personal trait, recent literature highlights that individual resilience is highly dependent on the context. Thus, resilience-enhancing factors successful in one context might not be relevant in another context. Furthermore, studies point to the importance of social support for individual resilience (Fletcher & Sarkar 2013, Bonanno 2004, Wilson & Ferch 2005).

Based on individual competences, team resilience enables the team to jointly sense and correct maladaptive tendencies. Abilities to cope positively with unexpected situations can arise from a team's positive orientation towards acquiring new skills, mastering new situations, and improving competences, and from collective efficacy, i.e. the group's shared belief in its conjoint capabilities to organize and execute the courses of action (Ortiz-de-Mandojana & Bansal 2016, Bandura 1998). The team needs to understand the full situation and to have the feeling of manageability. This asks for options of influence and action for every individual, for transparency of goals, impact factors, events and situations (Borgert 2013).

Organizational resilience can be defined as the organization's ability to rebound from adverse and unexpected situations towards the right path to success and is therefore understood as the capacity to resist major changes and endure perturbation without systemic change (Hamel & Välikangas 2003, Ortiz-de-Mandojana & Bansal 2016, Välikangas 2010). Resilient organizations are characterized by 'conceptual slack, ad hoc problem-solving networks and […] rich media to communicate' (Sutcliffe & Vogus 2003: 101). They reduce the degree of control; they lessen immediate activity and increase their requisite variety. Tasks are not understood as instructions or fixed responsibilities but are formed by coordinating activities. Against the backdrop of the shared goal, team members are encouraged to track possible misassumptions and to question known routines. Resilience on an organizational level also stems from processes that encourage mindfulness (Darkow & Geiger 2017, Sutcliffe et al. 2016).

Informed by organization theory and practice on resilience we define high-performing projects on three levels: They are led by highly resilient project managers together with highly resilient project teams which are embedded in highly resilient organizations. After a short view on selected literature, we will show how a project-oriented organization, its project managers and teams should act before, during and after unexpected events in their projects to enhance their overall project performance.

High-reliability and resilient projects – First insights

High-reliability organizing has originally focused on safety-critical environments only and on absolute reliability: Well-known application fields are nuclear power plants, aircraft carriers and air traffic control systems. These organizations share some characteristics, i.e. their technologies are risky and present the potential for error, the scale of possible consequences from errors or mistakes precludes learning through experimentation, and they are characterized by complex technologies and complex work. High-reliability organizations emphasize the necessary mindfulness and organizational preparation for the unexpected incident, as well as learning effects from such events (Weick & Sutcliffe 2007). High-reliability organizations strive for flexibility and delegate decision-making responsibility to the shop-floor level; they put knowledge and skills above hierarchy. Weick, Sutcliffe and Obstfeld (1999) recommend five principles for managing the unexpected: (1) preoccupation of failure, (2) reluctance to simplify, (3) sensitivity to operations, (4) commitment to resilience and (5) deference to expertise.

Research on resilient organizing, on the other hand, concentrates on emergency and rescue crews, police and SWAT units, military forces and similar groups. These organizations operate in turbulent and confusing fields with many surprising events, but still, they have to decide and react fast, reliably and confident (Farjoun & Starbuck 2007, Sutcliffe & Vogus 2003). The starting point was Weick's (1993) seminal study on the Mann Gulch firefighters' disaster that showed how structures are bound to fail when people do not understand what is going on in their environment and even more so, when they cannot make sense of the other one's actions. Recommendations comprise reducing the degree of (immediate) control, slowing down direct activity and increasing the required diversity. Tasks are not understood as instructions or fixed responsibilities but are formed by coordinating activities, and team members are encouraged to question known routines. Within teams, mindfulness and a shared situation awareness should be promoted (Darkow & Geiger 2017, Barton & Sutcliffe 2010). The incident-command system, characteristic for armed forces and emergency aid organizations, is more viable and successful in unexpected situations when there is also space for role-switching, authority migrating and system resetting (Bigley & Roberts 2001).

Saunders, Gale and Sherry (2016) analyzed project management responses to project uncertainty taken from high-reliability practices. In an empirical study based on 47 vignettes of safety-critical civil nuclear and aerospace projects, they found out that project managers had adopted high-reliability practices for managing uncertainty in projects. When drafting 'high reliability project organizing', Saunders (2015) has generated the following recommendations:

- High-reliability projects have clear high-level decision-making rules to enable the project team to make progress even in uncertain situations. A strong sense of mission needs to be developed and articulated in the team.
- High-reliability projects have a strong organizational culture built on openness, communities of practice, team learning from mistakes, knowledge sharing, multidisciplinary problem solving and trust.
- In high-reliability projects, the team is encouraged to discuss and negotiate its way to a plan of action matching the specific project situation; a flexible and staged conformance to project processes is possible.
- Complacency is a threat to project success: the project team is resilient and reluctant to simplify interpretations of project situations. Reflection, robust debate and even elements of anarchy are fostered in high-reliability projects.
- With an 'ability to prosper in the paradoxes', high-reliability project organizing is encouraging redundancy and conceptual slack in terms of processing multiple interpretations of events.

Another important strategy to manage uncertainty occurring in projects is based on (personal and team) experience: being explorative, associative, sensual and in intense relation to the project environment (Heidling 2015). Rather than following best practice project management models as the starting point of research, newer approaches, such as 'projects-as-practice' (Blomquist et al. 2010), highlight the everyday struggle of keeping projects on track while dealing with the unexpected. Atkinson, Crawford and Ward (2006) suggested that uncertainty management asks for trust building, sensemaking, organizational learning and an appropriate organizational culture. The exposure to the unexpected requires an open approach less oriented towards planning: 'projects are better described as journeys of exploration in given direction, rather than strict plan-following endeavors' (Perminova et al. 2008: 74).

A good example of this new thinking is the megaproject to build a 20-km long tunnel under the area north of Sydney Harbour, stated as having been broadly successful, managed to create 'a project culture that was explicitly designed and crafted to encourage shared behaviors, decision-making, and values' (Pitsis et al. 2003: 576). This project culture included rather Agile (or adhocratic) values by projecting the desired ends and visualizing the means to achieve the projected future, both being subject to constant revision. A formal statement of collaborative values was shared with the team focusing on producing solutions 'best for project' and having a 'no blame' culture, combined with monetarized key performance indicators (KPIs) and a risk/reward scheme that fostered project team collaboration.

Improving performance: Successfully managing the unexpected

Even though high-reliability organizing has originally focused on safety-critical environments only and resilient organizing primarily on field operations, we believe that important lessons can be drawn for managing projects. We expand on the ideas addressing the relevant roles in projects, namely project managers, project teams and the organization (top management) and identify their options for action when being confronted with the unexpected along the timeline:

(1) Anticipation: the phase before an unexpected event occurs.
(2) Coping: the phase during detecting, deciding and recovery.
(3) Adoption: the phase after having managed the unexpected.

In the phase of anticipation, individuals, the team and the organization focus on observation, identification and preparation for the unexpected. This is accompanied by the willingness to be surprised and by the reluctance to explain everything with well-known patterns – a modus that is particularly difficult for experts (Barton & Sutcliffe 2009). Focusing on possible misconceptions, on the questioning of known routines and on errors in general, various perspectives are deliberately included. Barton, Sutcliffe, Vogus, and DeWitt (2015) talk about anomalizing, taking proactive steps to become attentive to deviations, to understand them better and more fully, and to be less attached to history. Of importance is the awareness of the contingency: Any opposing decision or action could be equally acceptable in the first place.

The phase of coping starts with detecting and accepting the unexpected. While not every unexpected event triggers a crisis, the potentially threatening unexpected that requires a short-term response breaks up the organization's normal operations. Denying and repressing the need for change are common mechanisms that have to be overcome in this stage. The core of the second part of this phase, the search for and implementation of solutions, is a combination of sensemaking and targeted action.

The focus of the final phase, adaptation, is reflection, evaluation and learning from the event. Christianson, Farkas, Sutcliffe and Weick (2009) differentiate between learning for rare events as result-oriented consideration (lessons learned) and learning through rare events while dealing with the unexpected (experiencing). The second mode addresses the individual's and organization's ability to permanently anchor learning experiences in new organizational structures and structures of mind as well as in actions.

The three phases are interdependent and closely interlinked; neither the linear sequence nor clear demarcations of the phases are given. Nevertheless, it is helpful to consider the phase transitions in order to be successful.

Project manager's perspective: Empowering others

Before the unexpected occurs, the project manager should become aware of the inherent complexity and uncertainty of projects. Planners can fight this complexity and uncertainty, ignore it or try to use it. When trying to use it, seeing complexity and uncertainty as considerably irreducible, project managers should follow 'a science of navigation in which there is a balance between opening and closing a process and the content, between the certain and the uncertain, the simple and the complex' (Giezen 2013: 739).

Project managers need to use innovative actions by creatively designing action patterns such as re-shuffling of resources or outsourcing. To accomplish that they need to detach from other project activities and negotiate favorable project conditions to deal with unexpected events rather than just obeying the plan. In the same vein, Bertolini and Salet (2007: 6) recommend 'strategic incrementalism' when dealing with uncertainty and complexity. Project managers should be 'keeping in mind and frequently testing and actualizing the strategic mission of the project on the one hand and being adaptive, flexible and inventive in muddling through all small steps and daily worries on the other hand'.

What makes that even more difficult is the variety of stakeholders, with their different values, interests and power positions. Stakeholder engagement helps to understand the partner's interests and way of thinking and provides the chance to build up trustful relationships. This end can be pursued by different means, starting with simple communication and information efforts. More sophisticated strategies comprise co-optation: the tactic to bring influential outsiders into one's network, and representation: having an advocate at the stakeholder, either directly or − sometimes even more effective and reliable − via third parties (Bouquet & Birkinshaw 2008).

While encouraging trust and openness within the team, the project manager should strive to be undisputedly accepted as team leader − and not just as (project) manager. Charles Pellerin (2009), former National Aeronautics and Space Administration (NASA) astrophysicist, developed a team performance analysis tool named '4-D System', which targets technical project teams and overcomes their assumed reluctance to social team-building processes. He based his considerations on a far-reaching incident: When he was the responsible person for the Hubble Space Telescope project, he and his team oversaw that Hubble was launched with a flawed mirror, due to a leadership failure by unnoticing social shortfalls in the project. Pellerin simplifies leadership into four dimensions which have to be addressed to be an effective leader:

Cultivating: Leaders appreciate and care for others and want a better world.
Including: Leaders include others and bring integrity to relationships and build teams.
Visioning: Leaders vision the impossible while acknowledging difficult realities, and constantly create, needing to be best.
Directing: Leaders take organized action and direct others toward results.

Project managers should create a constructive team atmosphere in the beginning and empower the team to define its way to reach the project goals by itself. Project managers are responsible for creating a non-blaming culture and a culture of trust, depicting the existing diversity and reinforcing the awareness that every single person is of importance. Ex ante team-building efforts and face-to-face interactions in crisis situations help in generating intersubjective meaning and developing a common situational model for action. Ex ante team building is necessary, as there is simply no time left to create a common sense and a collective situation model of what happens during crisis situations. Weick (1993) gives us an impressive example of the importance of sensemaking in his famous interpretation of the Mann Gulch disaster. Structure, he concludes, is bound to fail when people do not understand what is going on in their environment and even more so, when they cannot make sense of the other one's actions. This process is necessarily in need of constant interaction with others. People in organizations spend much time on negotiating what is considered a decent representation of what is going on and what reality 'really' is (Weick 1995).

Since communication is crucial, it is important to have a clear picture of one's (virtual) communication network in advance. The form of communication should be clarified, i.e. when to use one-way or two-way communication, when and how to use feedback loops, the preferred communication channel for which (kind of) information and whom to inform on which aspects, to name but a few. It is equally important to have clear and comprehensive language at hand, i.e. common technical terms and concepts, mutual understanding of the semantic field – which might be a huge challenge in international projects.

During the management of the unexpected, project managers need to 'exercise the art of managing the unexpected parallel to executing the plan' (Söderholm 2008: 81). This is not to say that it is automatically the project manager's responsibility to make all the decisions. Rather, the project manager should quickly delegate the decision power to the one team member that can contribute the most to solving the problem by knowing the most about the unexpected situation. And it's the project manager's task to encourage fast solutions, as fast responses are worth more than correct but too late actions. Söderholm (2008) showed that project managers, while initiating extensive meetings to keep up team commitment and urgency, regularly detach from operative project activities. In the same vein, practices in resilient organizations such as the search for gaps, distancing (both physical and psychological) from the events, shifting of priorities and time-outs, are central to coordination and replace – at least in part – traditional coordination means (Darkow & Geiger 2017).

A second very important task of project managers is to stabilize the emotional situation which requires high emotional intelligence (Geraldi et al. 2010). Especially in a crisis, leaders should convey confidence and trust. Meaning management concentrates on stabilizing the emotional situation in the team and sensemaking of the (interacting) actions. The maintenance of interaction and engagement is important in order to facilitate the mutual reinforcement of meaning management and the team's responsiveness to external and internal requirements, while isolation and the feeling of vulnerability have a negative effect on this connection. Resilience is then not a resource but a constant process of relating to the environment through a process of understanding, responding to and absorbing variations (Barton & Sutctliffe 2017).

Researchers agree that more and open communication is crucial to address the unexpected; especially face-to-face interactions seem to be important to generate intersubjective meaning (Weick & Sutcliffe 2007, Sutcliffe & Vogus 2003, Barton & Sutcliffe 2010).

However, the tighter the time horizon, the more restricted communication must be to avoid information overflow and allow for quick reaction. To gain valuable information in a timely manner and to secure the coordinated action in response to the unexpected, it appears necessary to communicate at the same time more intensely, but also more specifically and selectively.

Stakeholder engagement is one major task of project managers in unexpected situations and includes proper escalation, negotiation and prioritization. The project manager needs full support from the top management and other important stakeholders but without time-consuming communication involved. Just because top management support is so crucial, it is important for the project manager to communicate with executives in an efficient and direct way, with oral reporting rather than lengthy reports in written form.

After handling the unexpected, the project manager needs to make sure that learning processes are brought into action so that the team can better deal with similar situations in the future. Too often, lessons learned are just seen as an unloved formality.. Lessons learned point to the need for a culture of social communication and decision-making, openness and transparency, readiness for curiosity and the acceptance of people as they are with all their mistakes. It is up to the project managers to instill a sense of utter utility of lessons learned and document mistakes.

Project team perspective: Shared situation awareness

Before the unexpected occurs, team-building efforts should become of utmost importance, with the goal to achieve shared points of reference for decisions and to become mindful and open towards uncertainty. There is a need to create a team culture that is sensible for the unexpected, closely connected to a no-blame or just-action attitude, a high transparency of task fulfillment and permanent and joint learning, especially regarding developing resilience. Mindfulness is highly welcome, i.e. paying attention to internal and external present-moment events, providing a basis for experiencing minor deviations from the normal course of action, that could be – in the long run – prove harmful (Sutcliffe et al. 2016).

Shared situation awareness allows the team to understand the initial situation in a collective image, to make appropriate conjectures and take the actions the new situation requires (Endsley 2003, Schaub 2012). Shared situation awareness calls for three things: appropriate visual preparations which are understood by all parties concerned; the willingness to raise and to allow critical questions on the team level, and an organizational culture that calls for contradictory observations and views and welcomes the opinions of unconventional thinkers. Somewhat contradictory, a better understanding of the unexpected can only be achieved by a diverse team with different views and approaches – and at the same time grounded on a shared view about aims and actions. Team members need to feel valued and included, need to have a realistic and hopeful future and to know what is expected of them and have the resources to succeed (Pellerin 2009).

The advantage of flexible reaction during the handling of the unexpected is lost if persons set existing knowledge, beliefs, expectations and skills absolute. If perception is a constructive process, we then should be critical and question why certain information is communicated redundantly and intensively, while another one is completely overlooked. Especially in situations of operational hustle and bustle, relevant information is ignored, action is more oriented towards reacting as quickly as possible, rather than approaching issues actively and plan-based. The team therefore needs a mental model that helps to portray reality fast and appropriate. For once, the 'wisdom of doubt' protects persons to apply existing knowledge without reflection to new situations (Weick & Sutcliffe 2007).

Recent approaches promote 'irrational' perceptions as a major source of information for quick decision-making and of quality of actions. They accept that information is not only based on rational, analytic and conscious thought but also on sensual perception. One could say that it is rational to act allegedly irrational. In complex situations of uncertainty and urgency, it is more important to have a quick and acceptable decision than an optimal one. Given the limited information-processing capacities, the costs for the improvement of information and the urgency to act, a 'good' decision then depends more on the perception and framings of individuals than on 'objective' criteria (Stingl & Geraldi 2017a, 2017b). Following gut feelings, heuristics and simple rules adapted to specific environmental situations is, in this perspective, not irrational, but a very rational handling of the scarcity of time and information (Neumer 2009, Gigerenzer et al. 2011, Sull & Eisenhardt 2015).

Professional toolsets should be expanded to include professional improvisation, understood as an unplanned, occasional regulation (Kamoche et al. 2002, Böhle & Porschen-Hueck 2014). 'When we cannot predict cause and effect any longer, we need to experiment' (Borgert 2015: 70, English translation). While in good times the possible room to maneuver should be agreed upon between different stakeholders, it should be clear in urgent situations where and to what extent improvisation is permissible and whether there is trust in the other person. Good improvisation lives from creativity and experiences, but also from good preparation, and mutual (blind) understanding and confidence – pointing at the importance of trust, courage in decision-making and a culture of compensation of losses. It is essential to make the decisions comprehensible for all team members to ensure understanding and commitment.

Not only project managers should apply interpersonal skills to manage stakeholders' expectations (building trust, resolving conflicts, active listening and overcoming resistance to change), but also the project team needs to engage better with external stakeholders, especially the affected public, environmental groups and regulators (Littau et al. 2015, Brookes et al. 2015). However, in urgent unexpected situations, communication paths to external stakeholders need to be defined well in advance, so that quick team reactions are possible. What is inherent in large complex projects is their dilemma between control and commitment (van Marrewijk 2005). While the project team might have no real power to act, the sponsor might use its control power for his own sake and thereby provoke low project team commitment.

Through mutual feedback, project teams can prepare themselves after having managed the unexpected to avoid similar mistakes in the future. We need a 'culture of errors' that allows talking about errors, failures and near misses rather than displacing them, a culture in which mistakes are accepted. Nevertheless, this shift to more open conceptions is very demanding, as decision in projects must be acceptable not only within the organization but more so beyond the organization's boundaries to meet the legitimacy requirements of the environment.

Organizational perspective: Accepting 'illegality'

To be able to decide fast, it is important to have a clear picture of one's communication network before the unexpected occurs that could be activated in crisis situations. It's equally important to know both power and expertise within the project and its relevant environment. Many authors ask for flat hierarchies and liquid, at least adjustable responsibilities. Concepts like Holacracy (Robertson 2015) promise to be better suited for a complex and fast-changing world with a bunch of daily surprises just because they reduce traditional hierarchies, duties and fixed responsibilities. More recent conceptions of project management like Agility (Beck et al. 2001, Laufer et al. 2015, Hobbs & Petit 2017) weaken the predominance of time, budget and scope for project success by concentrating more on client needs and involving stakeholder interests. This definitely influences the significance of risk and uncertainty for project management, i.e. replacing foresight and avoidance by consciously allowing for insecurity in favor of a look forward (Drury et al., 2012).

For managing unexpected situations, organizations should allow for flexible teams along informal knowledge and adaptable responsibilities. Decision power should migrate to the persons with the most expertise of the specific uncertain situation. This asks for a new hierarchical understanding where informal networks are given the competence to act. A closer look at flexible or 'flat' concepts shows that they do not abolish hierarchy in the original meaning, i.e. defined area of accountability, functional responsibility and communication flow patterns. Rather, they re-define them away from stable and formal norms to learning and adaptable structures. Even with flat hierarchies and open communication, coordination and common orientations are still necessary. Just because the unexpected can disrupt structures, it is even more important to have a clear basis to act on. To effectively balance structure and autonomy, organizations need to consider relationships in and between projects and units (Borgert 2015).

Shared situation awareness requires the willingness to raise and to allow critical questions, even invite team members to take the position of a 'devil's advocate'; and an organizational culture that calls for contradictory observations and views and welcomes the opinions of unconventional thinkers. In a stressful situation, we cannot always easily draw a clear line between acceptable improvisation and illegal action. Thus, recommending professional improvising, we have to go one step further and tolerate a certain degree of illegality, if this illegality is useful (Neuberger 1995). In fact, we can see that 'useful illegality' or 'creative disobedience' is widely accepted in business life – and embedded in still clear (formal and informal) structures.

Reducing the impact of more formal decision-making premises must be accompanied by a growing importance of persons (leaders, figureheads) and (organizational, team) culture. Organizational Culture defines what is understood as self-evident and taken-for-granted matter of course that everyone who is familiar with the organization understands and accepts. The importance of organizational culture is based on the observation that all other structural elements are interpreted (framed) against the background of (more or less) jointly shared considerations on how the world and its events are to be understood (Weick 1995).

Learning from the incidents in the confrontation with the unexpected requires an organizational and team culture that allows talking about mistakes and failures instead of concealing them, a culture that accepts mistakes. To reach out for resilient project organizations, single loop learning, i.e. correcting individual error corrections, or double loop learning, i.e. development of new working methods or optimizing prevailing work routines will not suffice. Deutero-learning means questioning previous patterns, values and strategies (Argyris & Schön 1978). However, norms, values, beliefs and, above all, organizational culture are normally resistant to learning. Initiating change is hard and constant work, and an ongoing process to be kept alive all along and deliberately.

Lessons learned: Examining select project cases

Taken from an empirical study conducted by the authors in Austria in spring 2018 amongst project managers, eight vignettes of incidents and companies, all of them ranked as large enterprises (more than 250 employees), were designed (Nachbagauer, forthcoming). All the respondents display long term and international experience as project managers, most of them having an additional function within their company besides managing projects.

In the case reports, no systematic connections between successfully managing the unexpected and features normally ascribed to project-oriented organizations, i.e. orientation towards the environment, sensitivity and mindfulness, readiness to accept diversity and equality in the team, were found. Even more so, successful organizations are overall characterized by a higher formalization grade, decision-making is centralized, and individualistic and bilateral information relations prevail. In addition, it was not the complex projects that were most likely to fail, as predicted by literature (Sanderson 2012, Saunders et al. 2015). However, organizations that defined themselves as project oriented are more apt to manage sudden incidents. Data suggests that project-oriented organizations are not more successful in handling sudden events because they show typical characteristics of project-oriented organizations, but because they respond smarter by making flexible use of these characteristics.

Smart project managers used to integrate the team in both the detection and analysis phase and in preparing the decision. Contrary to the rather flat and empowering features in the coping phase, communication about how to proceed after the decision was very efficiently organized and centralized again. Obviously, organizations managed swiftly to adapt their style of management to the needs of the situation. This behavior is in line with recent insights in research on organizational resilience and the suggestions presented above (Barton & Sutcliffe 2017).

In the cases, the surprises occurred mainly in those areas, which run counter to the basic assumptions of the respective organizational culture. Expectations can develop into blind spots where unexpected events can develop and become unmanageable. For example, process cultures were challenged by new and quick to implement regulations, and loss of clear-cut direction, whereas macho culture organizations took the risky road by ill-defined project charters.

When the first instabilities are visible, individuals, the team and the organization focus on tracing the unexpected by the application of a wide range of tools, including weak signals. Questioning known routines is crucial in this phase, and this might explain why project managers in complex projects are better prepared to handle the unexpected. Put simply, they are readier to expect the unexpected, while in simpler contexts they might stick to their well-trained routines for too long. Especially for stable organizations and strong organizational cultures, accepting a severe problem or a potential crisis is difficult. The final stage of the detection phase is sensemaking and the search for targeted action. In this situation, openness, team learning and knowledge sharing helped the team to discuss and negotiate its way to a plan of action matching the specific project situation.

Once decided on necessary actions, quick response and unquestioned direction is needed: Undisputed hierarchies and rules have a relieving and accelerating effect for decision makers, both subordinates and supervisors. To avoid information overload and allow for quick action, communication must be intensified and at the same time more restricted, specific and selective. Clear and bilateral communication structures and a shared language accomplish that. Smooth coordination, common orientations towards a new goal and a strong sense of mission instill both a basis to act on and stabilize the emotional situation.

Obviously, different capabilities and mindsets are necessary in the three phases, both of the organization and the individuals involved. Initially, attention and empathy for the little things are needed, while later clear and decisive actions and interactions should take place. Responsibilities also shift across the phases: although situation awareness is a task for the entire organization, intertwined data often requires a central hub with specialized observation tools and clear guidelines, thus centralized intelligence. However, as soon as an unexpected event occurs, decision-making powers within the organization should be able to move to those individuals who are actually on-site and competent in the specific situation. The subsequent learning process again included the entire project team, and in more important cases also the organization.

Challenges and pitfalls

In the best of all worlds, recommendations and hints to achieve resilient projects and project-oriented organizations seem to be trivial and accessible. However, things are easier said than done, and academics are in the comfortable situation of not having to go through the hassles of the level. To be sure, achieving resilience or high-reliability is a demanding endeavor. The checklist below specifies some considerations before starting:

First Step: Defining the criticality of the project.
- How is the environment shaped? Do we have to face volatile, fast-paced changes in the project environment? Are the value creation processes connected to temporary and knowledge-based co-operations, with integrated information and goods flows in real time? Are we facing diverse, powerful and interdependent stakeholders including a critical public? Do projects span organizational, cultural and professional boundaries? Do we lack clarity of project objectives and project constraints?
- What about the project? Is the project 'really' characterized by complexity? Are relationships unstable, system boundaries changing over time, and the system showing unexpected behavior not explained by the past? Alternatively, is it just a complicated undertaking that we happen to understand not fully now, but will be able to, if we just employ enough time and effort? Is the project unique or can we learn from (structural) similarities of related projects, even far related ones? Can we draw on our own experience; can we access someone else's experiences?

- Will urgency be an issue? Who is in charge to decide on the pace of the project? Can we influence deadlines, adapt milestones, slow down or speed up action? Can we prepare for urgent answers by building up organizational and conceptual slack?

Second Step: Assessing preparedness of the organization:

- Does the organization show a clear and consistent strategy for both the organization and the project? Is the business case unambiguously defined and known to all relevant team members, even down to the shop-floor level? Does the vision serve as a guide in the organization members' minds when the organization's architecture gets fluid?
- Are our structures both well-defined and flexible? Is the organization ready to accept projects as journeys of exploration rather than just following a plan? Are assignments and responsibilities (including informal ones) clear, outspoken and accepted? Is the organization ready to appreciate creative disobedience? Can we draw on determined and adaptable communication structures, allowing for quick and precise coordination?
- Is our organizational culture strong and at the same time built on openness, knowledge sharing and trust? Does the culture depict the existing diversity and reinforce the awareness that every single person is of importance? Is this culture underpinned by a structural change in human resources management (HRM) systems, most notably reward and career systems? Do the organization and managers concentrate on rewarding team performance and organizational reliability rather than pure individual performance?

Third Step: Enabling acting personnel

- Project managers: Are the project managers smart? Are they capable of sensing different situations, and able to adapt their leadership style and actions to differing demands? Are project managers emotionally stable, and can they convey trust and assurance? Are people in central positions experienced and equipped with leadership – and yet modest enough to step back when necessary? Do leaders really care for their team members as persons?
- Is the project team mature, both in terms of knowledge and motivation? Are the team and team members ready to take over responsibility and voice? Is the project team reluctant to simplify interpretations, welcoming reflection, robust debate and even elements of anarchy? Is the team encouraged to discuss and negotiate its way to a plan of action matching the specific project situation?

Conclusion

To make good decisions in unexpected situations, project managers and the organization have to make use of flexible and resilient team and organizational structures and acknowledge the importance of mindfulness and organizational culture. We showed that high-performing projects have to enact (at least) three equilibria to better face the unexpected: communication vs. time restriction; hierarchy vs. autonomy; and culture and vision vs. structure.

Intense and fast communication is crucial. To avoid messy communication and information overload, we need clear communication structures, a shared language and responsive managers when faced with high time-pressure. Thus, communication should be selective, specific and intense but in an efficient and oral manner according to a pre-defined communication form for each type of information.

The same holds true for decision-making structures: Complex projects need clear decision-making rules. Within such high-level decision-making rules, there should still be enough flexibility to act according to the demands of the situation. Intelligently handling formalized structures does not include abolishing them altogether, but redefining hierarchy. We need new chains of responsibilities, and a few, clear rules which empower the teams to act within them also in the case of unexpected events. This allows the project team to negotiate its way to actions adequate for handling the uncertain situation. Moreover, if necessary, a certain form of 'illegality' and breaking of rules should be accepted by the organization to find fresh solutions.

Because the unexpected can disrupt structures, it is even more important to have a clear basis to act on: Vision, aims and culture serve as a guide in the organization members' minds, when the organization's architecture gets fluid. Planning, ex ante team-building efforts and face-to-face interactions in crisis situations help generate intersubjective meaning and develop a common situational model for action. Resilient projects need a strong organizational culture based on an open error culture combined with the 'wisdom of doubt' and multidisciplinary problem solving, and a team which has developed resilience in crises and is trained in dealing with a sudden rise in urgency and speed.

To manage the unexpected demands the combination of apparent opposites: We ask both for a culture of clear decision-making and defined responsibilities and for a high degree of flexibility and open communication. Combining centralization with decentralization is one of the cornerstones to smart project management, deserving a unique equilibrium of structure and autonomy for each project.

Acknowledgments

This chapter is based on previous working and conference papers within the research project 'Der Beitrag der Human-Factors-Forschung zum Management von Unsicherheit in projektorientierten Organisationen' ('The contribution of Human Factors research for managing uncertainty in project-oriented organizations') at the University of Applied Sciences BFI Vienna, funded by the City of Vienna/Austria, MA 23.

Chapter 5

Leading without authority

Andrew Kallman, Jeff Kissinger and Ted Kallman

Project managers generally have no direct authority over their project teams. Many derive their authority indirectly from a manager, director, or a C-suite executive through a project charter, wherein they have it stated, or by proximity to whom they report. More often than not when a project manager is asked to manage a project, he or she must borrow resources over which he or she has no direct authority to complete the project. Some do this well, but many struggle with it.

What is authority? According to Merriam-Webster, authority is "The power to give orders or make decisions; the power or right to direct or control someone or something; power to influence or command thought, opinion, or behavior." Dictionary.com defines authority as "The power to determine, adjudicate, or otherwise settle issues or disputes; jurisdiction; the right to control, command, or determine." The key word is POWER.

There are several traditional methods that project managers use to gain authority on a project. Many will write the specifics of their authority into the project charter. Others develop the respect and trust of the project sponsor. Sometimes their project team reports to that project sponsor. However, these are all examples of provisional authority.

Leading without direct authority is just as much an art as it is a skill. There are four main areas of emphasis that a project manager should apply themselves to lead without direct authority. They are as follows:

1. Remove roadblocks and anti-Flow that inhibit the team's performance;
2. Get to know each other and build trust;
3. Promote team autonomy;
4. Be a human first and a project manager second.

Remove roadblocks and anti-flow that inhibit the team's performance

Teams that can attain Flow, or optimal performance, can produce their project deliverables on scope, on budget, and on time. Any roadblocks that impair their Flow is anti-Flow. Anti-Flow elements impede a team's ability to create and produce at its optimal level. It clogs the pipes of their capability, communication, creativity, knowledge, productivity, synergy, talent, and everything else they need to work well together and complete a project. Defining and eradicating anti-Flow elements in a project team is a very effective way for a project manager to lead without authority.

The Unified Vision Framework in Figure 5.1 defines the elements necessary to create and establish Flow among teams, as well as organizations. It emphasizes communication, having a common language, and creating a shared vision. Let's start with vision.

Teams without a clear and agreed-to vision are difficult to lead under any circumstances. The importance of vision to a project manager who must lead their project team without authority cannot be overstated, but it can easily be blundered. A vision that is not clearly known and understood by each team member will create fractures in the team, which will adversely affect how they work together, what they are working on, as well as how well they deal with the six constraints of any project: scope, time, cost, quality, resources, and risk.

Vision, itself, is often thrown around by leaders without them really knowing its importance. A clear and accurate vision provides direction to the team. It must be clear and memorable. Have you worked for a company that has a vision statement? If so, do you know it word for word? Chances are that you do not, because most organizational vision statements, although well intentioned, are overly wordy and poorly written. A vision statement must be seven words or less. It must be clear and memorable – even poetic. It must be understood by all who work to achieve that vision. Anything short of that, the organization will not be unified to the degree that it is misaligned.

The same is true for leading a project without authority. The project's vision must be clear and memorable (seven words or less) and connect to the organization's vision. Not only does this make the project more relevant, the organization's leadership will more likely prioritize it higher and be more likely to give it the resources it needs to succeed. What's more, a clear and memorable project vision fills the project team with purpose and clarity, which makes them a lot easier to lead.

A project manager can use the Unified Vision Framework in a number of ways to manage their project team. It can work within any project management methodology, whether it is Agile or Traditional. When applied, the foundations of the Unified Vision Framework support not only the team, it can be applied to support everyone from an individual to the entire organization. For the purposes of this chapter, this framework

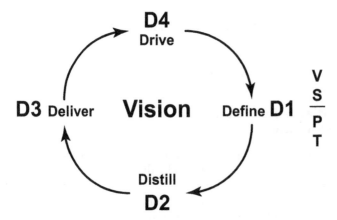

Figure 5.1 The Unified Vision Framework and the importance of vision.

People &
Relationships

VISION

Technology
& Tools

Knowledge &
Process

Figure 5.2 Foundations of the Unified Vision Framework.

will be applied to the project team and how the project manager can use this to remove anti-Flow – the roadblocks that prevent a team from obtaining its optimal Flow.

There are three supporting constructs that support vision at the base of the triangle: Knowledge and Process, Technology and Tools, and People and Relationships.

Knowledge and process

With respect to project management, knowledge and process is more about what a project team needs to complete their project. This includes knowledge about themselves, the team, and the product, service, or result they are working together to provide. Process development helps a team optimize how they work together to produce the project's deliverables. A common roadblock that project teams face is a lack of knowledge, which can come in many forms. Some teams may lack knowledge of the product or project they are working on, the tools they need to develop the product or manage the project, or they may lack knowledge about each other that impedes their ability to work together well as a team. All of these are forms of anti-Flow.

Project team members begin a project with their individual knowledge and processes, which may often be in conflict. An effective way a project manager can lead their team without authority is to resolve those conflicts by working with them to create common knowledge and processes that facilitate the development of the project deliverables. This includes helping them determine the knowledge they need about the product, project, of each other, as well as the processes necessary to build collective knowledge and to refine their use of it to complete the project's deliverables and achieve the vision of the project. It also includes helping the team determine which processes they need to be more effective and efficient and even map those processes, so the team can find agreement and move forward.

Identifying those needs and fulfilling them not only improves the team's ability to perform, but it also improves the project manager's ability to understand the team's dynamics and affords them the opportunity to help the team. This does not go unrecognized by the team. They will appreciate it, which makes it easier for the project manager to lead.

Providing knowledge to the team also allows the project manager to create opportunities for the team to learn more about each other. These opportunities can help increase cohesiveness, which makes it more likely for the team to communicate more effectively, which increases performance.

Of course, the project manager should continuously seek leadership knowledge and experience. A project manager is a leader. This requires them to seek more knowledge and experience if they wish to become a better leader. There are many books, seminars, coaches, and white papers available to increase one's knowledge of leadership. Learning from their successes and failures and honestly sharing those experiences with their teams provides a foundation for their teams to do the same.

Technology and tools

Using technology and tools that make working together easier can break some of the glut that makes it difficult to lead without authority. Scheduling and tasking tools that are familiar to the team makes it more likely for team members to work well together and accomplish the right tasks at the right time. Sometimes a team does not have a specific scheduling tool. In this case, consider introducing them to a new tool, but only if it is easy to use, exposes the work of the team, and it becomes their idea to use it. There are times, too, when there are multiple tools a team may use, but their use interferes with the productivity of the team. In this case, consider defining the elements of each tool that the team believes are the most important, and either determine which of the tools they use has the most important elements and work with them to use it or find a different tool that has these elements. The point is, the scheduling and tasking tools used to manage the work of the team should not interfere with the work of the team, because it only breaks their Flow, and thus impedes a project manager's ability to lead without authority.

The simplest tools tend to be low-tech. A simple Kanban board with sticky notes with clearly defined statuses of work and responsibility can do wonders. Plus, it requires very little training, it's visible, and it does not interfere with the team's productivity, because they're not spending time feeding and maintaining the tool that they could spend working on the project.

People and relationships

People and relationships are key to any project because it is not possible to have a project without people. People can be the greatest asset or liability to any project, depending on the people involved. One of a project manager's primary responsibilities is to get people pointed in the right direction and focused on the work at hand. This, coupled with trust in the team and supporting the team's autonomy to complete the work at hand, enables a project manager to lead without authority. This begins with defining and agreeing to the vision of the project and filtering the team's efforts through that vision.

Developing people and relationships leads to trust, which is the key to leading without authority. This is a constant, never-ending effort regardless of the people on your project team. The project manager who takes the time to know the people within his or her organization – their skills, opinions, values, strengths, weaknesses, etc. – and uses this information to understand them, so they can better engage them in the project at hand, will always have an advantage over those who do not do this. This requires a project manager to employ strong listening skills, empathy, and respect for each current

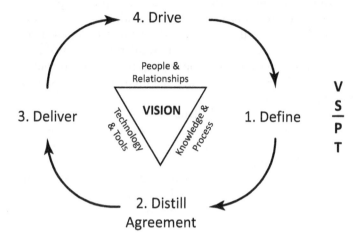

Figure 5.3 Foundations:The Four Ds.

and potential project team member. Those who do not do this will tend to utilize more aggressive or passive forms of leadership to "motivate" their teams, which do not work as well and have no long term value.

Define

When it comes to projects, definitions are often requirements. Unclear, incorrect, uncommunicated, or incorrectly assumed requirements will cause a project to fail. However, when it comes to leading without authority, definitions go well beyond product requirements; it also involves defining:

- The vision, mission, goals, and objectives of the project;
- What done looks like;
- The right people needed to carry out the project work;
- The proper project management methodology and tools that will maximize the team's productivity and quality, as well as to enable the project manager to manage the project's constraints most effectively.

Consistent effort must be taken to ensure that clear definitions are sought in all areas throughout a project. This will mitigate confusion, which, left unattended, will adversely affect the optimal performance and productivity of the project team.

Distill agreement

If there is no project vision, the project manager must work to define and distill agreement on what the vision really is (or should be) with the appropriate stakeholders. The project manager must understand, help the team to articulate, and keep the team focused on WHY they are doing the project.

An inability to understand and grasp how quickly politics can kill a project, product, service, or result is one of the major causes of project failure regardless of the methodology used to manage it. "Purists" in the Agile movement do themselves no favors by declaring "management" the source of all evil in the world. Similarly, traditional project managers that adhere with dear life to irrelevant project plans in an effort to control scope tend to neglect stakeholder needs and poorly defined requirements. The results of this behavior in either case is toxic and unfortunate.

Politics and a toxic project environment can easily demoralize a team and put a project at great risk of failing. When politics are present in a project team, the best way to resolve them is to find agreement. This may require the team to redefine the things they disagree about. They may have to determine if they have the right people involved to properly define the issues over which they disagree. It may even involve revisiting the vision. Whatever the case may be, wherever there are politics, there is disagreement, and this disagreement must be dealt with quickly before it erodes a project manager's ability to lead their team.

Deliver

A project team's ability to deliver or execute a project is necessary to a project's success. Anything that impedes their ability to do this is anti-Flow. One of the principles behind the Agile Manifesto is: "Simplicity – the art of maximizing the amount of work not done – is essential." Simplifying the process, the work, the schedule, issue definition and resolution – anything that could impede a team's ability to work together to complete a project – creates an environment that makes it more likely for a project manager to lead without authority.

It is puzzling that any organization would not immediately recognize the return on the investment available through simplification and start on the journey of simplifying everything they do at every level in the enterprise. However, many times the negative inertia of a corporate culture keeps things the way they are, regardless of how broken or misdirected. Simplicity is needed not only to deliver a project, but to make it more likely for future projects to be delivered well.

Drive

Driving the team and the organization forward, focused on the vision of the project and the organization, is necessary to complete the loop of the Four Ds. This helps to eliminate division amongst the team, which is necessary for their productivity to complete the tasks for the next milestone, sprint, or project, as well as to further the progress of the organization with greater unity and purpose. A team that is not divided is much easier to lead.

VS | PT

VS | PT stands for Vision, Strategy | People, and Tasks. This originated from West Point cadet training, but there it stands for Vision, Strategy | Projects, Tactics. The line between the VS and the PT defines the line that often separates leaders and skilled professionals; from those that develop the vision (the big picture that steers the organization) and those that are tasked with doing the work that drives the organization toward that vision.

A project leader's focus should always work to remove the line that separates VS and PT. This requires the project manager to act as a conduit between the organization's leadership and the project team members. One way this is done is to communicate the project team's work into the language of leadership, as well as to communicate the leadership's vision to the project team whose work helps to accomplish that vision. This is why vision and the focus on it is so important. Organizational leaders do not care so much about details, but if the details are focused on a clearly defined and accepted vision that is connected to the vision of the organization that they defined, the leaders cannot help but take notice. This makes it more likely that a project with a clear and connected vision is supported financially and politically, which clears two very important roadblocks a project manager typically faces. This makes it easier for them to lead without authority.

Successful team equation

$$\textbf{Vision} + \text{Right People} \left(\textbf{RP}\right) + \text{Definitions} \left(\textbf{D1}\right)$$

$$+ \text{Distilled Agreements} \left(\textbf{D2}\right) + \text{Delivery} \left(\textbf{D3}\right)$$

$$+ \text{Drive} \left(\textbf{D4}\right) = \text{Successful Team}$$

A team in anarchy is a team without vision

A vision that is unclear, poorly communicated, or completely missing is the number one anti-pattern blocking Flow, which has a devastating effect on a project manager's ability to lead without authority. A clear indicator that vision is absent or unclear is the presence of anarchy. Project managers experiencing anarchy with their project teams

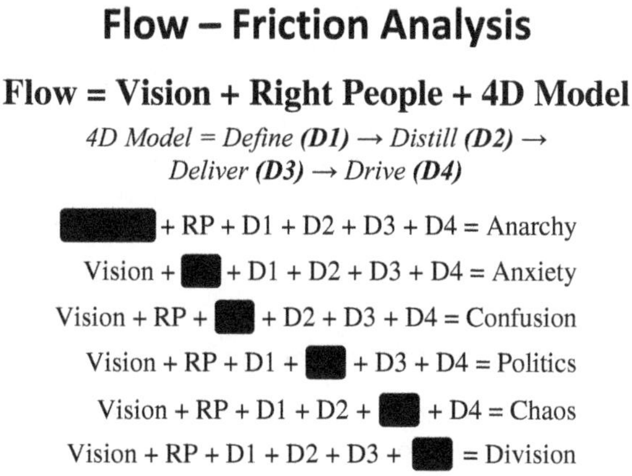

Flow – Friction Analysis

Flow = Vision + Right People + 4D Model

4D Model = Define (D1) → Distill (D2) →
Deliver (D3) → Drive (D4)

██████ + RP + D1 + D2 + D3 + D4 = Anarchy

Vision + ██ + D1 + D2 + D3 + D4 = Anxiety

Vision + RP + ██ + D2 + D3 + D4 = Confusion

Vision + RP + D1 + ██ + D3 + D4 = Politics

Vision + RP + D1 + D2 + ██ + D4 = Chaos

Vision + RP + D1 + D2 + D3 + ██ = Division

Figure 5.4 Identifying anti-Flow with the Team Issue Diagnostic Chart.

must look to the project's vision as the root cause. If the team doesn't know the project vision, understand it, or believe in it, the project they are working on has no clarity or purpose. This brings rise to anarchy within the team. Defining a clear, memorable vision and establishing a clear agreement among the team of that vision will remove this anarchy and replace it with purpose and clarity. And a team with purpose and clarity is much easier to lead.

A team experiencing anxiety has the wrong people involved

Anxiety can spring from many sources. But, along with vision and VS | PT, having the right people on the project team is vital to the project's success. Having the wrong people involved in the project nearly guarantees an anxious undercurrent for the team. Anxiety rises because confidence in eventual success is reduced. Lack of confidence among teammates or co-workers can increase anxiety among the team. If individual team members believe they or others on the team lack the skills, talents, and abilities necessary to get the job done, their anxiety and the anxiety of their teammates will increase. Having the wrong people in any functional area can weaken and even completely destroy Flow, and thus the ability to lead without authority. However, the most important "right" person needs to be the leader. This is true at the team level and every other level in an organizational structure.

A team in confusion is a team without clear definitions

Without exception, failed projects have one thing in common: poor, wrong, or non-existent definitions. Not having a clear definition for "done" is a good example of this. Another is not having an explicit link to vision, purpose, mission and/or the strategies of the organization. A lack of clear definitions is an early indicator of eventual project failure. A high level of confusion among the project team can almost always be traced back to this root cause.

Wrong definitions happen for many different reasons. For example, during the requirements gathering process, a team may either miss or omit requirements (functional or technical) that in the end may turn out to be key for completing the project. Many times the end users do not fully understand or are unable to clearly communicate exactly what it is that they need, so requirements can be missed or be poorly defined. Requirements should not be developed in a vacuum nor should they be assumed. Definitions generated by poor practices or processes will result in confusion.

Defining the skills, talents, and abilities of the people needed to deliver the organization's vision is key to its success. Improper definitions or poor agreements in this area will stifle Flow, and thus stifle a project manager's ability to lead their team without authority.

A team wrapped up in politics is a team without distilled agreements

Lack of clarity in definitions means that all relevant agreements are flawed. If the agreements are flawed, this often results in an incomplete or a completely undesirable outcome. When this occurs – and it will occur – the net result, organizationally, is politics. Politics diverts attention away from the needs of the project to secondary agendas and/

or tribal warfare among the team or with various internal entities. Fractures in the team's cohesiveness occur as a result, because the focus shifts away from the overarching true vision of the project to political skirmishes, which adversely affects a project manager's ability to lead the team.

When politics are identified as an issue among a project team, find where their team disagrees and work to resolve those disagreements. Oftentimes this can be achieved by stepping back to definitions. Perhaps there is a misunderstanding that has grown into a disagreement. Redefining the situation that led to the misunderstanding will eliminate the confusion, which will eliminate the disagreement.

What if the disagreement is the result of a team member whose very presence on the team creates disagreements? They may be unreliable, lazy, or possibly very capable, but often absent or too busy with other projects or operational responsibilities to concern themselves with the project. Or perhaps they are a perfectionist on a project where time is a critical constraint to a project. While the team is working tirelessly trying to get a product out the door, they are being held up by a perfectionist. In either case, these people may simply not be the right people for the team, which means that removing them is an option, if they are not willing or able to do the work and work well with the team.

But what if these team members cannot be removed? It is possible that a team member has not bought into the vision of the project. In this case, the project manager should address the vision with that team member and help them find meaning and purpose in that vision. If that does not resolve the problem, then work on better defining their needs and responsibilities to the project, and work with them to distill the agreements for the betterment of the project and the project team. This can be done with one-on-one discussions or with sprint retrospectives, which would involve the other team members honestly communicating to the difficult team member how they feel and work together to resolve the issues.

Politics are never fully avoided, but clear definitions and distilled agreements remove most of these anti-Flow patterns.

A team in chaos is unable to deliver/execute their plan

If there are faulty definitions and poor agreements, it is impossible to have a strong delivery plan and capability, which only results in chaos. Without fail, regardless of methodology used, one is likely to encounter an "oh, by the way" from a stakeholder that just realized that they forgot to include a definition from the start. When that happens, and it will, it is necessary to filter this "oh, by the way" with the lens of the vision for the product or project, since the project is being altered. This alteration could be slight or massive, but it should still be focused on delivering the vision regardless of the change. To not do so will create chaos.

But what if there are strong definitions, clear agreements, and the planning is done well? Is it still possible to end up with chaos and confusion? Yes. This is particularly true with very large projects that have multiple cross dependencies and integration points. The importance of keeping all of the work, regardless of the size to the project, in a big and visual format is imperative to success. Having a tangible, big picture is a good starting point for eliminating chaos and confusion. It exposes issues to the light of the team. It is also a tool that helps the leadership team maintain the focus and agreement.

Use a war room whenever possible, and keep it simple. In the same way, it is important to keep all of the tools simple and light. For example, project management offices (PMOs) or Portfolio Directors that focus on tool normalization are usually focusing on proxy variables instead of confronting and addressing the real issues. This is one of the primary reasons that PMOs fail to deliver on their promise and value-add.

A high-performing project team that is operating in Flow will experience the same environmental disruptions that many project teams experience. However, they are more likely to find the creative, innovation solutions to successfully navigate any challenge that rises as they drive towards fulfilling their vision. A project manager will gain the most respect, which increases their influence among the team and thus the ability to lead them, if they keep the team focused on the true vision and root out any chaotic roadblocks that could prevent them from achieving that vision.

A team unable to drive the project forward is a team divided

Driving a project based on command-and-control focus on production or profitability alone is an anti-Flow. The focus or vision needs to be on a higher purpose or more compelling "WHY" if it is going to succeed as a project team driver.

Another anti-pattern is creating or allowing a culture of fear. A fear-based culture, many times, uses shame and/or guilt as a motivator. But the reality is that fear, shame, and guilt demotivates and kills Flow. In a fear-based culture, failure is seldom accepted and almost never encouraged. This obviously stifles innovation and creativity that are the necessary fuel for achieving continuous improvement and always a vital part of high performance.

Here are some events and situations where a project manager can apply the Team Issue Diagnostic Chart to identify and root out anti-Flow in a project team that put the project and the project team at risk.

1. Status meetings – especially daily standup meetings in Scrum environments – presents an opportunity to identify anti-Flow that put the project and project team at risk. Any roadblocks identified are anti-Flow items, which makes them risks to the project – typically those of an immediate nature. This also affords a project manager the opportunity to identify risks in these meetings that could have an adverse effect on the long-term planning and execution of a project and even the maintenance of the deliverables.
2. Any anti-Flow identified that has long-term implications should be carefully considered and shared with the key stakeholders and the project sponsor/product owner during project and sprint planning. Risks, a form of anti-Flow, affects the other five constraints of any project: scope, time, cost, quality, and resources. Information resulting from this should be considered during planning and allow for the project manager to set a strategy if the mitigation or elimination of the identified risks require assistance outside of the project team.
3. Lessons learned and sprint retrospectives offer great opportunities to identify the anti-Flow inherent with the team's dynamics. These risks are often very personal and are not often exposed easily or fully unless the team is honest about what they think and feel. Honesty is essential to the success of these meetings. In fact, a project

manager can set a great example by being the first person to get honest about their mistakes and shortcomings. Getting honest first about what may be going wrong, what the issues are, or any other concerns that are apparent, will immediately set the tone for the team and make it okay for others to be honest. This will make it much more possible to break through any of the anti-Flow matters that have persisted. A lack of honesty during these meetings only increases the denial of the heaviness and tension in the room that is often the product of fear, anger, and resentment resulting from unaddressed issues and situations. Honesty not only breaks this tension and shows our humanity, but it also brings levity, which further helps connect the team and make them productive and much easier to lead.

4. Review meetings provide a great opportunity to identify elements of anti-Flow. One of the obvious opportunities is when increments or deliverables under review are rejected. What's good about this is the team has immediate feedback that they can use to work toward a solution. The real risk in this situation is having team members ignoring the feedback provided or having those reviewing the increments or deliverables not fully participating in the process either because they do not feel comfortable being honest or they simply do not care. Either way, the risks inherent to the project and the team of having people like that in the room is significant. They either need to engage enthusiastically or the project manager needs to get different people in the room.

5. Finally, use general observation and interaction outside the planned events while the teams are producing usable increments to identify anti-Flow. Take time to wander about, listen, and interact casually with the team members. Stop into the product owner's or project sponsor's office and do the same. Read their body language and piece together what may seem like irrelevant information if they begin to form personal or political patterns that could put the project at risk. Probably one of the more useful things one could do is to look above the surface of the project team level and identify what else is going on around in the department, other departments, and the organization as a whole and determine what effect these things could have on the project team and to what degree would these things put them at risk.

Get to know each other and build trust

Since authority and the issues surrounding it are plenty, it is best to identify authority issues with project teams at the outset. Specifically, identify authority issues with team members, the leadership, and yourself. They all present roadblocks to the team's performance. With respect to the team, focus on how the team members respond to authority both individually and collectively. For project managers that may not have had enough experience working with specific team members and/or how the team works together, one way to gather this valuable information is to play a game that forces the team to work together and allows them to observe their individual characteristics and team dynamics.

A game that the authors use that has proven most effective to gather this information quickly is simply called "The Candy Game." This game has very few rules, is easy to conduct, is time boxed, and, when played, has many benefits that include the ability to capture how the team responds to authority both individually and collectively.

Here is how you play The Candy Game:

1. Break the team up into teams of four and give them a pile of individually wrapped candy. (Lifesavers mints work great for this!)
2. Each team must pass the candy around in a circle. Each piece of candy that is not dropped equals one point.
3. When passing the candy, each teammate must touch each piece of candy and that candy must have air time as it passes from one teammate to the next.
4. Each team will have two minutes to plan how they will pass the candy, two minutes to execute the passing of the candy, and a minute to determine what worked, what didn't work, and what they will do differently next time to optimize their performance.
5. At the end of the planning phase and before execution, each team will state how many points they will have and how many drops they will have. At the end of execution, each team will report how many points and drops they actually had. The facilitator will record this information for everyone to see.
6. Repeat this process for a total of three iterations.

Here is what is often observed:

1. How well the teams learn from their mistakes and how they treat others who make them.
2. Who are the creative types? Who are the analytical types? Who is assertive, passive, aggressive, and anywhere in between? How people react to being told what to do? How well people can influence their team members to improve without offending them?
3. The teams will learn from their mistakes. How they learn and who points them out helps to determine who stands out as a leader, how well the others follow that leader, and the authority issues that may be apparent. This is especially useful information if employing autonomous teams.
4. The teams will communicate. How well or how poorly they will communicate is easily observed while watching the game unfold.
5. The teams will observe each other. How they do this and what they take from it is valuable information.

When the game is done, there are plenty of questions to ask, observations to discuss, and experiences that individuals and teams are very willing to share. This information varies based on the number of teams that participate, but, more often than not, here are the main takeaways:

1. The teams improve the accuracy of their predictions, dramatically increase the number of points, and reduce the number of drops. How they do this is the product of their teamwork dynamics.
2. The participants, with the help of the facilitator, quickly connect the game experience with their own project team experiences.
3. The facilitator has a rough understanding of how his or her project team will respond to iterative project work, time-sensitive deadlines, and, of course, how

well each of them respond to authority by how well they follow rules, how and why they are willing to bend or break the rules, and how that affects their team and the other teams that participate in the game.

Getting to know each other builds trust. Trust is key to leading without authority. You cannot have projects without people, therefore building and maintaining trusting relationships with the people involved with a project must be an active and ongoing effort. As mentioned earlier, people can be either the greatest assets or the greatest liabilities to any project. Whatever they are or become on a project will depend greatly on how well the relationships with these people are built and maintained. Leading without authority requires this.

A project manager without the trust of their team cannot lead well (or at all) either with or without authority. Trust is essential throughout the team dynamic. The team is more likely to work well together when they trust its leader. They not only will listen and take guidance and counsel from the leader, they will also be more likely to challenge the leader when they do not agree with them. This is healthy for the team, but it is not possible without trust.

The team members must also trust each other. Flow between team members is enhanced by trust, because trust makes it more likely for team members to communicate honestly, and honest communication enhances the quality and reliability of that communication. This makes it more likely for team members to plan, make decisions, execute their project deliverables, troubleshoot issues, and drive the team forward more effectively and efficiently.

The leader's trust in their team nurtures the team's trust in the leader, but only if the trust is earned. This is done in progressive stages, and sometimes these stages are wrought with difficult experiences and uncomfortable feelings. However, if handled well by the leader, these experiences become the building blocks of trust that makes it more likely for trust to proliferate throughout the team.

The best way for a leader to earn the trust of his or her team is to lead with honor and integrity. Nobody likes a hypocrite, let alone trusts one. A leader that demonstrates the values they expect from their team makes it easier to not only follow that leader, but it also provides a model for team members on which to base themselves. Here are some additional ways to build and sustain trust.

Clear roadblocks to progress

Team members respect and trust project managers who actively work to remove roadblocks to the team's success. There are several ways to do this without adversely affecting the autonomy of the team. One way is to do the mundane, yet painful parts of the project that teams often consider drudgery, such as taking meeting minutes and processing expense reports. There are times, too, when the team is working long hours leading up to a go-live when a project manager can improve the morale of the team. There are several simple, yet effective ways to do this.

Providing for the team's basic needs, such as ensuring there is plenty of food and drink available, is easy and goes a long way to keeping the team focused and happy. There are times when team members are too close to an issue and need a momentary distraction to allow them to regain their perspective. Humor is most effective here.

More often than not, a good 15-to-30-minute distraction is all it takes. Finally, just being present or at least available for the team and offering to assist with anything they need is helpful. You never know when you will work together again, and, whether you like it or not, your story will be told by others.

Another way to clear roadblocks is to build the processes under which the team operates. This involves defining the processes the team will follow, deciding on them by consensus, executing the processes, and reviewing them at regular intervals. This provides a team foundation on which to operate, that of and by itself avoids roadblocks. It also is a great way to build and sustain trust.

Show genuine concern for others

Genuine concern rings true. This requires a project manager to be honest and listen well to the project team members. Honesty is key, but it must be tempered with tact and concern. Realize that everyone is different, and their response to "the truth" will vary. Understanding each team member individually and collectively will guide how much truth they can handle and how it is communicated. Some people like blunt and direct while others need to be eased into the truth. The best guide is what is going to enhance individual and collective productivity.

In the end, it is important to remember that people are more important than the project. Therefore, being a human being first and a project manager second will center one's perspective when dealing with difficult team members. That said, this does not mean it is okay to be a people-pleasing pushover. Not only does this not garner much respect, but it also all but eliminates a project manager's ability to lead – with or without authority.

Find out what makes them feel alive

Each and every person has something that drives them; that makes them feel enthusias-tic and alive. Engaging project team members, listening to them, watching them, and learning about them and what makes them feel alive makes it more likely to determine what makes them feel happy and fulfilled and enthusiastic about their job. Once this is understood, harness the team's individual and collective enthusiasm and connect it to the vision of the project.

Recognize the team members' contributions and make the most of their failures

One of the best ways to increase enthusiasm for a project as well as the trust and respect of the team members is to honestly and publicly recognize each team mem-ber's contributions. In fact, project managers who give honest and public credit to the team, yet take honest and public responsibility for its failures, will not only endure themselves to the team, they will also infuse in future project team members a strong sense of respect and trust. However, this requires a project manager to act with humil-ity. This is in contrast to project managers who expect perfection and shame people for making mistakes, which not only stifles creativity, it also eliminates any benefits that mistakes can bring.

Humble project managers recognize and make known their own faults and mistakes. This makes it more likely that their team members will be more forthcoming about their own mistakes. This not only creates an environment where mistakes are okay and will be made, but also one where the team communicates mistakes freely (as opposed to hiding them and jeopardizing the team and the project), and works together to learn and improve from those mistakes. This builds strong camaraderie, trust, and creative effort. At the very least, shaming project team members makes them overly cautious and far less creative. At the most, it makes them rebellious and mutinous. In either case, project teams harboring these feelings are impossible to lead without authority.

Practicing humility is the key to managing mistakes and making the most of them. Project managers that are quick to recognize the ideas of their team members and give them complete ownership of those ideas provide encouragement to the team, which often leads to increased idea generation. However, this does not always lead to great ideas. In fact, it may lead to failures. However, these failures, when handled properly, always lead to important lessons that lead to new ideas, approaches, and perspectives that never would have been considered unless the mistakes were made in the first place. Paradoxically, allowing for mistakes to be made and working through them without shame emboldens the team's sense of adventure, creativity, openness, and productivity to the point where they are less likely to make significant mistakes.

Promote team autonomy

Self-managed teams are the cornerstone of Agile project management methodologies, such as Scrum. This differs from traditional project team environments, which, at their best, are hierarchical with varying degrees of respect for the team members' knowledge and abilities, and at their worst, are overly managed and held to unrealistic standards of perfection. Traditional project team environments also tend to follow a command and control structure. This stifles creativity, causes teams to produce just enough to not endure the wrath of the project manager or key stakeholders, work too cautiously, and are more likely to hide their mistakes. This is in contrast to self-managed teams, which are generally far more creative and productive. And when they make mistakes, they admit them, learn from them, and often find that the mistakes were necessary to learn and progress in unexpected ways that benefit the project greatly.

It is important to push authority to the team to lead better without authority, but it is even more important to ensure they are ready for it. For some people, team autonomy may be a very new concept, and one that they may not take too well at all. It is best to pay special attention to the team members' body language and actions, more than their words and status reports in the early stages of a project if it appears that they are not used to taking greater responsibility for the development of project deliverables. A clear indicator that team members are not handling their autonomy well is when there is a significant divergence between what they say and what they are actually completing. Another indicator is when they are frequently tardy or absent from daily standup or status meetings, or they are clearly uncomfortable being there.

If a project team is struggling with autonomy, there are several options to remedy this. One way is to adjust the team's expectations, which, in a Scrum environment is as simple as reducing the batch size of the work a team is doing. And, in doing so, ensure that work for the sprint is clearly within their capability and availability to complete.

This will give the team the confidence to continue. Oftentimes, teams new to Scrum and team autonomy will overestimate what they can do, which may indicate that the Scrum Master has done a poor job of showing them how to estimate work properly. Another way is to use the Scrum Retrospective to facilitate an honest discussion of the project and process. This presents a difficult but valuable opportunity on the part of the Scrum Master (i.e., project leader) to make the meeting effective by getting honest about their own mistakes and feelings, which makes it easier for the team members to do the same.

Be a human first and a project manager second

One of the most important things a project manager can do to lead without authority is to recognize and embrace their humanity, as well as the humanity of their project team. This takes a strong adherence to principles – particularly honesty, open-mindedness, willingness, patience, tolerance, perseverance, and acceptance – to manage this. To not do this creates rifts and anti-Flow within the project team that may quickly become too difficult to resolve.

Projects will always involve people. Everyone has strengths and weaknesses, joys and sorrows, achievements and tragedies. All of this affects performance, engagement, and Flow one way or another. As difficult as it may be, it is best to acknowledge and accept all of this. The problem is that people tend to overemphasize their strengths and minimize their weaknesses. However, we all have flaws.

Project leaders who are forthcoming about their limitations – to themselves, as well as to the team – will garner a great deal of respect and make it more likely that the project team members will do the same. This is valuable knowledge to have, because it paints a more accurate picture of the team's capabilities in relation to the six constraints that every project faces (scope, time, cost, quality, resources, and risk/opportunity). This makes it possible to identify potential solutions that the team works on together to improve, which increases the team's cohesion and trust for each other. However, teams that hide from or lie about their weaknesses will only exacerbate them to the point that they adversely affect their individual and collective accountability, creativity, and productivity.

Project leaders who acknowledge the humanity of their project teams, as well as their own, are more likely to stand up for what is right for the team and the project. They will shield their teams from unnecessary interference from problem stakeholders and work to mitigate, eliminate, or avoid anything that is rolling downhill, while still holding their team, as well as themselves, accountable to the agreements they have made to produce the project's deliverables.

In the end, a project manager does not need direct authority to lead a project; they need only to be a leader. Leaders put their team first; they respect the team's knowledge, understanding, and concerns; they watch, listen, and acknowledge their contributions; they are assertive and kind, but never a pushover; and they exhibit a true we mentality. But most of all, they remain humble, for authority, itself, is tenuous – even if it is granted organizationally – because teams will truly follow leaders faithfully who are principled, competent, and respectful of the team, themselves, the project, and the organization for which they work.

Section II

Processes, tools and techniques

Performance

A combined project and portfolio perspective

Jamal Moustafaev

Case study: The new Ashgabat airport

On September 17th, 2016, the president of Turkmenistan Kurbanguly Berdymukhamedov officially opened a new US 2.3 billion-dollar ultra-modern Ashgabat International Airport shaped in a form of a falcon. The entire complex is comprised of 190 buildings spread on a 1,200-hectare site. The airport is designed to handle up to 17 million passengers (remember that number!) combined with 200,000 tons of cargo every year.

At the opening ceremony, the president claimed that Turkmenistan has "all the opportunities to become a transport bridge facilitating economic cooperation between Europe, the Asia-Pacific region, and South Asia". He also added that the new airport was needed to accommodate a massive influx of tourists eager to visit Turkmenistan.

The official position of Turkmenistan is understandable since the country's income has heavily depended on the export of natural gas. As a result of plunging energy prices and foreign currency shortages, the government is now forced to develop the tourism and transportation sectors of the economy.

There is, however, an array of problems associated with the new Turkmen initiative. For starters, due to very restrictive visa regulations the country has been visited by anywhere between 7,000 (if you choose to believe World Bank) and 100,000 tourists (if you prefer to rely on official Turkmen government reports). For comparison, neighboring Kazakhstan had 4.5 million visitors, while Kyrgyzstan saw more than 2.8 million tourists in 2014.

Here is an additional compilation of facts about Turkmenistan if you are planning to visit that country anytime soon:

- Turkmenistan Airlines' air tickets for flights are not sold over the Internet. They promised to initiate that program by 2015 but failed to do so.
- Turkmen entry visa is one of the most expensive ones in the world, and it is almost impossible to obtain.
- You can't rent a car in Ashgabat.
- You can't walk with a camera around the city and, God forbid, you decide to take pictures of the government buildings.
- Internet access is limited and all of the popular social media sites like Facebook, Twitter, WhatsApp, Viber and others are blocked.
- Democracy index – 162nd place out of 167.
- Press Freedom – 178th place out of 180.

On the bright side, Ashgabat holds a Guinness World Record for the highest density of white marble-clad buildings as well as the largest indoor Ferris wheel.

So far, the official Ashgabat has not undertaken any steps to either address the tourism-related problems outlined above or initiate any trade deals to attract any transportation companies.

Was this project a success or a failure? On one hand it was completed (to the best of our knowledge) on-time and on-budget while delivering the entire planned scope. So, there should be no complaints to the project manager. However, on the other hand it completely failed to deliver the value it was expected to realize. This project is unlikely to assist in any way to bring more tourists into the country due to the above-mentioned reasons. Also, its capacity exceeds the potential demand by a wide margin. As a result, we will have to agree that while this project was a resounding success from a project management point of view, it was a failure from the project portfolio management perspective. In other words, it was a very bad idea, albeit implemented on-time and on-budget. Formulaically this phenomenon can be expressed in the following manner:

$$Success_{PM} + Failure_{PPM} = Failure$$

Keeping this particular story in mind, let us now try to define a project, study industry statistics, examine the opinions of industry's thought leaders on the subject and try to define our own understanding of project success and failure.

What is a project?

This is a seemingly simple question, at least, for a certified project manager. After all, we all know that a project is an "endeavor that has a definite start and an end, undertaken to deliver a unique product a service". Usually this definition is followed by a couple of illustrative examples:

- Creation of the first prototype of the Formula One car is a project since it does have a defined start, an end and produces a unique product.
- Mass production of, say, canned soup is not a project, since while it has a defined start it does not have a defined end. Also, thousands of cans can't be considered a unique product since all of them are identical.

Another aspect of the project definition that started to be mentioned fairly recently is "value". It is now implied that any temporary endeavor undertaken by a company must inherently strive to deliver some type of value to the organization. As a result of that the definition of project can be summed up as:

"An endeavor that has a definite start and an end, undertaken to create a unique product or service and to deliver value to the organization".

Having defined the essence of the project, let us now discuss the next set of questions:

- What are the domains of project vs portfolio management?
- What is project performance?
- How do we measure project performance?
- What is a successful project?

- What is a troubled project?
- What is a failed project?

Project vs portfolio management

Before we proceed further in this chapter, let us try to define the domains of both project management and project portfolio management. My purpose here is to provide the readers with a brief overview of both fields without going too deep in either subjects. First, I assume that the readers of this handbook already know the answers to these questions and second, plenty of reading materials can be found on the web including a recent book by yours truly titled *Project Portfolio Management in Theory and Practice: Thirty Case Studies from around the World.*

What is project management?

Project management is the practice of delivering projects on-time and on-budget by initiating, planning, monitoring, controlling and closing them. A project manager achieves that by focusing on the following knowledge areas (see Table 6.1):

- Project integration management
- Project scope management
- Project time management
- Project quality management
- Project cost management
- Project risk management
- Project human resources management
- Project communications management
- Project stakeholder management and
- Project procurement management

The idea here is that in general a project manager attempts to deliver the project product or service while trying to respect all of the above-mentioned constraints. He or she, as a rule, does not question the value of the project at hand or does not get involved in

Table 6.1 Overview of project management

	Initiation	Planning	Execution	Control	Close-out
Integration	X	X		X	
Scope	X	X		X	
Time	X	X		X	
Cost	X	X		X	
Quality	X	X	X	X	
Risk	X	X		X	
HR	X	X	X	X	
Communications	X	X	X	X	X
Stakeholder	X	X		X	
Procurement	X	X		X	X

its selection, prioritization and approval. Those three functions fall into the domain of project portfolio management.

What is project portfolio management?

Project portfolio management is defined as a methodology for analyzing, selecting and collectively managing a group of current or proposed projects based on numerous key characteristics, while honoring constraints imposed by management or external real-world factors.

The three key requirements that portfolio management professionals impose on every candidate are:

- Each project, as well as the portfolio of projects, should maximize the value for the company
- The candidate project should preserve the desired balance in the portfolio mix
- The final portfolio of projects is strategically aligned and truly reflects the business's strategy

The definition of "value" can vary from company to company and even from project to project but typically it includes certain economic measures (e.g. return on investment, net present value and payback), competitive advantage, market attractiveness, expected sales, probability of success, etc. Table 6.2 is an example of a matrix to determine project value at a European pharmaceutical company.

Table 6.2 Sample project portfolio scoring model

Selection Criteria	Points Awarded (Maximum possible 135)			
	1 point	*5 points*	*15 points*	*Kill?*
Market Attractiveness (How many patients are out there?)	Number of patients < X	X < Number of patients < Y	Number of patients > Y	Yes
Strategic Fit	Fits only 1 of the strategic fit criteria	Fits 2 of the strategic fit criteria	3–4 of the strategic fit criteria	Yes (if scores zero)
Innovativeness	Generic approach	Mixed approach	Unique approach	No
Risk (both technical and market)	10% < Probability of success < 25%	25% < Probability of success < 75%	Probability of success > 75%	Yes (if less than 10%)
Effectiveness	Low	Medium	High	No
Cannibalization	Will compete with several other company drugs	Will compete with 1 other company drug	No competition with other company drugs	No
Core competencies	No in-house knowledge	Some in-house knowledge	All knowledge is in-house	No
Competitors	More than 3 competitors with similar products	1–2 competitors with similar products	No competitors with similar products	No
Financial (Revenue)	Revenue < $A	$A < Revenue < $B	Revenue > $B	Yes (if revenue minimal)

The "balance requirement" ensures that the following situations are successfully avoided:

- Too many small projects and not enough breakthrough, visionary projects
- Too many short-term and not enough long-term strategic projects
- Certain business areas are receiving a disproportionate amount of resources
- Poor risk management (all eggs in one basket)

Finally, the "fit to the strategic goals" requirement makes certain that company finances and other resources are not wasted on ventures outside of the organization's sphere of strategic interests.

So, again, just to summarize two very important points:

- Project portfolio management is responsible for the selection and prioritization of the best projects for the company
- Project management is responsible for a successful delivery of the projects selected

What is project performance and how do we measure it?

In this particular section of the chapter I would like to examine the statistical data about project success and failure released by several reputable companies. Then, I want to discuss several opinions and definitions of project success and failure voiced by famous project management experts and thought leaders. And finally, we will examine the domains of project management and project portfolio management and attempt to come up with a final formula for project success.

Industry statistics

How are we doing with projects so far? According to a study of information technology projects published by Accenture[1] in 2008, our success rate is only 29%, with 56% of our venture going over budget and 84% ending up late.

KMPG[2] reveals that in 2010 in New Zealand, 70% of organizations had at least one project failure in the prior 12 months while 50% of respondents also indicated that their projects failed to achieve what they set out to achieve.

According to a study performed by McKinsey[3] in 2012, 50% of large IT projects ("large" being defined as having a budget more than US$15 mil) massively exceed their budgets. The report also adds that on average, large IT projects are 45% over budget and 7% are late. Finally, McKinsey reports that the projects in the study delivered on average 56% less value than expected.

Note: we will revisit this mysterious notion of the "project value" a bit later in this chapter.

---

1 Outsourcing: Industrialize your applications delivery to achieve high performance, Accenture, 2008
2 NZ Project Management Survey 2010, KMPG, 2010
3 Delivering large scale IT projects on time, on budget and on value, Michael Bloch, Sven Blumberg and Jurgen Laartz, McKinsey Quarterly, October 2012

Table 6.3 Project performance over the years

	2011	2012	2013	2014	2015	2016
Successful	29%	27%	31%	28%	29%	35%
Challenged	49%	56%	50%	55%	52%	46%
Failed	22%	17%	19%	17%	19%	19%

And finally, according to the Standish Group, a US-based company that has been assessing project performances for the last several decades, our project performance (see Table 6.3) hasn't improved much over the course of the previous decade. The number of successful projects has increased slightly (from 29% to 35%), while the number of challenged and failed projects remained pretty much the same, 49% vs 46% and 22% and 19%, respectively.

In my opinion, all of the above-mentioned studies suggest that we are a long way from having a robust project delivery system.

Opinions about project success and failure

Let us now discuss the definitions of project success and failure. I like to say that the very old school method of project management used to define project success as follows:

> *The project is completed on-time, on-budget and delivered the full scope promised.*

The example of Ashgabat new airport mentioned earlier in this chapter in my opinion completely disproves this theory, which brings us to a "new school" project success definition:

> *A successful project must deliver value to the company.*

One of the project management thought leaders, Harold Kerzner, suggests two alternatives for defining project success and failure.

Alternative 1:

Success: *Finished (more or less) on time, within budget and met all requirements.*
Challenged: *Reaches conclusion, but with cost overruns and schedule slippages; possibly not all specifications are met.*
Failure: *Project was abandoned or canceled due to project management failure.*

Alternative 2:

Complete Success: *Project met success criteria, value was created and all constraints were adhered to.*
Partial Success: *Project met the success criteria, the client accepted the deliverables, value was created, and all of the constraints were met.*
Partial Failure: *Project was canceled. But some IP was created that can be used on other projects.*
Complete Failure: *The project was abandoned and nothing was learned.*

Here are some other attempts to define project success and failure:

Product is unsuccessful in providing value.
A project that does not make the journey from conception to successful implementation.
Runaway project: significantly failed to meet its objectives and +30% over budget (KPMG).
Runaway project is +100% over budget (Robert Glass).

It is fairly easy to see that while the authors of these definitions make an honest attempt to define the boundaries of project success, they typically fail on one of the two fronts. They either focus entirely on project management aspects (e.g. on-time, on-budget, full scope, constraints, etc.) or they mention the portfolio management aspect (i.e. value) without providing definitions of what value is.

Let us now try to examine several case studies and attempt to develop our own definition of project success.

The combined project and portfolio management view

Over my close to 20 years of project management consulting and training experience, I have been involved in this discussion on more times than I care to remember. Some people claimed that as long as the project was completed on-time, on-budget and delivered a full scope as promised, it should be considered a success.

Others claim that it is OK to be somewhat late and over budget but deliver a great quality product. And yet there is another group of professionals that claims that – of course, within reason – budget and timeline are not that important as long as the project realizes the truly great idea behind it.

Let us try to analyze each one of the "project success" ingredients. Let us assume that we have a project at hand that has been completed on-time, on budget and delivered a full scope of excellent quality. Does this automatically imply that this was a successful project?

In order to assess this question, we would need to take a look at a couple of examples. Imagine that a real estate development company in 2018 commissioned a project manager and requested him to build a luxury condominium building near a local lake. The project manager had successfully completed the project on-time, on-budget and delivered the full scope requested. Having said that, shortly after the construction was finished, the executives discovered that due to a number of factors (including economic and demographic ones) they would be able to sell only 10% of the units built.

Can this project be considered a success? Most likely all of the readers will agree that it was not, since the company failed on the portfolio management end of the spectrum (i.e. selecting the projects with the highest possible business value). The resulting formula for this endeavor is:

$$\text{Success}_{PM} + \text{Failure}_{PPM} = \text{Failure}$$

Let us now look at the example of the Denver Airport Baggage Handling System that due to failures in the areas of requirements elicitation and proper planning required an additional 50% of the original budget – nearly \$200m – and has been delayed by almost 2 years. Was the original initiative to replace the outdated system a good idea? Most likely yes. Was it a successful project? Absolutely not, because of the cost and time overruns. So, in this particular case the formula looks like this:

$$\text{Failure}_{PM} + \text{Success}_{PPM} = \text{Failure}$$

Now we can turn our attention to a couple of projects that can be considered quite successful. The first one is a construction of the "world's only seven-star hotel" in Dubai, that started in 1994 with the blessing of the ruling family of Dubai. The construction took five years between 1994 and 1999. Since the building was commissioned by the Jumeirah Group, a wholly owned subsidiary of the government-owned Dubai Holding, very limited information is available about the financials of the project. However, one can reliably state that the project was on-time (five years), on-budget (US$650 million) and delivered the full scope promised.

Due to the fact that Dubai Holding does not publish its financial results, it is very difficult to calculate the ROI (return on investment) or NPV (net present value) on this project. However, it was known from the very beginning that this project was conceived at the very top of the UAE government as a venture that would assist in transforming the country and the state from the exclusively oil-based economy to the trade and tourism-based market.

The ruling family of Dubai gambled – and by all accounts won – that the conversion into international hub of trade and tourism should start with a "wow-type" project that would demonstrate to the rest of the world that the Gulf country can:

- Undertake ambitious projects and see them to completion
- Have a rich cultural and historic heritage
- Have the supply of and the demand for luxury hotel accommodations

Have the goals of this project been achieved? Absolutely yes. Burj Al Arab has become an iconic building in the minds of millions of people worldwide, it is firmly associated with Dubai in particular and United Arab Emirates in general. Moreover, one can argue that a significant portion of the tourist and business influx into the country can be directly attributed to the erection of the building. So, we can say for sure that this project was a success. The final formula looks like this:

$$\text{Success}_{PM} + \text{Success}_{PPM} = \text{Success}$$

Let us now venture into the paradigm of alternative realities. Would the Burj Al Arab project be considered a success if the construction took seven instead of five years? Probably yes. Would this project be considered a success if it cost $700 instead of $650 million? Again, absolutely yes.

As a matter of fact, I can think of a number of projects that fall into this category: the movie *Titanic* (cost – $200 million, revenues – $2 billion), the first iPhone (cost – $150 million, revenues – $2.7 billion), Grand Theft Auto 5 (cost – $265 million, revenues – US $1 billion in its first three days!), just to name a few. Would really reasonable deviations in their budgets make them less of a success? Absolutely not. Would the iPhone be less of a success if it was released three months later than the actual date? Most likely yes.

So, how can we derive a formula for a successful project? Based on our analysis it looks something like this:

- Project success is a function of:
  - Business value is realized
  - Project is delivered reasonably on-budget
  - Project is delivered reasonably on time
  - Project scope is delivered within reasonable limits
  - Note: "reasonable" = "does not negate the business value"
- We have to look at project success both from the project management perspective (on-time, on-budget, etc.) and the project portfolio management perspective (value)

Final definitions

Having discussed the role of both project management (PM) and project portfolio management (PPM) in the success of any endeavor, let us now try to define the difference between the successful, troubled and failed projects.

Since we are using a two-dimensional view of the topic, we would need to examine each potential project from both the PM and PPM perspectives (see Table 6.4). I also thought that it would be necessary to distinguish salvageable or fixable projects from unrecoverable or non-fixable ones. Also, for the purpose of understanding of this list:

- PM_{GOOD} – means the project is in great shape from the project management's point of view (i.e. it is delivering full scope and is more or less on time and on budget)
- PM_{BAD} – implies that there are certain problems with the project scope, timeline or budget
- PPM_{GOOD} – means that the project was a good idea to implement and will deliver significant value to the company
- PPM_{BAD} – indicates that either the project was a bad idea at the very inception, or due to an array of factors (potentially including project management issues) it is not expected to deliver any value to the organization

Successful Project – in the upper left corner (quadrant A) we have projects that are on track both from the project management and project portfolio management perspectives. These ventures should be just properly monitored and controlled until their successful completion.

Troubled Projects – the next layer (quadrants B, E and D) contains troubled projects (either on the PM and/or PPM side), but these projects can still be saved by adjustments to their scope, schedules, budget, governance, etc.

Finally, the last layer (quadrants C, F, I, H and G) is comprised of projects that are so deep in trouble from PM and/or PPM viewpoints that the only option available to the stakeholders is to kill them, unless they are "stay-in-business" or regulatory initiatives.

Table 6.4 Successful vs troubled vs failed projects

	PM$_{Good}$	PM$_{Bad}$ Fixable	Non-Fixable
PPM$_{Good}$	**A** 1. Project is reasonably on-time and on-budget 2. Project will deliver full scope 3. Project will deliver planned value	**B** 1. Project is significantly late and/or over budget 2. Project scope will have to be cut significantly 3. Above issues can still be addressed 4. Project will deliver planned value if above issues are addressed	**C** 1. Project is immensely late and/or over budget 2. Project scope will have to be cut drastically 3. Above issues can't be addressed 4. Project will not deliver planned value because of (1), (2) and (3)
PPM$_{Bad}$ Fixable	**D** 1. Project is reasonably on-time and on-budget 2. Project will deliver full scope 3. Project's ability to deliver planned value is in question but can be addressed	**E** 1. Project is significantly late and/or over budget 2. Project scope will have to be cut significantly 3. Above issues can still be addressed 4. Project's ability to deliver planned value is in question but can be addressed	**F** 1. Project is immensely late and/or over budget 2. Project scope will have to be cut drastically 3. Above issues can't be addressed 4. Project will not deliver planned value because of (1), (2) and (3)
Non-Fixable	**G** 1. Project is reasonably on-time and on-budget 2. Project will deliver full scope 3. Project will not deliver planned value	**H** 1. Project is significantly late and/or over budget 2. Project scope will have to be cut significantly 3. Above issues can still be addressed 4. Project will not deliver planned value	**I** 1. Project is immensely late and/or over budget 2. Project scope will have to be cut drastically 3. Above issues can't be addressed 4. Project will not deliver planned value

What are the root causes of poor project performance?

Many excellent compilations on the root cause of project failure can be found in project management literature. While agreeing with almost all of them, I suggest, especially in the light of previous discussions, to categorize (see Table 6.5) them into three distinct groups:

- Pure project management root causes
- Pure project portfolio management root causes
- Mixed project and portfolio management root causes

Pure project management causes involve the issues that can be addressed by the project manager alone, without intervention of the senior project stakeholders and champions. These include (but are not limited to) lack of user involvement, poor requirements elicitation and analysis potentially resulting in scope creep, poor cost and time planning, lack of smaller project milestones or lack of properly trained staff.

Pure project portfolio management causes are usually beyond the project manager's control and can only be addressed by the senior management. These include low value of the selected project, lack of strategic alignment, absence of proper resources in terms of quality and/or quantity or very high riskiness of the initiatives.

The final group of root causes can be attributed both to the project management and project portfolio management domains in a sense that on some projects these factors can be related to the errors on the project manager's behalf and on some endeavors the senior stakeholders should be blamed for them. For example, lack of executive

Table 6.5 Root causes of project failure

PM Project was a brilliant idea, but something went horribly wrong	PM + PPM Root causes can be attributed both to PM and PPM domains	PPM Project was a bad idea but we executed it brilliantly

• Lack of user involvement
• Lack of clear statements of requirements
  • Scope creep
• Lack of proper planning
• Lack of smaller project milestones
• Lack of competent staff
• Lack of ownership
• Lack of hard-working, focused staff
• etc.
	• Lack of executive management support
	• Lack of realistic expectations
	  • Schedule pressure
	  • Budget pressure
	• Rushed implementations
	• Underestimation of complexity
	• Lack of clear vision and objectives
	• Lack of resources
	• etc.
		• Project is not delivering any value
		  • Overestimated value
		  • Underestimated budget and timeline
		• Project is not strategically aligned
		• Project is not in line with available resources or mission
		• Project is not sound politically, socially or for business relationships
		• Project is not feasible technologically and/or economically
		• Involves excessive risk for our risk culture
		• etc.

management support can happen because of the executives distancing themselves for whatever reasons away from the project manager and not providing him/her with the feedback necessary for the success of the venture. However, on the other hand, the project manager himself may choose not to be proactive and follow up on the status reports he has disseminated earlier in the process.

It is very important in my opinion to distinguish these three categories of project failure root causes because later in the "Project Recovery Plan" stage we will need to know whether the problem at hand should be addressed from the project management or project portfolio management perspective.

What are the warning signs?

What are some of the telltale signs that your project could be in trouble? One of the most significant ones is when the key project stakeholders start abandoning their previous commitments with respect to overall support for the project, finances and human resources, to name a few. In addition, they may cease to refer to the project as "our project", instead calling it "your project".

Speaking of resources, you may suddenly discover that they are not as available to you as they were at the project's inception. You will be encouraged to produce "more with less", "work smart, not hard" and "trim the fat".

Some people may even start convincing you that there are more than 40 hours in a work week and there are more than 22 days in a month. As a result, you may discover that the overtime situation on your project is out of control.

Another sign that your project is in trouble is when one of the following scenarios occurs:

- No one is paying attention to your status reports sent to senior stakeholders
- You are being told in no uncertain terms to change the color of your status reports from red or yellow to green

Finally, you may start hearing voices questioning the value of the project to the organization, or – on the opposite end of the spectrum – you may be drowned in the overly optimistic sales forecasts regarding the final product of your project.

Saving troubled projects

Obviously, it is best to prevent the situations with underperforming projects by properly following both project portfolio management and project management procedures when selecting prioritizing, planning and controlling your company's ventures. But what can be done if your senior management suddenly feels that your project gets off track or slips into low performance? What can be done about it? Can the project get back on track? How?

First, senior stakeholders must agree that the project is, indeed, in trouble, and announce a troubled project audit. Then, they must assign a recovery project manager consultant. The recovery project manager should preferably be external to the company so that he or she are not affected by previous project history and intercompany politics. What are the steps that the RPM should undertake during the project audit?

1. Conduct expectations meeting with executive stakeholders in order to determine the exact expectations from the recovery project manager
2. Conduct meetings with the key project stakeholders including the project champion and key project sponsors
3. Analyze general project portfolio management and project management procedures at the company
4. Interview other project stakeholders, including key subject matter experts and decision makers
5. Review project documentation
6. Determine potential trouble areas, at least at a high level

Let us now focus on step 3 of the audit process. Here is a list of preliminary questions that a recovery project manager can direct at all of the stakeholders he/she is interacting with:

Project portfolio management questions

- How did you arrive at a decision to initiate this particular project?
- What value or benefits were you expecting to realize after a successful completion of this venture?
- Is there a project selection/prioritization process at the company?
- Are all project proposals subjected to robust, uniform and measurable selection criteria?

Project management questions

- Does the company have a well-defined project management process?
- Do you assign qualified, certified project managers to run their projects?
- Is there a robust line of communication between the project managers and the executives (i.e. are the status reports issued and are they read?)
- What is the minimum of key project documents that the project manager must produce?
- Does your project management conform to the industry's best practices?

Once the preliminary questions have been asked, the recovery project manager can identify high-level areas of interest to delve into more detailed inquiries regarding the project at hand.

Questions to ask – Project portfolio management domain

Here are some of the detailed questions from the project portfolio management domain that should be asked:

- Why did you decide to implement this project?
- What would have happened if this project had not been approved?
- What is the value of this project?
  - How do you measure project value?

- Is this project aligned with your strategy?
  - What is your company strategy?
- Did you have all the required resources (financial and human) to accomplish this initiative?
- Was this project sound politically, socially or for business relationships?
- Was this project feasible technologically and/or economically?
- Did this project involve excessive risk for your risk culture?
- Is this a regulatory or stay-in-business project?
- Did you achieve all of your project portfolio management goals?
  - What is missing?
- How in your opinion can this be remedied?
- What changes should be implemented in order to achieve your PPM goals?
  - Scope
  - Budget

Questions to ask – Project management domain

Below is the list of project management-related questions that a recovery project manager may ask of the project stakeholders:

- What are the issues?
- Why did they happen?
- How would you fix them?
- Who was managing the project?
  - Single qualified person
  - Single unqualified person
  - Management by committee
- Did s/he create a project charter?
- Did s/he create a Requirements Document?
- Did s/he create a Project Plan?
- Have all these documents been through:
  - Stakeholder walkthroughs
  - Technical team inspections
  - Peer reviews
- Was there any pressure applied to the project manager with respect to:
  - Deadline
  - Budget
- Did you have a predefined scope management process?
  - Has it been communicated to all stakeholders?
- Did you utilize change requests?
- Did the PM issue meeting minutes?
- Did the PM issue status reports?
- Were the stakeholders paying attention to status reports?
  - Especially "red" and "amber" ones?
- Did the executives provide sufficient support to the project team in general and to the project manager specifically?

- Did they keep their doors open to the PM?
  - Were they paying attention to the status reports?
- Were the project estimates based on calculations performed by experienced professionals?
- Did the executives provide the project manager with all the required, adequately-skilled resources?
- Did the executives grant the project manager sufficient authority to run the project freely with respect to:
  - Timeline
  - Quality
  - HR
  - Risks
  - Procurement

Documents to review

The recovery project manager should also request to review the following project documents:

- Project charter
- Requirements specifications
- Design documents (may need technical experts)
- Project plan
- Status reports
- Meeting minutes
- Change requests
- Any other important documents (depends on company maturity and complexity of the project)

The decision matrix

Based on the in-depth analysis of the documents and the information received during the interviews, the recovery project manager working together with the senior stakeholders should determine the answers to the following questions:

- Is this project still a good idea from the project portfolio management perspective?
- Is this initiative in good shape from the project management perspective?

If the answer to both questions is "yes", then no significant action is required. However, if the answer to any or both of the above questions is negative, the recovery project manager and the executives should consider the following questions (see also Table 6.6):

- Can the project portfolio issues the project is facing be addressed by adjusting its scope, implementing auxiliary projects or some other action?
- Can we fix the project management troubles affecting the project by cutting the scope, increasing its budget, assigning more resources, etc.?

TABLE 6.6 Recovery decision matrix

		PM$_{Good}$	PM$_{Bad}$ Fixable	Non-Fixable
PPM$_{Good}$		Do nothing	Implement full project management rescue	Kill the project, unless continuing is more profitable (or mission-critical/regulatory initiative
PPM$_{Bad}$	Fixable	Try to adjust scope, budget, timeline, quality, HR, risks, procurement in order to increase project value	Try to adjust scope, budget, timeline, quality, HR, risks, procurement in order to increase project value AND implement full project management rescue	Kill the project, unless continuing is more profitable (or mission-critical/regulatory initiative
	Non-Fixable	Kill the project, unless continuing is more profitable (or mission-critical/ regulatory initiative)	Kill the project, unless continuing is more profitable (or mission-critical/regulatory initiative)	Kill the project, unless continuing is more profitable (or mission-critical/regulatory initiative)

If the answer to any one of the above questions is "no", then the company should consider abandoning the project, unless, of course it falls into the category of "must-do" ventures (e.g. mission critical or regulatory).

If the project is deemed to be "saveable" at the end of this exercise, then the recovery project manager must develop a project recovery plan and present it to the Project Steering Committee.

Project Recovery Plan

Project recovery plan (PRP) usually consists of the following sections:

- **Introduction** – where the author is expected to provide a brief background on the project and to discuss challenges encountered, both from the project management and project portfolio management points of views
- **Proposed solution** – where the project manager should discuss proposed changes to project scope, schedule, budget, quality, team procurement and communications in order to address the problems mentioned earlier
- **Detailed project plan** – a regular project plan document that covers all ten project management knowledge areas mentioned earlier in this chapter:
- Project scope management plan
  - Note: will potentially require a new baseline requirements specifications document
- Project Time Management Plan
- Project Cost Management Plan

- Project Quality Management Plan
- Project Risk Management Plan
- Project HR Management Plan
- Project Communications Management Plan
- Project Stakeholder Management Plan
- Project Procurement Management Plan

Case study: Product company

Let us now try to illustrate the principles described earlier in the chapter by using a real-life case study with a software development company.

Introduction

Several years ago, I was approached by a CEO of a fairly small software company (about 150–200 employees in total) who wanted our help with his challenges. The company had gone through very rapid growth, but started experiencing severe problems with their new product release project.

Several conversations and one-on-one interviews ensued where we heard the following complaints from the senior stakeholders:

"We struggle with our main product"
"We are falling behind the industry leaders with respect to the richness of our features, but we want to be known as innovative leaders of the industry"
"We are constantly late and over budget"
"Whatever we deliver has serious quality issues"
"Our team morale is low"
"Six out of eight main customers told us not to call them again until we fix our problems with the product"

Audit findings

Further investigation discovered that from the project portfolio management's point of view, there was no prioritization of the features going into the final product design; all of the desired functionality would receive a "Must Have" rating and be added to the scope.

Also, the professional services team (i.e. the employees who installed and fine-tuned the company's platform at the clients' sites) were perceived as "money-earners" by the executives since they charged the company customers between $275 and $350 per man-hour of services, usually generating between $500,000 and $2,000,000 per project in professional services fees. On the other hand, the product development department was considered to be the "money-wasters" since they didn't generate any direct, tangible revenue for the organization. As a result of this "policy", the most experienced and talented technical members of the team would end up in the professional services department, while the inexperienced underachievers would be assigned to the product development team.

Project management issues identified by our team included:

- While the customer-facing professional services department was fairly mature from the project management and business analysis perspective, the product development team was a complete mess with an utterly ad-hoc approach to their projects
- Very vague and incomplete project charters, requirements documentation and project plans
- Project manager leading the product development effort had a programming background with no project management training (formal or informal) or experience
- Status reports were neither demanded by the executives, nor issued by the team
- There was a significant pressure applied to the team to deliver more scope for less time and money with the project manager yielding to the pressure almost every time

Recommendations

With respect to project portfolio management practices, our team urged the management of the company to establish a feature prioritization mechanism by developing a scoring model similar to the one described earlier in this chapter (see Table 6.2) and processing all of the features requested through it. Also, the management was advised to establish a so-called "available resources bucket" to assess the total resources available for the project. For example, if the product development team was expected to consist of 20 developers and the project was expected to last for 6 months, the total available resources bucket was calculated in the following manner:

$$\text{Total Available Resources Bucket} = 20 \text{ people} \times 22 \text{ days/month} \times 6 \text{ months}$$

$$= 2,640 \text{ man-days}$$

This implied that the total resource cut-off for the project was at around 26 hundred person-days and once the prioritized features filled this bucket, the rest of them should either be discarded or moved to the next phase.

Also, the cannibalization of the product development team had to stop immediately and several high-performing resources had to be reassigned to the PD team right away.

From the project management perspective, the following suggestions have been presented to the executive team:

- Establish a robust project management process at least for the flagship product development project
- Provide all team members with project management and requirements engineering training
- Assign external project manager and business analyst (qualified, experienced and certified)
- Senior development manager now reports to the project manager
- Explain the basics of successful project delivery to the executives
- Communicate with your external stakeholders (clients) on a regular basis

Results

The executive committee has accepted and implemented all of the above recommen-dations in a very short period of time. These actions resulted in significant cuts to the features that made it to the final scope, improved project planning, monitoring and control. As a result, the customers were able to receive the most desired features on-time and the company was able to stick to a 20-man product development team.

Conclusion

Just like in pretty much any endeavor, there are two ways of initiating and running any given project: to start and manage it properly right from the very beginning or to start and manage it poorly only to realize your mistakes at a later point of time, stop all the work and redo all of your tasks. Needless to say, the first approach is way faster and less expensive than the second one. Therefore, I strongly recommend the following method to project selection and management:

- **Step 1:** When assessing the new idea, ask yourself a question, "Will this project add significant value to our organization?" This step can be just an informal discussion between the key project stakeholders or a full-scale project portfolio management exercise with scoring models, portfolio balance and strategic fit assessments.
- **Step 2:** Properly initiate the project by assigning an experienced certified project manager. Ask the project manager to produce the project charter. Examine, discuss and, if necessary, improve this document.
- **Step 3:** Ask your project manager – with the help of other team members – to gen-erate a requirements specifications document. Examine, discuss and, if necessary, improve this document. Revisit your project selection criteria and try to assess if your initial project portfolio management assumptions have been impacted in any way.
- **Step 4:** Develop a project plan. Examine, discuss and, if necessary, improve this document. Revisit your project selection criteria and try to assess if your initial project portfolio management assumptions have been impacted in any way.
- **Step 5:** Execute the project while maintaining control over it by monitoring the team's performance. Constantly revisit your project selection criteria and try to assess if your initial project portfolio management assumptions have been impacted in any way.
- **Step 6:** Close out the project and produce Lessons Learned document.

Good luck on all of your future endeavors!

Chapter 7

Communications shape reality

Ann Pilkington

It is often said that the most common reason for project failure is poor communication. These days, every project manager must surely know the importance of communication – but what does good communication look like? What should a project manager expect from their communication lead?

This chapter sets out to answer those questions. But first, let's define communication in the context of projects.

First, communication is the same as stakeholder engagement. This is important to note as sometimes the two are viewed separately with communication seen as a process and the 'stuff' that is sent out. Sometimes in the world of public relations and internal communication this is known as SOS – 'Send out Stuff'. Stakeholders are at the heart of a good communication strategy, so when talking about communication on projects, you are also talking about stakeholder engagement.

Second, good communication is two-way. Think about defining it as 'the response you get back'. This simply reminds us that unless we check back with our stakeholder we have no idea how our communication has been received and interpreted. To take a quote attributed to George Bernard Shaw: 'The biggest problem with communication is the illusion that it has been accomplished'.

Communication on projects should be designed to help the project deliver its objectives by:

- Managing engagement with stakeholders
- Ensuring there is effective communication within the team
- Helping the project to identify and manage risks and issues
- Aligning activity and messaging with the wider organisation, where appropriate

Planning communication strategically

Communication is not a 'soft skill'. Every project should have a communication strategy that is informed by research, draws on theory and can be measured. A good communication strategy is a bit like a business case in that it sets out the rationale for a particular approach, with a budget. It is a written description of a strategic planning process that has taken place.

Communication strategies and plans are different. A plan is a collection of tactics with timings that are designed to deliver the strategy. It can sit as an appendix to the strategy document.

High-performing projects will plan communication strategically. This is important for the following reasons (Gregory 2010):

- Focuses effort
- Improves effectiveness
- Encourages the longer term view
- Helps demonstrate value for money
- Minimises mishaps
- Reconciles conflicts
- Facilitates proactivity

Writing from a public relations perspective, Dr Heather Yaxley (2017) says:

> For public relations to act as a strategic function, it needs to encourage development of capabilities in analysing issues and opportunities. The knowledge base of PR practitioners will not be respected if it is based predominantly on personal experience, intuition, common sense, methodologically weak research or habitual practice.

This is equally true when delivering communication to support project outcomes.

Watch out for plans that simply pull together a number of tactics without a strategy behind them – this won't be strategy and is really just a calendar. That isn't to say that such plans don't have a use; where a project is part of a wider programme it can be helpful to pull together the plans of all the constituent projects to spot conflicts and potential synergies.

Make sure that the communication strategy does not exist in isolation, it must always be designed to help the project deliver its objectives.

There are many communication planning models, for example the RADAR model by Ruck (2015). When the project is part of a wider organisation, there may be established planning models, for example with UK government the OASIS model is used (Figure 7.1).

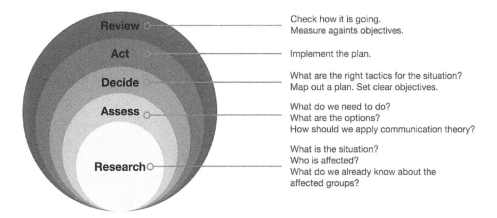

Figure 7.1 RADAR model of communication planning by Dr Kevin Ruck.

All strategic communication planning models follow a similar approach of:

* Research
* Stakeholder identification
* Objective setting
* Strategic approach
* Content
* Evaluation

Research

A project communication strategy should be based on research. This research should answer the following questions:

* What is the situation?
* Who is affected?
* What do we already know about the affected groups?

At this initial stage of planning, this research has two uses:

* To set benchmarks to inform communication objectives.
* Decide the strategic approach. For example, what will make people change their behaviour and what might the blockers/motivators be? Never assume that you know the answer.

It may not be necessary to do or commission original research (known as 'primary research'). Have a look within the organisation first. Then look outside the organisation. Go to reputable sources – that means someone or an organisation that is qualified to do research. Look closely at how the data was collected – is the methodology published? Who did it? Why did they do it? There is a lot of dodgy data out there.

Understanding the stakeholder and their motivations is key. This can be illustrated through this example:

> An American university wanted male students to start drying their washing outside on the line. Using the dryers went against their 'green' policy of cutting down on energy use. So they embarked on a campaign with an environmental theme – but nothing changed.
>
> Then they did some research with the male students. They learned that they wouldn't put washing on the line because it wasn't seen as 'manly'. No amount of green messaging was going to change their behaviour.

Who are the stakeholders?

It is during this research stage that stakeholders for the project need to be identified and mapped. High-performing projects will communicate from the perspective of the stakeholder, not project or programme structure. What the project wants to tell stakeholders may not be the most important thing to them.

The key is to segment stakeholders in as much detail as possible. There is no such thing as 'the general public' or 'all employees'. Even 'the local community' is too vague. Within that community could be community leaders, people of school age, activists, young mums – they may all have different needs from your project. The research done to understand the situation informs the stakeholder list. For example, if the project is to increase healthy eating, it may be discovered that the price of fresh food is a blocker in which case key stakeholders will include supermarket bosses and buyers.

Having decided who the stakeholders are, there are a number of ways of prioritising them. This is often done through a power/interest matrix where those stakeholders who are considered to be most powerful and most interested are prioritised over those thought to be less so.

However, care needs to be taken with the notion of power. In an age of social media, a stakeholder who at one time would have struggled to have a voice can now find one very easily online. A project should also consider how ethical it is to consider those perceived as less powerful – but still interested – of less importance.

It could be argued that this model of power/interest is outdated and it is far more useful to consider each stakeholder or group of stakeholders individually rather than shoehorn them into a matrix. This enables the project to look at things from a stakeholder perspective and design communications accordingly. The power/interest matrix can encourage a tick-box approach to stakeholder engagement with the matrix sometimes seen as the end in itself. It also fails to prompt projects to think about what is wanted from a stakeholder relationship. Too often the project sets out to seek a positive attitude to the project from stakeholders. Moving powerful, interested stakeholders to a positive position is thought to link strongly to project success. However, this approach drives effort towards a coterie of powerful, interested individuals in an organisation, who may have the strategic vision but may lack vital practical knowledge – knowledge which can make all the difference to a project (Horton and Pilkington 2014).

Stakeholders will vary through the life of a project. Another way to think about categorising them is in terms of what the project will want from them and what they will want from the project at different stages. It is the project's responsibility to help stakeholders understand why they are being engaged at each stage and what is wanted of them. This understanding can be used to inform a different way of looking at stakeholders – by role, proposed by Pilkington and Horton (2014):

> An effective project/stakeholder relationship relies on both parties being clear about what each needs from the other and in order to achieve this a role-based approach to stakeholder identification can be adopted.

The suggested roles are:

- Sponsors: they hold the budget and can release resources.
- Shapers: involved at the design stage (this could be the design of an IT system, new ways of working, policy or a product). Failure to engage this group during design is most likely to cause behaviours that exhibit the 'not invented here' syndrome, which challenge a successful implementation and adoption.

- Schedulers: often 'gatekeepers', they can get things done and make the implementation of the project happen. They are also often the group most likely to alert projects to practical risks and issues relating to plans.
- Users: change targets who will use the new service, adopt different ways of working, etc.

Finally, think about who is going to own each stakeholder relationship. It won't always be the project manager. This is where the project sponsor can have a key role. As well as approving the communication strategy itself, the sponsor will have a role to play in stakeholder engagement. They can talk peer-to-peer with stakeholders and often unlock difficult relationships. It is important that the sponsor understands that this is part of his or her role on a project.

Setting objectives

> 'Would you tell me which way I ought to go from here?' asked Alice. 'That depends a good deal on where you want to get,' said the Cat. 'I really don't care where,' replied Alice. 'Then it doesn't much matter which way you go,' said the Cat.
>
> Alice's Adventures in Wonderland (1865) by Lewis Carroll

Having worked out what the situation is, who the stakeholders are and the strategic approach, communication objectives can be set.

Devising the communication objectives can work well as a collaborative exercise. It helps to get buy in to the communication approach from the project team members and gives support to the communication lead.

Research done at the start of the process informs the objectives and helps to set the measures. Just like all objectives, the communication ones should be SMART: Specific. Measureable. Achievable. Relevant. Timed.

Two key things that the project manager should demand from a communication strategy are SMART objectives and measurements.

Setting objectives is essential. Without them, it isn't possible to measure success. If you can't prove how well your campaign went, then why should anyone take the PR and communication function seriously? Objectives focus effort and stop you from doing things that aren't of any value. They help to demonstrate that PR and communication is a function to be taken seriously.

An example of a SMART objective would be:

> By the end of the year, 80% of office-based employees know what they have to do to prepare for the office move.

There are some things to look out for when setting objectives:

- They must be about communication. It sounds obvious, but communication alone may not be able to achieve a successful office move. There will be many other factors!
- There should only be one thing per objective – otherwise the objective can't be measured accurately. An example of doubling up would be setting an objective

around awareness and behaviour change, e.g. '80% of office-based employees are aware of the office move and know what they need to do'.

- Objectives should be about outcomes. Too often objectives are only about process – issuing a number of newsletters, getting people to an event, for example. Think about what the project wants people to think, feel or do as a result of the communication activity.

Deciding on the strategic approach

The RADAR model (Ruck 2015) is different from most models in one key way – it prompts the communicator to think about the application of theory to achieve objectives. The model suggests communication theory, but this may also be an understanding of psychology.

It is at this stage that the strategic approach to communication will be decided. It can sound odd to have a strategy section in a document called a strategy but it simply means explaining what your strategic approach is going to be.

The strategic approach will guide the tactics. For example, there is no point in saying that you are going to give stakeholders a voice by adopting a two-way approach to communication and then delivering tactics that only broadcast information. The strategic approach is the golden thread that runs through the communication strategy linking everything together.

Tell or sell?

In any discussion about project communication it is common to hear the advice: 'We must tell people what's in it for them'. However, the truth is that sometimes there isn't anything 'in it' for some or all stakeholders. Thinking about project communication from this perspective engenders a 'sell' approach which is more associated with one-way communication than a genuine two-way dialogue.

A focus on selling a change can actually be a blocker to successful communication. For example, a line manager told to sell a change to his or her team, when there isn't really a clear benefit, is going to find this much harder than explaining the change and facilitating a conversation about it, perhaps with questions and feedback for the project. This fear of having to sell a message that they don't understand or feel uncomfortable with is a blocker to communication at this level.

Communicating change

All projects are, of course, about change. There is no mystery to change communication but there are some key things to be aware of:

- Communication must reflect the degree of change. It is important to assess the change impact on the different stakeholder groups – usually a role for the business change function. A project many be spending millions on a new IT system, but the impact of the change on users may not be significant. Elsewhere in the business, a smaller, low budget project could be having a much higher impact. The communication effort should go where the impact is greatest and that may not be where the most money is being spent.

- Be clear about which stakeholders need to be involved at each stage. Set out a clear timetable for engagement so that stakeholders know when they are going to be involved and how. Stakeholders will vary in importance throughout the lifecycle of a project, so the stakeholder approach must be reviewed regularly.
- Engagement works better than telling or selling the change. It is now established that employee engagement results from giving employees a voice that is listened to and project communication with stakeholders can adopt the same approach. But to make the most of that voice, stakeholders need to know what is going on and why. So, accurate and timely information (not propaganda) is essential. And their voice must be listened to. It is important to close the feedback loop by ensuring that stakeholders know how their feedback is being used and, if it can't shape the project, explain why.
- Ambiguity can be a challenge. Communicating change can be a difficult balancing act. It is unlikely that at the start of the project, the team will have all the answers about what is going to happen and when. This ambiguity can be unsettling for stakeholders, particularly employee stakeholders within organisations. The way to manage this is through signposting. Signposting involves pointing to stakeholders to when the project will have the answer and explaining why at present, it doesn't.
- Keep it stakeholder-centred. There may be a number of parts to the project or lots of projects within a programme, but what matters to the stakeholder? The approach must be built around them. Ask what it means for a line manager, HR colleagues and operatives on the shop floor and design the communication accordingly.

A common myth of change communication is that projects should communication 'early and often'. This sounds like common sense and good practice, but it is a simplistic statement that needs some thought. Communicating early in the change process may not be appropriate for all stakeholders. For some, the change may be sometime in the distance and not the most important issue for them. The other problem with communicating too early is that it starts something of a treadmill of communicating often when there may not be anything new to say. Sometimes it is OK not to communicate! Use the signposting technique above and ensure there is a place from where stakeholders can pull information if they want it.

Behaviour change: Using nudge in project communication

Projects are always about change and will sometimes require people to change their behaviour.

The concept of 'nudge' is a method of increasing the likelihood of behaviour change. The idea of a nudge comes from behavioural economics – a field dedicated to understanding why people and institutions make the decisions they do. It grew in the 1960s as scientific knowledge about the brain played a bigger role in psychology but it absolutely exploded in 2008 with the publication of a book called *Nudge* (The Guardian).

Nudge is about making small changes to 'nudge' people into a certain behaviour. There are many examples in practice including the UK government tax collector – HM Revenue and Customs (HMRC). A trial with HMRC showed how telling late tax payers that most people in their towns had already paid their tax increased payment rates by 15 percentage points. It was anticipated that when rolled nationally, the approach would generate £30m of extra revenue to the Exchequer annually.

The approach is not unlike Cialdini's 6 Principles of Influence which include:

- Commitment and Consistency: If people commit, orally or in writing, to an idea or goal, they are more likely to honour that commitment because of establishing that idea or goal as being congruent with their self-image. Even if the original incentive or motivation is removed after they have already agreed, they will continue to honour the agreement.
- Social Proof: People will do things that they see other people are doing.
- Liking: People are easily persuaded by other people that they like. Cialdini cites the marketing of Tupperware in what might now be called viral marketing. People were more likely to buy if they liked the person selling it to them.

Ethics in change communication

Persuasion techniques such as nudge, the work of Cialdini and other techniques such as the use of NLP (Neuro-linguistic programming, a sometimes controversial approach to communication, personal development and psychotherapy created by Richard Bandler and John Grinder in California), are powerful and can help a project to achieve its aims. But what are the ethical considerations?

Being in possession of the knowledge to deliver effective behaviour change communication programmes can put the project at an advantage, but how ethical is it to use these techniques to persuade?

Some may argue that it depends on the desired outcome – for example, getting people to eat more healthily may be seen as a good thing, but getting people to accept a pay cut or less advantageous working conditions may not.

The first approach is referred to as rule-based ethics and relies on the idea that human beings have a duty to do certain things or act in certain ways in all situations. This is also known as the deontological approach (the study of duty). A problem with this approach is interpreting the rules (Parsons 2008).

The second approach is known as situational ethics and as the name implies allows for consideration of the special circumstances inherent in each situation, while still using fundamental principles as guidelines. This is also known as the teleological approach (the study of ends). Unfortunately, it is often difficult to determine in advance what the consequences might be of a particular course of action. What if there are conflicting benefits such as something that is good for employees but bad for customers? Also, this type of thinking does risk tipping over into the ends justifies the means and a danger that minority views are screened out, i.e. as long as most people are happy with what is proposed then we are behaving ethically.

There is perhaps a conflict here between persuading stakeholders to a particular course of action versus engaging with stakeholders to enable them to influence the course of action. Having said that, there will be times when a project really needs people to work or act differently and will need to consider how comfortable it feels in adopting persuasion techniques.

Ethics should of course pervade the whole project and communication strategy. This must include presenting data accurately, using research and measurement to ensure the best use of project resources, avoiding 'spinning' facts and figures to make the project look good – everyone will see through it anyway!

Content and messages

Many communicators are moving away from the concept of 'key messages' to one of storytelling or narrative.

A key message approach involves creating consistent statements comprised of pre-determined words, phrases and/or sentences. They can be monitored as outputs to be deemed as a measure of successful communication.

Adopting a key message approach is useful for ensuring consistency, but can lead to the project focussing on the transmission of messages rather than engaging in dialogue with stakeholders.

Storytelling can be much more engaging (Pilkington 2018). Denning, writing for *Forbes*, says that storytelling is quick, powerful, free, natural, refreshing, energising, collaborative, persuasive, holistic, entertaining, moving, memorable and authentic.

Research undertaken at the Massachusetts Institute of Technology (MIT) demonstrated that students had a higher information retention rate when information was presented to them in the form of a story. Not everybody has a head for recalling numbers and detail. Presentations packed with facts and figures have their place but according to psychologist Jerome Bruner, facts are 20 times more likely to be remembered if they are part of a story (Harrison 2015).

However, this does not mean abandoning messages. Messages can form the framework for a story. On projects, storytelling is particularly useful as it can set out the rationale for change.

So what about narrative? Storytelling and narrative are different although the terms are often used interchangeably. In the context of a project, a story can explain the rationale for change and the narrative might be wider organisation's position on something.

A high-performing project will be able to tell a compelling story about why it is doing what it is doing. This story must be informed by the research at the start of the strategic planning process. It should reflect what stakeholders want to know and their concerns.

Projects should look for opportunities to tell joined-up stories. For example, within an organisation it is likely that a project is just one of a number of change initiatives. How are employees meant to make sense of it all? It can be rather like a piece of flat-packed furniture – there are lots of parts but it's not very clear how it all fits together. Setting the project in the context of what else is happening enables employees to make sense of all the change rather than leaving staff to work out how it all fits together. Doing this effectively means forging relationships with other communicators working on other projects and at a corporate level.

Storytelling techniques

Smith's (2012) CAR framework sets out a suggested structure for storytelling. His CAR model has three elements – context, action and result.

The context stage includes the introduction of a villain or challenge. The second stage, action, talks about what is done and includes a setback or failure along the way. The final stage, the result, includes a point of learning for the reader or audience.

Denning (2005) says that there is no 'right' way to tell a story but he sets out eight different types of stories, according to what the organisation wants to achieve. He calls these 'narrative patterns', four examples are set out here (Table 7.1):

Table 7.1 Denning's Narrative Patterns

What do you want to achieve?	Your story needs to...
Sparking action – springboard stories	Describe how it worked in the past while allowing people to see how it could work in their situation.
Communicate who you are	Provide drama and some strength or vulnerability from the past.
Transmit values	Feel familiar and prompt discussion.
Lead people into the future	Evoke the future.

Evaluation of communication

Evaluation should link back to the communication objectives set. This is why setting SMART objectives is so important. If there are well-constructed objectives, it is simply a case of seeing if the measures within them have been met. It really is as straightforward as that.

Having said that, leaving evaluation to the end is risky. The project may deliver a whole change communication campaign and then find out that it hasn't worked. The answer is to check at key points by setting some KPIs through the campaign. These may check outputs as well as outcomes. If something isn't working there is time to change it.

Getting the most from your communication lead

Communication is a specialist skill underpinned by theory. While everyone can communicate, designing effective communication programmes is a job for a specialist. Project managers should seek out communicators with not only experience, but appropriate qualifications.

As discussed earlier in the chapter, the role of communication is not simply to 'send out stuff' or make things look nice. It isn't a soft skill, it is a strategic function key to project success and therefore worth investing in. The communication role is a demanding and varied one. It involves (Pilkington 2015):

- Scoping and understanding the communication requirement
- Developing and maintaining a fit-for-purpose communication strategy and plan
- Taking an audience/stakeholder–centred approach
- Ensuring there is a clear vision and narrative
- Coaching and advising project leaders on personal communication style and messaging
- Providing accurate and timely information to stakeholders and project team
- Encouraging and facilitating feedback to help achieve mutual understanding between the project and its stakeholders
- Producing communication products that are accurate, on-brand and meet a communication need
- Evaluating the effectiveness of communication
- Building relationships with other communicators
- Monitoring the environment to 'gauge the mood' of stakeholders

When to involve communication

While the project communicator should be involved in discussions at all times on a project, there are some points when input is key. Involving communication at the following times will benefit the project and stakeholders.

Change control. The project communication lead should be part of any change control process. A good communicator can advise on how a change may be perceived by stakeholders. It also means that the function gets early sight of potential changes which need to be communicated.

Risks and issues. Project managers are concerned with risks to the delivery of their projects. The communication function will take a wider view and think also about risk to the reputation of the organisation of which the project is a part. An understanding of the external implications of a course of action may sometimes be needed – for example, how will something be perceived by the media or politicians. The communication function adds real value here.

On a day to day basis, communication should be considered at all project and programme meetings. Don't leave it as a standalone item at the end of the agenda. While there should be regular reporting from communication on progress against plan, high-performing projects will consider the communication implications of all decisions. Sometimes there won't be any implications but when there are it can be decided quickly which stakeholders are affected and who is going to have a conversation with them about it.

Having said all of the above, perhaps the most important point is to involve communication from the word go. This will mean better outcomes for the project and stakeholders. Communication should be there at the start of the project helping to develop the narrative. Bring communication in too late and there is a danger that time will have to be spent in catching up, unpicking muddled messaging and re-engaging stakeholders.

Equally important in getting the most from your communication lead is to go to them with problems – not solutions.

> Ask your communicator to come up with the solution. One thing that really bugs the communicator is being brought a solution rather than the problem. Communication is most effective when the solution is designed once the problem is understood fully. Sometimes the answer may not even be a communication intervention. Good communicators have a range of tools in their toolkit and should be able to select the most appropriate. So, seek their advice and counsel and don't be surprised if they ask 'why?' a lot! (Pilkington 2016)

Also, don't be surprised if the answer to the problem isn't communication. Communication should never be a sticking plaster to cover a poor process or bad decision.

Who is your spokesperson?

Part of the role of communication on a project is to guide and coach whoever the spokesperson for the project is. This may be the project manager and/or the sponsor. It is important to select the right person for this role and this won't necessarily be the most senior person.

Perloff (2017) has looked at a number of studies on what makes someone a credible communicator and summarises studies into three attributes:

- Expertise: special skills or know how
- Trustworthy: perceived honesty, character and safety
- Displaying goodwill: caring

Storytelling is an effective way for project leaders to position themselves as credible communicators. The approach is to tell a personal story that illustrates these attributes. However, there are some things to think about:

Expertise. During the Brexit debates in the UK, the claim was made that 'we have all had enough of experts'. The point is to select an expert who will have resonance with the audience. An expert does not need to have letters after his or her name; that expertise may have been gained through experience.

Trustworthy. In her book on change, Julie Hodges talks about Andrea Jung, CEO of Avon Products until 2012, who had to take the organisation through a structure. She decided against cascade communication and instead travelled the world telling a compelling story of how she saw the future of the company. The approach was credited with making the harsh reality of job losses easier to accept and she was seen as open and honest.

Goodwill. Being an expert is no good if there is no empathy – Perloff uses the example of the doctor/patient relationship to illustrate this. The doctor may be an expert, but without empathy he or she would not be thought of as a credible communicator.

Personality

The Myers–Briggs Type Indicator (MBTI) assessment is a psychometric questionnaire designed to measure psychological preferences in how people perceive the world and

Extraversion	Introversion
Face to face is preferred to written communication	Written communication is preferred to face to face communication
Likes to communication in groups	Likes to communicate one to one
Sensing	**Intuition**
Likes suggestions to be straightforward and feasible	Likes global schemes with broad issues presented first
Likes specific examples	Refers to general concepts
Thinking	**Feeling**
Want the pros and cons of each alternative to be given	Want to know why an alternative is valuable and how it affects people
Judging	**Perceiving**
Expect others to follow through and count on it	Present their views as tentative and open to modification

Figure 7.2 Myers-Briggs Type Indicator (MBTI), contrasting communication preferences.

make decisions. MBTI is based upon the theory of psychological type as originally developed by Carl Jung.

There are many personality profiling techniques, but MBTI is perhaps the most useful from a communication perspective. If the project spokesperson understands his or her profile, they can understand how to adapt their communication style to appeal to a wider range of stakeholders.

Figure 7.2 provides some of the contrasting communication preferences.

From the figure of contrasting communication preferences, it is possible to see how, for example, someone with a strong 'intuition' preference may need to adapt their style when talking to stakeholders to provide more detail and specific examples.

This understanding of personality should also be factored into the broader communication strategy, for example, by providing a range of different products and events that meet the needs of different communication styles.

In conclusion

Good communication can mean the difference between success and failure on a project. It must be planned strategically. The days of it being seen as a 'soft skill' are over. A good project communication strategy is informed by research, built on theory and evaluated using a recognised methodology. Look for SMART outcome objectives, detailed stakeholder analysis and a compelling narrative. Make it stakeholder centred – it may be costing big money, but what is the change impact? This is what should dictate the level of communication input.

Embed communication across the project. Every time a decision is made, stop and think about the communication implications. Who is affected? Who owns that stakeholder relationship and what do they need to do?

A project communication lead likes to be brought problems, not solutions. Make the most of their expertise – the answer isn't always a newsletter!

There is nothing more satisfying than a project that delivers its benefits or hearing a stakeholder say how engaged they were in the process.

Chapter 8

Knowledge management shapes culture

Stephen Duffield

> Those that fail to learn from history are doomed to repeat it.
>
> Winston Churchill (1874–1965)

Introduction

The process of managing project knowledge is a new addition to the PMBOK® Guide Sixth Edition (Project Management Institute, 2017). The concept of knowledge management (KM) is for most project managers, a new journey. They may be familiar with the organisation problems from their daily experiences and may have some understanding of the flow of knowledge in the organisation. Management as a whole need to be more involved in learning about KM, as KM initiatives and practices have overall strategic implications. A high-performing project is one where organisational project knowledge and lessons learned are well integrated and managed.

In this chapter, you will discover the integration of organisation learning, knowledge management and lessons learned within the project management organisation environment. The chapter presents the Systemic Lessons Learned Knowledge (Syllk) model. When applied, the Syllk model can enable management to conceptualise (and illustrate) how an organisational know-how is wired (distributed) across various people and system elements of an organisation. Learn how storytelling integrated with the Syllk model is an effective knowledge management tool.

Organisational learning

There is a real organisational need to successfully manage projects and day to day business activities, to learn from success and failure, and to capture, disseminate, and apply lessons learned (Shergold, 2015). In today's business environment, ensuring the business margin is becoming harder to achieve. Competition keeps margins lean and projects are becoming more complex. As knowledge is taking on a business role, an increasing number of organisations are expecting their KM to be sufficient to transform organisational knowledge into a competitive advantage. Organisations need to become knowledge-intensive, as KM should be able to support the core tasks of project management, including decision-making, planning, control, and production. An organisation will often document its KM experience as lessons learned (APM, 2006). The use of lessons learned, capturing, and sharing relevant experience and implementing mechanisms for enhancing the reuse and sharing of project knowledge are fundamental elements that can improve project management practices. Organisational learning is a field of practice that is focused on how groups and companies learn. Organisational learning from projects rarely happens, and when it does it typically fails to deliver the intended results (Williams, 2008). KM should enhance individual, group, and organisational learning, improve information circulation, and support innovation. A KM system in an organisation is seen as a means of identifying and exploiting organisation knowledge assets such as individual experiences, lessons learned, and best practices.

Organisational knowledge plays a vital role in the development of both enterprise and project risk management controls and treatments by first searching and learning what others have done (what has worked and what has failed), so the wheel is not reinvented (Liebowitz and Megbolugbe, 2003). An organisation cannot manage its risks without managing its knowledge (Neef, 2005). Projects frequently fail due to a lack of lessons learned from the project team or lack of knowledge sharing. KM tools and techniques can be used to communicate appropriate risk treatments and decision-making among members of a project team. It is essential that the organisation manage knowledge including the identification, dissemination, and application of knowledge related to potential enterprise, portfolio, program and project risks to contribute to risk assessment and response analysis.

Reflection learning has also been recognised as playing a crucial part in project learning (Raelin, 2001, Williams, 2007). Learning is not only about acquiring information and knowledge but also socialisation (Duffield and Whitty, 2015). Reflection "is the practice of periodically stepping back to ponder the meaning to self and to others in one's immediate environment about what has recently transpired" (Raelin, 2001, p. 11). Raelin (2001) concludes that learning through reflection provides the what, why, and how to do it and that it is pertinent to learning from projects. Single loop learning engages the generation of new actions to achieve governing variables whereas double loop learning involves adaption and modification of the governing variables. Governing variables are the actions of individuals in the organisation (Argyris, 1999). Reflection learning is often used in double loop learning as reflection is based on how they think (Argyris, 1999). Organisational learning re-enforces the people factors influence and the success of the lessons learned process and that having a learning organisation culture is critical to the successful dissemination of lessons learned.

All learning takes places inside individual human heads; an organisation learns in only two ways: (a) by the learning of its members, or (b) by ingesting new members who have knowledge the organisation did not previously have. ... What an individual learns in an organisation is very much dependent on what is already known to (or believed by) other members of the organisation and what kinds of information are present in the organizational environment. ... Individual learning in organizations is very much a social, not a solitary, phenomenon. (Simon, 1991, p. 125)

There are five main activities to becoming a learning organisation (Garvin, 1993):

- Systematic problem solving (based on quality plan, do, check, act (PDCA) cycle)
- Experimentation (use of demonstration projects)
- Learning from what went before (companies need to review both failures and success and document the lessons learned, unfortunately, most fail to learn and allow knowledge to leave)

- Learning from others (benchmarking and applying best practice)
- Transferring knowledge (knowledge needs to spread rapidly and efficiently).

Some say that an organisation knows something if just one person knows it and that the organisational culture and structure enables that knowledge event to be used effectively. Individuals are learning; knowledge storage (checklists and work processes); organisational changes that re-focuses knowledge; culture changes to open and act on problems; and relationship building that enables skills and knowledge to deal with organisational problems are all effective KM actions. Another way to explain it is that people learn by processing information using the human central nervous system. However, as an organisation does not have a central nervous system, it needs to create analogue structures to enable its personnel to learn as one holistic group (Duhon and Elias, 2008).

Culture per se plays a significant part in KM, organisational learning, and in the effectiveness of learning mechanisms. As Dvir and Shenhar (2011, p. 20) point out, "Great projects create a revolutionary project culture. The execution of great projects often requires a different project culture, which can spread to an entire organization". It is critical to understand the culture of an organisation before implementing or using lessons learned processes (Williams, 2008). Furthermore, surveys consistently reveal that the main obstacles to project success are organisational people (social and culture) factors (O'Dell and Hubert, 2011, Milton, 2010). Organisational knowledge or know-how of how to respond to the business environment are behaviours and actions that are embedded in and distributed across organisational artefacts, system and processes, and cultural practices and rituals. They are networked elements that together generate a particular organisational response.

Lessons learned

O'Dell and Hubert (2011, p. 69) stated that the lessons learned approach typically focuses on a few fundamental questions:

> What was supposed to happen?
> What actually happened?
> Why was there a difference or variation?
> Who else needs to know this information?

The challenge is to get employees to participate and reuse the captured knowledge "lessons learned" (O'Dell and Hubert, 2011, Milton, 2010, O'Dell et al., 1998). The literature on the lessons learned process model provides many variations on essentially three process phases (Williams, 2007). The three phases of practical lessons learned process model are creating, dissemination/transferring, and application. Creating/identifying the knowledge consists of observing, collecting, and understanding the facts and information. An element of this phase is to document the findings and provide sufficient information regarding the situation, action taken, results observed, and recommendations. The next phase provides for the dissemination of information through codification/verification, storage, sharing for easy access and transferring knowledge to organisational members, improvements to standard processes, and procedures to reflect changes in identified best practices. The final element is where we adapt and use knowledge (Bresnen et al., 2003, Bresnen et al., 2004, Cowles, 2004, Liebowitz and Megbolugbe, 2003, O'Dell and Grayson, 1997, Schindler and Eppler, 2003, Williams, 2008).

The literature on knowledge identification and creation mention several ways project temporary organisations or individuals reflect on their experiences. Standard techniques are lessons learned sessions; after-action reviews; project debriefings; close out meetings; post project appraisals/reviews; case study exercises; project reviews; project histories; project health checks; and project audits (Williams, 2007, Schindler and Eppler, 2003, Koners, 2005, Reich et al., 2008, Anbari et al., 2008, Von Zedtwitz, 2002, Bakker et al., 2010, Busby, 1999, Maqsood et al., 2004). Each method has many different features and characteristics. However, they all essentially capture-disseminate-apply knowledge.

The literature on knowledge disseminating and transfer often refers to codification, verification, storing, searching, retrieving, knowledge sharing, and training (O'Dell and Hubert, 2011, Williams, 2007, Firestone and McElroy, 2003, Schindler and Eppler, 2003, Cowles, 2004, Boh, 2007). Schindler and Eppler (2003) report that if projects do not frequently disseminate their experiences, the project knowledge could be forgotten by the end of the project. The literature provides many technological ways of storing and recording the knowledge; the key is to identify what works for an organisation and continuously monitor, update, and keep it current and relevant (Williams, 2007, Williams, 2008). Technology is a critical element to knowledge dissemination. Quite often technology is blamed for failure in knowledge dissemination (Williams, 2007). Most organisations maintain their lessons learned in-house for competitive advantage, although some organisations make their lessons learned available to the public (Basili et al., 2002, Li, 2001, Li, 2002, Madden, 1996, NASA, 2011).

The disseminate knowledge phase uses two methods of interest: 1) process methods and 2) social-based methods. Process-based methodologies are those lessons learned where the knowledge is reflected in an organisation's policies, processes, and procedures. If projects follow the process, then the chance of repeated mistakes should be minimised (Midha, 2005, Schindler and Eppler, 2003, Williams, 2007, Keegan and Turner, 2001, O'Dell and Grayson, 1997). Social- based methodologies are those lessons learned that are not easy to break up and transfer knowledge from one person to another (Fernie et al., 2003, Bresnen et al., 2003). Fernie et al. (2003) argue that knowledge sharing is performed through the communication of individuals. Two social-based processes are networking and mentoring (Huang and Newell, 2003, Bresnen et al., 2003). A critical component of success for social methods is to ensure that an organisation's culture and environment provide the support (Hoegl et al., 2003).

Knowledge dissemination is an essential step in the process, and the work of Dixon (2000) helps to understand different strategies when dealing with the transfer of tacit or explicit knowledge. Dixon (2000) identifies five types of knowledge dissemination strategies: Serial Transfer, Near Transfer, Far Transfer, Strategic Transfer and Expert Transfer (Dixon, 2000). Literature reviews on knowledge application often state that a significant effort, commitment, and understanding of people behaviour is required for both the organisation and individuals, as this is the area where the process typically breaks down and fails (Williams, 2007, Williams, 2008, Keegan and Turner, 2001, Duhon and Elias, 2008).

PMBOK® Guide

Up until the PMBOK® Guide Sixth Edition (Project Management Institute, 2017), there has been a disregard to KM processes and lessons learned methods. The PMBOK® Guide Sixth Edition has a newly defined process – "Manage Project Knowledge". Manage Project Knowledge "is the process of using existing knowledge and creating new knowledge to achieve the project's objectives and contribute to organizational learning" (Project Management Institute, 2017 p. 98). The key benefit of this process is that existing knowledge and new knowledge are used in the project and knowledge created by the project is available to support organisational operations and future projects or phases (Project Management Institute, 2016). The author's observation of this newly defined process is that this would appear to be a significant step in the right direction as KM is more than lessons learned and the project manager should be aware of all the knowledge/lessons learned across the ten knowledge areas of the PMBOK® Guide.

Earned value management

Earned Value Management (EVM) methodology involves the systematic tracking and recording of project cost and schedule performance. It involves the PDCA cycle at the work package level of projects and should include the identification and recording of causes of performance anomalies and the identification of mitigation steps (Halse et al., 2014). Performance knowledge is invaluable to an organisation and should be captured thoughtfully to enhance planning, estimating, management, and control of future projects. EVM performance information needs to be linked to other knowledge resources (such as lessons learned, best practices, and project manager's expertise) to adapt quickly to making changes to counter adverse trends and resolve project issues. Project performance can be enhanced when people communicate and share best practices, lessons learned, experiences, and insights. With today's data and information processing capabilities, the opportunity for EVM performance data to be stored and analysed to provide meaningful insights for future projects is vast. Earned value data can easily be sliced and diced to create graphical visualisations that can become the backdrop for the storytelling of what worked well and what has not. Regression analysis can be performed to identify the relationships and correlations between different project parameters and actual performance.

Diverse teams

Diverse teams generally have more knowledge to draw on than teams of similar individuals. Organisations are increasingly utilising interdisciplinary organisational structures, such as integrated product teams, in which employees share knowledge and expertise within and between groups to cope with complex tasks. The challenge in a project environment is to capture, reuse, and share this knowledge and expertise (Duffield and Whitty, 2015). We typically see knowledge sharing within an organisation. However, knowledge acquisition from the outside is a competitive factor that the organisation needs to narrate (Davenport and Prusak, 1998). To be able to use the knowledge acquired from outside the organisation, the organisation first has to have a successful knowledge capability for converting the newly acquired knowledge into action.

Storytelling

Storytelling is one of the oldest and traditional means of passing on wisdom and culture and is a mechanism for sharing knowledge within organisations. An organisational story is defined as, "a detailed narrative of past management actions, employee interactions or other intra- or extra-organizational events that are communicated informally within the organization" (Swap et al., 2001, p. 103). Stories usually include characters, plots, twists, and narrative perspectives and reflect skills, organisational norms, values, and culture. Well-told stories can convey knowledge, information and emotion, both explicit and the tacit, and are a powerful way to represent and communicate complex, multi-layered thoughts (Snowden, 2000). Stories can increase organisational lessons learned, communicate universal values, and support a system to capture and share tacit dimensions of knowledge (Dalkir, 2005, Swap et al., 2001, Hayes and Maslen, 2014). However, some storytelling conditions such as authentic, believable, and compelling needs to be in place to ensure value for the organisation (Dalkir, 2005). Furthermore, Swap et al. (2001) conclude that if a story is understandable, it will almost positively stimulate a cognitive connection to the listener's personal experiences providing an experience that increases the likelihood of being remembered (Sims et al., 2009, Parry and Hansen, 2007).

The telling of stories is an appropriate social method for identifying and capturing lessons learned, especially those related to tacit knowledge (Williams, 2008). The social process of storytelling and recording is an effective way to explore project issues, capturing their complexity and behaviours outside organisational norms. Stories are often used in project lessons learned reviews to explain problem-solving, product specifications, and project performance management (Goffin and Koners, 2011). A story can support a lesson learned by providing valuable background and context, and therefore, stories are most natural to learn from when they carry a lesson learned that is explicit and actionable (Milton, 2010).

Desouza et al. (2005) compared two ways of conducting project post reviews, via anecdotal reports and stories. Desouza et al. (2005) found that stories are high in knowledge richness and are easy to recall. Storytelling provides an excellent means to communicate norms, core beliefs, values, and culture of the organisation, however, they are less suitable for lessons learned on rules or policies (Desouza et al., 2005, Parry and Hansen, 2007). Milton (2010) suggests that storytelling alone with no analysis of the learning points, identification of the lesson, and movement into action is not an efficient way of conveying a lesson learned. Milton recommends that every story should have a definite conclusion so others can gain knowledge from the story. Linde (2001) highlights the evidence that suggests lesson learned databases are not useful in collecting and archiving stories as they have not considered that learning from stories is primarily a social process (Prusak, 2005). Where there are successful lessons learned systems, a significant effort has gone into the translation of oral stories or story reports into functional written texts (Linde, 2001).

Both Peet (2012) and Linde (2001) suggests that new leaders become accustomed to their roles by learning the stories of their organisation. However, with an increasing prominence on storytelling, relatively little is known about the kinds of stories and narratives that need to be told, how those stories should be encouraged and captured, or the ways in which people need to be guided to enable knowledge sharing to occur (Peet, 2012). Boje's (1991) study of the organisation as a storytelling system demonstrated that skilled storytellers and story interpreters are effective organisational communicators, are vital to understanding the organisational culture and history, and possess skills that managers dealing with rapid change should develop. Boyce (1996) concludes that storytelling clearly expresses organisational culture and that storytelling is a useful tool for organisational renewal and workforce participation. Stories can play a central role in the change process (Taylor et al., 2002).

Harris and Barnes (2006) demonstrate the relevance of management storytelling skills to the practice of leadership. Harris and Barnes (2006) found that leaders who tell stories communicating key messages in an unforgettable way show a pathway to leadership and develop more effective relationships with those they lead and can generate an inspirational culture in their organisations. Leaders should research their own history and experience for *lessons learned* that could be communicated in the form of a story or narrative and learn to tell them with charismatic and visionary refinement at appropriate times (Parry and Hansen, 2007). When telling stories, the leader needs to be clear on why they are using them and to use more than one medium (Sole and Wilson, 2002). Taylor et al. (2002, p. 322) highlight that

> managers can be both monitors and disseminators by using stories to help employees be aware of and make sense of changes, to allow an opportunity to reflect on and reassemble information to make it actionable, and to reveal unspoken or unconscious norms of the organization.

Parry and Hansen (2007) report on conceptual similarities between leadership and organisational stories.

Sanne (2008) reports on how railway workers use simple storytelling within the operational communities and the need to make an incident reporting scheme integrated with an existing storytelling practice to address the systemic causes of accidents. The storytelling of incidents and accidents is critical for sharing knowledge about recent events and what one might appropriately learn from them (Sanne, 2008, Hayes and Maslen, 2014). Incident reporting schemes and narrative storytelling are both critical in the organisational communication of safety culture (Coan, 2002, Hayes and Maslen, 2014). Aviation accident investigators actively share safety stories and their collective knowledge of risks and to summarise lessons learned. The investigators disseminate stories at air safety seminars, industry forums, visits to partner airlines, accident and incident reports, safety publications, and their personal networks in the industry. Investigators use stories as a way to converse knowledge and also to refresh and contextualise their current concerns with lessons learned from the past. Stories and narratives take up a central place in communicating investigators' knowledge of safety (Macrae, 2014).

The use of storyboards and images as a way of telling a story is an active know-how medium to facilitate the learning process (Duffield and Whitty, 2016b). The skill of storytelling and having appropriate storytelling learning and development tools available were essential capabilities that enabled storytellers to be effective at communicating lessons learned. Those leaders that are telling stories have an impact on the audience that is in line with the leadership aims of the leader creating the story. The moral of the story is in effect the essence of the message that the listener takes away.

Finally, the means by which a story is communicated is also an essential factor. Stories are powerful in verbal form; their effect can be enhanced through the use of multimedia such as graphical performance trends, dashboards, pictures, art-based and recorded clips (Pässilä et al., 2013). Although stories flow informally within organisations, it requires a skilled workforce to provide stories and even more experienced workforce to capture, record, and make appropriate stories available for dissemination in a usable format. A recorded story may or may not be useful, depending on the skills of the storyteller (Linde, 2001). Through the establishment of a well-structured project controls database, including systematic measurement and analysis of trends, an organisation can efficiently produce graphics and visualisations based on factual performance data as the backdrop for stories. These stories can either celebrate success or provide learning about the causes of problems and what should have decisions or behaviours that should have taken place.

Systemic Lessons Learned Knowledge model

Life cycle models are used to organise one's thinking about KM in an organisational environment. There are several KM life cycle models available that outline the key aspects and processes of KM. The model proposed in this chapter describes the key aspects of KM in the organisational learning context. A conceptual model is presented, hereafter referred to as the Systemic Lessons Learned Knowledge model or Syllk (pronounced Silk) model (See Figure 8.1), which is a variation of Reason's (1997) Swiss cheese model (Duffield and Whitty, 2015).

Whereas the Swiss cheese model appropriately fits accident causation, the Syllk model is better suited to the organisation managing projects and day to day business activities. In line with the complex adaptive systems theory, the Syllk model represents the various organisational systems or functions (in terms of elements) that collectively drive the

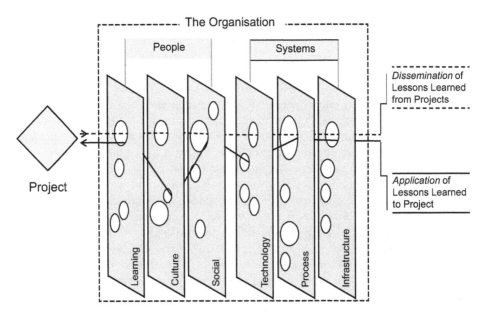

Figure 8.1 The Systemic Lessons Learned Knowledge model.

Source: (Duffield and Whitty, 2015).

overall behaviour and responses of the organisation. The Syllk model replaces Reason's defence barrier layers (person, workplace, organisation factors (policies and procedures), and defences (technology, training, and regulations)) with the organisational elements of learning, culture, social, technology, process, and infrastructure. The reverse relationship refers to the fact that the open holes (facilitators) in each element represent the various facilitators (lessons learned practices). These elements need to be aligned to enable the effective dissemination and application of the lessons learned. Barriers need to be overcome for effective lessons learned, and the Syllk model can assist in identifying these.

An earlier version of the Syllk model (Duffield and Whitty, 2012) supports the construct of information sharing and knowledge integration where information and knowledge are exchanged between an organisation and its suppliers, customers, and partners (Leal-Rodríguez et al., 2014). The Syllk model elements of people and culture play an important role in learning from projects (Virolainen, 2014). The alignment of the people and system elements positively influence an organisation's capability for storytelling, and, therefore, learn and accumulate lessons from stories of past project experiences (Duffield and Whitty, 2016b). The Syllk model shows that for organisations to learn, people and systems (processes and technology) need to be aligned and that this combination is the best way of organisational learning (Hedman et al., 2015). The Syllk model has been shown to support an online Community of Practice (Duffield, 2016) and has also been implemented in an organisation (consisting of 200 capital projects with project budgets ranging from approximately $1 million to $1.7 billion) in implementing a KM framework to manage the knowledge gathered during the planning, design, and delivery of capital projects, including lessons learned (Duffield, 2015, Duffield and Whitty, 2016a).

Wiring an organisation with knowledge and lessons learned

It has been shown by action research that the identified Syllk model facilitators and barriers need to be well understood and managed to connect effectively or couple up (or conceptually wire) organisational systems together. Understanding organisational facilitators/barriers and the associated KM practices and tools offer an opportunity to reflect and learn from past experiences (Duffield and Whitty, 2015).

An organisation can be effectively wired to acquire and accumulate knowledge and lessons learned. Figure 8.2 is an example of how the Syllk model can enable management to conceptualise and illustrate how organisational know-how (project delivery capability) is wired across various systems of an organisation for storytelling. The highlighted knowledge variables of the Syllk model elements shown in Figure 8.2 were found to be the most dynamic and influential in an organisation under a study. The outcomes showed that an organisation is not a simple structure but rather a complex interweaving and coupling (through the Syllk elements) of people and systems.

To explain Figure 8.2, the knowledge and lessons learned know-how commences with learning where storytelling and storytelling skills come together. One of the features of storytelling is mostly to reinforce the values and behaviours that align with the organisation's culture. Those in leadership roles should be encouraged and developed to improve their storytelling techniques. To implement storytelling effectively, we need an identifiable organisation culture; the stories then need to be heard and felt

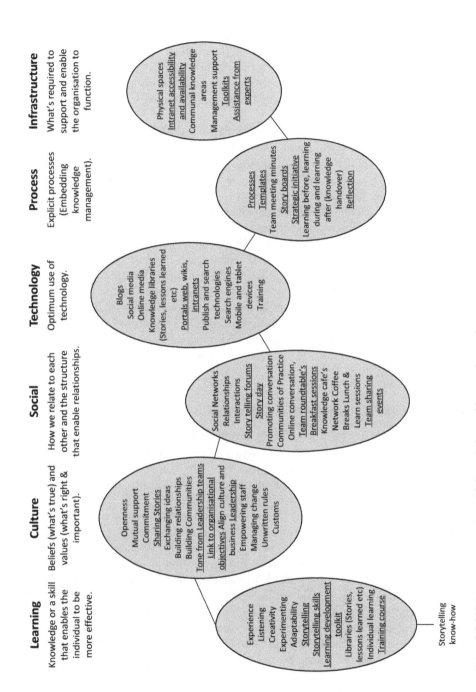

Learning

Knowledge or a skill that enables the individual to be more effective.

Experience
Listening
Creativity
Experimenting
Adaptability
Storytelling
Storytelling skills
Learning development toolkit
Libraries (Stories, lessons learned etc)
Individual learning
Training course

Storytelling know-how

Culture

Beliefs (what's true) and values (what's right & important).

Openness
Mutual support
Commitment
Sharing Stories
Exchanging ideas
Building relationships
Building Communities
Link to organisational objectives Align culture and business Leadership
Empowering staff
Managing change
Unwritten rules
Customs

Tone from Leadership teams

Social

How we relate to each other and the structure that enable relationships.

Social Networks
Relationships
Interactions
Story telling forums
Story day
Promoting conversation
Communities of Practice
Online conversation,
Team roundtable's
Breakfast sessions
Knowledge café's
Network Coffee
Breaks Lunch &
Learn sessions
Team sharing events

Technology

Optimum use of technology.

Blogs
Social media
Online media
Knowledge libraries (Stories, lessons learned etc)
Portals web, wikis, intranets
Publish and search technologies
Search engines
Mobile and tablet devices
Training

Process

Explicit processes (Embedding knowledge management).

Processes
Templates
Team meeting minutes
Story boards
Strategic initiative
Learning before, learning during and learning after (knowledge handover)
Reflection

Infrastructure

What's required to support and enable the organisation to function.

Physical spaces
Intranet accessibility and availability
Communal knowledge areas
Management support
Toolkits
Assistance from experts

Figure 8.2 **Wiring an organisation with knowledge and lessons learned.**

across the organisation. This comes through in the conversations (and actions) from senior management and leaders as they demonstrate that they believe sharing stories, exchanging ideas, building relationships and communities is essential, and they invest in activities that enable it.

The cultural message is that we think there is significant value in sharing stories and anecdotes of our experiences, and we are going to make time for that activity. Social is where the organisation invests in social structures that enable knowledge and lessons learned to take place. These might be regular or periodical storytelling forums and team sharing events. There might be other structures such as team roundtable meetings and breakfast sessions. A storytelling forum, story day, is not going to just happen; it requires all the other elements to align and work together. Technology is needed to help facilitate the storytelling know-how, and in this organisation, an intranet web portal and Yammer platform met the needs. Technology provides a knowledge library home, a communication medium, links to process and templates, links to where storytelling knowledge can be found in the organisation and learning development tools. Without the physical space for valued and open storytelling (remember our cultural values and beliefs) to take place, all the other activities will go to waste. Without high-quality intranet accessibility and availability, the storytelling knowledge and lessons learned sharing medium will be affected. There is a need for management support, experts, and leaders to enable the learning, culture, and social elements.

Implementing the Syllk model in project organisations

The implementation of the Syllk model in project organisations involves the organisation teams to identify the barriers and facilitators that exist in the organisation against the Syllk model elements. KM practices are then aligned with these elements. Figure 8.2 is an example of the Syllk aligned KM practices. However, this alignment will be different for each organisation and projects within the organisation. The alignment of the practices across the Syllk elements is the critical part of the process. Often we see only partial alignment and lessons learned become lessons identified and not learned, due to a breakdown of the Syllk elements (Duffield and Whitty, 2015).

During workshops where the Syllk model has been applied, a participant stated that

> when we did our workshop to capture the blockers [barriers] ... we then further looked at the Syllk model for our project... what is becoming clear is having a system to capture [stories] and retrieve [stories], because, without that, the project was going nowhere. So for us having a platform was using the Syllk model. The technology became the critical element to get right, then ...the other elements could happen at their timeframe, but without technology, nothing gelled together.

Another workshop participant stated that

> when you think about a slice of cheese ... and how storytelling works ... all those barriers and infrastructure just were there still. They were not going away, so now you perhaps reshape your whole storytelling focus around the ones that are working. ... I can see all this stuff working. I mean, you have got excellent coverage;

you have got all the support, you have got all the processes in place; you have got the tools in place.

Once the project team understands how the organisation is wired for knowledge and lessons learned, then KM within the project environment can be more successful.

Conclusion

The chapter highlights the integration of organisation learning, knowledge management, and lessons learned within the project management environment and presents the Systemic Lessons Learned Knowledge (Syllk) model. When applied, the Syllk model can enable management to conceptualise (and illustrate) how organisational know-how is wired (distributed) across an organisation. Storytelling integrated with the Syllk model can be an effective knowledge management tool and influence organisation learning. This chapter and associated references show how the Syllk model enables organisational know-how distributed across various people and system elements of an organisation. The alignment of the people and system elements (learning, culture, social, technology, process, and infrastructure) can positively influence organisation learning within the project management domain.

Chapter 9

Risk management principles

Glen B. Alleman, Tom Coonce and Rick Price

> All projects are affected by cost, schedule, and technical risks, created by reducible and irreducible uncertainty.
>
> Virine and Trumper (2013)

Cost and schedule growth for complex projects is created when unrealistic technical performance expectations, unrealistic cost and schedule estimates, inadequate risk assessments, unanticipated technical issues, and poorly performed and ineffective risk management contribute to project technical and programmatic shortfalls, shown in Figure 9.1 and documented in a wide range of sources. (SMC, 2014; Charette et al., 2004; Clemen, 1996; Davis and Philip, 2002; van Dorp and Duffey, 1999; Grady, 2006; Hofbauer et al., 2011; Hulett and Hillson, 2006; Lorell et al., 2006; Lorell et al., 2017; Rendleman and Faulconer, 2011; Scheinin, 2008; Schwartz, 2014; Williams, 2017; Younossi et al., n.d.).

Root causes of this cost and schedule growth and technical shortfalls on projects start with not adequately specifying what **Done** looks like in Measures of Effectiveness (MOE) for the project's outcomes prior to issuing the Request for Proposal, not quantifying uncertainty, and failing to manage resulting risks for the Measures of Performance (MOP) associated with these MOE's during execution of the project (Acker 1979; Bolten et al., 2008; Dezfuli et. al., 2010; Leveson et al., 2005; NASA, 2011a, b; USAF, n.d.

Applying Continuous Risk Management (CRM) (Alberts et al. 1996) to projects provides the needed discipline to produce risk-informed actionable information to address these issues, by: Bilardo et. al. (2008), Dezfuli et. al. (2010), Dezfuli (2010) and SMC (2014).

- **Continuously managing** risks produced by uncertainty has shown positive correlations between risk management and increasing the probability of project success (Conrow, 2003; Dwyer et al., 2015; Dezfuli et al., 2010; Public Works and Government Services Canada, 2015).
- **Determining which risks are important** to deal with in a prioritized model, their interactions, statistical interdependencies, propagation, and evolution (Alleman et al., 2014; van Dorp and Duffey, 1999; Perez, 2016; Rogers et al., 2003).
- **Implementing strategies to handle risk** with mitigation, correction, prevention, and avoidance, derived from Root Cause Analysis, to remove and prevent the conditions and actions creating the risks (Gano 2008; Helton and Burmaster 1996). Continuous Risk Management increases the probability of project success by ALTESS (2007).

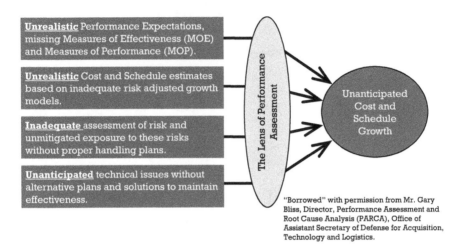

Figure 9.1 Root causes reducing probability of success on complex programs.

- **Preventing problems before they occur** with a *pre*-mortem to identify cause, take corrective and preventive actions to remove the conditions and actions of the root cause before the risk becomes an issue (Gano, 2008; Scheinin, 2008).
- **Improving product quality by focusing on project objectives** and consciously looking for risks that affect cost, schedule, and performance throughout the project's lifecycle (Conrow, 2003; NASA, 2011, 2015).
- **Enabling better use of resources** through early identification of problems and providing input to management decisions regarding resource allocation (Dezfuli et al., 2010; NASA, 2014).
- **Promoting teamwork** by involving personnel at all levels of the project and focusing their attention on a shared vision of the mission to provide a mechanism for achieving the MOEs and MOPs as planned (Table 9.1).

Overview

This chapter describes how risks are created by uncertainty (reducible and irreducible), the identification of the risks, and the corrective and preventive actions needed to mitigate these risks to increase the probability of project success (Salado and Nilchiani, 2014; Walker et al., 2003; De Meyer et al., 2002).

Uncertainty is the consequence of all complex systems. It is the lack of needed knowledge of the state of the system in the present or in the future that creates risk (Marle and Vidal, 2011; McManus and Hastings, 2005).

Adaptability, flexibility, and other systems "–illities" are devoid of meaning in a deterministic world (Rogers et al., 2006).

In the non-deterministic world, risk management is a critical success factor for increasing the probability of project success (Riesch, 2011).

Risk Never Occurs without a Cause, that Cause is Uncertainty – Risk is the Outcome of Uncertainty

One contributing factor to the probability of a project successfully delivering capabilities needed to accomplish its mission is determined with integrated data and processes used by project controls and engineering staff to track and manage technical and programmatic performance, and risks to that performance.

Table 9.1 For complex projects, Root Causes (Condition, Action, Outcome) have been shown to reduce the Probability of Project Success

Condition or Action (Cause)	Undesirable Outcome (Effect)
Probability of Project Success Reduced by Programmatic Uncertainties	
The acquirer fails to define what Done looks like in units of measure meaningful to the decision makers prior to the RFP (Blickstein et al., n.d)	Delivered Systems don't provide the needed capabilities, effectiveness and performance, arrive too late, and cost more than budgeted.
Different participants in the acquisition process impose conflicting demands on project structure and processes Gerstein et al. (2015)	Participants do what is in their own *best interest* versus the *best interest* of product, cost, and schedule.
Budget process forces funding decisions to be made in advance of project decisions (Charette et al., 2004; Younossi et al., n.d.)	Budget process encourages undue optimism that creates project risk for cost, schedule, and technical performance.
Project managers' short tenures, limitations in experience, and formal training create shortfalls in management skills (Arena et al. 2013; H.A.S.C, 2013)	The project manager focused on minimizing risk to *Keep the Project Sold* and creating the opportunity for career advancement.
Probability of Project Success Reduced by Cost, Schedule, and Technical Uncertainties	
Schedule and Cost Margin not defined and related to schedule and cost risk. Schedule margin tasks not assigned to protect end-item deliverables against uncertainties (Blickstein et al., n.d.; Dezfuli, 2010; DOD, 2012; Kerzner, 1998)	Lack of validated cost and schedule margin causes the project to under-deliver technical, go over budget, and deliver late.
Technical Plan not aligned with Budget and Spend Plans, with missing Schedule Margin and risk buy down plan (Younossi et al., n.d,)	Lack of integrated cost, schedule, technical progress gives wrong performance information of future performance.
Alternative Points of Integration (APOI) not considered in IMS (Price and Alleman, 2016)	Missing Plan-B means Probability of Success is reduced.
Cost, Schedule, and Technical Uncertainties impact Probability of Project Success without handling plans (Hamaker, 1994; Lorell et al., 2017)	Without a credible risk strategy, there is no credible plan for success.
Missing Resource Loaded Schedule to assure staff, facilities, and other resources available when needed (Navy, 2008)	If resources are not available when needed, there is no credible plan for success.
Propagation of Aleatory and Epistemic Uncertainty not considered in risk profile or handling plans (Fang et al., 2016; Maier and Rechtin 2009; Virine and Trumper, 2013)	Without understanding the dynamics of risk, there is no credible plan to Keep the Project Green (Cox, 2008)

Each project performance factor identified in this is used to inform one or more of the Five Immutable Principles of Project Success and enable the modeling of this probability in units of measure meaningful to the decision makers (Alleman, 2014; Lehman et al., 2012; Razaque et al., 2012; Reeves, 2013).

1. What does Done look like in units of measure meaningful to the decision maker?
2. What is the Plan and Schedule to reach Done with needed Capabilities, at needed time, for needed cost?
3. What time, money, and resources are needed to reach Done and in what period are they needed?
4. What impediments will be discovered on the way to Done and what are their corrective or preventative actions?
5. What are the units of measure needed to credibly describe how progress is being made toward Done?

Risk, created by uncertainty, and its management, is the central paradigm in a wide range of fields, from engineering to medicine, from life sciences to economics (Roedler and Jones, 2005; Zio, 2007). This chapter presents a background on risk, its impact on the probability of project success, and the preventative and corrective actions needed to increase that probability. The structure of this is modeled after *Beyond Bullet Points*, guided by the following framework: Atin (2016).

- **The Setting** – Many projects have not successfully delivered the effectiveness and performance needed to achieve the capabilities paid for by the user.
- **The Protagonist** – Project Managers and their supporting Engineering, Project Controls, and Finance and Business Operations staff.
- **The Imbalance** – Many times project management is incentivized to downplay the technical difficulties of development projects (Karim, 2014). This leads to overlooking the principles, processes, and practices that would have revealed the risk to cost, schedule, and technical performance and identified the corrective and preventive actions needed to keep the Project Green.
- **The Balance** – Prior to committing to a project, management needs to have a clear understanding of what Done looks like in units of measure meaningful to the decision makers, informed with analysis of the technical, schedule, and cost risks affecting the probability of project success (Lorell et al., 2015).
- **The Solution** – Project Management creates a Master Plan, approved prior to Milestone B, containing Measures of Effectiveness (MOE), Measures of Performance (MOP), Technical Performance Measures (TPM), and Key Performance Parameters (KPP) for each deliverable in support of the Mission or Business Strategy. Industry's proposal then shows how each measure will be achieved for each deliverable in a Master Plan and Master Schedule.

Framing assumptions

A framing assumption informs acquisition leaders about key project assumptions, enables discussion of their validity, and establishes a context for project assessments. A framing assumption (FA) is any supposition (explicit or implicit) that is central in shaping cost, schedule, or performance expectations of an acquisition project.

> Delays in schedule, overruns in cost, and shortfalls on technical capabilities are often traced to difficulties in managing technical risk, initial assumptions or expectation that are difficult to fulfill, and funding instability.
>
> (Riesch, 2011)

One purpose of this is to identify the explicit and implicit framing assumptions of risk to the cost, schedule, and technical performance that decrease the probability of project performance.

With this starting point, there are several framing assumptions that are needed when applying the Five Immutable Principles. Different domains will have different approaches to answering the questions posed by the Five Principles. The fundamental assumptions for how risk impacts the answers to each question remains the same (Table 9.2) (Alleman, 2014).

Table 9.2 Framing assumptions for Principles of Project Success

Immutable Principle	Framing Assumption
What does Done look like in units of measure meaningful to the decision makers?	To define Done, there needs to be Measures of effectiveness, Measures of Performance, Technical Performance Measures, and Key Performance Parameters traceable to the Capabilities needed for mission success.
What is the Plan and Schedule to reach Done, at the needed time, for the needed cost, with the needed Capabilities?	Plans are strategies for the successful delivery of the needed capabilities. These plans come in a variety of forms: <ul><li>Integrated Master Plan (Dezfuli et al., 2010)</li><li>Product Roadmap (Dezfuli et al., 2010; USAF, 2008)</li><li>System architecture process plans Section 32 of TOGAF (2011)</li><li>Narratives in long term agency planning guidance (Davis, 2002, 2012)</li><li>Concept of Operations Kim et al. (2015).</li></ul> In all cases these plans must describe the increasing maturity of the deliverables needed to fulfill the mission capabilities
What time, money, and resources are needed to reach Done?	Some form of a *master schedule* showing deliverables is needed, the dependencies between the deliverables and measures of performance, technical performance measures and quantifiable backup data for these deliverables to assess the *physical percent complete*.
What impediments will be encountered on the way to Done and what are their preventive and corrective actions?	All risk comes from uncertainty. Uncertainty comes in two forms – epistemic (reducible) and aleatory (irreducible). Risk from epistemic uncertainty can be *bought down* with work on the project to *handle* the results of the risk. Risk from aleatory uncertainty requires *margin* to protect the deliverable from this variance.
What are the units of measure describing physical percent complete to plan?	Physical percent complete must be in some unit meaningful to the decision maker for the technical performance measures, Measures of Performance, and Key Performance Parameters for the project deliverables.

Source of the imbalance

> Risks Identified are rarely realized, risks realized were rarely identified.
> All unidentified risks are accepted risks.
>
> (Frazier et al., 2014)

Research shows that the root causes of a system's failure to deliver the needed capabilities, for the needed cost, at the needed time, have many sources[1]. Primary sources of the imbalance are technical and programmatic complexity and weak implementation of formal risk management. On failed projects, these conditions have been routinely ignored or minimized while not questioning or defining the framing assumptions for cost, schedule, and performance expectations that create the risks in the first place (Alzaharna, 2012; Cooke-Davies, 2011; Hubbard, 2009). The corrections needed for the sources of this imbalance are not addressed here[2]. This chapter does address the principles, processes, and practices for handling the consequences of the lack of risk management in the imbalance and the impact on the Probability of Project Success.

Problem statement for increasing probability of success in the presence of risk

How can the uncertainties for the project be identified and classified, with the needed level of confidence, to enable appropriate corrective or preventative actions to improve the probability of successfully completing projects on time, on budget, with the needed mission Capabilities?

The four summary areas affecting the success of projects shown in Figure 9.1 are associated with unmitigated or unanticipated risk to cost, schedule, and technical performance.

There are thousands of ways to fail … most have not been explored (Jolly, 2009).

What is risk?

> Risk is the effect of uncertainty on objectives. Uncertainty is a state or condition that involves a deficiency of information and leads to inadequate or incomplete knowledge of understanding. In the context of risk management, uncertainty exists whenever the knowledge or understanding of an event, consequence, or likelihood is inadequate or incomplete
> – ISO 31000:2009, ISO 17666:2016, and ISO 11231:2010

> Risk is Uncertainty that Matters
>
> (Hillson and Simon, 2007)

---

1 IDA, MITRE, RAND, NASA, NRO, Naval Postgraduate School, Air Force Institute of Technology, Aerospace Corporation, all have research on the root cause analyses of acquisition problems.
2 Perverse Incentives create unintended and undesirable results contrary to the interests of the incentive makers (Galway, 2004).

Risk is the potential consequence of a specific outcome affecting a system's ability to meet cost, schedule, and/or technical objectives. Risk has three primary components:

- Probability of the activity or event occurring or not occurring, described by a Probability Distribution Function.
- Consequence or effect resulting from the activity or event occurring or not occurring, described by a Probability Distribution Function.
- Root Cause (condition and action) of a future outcome, which when reduced or eliminated, will prevent occurrence, non-occurrence, or recurrence of the cause of the risk.

For the project manager, there are three risk categories that must be identified and handled:

- **Technical** – risks that may prevent the end item from performing as intended or not meeting performance expectations. Measures of Effectiveness, Measures of Performance, Technical Performance Measures, and Key Performance Parameters describe the measures of these expectations.
- **Programmatic** – risks that affect the cost and schedule measures of the project. The programmatic risks are within the control or influence of the Project Management or Project Executive Office, through managerial actions applied to the work activities contained in the Integrated Master Schedule (DOD, 2012).
- **Business** – risks that originate outside the project office or are not within the control or influence of the Project Manager or Project Executive Office.

Uncertainty comes from the lack of information to describe a current state or to predict future states, preferred outcomes, or the actions needed to achieve them (Garner, 1962; Public Works and Government Services Canada, 2015; Zack, 1999). This uncertainty can originate from the naturally (randomly) occurring processes of the project (Aleatory Uncertainty). Or it can originate from the lack of knowledge about the future outcomes from the work on the project (Epistemic Uncertainty).

(Laitonen et al., 2013)

Root Cause Analysis Reveals Source(s) of Uncertainty and Resulting Risk

When gaps in performance, shortfalls in benefits, unanticipated cost, schedule, and performance variances, faulty products, or any undesirable outcomes appear, blame the process, not people.

Root Cause Analysis is the means to fix the root cause, rather than treat the symptom.

(Hahn, 2015; Jaber, 2016)

To fix a symptom the root cause must be identified. This starts with defining the problem, determining the causal relationships including the actions and conditions that create the symptom, providing evidence of the cause, determining the actions and conditions that allowed the cause to create the symptom, providing solutions that remove, change, or control one or more causes, and finally implementing and tracking the effectiveness of each solution (Gano, 2008).

Project performance solutions applied in the absence of a Root Cause Analysis of the source of a problem have little chance of improving project performance (Gano, 2008). The Root Causes need to be found for the uncertainties that create risks that impact the nine areas of project management success shown in Table 9.3, and the corrective or preventive actions needed to remove these causes: Tzeng (2007).

Table 9.3 Nine programmatic risk areas to program success. (Nilchiani et al., 2013). Each area has measures that provide evidence of compliance to a planned reduction in uncertainty needed to increase the probability of project success

Source of Uncertainty	Description of Uncertainty
1. Scope	The project work scope defined from the Concept of Operations, Statement of Work, Statement of Objectives, or similar documents. This work description is next captured in the Work Breakdown Structure, traceable to the Capabilities described in the ConOps, SOW, and SOO. The units of measures of the Capabilities are Measure of Effectiveness and Measures of Performance.
2. Time	The Integrated Master Schedule representing the defined deliverables that fulfill the Capabilities of the project, to include all work activities, in the proper sequence, with the needed staffing and budget. All these are risk adjusted for reducible and irreducible uncertainties.
3. Cost	The planning, estimating, budgeting, and control of costs assigned with each scope element at the specific time in the project.
4. Staffing	The planning, acquiring, development, and management of the project team, with the reducible and irreducible uncertainties assigned to labor categories or even individual staff.
5. Risk	The planning, identifying, analysis, management, control, and communication of risk, created by the reducible and irreducible uncertainties. This risk management process has risk itself, so lack of confidence in the risk process is itself a risk.
6. Procurement	The planning, execution, and control of procuring materials, services, and resources. Lead times, product quality, fit for purpose, fit for use are all risks to the supply chain.
7. Communication	The planning, management, and control of project communications. *Noisy* communication channels are a risk to project success. Failure to understand, failure to follow guidance, confusion in the work processes, lack of coordination, duplication of work and missing work all have the potential root cause of failing to communicate.
8. Integration	The Development of charter, management plan, directing and managing work, monitoring, and controlling work, managing change control, and closing out the project. Integrated Project Performance Management (IPPM) means all components of performance management are seamlessly integrated to provide the decision makers with actionable information.
9. Quality	The planning, assurance, and control of the effectiveness and performance of the project outcomes. The units of measure of *quality* are Technical Performance Measures and Key Performance Parameters.

Root Cause Analysis asks and answers the following:

- What condition(s) and what action(s) allowed the gap or mistake to appear or happen?
- Both the condition and action are required in accordance with the Apollo Root Cause Analysis method (Gano, 2008).
- What removes the condition(s) and prevents the actions from recurring or occurring in the future?
- Removal of the condition(s) and the action(s) is the foundation of correction and/ or prevention of undesirable outcomes from recurring.
- When errors, faults, undesirable outcomes (the Primary Effect in Apollo Root Cause Analysis) are encountered or continue to occur, through people or processes, build fault–tolerance into the root cause corrective or preventive processes.

Building fault–tolerance into the process protects the outcomes from the misuse of the process.

This approach is based on four elements of the *cause and effect* principle:

- Cause and Effect are the same things
- Every effect has at least two causes – actions and conditions

- Cause and effect are part of an infinite continuum
- An effect exists only if its cause exists at the same point in time and space

---

The biggest single risk for any organization is the risk that its risk management process doesn't actually work.

It is the ultimate common cause failure mode.

(Ho, 2010)

Measuring project success

Without a programmatic architecture (cost, schedule, risk management) supporting the technical architecture, risks and their corrections and preventions to deliver needed technical capabilities cannot be defined, assessed, or measured, reducing the probability of program success.

(Maier and Rechtin, 2009; NASA, 2014)

Measuring progress to plan in the presence of uncertainty requires probabilistic modeling of the uncertainties of cost, schedule, and technical performance in units of measure meaningful to the decision makers. This meaningful information of the status of the project during its development is critical input to decision making in the presence of uncertainty. The established principles of this process have been around for decades. It's time these are put back to work (Timson, 1968). In the presence of uncertainty, all projects have several important characteristics:

- The development of new, operational systems involves combining subsystems and component technologies to produce a new systems capability. Early in the project, two types of information are available – the design basis of the general class of systems and some knowledge about newer or improved technologies to be incorporated into the components or subsystems.

- The status of the development can be a measure of uncertainty and progress can be measured by change in this uncertainty. Physical *progress to plan* can be measured by the reduction of uncertainty, when it is reducible, and by the assessment of remaining margin when the uncertainty is irreducible. This process has been described – long ago – as *the sequential purchase of information regarding some object about which the state of knowledge is incomplete*[3]. This *knowledge* is periodically assessed to confirm risk is being bought down at the planned rate, and margin is being consumed according to plan.
- The system's variables defining the performance characteristics must indicate an increasing mature *capability* to fulfill a prescribed mission, in the Concept of Operations and other documents, in units described in the next section.
- Acquiring these measures requires a method of systematically analyzing the implications of this knowledge at the subsystem and component levels of the project.
- Since the development of complex projects is not a random process, but a directed engineering process in the presence of uncertainty, *subjective probability distributions* are needed for measuring this technological uncertainty. When an *objective* measurement is possible, it will be used to inform the decision maker. When this measure is not directly available, a *subjective* measure must be made with a model containing a degree of uncertainty[4].

Measures of progress to plan

To assess the increasing or decreasing project probability of success for the characteristics described above, *units of measure* are needed to define this success[5].

- **Measures of Effectiveness** (MoE) – operational measures of a desired capability whose success is related to the achievement of the mission or operational objectives, evaluated in the operational environment, under a specific set of conditions.
- **Measures of Performance** (MoP) – measures that characterize physical or functional attributes relating to the system operation, measured, or estimated under specific conditions.
- **Technical Performance Measures** (TPM) – attributes that determine how well a system or system element is satisfying or expected to satisfy a technical requirement or goal.

---

3 "Military Research and Development Policies," Klein, B. H. Meckling, W. H., and Mesthene, E. G., *The RAND Corporation*, R-333-PR, *December 4, 1958.*

4 When a direct measure is available, and *objective* measure is possible. When predicting an outcome, a *subjective* measure is used. The likelihood of the possible outcomes can be expressed quantitatively in terms of probabilities to indicate the degree of uncertainty. These probabilities can be *objective* when the events they predict are the results of *random processes.*

5 Measures of Effectiveness (MOE), Measures of Performance (MOP), Technical Performance Measures (TPM), and Key Performance Parameters (KPP) are measures of project success (NASA 2014).

- **Key Performance Parameters** (KPP) – represent the capabilities and character-istics so significant that failure to meet them can be cause for reevaluation, reassess-ing, or termination of the project.

Each of these measures provides visibility to *Physical Percent Complete* of the development or operational items in the project.

These measures of progress to plan have been developed and applied since the mid- 1960s.

(Acker, 1979; Browning, 2002; Petković, 2012; Timson 1968)

The challenge is government connecting the Technical Plan, with its MOEs, MOPs, TPMs, and KPPs with the Cost and Schedule Plan for any complex program before issuing the RFP.

(Leveson et al., 2005; Razaque et al., 2012; Riesch, 2011; Roedler et al., 2010)

Framework for technical, cost, and schedule uncertainties

Uncertainties have many sources and drivers. Some are model related, some are parameter related.
Parameter related uncertainties come in two categories – aleatoric and epistemic.

(Leveson et al., 2005)

How Is the Degree of Uncertainty Modeled for the Probability of Project Success?

To answer this question, uncertainties impacting the probability of project success need to be separated into two categories. If the uncertainty can be reduced with work effort, it is labeled *Epistemic*. If there is a random process creating the uncertainty, no possibility of reducing the uncertainty, it is labeled *Aleatory*.

Major development projects contain complex data and process relationships. Models that attempt to simulate the risks to project success are many times simplified mathematical representations of complex phenomena (Nilchiani and Puglises, 2016) This risk assessment uses probabilistic models for future events, identifying needed corrections and preventions of the risks created by these uncertainties. This tradi-tional approach to risk analysis and management constructs a Risk Management Plan containing probabilistic events, where the probability of occurrence of these events are reduced with explicit work activities captured in the Risk Management Plan as Handling tasks.

On complex projects, there are also statistically random processes affecting work durations, technical attributes, labor and facilities, and cost. These naturally occurring deviations from a desired state, a planned duration, or some technical performance parameter are irreducible. It is useful to separate these two types of uncertainties in the risk model in order to be clear on which uncertainties have the potential of being reduced or not (Lehman et al., 2012). More importantly, reducible uncertainty, *Epistemic*, may introduce dependencies between probabilistic risk events that may not be properly modeled if their character is not correctly identified (Acker, 1979).

Uncertainty can be modeled as knowable in principle, fundamentally unknowable (random), or a combination of the two.

Uncertainty must be properly modeled to quantify risk between the inherent variability with sufficient data (Aleatory) and uncertainty from the lack of knowledge (Epistemic).

Risks, their sources and their handling strategies

Risk identification during the early design phases of complex systems is commonly implemented but often fails to identify events and circumstances that challenge program performance. Inefficiencies in cost and schedule estimates are usually held accountable for cost and schedule overruns, but the true root cause is often the realization of programmatic risks. A deeper understanding of frequent risk identification trends and biases pervasive during system design and development is needed, for it would lead to improved execution of existing identification processes and methods.
(Raiffa, 1968; Razaque et al., 2012; Reeves, 2013)

Risk management means building a model of the risk, the impact of the risk on the project, and a model for handling of the risk. Since it is a risk and not an issue, the corrective or preventive action has not yet occurred (Gano, 2008; der Kiureghian, 2007; Vrouwenvelder, 2003).

Probabilistic Risk Assessment (PRA) is the basis of these models and provides the Probability of Project Success. Probabilities result from uncertainty and are central to the analysis of the risk. Scenarios, model assumptions, with model parameters based on current knowledge describe the behavior of the system under a given set of uncertainty conditions (NASA, 2011).

The source of uncertainty must be identified, characterized, and the impact on project success modeled and understood, so decisions can be made about corrective and preventive actions needed to increase the Probability of Project Success.

Since risk is the outcome of uncertainty, distinguishing between the types of uncertainty in the definition and management of risk on complex systems is useful when building risk assessment and management models (Bartolomei et al., 2012; Grady, 2006; Helton and Burmaster, 1996; der Kiureghian, 2007; Zarikas and Kitsos, 2015).

- **Epistemic uncertainty** – from the Greek επιστημη (episteme) is uncertainty from the lack of knowledge of a quantity or process in the system or an environment. Epistemic uncertainty is represented by a range of values for parameters, a range of workable models, the level of model detail, multiple expert interpretations, or statistical confidence. The accumulation of information and implementation of actions reduce epistemic uncertainty to eliminate or reduce the likelihood and/or impact of risk. This uncertainty is modeled as a subjective assessment of the probability of our knowledge and the probability of occurrence of an undesirable event.

Incomplete knowledge about some characteristics of the system or its environment are primary sources of Epistemic uncertainty.

- **Aleatory uncertainty** – from the Latin *alea* (a single die) is the inherent variation associated with a physical system or environment. Aleatory uncertainty comes from an inherent randomness, natural stochasticity, environmental or structural variation across space and time in the properties or behavior of the system under study (Ali et al., 2012). The accumulation of more data or additional information *cannot* reduce aleatory uncertainty. This uncertainty is modeled as a stochastic process of an *inherently* random physical model. The projected impact of the risk produced by Aleatory uncertainty can be managed through cost, schedule, and/ or technical *margin*.

Naturally occurring variations associated with the physical system are primary sources of aleatory uncertainty.

There is a third uncertainty found on some projects not addressed by this chapter, since this uncertainty is not correctable.

- **Ontological Uncertainty** – is attributable to the complete lack of knowledge of the states of a system. This is sometimes labeled an *Unknowable Risk*. Ontological uncertainty cannot be measured directly.

Ontological uncertainty creates risk from inherent variations and incomplete information that is not knowable.

Separating aleatory and epistemic uncertainty for risk management

Knowing the magnitude of reducible and irreducible uncertainty is needed to construct a credible risk model.

Without the separation, knowing what uncertainty is reducible and what uncertainty is irreducible inhibits the design of the corrective and preventive actions needed to increase the probability of project success.

Separating the uncertainty types increases the clarity of risk communication, making it clear which type of uncertainty can be reduced and which type cannot be reduced. For the latter (irreducible risk), only margin can be used to protect the project from the uncertainty (Beer, 2016; Laitonen et al., 2013).

As uncertainty increases, the ability to precisely measure the uncertainty is reduced to where a direct estimate of the risk can no longer be assessed through a mathematical model. While a decision in the presence of uncertainty must still be made, deep uncertainty and poorly characterized risks lead to the absence of data and risk models in many domains (Lempert and Collins, 2007; NASA, 2011).

Epistemic uncertainty creates reducible risk

The risk created by Epistemic Uncertainty represents resolvable knowledge, with elements expressed as probabilistic uncertainty of a future value related to a loss in a future period of time (Apeland et al., n.d.; Zhang et al., n.d.). Awareness of this lack of knowledge provides the opportunity to reduce this uncertainty through direct corrective or preventive actions (Kwak and Smith, 2009).

> Epistemic uncertainty, and the risk it creates, is modeled by defining the probability that the risk will occur, the time frame in which that probability is active, and the probability of an impact or consequence from the risk when it does occur, and finally, the probability of the residual risk when the handing of that risk has been applied.
> Epistemic uncertainty statements define and model these event-based risks:

- **If–Then** – if we miss our next milestone then the project will fail to achieve its business value during the next quarter.
- **Condition–Concern** – our subcontractor has not provided enough information for us to status the schedule, and our concern is the schedule is slipping and we do not know it.
- **Condition–Event–Consequence** – our status shows there are some tasks behind schedule, so we could miss our milestone, and the project will fail to achieve its business value in the next quarter.

For these types of risks, an explicit or an implicit *risk handling plan* is needed. The word *handling* is used with special purpose. "We *Handle* risks" in a variety of ways. *Mitigation* is one of those ways. In order to mitigate the risk, new effort (work) must be introduced into the schedule. We are *buying down* the risk, or we are *retiring* the risk by spending money and/or consuming time to reduce the probability of the risk occurring. Or we could be spending money and consuming time to reduce the impact of the risk when it does occur. In both cases actions are taken to address the risk.

Reducible cost risk

Reducible cost risk is often associated with unidentified reducible technical risks, changes in technical requirements, and their propagation that impacts cost (Becerril et al., 2016). Understanding the uncertainty in cost estimates supports decision making for setting targets and contingencies, risk treatment planning, and the selection of options in the management of project costs. Before reducible cost risk can take place, the cost structure must be understood. Cost risk analysis goes beyond capturing the cost of Work Breakdown Structure (WBS) elements in the Basis of Estimate and the Cost Estimating Relationships. This involves:

- Development of quantitative modelling of integrated cost and schedule, incorporating the drivers of reducible uncertainty in quantities, rates and productivities, and the recording of these drivers in the Risk Register.
- Determining how cost and schedule uncertainty can be integrated in the analysis of the cost risk model.
- Performing sensitivity analysis to provide understanding of the effects of reducible uncertainty and the allocation of contingency amounts across the project.

Reducible technical risk

Technical risk is the impact on a project, system, or entire infrastructure when the outcomes from engineering development do not work as expected, do not provide the needed technical performance, or create higher than planned risk to the performance of the system. Failure to identify or properly manage this technical risk results in performance degradation, security breaches, system failures, increased maintenance time, and significant amount of technical debt[6] and addition cost and time for end item delivery for the project. A good example of implementing reducible risk mitigation is deciding to build and test engineering models to gain early understanding of design viability and performance characteristics and avoid downstream issues.

Reducible schedule risk

While there is significant variability, for every 10% in Schedule Growth there is a corresponding 12% Cost Growth.

(Blickstein et al., n.d.)

Most reducible schedule risk is directly linked to reducible technical risk. Avoiding a technical risk avoids the associated schedule risk. But there can be epistemic schedule uncertainty that drives reducible schedule risk. For example, obtaining rare materials may by a potential long lead issue that can drive out end item delivery. Taking specific actions to reduce the likelihood or impact presented by this rare long lead material should be included as risk reduction activities.

Reducible cost estimating risk

Reducible cost estimating risk is dependent on technical, schedule, and programmatic risks, which must be assessed to provide an accurate picture of project cost. Cost risk estimating assessment addresses the cost, schedule, and technical risks that impact the cost estimate. To quantify these cost impacts from the reducible risk, sources of risk need to be identified. This assessment is concerned with three sources of risk and ensure that the model calculating the cost also accounts for these risks: Galway (2004).

- The risk inherent in the cost estimating method. The Standard Error of the Estimate (SEE), confidence intervals, and prediction intervals.
- Risk inherent in technical and programmatic processes. The technology's maturity, design and engineering, integration, manufacturing, schedule, and complexity (Wood and Ashton, 2010).

---

6 Technical debt is a term used in the Agile community to describe eventual consequences of deferring complexity or implementing incomplete changes. As a development team progresses there may be additional coordinated work that must be addressed in other places in the schedule. When these changes do not get addressed within the planned time or get deferred for a later integration, the project accumulates a debt that must be paid at some point in the future.

- The risk inherent in the correlation between WBS elements, which decides to what degree one WBS element's change in cost is related to another and in which direction. WBS elements within the project have positive correlations with each other, and the cumulative effect of this positive correlation increases the range of the costs[7].

Unidentified reducible technical risks are often associated with reducible cost and schedule risk.

ALEATORY UNCERTAINTY CREATES IRREDUCIBLE RISK

Aleatory uncertainty and the risk it creates comes not from the lack of information, but from the naturally occurring processes of the system. For aleatory uncertainty, more information cannot be bought nor specific risk reduction actions taken to reduce the uncertainty and resulting risk. The objective of identifying and managing aleatory uncertainty is to be prepared to handle the impacts when the risk is realized.

The method for handling these impacts is to provide margin for this type of risk, including cost, schedule, and technical margin.

Margin is the difference between the maximum possible value and the maximum expected value and is separate from contingency. Contingency is the difference between the current best estimates and maximum expected estimate. For systems under development, the technical resources and the technical performance values carry both margin and contingency.

Schedule margin should be used to cover the naturally occurring variances in how long it takes to do the work for known but uncontrollable likely delays. Weather delays during storm season is an example. Cost margin is held to cover the naturally occurring variances in the price of something being consumed in the project. Technical margin is intended to cover the naturally occurring variation of technical products.

Aleatory uncertainty and the resulting risk is modeled with a Probability Distribution Function (PDF) that describes the possible values the process can take and the probability of each value. The PDF for the possible durations for the work in the project can be determined. Knowledge can be bought about the aleatory uncertainty through Reference Class Forecasting and past performance modeling (Bordley, 2014; Fleishman–Mayer et al., 2013; Zarikas and Kitsos, 2015). This new information then allows us to update our forecast using our past performance on similar work to provide information about our future performance. But the underlying processes is still random, and our new information simply created a new aleatory uncertainty PDF.

The first step in handling Irreducible Uncertainty is understanding the need for schedule margin. An effective method of determining the necessary margin is by performing a Schedule Risk Assessment (SRA). Schedule Risk Analysis (SRA) is an effective technique to connect the risk information of project activities to the baseline

---

7 The use of Design Structure Matrix provides visibility and modeling of these dependencies. Many models consider the dependencies as statistic or fixed at some value. But the dependencies are dynamic driven by non-stationary stochastic processes, that evolve as the project evolves.

schedule, to provide sensitivity information of individual project activities to assess the potential impact of uncertainty on the final project duration and cost.

Schedule risk assessment is performed in four steps:

1. Baseline Schedule – Construct a credible activity network compliant with GAO–16–89G, "Schedule Assessment Guide: Best Practices for Project Schedule."
2. Define Reducible Uncertainties – for activity durations and cost distributions from the Risk Register and assign these to work activities affected by the risk and/or the work activities assigned to reduce the risk.
3. Run Monte–Carlo simulations – for the schedule using the assigned Probability Distribution Functions (PDFs), using the Min/Max values of the distribution, for each work activity in the IMS.
4. Interpret Simulation Results – using data produced by the Monte Carlo Simulation.

Schedule margin, cost margin, technical margin, to protect the project from the risk of irreducible uncertainty. Margin is defined as the allowance in budget, programed schedule … to account for uncertainties and risks (NASA, 2014).

Margin needs to be quantified by:

- Identifying WBS elements that contribute to margin.
- Identifying uncertainty and risk that contributes to margin.

Irreducible schedule risk

Projects are over budget and behind schedule, to some extent because uncertainties are not accounted for in schedule estimates. Research and practice is now addressing this problem, often by using Monte Carlo methods to simulate the effect of variances in work package costs and durations on total cost and date of completion. However, many such project risk approaches ignore the significant impact of probabilistic correlation on work package cost and duration predictions (Karim, 2014).

Irreducible schedule risk is handled with schedule margin which is defined as the amount of added time needed to achieve a significant event with an acceptable probability of success (Alleman et al., 2014). Significant events are major contractual milestones or deliverables (Petković, 2012).

> With minimal or no margins in schedule, technical, or cost present to deal with unanticipated risks, successful acquisition is susceptible to cost growth and cost overruns.
>
> (Rogers et al., 2006)

The project manager owns the schedule margin. It does not belong to the client nor can it be negotiated away by the business management team or the customer. This is the primary reason to CLEARLY identify the schedule margin in the integrated master schedule (DOD, 2012). It is there to protect the project deliverable(s). Schedule margin is not allocated to over-running tasks, rather is planned to protect the end item deliverables.

The schedule margin should protect the delivery date of major contract events or deliverables. This is done with a task in the IMS that has no budget (BCWS). The duration of this task is derived from Reference Classes or Monte Carlo Simulation of aleatory uncertainty that creates risk to the event or deliverable Bordley 2014; Pawlikowski et al., 2012).

> The IMS, with schedule margin to protect against the impact of aleatory uncertainty, represents the most likely and realistic risk-based plan to deliver the needed capabilities of the project.

Cost contingency

> Cost Contingency is a reserved fund held by the Project Management Office or business sponsor, added to the base cost estimate to account for cost uncertainty. It is the estimated cost of the "known–unknowns" cost risk that impact the planned budget of the program. This contingency is not the same as Management Reserve, rather this Cost Contingency is not intended to absorb the impacts of scope changes, escalation of costs, and unforeseeable circumstances beyond management control. Contingency is funding that is expected to be spent and therefore is tightly controlled.
>
> Contingency funds are for risks that have been identified in the project[8].

Irreducible cost risk is handled with management reserve and cost contingency for project cost elements related to project risks and are an integral part of the project's cost estimate. Cost contingency addresses the ontological uncertainties of the project. The confidence levels for the management reserve and cost contingency are based on the project's risk assumptions, project complexity, project size, and project criticality (Davis et al., 2017).

When estimating the cost of work, that resulting cost number is a random variable. Point estimates of cost have little value in the presence of uncertainty. The planned unit cost of a deliverable is rarely the actual cost of that item. Covering the variance in the cost of goods may or may not be appropriate for management reserve.

Assigning cost reserves needs knowledge of where in the integrated master schedule these cost reserves are needed. The resulting IMS, with schedule margin, provides locations in the schedule where costs reserves aligned with the planned work and provides the ability to layer cost reserves across the baseline to determine the funding requirements for the project. This allows project management to determine realistic target dates for project deliverables and the cost reserves – and schedule margin – needed to protect those delivery dates (NASA, 2013).

---

8 FAR 31.205–7 defines "contingency" as a probable future event or condition arising from presently known or unknown causes, the outcome of which is indeterminable at the present time. In "An Analysis of Management Reserve Budget on Defense Acquisition Contracts," David Christensen and Carl Templin, *9th Conference on the Society of Cost Estimating and Analysis*, June 13–16, 2000.

Irreducible technical risk

> The last 10% of the technical performance generates one-third of the cost and two-thirds of the problems.
>
> – Norman Augustine's 15th Law (Atin 2016)

Using the NASA definition, margin is the difference between the maximum possible value and the maximum expected value, whereas contingency is the difference between the current best estimates and maximum expected estimate. For systems under development, the technical outcome and technical performance values both carry margin and contingency.

- Technical margin and contingency serve several purposes:
  - Describe the need for and use of resource margins and contingency in system development.
  - Define and distinguish between margins and contingency.
  - Demonstrate that, historically, resource estimates grow as designs mature.
  - Provide a representative margin depletion table showing prudent resource contingency as a function of project phase.

For any system, in any stage of its development, there is a maximum possible, maximum expected, and current best estimate for every technical outcome. The current best estimate of a technical performance changes as the development team improves the design and the understanding of that design matures.

For a system in development, most technical outcomes should carry both margin and contingency. The goal of technical margin (unlike Cost and Schedule Margin) is to reduce the margins (for example size, weight, and power) to as close to zero as possible, to maximize mission capabilities. The technical growth and its handling include:

- Expected technical growth – contingency accounts for expected growth
  - Recognize mass growth is historically inevitable.
  - As systems mature through their development life cycle from conceptual to detailed design, variability is reduced and better understanding of the design is achieved.
  - Requirements changes often increase resource use.
- Unplanned technical growth – margins account for unexpected growth
  - Recognize any complex project or project development is challenging
  - Projects encounter "unknown unknowns" with the use of new technology that is difficult to gauge, that develop into uncertainties in design and execution of the project, all the way to manufacturing variations.

Chapter 10

Risk management practices

Glen B. Alleman, Tom Coonce and Rick Price

The principles of effective risk management were presented in the preceding chapter. There we learned that successful projects begin with careful customer analysis and assessment of what Done looks like before releasing a request for proposal (RFP) and continues through implementation. Before the release of the RFP, the customer must have a very clear picture of how the end user will apply the developed system to accomplish their missions. This vision is quantified with Measure of Effectiveness (MoE) and Measures of Performance (MoP) for the various user application scenarios. The customer must also specify the associated Technical Performance Measures and Key Performance Parameters within those scenarios prior to release of RFPs. Additionally, the customer must develop a notional top level-funded implementation plan that has been informed by historical uncertainty and known specific risks.

Root causes of cost and schedule growth and technical shortfalls on projects start with not adequately specifying what *Done* looks like in MoEs for the project's outcomes prior to issuing the RFP, not quantifying uncertainty, and failing to manage resulting risks for the MoPs associated with these MoEs during execution of the project.

The principles of effective risk management start with applying Continuous Risk Management providing the needed discipline to produce risk-informed actionable information by:

- **Continuously managing** risks produced by reducible and irreducible uncertainty.
- **Determining which risks are important** to deal with in a prioritized model, their interactions, statistical interdependencies, propagation, and evolution.
- **Implementing strategies to handle risk** with mitigation, correction, prevention, avoidance or acceptance, derived from Root Cause Analysis, to remove and prevent the conditions and actions creating the risks.

Continuous Risk Management increases the probability of project success by:

- **Preventing problems before they occur** with a *pre*-mortem to identify cause, take corrective and preventive actions to remove the conditions and actions of the root causes before the risk becomes an issue.

- **Improving product quality by focusing on project objectives** and consciously looking for risks that affect Cost, Schedule, and Performance throughout the project's lifecycle.
- **Enabling better use of resources** through early identification of problems and providing input to management decisions regarding resource allocation.
- **Promoting teamwork** by involving personnel at all levels of the project and focusing their attention on a shared vision of the mission to provide a mechanism for achieving the MoEs and MoPs as planned.

Five questions were defined in the beginning of the *Principles of Risk Management* chapter that require tangible evidence as answers before those Principles can be put to work on actual projects.

Answers to the five questions form the basis of the practices and processes in this chapter to address four classes of risk below that impact the probability of success for the project.

1. Unanticipated technical issues without alternative plans and solutions to maintain the MoEs and MoPs of the project's deliverables.
2. Unrealistic cost and schedule estimates based on inadequate risk-adjusted growth models resulting from the risks.
3. Inadequate assessment of risks and unmitigated exposure to these risks without proper risk handling plans.
4. Unrealistic performance expectations with missing MoEs and MoPs.

Data and processes needed to reduce risk and increase the probability of success

The data and processes needed to increase the probability of project success for each item related to each other are shown in Figure 10.1. The connections between the data and the process is representative of the typical project over its lifecycle. These connections and data are the basis of the Business Rhythm. Each input data item should be included in the contractor's Performance Measurement Baseline (PMB) and supporting documents. Each process should be defined in some form of procedure and process description implemented by the contractor. Each outcome should be used to inform the decision makers on the increasing probability of project success.

For each of the data items and processes that consumes or produces this data, there is both reducible and irreducible risk. Figures 10.2 and 10.3 describe the source of uncertainty as Aleatory or Epistemic. Figure 10.4 describes the outputs from the processes using the Input data. Each of these outputs has uncertainty as well which creates risk that must be handled.

Each Input, Process, and Output needs to be assessed for uncertainties and their impact on the probability of program success. If there is impact, a handling plan or margin needs to be in place to reduce the uncertainty to an acceptable level.

Each data and process item in Figure 10.1 has risk created by the Aleatory and Epistemic uncertainties shown in Table 10.1, Table 10.2, and Table 10.3.

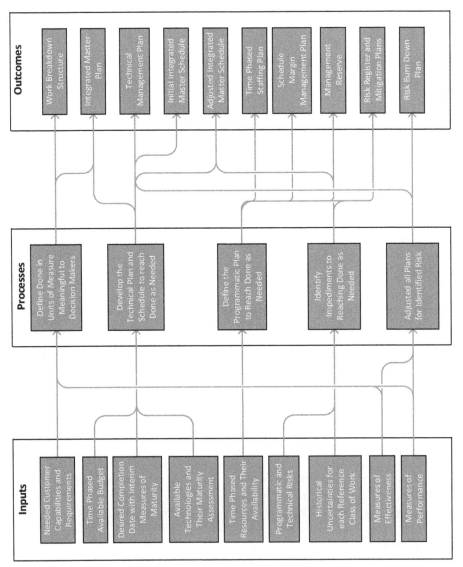

Figure 10.1 Data and processes to increase probability of success.

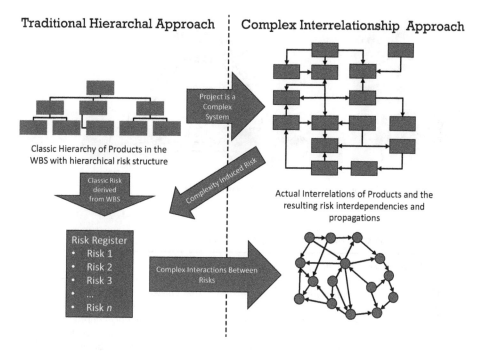

Figure 10.2 Modeling non-traditional risk relationships.

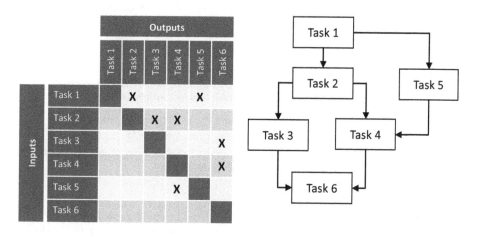

Figure 10.3 Design structure matrix connecting risk drivers to task risks.

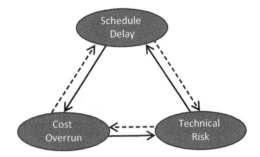

Figure 10.4 Modeling loops not captured in traditional risk models.

Table 10.1 Risks to inputs of increased probability of success

Input Data Needed to Increase Probability of Project Success

Inputs	Aleatory Risk	Epistemic Risk
Needed Customer Capabilities and Requirements	Aleatory uncertainties derived from Reference Classes and other models applied to Capabilities.	Epistemic uncertainties derived from system engineering model of needed Capabilities
Time Phased Available Budget	Variance in time-phased budget does not match time-phase plan to produce value must have margin to assure sufficient budget is allocated to produce the planned product value for the planned cost.	Probabilistic risks require planned work effort to reduce the uncertainty and buy down the risk at the planned point in the schedule.
Desired Completion Date with Interim Measures of Maturity	Confidence intervals around the delivery dates in the Schedule and other planning documents must be produced with modeling processes using both reducible and irreducible uncertainties.	
Available technologies and their maturity assessment	Unaddressed Variances in the maturity of the technologies.	Unmitigated risks in the technology.
Time phased skills mix and their availability	Variances in the availability of the skills and the efficacy of those skills to produce the needed value.	Unaddressed efficacy of staff.
Historical Uncertainties for each Reference Class of Work	Past performance of efficacy of labor inaccuracies.	Past technical performance of products, services, components, or systems.

Table 10.2 Risks to processes of increased probability of success

Processes Needed to Increase Probability of Project Success

Source	Aleatory Risk	Epistemic Risk
Define Done in Units of Measure Meaningful to the Decision Makers.	Naturally occurring variances in each of the measures – MoE, MoP, TPM, KPP.	Event-based uncertainties in each of the measures – MoE, MoP, TPM, KPP.
Develop the Plan and Schedule to reach Done as planned.	For both reducible and irreducible uncertainties, the Plan and Schedule must include the margin and risk reduction work activities. These processes must be captured in the Risk Register, but work needed to deal with them must be shown in the Plan and Schedule.	
Define the Resources needed to reach Done as planned.	For both reducible and irreducible uncertainties, the resource management processes must assure the margin and risk reduction work activities are properly staffed. These processes must be captured in the Risk Register, but work needed to deal with them must be shown in the Plan and Schedule.	
Adjust Plan for reducible and Irreducible risks.	With the identified reducible and irreducible uncertainties, vertical and horizontal traceability must be visible in the Plan and Schedule.	
Finalize the Risk-adjusted measures of progress toward Done	For each identified uncertainty and resulting risk, assess impact on the MoE, MoP, TPM, and KPP in the Plan and Schedule and provide reduction plan or margin to assure risk is reduced as needed to increase the probability of project success.	

Dependencies, structures and correlations of risk

When risk is modeled as a collection of non-stationary or stationary stochastic processes[1] interacting with each other and other elements of the project modeled in the Integrated Master Schedule, the risk that impacts the probability of project success is no longer static. The risks and the relationships are dynamic.

(Jaber, 2016)

The relationships between work activities in the Integrated Master Schedule (IMS) and the Work Breakdown Structure (WBS) are dynamic and change over time. This means risk management must be a continuous process. (Ho, 2010; Latouche, 1987]. The first step in addressing the management of risk created by aleatory, epistemic, and ontological[2] uncertainty – modeled by their distribution and density functions – is to develop a model of the structure of the risks, their interrelationships, correlations, propagation to the future, and the impact on the elements of the project (Marle, 2010).

---

1 A stochastic process is stationary if its statistical properties do not change over time. This means the underlying processes are identically distributed and independent of each other. A non–stationary stochastic process has a time–varying mean and variance or both.

2 Ontological uncertainty represents a state of complete ignorance. Not only do we not know, we do not know what we do not know.

Table 10.3 Risks to outputs of processes for increased probability of success

Output Data Needed to Increase Probability of Project Success

Output	Aleatory Risk	Epistemic Risk
Work Breakdown Structure	Identify aleatory risks by WBS element.	Identify Epistemic risk by WBS element.
Integrated Master Plan	Identify aleatory risks by Plan element.	Identify Epistemic risk by Plan element.
Technical Performance Plan with TPMs	Define Technical Performance Plan assurance in the presence of aleatory uncertainties.	Define epistemic risk buy down plan for each Technical Performance Measure.
Initial Integrated Master Schedule	The Schedule at Authorization to Proceed and possibly Integrated Baseline Review will not have sufficient *reference class* data to a credible assessment of Aleatory uncertainty.	Event-based uncertainty are likely in the future, so credible modeling of Epistemic uncertainty requires more maturity.
Adjusted Integrated Master Schedule	As the project proceeds the fidelity of the Reference Class Forecasting data improves.	As knowledge is acquired reduction in the Epistemic takes place – this is the *Cone of Uncertainty* paradigm.
Time Phased Staffing Plan	Natural variances in the productivity of the staff creates uncertainty and resulting risk.	Event-based uncertainty, turnover, reassignment, and other disruption impact productivity.
Schedule Reserve	Naturally occurring variances in the work productivity creates risk to completing work as planned	Event-based uncertainties associated with the work processes.
Management Reserve	Management Reserve early in the project is usually based on models built during the proposal. As the project proceeds better models of aleatory uncertainty emerged.	Management Reserve models of epistemic uncertainty mature as the project proceeds.
Risk Register with Mitigation Plans	The Risk Register must contain the range of uncertainties for work in the Schedule.	Risk Register must contain the event-based risks, their mitigations, and residual risks contained in the Schedule.
Risk Burn Down Plan with Quantified Measures of Risk	Reduction in the aleatory uncertainties modeled as the *Cone of Uncertainty*, showing the planned risk reduction as the project proceeds.	Measurement of the risk burn down is subject to epistemic uncertainty in the measurement process. As well subject to calibration of the risk ranking in the burn down process.

The categorization of risk starts with the categorization of the uncertainties that create the risk. These risks are usually started in the requirements stage of the project, covering technical, cost, and schedule requirements (Grady, 2006; Salado and Nilchiani, 2013). Most important are the dynamic correlations between risks. Since risk is created by uncertainty, these correlations are not static, they are dynamic. They drive risk but also drive the schedule of work (MacKenzie, 2014).

Modeling risks as *trees* in the Risk Breakdown Structure (RBS) fails to identify interactions between these risks. The same is true for Failure Modes and Effects Analysis (FMEA) and Bayesian Belief Networks, which model risk interactions, from multiple inputs through the risk generating processes, to multiple outputs as static relationships. The growing complexity of projects requires models of complex interacting risks, creating *loops* of propagating risks that amplify the original risk (Marle n.d., Marle and Vidal, 2008; Stewart, 1981).

In traditional risk management, a list of *reducible* uncertainties and the risks they create are captured in a Risk Register, analyzed for the probability of occurrence, probability of impact, probability of residual risk once handling has been applied. The *irreducible* uncertainties and the risks they create are modeled with statistical processes.

These approaches are based on identifying the risks and sometimes the *drivers* of the risks and the outcomes to the project when the risk turns into an issue. But there is more going on in the project than this paradigm captures (Figure 10.2) (Marle n.d.; Marle and Vidal, 2008; Marle, 2010; Marle and Vidal, 2011).

Managing complex interrelated risks requires integrating multiple dimensions of the risks, using the classical characteristics of probability and impact. Risk interactions need to be analyzed to make decisions based on project complexities. An effective method for doing this is through a Design Structure Matrix (DSM), simulating the interactions and taking corrective and preventive actions to reduce the impact of risk in the following five steps:

1. Identify potential interactions between risks. This is a binary identification of a potential cause and effect relationship between two events. This is done using a risk matrix based on the DSM (Petković, 2012)
2. Assess the strength of each interaction of the risks identified in Step 1.
3. Model the network based on risk interactions in the simulation context with the software such as Arena (Carroll and Burton, 2012; Kelton et al., 2014; Price and Alleman, 2016).
4. Design simulation experiments that will be run in order to test different parameters and to anticipate different propagation scenarios.
5. Analyze the simulation results of the mitigation plan (or response plan) and determine where the changes in terms of risk assessment or risk ranking are, and where the mitigation possibilities in terms of actions are.

This approach extends the traditional risk management process by simulating risk on risk effects. These effects may be different than the initial values captured in traditional risk management processes. This approach then takes non-traditional mitigation actions, by modeling the mitigation of the propagation links, instead of mitigating risk occurrence as a standalone process.

Design Structure Matrix topology

The DSM method was introduced by Stewart for task-based system modeling and initially used for planning issues (Eppinger and Browning, 2012; Stewart, 1981). It has been widely used for modeling the relationship between product components, projects, people, and work activities. (Bronson, n.d.; Yao et al., 2010). DSM relates entities with each other in ways schedules cannot. It can be used to identify appropriate teams, work groups, and a sequence of how the tasks can be arranged. Risk interaction within systems and subsystems, between functional and physical elements can also be modeled with DSM (Banazadeh and Haji Jafari, 2012).

A DSM is a square matrix, with labels on rows and columns corresponding to the number of elements in the system. Each cell in the matrix represents the directed dependency between the related elements of the system. The DSM allows self-loops (an element is directly linked to itself). These self-linked relationships appear in diagonal cells.

Figure 10.3 shows the structure of a DSM relating entities of one kind to each other. The tasks that constitute a complete project can be used to identify appropriate teams, work groups, and the sequence of how tasks can be arranged. In the same way, the DSM and the multiple-domain matrix (MDM) (Bickel et al., 2011) can be used to identify risk interactions across different domains of project, where a standard DSM can model a single domain.

Uncertainties between element relationships can be modeled to represent technical performance or uncertainties related with the risk of the element's reducible or irreducible risk.

DSM and risk management

Managing in the presence of uncertainty requires the coordination of potentially hundreds of *moving parts* at any one time, the deliverables from these activities and the risks associated with the work. Dependencies between project elements which increase risks are part of any complex project. Problems in one element can propagate to other elements directly or indirectly through intermediate elements – risk propagation. This complexity creates a number of phenomena, positive or negative, isolated or in chains, local or global, that will impact the success of the project if not properly handled.

Risks associated with project complexities, from design changes, to technical shortfalls, to the mismatch of available resources with the plan, can be reduced by increasing the visibility of this complexity and its propagation associated with each system element (Oduncuoglu and Thomson, 2011). This starts with analyses of complexity-related interactions, measurement, and prioritization of the *handling* of these risks. DSM can be used to model the risk structure between each element and across the project (Jaber, 2016; Mohan, 2002).

Modeling risk drivers and risk propagation with DSM

Risk is directly related to the complexity of the underlying system (Nilchiani et al. 2013). For engineered systems, risk is defined as: Davis et al. (2017).

Risk is a measure of future uncertainties in achieving project performance within defined cost, schedule, and performance constraints. Risk is associated with all aspects of a project (threat, technology maturity, supplier capability, design maturation, performance against plan). Risk addresses the potential variation in the planned approach and its expected outcome.

The DSM method is an information exchange model of the representation of complex task (or team) relationships to determine a sensible sequence (or grouping) for the tasks (or teams) being modeled.

(Yassine, 2004)

No matter how the project is organized, there are always intersections between the components needed to share information on risk impacts on other components. DSM provides visibility and insight to risks created by the complexity found in engineered systems where these unavoidable interdependencies exist.

The risk DSM paradigm has three components.

- The **undesirable effect** that creates risk has two components. (1) the condition that allows the root cause to occur and activity. (2) Root cause for occurrence of the risk by determining the known causal relationships to include the actions and conditions for the effect. (Gano, 2008)
- A **probability of occurrence** or natural occurring statistical process that is the source of risk to the project.
- A **consequence from this occurrence** – event or naturally occurring process – modeled in a similar way, along with the residual risk from the handling processes (Filippazzo, 2004).

Beyond the probability of occurrence and its impact of a risk, it is critical to model the connectivity of the evolving risk processes. Risks are typically modeled as independent activities. When the propagation of a *risk chain* and their interactions is not properly modeled, the consequences of this propagation cannot be clearly identified or managed (Marle and Vidal, 2011; Yassine, 2004). The design and development of complex systems require the efforts of hundreds of systems and subsystems. The interactions between the elements and the risks associated with each of those interactions are modeled with DSM. The probabilistic (reducible) correlations between the risks and the irreducible risks due to the propagation of uncertainty is represented by DSM and the details of those interactions. This matrix-based (DSM) risk propagation is used to calculate risk propagation and reevaluate risk characteristics such as probability and criticality as the project proceeds (Chapman and Ward, 2003; Schwabe et al., 2015).

DSM and the resulting Risk Structure Matrix (RSM) can model the loops and risk propagation needed to assess the actual impacts of risk on the Probability of Project Success on actual projects, shown in Figure 10.7.

The DSM for an example project, the SAMPEX satellite in Figure 10.4, can be used to construct RSM and define the probability of occurrence outcomes of the risk handling for a complex project using the Arena tool.

This starts with building the DSM of the system components listed in the left-hand column. The loops can then be modeled from this DSM into a Risk Structure Matrix (RSM), directly derived from the DSM. Figure 10.8 shows risk modeling using a DSM of NASA SAMPEX (Solar Anomalous and Magnetosphere Particle Explorer) Space Craft. The network of connections is shown in Figure 10.5 showing the loops in the propagation of risk between individual elements of the spacecraft.

		1	2	3	4	5	6	7	8	9	10	11	12	13	14	15	16	17	18	19	20
Antenna	1	■	X	X	X				X					X			X	X			
Coupler	2		■	X	X									X				X			
Diplexer	3		X	■				X			X							X			
Transponder	4				■			X	X		X			X		X		X			
1773 Data Bus	5					■			X		X			X		X		X			
Data Processing Unit	6						■		X		X							X			
Low Energy Ion Analyzer	7			X				■			X							X			
Heavy Ion Large Telescope	8			X			X		■		X					X					
Proton/Electron Telescope	9									■				X							
Mass Spectrometer Telescope	10							X			■					X		X			
Attitude Control Electronics	11							X	X			■				X		X			
Attitude Control Sensors	12							X					■			X					
Attitude Control Actuators	13										X			■		X		X			
Mechanisms and Pyros	14													X	■	X		X			
Solar Arrays	15							X								■		X			
Battery	16							X	X					X		X	■	X			
Power Supply Electronics	17							X						X		X		■			
Passive Thermal Controls	18													X		X			■		
Scout Launch Vehicle	19						X	X	X		X			X						■	X
Space Craft Structure	20						X	X	X		X				X			X	X	X	■

Figure 10.5 Risk modeling using a design structure matrix (DSM).

Representing risk interactions using DSM

There are three types of risk interactions between pairs of risk in the Design Structure Matrix.

- Dependent risks – that are engaged in precedence relationships.
- Interdependent risks – that are engaged in mutually dependent relations, or within a large loop.
- Independent risks – that are not related to other risks but impact the project independently.

These interactions can also be classified into several categories using a model to identify different kinds of relationship links between risks.

- Hierarchical link – divides the system into subsystems or modules divided into components.
- Contribution link – a modeling element can influence a soft goal positively or negatively.
- Sequential link – link between risks that are dependent on each other.
- Influence link – links that influence other elements of the matrix, but are not directed connected.
- Exchange link – links in which an exchange in state takes place, either bi-directional or uni-directional.

Several links with different natures can exist between two risks. These can be expressed as causal relationships.

With existing methodologies, individual risks are identified and analyzed independently. The relationships between risks in actual projects are more complex in both structure and context. Organizational and technical complexity must also be included in the model. This introduces complexity in an interacting risk network (Marle n.d.). In a complex project there can be propagation from one *upstream* risk to several *downstream* risks. The resulting *downstream* impacted risk may create additional *upstream* risks. This result is a *domino effect, chain reaction* or *looping* risk structures (Aroonvatanaporn et al., 2010)

The traditional Risk Register, and sequential risk driver paradigm, cannot model these risk conditions, which occur very often on complex projects (Marle, n.d.).

Using DSM as the basis of risk modeling in an RSM provides a technique to model these looping structures.

Simulating a risk network in Arena

Calculating the risk resulting from these interactions in Figure 10.6 is difficult with a modeling tool, since the model is complex and contains loops. Static Risk Registers, Monte Carlo Simulation, or Method of Moments (Bickel et al., 2011) modeling in the Integrated Master Schedule (DOD, 2012) will show the impact of risk on cost and schedule. But these processes don't show impact of one risk on other risks, through their interactions with each other. Figure 10.9 shows risk interactions modeled as a network from the Risk Structure Matrix in Figure 10.8, including loops that create a

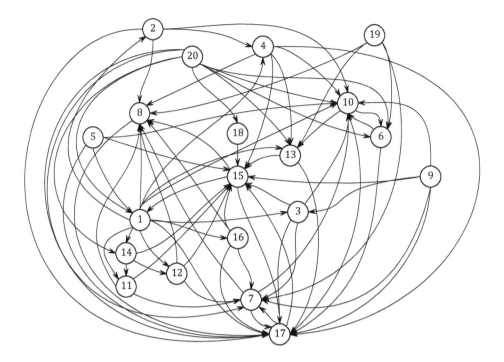

Figure 10.6 Risk interactions modeled as a network.

domino effect from one risk to another, that propagate from one portion of the project to another impacting Cost, Schedule, and Technical risks and finally impacting the Probability of Project Success. Each node has a probability of occurrence and each arch has a probability of impact.

These risk interactions can be modeled with the Arena tool for the network of risks, the risk probability parameters, and the transition (propagation) probabilities to each interaction link.

- **Transition probability.** In the simulation model, evaluated causal conditional probability can also be interpreted as transition probability between two risks. In the network with *n* risk nodes, transition probabilities are in a square matrix with *n* × *n* elements of probability.
- **Spontaneous probability.** In project risk networks, risks may be caused by an external event or a risk that has not been identified. These risks may also occur spontaneously due to some unknown or undefined reason outside the system. Spontaneous probability can be interpreted as the evaluated likelihood of a risk, which is not the effect from other activated risks.

Spontaneous risks and their probabilities are the starting point for modeling of the network of risks. In the traditional Risk Register or Static Risk Driver paradigms, this *spontaneous* risk model represents the Probability of Occurrence for an Epistemic uncertainty or the statistical behavior of an Aleatory uncertainty, both creating a risk.

While these traditional approaches are useful, they cannot model the propagation of risk through the system in a statistically sound manner needed to not only correct the impact of risk but prevent risk from occurring in advance.

Effectiveness of risk assessment

Several risk analysis tools and risk modeling methods are available in the complex project domain, including fault tree analysis, failure mode and effects analysis, and modeling and simulation. Risk analysis results are used in risk assessments where the goal is to assess the confidence in the analysis results and determine if the level of risk is acceptable, tolerable (operationally manageable), or unacceptable. These assessments directly contribute to the Probability of Project Success.

The effectiveness of risk assessments is impacted by three major factors limiting the accuracy of the outcomes (Bellos et al., 2004). These include the evolving understanding of the cost, schedule, and technical domain and its uncertainties, the inherent random nature of cost, schedule, and technical phenomena, and learning from experience involving untestable assumptions in rational processes of inductive reasoning about this world.

Considerations of ontological uncertainties (what exists and its nature) and epistemological uncertainties (acquisition and thoroughness of knowledge about what exists) complicate the assessment of risk since any truly objective and accurate assessment of risk is not possible, except for the simplest of situations. Situations involving complexity, uncertainty, and ambiguity require subjective judgments and considerations of stakeholder values and preferences to arrive at a decision.

> The approach is to model these uncertainties, the connections between them, the propagation of these connections, the resulting risks, the impacts of each risk, the propagation of those risks, and that risk's impact in the Probability of Project Success.

A risk-adjusted schedule

Starting with the WBS, a credible Schedule that produces the system elements must address reducible risk through risk mitigation activities. This Schedule must also address the irreducible uncertainties and those discrete risks that remain in the Risk Register that could not be mitigated through work activities. These uncertainties are categorized as known–unknowns because they are known, but not known for certainty they will occur.

Projects can protect against these uncertainties by setting cost and schedule margin for the irreducible uncertainties, and management reserves for the reducible risks that were not mitigated.

Reducible risk management processes are held in the schedule

All reducible risks identified in the Risk Register need to be assessed for *reducibility* in the Schedule. If the risk – the uncertainty that is event based – can be reduced, then that work is assigned to work packages and activities in the Schedule and placed on baseline. These *risk buy down* activities are managed just as ordinary work, funded by the CBB, measured for performance just like any other work.

The risk reduction mitigation activities are planned to achieve a specific level of risk reduction at a specific time in the Schedule. Meeting the planned risk reduction level at the planned time is a measure of performance of the risk retirement activities.

Irreducible risk management processes include use of margin and alternate points of integration

With the reducible risks from the Risk Register handled with risk reduction activities in the schedule, the irreducible risks now need to be identified and handled in the Schedule. Since the irreducible risks are actually *irreducible*, only margin or alternate points of integration (changing logic sequence) can be used to protect the system elements from this naturally occurring variance. No actual work can be done to do this.

Monte Carlo Simulation of the schedule is the primary tool for assessing how much margin is needed for each irreducible risk type. Schedule margin is a buffer of time used to increase the probability that the project will meet the targeted delivery date. Schedule Margin is calculated by starting with a Probability Distribution Function (PDF) of the naturally occurring variance of the work duration of the *Most Likely* value of that duration. With the *Most Likely Value* and the PDF for the probability of other values, the durations of all work in the Integrated Master Schedule and the probabilistic completion times of this work can be modeled with a Monte Carlo Simulation tool.

This modeling starts with the deterministic schedule, which includes work for the Reducible Risks. The schedule margin is the difference in the initial deterministic date and a longer duration and the associated date with a higher confidence level generated through the Monte Carlo Simulation.

A practical example of schedule margin

Schedule margin was used in a project we can all recognize. Immediately after the Wright Brothers made their first powered flights in 1903, they begin to develop their experimental aircraft into a marketable product. By 1905 they had the basis of a "practical flying machine." Other experimenters learned of their work and began to build on their success.

By 1906, other pilots were making tentative hops in uncontrollable aircraft. By 1909, after watching the Wrights' flying demonstrations, they grasped the brilliance and necessity of three–axis aerodynamic control. The performance of their aircraft quickly caught up to and then surpassed the Wright Flyers. The capabilities and uses for aircraft expanded as designers and pilots introduced float planes, flying boats, passenger aircraft, communication and observation platforms, fighters, and bombers.

As World War I approached, aircraft become an essential part of war and peace. In 1907 the U.S. Army renewed its interest in the Wright Brothers. The Board of Ordnance and Fortification and the U.S. Signal Corp announced an advertisement for bids to construct an airplane. However, the design and performance specifications were such that the Wrights were the only viable bidder. A price of $25,000 was set for the brothers' airplane if they could meet the performance criteria in actual flight trials.

These flight trials were scheduled for late summer 1908 at Fort Myer, Virginia, a military post outside Washington, D.C. With commitments in Europe, the brothers had to separate for the first time. With Wilbur off to France, Orville did the flying for the Army.

Table 10.4 Wright Brothers metrics to increase probability of success

Historical Document	Project Performance Measure
The flying machine must be designed to carry two people having a combined *weight of no more than 350 pounds,*	MoP
Also, sufficient fuel for a *flight of 125 miles*	MoP
The flying machine should be designed to have a *speed of at least 40 miles per hour in still air for at least 125 miles*	MoP
The flying machine should be designed so that it may be *quickly and easily assembled* **and** *taken apart* **and** *packed into an Army wagon.*	KPP
It should be capable of being *assembled and put in operating condition within one hour*	KPP
Before acceptance, a *trial endurance flight* will be required *of at least one hour* during which time,	MoP
The flying machine must remain continuously in the air without landing.	MoE
It shall *return to the starting point* **and** *land without any damage* **that would** *prevent it immediately starting upon another flight.*	MoE
During this flight of one hour, it *must be steered in all directions without difficulty* **and at all times** *under perfect control and equilibrium.*	MoE
It should be *sufficiently simple in its construction* **and** *operation* **to** *permit an intelligent man to become proficient* **in its use within a reasonable length of time.**	KPP

From the source document in the *U.S. Signal Corps Agreement and Specifications for a Heavier-Than-Air Flying Machine* in the Smithsonian aviation archives, we have Measures of Effectiveness, Measures of Performance, Technical Performance Measures, and Key Performance Parameters. These were all part of their project increase the probability of success to meet the requirements for the US Army contract (Table 10.4).

Development of schedule margin

Schedule margin is a buffer of time used to increase the probability that the project will meet the targeted delivery date. Schedule Margin is calculated by starting with a Probability Distribution Function (PDF) of the naturally occurring variance of the work duration of the *Most Likely* value of that duration. With the *Most Likely Value* and the PDF for the probability of other values, the durations of all work in the Integrated Master Schedule and the probabilistic completion times of this work can be modeled with a Monte Carlo Simulation tool.

This modeling starts with the deterministic schedule, which includes work for the Reducible Risks. The schedule margin is the difference in the initial deterministic date and a longer duration and associated date with a higher confidence level generated through the Monte Carlo Simulation.

In Figure 10.7, the deterministic delivery date is 8/4/08 with the contract delivery date of 8/31/08. Using the historical variability of the task durations resulted in a 5% confidence level of completing *on or before* 8/4/14 shown in the deterministic schedule. This says that with the deterministic schedule – no accounting for the natural variability in work durations, the probability of completing on or before 8/4/08 is 5%. These dates are taken from the Wright Brothers development efforts of the *Heavier-Than-Air* contract issued by the U.S. Army at the turn of the twentieth century.

To increase the confidence level of meeting the contractual date, the contractor needs to increase the probability of completing *on or before* to 80%. The difference in duration between the deterministic schedule's completion date of 8/4/08 and the 80% confidence of completing *on or before* 8/14/08 is 10 calendar days, still earlier than the contractual date of 8/31/08. The Schedule Margin is added in front of key system elements to protect their delivery dates to meet the contractual need date of 8/31/08.

Assigning schedule margin to protect key deliverables

Using schedule margin to protect against schedule risk – created by the natural uncertainties in the work durations – enables on-time contractual end item deliveries.

There are two schools of thought on how schedule margin should be managed.

- Place all schedule margins at the end of the project or system elements.
- Distribute margin at strategic points along critical paths where there are known schedule risks.

Placing all the margin at the end appears effective in short duration or production efforts where the primary schedule risk is not driven by technical complexity. The same objective can be achieved when a disciplined process is followed for control and consumption of distributed margin. Paramount to this approach is accelerating downstream efforts when margin is NOT consumed.

Most schedule risk in a development project is encountered when project elements are integrated and tested. Even when margin is distributed, margin is often kept at the

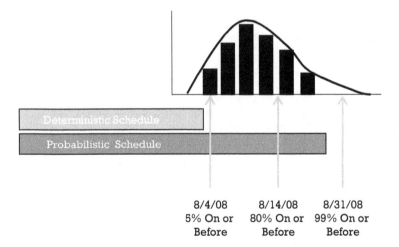

8/4/08	8/14/08	8/31/08
5% On or	80% On or	99% On or
Before	Before	Before

Figure 10.7 Monte Carlo and schedule margin on Wright Brothers schedule.

end of the schedule to help protect against risk when all paths come together during final integration and test. This approach enables on-time end item delivery with realistic cost and schedule baselines that provide accurate forecasts and decisions based on current status, remaining efforts, and related schedule risks.

There are several valid reasons for distributing schedule margin earlier in the IMS including:

- Protecting use of critical shared resources so that being a few weeks late doesn't turn into a several month schedule impact. An example in space projects is use of a thermal vacuum chamber shared across multiple projects at critical times in their schedules. If a project is unable to enter the chamber at their scheduled time, the ultimate delay may be an exponential factor of their original delay.
- Protecting highly visible milestones that are difficult and undesirable to change like a Critical Design Review (CDR).
- Establishing realistic performance baselines accounting for schedule risk at key points provides more valid data to make project decisions.
- Establishing realistic baselines that are cost effective.
- Placing margin where we believe it will be needed and consumed provides the most realistic schedule baseline possible for succeeding efforts and enables more accurate resource planning for prime contract, customer, and suppliers.

Key insertion points for schedule margin

Schedule Margin is not the same as Schedule Slack or Schedule Float as stated in the GAO Schedule Assessment Guide. Margin is preplanned and consumed for known schedule irreducible uncertainty and float is the calculated difference between early and late dates. In many ways margin is much like management reserve and float is similar to underruns/overruns.

- Schedule margin is placed where there is known irreducible schedule risk. It is never consumed because of poor schedule performance. In this case, Schedule Margin is managed like Management Reserve.
- Schedule margin is not budgeted – it does not have an assigned Budgeted Cost of Work Scheduled (BCWS). If the risk the margin is protecting comes true, new tasks need to be identified and budgeted. If the risk is not realized, the schedule margin is zeroed out and the succeeding tasks accelerated – *moved to the left*.
- Allocating margin for known risks at key points prevents this margin from being used to cover poor schedule performance. This forces an immediate recovery action to stay on schedule instead of degrading margin as if it was schedule float.
- Inclusion of margin – either distributed in front of key system events or at the end of contractual end item delivery – does not affect contractual period of performance. The period of performance is defined by the contract. The Schedule Margin activities in the deterministic schedule are represented in the Schedule, using the task label defined as *Margin* for all to know this is a task that doesn't produce an outcome, but is in the schedule as *margin* to protect the delivery dates for the outcomes.
- Inclusion of schedule margin for known schedule risk provides a realistic baseline and accurate resource planning (including the customer). If not consumed the effort is accurately represented as "ahead of schedule."

Identifying and managing Alternate Points of Integration (APOI)

Risks from aleatory uncertainties can also be managed by identifying and using Alternative Points of Integration in the Integrated Master Schedule (MS) (Price and Alleman, 2016). When an IMS is developed, it is usually based on specific preferred relation-based logic between work tasks that deliver contractual end items. For any IMS there are alternate ways of defining the logical connections between tasks. If one element of a complex system is driving the schedule unacceptably based on initial logic, it may be acceptable to integrate that element at a later point in the schedule and preserve an end item delivery date. This technique provides valuable insight into realistic and supportable schedule confidence levels.

This concept starts with the alternatives defined in Table 10.5. Defining acceptable alternative points of integration for each subsystem provides options for when things don't go according to plan and they increase schedule confidence intervals. Two Monte Carlo Simulations are shown in Figures 10.8 and 10.9, where the probability of completing as needed goes from 61% to 94% by rearranging the logic with Alternate Points of Integration.

The original showed a 61% probability of completing *on or before* the need date of 8 June 2018, using the Monte Carlo Simulation for the Integrated Master Schedule for the Spacecraft.

Development of cost margin or contingency reserve

The cost margin is the amount of cost *reserve* needed to address irreducible cost variances of the project's work efforts and improve the probability of meeting the target cost – the contract cost. Cost margin is calculated in the same manner as schedule margin. The contractor develops a probability distribution of the final cost based on the natural variances contained in the historical databases. The confidence level of meeting the target contracted cost in the IMS is noted. If the confidence level is too low, cost margin may be added to the baseline in the same manner as schedule margin, to bring the baseline up to a desired cost confidence level.

However, currently, there is no generally agreed mechanism to do so. If the Confidence Level is unacceptably low, the contractor must redo the IMS and try to reduce costs for time dependent and time independent costs to raise the cost confidence to an acceptable level. Re-planning would result in re-calculating the schedule margin. If after re-planning, the cost confidence level is still unacceptably low, the contractor should report the Confidence Level to the customer at the time of the Integrated Baseline Review (IBR). If the customer agrees the Confidence Level is too low, resources could be added, and the contractor would update the IMS or de-scope the contract to improve the Confidence Level. Alternatively, the customer would hold the cost margin as a contingency for overruns.

Development of management reserves

Management reserves are financial resources needed to address the reducible risks that were not mitigated. The optimal way to develop management reserves is to re-run the Monte Carlo Simulation tool with only these risks against the resource-loaded IMS. The difference between the deterministic cost estimate and the point on the cost distribution curve for the desired cost confidence level is the management reserve.

Table 10.5 Defining acceptable alternative points of integration

Component	Planned POI	Alternate POI	Must Have POI	Other Contingency Factors
Structural Panels	Assemble Bus Structure	None	Assemble Bus Structure	Ned at Least 2 of the 6 Panels
Solar Array Development Mechanisms	Assemble Bus Structure	Payload and Solar Array Installed	Spacecraft Mass Properties	No Engineering Design Units
Propulsion Tanks	Assemble Bus Structure	None	Assemble Bus Structure	Need Prior to Last Panel Assembly
Thrusters	Assemble Bus Structure	Install External Components	System Level Tests	No Engineering Design Units
Tubing	Assemble Bus Structure	Bus Functional Tests (1)	Bus Functional Tests (2)	Need Prior to Last Panel Assembly
Avionics	Assemble Bus Structure	Bus Functional Test (2)	Spacecraft Mass Properties	Can Use Engineering Design Units
Attitude Control Systems	Assemble Bus Structure	Bus Functional Test (2)	Spacecraft Mass Properties	No Engineering Design Units
Solar Arrays		Spacecraft Mass Properties	System Level Tests	No Engineering Design Units
Batteries	Install Internal Components	Spacecraft Mass Properties	Prior to Launch	Can Use Workhorse Batteries
Harnesses	Assemble Bus Structure	Bus Functional Test (1)	Bus Functional Test (2)	No Engineering Design Units
Thermal Control System	Assemble Bus Structure	Bus Functional Test (2)	System Level Tests	No Engineering Design Units
Communications System	Assemble Bus Structure	Bus Functional Test (2)	System Level Tests	No Engineering Design Units
Flight Software	Bus Functional Test (1)	Bus Functional Test (2)	System Level Tests	Specific Drops for Functional Tests
Payload 1	Payload Installation	None	Payload Installation	Minor Modification Development
Payload 2	Payload Installation	None	Payload Installation	High Risk Development

Next steps to increase the probability of project success

The risk management process requires information exchange among all project domains and provides visibility over risks, with a ranking according to their criticality for the project; these risks are monitored and controlled according to the rules defined for the domains to which they belong.

(Innal et al. 2013)

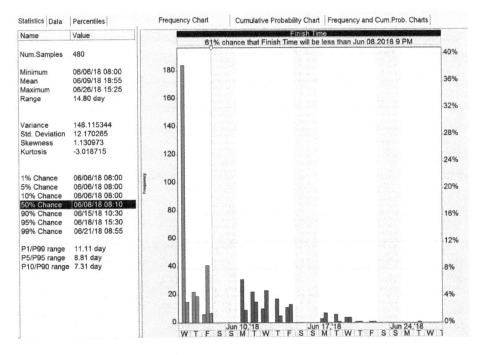

Figure 10.8 Monte Carlo schedule risk assessment.

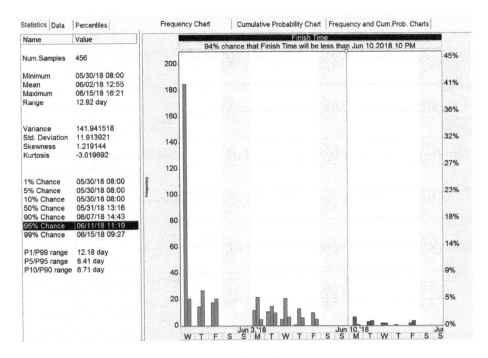

Figure 10.9 Monte Carlo showing 94% probability of completing on time.

Uncertainty Quantification

Uncertainty has been called "an unintelligible expression without a straightforward description."

Quantification of Margins and Uncertainty (QMU) is a decision-support methodology for complex technical decisions. QMU focuses on the identification, characterization, and analysis of performance thresholds and their associated margins for engineering systems that are evaluated under conditions of uncertainty, particularly when portions of those results are generated using computational modeling and simulation.

(Petković, 2012)

Uncertainty Quantification (UQ) is the quantitative characterization and reduction of uncertainties as part of a decision-support method for complex technical decision processes (Petković, 2012) UQ attempts to determine how likely certain outcomes will be if some aspect of the system is not exactly known. Risk management may be well developed in many complex project domains. Applying the formality of UQ is not (Acker, 1979).

Capturing the risks resulting from reducible and irreducible uncertainties is the first step in increasing the probability of project success. But these uncertainties must be properly modeled to quantify risk and design robust and reliable systems from both the technical performance and projectmatic performance point of view.

Quantification of margins and uncertainties

In the presence of Aleatory uncertainty, margin is needed to protect the project from naturally occurring uncertainties. For Epistemic uncertainty, assessment of the probability of occurrence, probability of impact, and probability of residual uncertainty is needed. QMU is a risk management decision-support method for complex technical decisions. QMU focuses on identifying, characterizing, and analyzing performance thresholds and their margins are evaluated under conditions of uncertainty, particularly when portions of those results are generated using computational modeling and simulation (Helton and Burmaster, 1996; Petković, 2012).

QMU is focused on characterizing the detail of sources of uncertainty in a model, quantifying the uncertainty in the system response output variables. These sources are described in terms of probability distributions to account for the stochastic nature of complex engineering systems. The characterization of uncertainty provides for the comparisons of margins for key system performance metrics to the uncertainty associated with their models. QMU provides risk-informed decision-making processes where simulation (Monte Carlo Simulations, Method of Moments) provides inputs to the decision-making authority.

Uncertainty Quantification approaches

Model Based Uncertainty Quantification is the next step in applying risk management to the Integrated Project Performance Management system in the Defense Acquisition domain.

Quantifying of the uncertainty creating risk is needed before uncertainty reduction can take place (Helton, n.d.; Holley et al., 2014; Lin et al., 2012; Litvinenko and Matthies, 2014; Pilch et al., 2006; Schwabe et al., 2015; Schwabe et al., 2015; Walker et al., 2015; Whitley, 2014).

- Forward Uncertainty Quantification – is the quantification of uncertainties in system output(s) propagated from uncertain inputs. This assessment focuses on the influence on the outputs from the parametric variability listed in the sources of uncertainty in Figure 10.1.
- The targets of forward uncertainty propagation analysis include:
    - Evaluate low-order moments of the outputs, the mean and variance of the uncertainty and resulting risk.
    - Evaluate the reliability of the outputs. This is especially useful in reliability engineering where outputs of a system are usually closely related to the performance of the system.
    - Assess the complete probability distribution of the outputs. This is useful in the scenario of utility optimization where the complete distribution is used to calculate the utility.
- Inverse Uncertainty Quantification – estimates the variance between the actual outcomes and the estimated model of the risk (bias correction) and estimates the values of unknown parameters in the model if there are any (parameter calibration or simply calibration).

Methods of Uncertainty Quantification

For several decades, research shows how to solve uncertainty quantification problems (Walker et al., 2003). The focus has been on uncertainty propagation. Recently several approaches for inverse uncertainty quantification problems have been developed and been shown to be useful for most small to medium scale risk management problems.

Uncertainty implies lack of information. This can be lack of understanding about a probabilistic event (Epistemic) or about the range of outcomes of a process (Aleatory).
- Methods for forward uncertainty propagation
    - Monte Carlo Simulation – schedule network of work with aleatory uncertainties assigned to task duration and epistemic uncertainties assign technical performance measures and cost models.
    - Adaptive sampling – is a general technique for estimating properties of a distribution – in this case the behaviors of the underlying risk process – while only having samples generated from a different distribution from the distribution of interest.
    - Fuzzy theory risk estimates – is a form of many-valued logic in which the truth values of variables may be any real number between 0 and 1. It is employed to handle the concept of partial truth, where the truth value may range between completely true and false (Wierman, 2010).
- Methods for inverse uncertainty quantification
    - Frequentist – using regression analysis, least square assessment to produce standard error parameter estimates of the risk and its reduction as a function of time.
    - Bayesian – using a modular Bayesian approach to solve the bias correction and parameter calibration (Kennedy and Anthony, 2001).

Event Chain Method for propagation assessment

Epistemic and Aleatory uncertainty and resulting risk affect project cost, schedule, and technical performance differently. These uncertainties can be correlated in any complex project. The same risk may have different impacts, and require different handling plans because of the interdependencies of the risks (van Dorp and Duffey, 1999).

The accuracy and precision of cost and scheduling can be improved by constantly refining the original plan using actual project performance measurement (Williams, 2017). This can be achieved through analysis of uncertainties during different phases of the project and incorporating new knowledge into the project schedule.

Event Chain Method (ECM) is a stochastic modeling method applied to schedule and cost risk analysis. Risks are assigned to activities or resources. ECM models relationships between project risks by identifying risks that cause or trigger other risks. All risks and relationships between them are modeled in the project using event chain diagrams (Innal et al., 2013).

After risks are assigned to the IMS, Monte Carlo Simulation is performed (DOD, 2012). Statistical distributions of project cost, duration, finish time, resource allocation, and other parameters help to determine the chance that the project can be completed on time and on budget. Risk impact is calculated based on a correlation between the incremental increase of a task's cost or duration and project cost, duration, and other parameters. Risks within a Risk Register are ranked based on calculated impact and probabilities. The method simplifies complex risk analysis process, which in most cases is performed by project schedulers (Virine and Trumper, 2013).

Adding processes and practices to the principles

With the Five Principles of Increasing the Probability of Project Success in place, a set of processes and practices for quantitative risk assessment and risk reduction are needed to answer the questions – before the issues arise from the potential root causes. This is referred to in other domains as *pre-mortem* (Tables 10.6 and 10.7) (Scheinin, 2008).

There are Practices Supporting the Five Processes. For each of these practices, risk continues to influence the outcomes, so risk management continues to influence activities following the business rhythm (Plan of the Week) for the monthly performance reporting cycle (Table 10.8).

Table 10.6 Questions for managing risk

Question	Answer
1. What can go wrong?	Look in the Risk Register that contains both epistemic and aleatory uncertainties. Models of both are needed for both reducible and irreducible uncertainties that create reducible and irreducible risks to project success
2. What might be the cause of the problem?	Perform Root Cause Analysis and develop corrective or preventive actions to remove the risk or break the causal chain for reducible risks and provide *margin* for irreducible risk.
3. What might prevent the problem from happening?	Implement the corrective or preventive action plan for each identified risk or provide needed margin to protect the project from the naturally occurring variances.
4. What might we do if the problem occurs?	Develop a risk handling plan for each risk created by the identified uncertainties. This plan has direct action to correct or prevent, or margin to protect.
5. What are the consequences of going wrong?	Model risk propagation to other components and subsystems. Address the reducible risks at the boundaries of the propagation. Provide margin between the boundaries for the irreducible risk.
6. What is the confidence in the answers to each of the five questions?	Build a model of the uncertainties that create the risks, with the probabilistic occurrences of the epistemic uncertainty and statistical behaviors of the aleatory behaviors. Connect the elements of this model in a Risk Structure Model (RSM) to make visible the propagation of risk as well as the individual risk elements.

Table 10.7 Processes supporting five principles of success

1. Identify the needed technical and operational Capabilities of the system.	Develop a Risk-adjusted Integrated Master Plan which shows the impacts to the increasing maturity of the project's capabilities.
2. Establish Technical, Schedule, and Cost Requirements in support of needed Capabilities.	Risk-adjusted Integrated Master Schedule, with risk handling tasks and margin assigned to protect End Item Deliverables.
3. Integrate Cost and Schedule, Risk Register and risk modeling tools.	Risk-adjusted Performance Measurement Baseline to produce products that meet the project requirements assessed with MoEs, MoPs, TPMs, and KPPs.
4. Execute Performance Measurement Baseline.	Continuous Risk Management applied to reducible and irreducible uncertainties and the propagation of these uncertainties to other elements of the project.
5. Perform Continuous Risk Management.	Risk Management Plan shows how risks are being handled and how Ontological Uncertainty will be handled when it is discovered.

Table 10.8 Conditions and outcomes for the 10 practices

Condition	Outcome
1. Capabilities Drive Requirements.	Systems engineering capabilities structure with Measures of Effectiveness and Measures of Performance in the Master Plan.
2. Requirements Identify Deliverables.	Measures of Performance, Technical Performance Measures, and Key Performance Parameters.
3. Work Packages Produce Deliverables.	Risk-adjusted Work Package Exit criteria used to update Risk Assessment model
4. Master Schedule Sequences Deliverables.	Event Chain and Uncertainty propagation assessment.
5. Progress Measured as Physical Percent Complete.	Define measures of progress to plan defined in Quantifiable Backup Data.
6. Compliance with Technical Performance Measures Adjust EV.	Adjust EV (BCWP) for Physical Percent Complete with risk-adjusted assessment of future performance.
7. Performance Feedback Adjusts Work Sequencing.	Develop Alternative Points of Integration and Event Chain modeling.
8. Future Performance Based On TCPI.	Risk-adjusted TCPI, EAC, and ETC.

Chapter 11

Act fast and think fast

Agile schedule performance

Robert Van de Velde

> "Only when performance is described by objective measures can project[s]...truly gain deeper understanding and formulate reasoned tactics for improving the opportunity for success."
>
> (Lipke, 2013)

> "Even if you get numbers, is it not more important to actually produce 'useful deliverables'?"
>
> (JFG, personal communication, 2013)

Here is the dilemma faced by Agile practitioners. On one hand, they are philosophically committed to the priority of fast delivery. After all, the first principle of the Agile framework states: "Our highest priority is to satisfy the customer through early and continuous delivery" (Beck, et al., 2001b).[1]

On the other hand, projects almost always operate in the context of scarce resources and limited time—a context that breeds uncertainty and risk. There, decision-making on what to do (or not do) must carefully weigh project performance on costs and timeline. Without objective measures of performance, project decisions are subject to cognitive bias, logical fallacies, and statistical faux pas.[2]

In short, Agile practitioners feel caught between acting fast and thinking slow. How do you resolve the dilemma? How do you improve performance, specifically schedule performance, with reasoned tactics while maintaining a fast pace of delivery?

The **Chapter Roadmap** outlines the answer: Earned Schedule for Agile projects.

---

1 Citations are included in the text with References collected at the end. Jargon is defined in a footnote, unless the text makes its meaning clear.

2 The problems of intuitive decision-making were detailed by Kahneman and Tversky (see References). Although not without controversy, their views are widely accepted as describing systematic errors that frequently occur when quick, intuitive judgements are made. The antidote to such errors is deliberate, rational thinking attended by objective data. The difference is popularized in Kahneman's book, *Thinking, Fast and Slow* (Kahneman, 2011).

Chapter roadmap

First things, first: what is meant by "schedule performance"? Here, the view is that **Schedule Performance Is the Efficiency of Value Delivery**. Consistent with the Agile framework, efficiency relates to the volume of delivery, rather than conformance with a predefined sequence of delivery. Extending the Agile framework, delivery encompasses both the objects and value that are produced.

How do you **Measure Agile Schedule Performance**? The short answer is, with both absolute and comparative metrics expressing how well time is being used on the project. The metrics look back and also ahead, reflecting past performance and predicting future performance.

To accelerate evaluation of performance, you need to **Set Schedule Performance Levels** at the start of the project. Subjectivity and its associated problems are avoided by using objective data. Allowances for uncertainty and risk are used to ground threshold values between levels of performance.

With metrics for schedule performance and thresholds for evaluating them, you're ready to **Improve Agile Schedule Performance**. The improvements depend in part on expectations, which need to be set before and re-enforced during project execution. As the project proceeds, data needs to be gathered—the same data normally captured during an Agile project, with a small twist.

The data is used on some new calculations—don't worry, they take little time and can easily be automated, if you prefer. The results are matched against performance thresholds to determine what and when action is required. Action recommendations feed into the normal Agile planning cycle.

Implementing this technique on an individual project is a relatively small change, but even so, there are significant **Agile Challenges to Earned Schedule**. Some Agile practitioners resist using Earned Value itself. Judging by social media and blog postings, there is also widespread resistance to the estimation that supports the metrics and to the status reporting of results.

On the other hand, there are impressive **Agile Benefits from Earned Schedule**. The technique offers insights into schedule performance that are not available through typical Agile metrics such as Burn Charts. Beyond that, you can **Leverage Earned Schedule for Agile Projects**. That is, you can extend the techniques for an even deeper understanding of schedule performance.

A brief **Conclusion** wraps things up, but before you start the journey, you'd better check whether or not yours is one of the **Target Projects** for the chapter.

Target projects

Projects using the Agile framework are obvious targets for this chapter. That is not to say that plan-driven projects cannot also benefit. There are a couple of techniques adapted from Agile that can equally be applied to plan-driven projects. Still, the primary audience is one schooled and practised in Agile.

It is equally helpful if projects are already using Earned Value Management. That method objectively measures and estimates project performance on costs and schedules. If your project does not currently employ Earned Value Management, check out the section on challenges to Earned Schedule. It contains guidance on how to fill in the gap.

Most important, the targets are mission-critical projects with hard deadlines. Certainly, project costs must also be managed, but for the target projects, timeline is critical. That makes it imperative for them to have a deep understanding of and reasoned ways to improve schedule performance. Typical Agile measures will not do—a more robust assessment of how time is being used on the project is required.

Schedule performance is the efficiency of value delivery

The phrase "how time is being used on the project" is important but ambiguous. True, it highlights schedule performance as a function of time, but it glosses over the type and content of that performance.

Schedule performance as efficiency

Schedule performance is most commonly tied to the efficiency of delivery, but it can also relate to the sequence of delivery. The difference is like gas mileage versus wheel alignment of a car.

Mileage indicates how far you can travel on a certain amount of gas. From the mileage, you know if you are where you should be given the fuel that has been burned. Your actual mileage on a trip can be above, below, or at the rated capacity of your vehicle.

By contrast, for your car to run straight, its wheels must be properly aligned. The wheels are either in alignment, or they are not. Although wheels can be wildly out of line, they cannot be better-than-aligned.

Like fuel efficiency, schedule efficiency tells you whether the volume of delivery meets the plan and whether that puts you where you should be on the project timeline. By contrast, schedule adherence is either on-plan or off-plan. It matters very much which deliverables are completed. If the completions exactly align with the plan, the adherence is perfect. Otherwise, it is out of line.

Agile projects cannot guarantee that a fixed network of deliverables exists. The principle of Independence means that equivalent Backlog Items can be substituted for one another.[3,4] In theory, the order in which deliverables are scheduled is determined on-the-fly.

Even though complete independence is not realistic, there are times when equivalent Backlog Items can be substituted for one another dynamically. That possibility undercuts the assumption behind adherence.[5] So, for Agile projects, schedule performance means the efficiency of delivery.

---

3 The principle of Independence is taken from the INVEST mnemonic. The mnemonic characterizes the quality of a Backlog Item. Independent Items can be moved around because they do not depend on one another (Wake, 2003).

4 "Backlog Item" is a familiar term in the Agile framework. A Backlog (aka, Product Backlog) lists the requirements that the project is to deliver. The list is prioritized and sized. An Item is one of the deliverables listed in the Backlog.

5 It should be noted that some implementations of Agile retain the notion of a fixed network of activities, at least for the next "wave" in Rolling Wave plans. In those cases, measures of schedule adherence are relevant to the project. For more information on adherence metrics, see Van De Velde (2018).

Schedule performance as value delivery

What is the unit of measure for delivery? For Agile projects, it is customary to use Points (aka, Story Points or Release Points) as the unit of measure. Points are variously interpreted as arbitrary units of relative size (A is twice the size of B) or as absolute units of work (A is 20 work hours and B is 40 work hours). I have shown elsewhere that relative measures fall short—only absolute units of work are sufficient to ground decisions on schedule performance (Van De Velde, 2017a, b, c).

Typically, Agile projects infer schedule efficiency from Point counts: the number of Points completed is compared to the number expected to be complete. If the actual count exceeds expectation, the project is taken to be early. If the actual count does not meet expectation, the project is assumed to be late. In the rare case that the two counts are equal, the project is considered to be exactly on time.

The central problem with this view is that the number of Points alone does not reflect the value being delivered. Projects need to know whether the time invested is returning the value needed, regardless of the simple quantity of Points completed. That is to say, completing five high-value Points has more impact than finishing five low-value Points.

Caution is warranted on the term "value". Agile practitioners often understand value to mean Business Value, but that value is related to the achievement of the business vision or business objectives. The Project Sponsor and Stakeholders evaluate the effectiveness of the schedule in delivering value to the business. They use techniques such as Balanced Scorecard to do so (Alleman, 2014).

In contrast, there is value to the project. That is the value of the work required to produce a project deliverable. Such value is related to the planned work and cost for a deliverable. On one hand, it represents work *planned to be completed* at a planned cost. On the other hand, it signifies work *completed* at a planned cost.

In this sense, efficiency derives from the volume of project value delivered. Performance is assessed by comparing the value actually earned versus the value that should have been earned. If value is then linked to time, there is a way to measure the project's schedule performance directly.

Measure Agile schedule performance

For Earned Schedule, the linkage of value to time is simple and elegant: "the amount of time earned on a project is the time at which the value currently earned should have been earned" (Lipke, 2003 and Lipke, 2009b). A graph illustrates the point.

In Figure 11.1, the current value earned is mapped back to the value planned (the horizontal dotted line). By dropping a line from that point to the timeline, the amount of schedule earned is marked out. It extends from the project's starting point to Sprint 5.[6] As Sprints run for a fixed period of time, say 2 weeks, this is equivalent to saying that, as of week 12, 10 weeks have been earned.

Performance measures flow readily from this basic idea. First, compare the amount of time earned to the amount of time spent. If the Earned Schedule exceeds the Actual

---

6 A "Sprint" is a timebox (a fixed period of time usually one to four weeks in duration) in which a product increment is done.

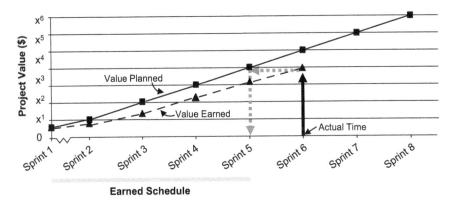

Figure 11.1 Earned schedule definition.

Time, the project is ahead. If the Earned Schedule does not meet the Actual Time, the project is behind. If the two are equal, the project is exactly on schedule. In contrast to Point counts, the relationship here is natively in terms of time.

Still, the measurement tells us only that the project is early, late, or on time. It does not tell us the significance of any variation. What's missing is a sense of proportionality.

For that, first compare the Earned Schedule to the Actual Time. The ratio, formally called the Schedule Performance Index for time or SPIt, quantifies the relative performance as a fraction (Henderson, 2004). That's one step toward determining significance.

Next, leverage the SPIt to estimate when the project will finish. Compare the planned duration of the project to how well it has used time thus far. That is, divide the planned duration by the SPIt. The result indicates how long the project is going to run (called the Estimate at Completion for time or EACt). It says, given the performance thus far and assuming that the same pace of delivery will continue, the project is going to take *this* long.

Figure 11.1 can be used to illustrate these points. As just mentioned, 10 weeks have been earned as of week 12. So, the SPIt is the ratio between 10 weeks and 12 weeks. That is, it equals 0.83. The planned duration is 8 Sprints. At 2 weeks per Sprint, that's 16 weeks. To complete the project, it will take 16 divided by 0.83, or a little over 19 weeks.

The power of the schedule performance measures begins to emerge. A performance index of 80% means that 20% of the deliverables are not being completed on time—leaving that much undone can't be good. The implications are highlighted by the estimated delivery date: the project is headed for a delay of at least three weeks. Again, that's not good news, especially at Sprint 6 of 8.

The amount of Earned Schedule, the comparative performance efficiency, and the estimated completion date provide a basis for determining the significance of variations. To deepen insight into project performance and to guide decision-making, these numbers need to be operationalized. That is, there needs to be a systematic way to identify the performance level indicated by the metrics.

Set schedule performance levels

The key to identifying performance levels is thresholds. Thresholds, or more precisely, threshold values, mark the boundaries between levels. The boundaries differentiate between high, medium, and low performance.

In the past, threshold values for the metrics have been based on intuition and experience. As a result, the values have varied widely from one practitioner to the next. The subjectivity undermines confidence in thresholds. What is needed, instead, is an objective basis for threshold values.

Consider the earlier observation that all projects facing scarce resources and limited time breed uncertainty and risk. Some uncertainties are epistemic—they reflect our lack of knowledge. These uncertainties can be addressed by gaining knowledge, and the work behind the gains can be quantified. That's the role of Contingency (Alleman, 2017).

Other uncertainties are aleatory—they reflect random, naturally occurring variations that cannot be known in advance (Ibid.). They are addressed by including a reserve based on similar situations in the past. That's the role of Margin.[7]

When loss is attached to an uncertainty of either type, the result is risk. Contingency and Margin include allowances for uncertainties and their associated risks. For simplification, this chapter generally refers just to uncertainty.

Finally, there needs to be a yardstick against which values can be compared. Agile provides a good starting point for such a benchmark: velocity. Velocity measures the estimated work effort to produce the Points for each Sprint ("Velocity", n.d.).

In a departure from the Agile canon, velocity is used here to mean "look forward", i.e., it sets the pace of delivery for the whole timeline. The delivery, moreover, is not measured in Points but in Earned Value.[8]

The velocity yardstick covers all planned work, including Contingency but excluding Margin. (Margin is excluded because it is not tied to specific work.)

Thresholds are based on uncertainty allowances. High performance is defined as any variation in the metric that is within the Contingency allowance. Medium performance is variation beyond Contingency but within Margin. Low performance is any variation beyond Contingency plus Margin.

For an example of the thresholds in action, see the following section.

Improve Agile schedule performance

With metrics for schedule performance and thresholds for assessing them in place, the next consideration is how they are used to improve performance.

There are five rungs to the performance-improvement ladder: *Setting Expectations, Capturing Empirical Data, Calculating Metrics, Assessing Results,* and *Improving Performance.*

---

7 Management Reserve can also be included with Margin. Management Reserve is an allowance for unspecified epistemic uncertainties—what have been called "unknown unknowns".

8 The Agile Alliance defines velocity as "a 'measurement' made after the fact" ("Velocity", n.d.). Hence, it is not a forecast, and "phrases such as 'setting the velocity'" are considered to be a mistake (Ibid.). In practice, it is common for velocity to be used as a uniform pace of delivery. (See, for instance, Brodinski, n.d.) There are even cases where the unit of measure is Earned Value (Sulaiman, et al., 2006).

Setting expectations

Both actual and perceived performance improvement depends in large part on expectations. The expectations are initially set before schedule execution begins. In Agile projects, the performance expectation is expressed by velocity—the rate at which Points are expected to be finished in a Sprint. Dividing the total number of Points by the mean velocity yields the number of Sprints in the project.

In Agile projects that use Earned Schedule, expectations are similarly shaped by velocity—here, the rate at which value is expected to be delivered in a Sprint. Dividing the total planned value by the mean value yields the number of Sprints. In practice, there is usually cycling between Points and value to synchronize the expected number of Sprints.

Conceptually, the planned value and earned value should be the same at the end of a Sprint. So, for each Sprint that is planned, a Sprint is expected to be earned. The number of Sprints and the planned Start Date determine the Finish Date. With start and finish set, the performance baseline follows. It is typically expressed in a manner familiar to Agile practitioners: a Burn Chart.

Here is an example from a recent project. It will be used throughout this section for illustrations.

Figure 11.2 displays the Baseline Earned Schedule (ES) Burndown. The total baseline duration, including Contingency, is 9 Sprints. An additional Sprint is included to represent the Margin allowance for the project. In the actual project, each Sprint spanned two weeks.

The burndown shows that for each Elapsed Sprint, 1 Sprint is planned to be earned. Thus, at the end of Sprint 1, the remaining number of baseline Sprints would be 8. By the end of Sprint 9, all baseline Sprints should have been completed. Hence, there would be 0 remaining Sprints.

Most Agile projects have an estimated velocity of Points for a Sprint. Currently, most lack a similar estimate for the velocity of value. If your project lacks estimates, check out the section on **Agile Challenges to Earned Schedule**. It contains tips on how to fill in the gaps.

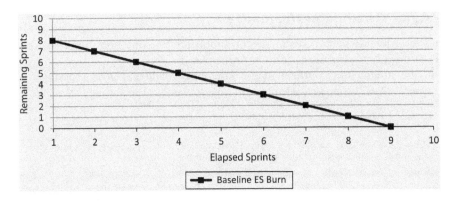

Figure 11.2 Baseline earned schedule burndown.

Capturing empirical data

Performance expectations are expressed by the baseline. Performance results are grounded in empirical data—the same data that is ordinarily collected on an Agile project: Points that are done.

But, there's a small "twist". Earned Schedule places two additional demands on empirical data. First, the definition of "done" must be clear and definitive (Alleman, 2009). A deliverable is either "done" or "not done", and there is tangible evidence of completion (Alleman, 2010).

Second, Points must be costed. Doing so weighs the Points in units familiar to businesses, namely, money. Applying rates to the work required to produce deliverables expresses their value to the project.

Keep in mind that new Points and even new Backlog Items often emerge during a Sprint. When they do so, the total number of Points and the Backlog must be adjusted to reflect the change. It is also possible for Points and Items to no longer be required. Again, the total and Backlog must be updated.

Agile projects routinely collect empirical data on the Points that are done and update Point totals and Backlogs. The only incremental data capture required by Earned Schedule is the value of the work associated with the Points.

Calculating metrics

Calculation of the metrics is also done quickly.

To determine the amount of schedule earned (called the Earned Schedule metric, or simply, ES), count the number of Sprints in which the current total of value earned is greater than or equal to the cumulative value planned. After the last full Sprint is counted, there is usually some earned value left over. The fractional time earned equals the ratio between the left-over value earned and the value planned for the next Sprint beyond the last full one. Add the Sprint count and the fraction to get the total amount of Earned Schedule.

To find the comparative performance (SPIt), divide the Earned Schedule by the Actual Time.

To calculate the estimated completion date, first get the estimated duration (the EACt). It equals the ratio between the baseline duration and the current time (i.e., the number of the Sprint just completed). Then, multiply the result by the number of time periods (weeks, months) in a Sprint. Finally, add that amount to the project start date. The result is the estimated end date (known as the Estimated Completion Date for time or ECDt).

A wide range of Earned Schedule calculators are available both as free-ware and commercial packages. Available tools use various technologies, have widely different scopes, and fall into a broad spectrum of price points.

On small projects, the calculations can easily be done by hand or in a spreadsheet. Larger projects benefit from automation, as the calculations can be done more quickly and accurately.

Assessing results

Thresholds make quick work of assessing results. Compare the amount of schedule earned, the comparative performance achieved, and the estimate to complete against thresholds for each. The amount of deviation from the baseline determines what, if any, thresholds are breached and what, if any, actions are required.

Graphical representations are often used to accelerate assessment and ease communications. Details follow on assessing each metric.

Earned Schedule metric

The Earned Schedule (ES) metric offers a quick, easily understood reading on schedule performance. The Baseline Earned Schedule Burndown mentioned above is the starting point. Here is the chart for the sample project. The chart is updated with results after the third Sprint. Figure 11.3

In this version of the chart, the Sprints have been rendered as dates. Dates add context to the chart and ease communication, especially outside the project. The vertical axis remains the same.

The Baseline ES Burn line (solid line with square markers) is the estimated track for time utilization, running straight from the end of the first Sprint to the end of the final baselined Sprint. The ES Burn line (dashed line with round markers) shows how much time has actually been earned, extending from the first Sprint to the last completed Sprint.

The Baseline ES Burn line equals the total number of remaining Sprints decremented by the number of elapsed Sprints. The ES Burn equals the total number of remaining Sprints decremented by the amount of schedule earned up to the end of each completed Sprint.

The threshold value is the amount of schedule estimated to be earned by the end of each Sprint. Schedule performance is assessed as early, on-time, or late based on whether the ES Burn line is below, on, or above the Baseline ES Burn line.

In Figure 11.3, the ES Burn line is above the baseline, and the gap is widening. The project is late, and the situation is getting worse.

Although an effective high-level communication tool, the ES Burn Chart does not go far enough. It does not tell how well or poorly time is being used. In other words, it does not measure the proportionality of variance.

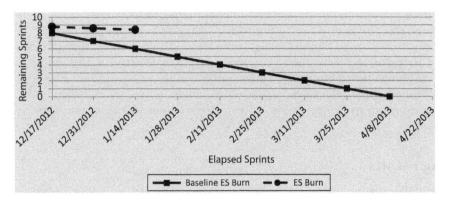

Figure 11.3 Earned schedule burndown.

Comparative performance metric

The Schedule Performance Index for time (SPIt) measures schedule performance efficiency, indicating how well or poorly the volume of value delivery is tracking the estimate. Here is the chart with the additional data on the secondary axis.

In Figure 11.4, the Efficiency (i.e., SPIt) axis on the right runs from 0 to a maximum value of 1.00. If the reported SPIt were to exceed 1.00, the maximum value achieved would become the end point. In the example, the maximum is set to 1.00 because it shows the efficiency of a project that is on schedule, which the example decidedly is not.

The SPIt (dotted line with triangles) achieved at the end of each Sprint is plotted on the chart. At around 0.20, it runs well below the nominal value of 1.00.

The project's performance level is determined by comparing the SPIt value to the thresholds for the project. Note that the SPIt is calculated taking account of Contingency. That is, the SPIt measures performance against the baseline schedule. Thresholds are calculated as a percentage allowance given Contingency, Margin, and beyond (both positive and negative).

In the example, the Contingency allowance was set at 10% and Margin at 5%. The SPIt threshold values (rounded) and associated performance levels for the project are outlined in Table 11.1

Table 11.1 depicts efficiencies not only below thresholds but also above them. Although efficiency greater than the estimate is often viewed positively, it can indicate

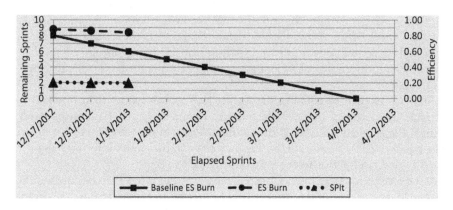

Figure 11.4 Earned schedule burndown and performance efficiency.

Table 11.1 Sample threshold values for schedule efficiency

SPIt Threshold	Performance Level
< 0.80	Low
>= 0.80 and <0.90	Medium
>= 0.90 and <= 1.00	High
>1.00 and <= 1.10	High
>1.10 and <= 1.20	Medium
> 1.20	Low

that the estimate was "low balled". Keeping expectations artificially low is just as bad as failing to deliver at the expected rate. Given that the plan was developed as the best way forward, it should be the project's goal to follow it.

Assessing comparative schedule performance includes visually inspecting the chart and reviewing the performance levels being achieved. The chart makes trends readily visible. The table indicates the seriousness of deviations.

In the example, there is a clear trend: the SPIt hovers around 0.2, well below the 0.80 threshold for Low performance. The next step on the performance ladder, *Improving Performance*, describes the response to such an assessment. Before addressing it, there's one more metric to consider.

Estimate to complete

The Estimate to Complete for time (EACt) and the Estimated Completion Date for time (ECDt) are estimates of when the project will finish. The following terminology is used for dates. The Baseline Finish Date includes Contingency. When Margin is added, the date is referred to as the Deadline. If both Contingency and Margin are removed, the date is called the Target.

EACt and ECDt are used interchangeably below because the ECDt is simply the project Start Date plus the EACt.

In Figure 11.5, the Target, Baseline, and Deadline are portrayed as a set of vertical lines at the right side of the graph. Thresholds for EACt cluster around those dates.

The thresholds are expressed in Sprints. The number of Sprints is calculated from allowances for Contingency and Margin. In the example, the Contingency allowance is 10%, and the Margin allowance is an additional 5%. If the Target is Sprint 8, Contingency adds (rounded) one Sprint and Margin (rounded) one Sprint.

Here are the EACt threshold values and associated performance levels for the example. Table 11.2

If the EACt is later than or equal to the Target (>= 8), but earlier than or equal to the Target plus Contingency (<= 9), the outlook for meeting the Baseline is good, and performance is labelled as High. If the estimate is earlier than the Target (< 8) but later than or equal to the Target less Contingency (>= 7), the outlook for meeting the Baseline is also good, and performance is again labelled as High.

If the EACt exceeds the Target plus Contingency (> 9) but is less than or equal to the total including Margin (<= 10), the project is not on track to meet the Baseline, but it should still finish by the Deadline. So, performance is labelled as Medium.

SPIt Threshold	Performance Level
< 0.80	Low
>= 0.80 and <0.90	Medium
>= 0.90 and <= 1.00	High
>1.00 and <= 1.10	High
>1.10 and <= 1.20	Medium
> 1.20	Low

Figure 11.5 Earned schedule burndown, performance efficiency, estimated dates.

Table 11.2 Sample threshold values for EACt

EACt Threshold	Performance Level
> 10 Sprints	Low
> 9 Sprints and <=10 Sprints	Medium
>= 8 Sprints <= 9 Sprints	High
>= 7 Sprints and < 8 Sprints	High
>= 6 Sprints and < 7 Sprints	Medium
< 6 Sprints	Low

If the EACt is earlier than the Target less Contingency (< 7), the project is again not on track to complete as baselined and is labelled as Medium. In this case, it is Medium not because the Baseline is likely to be exceeded but because the plan is unsound. After all, an allowance should have been made for early delivery, and the estimate makes it appear that something was mistaken. Either the uncertainties relevant to early delivery were incorrectly identified, or the Contingency allowance for early delivery was too small.

Finally, if the EACt exceeds the Margin (> 10), the project will not meet the Deadline, even if both Contingency and Margin are used. Performance is labelled as Low. By the same token, if the EACt is earlier than Target less Contingency and Margin (< 6), it appears that there are serious flaws in the plan, and performance is labelled as Low.

Normally, the ECDt (which is Start Date + EACt) is drawn on chart along with the threshold dates. In the example, however, the EACt ranged from 44 to 46 Sprints (and ECDt maximum was 10 October 2014), far beyond allowances for Contingency and Margin. The values were so far beyond the limits of the chart that the estimated dates appear only as a comment in the lower right corner of the graph. Clearly, performance efficiency is Low.

Again, the response to such a deviation will be described in the next section.

Improving performance

Data collection, metrics calculation, and performance assessment consume little incremental time on an Agile project. Once variances are identified, the next and final step toward improving schedule performance is action.

The action takes place as part Sprint Planning. During project execution, Sprint Planning sets the goal for the next Sprint, identifies the Backlog Items to be delivered, and details the tasks and responsibilities for the work to be done.[9]

9 Earned Schedule metrics fit into two other common Agile practices. (1) Sprint reviews. They reflect on the previous Sprint with a view to improving project processes. The same performance levels, threshold values, and generic action steps are used to assess and adjust Sprint processes during the Reviews. (2) Initial planning and estimating. They can use metrics from other, similar projects as guides. See the section on **Agile Challenges to Earned Schedule** for more information on estimation techniques.

In the Agile canon, input to Sprint Planning comprises the following: "the Product Backlog, the latest product Increment, projected capacity of the [Project] Team during the Sprint, and past performance of the [Project] Team" ("Sprint Planning", 2014).

The Product Backlog and latest increment are used in Sprint Grooming. The Grooming ensures that the Backlog is up-to-date. Using the latest increment as the starting point, Sprint Planning adds new Backlog Items and Points, removes Items and Points no longer required, and flags Items and Points that have been completed.

Measures of projected capacity and past performance are enhanced by Earned Schedule metrics. They offer quantitative measures of schedule performance efficiency (the ES and SPIt) and estimates of future performance (EACt and ECDt). The quantification means that thresholds can be set and monitored to guide Sprint planning.

The response most commonly triggered by an identified variance is the following: root-cause analysis, remediation planning, and communication both inside and outside the project team.

Root-cause analysis tracks variance back to its source. The analysis reveals the cause(s) of the problem, supported by evidence. Once the cause(s) are known, remediation follows.

The details of remediation vary depending on root-cause, but they often involve rapid, and sometimes large, shifts in the number and size of Backlog Items in a Sprint, changes in the number and expertise of team members, and/or revisions in the timeline. Remediation is implemented in following Sprints, which are monitored to ensure the fix works.

Communication of variances, root causes, and remediation occurs both inside and outside the team. The charts described above not only support performance assessment but also its communication. Challenges associated with communications will be dealt with in the next section.

Sprint Planning uses Earned Schedule metrics to identify and triage variances in schedule performance. Knowing when variances demand a response is not always obvious. Here are some rules-of-thumb to guide responses.

Individual readings of the metrics often hover around the baseline, rather than falling exactly on schedule. As long as individual readings are within the Contingency allowance, they do not need to invoke the response just described.

For individual readings that occur outside Contingency, the reaction is different. Within Margin and, even more so, beyond it, the lagging performance might not be redeemable by future high performance. Such readings indicate a serious shortfall in productivity and require further action.

Even if the project appears to be highly efficient, there might be problems. If efficiency exceeds Contingency, and especially if it goes beyond Margin, the estimate was probably understated. If so, the plan for the next Sprint must be adjusted.

Dramatic changes in the value of a metric (say, 20% or more) from one Sprint to the next are another sign of problems. While these differences are frequently caused by failures in reporting, there are cases where the project team has made a sudden change in tactics, causing productivity to dive or to soar. Such tactical changes warrant further action.

Threshold breaches are another worrisome type of change. Even if the Sprint-over-Sprint change is small, when a metric moves into an efficiency-level other than High performance, follow-up action is required.

Finally, a series of related readings indicates a trend. At ProjectFlightDeck, we generally build action plans based on trends, rather than on individual readings. For long-running projects, we require three or more consecutive readings headed in the same direction to mark a trend. For short-term projects, we reduce the required number of consecutive readings.

In most cases, if the performance level is Low, the response is immediate. For other performance levels, the response is moderately paced, involves smaller adjustments, and employs low-key messaging.

In summary, the time required to prepare and use Earned Schedule to manage Agile schedule performance is minimal. Yet, the insight it provides goes well beyond what is available through canonical techniques such as the Burn Chart. Earned Schedule enables the project team to think and act fast.

That is not to say, however, that using Earned Schedule on an Agile project is a cakewalk. The next section addresses its challenges and how they can be met.

Agile challenges to Earned Schedule

There are three major challenges to using Earned Schedule on an Agile project: *Earned Value*, *Estimates*, and *Project Communications*.

Earned Value

The most comprehensive challenge is the introduction of Earned Value itself. Agile resistance to Earned Value methods rests on the view that they are "heavyweight" processes inconsistent with Agile's valuing "individuals and interactions over processes and tools" (Beck, 2001a).

In a strict sense, Agile and Earned Value are formally consistent. It has been shown that both Earned Value and Earned Schedule metrics can be mathematically deduced from Agile metrics (Sulaiman, et al., 2006 and Van De Velde, 2014).

Of course, there's more to Earned Value adoption than the force of logic. Earned Value methods demand a mind-set change. Rather than measure performance only in Points, Agile projects need to consider value as well. Value, moreover, means the planned cost of work that is to be done and that has been done to produce deliverables.

At the enterprise level, this is a significant shift. It has all the risks and potential rewards of a major change initiative. Unfortunately, such initiatives have "a dismal track record" (Hamel & Zanini, 2014). Classic guidance on change programs is still worth reviewing (see Kotter, 1996), but if enterprise adoption is the goal, check out more innovative approaches (for example, Little, 2014).

At the project level, it's a different matter. The change is a relatively small one. Agile projects are already thinking of value delivery, albeit Business Value. They also have access to all base data required to calculate and track planned value, earned value, and Earned Schedule. How so?

Through the Backlog, Agile projects have a list of deliverables. To estimate velocity, Agile projects need to have an understanding of the work required to produce the deliverables. Given a budget and a timeline, Agile projects generally create a Release Plan that shows a way to get from the project start to the finish.

Given Agile's value of people over process, Agile projects are well aware of the team to do the work. Costs associated with team members are either known or can easily be calculated from the budget and amount of work.

From this data, the planned value, earned value, and Earned Schedule are just a calculation away.

For Agile projects, adoption of the Earned Value perspective is easier than it is for enterprises. All that's missing is the motivation. The benefits of Earned Schedule, which will be discussed presently, offer plenty of reason to make the change.

Estimates

Another common challenge is to estimates, as they seem to conflict with Agile fundamentals. Neither the Agile Manifesto nor the 12 Principles make any references to estimates. Popular Agile hashtags, blogs, and books take the omission a step further: "Estimates are a waste of valuable time" (Issacs, n.d.).

Underlying the objection are several beliefs: that estimates are always wrong, that they are used to bully project teams, that they are hard to do, and that they are done only because they have always been done.

There is an element of truth in these beliefs, and that is, no doubt, an on-going inspiration to the #NoEstimates camp. But counter-arguments abound (see Alleman, 2018).

They focus on two points. First, there is little, if any, systematic data that supports dropping estimates. Anecdotal evidence is vague about how to manage performance successfully without estimates. So, duplicating success without estimates, especially on large initiatives, is practically impossible.

Second, the "micro economics" of project decision-making demands estimates. Micro economics describes how individuals and organizations make decisions in the presence of scarce resources and uncertainty.

Projects that are constrained by time and budget face uncertainty. To make micro economic decisions, projects need a yardstick for assessing current performance and a basis for future planning. Estimates support prioritization of work, analysis of how changes affect the schedule, (re-) allocation of resources, and reporting on past performance and likely future outcomes.

Apart from the academic debate, Agile projects in practice continue to be asked for estimates. Business managers need to prioritize investments and pick initiatives to go forward or be held back. Without estimates, they find it impossible to manage project portfolios. Beyond internal project decisions, therefore, estimates support broader business decision-making.

All of that said, what if a project has no estimates, even base estimates of the work required to produce its deliverables? Full treatment of estimating techniques warrants "deep dive" research that goes beyond the scope of this chapter. Still, here are some tips on how to estimate and references to use as a starting point for the research.

Look for similar projects—the "Reference Class" (Kahneman, Slovic, & Tversky, 1982 and Flyvberg, 2008). In those projects, find the values of specific parameters such as duration and cost. The values will be scattered over a range—the "probability distribution". Finally, compare the current project to the Reference Class. See where it fits best into the probability distribution. The outcome is an estimated duration and cost for the target project.

Alternatively, look at historical projects in the same domain as the current one. In those projects, find durations and costs of typical units of work (International Society of Parametric Analysts, 2008 and Goodrich, 2014). Then, identify the number of comparable units of work in the target project. Scale the durations and costs to fit the target project, and apply the adjusted figures to the units in the target project. Again, the outcome is an estimate for the project.

Either way, ensure that the estimate includes allowances for uncertainty and risk.

Project communications

Consistent with canonical Agile practice, project teams can create and use Earned Schedule metrics as part of Sprint Planning. The team thereby has first-hand knowledge of the metrics. Communication occurs through participation. No additional time is required.

As for communication outside the team, the Agile canon is silent—there is no mention of Stakeholder communication or status reporting.[10]

Agile blogs are not so taciturn. They are filled with vigorous attacks on anything that smacks of outside communication such as status reporting: "... the idea of a 'project status' is utter nonsense in a Scrum or Open Agile setting because it presupposes that you're working toward some enormous Big Bang release or similar milestone. If that's the case, you're simply not doing Agile" (Aaronaught, 2013a).

Many in the Agile community believe that participation in Sprint Planning is the only way for Stakeholders to understand how things are going. Doing so eliminates the need for the team to spend any time on outside communication because there is no "outside".

As noted in one blog: "Someone who cannot be bothered to participate in any of these events [e.g., Sprint Planning] is generally someone not worth involving in the project" (Aaronaught, 2013b).

Granted, "pointy-haired" managers à la Dilbert exist, but many more managers take seriously the fiduciary responsibility of their position.[11] They have a duty to understand how their (or, more often, their shareholders') money is being spent. That means they need to understand how things are going on projects in their portfolio—and, not just on major releases but on each Sprint.

At the same time, managers often have a wide span of authority, especially given the down-sized organizations that are the rule today. The size of project portfolios makes it practically impossible for managers to participate as team members on all projects. It is, therefore, up to project teams to provide managers and related Stakeholders with the information they need to perform their duties.

Agile teams sometimes meet the need through demonstrations of working products. Undoubtedly, demos engage Stakeholder interest and give them a sense of progress, but

---

10 A "Stakeholder" is a person who is involved with a project and has responsibilities towards it and an interest in its success. Project Stakeholders often include executives, managers, customers, or investors who are not directly part of the project team.

11 For those unfamiliar with the Dilbert comic strip, the "pointy-haired Boss" is grossly incompetent, prone to adopt management fads, yet somehow retains his position, making life miserable for project teams.

they take time to prepare and deliver. They also may not reflect the overall project status. For instance, they do not show work done on infrastructure requirements.

Earned Schedule gives project teams a way to meet Stakeholder needs for status information on the whole project and to do so with no incremental impact on the team's time. The Earned Schedule Burndown Chart is already being produced as one of the inputs to Sprint Planning. It can easily be re-purposed to provide Stakeholders with the information they need.[12]

Summary of challenges

Earned Schedule offers a way to satisfy the needs of Stakeholder communication such as Status Reporting with little incremental demand on the project team's time.

Estimates are needed to support decision-making in the face of scarcity and uncertainty. The decisions pertain to both the conduct of the project and of the surrounding business.

Finally, the introduction of Earned Value at the enterprise level is a big challenge, but its introduction into an Agile project is a small step, as long as the project team has the motivation to make the change. Earned Schedule benefits provide the motivation.

Agile benefits from Earned Schedule

Earned Schedule offers insights into Agile schedule performance not otherwise available. A striking example occurred on a recent project.

Consider, first, the Point Burndown chart for the project. Such charts are frequently used on Agile projects to assess schedule performance.

As already mentioned, if the Point Burn line is above the Planned Point Burn line, the project is considered to be late, as the Point count is less than expected. If the Point Burn is below the plan line, the project is taken to be early, as the Point count is greater than expected (thus lowering the number of remaining Points below the planned count). If the actual count and planned count are the same, the project is on schedule.

Given this explanation and the apparent convergence on the chart, it would be natural to conclude that, as of Sprint 6, the project has been tracking on or slightly behind schedule.

Now, consider the Earned Schedule Burndown chart from the same project. 11.7

A different impression of performance emerges when value is taken into account. From Sprints 3 through 5, schedule performance clearly lagged, which is information not available through simple Point counts.[13]

---

12 For Stakeholders, start with the simplest version of the chart (see Figure 21.3). It is easy to explain and understand.

13 Point counts usually number in hundreds or thousands. Earned Schedule amounts, expressed in Sprints, rarely get higher than tens. The differences in scale can skew comparisons between Point Burn Charts and Earned Schedule Burn Charts. To check the example, the data was normalized to the per cent of variance each parameter had from its baseline. In Sprints 3 through 5, the Point variance ranged from less than 1% to 6%, and the Earned Schedule variance ranged from 8% to 18%. In this case, appearances were not deceiving.

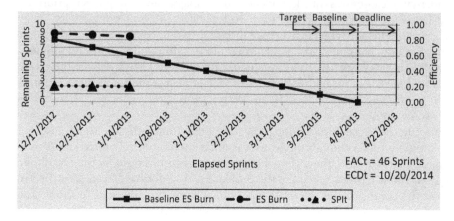

Figure 11.6 Point burndown convergence with plan.

EACt Threshold	Performance Level
> 10 Sprints	Low
> 9 Sprints and <=10 Sprints	Medium
>= 8 Sprints <= 9 Sprints	High
>= 7 Sprints and < 8 Sprints	High
>= 6 Sprints and < 7 Sprints	Medium
< 6 Sprints	Low

Figure 11.7 Earned schedule burndown divergence from plan.

Table 11.3 SPIt and EACt divergence from plan

Sprint	1	2	3	4	5	6
SPIt	0.71	0.97	0.82	0.74	0.83	0.99
EACt	12.76	9.26	11.03	12.20	10.90	9.05

Beyond the impression given by the charts, Earned Schedule offers a quantitative view that indicates how well or poorly the schedule is performing. It gives us a way to determine if the gap between plan and actual is large enough to warrant further action.

Here is a snapshot of two metrics for the project as of Sprint 6: the comparative performance measure (SPIt) and the estimated impact on the completion date (EACt). Table 11.3

The figures from Sprint 3 represented a dramatic change that breached thresholds to lower-performance levels for both the SPIt and EACt. When the trend continued in Sprint 4, root-cause analysis was initiated.

The underlying cause was quickly identified: a major shift in project priorities. Concerned by a slow start, the project team had decided to boost productivity. They revised their Release Plan to target deliverables that were easy to complete but of low value.

Reaching for "low hanging fruit" is a familiar tactic. Although it can build momentum, it risks future rework. In this case, many of the completed deliverables were expected to be done later. By tackling them early, the project team had to make assumptions to fill in missing information. If the assumptions were incorrect, deliverables would have to be revised.

By identifying the variance early, the project was able to identify the root-cause and implement a timely fix. Although the team was unable to completely recover lost time and missed the Baseline date, they were able to finish within Margin by the Deadline.

Arguably, without Earned Schedule, the problem would not have been identified in time to meet the commitment. After all, the Point Burndown appeared to show little variance from the planned velocity. The problem was recognized once earned value was taken into account.

Granted, this is a single anecdote, but it is used here only as an illustration. The underlying benefit and ultimate motivator is a principle, namely, the principle of microeconomics: to make credible decisions in the face of scarcity and uncertainty, projects need to know not only the Points being done but also the value being delivered.

Point counts are useful but insufficient for decision-making because projects need to understand what it costs to deliver the Points. Think of it this way: the money is being used to buy time. It's natural to then ask: Is the investment paying off? Earned Schedule metrics give the answer, and in doing so, they support microeconomic decision-making about the schedule. That is the real benefit of and motivation for using Earned Schedule on Agile projects.

Leverage Earned Schedule for Agile projects

Let's say that your project has implemented Earned Schedule. What's next? The basic metrics can be leveraged to provide further insight into schedule performance. Here are a couple of opportunities to explore in the future.

Estimating future schedule performance

As described previously, the estimate to complete for time (EACt) tells the team when the project will finish, given that future performance is at the same level as past performance. If the project is late, higher future performance might salvage the target date. But, what level of performance will be required?

Using the metrics already described, the project can answer the question. First, find the difference between the planned duration and the amount of schedule earned—that equals the remaining time to earn. Then, find the difference between the planned duration and the current time—that equals the remaining time to spend.

Compare the time-left-to-earn to the time-left-to-spend.[14] If the two times are equal, it will take one unit of earned time for each unit left, i.e., a ratio of 1. If the time

---

14 Formally, this is called the To-Complete Schedule Performance Index or TSPI. See Lipke (2009a).

to earn is larger than what's left to spend, it will take more than one unit of earned time for each unit left. How much more? The fractional amount of the ratio answers that question. (The same principle works when the time to earn is smaller than the time left.)

Knowing what level of future performance is required, projects can assess whether current performance levels are sufficient to meet the planned end date. That is useful in cases like the example cited in the previous section.

There, schedule performance recovered once the deviation's root-cause was identified, and remediation was applied (see Sprint 6 in Figure 11.7 and Table 11.3). Performance became good enough to be rated as "High", according to the project's thresholds. But, was that good enough to recover the lost time? Although the rating remained "High" throughout the rest of the project, it was consistently below the future performance ratio—"High" was not "High Enough".

Research has shown, moreover, that there is a single threshold value for the ratio (Lipke, 2009a and Lipke, 2016). When the ratio exceeds a value of 1.10, projects are unlikely to finish on time.

Given the additional insights available, it is worth investigating the estimation of future schedule performance.

Statistical variation of schedule performance

Basic Earned Schedule metrics provide a point estimate for project duration—the EACt. The credibility of that point estimate derives from its pedigree: the amount of schedule actually earned and the level of schedule efficiency achieved thus far on the project. Although historical performance on a specific project offers prima facie support for the estimate, it does not tell a full story.

The point value is only one of many possible values. What's missing is a fix on the underlying distribution of the values in the problem space. With knowledge of that variance, the project knows how confident to be in the estimated duration.

Statistical analysis identifies an estimate's variance (Lipke, 2006). That variance can be checked against the project's allowances for uncertainty. If the boundaries of the variance exceed the allowances, the planned completion date is at risk. The size of the threat depends on the amount of variance.

Furthermore, trends in the boundaries of the variance reflect schedule performance (Lipke, 2009b). If both the upper and lower boundaries rise over time, that indicates the estimated finish is growing later. Schedule performance is lagging.

The opposite trend indicates that the estimated finish date is drawing closer. Schedule performance is improving over time.

If the upper and lower boundaries remain symmetrical around the nominal value (which is the EACt point estimate), the nominal forecast is close to the final duration.

On long-running projects with frequent Sprints, statistical analysis is especially useful. The analysis depends on having a significant number of observations. A rule-of-thumb is 30 observations as a minimum.

Also, it is necessary to have the Earned Schedule metrics for all of the Sprints, as those metrics, in particular the comparative performance measure (SPIt), are the raw material used in the analysis.

For relevant projects, the added accuracy and insights provided by statistical analysis make it worthwhile to investigate the details on how to perform the analysis and what tools to use.

Conclusion

Agile projects that face time and budget constraints must deal with uncertainty and risk. In that context, project decisions must take account of historical and forecasted performance on timeline and costs. Without objective measures of performance, intuition and "gut feeling" take over, opening the project to systematic errors in judgement.

To the Agile mindset, objective measures appear to be diversions from what's really important: producing useful deliverables. So, how can Agile projects maintain focus on delivery but still make sound project decisions?

Earned Schedule has an answer. It leverages data already available on most Agile projects: Points (and associated work) and velocity (and associated estimates). By costing the work required for deliverables, the volume of value delivery can quickly be determined across the timeline.

Then, thresholds for performance levels can be set using allowances for uncertainty and risk.

Calculation of basic metrics is straight-forward and easily automated. Assessment of results against thresholds and action planning is well-defined and fast. Applying Earned Schedule, therefore, requires little incremental time during project execution.

Resulting insights into schedule performance go beyond familiar Agile metrics. Point counts and Burn Charts are useful but insufficient for microeconomic decision-making. Projects need to understand the value being delivered for the time invested. Earned Schedule gauges the return on the investment, telling how well time is being used and its impact on the end date.

The quantitative measures, moreover, can be extended. They can forecast the future performance required to meet planned end dates and indicate the likely variance around the estimate. That, in turn, tells the project how confident to be in the numbers.

In short, Earned Schedule gives Agile projects a way to think and act fast to improve schedule performance.

Chapter 12

Monitoring and controlling
Understanding your project's status

Kristine A. Hayes Munson

Introduction

Monitoring and controlling processes can be the most underappreciated of the project management processes (PMP). Think about a project manager preparing for the PMP exam. She enrolls in a PMP preparation class or purchases commercially available test preparation material. Hours are spent learning the planning processes which result in the project management plan and its associated scope, schedule and cost baselines. Finally, she comes to the monitoring and controlling processes in each knowledge area at the end of the knowledge area chapter. Our student is tired from a long study session. She quickly reviews the processes believing that they seem pretty simple and straightforward and seeing the end to her study session rapidly approaching. The exception occurs when she hits Earned Value Management. Then she spends hours memorizing formulas because she has heard through the grapevine that knowing Earned Value Management is the key to PMP exam success. Does this scenario seem familiar?

This scenario is the opposite of real life. Frohnhoefer asserts that "controlling is only second in importance to planning" (Frohnhoefer, 2018, position 1239. Kindle Edition). I would argue that monitoring and controlling are of equal importance to planning as these processes are completed in conjunction with both planning and executing processes. Stakeholders measure project success by the project's ability to deliver the entire scope, on time (or early) and on budget (or under). Determining where a project is compared to the scope, schedule and cost baselines is a function of monitoring and controlling. Stakeholders expect that project managers continuously and actively monitor and control their projects in order to know the project's status at any point in time. It sounds simple enough.

Take a minute and honestly answer these questions regarding your project management practice. How do you know the current status of your project? Can you look a stakeholder in the eye and say the project is completely on track in each of the triple constraints? Or is the project encountering a challenge or two? How do you decide to report the project's summary status as green, yellow or red on a weekly status report? When do you take corrective action based on the project's current status? How do you decide when to introduce other changes such as adding new scope requirements into the project? When do you decide to allow the project to continue "as is" with no changes being introduced? In my experience, I find these to be the most difficult questions faced by project managers.

This chapter applies systems thinking concepts to the Monitoring and Controlling Process Group. Its goal is to help each of us develop new tools and techniques while re-emphasizing the basics found in *A Guide to the Project Management Body of Knowledge (PMBOK® Guide)*. We will rediscover the works of W. Edwards Deming, Peter Senge and other systems thinkers to see how systems thinking can be applied to monitoring and controlling. We will also explore the concept of situational awareness to gain an understanding of which obstacles within our projects we may be blindly missing. Together we will gain an understanding of our project's status and tackle the question of whether to change or not to change the project.

Back to basics: Systems, projects and the *PMBOK®* Guide

Meadows defines a system as "an interconnected set of elements that is coherently organized in a way that achieves something" (Meadows, 2008, p. 11). A project is a system made up of multiple processes undertaken to deliver business value in the form of a product, service, process improvement, etc. Meadows uses a Slinky to illustrate the relations between a systems structure and behavior (Meadows, 2008, p. 1). A Slinky is a childhood coiled spring toy made of metal or plastic that uses gravity to move. Recall how a Slinky climbs down stairs. The entire Slinky moves together to reach the floor below.

A Slinky is a good representation of the system known as a project. Think back to the *PMBOK® Guide's* definition of a project as "a temporary endeavor undertaken to create a unique product, service or result" (PMI, 2017, p. 715). Both a Slinky and a project have a defined start and stop. Each coil of the Slinky and each project management process works together, especially when moving in a certain direction. An expert must identify a stair with the correct height and position the Slinky in the right spot on the stairs for the toy to descend. The expert can use the Slinky in other tricks such as the energy beam, the escalator, and slingshot and flip. A project requires the project manager's expert guidance to move forward towards the desired goal. How a project team functions and interacts is directly related to the management techniques used by the skilled project manager. If only one coil of a Slinky is damaged, the ability of the whole slinky to climb down the stairs is impacted. A broken or damaged coil also results in a visible gap, shown when the slinky sits on the shelf or in your hand. A project behaves similarly in that if one of the project management processes encounters an issue, the entire project is impacted.

Systems thinkers break systems into multiple defined processes to better understand how the system works. They study how each process interacts and impacts other processes within the system. The *PMBOK® Guide* defines the process found within the system, called a project. The volunteers who compile the *PMBOK® Guide* carefully name each individual process with a name that reflects what each process does and how it impacts the project or the system. The names are reviewed and modified as required with each new *PMBOK® Guide* edition. For ease of reference, the *PMBOK® Guide* classifies these project management processes into one of five process groups: initiating, planning, executing, monitoring and controlling, and closing.

The monitoring and controlling process group is how we as project managers study how each process interacts and impacts the others. The *PMBOK® Guide* states that monitoring and controlling processes accomplish three things:

- Track, review and regulate the progress and performance of the project
- Identify any areas in which changes to the plan are required
- Initiate the corresponding changes (PMI, 2017, p 23)

The *PMBOK® Guide* names 12 monitoring and controlling processes in each of the 10 knowledge areas. The sixth edition of the *PMBOK® Guide* marks the first time that each knowledge area contains at least one monitoring and controlling process. Historically, the Project Human Resources Management Knowledge Area lacked a monitoring and controlling process. The renaming of that knowledge area to Resource Management expanded the knowledge area's focus to include people, materials and equipment, resulting in a new monitoring and controlling process. The majority of monitoring and controlling process names contain either the verb "monitor" or the verb "control." The *PMBOK® Guide* glossary makes it clear that these are not interchangeable terms.

Let's take a look at how the monitor processes differ from the control processes. Keep in mind throughout this review that the project manager oversees each of these processes, ensures the completion of each process of the project's duration and uses the insights gained from these processes to guide the project to successful completion. Ask yourself: "How do I conduct each of these processes individually in each project I manage? How does each process help me understand my project status?"

Monitor processes

To monitor a project is to "collect project performance data, produce performance measures, and report and disseminate performance information" (PMI, 2017, 711). In other words, planning and executing the project results in a set of data collected by the project manager and the project team. The marketing team member sent out a press release on Friday. The procurement team purchased a cybersecurity insurance policy on Tuesday. These data points are interesting, but on their own, mean nothing. The project manager must provide context for the data. The project manager shares the data and context with stakeholders according to the communications management plan. The marketing team distributed as planned on Friday a press release to the local media contacts detailing the cost savings realized from successful completion of the first project phase resulting in positive media coverage and an increase in the stock price. The procurement team purchased the agreed-upon cybersecurity insurance policy on Tuesday to mitigate the residual cybersecurity risks documented on the risk register. The project manager uses defined tools to complete the monitor processes.

Only three processes within the monitoring and controlling process group exclusively contain the verb "monitor" in their name.

Control processes

Six processes exclusively contain the verb "control" in their name. To control is "comparing actual performance with planned performance, analyzing variances, assessing trends to effect process improvements, evaluating possible alternatives, and recommending appropriate corrective action as needed" (PMI, 2017, 702). Control processes start in a similar fashion as monitor processes. Raw data is collected from project execution. We completed 10 user acceptance test cases to validate the newly developed application code. As before, the project manager provides context for the data. We completed 10 of 20 planned user acceptance test cases with one bug found and testing was placed on hold. The monitor

Table 12.1 Monitor processes

Process	Definition	Sample Tools
Monitor Communications	Determining if stakeholders receive the information required to maintain or increase their support of the project	• Project reporting • Meetings
Monitor Risks	Ensuring stakeholders understand the current risk exposure by tracking identified risks, implementing an agreed upon risk response plans if a risk trigger occurs and analyzing new risks as they arise	• Technical performance analysis • Reserve analysis • Audits • Meetings
Monitor Stakeholder Engagement	Managing stakeholder expectations by addressing issues and clarifying concerns throughout the project's duration to maintain their support of the project	• Stakeholder analysis • Root cause analysis • Alternatives analysis • Decision making • Meetings

processes stop at this point. The control processes require that the project manager analyze the variances and recommend changes as necessary. This is the first significant bug found to date via user acceptance testing. It must be mitigated prior to production deployment. The development team anticipates one week is required to mitigate the issue. Testing will resume upon receipt of the modified code. Notice that the project manager uses more analysis tools to complete the control processes than in the monitor processes.

Monitor and control process

One process contains both the verb monitor and control in its name—Monitor & Control Project Work. Monitor & Control Project Work is found in the Project Integration Management knowledge area. It integrates the performance information from the other monitor processes along with the data analysis and recommended corrective actions from the control processes. Of the monitoring and controlling processes discussed thus far, only Monitor Risk is considered an output of Monitor & Control Project Work rather than an input.

Validate and perform

Verbs other than monitor and control are used to name the last two remaining monitoring and controlling processes—Validate Scope and Perform Integrated Change Control.

As every PMP recalls, Validate Scope is closely tied to Control Quality. An output of Control Quality is verified deliverables where the project team confirms the correctness of the deliverable based on the deliverable's requirements. Validated deliverables or deliverables accepted by the project's customer based on previously defined acceptance criteria is the output of Validate Scope. Both Control Quality and Validate Scope are inputs into the Monitor & Control Project Work process.

Perform Integrated Change Control is the second Project Integration Management monitoring and controlling process and is an output of the Monitor & Control Project

Table 12.2 Control processes

Process	Definition	Sample Tools
Control Scope	Maintaining the scope baseline and avoiding scope creep	• Variance analysis • Trend analysis
Control Schedule	Maintaining the schedule baseline specifically focusing on the critical path	• Earned value analysis • Iteration burndown chart • Performance reviews • Trend analysis • Variance analysis • What-if scenario analysis
Control Costs	Maintaining the cost baseline	• Expert judgment • Earned value analysis • Trend analysis • Reserve analysis
Control Quality	Verifying deliverables are complete and correct based on stakeholder requirements	• Checklists/inspection • Statistical sampling • Questionnaires and surveys • Performance reviews • Root cause analysis • Testing/production evaluations • Data representation diagrams • Meetings
Control Resources	Ensure the project resources are assigned and released at the right time and place	• Alternatives analysis • Cost-benefit analysis • Performance reviews • Trend analysis • Problem solving
Control Procurements	Managing vendor relationships, contracts and closing contracts	• Expert judgment • Performance reviews • Earned value analysis • Trend analysis • Inspection • Audits

Work process. The majority of executing and monitoring and controlling processes are an input into this process with recommended change requests. It is here where the change control board approves, defers or rejects changes. Only approved changes can be implemented by the project manager and the project team. This can be compared to the game Simon Says. A leader asks players to take certain actions like raising their right hand or standing on one foot. Players only execute approved instructions indicated by the phrase "Simon Says" being stated before the instruction is given. A player is out if she executes an instruction not proceeded by the "Simon Says" approval.

Table 12.3 Monitor and control process

Process	Definition	Sample Tools
Monitor & Control Project Work	Determining the project's overall progress towards meeting the project's stated performance objectives and aligns with the business needs	• Variance analysis • Trend analysis

Table 12.4 Validate scope

Process	Definition	Sample Tools
Validate Scope	Completing the formal acceptance of completed deliverables by customers	• Inspection • Decision making

Table 12.5 Integrated change control

Process	Definition	Sample Tools
Perform Integrated Change Control	Reviewing, accepting, rejecting and/or deferring recommended change requests	• Expert judgment • Alternatives analysis • Cost-benefit analysis • Decision making • Meetings

Did you see the gorilla?

Monitoring and controlling processes produce an overwhelming amount of project performance information. Do we really know the status of our project? What are we missing or unable to see?

Consider the famous invisible gorilla research. Researchers made a short film (yes, this was before video) of two teams passing a basketball around. White shirts and black shirts distinguished one team from the other. Viewers were asked to count the number of passes made by only the white shirt team, ignoring the black shirt team's passes. Watch the video yourself and count the passes at www.theinvisiblegorrilla.com before reading the rest of this description. I'll wait for you...

Did you notice the gorilla when you watched the video? At the halfway point of the film, a person dressed in a gorilla suit walks into the middle of the teams passing the basketball, stops and looks at the camera, pounds its chest and exits. The basketball passing continues uninterrupted while the gorilla is in view and after the gorilla leaves. Approximately half of the viewers miss the gorilla's appearance completely. (I missed the gorilla the first time I saw the video.)

According to Chabris and Simons, the gorilla's invisibility results from "a lack of attention to an unexpected object," which is called "'inattentional blindness'...In other words, the subjects were concentrating so hard on counting the passes that they were 'blind' to the gorilla right in front of their eyes" (Chabris and Simons, 2010, p. 6).

They continue: "The fact that people miss things is important, but what impressed us even more was the *surprise* people showed when they realized what they had missed" (Ibid, emphasis in original). Viewers saw the gorilla when watching the video a second time. Chabris and Simon conclude,

> For the human brain, attention is essentially a zero-sum game: If we pay more attention to one place, object or event, we necessarily pay less attention to others. Inattentional blindness is thus a necessary, if unfortunate, by-product of the normal operation of attention and perception.
>
> (Chabris and Simons, 2010, p. 38)

What monitoring and controlling information are you watching so closely on your project that may be causing you to miss the figurative gorilla? Recall the Central Artery/Tunnel Project or the Big Dig, which rerouted Boston traffic into a series of tunnels. If you have traveled from downtown Boston to Logan airport, you've probably driven a tunnel built by the Big Dig. The project successfully delivered the scope of reducing traffic congestion and replacing aging infrastructure. Yet it is famous for its schedule and cost overruns. The project placed a strong emphasis on monitoring and controlling. Greiman writes:

> The management, coordination and scheduling of this massive project emanated from the Central Artery/Tunnel Project's Control Center. The project's Control Center...contained numerous diagrams and maps and dealt with the daily confusion of coordinating the activities of the joint-venture engineers and extensive network of contractors and consultants.
>
> (Greiman, 2013, p. 196)

The Control Center tracked schedule and costs daily using tools including Earned Value Management. Yet they missed the gorilla (or gorillas). The project finished in 2006, or eight years after its original 1998 target date, costing approximately $14.8 billion. This is a sobering tale for each of us as project managers, regardless of the size of projects we manage.

Early warning signals

The gorilla we are missing could be those early warning signals of future project challenges. An early warning signal can be something as simple as seeing clouds on the horizon and realizing that a storm is approaching. Williams states that "Traditionally, project performance measures are lagging indicators—consequences of activities and incidents—not leading indicators that can provide more relevant and valuable information" (Williams et al, 2012, p. 38).

Proponents of Earned Value Management would disagree with Williams. They argue that earned value provides an early warning as to the project's overall health. Fleming and Koppelman write:

> Earned value provides the project manager with a type of "early warning" buzzer that sounds when faced with impending problems, allowing him or her to take

necessary corrective actions...Such warning signals become available to management as early as 20 percent into a new project. (Fleming and Koppelman, 2010, loc 496—Kindle Edition)

The challenge with using earned value is the planned value baseline. It must be solid and valid with few uncertainties or unknowns. If you are unknowingly measuring against a weak baseline, then you could miss the gorilla of challenges ahead because the earned value numbers provide you with a false sense of security. Initial project baselines are frequently created with a sense of optimism or overconfidence as to how fast something can be accomplished and how much it will cost. The optimistic baseline may be viewed by the project manager and team as necessary in order to obtain approval and funding for the project. Greiman asserts that megaprojects such as the Big Dig are regularly underestimated for this very reason (Greiman, 2013, p. 215).

Williams advocates using a combination of a formal project assessment and gut-feeling to detect early warning signals. Signals to be determined by formal project assessment include unclear roles and responsibilities for sponsors and project team members, lack of a thorough business case, incomplete or missing project documentation, optimism bias in cost and schedule baselines, and incompetency found in the project team. Gut-feeling should be used to identify leadership/sponsorship issues, uneasy comments or body language, strained atmosphere, unwillingness to make a decision and lack of trust in the project organization (Williams et al, 2012, p. 50). Any one of these could be our gorilla.

Too many reports, use a feedback loop

Now that we've found our gorilla, can we make change in the project? Not so fast. We probably found the gorilla at the same time we need to create our daily/weekly/monthly status report based on metrics obtained from traditional monitoring and controlling processes. Are we reporting on too much time collecting and reporting data regarding our project? Do these reports capture the right data? After all, would we include one of gut-feeling early warning signals on a status report?

Morieux and Tollman think we write too many reports containing the wrong information. They assert that "managers in the top quintile of the most complicated organizations spend more than 40 percent of their time writing reports and between 30 percent and 60 percent of their total work hours in coordination meetings—work on work" (Morieux and Tollman, 2014, p. 6). They argue that the majority of this is non-value adding work. Even though their statement is regarding managers in general, I'm sure as a project manager you strongly relate to their sentiment. Time spent writing reports is time not spent working directly with the team or with other stakeholders.

In a 2013 TED Talk, Morieux says the root cause for spending so much collecting metrics and reporting on them is complexity within the organization. He states, "When there are too many layers people are too far from the action, therefore they need KPIs, metrics, they need poor proxies for reality. They don't understand reality and they add the complicatedness of metrics, KPIs" (Morieux, 2013). To resolve this issue, he advocates empowering managers to use their judgment by creating "feedback loops that expose people to the consequences of their actions" (Ibid.).

Feedback loops take us right back to systems thinking. Remember by definition a system exists to achieve a goal. Think about a heating, ventilation and air conditioning (HVAC) system. It exists to maintain air quality while keeping your home's temperature an ideal level—somewhere between 70 and 78 degrees Fahrenheit based on your individual preferences. The input into the HVAC system is air in your home. Inside of the system the air is cleaned of particulates, exchanged with outside air and heated/cooled to the desired temperature. The output is "perfect" air for your home. What happens when environmental conditions change within your home because someone opens a window? A feedback loop takes over and notices the change. The feedback loop notices the temperature discrepancy and instructs the HVAC system to make appropriate changes.

Feedback loops look to the future and affect the system's future behavior. Feedback loops ask the system to take corrective actions based on the current situation. There will be a delay—no matter how short—before the corrective action can take effect. If the room temperature suddenly drops because you open the window and allow 32 degree Fahrenheit air into the room, you can hypothesize that the heater will start in order to bring the room's temperature to the desired level. You can prove your hypothesis only after the future action occurs or a different, unanticipated future action occurs.

Now we are ready to talk about making changes in our project.

To change or not to change?

The necessity of change is an implicit bias in the monitoring and controlling process group. We observe a variation from an established baseline or we discovered our gorilla. We know we can "fix" this. We know we can do better. We instinctively want to make a change. The *PMBOK® Guide* specifies three reasons why change requests are submitted:

- Corrective action to realign the project's performance with the project management plan
- Preventative action to ensure the project's future performance aligns with the project plan
- Defect repair to fix a nonconforming deliverable (PMI, 2017, p. 112)

I would add a couple more reasons why change requests should be submitted:

- Baseline optimization to remove the optimistic biases introduced during the initial project planning and to address scope creep
- Continuous process improvement to improve the overall operations and processes used by the project team to produce deliverables
- Business value rationalization to appropriately respond to changes in internal and external enterprise environmental factors which impact the business reasons for which the project was undertaken

Project managers use Perform Integrated Change Control so that the change control board can approve, defer or reject a change. There is a space between when we identify the potential need for a change and submit a formal change request to the change control board which is omitted from the *PMBOK® Guide*. The step is to determine if the change is truly necessary and what impact it will have on the project. In other words:

- How do we decide a change to the project is required?
- How do we know we are making the right change to the right element of the project to obtain the desired result?
- How do we determine if a change will positively or negatively impact the project?
- How do we minimize the risk of unintended consequences from the change?

Common cause vs special cause variation

A control chart can help us understand if what we believe needs to be changed is a common cause or special cause variation. A control chart is the Six Sigma tool used for Statistical Process Control. Results of a process are charted over time. The results are compared to the statistical mean of the process with an upper and lower control limit set three standard deviations from the mean. The control chart's user examines where each event falls in relationship to the mean and control limits. The user expects to see common cause variation where events fall inside the upper and lower control limits. This shows that under control and no modifications to the process are required. The user observes a special cause variation when an event falls outside the upper and lower control limits on a control chart. These events are unexpected and indicate a change is required.

Let's use my daily commute to illustrate how a control chart works. Some days I drive to work and others I take the train. Regardless of how I choose to commute, I need to arrive before the scheduled start of my workday. Some days I arrive earlier than others. Yet my arrival times are clustered around the mean inside of the upper and lower control limits. This is common cause variation. No change is required. One day my car has a flat tire, which extends my daily commute time outside of the upper control limit. This is a special cause variation. I must fix the flat tire in order to ensure my arrival time returns the acceptable variation.

Deming reminds us there are two common mistakes made when working with variation:

- Mistake 1: To react to an outcome as if it came from a special cause, when actually it came from common causes of variation
- Mistake 2: To treat an outcome as if it came from common causes of variation, when actually it came from a special cause (Deming, 1994, p. 174)

In other words, Deming is warning us to be cautious when considering whether to make a change. We as project managers need to clearly understand the root cause behind the problem symptom we are seeing to determine if we should make a change or continue "as is."

Making no change and the funnel experiment

Deming's funnel experiment demonstrates what can occur when the variation seen is common cause variation requiring no change vs. special cause variation requiring change. This experiment requires a funnel, a marble and a target on which to mark the marble's resting place. (I've also been known to use chocolate chips for this experiment as they don't roll when hitting a paper target.)

Round 1: The participant lays the target on a flat horizontal surface such as a table or floor. The funnel is aligned over the top of the target. (Think bulls-eye used for bow and arrow target practice.) Keeping the funnel at the same height and location, the participant drops 50 marbles through the funnel. The initial landing spot of each marble is marked in relationship to the target. The marble drops form a clustered circle around the original target.

Round 2: The participant attempts to compensate for the variation. After the first marble drop, the participant moves the funnel from its last position to compensate for the variation. The first marble will land at position x. The funnel is then moved to position -x, keeping the same height. For example, if the marble comes to rest 6 centimeters southeast of the target, the participant moves it 6 centimeters northwest from its last position. A corresponding adjustment is made each time one of the 50 marbles is dropped—always moving the opposite direction from the landing location. The variation increases from the first round. The diameter of the circle containing the marble drops is greater than the first circle.

Round 3: Still not satisfied, the participant moves the funnel using the target as a reference. The first of 50 marbles lands at location x. The funnel is now moved -x using the target as a reference point rather than the marbles location as in round 2. The pattern now takes the shape of a bow tie.

Round 4: The participant moves the funnel to be over the location of the last marble drop. The drops move farther and farther away from the target in a pattern Deming calls the "Milky Way," eventually going off in one direction.

The experiment results show that Round 1 where the funnel remained positioned over the target was indeed the best way to drop the marbles. Round 1 produced the least amount of variation. The main lesson learned is that sometimes the project should just be left alone. Deming calls the three attempts at moving the funnel management tampering.

By the way, Deming suggests two process improvement changes to minimize variation. The first is to move the funnel down closer to the target. The second is to use a terry cloth to keep the marble from rolling (Deming, 1994, pp. 190–206).

Change the right thing and the red bead experiment

Like all systems, projects are sensitive to change. Making change when change is not required can disrupt the project. So too can making the wrong change. Think back to my flat tire. What if I changed the left-front tire rather than the flat right-front tire? If I continue to drive the car with the incorrect repair, I would damage the rim and significantly slow my forward progress, costing me time and money.

Deming's red bead experiment demonstrates the dangers of making the wrong change. The demonstration is based on a role-play using members of the audience. He asks six willing workers to remove beads from a bin containing a mixture of red and white beads. The willing worker inserts a paddle with pre-drilled holes into the bin to remove beads. The goal is to only remove white beads with the paddle because red beads are considered defects. The willing worker can only use the paddle. No human hands may touch the beads. Three inspectors count the number of red beads on the paddle. A recorder documents the number of red beads. The supervisor rewards the person with the lowest red bead count and punishes the person with the highest red bead count.

The bead extraction, inspection and tracking processes are repeated multiple times to represent multiple days. Obviously, it is impossible to meet the goal of only removing white beads from the container because the willing worker exercises no control over how many red beads are on the paddle. The mixture of white and red beads on the paddle is determined by chance.

However, this does not hinder the supervisor from rewarding or punishing the willing worker based on red bead count each day. The supervisor also introduces new management-sponsored programs, such as Zero Defect Day and bonuses, to incent workers to lower the red bead count.

After Day 4, the management (aka the experiment facilitator) decides to implement a significant change in the project by firing the three worst-performing workers and retaining the three top performers. The remaining three workers execute the task and the variation continues. The results are disappointing, causing the management to announce the firm will be shut down.

Deming's lessons learned from this experiment apply to project management. These include:

- Ranking people is wrong and demoralizing. What is really being ranked is the effect of the process or project on people.
- Paying for performance is futile as it is merely rewarding and punishing the process or project.
- Rigid procedures to accomplish assigned tasks are a display of bad management. Workers should be allowed to continuously improve their performance and the performance of others.
- The root cause of the issue was never tackled by working with the supplier of the beads to eliminate or reduce the red beads in the container.
- No basis existed to assume that the best team member today would be the best in the future (Deming, 1994, pp. 154–171).

Time to implement the change

So how do we as project managers avoid making a change when something should stay "as is" or making the wrong change? Deming's Plan-Do-Check-Action (PDCA) cycle allows us to gain an understanding of the proposed change prior to implementing the change universally. (Figure 12.1).

Deming's Plan-Do-Check-Act cycle allows us to test the hypothesis that the proposed change will positively rather than negatively impact the project. The project manager prepares a plan in conjunction with the project team during the model's first step. The plan details or scopes the change to be tested, how the change will be tested and the expected results. If multiple options exist, the project manager and the project team will need to select which option to test prior to writing the test plan. The selected option should be the lowest negative risk and/or highest yield change.

The project team executes the test plan in the Do phase on a small scale or prototype. The test's duration should only be as long as necessary to confirm or invalidate the hypothesis.

Figure 12.1 Deming's PDCA cycle.

The Check phase involves the project manager and project team reviewing the test results and completing a lessons learned debrief, asking questions such as:

• How does the actual result compare with the anticipated result?
• What did we learn from implementing the change on a small scale?
• What went wrong?

The last phase involves deciding whether or not to Act. The change can be adopted/approved, revised/deferred or abandoned/rejected. The change control board makes the final decision considering the testing results. If the revision option is selected, the cycle is repeated. Remember to involve the change control board throughout the entire PDCA cycle. The first time they hear of the proposed change should not be the same day they are asked to approve it.

Stuff happens

No matter how much testing or pre-planning goes into making a change, sometimes stuff or unintended consequences happen. Senge defines unintended consequences as "fixes that backfire" (Senge, 1994, p. 125). These are the unknown unknowns, which negatively impact the project later. Senge attributes unintended consequences to a failure to understand the issue's root cause. The change is a "fix" to only a symptom of the variation. Systems thinkers frequently reference unintended consequences of layoffs. Profits go up in the short term, while the company may struggle in the long-term due to the loss of experienced workers.

Conclusion

Expert use of the processes contained in the Monitoring and Controlling Process Group allows the project manager to guide the project to successful conclusion realizing the intended business value on time and on budget. The project manager should constantly be looking for the gorilla or hidden issues that may be missed when looking at more traditional monitoring and process results, which may provide a false sense of confidence on the project's status. Formal or gut-feel early warning indicators can help identify the gorillas. Preparing for and implanting change couples the science and art of project management. Truly great project managers understand the difference between special cause variation and common cause variation. Project managers test change options to determine what change should be made or if the project should continue "as is" rather than make unnecessary or detrimental changes. The Standish Group founder, Jim Johnson, writes: "Learning the word 'no' is the hardest lesson for many project managers" (Johnson, 2006, p. 92). Mastery of monitoring and controlling processes separates the average project manager from the truly great ones.

The Project Management Office (PMO)

Emma-Ruth Arnaz-Pemberton

PMO can be defined as a function that 'provides enabling processes to continuously support management of project, program or portfolio work throughout the organisation' *(PMI)*. The concept of PMO is not new; however, the rate of change within the industry has seen the remit of PMO grow and develop exponentially as economies change and organisations expect more for less.

Just like running projects, during times of change, the basics often stay the same for PMOs in terms of core services; the change comes in the form of expectations of additional services needed in order for them to remain current and value-adding in the workplaces of today.

Note: while it is recognised that PMOs can take a multiplicity of forms (e.g. Centre of Excellence, EPMO, PSO, etc.), for the sake of simplicity, this chapter refers to PMO as a 'catch-all' term.

A high-performing PMO demonstrates several traits ensuring they support delivery teams' projects effectively:

- They work with Customers to understand their needs and expectations
- They deliver services which enable the organisation to not only do the right work but to do that work right
- They see maturity as a journey, and recognise the need for pragmatism in delivery methods and ways of working
- They measure progress and performance, including their own to support continuous improvement
- They communicate transparently and often with their Customers and wider Stakeholders

The State of Project Management survey 2018 identified that 85% of organisations cited having one or more PMOs. This number has been increasing year on year demonstrating that the value of having a function that provides the services affiliated with PMOs is growing. Unfortunately, the amount of PMOs that believe they have realised their full potential as a value-adding business partner sits at just 45%.

With that in mind, what happens if a PMO doesn't exist in an organisation? Do projects stop happening? No. In fact, projects continue because of the existence of project managers. So, if that is known to be the case why do we need PMOs in the first place? I was asked this question some years ago and it really made me think what benefit a PMO really brings to (ignoring the organisation for a minute) the projects themselves.

There are several well-known benefits to installing a PMO function (of whatever form suits the organisation) that directly impact delivery:

Knowledge re-use leading to a Decrease in Non-Value Adding Activities (often during the start-up stage)

- Decreased Project Lifecycle Time
- Earlier Identification of risks and issues
- Reduced Cost to Deliver Projects
- Increased Quality of Lifecycle and Project Products

Some of the benefits mentioned above that directly impact projects are very tangible even for the project teams. However, there are many benefits that are *peripheral* and circumstantial (that shouldn't be ignored even though they are uncharted and often happen by accident). There are also a few benefits that happen by *stealth* (those that add value in the background without project teams noticing).

Keeping those types of benefits in mind and changing the lens to think about what gets missed when projects are not supported by a PMO, it all starts to become a little clearer.

When practitioners are asked what the PMO role is in their organisation, there are a few key themes that always appear *(source: State of Project Management 2018)*. These themes can help us understand the value that PMOs add to projects themselves:

Data and Reporting activities appear at the very top of the list. Ensuring that information from the projects is appropriately aggregated for Senior Leadership is a fundamental role of the PMO because it assures the organisation that the activities undertaken by the change community are being delivered in the right way.

Peripheral Benefits: From a project perspective, data and reporting provide insight into other activities happening around the organisation which can provide an opportunity for sharing and collaborating. However, this is dependent on the organisation and the individuals involved – everyone knows someone who lives and works in their own bubble and rarely steps outside to see the wider view.

Stealth Benefit: To live the PMO Principle of One Version of the Truth and create credible information, a PMO must have a regular flow of consistent data. To achieve this, most PMOs provide project teams with several templates that allow the project teams to focus on delivery rather than how to collate information for different audiences.

The data and reporting function of a PMO supports successful delivery by enabling a reduction of non-value adding activities such as the need for days spent collating and consolidating only to find that it is out of date as soon as it is prepared.

Maintaining Portfolio Registers is a very common function for PMOs. Organisationally, it is important that visibility of the change activity (past, current, and future) is recorded. The PMO is an integrator and typically has access across the organisation, so is best placed to provide a realistic view of what change is happening across the board.

Peripheral Benefits: Business acumen is developed through various channels. Information maintained by the PMO to provide an overview of activities allows project teams to understand both the current tone and the direction of the organisation through what they are attempting to do. Individuals can develop and flex their political astuteness when dealing with unexpected situations and requests by understanding the wider context in which their project sits.

Stealth Benefits: Change in organisations is cyclical. Like fashion, what goes around, comes around and change that was a good idea some time ago, but failed, often comes up again in the future following personnel changes or strategic moves. Most project managers have been involved in a project that was 'doomed to fail' because of historical attempts to do something similar. To live the PMO Principle of Supporting a Learning Organisation, the activities relating to maintaining registers allow the PMO to help the organisation and its Delivery Managers avoid these kinds of activities starting in the first place thanks to learning lessons and managing how knowledge is disseminated into the organisation.

Methods and Standards is the first place that PMOs usually turn to when implementing or transforming themselves and is high on the list of functions that a PMO performs. Although not entirely necessary on day one, developing a consistent way of working allows the PMO to both engage with the project teams and provides them an opportunity to make a tangible, positive change.

Peripheral Benefits: Most organisations appreciate Organisational Maturity and work towards a desired state with a defined roadmap. Embedding standard ways of working underpinned by industry best practice supports the journey. With maturity comes increased recognition of PPM as a value-adding business function and a career choice for individuals.

Stealth Benefits: Enabling Capability is one of the PMO Principles that makes a PMO a PMO. By focusing on the maturity journey rather than just on the immediate needs, project teams are upskilled through the activities defined in the roadmap. This means that as the organisation matures, its people go on the same journey.

Process Facilitation is a staple responsibility of many PMOs and includes financial, resource, and approval processes. The ability to support the project delivery teams working through the relevant interfaces needed to get the project to completion is always a true value-adding service provided by the PMO.

Peripheral Benefits: Sub-cultures exist in every organisation as each team has a different set of people, who all have their own characteristics. The PMO having enough business acumen to navigate the needs of each independent team allows for the PPM community of practice to develop through enabling positive interactions and building relationships.

Stealth Benefits: An active community of practice is a key enabler for PPM maturity. Through the management of relationships, the community can become self-sufficient (an eco-system) as those both involved directly through delivery teams and through process take responsibility for sharing best practice and supporting each other.

Assurance is a buzz word that Senior Teams like to hear about in their PMO. If PMO enables the organisation through the principle of One Version of the Truth, assurance ensures decision making is informed and appropriate; whilst the delivery teams benefit from knowing that the right projects are being managed right, and the level of governance is appropriate for the nature of the change.

Peripheral Benefits: Assurance is often confused with audit. If the PMO can provide a clear line of what assurance is in their organisation, how it will be applied to the change space, and that it will be done so fairly, expectations are managed; delivery teams know what is expected of them, have confidence in the process, and can plan for the appropriate level of governance transparently.

Stealth Benefits: PMOs are constantly looking at ways to make things run more smoothly. The delivery teams may not be aware of this as changes to standards and practices tend to be scheduled, but assurance provides a set of analysis data that is utilised by the PMO to make the delivery teams' life easier over time.

Knowledge Management is defined as 'Any process or practice of creating, acquiring, capturing, sharing and using knowledge, wherever it resides, to enhance learning and performance in organizations.' *(Scarbrough, Swan, and Preston, 1999: 1)*

A key principle of what makes a PMO a PMO is that of Enabling a Learning Organisation. Knowledge management takes many forms but in two key ways: Codified knowledge that can be recorded or transmitted, and Tacit knowledge which is acquired via the informal take-up of learning behaviour and procedures (know-how).

The balance between Tacit and Codified knowledge of change in an organisation is often managed by the PMO; this ensures that the organisation and the delivery teams can learn and evolve using justified true beliefs rather than a personal perspective.

Peripheral Benefits: Knowledge management supports project delivery through ensuring opportunities are leveraged and lessons are learned. This is done primarily through early risk and issue identification and assigning historical and cultural impact statements to emerging work to provide the most informed view for the delivery teams to take ownership of the work.

Stealth Benefits: Communities of practice are founded on knowledge. Codified knowledge is an absolute, but the real value add comes from harnessing the tacit knowledge that exists in the minds of the people. Communities need three things to deliver true Collective Learning; domain (an area of interest), practitioners (experienced in the domain), and activities (opportunities to share). A community of practice allows project teams to develop their skills informally and through practice.

Benefits Tracking is cited as the most difficult process to embed in organisations. One of the reasons it eludes organisations is that benefits realisation happens after project delivery. This means that the focus for the delivery teams moves to their new assignment and there is a lack of ownership of the tracking of the benefits, except in very structured and mature organisations.

If the PMO facilitates that tracking (note; not owns) it ensures that the focus remains on achieving those benefits on behalf of the Sponsor and delivery team.

Peripheral Benefits: Benefits realisation is appreciated as having real-world value in that if done well, it will be commercially beneficial for an organisation; although there are also many other benefit types that (if embraced) add more impact longer term.

Project success is often perceived solely on the benefits achieved after the fact; see the case study of the Sydney Opera House whose final budget was a staggering seven times over the original estimate. Project Fail? Absolutely not. The Sydney Opera House is one of the most recognised buildings in the world, the economy benefits from the tourism it brings to the country, and it has won countless awards.

Stealth Benefits: The PMO facilitating the tracking of benefits provides delivery teams with tangible experience that allows them to develop their career both internally and externally to their current organisation. Without the PMO carrying out this task, there is a risk that individuals 'float' from one project to the next without really understanding how successful (or not) they may be; leading to unconscious incompetence in their chosen career path.

Why it's more important now than ever to consider how PMO supports Project Delivery

We live in a VUCA world. It is Volatile, Uncertain, Complex, and Ambiguous. In the world of PPM, this is seen most clearly in the methodologies space. We see Waterfall being 'set aside' in some organisations in support of more Agile approaches, alongside the misunderstanding of how and why fashionable methods can be applied to real-world organisations.

The rise of Bricolage is well on the way. The 'whatever works' method is gaining traction as delivery teams are able to define the approach as part of the kick-off process; need a bit of Waterfall to get the business case signed off, followed by some lean process work, Agile development, and change management to implement? Sure, whatever works.

This new way of thinking (note; not working) encourages organisations to exploit the skills they already have in-house and provide an opportunity to develop individuals in new and innovative topics. All facets of the business are affected, most notably team engagement, motivation to deliver, and desire for knowledge. All organisations benefit from this and demonstrate a modern culture of innovation and change to their Customers and competitors alike.

With clean transitions from one method to another, projects benefit from best fit practices that support the nature of the activity and teams rather than retrofitting a team into a particular way of working. A healthier experience all around.

The key to successful Bricolage is to have a PMO that is able to support all the methods that exist in the organisation; through specialists or generalists that are able to coach project teams through the importance of the transitions between methods, provide guidance on approach, as well as all the aforementioned benefits.

A high-performing delivery team demonstrates several traits that utilise the PMO service catalogue to their benefit:

- Pragmatism in approach
- Supportive and approachable attitude
- Enthusiastic about change
- Work with transparency

The PMO can ensure that projects get the very best chance of success, as long as they don't bring with them a command and control structure that project delivery teams will not appreciate or buy into.

Chapter 13

Managing change

From adoption to completion

Jim Young

He aha te mea nui o te ao
What is the most important thing in the world?
He tangata, he tangata, he tangata
It is the people, it is the people, it is the people.
Māori Proverb

In recent years change has become more frequent and more dynamic, so much so that a whole new branch of management has been developed to address the subject. A lot of what we as project managers (PMs) do are transformation projects that involve people working and behaving in a different way. Change management is key to embedding any change. Thus, PMs, to be effective, must be competent change managers, but in PM lexicon to confuse the unwary, change management has two meanings:

1. **Variations.** Managing changes to the scope of our project is often needed to accommodate risk, revised requirements and new product performance standards. Also, change might be driven by external factors, such as new legislation. But most often a change request arises when our client wants an addition or alteration to the project product to secure some extra benefit. Because change requests are beyond the scope of the initial agreement, they generally mean that the client will have to pay for the additions and possibly accept a later project completion date. Of course no such change should proceed unless the associated benefits exceed the costs involved. Change control is the process by which all such change requests are captured, evaluated and then approved, rejected or deferred.

2. **Product Adoption.** Managing the transitioning of individuals and organisations as they adopt new project products is another type of change management that is becoming integral to the PM function. We aim to bring stakeholders from awareness to acceptance of the new reality that the change creates. We build support, address resistance and develop the required knowledge and ability to properly implement the change. Ineffective management of people during such change is a top reason for unsuccessful projects across all industries. While there is no progress without it, change often freaks us out. The conversion of project products into outcomes and benefits invariably requires some form of behavioural change. So we need to spend time understanding what the desired behaviours are and how we might encourage our product users to adopt these behaviours. Managing such change in a controlled manner is essential if business case benefits are to be realised.

This chapter is about the latter type of change management – "product adoption" for want of a better name. PM and change management both aim to increase the likelihood that projects deliver their intended results. Although each discipline can function independently, the most effective approach is to integrate change management and PM.

Gone are the days of one large change every three years. Today's organisations are facing faster, more complex, more interdependent and more cross-functional change than ever before to survive and thrive in today's changing landscape. Even small projects require changes that include new behaviours, new skills, new jobs and often with new staff. To an increasing extent PMs are no longer asked to just manage tasks and people, and focus on project products, but we're also expected to help manage change to ensure our project products are properly embedded in order that they produce their forecasted benefits. We need to ensure that our project products become part of how our people work, and that there is a clear and beneficial difference between the business-as-usual before the project and the business-as-usual after the project.

While this integration of PM and change management increases the workload for us PMs and adds some cost to our projects, it's worthwhile if more projects then realise their promised benefits. The more dependent a project's benefits are on project product adoption and usage, the larger contribution change management makes.

This means that transition activities must be included in our PM plan. Yet, in many organisations change management is entirely reactive, and only applied as a last resort when employee resistance jeopardises project success.

When we undertake projects to improve performance, seize opportunities or address key issues, they often require changes to processes, job roles, organisational structures and the use of technology. More particularly, it's employees who have to change. If our people are unsuccessful in their personal adjustments the project will likely fail. However, if our employees adapt to the required changes, the project is much more likely to deliver the required results.

In effect, our project is a vehicle for delivering change and successful change is about getting people ready, willing and able to properly use our project products. Change is very much a psychological disturbance, as people lose the certainty and comfort of their familiar situation and have to swap this for the uncertainties of new ways of working. A successful change initiative requires we prepare people for the change, obtain their buy-in and engage our project sponsor and functional managers to champion and support the change before, during and after product launch.

In the diagram in Figure 13.1, PM and change management are shown as parallel activities. They both support moving operations from a current state, how we do things today, through a transition state to a desired future state – the new skills, attitudes, behaviours, equipment, processes, organisation structures and job roles needed for the proper adoption and exploitation of our new product. Thus the movement from the current to the future state occurs on two dimensions:

- The product is designed, developed and delivered – project management.
- The product is adopted and used to realise benefits – change management.

While all changes are unique and all individuals are unique, decades of research show there are actions we can take to influence people in their individual transitions. Change management provides a structured approach for supporting the individuals in

Project and Change Management Integration

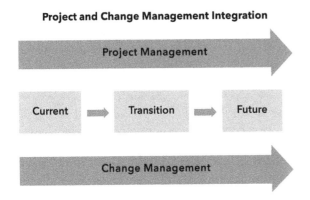

Figure 13.1 Project and change management integration.

our organisations to move from their own current states to their own future states, although the behavioural effects of change are not always predictable and are sometimes impulsive.

Even the most carefully planned and structured change is likely to have elements of emergent change, as the unpredictable surfaces during the change process, which emphasises the need to be responsive and adaptive in the implementation of change. With any change initiative there needs to be space and time to adjust or amend direction and expectations in the light of what is actually taking place. There has to be a balance between planned and emergent change. Organisations and people are so complex that it's nonsensical to imagine that every aspect of change can be precisely anticipated, planned and controlled.

There are many change management models and organisations need to avoid seeking the "one best way" approach to change. Nevertheless, as Figure 13.1 shows, one long-standing, simple and practical approach to planned change management (Professor Kurt Lewin's model) is to break the change into three stages, although the process may not proceed in an entirely linear manner as the diagram suggests and the effectiveness and time needed for the change process will vary depending on the extent of the change and the degree of resistance encountered.

It's the third stage of this classic model, the "future" stage (previously referred to as the "refreeze" stage) that has provoked some recent criticism from those who argue that the modern world is changing at a pace and frequency that gives us no time to settle or freeze before further changes occur. While there are other change management models, such as Kotter's eight-step model, Bridges' transition model or Prosci's ADKAR model, I suggest that Lewin's simple change management approach, which is endorsed by the NZ Change Management Institute (CMI), is still valid and particularly so for smaller projects.

There is a lot of cross-over between the skills needed for PM and those needed for change management. In particular, both need strong stakeholder engagement skills. Also, PMs who become effective change managers have tapped into their emotional intelligence. They appreciate the challenges, fears and anxieties that projects generate and are willing to spend time listening to those affected; letting them talk their way through their concerns.

Some organisations prefer the rapid, disruptive and riskier "big bang" approach to change whereby simultaneous initiatives are implemented on many fronts on a specified date, whereas other organisations prefer incremental change or a "phased" change over a longer period at a speed that ensures change can be properly managed and timely corrective action taken as needed. Both approaches have their advantages and disadvantages, although a product implementation strategy doesn't have to be limited to these two options. Sometimes a big bang approach can be used to implement the "must-have" functionality, followed by phased implementation of the "nice to have" functionality. Change management is often political, emotional and error-prone and when change occurs too quickly or is undertaken ineffectively we might expect any of the following consequences:

- Change may exceed people's capacity to cope.
- Organisation and individual productivity may dramatically decline.
- Passive and active resistance may escalate.
- Frustrated employees may leave the organisation.
- Employee morale and motivation may deteriorate.
- Employees may revert to their old way of doing things.
- Disagreements may occur between those with differing attitudes to the change.

Let's consider in more detail what needs to happen during each of these three stages or states to help ensure effective change:

Current State is the collection of behaviours, processes, tools, techniques, organisational structures and job roles that constitute how work is done at present. This current state may not be working well, but it's usually stable, predictable and familiar, and it's where we have been successful and where we know how we will be measured and evaluated. Above all else, the current state is the comfortable known. So, communication of change needs to start as early as possible so that people have time to understand and accept the change before they have to start working in new ways. During this state we prepare for the pending change, and in particular we should:

- Clarify exactly what will change and what will remain the same, so that we minimise confusion and prevent rumours from developing about the likely extent and impact of the change. Project team members and users work collaboratively to identify what needs to change and what can be retained from the current business-as-usual environment.
- Ensure there is strong support for the change by creating wide awareness of the reasons for the change and the anticipated benefits. We need to communicate a compelling and positive vision of what things will look like once the project is completed.
- Consider how to manage risks associated with the change and resistance to the change. Ignoring this and pretending that there are no downsides to change is naïve. People are likely to adjust quicker when we are honest about the losses involved as well as the gains.
- Communicate often, describe the anticipated benefits, explain how the change will affect those involved, listen to their concerns, and answer questions fully to provide the facts, and thus help dispel the rumours. Being upfront and clear with our

employees about what the change means to them and the way they work is a biggie in the lead up to the transition stage.

- Provide training, coaching and mentoring to those who will affect the introduction of the new product. This includes preparatory training on the use and maintenance of the new product, and the development of user guides. These tasks need to be captured in the PM plan and appropriately resourced.

Transition State is sometimes disorganised and unpredictable, and may create emotions such as despair, anxiety, anger, fear or relief. During the transition state, productivity may decline while users learn new ways of working, while we create an environment that encourages experimentation and minimises the fear of failure. Thus, in summary, this often challenging state is when we:

- Involve users in the testing of project products, which enables us to benefit from their input and provides them with some feeling of ownership.
- Monitor change reaction and progress, encourage learning, tolerate mistakes, proactively search out anything that could impede product uptake, and deal with emerging changes, risks and issues promptly and effectively.
- Gain and publish information about progress and success stories to reinforce the value of the change, and continue to answer questions and provide facts to avoid or help dispel rumours.
- Provide on-going training, coaching, mentoring and counselling to those affected.

Future State is the new norm and where we wish to go. Without this step, people may revert to their old practices and behaviours. This new state is sometimes not fully defined, and with user feedback might have shifted while we were going through the transition state. The future state is most likely to be better than the current state in terms of organisation and individual productivity. However, the future state can be worrisome. It may not match our personal and professional expectations and goals, and there is a chance that we may not be as successful in this new state. Above all else, the future state is somewhat unknown. Our goal is to reach the point when we have stopped thinking about the project product as anything other than normal practice. Useful strategies during this period of reorientation and familiarisation are:

- Ensure that the handover to business-as-usual operations is complete.
- Make sure that the new product is recognised across the organisation.
- Acknowledge, reward and celebrate change successes.
- Develop and reinforce ways to sustain the change.
- Provide for on-going training, coaching, mentoring and counselling.
- Assess the success of the change initiative and take corrective action as required.
- Watch for signs of a relapse to the old ways.

Having a project product that is the "right" answer is important, but this does not guarantee that employees will make the necessary changes in their behaviours and work processes. It takes more than the right solution to move employees out of the current state that they know well and into an unfamiliar future state. Today's workforce is often sceptical and questioning. Embracing change and helping others embrace change is often very difficult depending mainly on the degree of change involved. Fortunately, change management is not rocket science, and here are some well-proven principles to help ensure that the change process works effectively:

- **People issues.** Whatever the level or degree of organisational change, the people on the receiving end are the ones who will ultimately cause the change to be a success or a failure. Invariably, changes create people issues. For example, new leaders may be asked to step up, jobs may be created, changed or eliminated, new skills and capabilities may be needed, and as a consequence some employees may be uncertain and resistant. Dealing with these concerns on a reactive basis usually puts morale at risk, so a proactive approach for managing change risks is much preferred.
- **Start at the top.** Because change is often unsettling for people at all levels of our organisation, our eyes are likely to turn to the CEO and the organisation's leadership team for strength, support and direction. So our leaders themselves must be committed to the change, speak with one voice, and model appropriate behaviours. One of the worst possible scenarios is to have the leaders ignore the process rather than participate actively and visibly throughout. Also, sponsors cannot disappear once they've attended the project launch. Their sustained presence is necessary to build and maintain change momentum.
- **Make the case.** Most people will question to what extent change is needed, whether the change is headed in the right direction and whether they want to commit personally to making the change happen. Thus, the development of a sound business case for change is essential. But we should not mistake natural, normal, healthy resistance to change as a subversive attempt to destroy what we're trying to accomplish. Some individuals oppose change simply because they don't like the idea of an upset to their routine. Others might oppose the change because they feel it threatens their status within the organisation. As an example, someone who is considered a subject matter expert for a particular software program may feel ill at ease at the prospect of a new, unfamiliar application replacing the current system. In cases like this, it's important to identify why this individual feels ill at ease, so their concerns may be addressed, and in this example timely retraining might help.
- **Create ownership.** Leaders of change must over-perform during the transformation period and be the zealots who create a critical mass among the workforce in favour of the change. This usually requires more than passive agreement that the change is acceptable. It demands ownership by leaders and willingness to accept responsibility for making change happen in all of the areas they influence or control. Ownership is often best created by involving people in identifying benefits and implementation problems, and together then crafting solutions.
- **Communicate the message.** The first step toward change is awareness. The second step is acceptance. Too often, change leaders make the mistake of believing that others understand the need for change. The best change strategies reinforce core messages through regular, timely communication that is both inspirational and practical, and solicit timely input and feedback from users. Be wary of expressions like "mindset change", and "changing people's mindsets" or "changing attitudes", because this language often indicates a tendency towards imposed or enforced change, and it implies that the organisation believes that its people currently have the "wrong" mindset, which is seldom the case.

- **Provide end-user training.** Some organisations sabotage their own productivity by skimping on end-user training. End-user training is a very important requirement for the successful implementation of any new project product. Thus, in anticipation, we need to provide training for the users and for those involved in maintaining the new product. A training needs analysis (TNA) will help identify those who need training, what kind of training they need and what training materials and facilities are required. To adequately resource training helps ensure employee buy-in, confidence and productivity.
- **Risk management.** No change process goes completely according to plan. There will be unexpected issues and teething problems. Effectively managing change requires continual monitoring of its impact. As far as possible, change impediments should be identified, prioritised and responded to proactively. Contingency plans might also be developed in anticipation of some issues. In determining the risk involved in the change, the following factors are often relevant:
  - Few employees impacted versus many employees impacted.
  - Few aspects of work impacted versus many aspects of work impacted.
  - Small departure from current state versus large departure from current state.
  - Something similar versus something vastly different.
  - Few recent disruptive changes versus many recent disruptive changes.
- **Speak to individuals.** Change can be a very personal thing. People often spend many hours each week at work and may think of their colleagues as family. People need to know how their work will change, what is expected of them during and after the change, how they will be measured, and what success or failure will mean for them in the new state. Providing personal counselling to alleviate any change-related fears is appropriate. We need to recognise that for some, change may affect people in ways that we may not have foreseen. For example, people who have developed expertise in (or have earned a position of respect from) the old way of doing things, might see their status undermined by change.
- **Recognise success.** Change won't last long without confirmation that it's benefiting the organisation. Visible rewards, such as promotion, recognition and bonuses, could be provided to those who embrace the change. Early adoption and successes should be recognised, advertised and celebrated.

Most stakeholders who resist change do so for genuine reasons. They have real concerns that need to be addressed, such as:

- **Change seems unnecessary.** Employees cannot understand why the change is needed when the status quo seems to be satisfactory and has not previously been questioned. Expressions such as "this is a waste of time, it was working well before, and they never tell us what's going on" might be the immediate reaction from some of those affected.
- **Personal status threatened.** Employees are anxious that their current status in the organisation will be diminished or undermined, or that they may be made redundant. The association people have with their routine work defines them to some degree. People who have been improving their work methods for years to become very good at what they do are likely to resist planned change or possibly only comply to prevent disputes. They may also be concerned about the "what's

in it for me" (WIIFM) factor. On balance, the change may appear to be to their disadvantage.

- **Fear of the unknown.** Employees may be unsure what the future holds for them. Their jobs might be dis-established and they might be "let go" or their job descriptions might be altered in some way to their personal disadvantage. They will recognise that not all change is for the better and perhaps recall some previously bad experiences with change. In the absence of complete, accurate and timely information, unsettling rumours may proliferate.
- **Coping anxiety.** Stakeholders are unsure that they will be able to cope with the change – that their current skills may be obsolete and the new work required of them will be well beyond their comfort zone. Acute and chronic stress can be a consequence. If an employer fails to adequately address workplace stress, they could face a claim under our Health and Safety in Employment legislation.

We might consider which of the following reasons are behind an employee's negative reaction to the proposed change:

- Change threatens feelings of competence, and/or commitment.
- Not enough information is available.
- Individuals have a low tolerance for change and ambiguity.
- Misunderstandings about the change and its implications.
- Desire not to lose something of current value (e.g., security, position, title, status).
- Belief that the change does not make sense.
- Concern that the change will have a negative effect.
- Fear of having to learn new skills.
- Feeling overwhelmed due to too much change.
- Concern that there will be insufficient support to help them deal with change.

The reality is that change is never foolproof. There will be doubts about the wisdom of the change, the change will most likely disrupt work, may take some time to implement and may be even longer than originally thought, there will be risks to contend with, unforeseen issues to resolve, and while the change will likely be overall beneficial, some stakeholders may be disadvantaged as a consequence of the change.

We should encourage those impacted by the change to make suggestions and become involved in the change process. Other than participation, some further strategies to help obtain buy-in might be to sell people on the benefits (WIIFM), be positive ourselves about the change, publish early change successes, be approachable, welcome ideas, keep everyone updated, anticipate and prepare for objections, explain the consequences of change success or failure, get key stakeholders on side, and appoint visible and powerful change advocates. The change curve is a popular model used to understand the stages of personal transition and organisational change.

Faced with resistance to change, some leaders might attempt to drive through change regardless, but this often deepens the resolve of the "resisters" and can lead to outcomes that are in nobody's interest. To help overcome or reduce resistance to change, the PM must become a change leader or appoint others to this role to communicate the change, help those affected understand the purpose and benefits of the change, plan for the change, seek input and ideas to improve the change process, and support those impacted

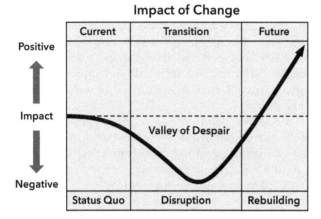

Figure 13.2 Impact of change.

by the change. Possible approaches to address the four most common reasons for resistance to change are these: Figure 13.2.

- **When change seems unnecessary.** To help overcome this concern we need to acquaint those involved with the actual problem or opportunity that has caused the project to be initiated. To be convincing, accurate figures and information will be needed rather than adjectives and rhetoric. We might also demonstrate that there are negative consequences if the change doesn't proceed.
- **When current status is threatened.** As far as possible we would assure stakeholders that they are highly valued and their positions and relative seniorities will be respected, and any proposed changes to their job descriptions would be freely negotiated, agreed with them and accompanied by appropriate training as required.
- **When there's fear of the unknown.** As appropriate, we would reassure staff that current remuneration rates and other conditions of employment would continue and that no redundancies were planned and that any changes to current policies, procedures and processes would be thoroughly discussed with them and all questions fully answered. If necessary, we would explain that should any staff members leave or wish to leave as a consequence of the change, they will be given adequate warning, be appropriately compensated and provided with a reference or detailed record of their service.
- **When there's coping anxiety.** Where appropriate, we would emphasise that few changes were likely to current job descriptions, and any changes in which new skills were needed, these skills would be taught to them through formal courses and on-the-job training. However, if we identify or have been notified about anyone who is suffering stress caused by the change, we might allow them time off to recuperate and later ease them back into work (maybe part-time, or reduced hours), or identify alternative less stressful roles for them.

In summary, while projects may successfully produce a new product, the management of change needed for the successful adoption of this new product is often poorly planned and executed, such that business case benefits that justified the investment are not realised or fully realised. Many projects fall short of their objectives because we PMs often don't see ourselves as change agents. We need to become more educated about change management and the approaches necessary to ensure its part of all our project initiatives. Accordingly, our job as PMs is broadening from that of product delivery to include the management of change.

A robust change management approach assesses the readiness for change and will only authorise projects to go-live when our organisation has properly prepared for the change and has sufficient capacity to cope with any initial fall in productivity as employees adapt to new ways of working.

Reality is that some staff may not be able to pick up the new skills or cope with the change, or despite assurances, they may have little faith or confidence in their own ability to adjust to the new ways of working. For them, the prospect of having to learn and apply new skills and knowledge may have little appeal.

Projects may conclude with the delivery of a product that is handed over to the client or user organisation other than our own organisation who then take responsibility for any change management required to ensure that product benefits accrue.

The next chapter discusses benefit realisation. It's important that changes are successfully embedded in order to deliver benefits, which are the measurable improvements resulting from our project outcomes. The achievement of project benefits depends on the speed and extent to which employees embrace, adopt and use the new product, which is more likely with effective change management. Benefits will particularly be put at risk if we don't proactively address the people side of change.

Thus, change management and benefit realisation have a symbiotic relationship. Benefits come only with change, and change must be sustained by benefits. Benefits are realised when something changes. This usually involves permanently changing attitudes and behaviours as well as physical workplace changes. The failure to embed new attitudes and behaviours so that they become normal practice is often the greatest risk to the realisation of project benefits.

Chapter 14

Securing benefits

Jim Young

While this integration of PM and change management, as discussed in Chapter 13, increases the workload for us project managers (PMs) and adds some cost to our projects, it's worthwhile if more projects then realise their promised benefits. The more dependent a project's benefits are on project product adoption and usage, the larger contribution change management makes.

This means that transition activities must be included in our PM plan. Yet in many organisations change management is entirely reactive, and only applied as a last resort when employee resistance jeopardises project success.

Traditionally, projects were considered finished when their products were completed. However, benefit realisation doesn't occur until products are used. Traditionally, it's us PMs who produced the products and the project sponsors who ensured that benefits accrue. This conventional division of responsibilities between project sponsor and PMs has its close equivalent in New Zealand (NZ) government where Ministers of the Crown are accountable for outcomes and our public service is accountable for outputs. The principle behind this split is that managers should only be held accountable for things they can control. Outcomes, while supremely important, are seen as more difficult to control because they are affected by many external factors that better reside in the political arena. This similar historical division of responsibility between project sponsors and us PMs was understandable, since:

- Immediate PM success, rewards and recognition are usually measured in terms of project objectives (scope, time, cost and quality) and not whether products yield their intended benefits.
- Most organisations have no formal process for managing benefits. Like their PMs, the organisation is often preoccupied with producing products, while benefits are left to chance.
- Most or all benefits arise after project closure when PMs are likely to have resumed their involvement with business-as-usual activities or refocused on other projects – new projects and on-going projects.

However, in today's environment, we PMs are now expected to understand the project business drivers, and help ensure that our projects deliver the benefits that were specified in the project business case, which is how an increasing number of organisations now view project success. Yes, it's becoming more common to assess project success according to benefits realised rather than evaluating success solely in terms of the traditional measures of scope, time, cost and quality. Few could dispute that PMs are in the best position to monitor if a project is on course to deliver such benefits.

Although "benefits" may sound more like health insurance or something obtained from NZ Work and Income, rather than anything to do with PM, every project is an investment with the purpose of obtaining benefits. Even when projects are completed on time and on budget, they may not deliver sustainable benefits. When that happens we are left asking, "What was the real value of our investment? What can we now do that we couldn't do before? Did we just waste our time and money?"

Without properly identifying benefits, there is no clear basis for planning or measuring project success, yet most organisations still have no formal process for securing and measuring project benefits. Benefits realisation is probably the most ignored area of PM except perhaps at the start of a project when sponsors might highlight or even exaggerate the anticipated benefits of their project propositions and downplay the costs to help get their projects approved. As a consequence, any benefits to the management regime is then built on unsafe foundations.

While project benefit estimation is of pivotal importance during project acceptance decisions, once the project is underway many PMs are then exclusively focused on specifications, timelines, budgets and products. Also, many organisations, including those keen to describe themselves as learning organisations, have no formal process in place to manage and realise benefits, don't appoint anyone responsible for their tracking, have no post-implementation benefits review and consider the project finished when project products are released. However, the mark of a more mature PM culture is that their PM methodology is extended to include a benefits realisation phase.

Thus, our understanding of a project's ultimate success is changing from products to benefits. Also, there is growing agreement that we PMs must assume greater responsibility for change management and benefit delivery. As a minimum, we should include measures for managing change and securing benefits in our project plans, and appreciate the impact of proposed variations on anticipated benefits, which encourages us to stay focused on why the project was initiated in the first place.

Nevertheless, project delivery still remains a vital step to achieving benefits. Completing our projects on time, within budget, and to expected standards of quality sets the platform for on-going success, but ultimately it's the realisation of expected, and sometimes unexpected benefits that determines project success, and such benefits should outweigh the costs of achieving them if the project is to add value.

To better understand the process we need to define some terms, including project goal, objectives, processes, outputs, outcomes and benefits, where:

- **Project goal** is a single SMART target to achieve something of value.
- **Project objectives** are measurable parameters or constraints of scope, time, cost, quality, risk tolerance and benefits, in keeping with which us PMs must build our creations.
- **Processes** are a series of actions or steps taken in order to transform one or more inputs into one or more outputs.
- **Outputs** or deliverables are created by PM processes and may be any of the project's products (interim or final, tangible or intangible). An output has no intrinsic value because it's the change caused by the use of the output that brings value and not the output itself. The project's outputs are used to create outcomes.

- **Outcomes** are the results of the change caused by integrating the new output into the operation of our own or our client's business. Such change needs to be managed to ensure that planned benefits emerge.
- **Benefits** are measurable improvements or positive impacts resulting from outcomes and are perceived as advantages by one or more stakeholders, such as a reduction in business costs by say 10% over the next six months, or an increase in sales by say 15% per annum. Benefits answer the question "What value is derived from this outcome?" and should be supported by key performance indicators (KPIs).
- **Benefits Realisation Management (BRM)** includes the activities of identifying, defining, planning and tracking to achieve and sustain benefits throughout the life of the project and its product. Benefits are tracked to ensure they're delivering value Figure 14.1.

By themselves, products do nothing. When that product is used it causes changes which are outcomes. Measured outcomes are benefits that add value through improvements.

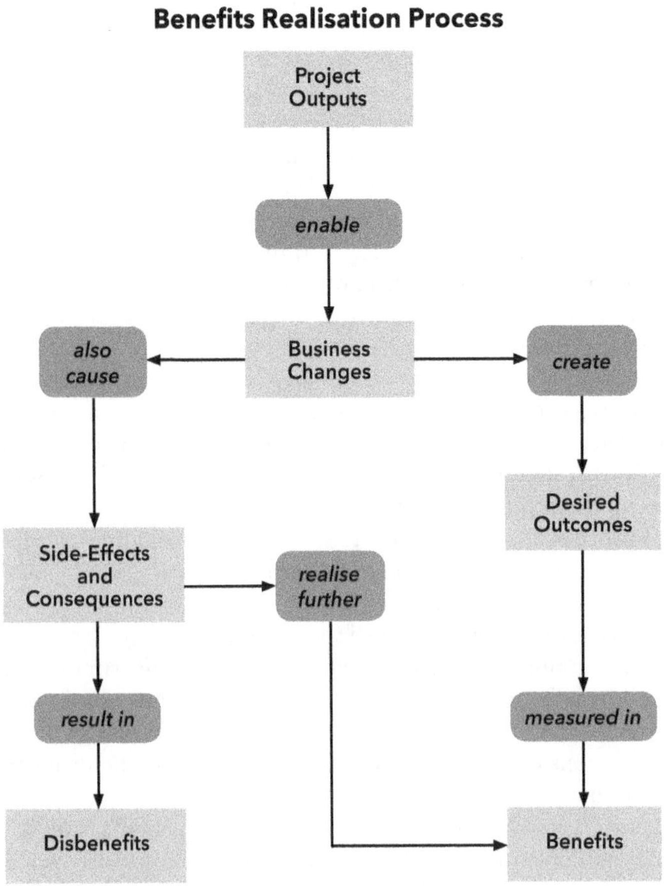

Benefits Realisation Process

Figure 14.1 Benefits realisation process.

Benefits may be quantitative or non-quantifiable (qualitative), monetary or non-monetary, direct (primary) or indirect (secondary), anticipated or unforeseen, one-time or recurring, and immediate or longer-term. Also, benefits are not necessarily assured – they possess uncertainty and have different likelihoods of realisation. Benefits anticipated at the commencement of the project may change during the project life and/or during the product life, often due to uncontrollable external factors. Thus, the project business case needs to be regularly reviewed and updated. Of course, not every benefit carries the same weight with every stakeholder. Here are some common benefit categories:

- **Direct monetary benefits (tangible)** are those benefits that can be quantified and valued in financial terms, such as cost savings and revenue generation. These readily dollarised benefits are usually the most persuasive. Examples are:
  - To increase revenue by 30% over the next 12 months.
  - To reduce costs by 15% within 12 months after product launch.
- **Direct non-monetary benefits (tangible)** are those benefits that can be quantified but are difficult, undesirable, insensitive or impossible to value in financial terms, such as fewer customer complaints, lower staff turnover, reduced lead times and improved response times. Specific examples are:
  - To reduce customer complaints each month by 80% by 1 June XX.
  - To gain 20% more customers over the next year.
- **Indirect benefits (intangible)** can be identified but cannot be easily quantified, such as enhanced end-user satisfaction, better access to information, enhanced organisational image and better morale. Further examples are:
  - To improve customer and staff satisfaction, morale and motivation.
  - To improve our business image.
  - To promote the company's trade brand.
  - To enhance our users' experience.
  - To increase favourable press coverage.
- **Disbenefits**, a clumsy expression, are seen by one or more stakeholders as negative outcomes from the intended change. We should ensure that disbenefits represent a price worth paying in the process of obtaining the positive benefits. For example, a road repair or upgrade project increases peak period congestion or requires traffic to be diverted onto other roads, to thus increase travel times, which some road users would see as a disbenefit.

Some may argue that indirect benefits are too tenuous to legitimately include in our project business case and if a benefit can't be measured numerically it shouldn't be claimed. I suggest any benefit might be relevant, providing we also consider the associated cost and include a realistic assessment of their probability. For example, if an indirect benefit has an estimated 70% likelihood of occurring, assuming a direct or primary benefit of similar likelihood first occurs, the secondary or indirect benefit would then only have an estimated 49% likelihood of occurring (i.e., $70\% \times 70\% = 49\%$). However, such probability predictions are usually very difficult to make and particularly so for pioneering projects about which we have no history.

Since benefits are not certainties, best and worst-case benefit scenarios may be developed and risk management techniques employed to help safeguard or enhance potential benefits. Also, the likelihood and impact of anticipated disbenefits should be mitigated. Disbenefits should be identified and analysed as part of the project business case to ensure that they don't outweigh expected benefits. If managed proactively some disbenefits could be nullified or even turned into benefits (Table 14.1).

Also, benefits might also be measured in terms of the "triple bottom line" where they are categorised as:

- **Economic or financial benefits** determined through such techniques as cost-benefit analysis, net present value, internal rate of return and economic value added computations.
- **Social and community benefits** that encompass health and safety, cultural factors, improved social justice, welfare and environmental impact factors.
- **Corporate benefits** such as revenue, profitability, innovation, growth, market share, shareholder value, community perception, and ethical and probity considerations.

"A benefits-lead change initiative" is a pertinent and concise way to describe a project. This definition emphasises the rationale for any project – to realise benefits that hopefully, sooner rather than later, considerably exceed the costs involved and thus add value, where:

$$\text{NET VALUE} = \text{BENEFITS} - \text{COSTS}$$

$$\text{ROI} = (\text{BENEFITS} - \text{COSTS}) / \text{COSTS}$$

Financial benefits such as cost savings and increased revenues are readily quantifiable. However, non-financial benefits such as a reduction in hospital emergency wait times, an improvement in educational outcomes or compliance with government legislation may be more difficult to quantify, but can usually be measured by way of surveys. However, if a benefit is definitely not measurable perhaps it should not be recognised,

Table 14.1 Project products, outcomes and benefits

Products	Outcomes	Tangible Benefits
New order processing software installed.	Faster processing of customers' orders.	Reduce the average processing time for customer orders by at least 20% from the current average of 15 minutes.
Sales campaign revitalised.	Attract new customers.	Add a minimum of 20 new customers each month for the next year.
Website updated.	Attract more viewers.	Increase visitors to the website by an average of at least 5% each week for the next year.
Core values published.	Enhanced culture, morale and image.	Staff absences and turnover reduced by at least 30% during the next year.
Team-building programmeintroduced.	Improved teamwork.	Team productivity increased by at least 20% during the next year.

Table 14.2 Benefit variance

Project Benefits	Net Baseline	Actual to Date
1. Disposal of redundant kit	$5,000	$5,000
2. Faster response	$12,000	$14,000
3. New customers sales	$40,000	$25,000
4. Headcount savings	$100,000	$100,000
Project Benefits	**Net Baseline**	**Actual to Date**

as there will be insufficient evidence to prove that it has been achieved. Thus, ideally, benefits should be measurable and evidence-based to show that they provide value, but if all project benefits are not measurable, then arguably we should accept that there is insufficient evidence to justify the investment Table 14.2.

While projects have benefits, some projects don't have obvious benefits, such as compliance projects that are undertaken in response to changing legislation when deadlines are fixed and set externally, although perhaps one benefit might be we avoid court cases and fines. Incidentally, compliance benefits can be measured immediately at the end of the project when we know straightaway we are now compliant. Also, there are enabling projects that don't have benefits themselves, such as the installation of a new computer network that allows other projects to run that do deliver benefits. Perhaps reading this book is an enabling project.

The process for benefit realisation starts with the end in mind. Obtaining some sort of benefit, whether financial, economic or otherwise is the reason we undertake our projects. If no worthwhile benefits are envisaged we should not embark on the project. Also, our project should not include any products that don't produce sought-after benefits. A benefits map, benefits flowchart or benefits dependency network is occasionally used to illustrate and track outcomes and benefits, particularly when benefits lead to more benefits, an example of which aimed to increase sales revenue is shown in Figure 14.2. To develop this map, we work backwards, or right to left, from the ultimate benefit or benefits that are desired. Benefit mapping should involve key stakeholders and might be undertaken as a workshop at which we identify benefits and their dependencies to each other and to the changes required to achieve them.

We can't expect benefits to materialise without some effort. Benefits evolve over time as people adapt to and use the new product. However, some projects declared successful never deliver the benefits originally envisaged. Also, different projects sometimes claim the same benefits. In fact, if any two projects claim the same benefits they are arguably the same project. Also, we need to recognise that one benefit may be dependent on first achieving another benefit as illustrated by a benefits map. Benefits management is essentially about remembering why we are doing the project and the process typically involves the steps outlined in Figure 14.3.

1. **Define benefits management plan.** A misunderstanding is that benefits just happen. Rather, they need to be planned for. We must determine how and when benefits will be managed and by who. Unless benefits are assigned, progressively tracked and reported there is no opportunity for management to recognise and

Example Benefits Map

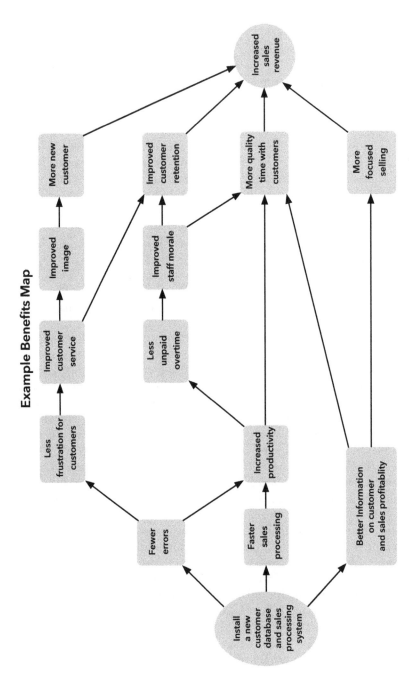

Figure 14.2 Example benefits map.

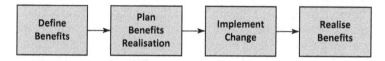

Figure 14.3 Benefits realisation process.

implement corrective measures to ensure benefits will be delivered in full and in a timely manner. Priority is usually given to those benefits with the greatest potential value. Benefits are identified by users and other stakeholders and depend on the delivery of outputs and the achievement of outcomes. Both benefits and disbenefits need to be measured. Informed and accurate decisions around business cases cannot be made unless disbenefits are also identified and measured. Each benefit (and disbenefit) should be documented in terms of their priority, value, timescale and ownership.

2. **Plan benefits realisation.** This step requires we first determine baseline measurements and agree on targets. Baseline measurements identify the current performance of an operation so that post-project improvements can be measured. This will enable the success (or otherwise) of the initiative to be established. The benefits plan identifies the anticipated benefits and our confidence level in them being achieved, assigns responsibilities and timelines for their achievement, and identifies their relationship to project outputs. Accountability and responsibility for benefit realisation is key to successful benefits management. Benefits are owned by project sponsors and business managers and not usually by PMs Table 14.3.

3. **Implement change.** Benefits only happen when something changes. This usually involves changing individual attitudes and behaviours as well as material changes. While implementing change, new opportunities for additional benefits might also become evident. Unless benefits are progressively tracked and reported, there is no opportunity for us to implement timely corrective measures (if needed) to ensure benefits are delivered in full.

4. **Realise benefits.** Each benefit should be given an overall benefit ranking based on its total impact and importance to the project, and the highest priority benefits should receive the greatest attention, resourcing and monitoring. Required changes to the way people work need to be embedded to ensure that benefits continue to be realised. Failure to formally assign accountability and responsibility for benefits creates a significant risk that benefits will not be properly measured or tracked. And

Table 14.3 Example benefits

Required Outcome	Benefit Owner	Benefit KPI	Achievement Timeframe
Increased income from sales	Sales Manager.	$10,000 additional revenue from monthly sales.	Each month for a 12 month period commencing in two months' time.
Improved customer service	Customer Service Team.	Elimination of customer complaints.	No customer complaints received during the next year.

it's important that responsibility for benefit realisation remains with those business units affected. The project sponsor, specifically appointed change managers, and/ or operations managers should track benefit realisation and ensure that changes are permanent. Actions needed for continued benefits realisation should be agreed and documented as part of the product handover process. Benefit owners are ideally assigned at the start of the project but aren't usually part of our project team. Typical responsibilities for benefit owners are:

- To provide input for the benefit realisation plan.
- To organise benefit measurement and reviews.
- To identify and remove obstacles to benefit realisation.
- To report benefit realisation progress.

The new product progresses through stages known as the product lifecycle during which time enhancement projects may be undertaken to extend the life of the product by upgrading it to create new benefits in terms of product functionality and features, ergonomics, environmental friendliness, sustainability, technology, features, supply or pricing. Eventually our product will reach the end of its useful life. For some products there may then be some residual, salvage or scrap value, although as a general rule, the longer a product's useful life, the lower these final values are likely to be. Many high-technology products now have a very short lifecycle – rapid introduction and growth stages, steep decline stage and no maturity stage. Despite our recycling efforts, detritus is piling up in vast electronic rubbish dumps. Figure 14.4.

There are several reasons why project benefits may not be realised, fully realised or sustained, including:

- An unsatisfactory business case that doesn't properly identify benefits and/or over-states benefits, which occasionally might be deliberate to help ensure a project's approval. Also, some benefits are described in only vague terms with plenty of adjectives and adverbs that make their objective measurement difficult or impossible. Such business cases have usually not been subject to robust and objective scrutiny.

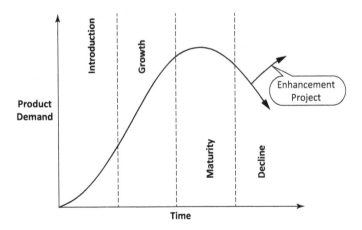

Figure 14.4 Product lifecycle.

- Over-emphasis on products, without thinking much, or at all, about the benefits that the products are intended to create, and no mechanism in place for benefit tracking and harvesting. Sometimes this is the consequence of lethargic sponsors or overly product-driven PMs.
- Product users aren't properly trained in the use of the new product, have no or little buy-in, and/or are reluctant to make the necessary changes.
- Project sponsors and champions leave the organisation or become preoccupied with other responsibilities including new projects.
- Believing that the project is over once the final product is produced, expecting benefits to automatically occur without further effort or expecting benefits when there's been no change.
- Changed external factors (e.g., politics, economics, social factors, new technology, new legislation, and competition) diminish or cancel anticipated benefits. Such external impacts are more likely and significant when benefits are to be realised over a period of years rather than within weeks.

Some argue that PMs should assume greater responsibility for benefit delivery. As a minimum, we PMs should include strategies for benefit tracking and realisation in our project implementation plans. And whether it's the business analyst's, sponsor's or the PM's responsibility, the first step is to ensure that the following foundations for benefits realisation are in place:

- That the business case clearly identifies anticipated benefits.
- That business case reviews are scheduled to validate benefits.
- That stakeholders who will be affected by each benefit are identified.
- That outcomes required for the realisation of each benefit are identified.
- That measures are in place for each benefit.
- That responsibilities for delivery of benefits are assigned.
- That benefits are prioritised according to their anticipated impact.

Since benefits are mainly realised or not realised after project closure, perhaps benefit realisation is therefore most appropriately a job for our project sponsor whose responsibility for the project should therefore extend into the product lifecycle until benefits are realised or not realised. The growth in other specialisations such as business analysis and change management mean that PMs are somewhat removed from the business consequences of their actions. Nevertheless, we PMs should manage the project with the anticipated benefits clearly in mind and navigate our project to help ensure that the intended benefits will materialise.

As PMs, our early involvement in a project means that we will better understand the rationale for the project and the required benefits, and we may then be able to inject some timely, rational thinking, given our project is to deliver these anticipated results should the endeavour be approved. In particular, we might ensure that the business case and initial estimates are realistic. Sponsors and other key stakeholders are often very keen for their project propositions to be approved, have been known to overestimate benefits, ignore disbenefits, under-estimate project costs, downplay the risks involved and promise amazingly optimistic delivery dates for products and their benefits.

The benefits part of our PM plan should contain the following information:

- What benefits will be measured.
- Who is accountable for the expected benefits.
- How to measure expected benefits.
- When to measure expected benefits.
- What resources are needed to review the benefits.
- Baseline measures from which improvement may be calculated (Table 14.4).

Thus, the main focus of every project should be on the benefits and not merely on the products. The products are the vehicles upon which benefits are delivered. Benefits are the rationale for undertaking the project and are identified in the project business case, which is a core reference document throughout the project life and subsequent product lifecycle. Benefits need to be clear, relevant and measurable, and the business case, which is a "living document", needs to be updated as circumstances change. Sometimes the rationale or value proposition for the project significantly diminishes, resulting in project cancellation, and this might even occur when project implementation is proceeding well in terms of schedule and budget performance.

A common misconception is that if we build the project, the benefits will come. Benefits management is seen as an unnecessary overhead, and once projects are approved, no further justification is sought. Therefore, not only are the claimed benefits not leveraged, but additional potential benefits are also missed. However, benefit realisation has become a vital driver for projects and it's now more common to assess the success of a project in terms of benefits achieved, rather than evaluating success only in terms of the traditional measures of time, cost and quality.

We need to raise our game so that managing benefits is regarded as a distinct and central component of PMs, ingrained in the culture of our organisations. The realisation of benefits to create value must be a core competence of every successful organisation, where the following good practices for managing benefits are evident:

- We PMs, sponsors and line managers work together.
- We assign clear responsibilities for benefit delivery.
- We involve all stakeholders in planning benefit delivery.
- We include benefit delivery in our PM plan.
- We develop benefit metrics for every project.
- We integrate risk management with benefit management.
- We communicate the benefit delivery plan to all stakeholders.

Benefits realised should be viewed against the business case. Only by comparing results against the business case can the degree of project success be fully determined and our

Table 14.4 Benefits planning template

Benefit Description	Benefit Owner	How Measured	When Measured	Resource Needs	Baseline Measure

future business cases improved. A comprehensive benefits report might include mention of benefits planned, benefits realised, disbenefits, benefits not yet achieved and why, actions to retrieve unachieved benefits, benefits discarded, further benefits available, and lessons learned. User surveys are very helpful for gauging benefit realisation progress and effectiveness.

Product users could be required to track, record and report performance against anticipated benefits. We also need to think about when we are going to stop measuring benefits. For example, we could take the benefit in this financial year and then not track it next year, considering it a business-as-usual situation by then. But it is not unlikely that some organisations will select a "benefits sampling period" that is favourable rather than representative. Sometimes enhancement projects are implemented when benefits don't materialise as planned or products under-perform. A post-project product implementation report that assesses benefits realised may be prepared by the project sponsor or project manager in co-operation with operational managers and product users.

Where a project is delivering a product for an external client under contract, we PMs usually have no formal involvement in benefit realisation. However, we should be familiar with the client's business case. The contract with the customer is to produce the project product, and it will be the customer who then obtains the benefits from the product's use.

In conclusion, contemporary PMs aim to transition project outputs into new operational business-as-usual capabilities and follow through to the achievement of outcomes, benefits and finally the organisation's strategic objectives. Benefit realisation has become a vital driver for projects and it is increasingly common to assess the success of a project by achieved benefits rather than evaluating success based entirely on the traditional measures of time, cost, quality and scope.

Remember that the ultimate purpose of our project is to deliver product(s) into the business-as-usual or operational area of our customer, and that this product will ultimately realise the benefits that have been described in our business case.

Although benefits are not the only criteria used to evaluate project success, they are a very good measurement of how valuable a project is. A project is truly successful only if it delivers the required benefits. That's why benefits realisation is now an added focus for us PMs and as a minimum we must consider the benefits and their realisation as they influence our decision-making throughout the life of the project. But, while project benefits are always listed in the project business case, many PMs still drive their project toward generating a specified product, while not giving enough attention to the expected benefits, on which thought I conclude this chapter.

Chapter 15

Beyond the triple constraints

Creating conditions for optimal performance

Marisa Silva

Introduction

It is undisputable that the subject of project management experienced an increasing level of interest recently. Despite this, projects keep failing and although more knowledge is created and is available to practitioners, we are still far from an ideal situation where all projects would succeed. With just 29% of projects being successful in 2015 (Hastie and Wojewoda, 2015), the overall performance of project management is questionable. What is missing?

In fact, what is project performance and where are the boundaries between performance and success? Let us take the example of the Sydney Opera House, for instance. Budgeted at an initial cost of $7 million, the Opera House ended up costing more than $100 million and took more than a decade to construct, making it the most expensive cost blowout in the history of megaprojects around the world (Flyvbjerg, 2009) and a classic case study of poor project management performance. However, it is a renowned building which attracts millions of visitors every year. Success, as it stands, is therefore a tricky concept.

This chapter uses the lens of the "management for projects" theory to challenge the traditional perspective of project performance as the evaluation of projects as per specifications, on time, and on budget, which the author perceives as a misleading driver. Indeed, other factors can strongly influence and even determine the success or failure of a project, pre and post-execution, yet, the dominant paradigm is still execution-orientated, where the role of the project manager is one of a mere doer.

To do so, the chapter starts by presenting and proposing a critic stand towards the traditional view of project performance, highlighting its limitations as acknowledged in project management literature. Following, the three levels of the management of projects are discussed with an emphasis on their viewpoint of project performance. Finally, the chapter elaborates on the importance of not just managing projects but also of managing *for* projects, providing insight into some of the contextual conditions which can contribute to optimal project performance.

1. The triple fallacy of project performance

Ultimately, one can say that projects have existed from the moment human beings existed in the planet. Over the centuries, from the Pyramids to the Incas, with more or less sophisticated tools and techniques, creativity or engineering, strict planning or rich imagination, buildings were erected, cities were built, lands were discovered, and skies were conquered. However, it is generally accepted that project management as a discipline with a scientific basis was only initiated during the sixties (Morris, 2013), in a time when the Race to the Moon and The Cold War prompted several projects in the government and defence industries.

While the world moved on, the way the majority still perceives projects has not and we are now left with a "hangover" from that time. In fact, most of the current literature describes project management as planning, implementing, and controlling a group of activities intended to deliver a unique product or service (PMBOK Guide, 2017). Because of this dominant model, project management is still seen as an execution-oriented discipline (Morris, 2013), whose focus is on delivering projects on-time, on-budget, and to scope – the infamous iron triangle, or triple constraint of project management.

The traditional view on the performance and the success of projects is therefore much guided by the attainment of the objectives of the project within these three parameters, a situation clearly demonstrated by the development and use of performance measurement techniques such as Earned Value Analysis, which combines measures of scope, time, and cost. While the level of transparency and rigour obtained through such techniques is valuable, I claim that it is not enough and, indeed, can cause more harm than good to the project if not supported by appropriate context and a long-term thinking mindset. The triple constraint can easily become a triple fallacy.

There are numerous cases available in the literature of projects which were challenged in their performance and even deemed unsuccessful considering the traditional project management metrics and yet are perceived as a success (e.g. Sydney Opera House, Porto's Casa da Música, the British Library, etc.). On the other hand, there are also multiple examples of high-performance projects which didn't manage to be successful in meeting the expectations of the project's client, hence, denoting a significant difference between project management success and project success. After all, no one wants to hear that the surgery was successful but the patient died.

Hodgson (2002) tells us that "projects fail – that's the fact of life. Too many fail because the average project is like an iceberg – 9/10ths of it lay hidden from view". To this point, to reduce success to project management success and to condense project performance in the triple constraint is to address just the tip of the iceberg.

Also, Morris (2013) strongly criticized this narrowed mindset, as it neglects the front-end aspects of a project, its definition and its interfaces with strategy, procurement, finance, and similar crucial elements that make the management of projects a pluralistic discipline, much more comprehensive than the management of the triple constraint. Likewise, authors of the Critical Management Studies (Cicmil and Hodgson, 2006) highlighted the perils of an instrumental rationality, too focused on efficiency and efficacy, and tools and techniques, but not in its context, thus ignoring the role of ethics, relationships of power, political issues, or interdependencies between project actors. Yet, Koskela and Howell (2002) are even more drastic in their views, by arguing that there is no explicit theory of project management, but a weak underlying foundation because its model is borrowed from other disciplines.

According to these authors, because of the lack of a well-defined, and unique theoretic basis, there is no distinct body of knowledge that could legitimize yet the project management discipline, and future advancement is hence dependent on a new, firm, theory that could allow the discipline to gain its own academic position and autonomy, as well as be translated into effective and consistent performance on delivering projects.

2. Project management, management of projects, and management for projects

Addressing the concerns regarding the present and future of project management as a discipline, Morris and Geraldi (2011) suggest that three levels of management of projects should be integrated:

> "Level 1: technical: that is, operational and delivery oriented;
> Level 2: strategic: managing projects as organizational holistic entities, expanding the domain to include their front-end development and definition and with a concern for value and effectiveness;
> Level 3: managing the institutional context; creating the context and support for projects to flourish and for their management to prosper".

The first level parallels the traditional view of project management, which is still much perceived as delivering a piece of defined scope within agreed boundaries of time and budget. At this level, project managers are doers and projects are instruments, part of a simplistic and mechanist view whose main purpose is to maximize efficiency.

Acknowledging this limited, although dominant, project management paradigm, Morris (1994) proposed a new model, coined management of projects. This revolutionary perspective argues that the triple constraint of scope, time, and cost should not be thought of as a given but as something that is built. More importantly, the management of projects positions projects as strategic units, part of a wider picture, where context has a significant role to play and where properly setting up the project front-end determines its conditions of success. Aspects such as agreeing with the project sponsor what value is the project to bring, where does it fit in terms of strategy, addressing procurement or the commercial side of projects, are key considerations at this level.

However, no project – and no organization – is an island. Projects do not exist in a vacuum but in a world of habits, norms, institutions, and other organizations. The traditional perspective of projects as a "distinct, manageable activity system that, once having been designed using the proper scheduling techniques, can be isolated from the environment" (Blomquist and Packendorff, 1998:38) is therefore detached from reality and should be challenged.

In fact, this conceptualization of projects fails to address projects as organizational entities that are part of a business and social setting which, likewise, requires managing (Engwall, 2003; Winter et al., 2006; Gann and Salter, 2000). To this end, Morris and Geraldi (2011) stressed that a third level of conceptualization about projects – the institutional level – has been poorly addressed but is of substantial importance.

By shedding light over the interplay between projects and institutions, focus shifts from managing in or of projects to managing on or for projects (Morris and Geraldi, 2011), in this way enabling a better understanding of how the setting outside and around projects can constrain or support the management of projects and their success. Managing for projects is not simply concerned in protecting the project and business environment from disruptions. Instead, management is focused on aligning project arrangements with their institutional environment (Miller and Lessard, 2000) and in creating a supportive setting that allows projects to flourish, both in its parent organization and its external environment, in line with what Cooke-Davies (2002) defined as consistent project management success.

As put by Grabher (2002:212), the excessive focus on projects as individual temporary settings detached from their context obscures our perception of surrounding structures "that are nourishing, linking, sponsoring, suspending and preventing projects". Without acknowledging the institutional context in project management, we are left to not see the forest for the trees.

Which conditions for optimal project performance?

To the above, it is then pertinent to pose the question: what are the conditions that need to be present for projects to flourish? Examples mentioned in the literature include but are not limited to the establishment of an organizational project management culture, focused on "best practices" and promotion of organizational learning; the direction provided by the sponsor; the support of enabling support structures, such as the PMO; the way resources are managed; portfolio management and the political context; and appropriate leadership styles. In the sections below, further analysis of how some of these contribute towards project performance is provided.

2.1. Organizational project management culture

The old adagio attributed to Drucker, "culture eats strategy for breakfast", remains as valid today as when it was first formulated. In fact, the organizational culture prevails over the most well-defined strategic intent and therefore is a consideration of utmost importance for projects and their performance.

In its most obvious form, organizational culture is "the way we do things around here". In its less visible form, it encompasses several factors that drive employee's perception of their role in the organization and their different interfaces, their place in the social system, and resulting beliefs, behaviours, and expectations. These factors can include (PMBOK Guide, 2017):

- System of beliefs, social norms, and behaviours
- Overall tone of the shared employee experience
- Shared visions, mission statements, and expectations
- Motivation and reward systems
- Views on leadership and authority relationships
- Risk tolerance and appetite
- Work ethic and codes of conduct
- Environmental factors

When people work together towards a common specific objective over a period of time, which is the case of projects, subcultures can be formed as well. In this way, projects are not just shaped by the organizational culture but can in turn influence that culture by adding to it through projects. Nevertheless, it is the alignment between these two – organizational culture and the project (management) culture – that will dictate the extent of success of the project. Projects that are seen as aligning with organizational culture are likely to have a less challenging implementation and higher success rates compared to projects that conflict with those cultural norms.

According to Suda (2007), projects have a higher probability of succeeding when they:

- Understand organizations as living social systems, with core and subcultures
- Assess, identify, work with and align with the organization's core culture
- Are designed, in the front end, with a system focused perspective and are implemented as to that design
- Tie directly to the organization's strategy
- Align with culture and leadership initiatives
- Understand that the project culture must function in service of the organization's core culture

To the above, Yazici (2009) maintains that cultures where premium is premium placed on participation, commitment, and shared values have better chances of dealing with project time, budget, and expectations issues. This view is shared by a recent study by the Project Management Institute (2015) where, according to participants, by "embedding the project management mindset in organizational culture" firms are more likely to have higher levels of performance in project management and therefore generate long-term benefits in a competitive environment, moving from temporary efficiency and efficacy gains towards lasting business results.

2.2. Organizational learning

An organization which learns and uses knowledge gained from projects to improve the performance of new initiatives is also a critical success factor in the management for projects, as it accelerates the learning cycle and prevents project teams from having to "reinvent the wheel" every time a new project is initiated in the organization.

Arguably, one of the most important contributes to the theory of Knowledge Management lies in Nonaka and Takeuchi's SECI Model (1995), which proposes an approach for knowledge creation, conversion, and transfer in organizations. While in practice knowledge can take different forms, being most of the time a combination of both explicit and tacit elements more than just one or the other, it is important to distinguish these two contrasting concepts in order to allow a comprehensive understanding of the SECI model. Explicit knowledge, also referred to as know-what (Brown and Duguid, 1998), is formalized and codified, captured in procedures, documents, and other artefacts which make use of language as the basis of their codification, thus making it relatively easier to transfer that knowledge between individuals. On the other hand, tacit knowledge, sometimes referred to as know-how (Brown and Duguid, 1998), is rooted in experience, hence being highly contextual and personal and making it more difficult to communicate through words (or, as Polanyi (1967: 4) puts it "we can know more than we can tell"), resulting in it also being more difficult to transfer.

Having investigated the relationship between the concepts of explicit and tacit knowledge, Nokaka and Takeuchi identified four modes of knowledge conversion, typically represented over the form of a spiral, to denote the continuous and dynamic act of knowledge creation. According to the authors, one of these four is socialization, involving the conversion of tacit to tacit, where knowledge is passed on in an apprenticeship environment through imitation, shared experiences, and using face to face mechanisms, such as meetings or brainstorm. The conversion from tacit to explicit is called externalization and, since it aims to codify a type of knowledge that is deemed difficult to codify, it is considered to be a particularly challenging endeavour, with metaphors, concepts, and images being cited as possible mechanisms to overcome that issue. Combination is potentially the simplest mode of transfer of the four, involving the conversion from explicit to explicit, where codified knowledge is combined or processed with other codified knowledge sources to create new knowledge. Finally, the conversion from explicit to tacit knowledge is referred to as internalization, where the knowledge from an explicit source is used and embedded in the user practices, being aligned to reflective practice and learning by doing.

While the SECI model has almost achieved a paradigmatic status in the field of Knowledge Management, critiques have emerged over the linearity of the concept and its applicability in practice (Gourlay, 2003). Regardless, the model opens the path to the role knowledge plays in inter-organizational relationships, particularly evident in the socialization route where, on one hand, the existence of relationships between individuals can favour experience sharing, hence facilitating the transfer of tacit knowledge while, on the other hand, the experience sharing exercise can also lead to a relationship built since a common denominator between individuals comes into existence. The practicality of this scenario is visible through processes such as the sharing of project lessons learned, project mentoring and coaching, or the induction of new team members.

In fact, the conversion of tacit knowledge into best practices, at the organizational level, is still perceived as a key challenge due to the difficulty of internal stickiness (Szulansky, 1996; Jensen and Szulansky, 2004). However, learning in project settings is strongly related to social practices and processes, which suggest that a community-based approach to knowledge management can help capture and transfer knowledge intra and inter-projects, therefore minimizing the challenge of "organizational amnesia" (Othman and Ashim, 2004). To this end, the establishment of communities of practice as a catalyst for interacting and learning together in project-based settings is certainly a factor that should be considered in the enabling of learning organizations and, in turn, in the achievement of greater project performance.

2.3. Project management bricolage and best-fit practices

The Principles of Scientific Management that reined in the previous century advocated a unique and optimal manner of work which was for decades considered the best approach. Yet, much has changed since Taylor's "one best way" approach, such as the dominance of the customer's role, the dynamic and unpredictable environment, or the nature of tasks which are now mental, unique, and complex, just to name a few.

Effectively, the standardization of processes, procedures, and tools is based on a critical need – prevent reinventing the wheel every time a project initiates and thus save time and energy, reduce rework, and increase quality, among others. Moreover, the existence of a standard removes ambiguity and constitutes itself as a factor of internal stability capable of providing the main conduct guidelines or modus operandi in the context of a project. However, some authors have recently alerted that Project Management standardization may obstruct the success of the project since its reduced elasticity peril an effective response to the dynamics and uncertainty surrounding projects, which are not as standard or stable.

In fact, any Project Management methodology implicitly presumes a single approach based on best practices, which can have led to the assumption that all processes and procedures must be carried out exactly as prescribed, a scenario referred to as "project is a project is a project syndrome" by Shenhar & Dvir (2007). Likewise, Milosevic and Patanakul (2005), who studied the influence of standardized project management in a project's success, concluded that:

> deploying a standardized Project Management process from the Organizational Project Management level may increase project success but only to a certain point. Increasing standardization further beyond this point – which we referred to as an inflection point – may actually stifle project success.

A shift from "practitioners as trained technicians" to "reflective practitioners", as proposed by Winter et al. (2006), is therefore recommended as an approach that brings together theory and practice through "the capacity to reflect on action so as to engage in a process of continuous learning" (Schon, 1983, pp. 102–104). Reflective practice enables a practitioner to critically analyze and evaluate his practice against the theory, and incorporate his reflection into practice, therefore allowing for continuous improvement and for the generation of new knowledge that can, in return, be useful for his praxis and leading to greater project performance.

Bearing in mind that "one size does not fit all", it is up to the project manager as a reflective practitioner to balance the project management approach to the organization's maturity, capacity, and type or scale of the projects, in this way not disregarding best practices but instead pursuing best-fit practices and not restraining from combining and re-arranging the different toolkits at hand as needed (e.g. Kanban, PRINCE2, Six Sigma), which could best serve the project in a sort of project management bricolage (De Hertogh et al., 2011; Ciborra, 1992). The exercise of tailoring methodologies and approaches to the project setting is therefore a critical factor for project performance since organizations need to have sufficient formal and standardized processes to achieve efficiency and consistency, but also must have the ability to provide themselves with sufficient informal and flexible processes that allow them to innovate and be Agile in their adaption to changing conditions.

2.4. Project management office

The establishment of supporting project management structures, such as project management offices (typically referred to as PMOs), is another factor that can contribute to greater project performance, particularly when the PMO is formed of staff dedicated to a single project (e.g. planners, risk specialists), or when involved in capability development functions, in this way removing some of the workload of the project manager, handling the project administrative activities, and/or ensuring that the project teams are equipped with the right competencies for the project.

While there is no one size fits all when it comes to PMOs, the following are generally accepted as domains of work of a PMO (PMI, 2013):

- Standards, Methodologies and Processes: methodology definition; metrics definition; process development and improvement
- Project/Program Delivery Management: define the business goals; resource management; schedule/cost/scope management; business realization management; risk management; stakeholder management; communications; project integration
- Portfolio Management: prioritization; strategic alignment; portfolio reporting; resource management allocation; opportunities and investment analysis; risk management; benefits realization tracking/reporting
- Talent Management: training; career paths; career development; capability/skills development and certifications/qualifications/credentials
- Governance and Performance Management: performance reporting; issue escalation; information distribution; metrics/KPIs; compliance; financial management; PMO performance management
- Organizational Change Management: customer/stakeholder satisfaction; managing resistance; readiness assessment; stakeholder management; communications
- Administration and Support: tools (provisioning/implementation/support); consulting; IT/IS support
- Knowledge Management: defining knowledge management policies; managing intellectual collateral/property; lessons learned; content management and collaboration
- Strategic Planning: confirming strategic priorities; defining business goals and aligning to initiatives; environmental scanning; opportunity analysis

PMOs can bring value to an organization in several ways and, while this is dependent on a number of factors, ten key benefits of having a PMO include (Aubry et al., 2007; Hobbs and Aubry, 2007):

- Consistency: of best-fit-practices, terminology, and processes, leading to discipline and alignment of expectations and behaviours
- Visibility: over the status and progress of projects that enables Senior Management to gain a general overview of the portfolio and decide with lights-on
- Transparency: through independent, objective, and unbiased audits and recommendations, able to act as a sole source of truth based on facts
- Quality: through quality reviews of project deliverables and management products, that ensures that products are complete, delivered according to acceptance criteria, and fit for purpose
- Assurance: enabling confidence, management by exception, and informed decision-making, by performing rigorous reviews, providing recommendations, and challenging assumptions, estimates, and approach
- Predictability: of delivery timescales and costs, and of resource requirements, enabling agility, foresight, and capacity planning
- Accountability: through a clear definition of roles and responsibilities, allowing people to be held accountable for project delivery and benefits realization

- Alignment and focus: so that effort and resources are put in the right initiatives, and only projects that contribute to the organization's strategic objectives are carried out
- Organizational learning: of what is to be replicated and what is to be avoided in the future through the establishment of risk and knowledge databases that enable knowledge transfer across projects
- Resilience: by running what-if scenarios, exploring project dependencies, and ensuring mitigation/exploitation strategies are covered so that the organization can leverage their risks and opportunities and become resilient

It is not sufficient to have a PMO in place to automatically achieve better project performance and organizational value – the performance and maturity of the PMO itself is a determining factor. For high-performance PMOs, due to its positioning in the organizational structure, typically close to Directors or the C-level, these can act as a communicating bridge between strategy planning and strategy execution (PMI, 2013a), allowing this entity to be a business-driven strategic partner and an instrument of integration in the organization, bringing together people, processes, and departments for the achievement of project results. In fact, according to PMI's Pulse of the Profession Report (2017), organizations that align their PMO to strategy (i.e. have a strategic Enterprise PMO), report 38% more projects meet original goals and business intent and 33% fewer projects are deemed failures, a strong indicator of the role PMOs can play in project performance.

Conclusion

As a mindset, managing for projects brings new opportunities for project practitioners who now have a wider responsibility towards project performance, which goes beyond the management of the triple constraint. No longer is the environment deterministic of the success or failure of projects, but responsibility is shifted from institutions to individuals, where all of us are positioned as agents of change. Project actors are called to actively engage in activities that can improve the context for projects, creating a supportive setting for project performance, in the short and long-term.

Section III

Experience

Chapter 16

Critical success and failure factors in large-scale complex projects

Azadeh Rezvani and Pouria Khosravi

16.1 Introduction

Large-scale complex projects are known to be the prime enablers of business and social change; they are also vital contributors to future business success, although they are notoriously difficult to manage (Whitty and Maylor, 2009). Despite the growing number of complex projects implemented around the world, most complex projects fail to meet their objectives and experience substantial cost and schedule overruns (Brady and Davies, 2014; Flyvbjerg, 2014; Molloy and Chetty, 2015). For example, the Summer Olympics in Rio de Janeiro ended up costing $16.4 billion over the 2008 budget of $4.6 billion (Flyvbjerg et al., 2016). Another example of project cost and schedule overrun is the Sydney Opera House, which exceeded the original budget by 14 times, costing AU$102 million, and was delivered 10 years over schedule (Söderlund and Lenfle, 2013). These disappointing outcomes motivate further investigation into identifying the best practices for succeeding in complex projects (Toor and Ogunlana, 2009a; Zhang and Fan, 2013). Different project success indicators have been identified in prior reviews (e.g. Cooke-Davies, 2002; Davis, 2014; Jugdev and Müller, 2005). Davis (2014), for example, described the evolution of the idea of project success over successive decades, paying particular attention to different stakeholders' perceptions of success. Jugdev and Müller (2005) produced a historical review and focused on the development of project success at different time periods in the project life cycle. These prior reviews illustrate that success indicators have been identified and reproduced in various studies; however, project management literature has not considered the importance of identifying project success indicators across different types of projects, specifically complex projects. The unclear view of success and failure factors in complex projects has therefore created a gap to further identify success and failure factors in complex projects (Adoko et al., 2015; Liu and Wang, 2016).

This review extends our understanding in the field by first focusing on complex projects, owing to their specific features, including multiple joined organizations with often dissimilar objectives; a large scope, timeline and budget; a high level of technology advancement; a high degree of interdependency; and a high degree of uncertainty (Chang, 2013). These specific features make complex projects much more challenging to manage than smaller-scale projects (Toor and Ogunlana, 2009a).

We argue that evaluating success and failure factors in complex projects are important, as the meaning of success may vary in complex projects (Hyväri, 2006; Ika, 2009). Recent empirical research into complex projects suggests that complex projects may require different success factors (Alshawi et al., 2012; Chang, 2013; Toor and Ogunlana, 2009a; Turner and Zolin, 2012; Williams, 2016). This is mainly due to the differences in environmental variables, the nature of the project, the nature of the participant organizations and the prioritization of project goals (Toor and Ogunlana, 2010).

We also conduct a systematic review of *failure factors* in complex projects to broaden the understanding of the best ways to deliver successful projects. Recognizing and understanding the potential failure factors in complex projects are essential for acquiring and preserving the capabilities that are needed to perform well in dynamic, uncertain and constantly changing environments. Some failure factors have already been identified in the literature. For example, Thamhain (2013) revealed that the main causes of project failure stem from a lack of competent and effective leadership, lack of management commitment, instability of project team and redesign or changing project requirements. Shenhar et al. (2016) indicated that major causes of project failure arise from underestimating project requirements, material procurement and incorrectly installing software. A systematic review is needed to integrate the literature and to provide a comprehensive view of barriers specific to the success of complex projects. This study, therefore, aims to answer the following research questions:

Research Question 1: What are the project success factors in complex projects?
Research Question 2: What are the failure factors in complex projects?

16.2 Methodology

Following guidelines offered by Tranfield et al. (2003), we conducted a systematic review to identify and synthesize all the available research evidence of sufficient quality over three stages: planning, conducting and reporting the review. In the planning stage, we identified a need for a review and developed research questions and the review protocol. In the conducting stage, we performed searches, identified included studies, extracted data from studies and synthesized the data. In the reporting stage, we reported the results.

16.2.1 Search terms

This systematic literature review was guided by the research questions investigating complex project success and failure factors. A three-step search strategy was used. An initial search of Science Direct, Wiley and ABI/INFORM databases was undertaken to determine optimal search terms, followed by a second search using all relevant keywords. In the second search, following discussions between the co-authors and focusing on the key papers related to complex project success, a number of search terms were identified and grouped into two categories: ("complex project★" OR "mega project★" OR "large-scale project★" OR "large project★" OR "major project★") AND ("success" OR "project success factor★" OR "project performance" OR "project success criteria" OR "performance" OR "project success" OR "project failure" OR "barrier★" OR "project risk★" OR "poor performance" OR "cost overrun" OR "time overrun"). Finally, the selected terms were searched for across publication keywords, titles and abstracts. In total, the search identified in excess of 8660 papers. It was possible to get a large number of papers, even with some limitations to the search, while performing searches in databases with search strings. However, most of these papers were discussion papers, duplicate papers or contained one of the review search terms but did not address project success or barriers to success in complex projects. Therefore, once all studies had been retrieved from the databases, the inclusion and exclusion criteria were used to determine whether the study was relevant to the review, leaving a total of 513 publications for further analysis. After removing duplicates and unrelated papers, the authors applied a two-stage filtering process previously adopted by Yang et al. (2011) and Mok et al. (2015) in their literature review. In the first stage, the authors reviewed the abstracts and introductions of the remaining 513 papers that addressed project success indicators and barriers to success in complex projects. This process led to the extraction of 435 papers, leaving 78 papers for further review. In the second stage, the authors excluded irrelevant papers after the full text was retrieved and thoroughly assessed. As a result, 50 articles were included in this study and were considered to offer insights about project success and failure factors in complex project environments based on the inclusion criteria. We believe the articles identified for the systematic review are demonstrative of the literature, owing to the rigorous search process employed.

16.2.2 Inclusion/exclusion criteria

We limited our review to papers that: (1) were published in peer review journals, (2) were published between 2000 and mid-2016 and (3) provided empirical evidence regarding the success/ failure of large-scale complex projects. Studies in languages other than English, conceptual papers, conference papers, unpublished full-text documents and review papers were excluded from the search. Following the Global Alliance for Project Performance Standard (GAPPS, 2007) guidelines and prior studies in complex projects (Ahern et al., 2014; Chang, 2013; Locatelli et al., 2014; Rezvani et al., 2016) we consider a project as being "complex" if it has at least one of the following characteristics: a high degree of uncertainty and mixture of joined organizations and sub-contracting (Ahern et al., 2014); rapid change of technology (Davies and Mackenzie, 2014); high degree of interdependency between a number of system parts and organizations involved (Locatelli and Mancini, 2012); strong legal, social or environmental implications from undertaking the project (Chang, 2013); strategic importance of the project to the organization or organizations involved (Mazur et al., 2014; Rezvani et al., 2017); stakeholders with conflicting needs regarding the characteristics of the project's product (Locatelli et al., 2014) and newness of technology (Robinson Fayek et al., 2006).

16.2.3 Data synthesis

This chapter used a combination of analytical approaches to guarantee a rigorous research process and to increase the validity and reliability of the systematic literature review (Levy and Ellis, 2006), namely descriptive and thematic analysis (Morgan and Smircich, 1980; Ritchie, 2013). The descriptive analysis allows the main characteristics of the field under investigation to be identified (Dey, 2003) such as a year of publication, countries, methodology and study design. The thematic analysis consists of synthesizing the main outcomes extracted from the literature and condensing the text into fewer content-related categories of qualitative data via content analysis (Braun and Clarke, 2006; Guest et al., 2011). Content analysis is a method used to determine the major facets of a data set by counting the number of times a topic appears (Neuendorf, 2002). According to the literature, this is a valid method to undertake a systematic literature review (Levy and Ellis, 2006). Following Ritchie et al.'s (2013) method, a series of steps were undertaken in order to conduct a thematic analysis. First, the literature was read and textually analyzed to derive a set of suitable success and failure factors. This led to identifying recurring themes from the collected literature with specific reference to complex projects and their success and failure factors in order to answer the first and second research questions. After the themes were identified, the first author arranged the factors and their attributes using a Microsoft Excel spreadsheet. Finally, the results of the complete success and failure factors were condensed into a table to answer the research questions and were revised as necessary by all authors. Any discordances were settled during meetings with authors and the complete set of final success and failure factors in complex projects were finalized. Section 4 of this chapter, the results section, provides the final detailed success and failure factors in complex projects.

16.3 Overview of selected publications

16.3.1 Annual publications

As shown in Figure 16.1, a rapid increase of publications on complex projects began in 2006, which then progressed to a peak of eight publications from 2012 to 2016. The fast pace of research into complex or large projects can be attributed to the advanced technology, rapid globalization and gradual increase in interest in exploring the best ways to deliver successful complex projects (Williams, 2016).

16.3.2 Projects per country

In order to ascertain countries with the most research on complex projects, we conducted a simple counting of papers. There were a number of papers that focused on complex projects which were not attributed to any specific country or were focused on multiple countries; these were considered to be "International" papers. Figure 16.2 presents research into complex projects based on countries. The vast majority of studies investigating complex projects came from the United States, which had the highest number of publications (n=10), followed by China, Australia and International (five

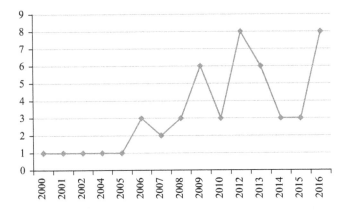

Figure 16.1 Publication per year.

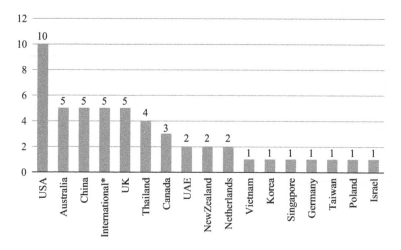

Figure 16.2 Projects per country.

* International category contains studies that were focused on multiple countries.

publications each). It is noticeable that contributions from researchers investigating complex projects in other countries are very low. This could be due to a limited number of complex projects in those countries or could be due to publications being in a language other than English, which were not considered in this study.

16.3.3 Research methods of included studies

In our attempt to understand the methodological diversity in research related to project success and barriers, we found that researchers have used multiple research methods to study project success in project management literature. Figure 16.3 shows a summary of the various research methods used by researchers; these include survey (20), case study (18), mixed methods (7), document analysis (1) and interview (4). The most preferred

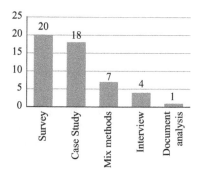

Figure 16.3 Research methods.

Table 16.1 Academic journals and number of publications

Journal Name	Number of Publications
International Journal of Project Management	16
Project Management Journal	8
Engineering, Construction and Architectural Management	3
Construction Innovation	2
Information System Journal	2
Construction Management and Economics	1
Cost Engineering	1
Decision Science	1
Journal of Enterprise Information Management	1
Engineering Applications of Artificial Intelligence	1
The Journal of High Technology Management Research	1
Communications of the ACM	1
Interfaces	1
Interlending & Document Supply	1
European Planning Studies	1
Journal of Business Research	1
Government Information Quarterly	1
MIS Quarterly	1
Progress in Planning	1
Public in Administration	1
IEEE Transactions on Engineering Management	1
System Dynamics Review	1
Utilities Policy	1
Information Systems Management	1

research method adopted by researchers is the quantitative and case study approaches (see Figure 16.3). This could be due to the findings being generalizable to similar projects.

16.3.4 Journal name and number of publications

This review identified a number of publications from academic journals which could be useful to researchers seeking to conduct future studies in complex projects. As Table 16.1 shows, the IJPM and PMJ have the most published articles in this area.

16.4 Results

16.4.1 Critical success factors in complex projects

Table 16.2 highlights the critical success factors in complex projects. The total number of critical success factors identified from the 27 publications is 28. As shown in the figure, the publications are indicated in numbers with their respective paper representatives presented in the Appendix section. Additionally, the number of times a CSF is identified by author(s) is accumulated and presented. The accumulation was, however,

Table 16.2 Success factors

Success Factors	Toor and Ogunlana (2009a)	Zhang and Fan (2013)	Ogunlana (2008)	Locatelli and Mancini (2012)	Dimitriou et al. (2013)	Tai et al. (2009)	Alshawi et al. (2012)	Liu and Leitner (2012)	Toor and Ogunlana (2010)	Hui et al. (2008)	Williams (2016)	Chang et al. (2013)	Mazur et al. (2014)	Lynels et al. (2001)	Turner and Zolin (2012)	Dvir et al. (2006)	Kwak and Smith (2009)	Adoko et al. (2015)	Rezvani et al. (2016)	Art Gowan and Mathieu (2005)	McGillivray et al. (2009)	Yetton et al. (2000)	Ferratt et al. (2006)	Sauer et al. (2007)	Chua et al. (2012)	Lech (2013)	Liu and Wang (2016)	Total
Stakeholders satisfaction	✓	✓					✓				✓				✓											✓	✓	7
Communication		✓	✓				✓					✓	✓		✓						✓							6
Project planning	✓	✓			✓										✓													5
Meeting users/customers/owner's requirement	✓	✓	✓													✓					✓							5
Top management support													✓						✓			✓	✓					4
Training												✓									✓		✓					3
Health and safety		✓							✓												✓							3
Meeting design goals												✓				✓			✓									3
Problem-solving												✓	✓						✓									3
Staff commitment			✓																		✓							2
Technical capabilities							✓											✓										2
Defense capability												✓				✓												2
Technical support																			✓							✓		2
Mission clarity												✓	✓						✓									2
Project member wellbeing												✓																1
Achieve business goals																									✓			1
Software selection																							✓					1
Team contributions																							✓					1
Consulting capability																							✓					1
Achieve organizational goals																										✓		1
Involvement of the client	✓																											1
Project control	✓																											1
Risks management		✓																										1
Claim management		✓																										1
Absence of conflicts		✓																										1
Standardization of the project delivery				✓																								1
Competence		✓																										1
Project efficiency																				✓								1

used to rank the CSFs identified from 2000 to mid-2016. It is observed from Table 16.2 that several factors account for successful large-scale projects, however, the top factors are stakeholder satisfaction, specific plans, open communication, Meeting users/ customers/owner's requirement and top management support. Each of these factors was identified 7, 6, 5, 5 and 4 times by the 27 papers considered in this study, respectively. This reveals how important these factors are to the success of large-scale projects irrespective of jurisdiction, the stage of project, sector or project model

16.4.2 Failure factors in complex projects

The total number of failure factors identified from the 28 publications is 44. As shown in Table 16.3, the publications are indicated in numbers with their respective paper. Additionally, the number of times a factor is identified by author(s) is accumulated and presented. The accumulation was, however, used to rank the failure factor identified from 2000 to 2016. As Table 16.3 shows, of the 44 factors that impede the successful delivery of complex projects, the topmost three factors are poor communication, poor planning/unclear initial requirements and redesign/rework/changing project requirements are the most frequently cited barrier factors in complex projects. This reveals how important these factors are to the failure of large-scale complex projects irrespective of jurisdiction, the stage of project, sector or project model.

Poor project planning, redesign or changing project requirements and poor communications – ranked first and second among the important failure factors identified in the literature and was identified in nine and eight different publications as the most frequently cited (see Table 16.3). While this may highlight the lack of clear initial requirements, it also reflects the nature of complex projects, which includes ambiguous project goals, a long time horizon and complex relationships. It has been argued that without a clear project design and documented requirements there is a high possibility of new requirements being added to the project and existing requirements being discarded (Patanakul, 2014), undermining the chance of project success (Hall et al., 2012; Ling and Lau, 2002; Thamhain, 2013; Rezvani, Khosravi and Ashkanasy, 2018).

Large projects cannot be completed without detailed planning from the start as the complexity is very high, which in turn may influence their development (Janssen et al., 2015 ; Rezvani and Khosravi, 2018). In order to overcome project design and implementation barriers, one solution would be to start out with a sufficient front-end plan that accounts for likely changes in the project direction or changes in technology and the legal environment, since most complex projects have little flexibility after initiation due to their high degree of regulation (Van Marrewijk et al., 2008). Studies have highlighted that projects with better initial design processes show a higher success rate than those with insufficient front-end plans (Davies and Mackenzie, 2014; Robinson Fayek et al., 2006). Investment in the early stages of the project can help to maintain the schedule and improve quality. Therefore, cost reduction is secured and better outcomes are achieved (Davies and Mackenzie, 2014).

Improper communication or failure to communicate effectively with internal and external stakeholders was considered a hindrance factor for project success in complex projects (Mazur et al., 2014; Rezvani et al., 2016; Rezvani, Barrett and Khosravi, 2018). This could be due to organizations engaged in complex projects focusing primarily on the technical aspects of a project, but lacking an emphasis on communication with

Table 16.3 Failure factors

Failure Factors	Lech (2013)	Alshawi et al. (2012)	Patanakul (2014)	Hall et al. (2012)	Rose and Schlichter (2013)	Yetton et al. (2000)	Locatelli and Mancini (2012)	Hui, et al. (2008)	Robinson Fayek et al. (2006)	Dimitriou et al. (2013)	You and Yang (2012)	Toor and Ogunlana (2009b)	Tai et al. (2009)	Thamhain (2013)	Ling and Lau (2002)	Flyvbjerg (2008)	Van Marrewijk et al. (2008)	Koppenjan et al. (2011)	Liu et al. (2016)	Long et al. (2004)	Brookes and Locatelli (2015)	Giezen (2012)	Han et al. (2009)	Anthopoulos et al. (2016)	Shenhar et al. (2016)	Akkermans and van Oorschot (2016)	Jansen et al. (2015)	Davies and Mackenzie (2014)	Number of references
Poor planning/unclear initial requirements	✓	✓	✓	✓			✓				✓					✓	✓							✓		✓			9
Redesign/Rework/Changing project requirements			✓	✓										✓									✓	✓	✓	✓	✓		8
Poor communication/relationship with stakeholders								✓				✓	✓	✓	✓		✓									✓	✓		8
Lack of a competent and effective leader			✓									✓		✓															3
Instability of the project team		✓				✓							✓											✓					3
Poor risk management		✓		✓																									2
Poor project control																		✓						✓					2
Conflict in the project team						✓								✓															2
Contractual disputes		✓	✓																										2
Governmental processes		✓									✓																		2
Undervaluation/changing of regulation requirements							✓							✓															2
Price increments		✓												✓															2
Unavailability of resources		✓																							✓				2
Technical difficulties						✓								✓															2
System complexity																						✓						✓	2
The newness of the project							✓		✓																				2
Lack of organizational structure													✓																1
Lack of uniform standards for information												✓																	1
Lack of access to relevant information										✓																			1
Changing organizational priorities														✓															1
The disproportionate focus on policy setting			✓																										1

(Continued)

Table 16.3 Continued

Failure Factors	Lech (2013)	Alshawi et al. (2012)	Patanakul (2014)	Hall et al. (2012)	Rose and Schlichter (2013)	Yetton et al. (2000)	Locatelli and Mancini (2012)	Hui et al. (2008)	Robinson Fayek et al. (2006)	Dimitriou et al. (2013)	Yau and Yang (2012)	Toor and Ogunlana (2009b)	Tai et al. (2009)	Thamhain (2013)	Ling and Lau (2002)	Flyvberg (2008)	Van Marrewijk et al. (2008)	Koppenjan et al. (2011)	Liu et al. (2016)	Long et al. (2004)	Brookes and Locatelli (2015)	Giezen (2012)	Han et al. (2009)	Anthopoulos et al. (2016)	Shenhar et al. (2016)	Akkermans and van Oorschot (2016)	Jansen et al. (2015)	Davies and Mackenzie (2014)	Number of references
Excessive and misplaced trust in commercial partners	✓																												1
Use of unproven vendors									✓																				1
Change management																								✓					1
Outsourcing structures where owner firms do not maintain high levels of dominance over the activities								✓																					1
Lack of management commitment														✓															1
Wrongful use of power												✓																	1
Complexity in managing contract																											✓		1
Lack of trust to team members					✓																								1
Unqualified engineers		✓																											1
Lack of teamwork experiences												✓																	1
Ineffective response plan			✓																										1
The inaccuracy of project information															✓														1
The inadequate business process model				✓																									1
Inadequate security measures for the eventual operation of the scheme				✓																									1
Lack of coordination with local governments		✓																											1
Political intervention											✓																		1
Lack of political antennae																	✓												1
Changing market or customer needs														✓															1
Difficulty in land acquisition or site availability																			✓										1
Inappropriate scheduling tools																							✓						1
Technology change														✓															1
Incorrect installations																									✓				1
Software delay																									✓				1

internal and external stakeholders. Lack of communication as one of the frequently cited barrier factors can be overcome by ensuring more effective communication focused on setting clear goals and requirements, and upholding the principles of transparency and open communication among all the stakeholders involved in complex projects (Liu et al., 2016; Remington and Pollack, 2007). This will help to ensure the commitment of all organizations, allow all possible requirements to be identified and all voices to be heard (Janssen et al., 2015).

16.5 Discussion and recommendations

This study was designed to conduct a systematic literature review in order to develop a comprehensive list of project success and failure factors in large-scale complex projects. In order to achieve this aim, we consolidated the literature on complex project settings from over the past 16 years.

To answer our first research question, we systematically reviewed project success factors in large-scale complex projects. In contrast to previous project success reviews, which classify success indicators into decades with a focus on the time frame of the project lifecycle (e.g. Jugdev and Müller, 2005; Davis, 2014). Our results show that stakeholder satisfaction, specific plans, open communication, meeting users/customers/ owner's requirement and top management support are mostly identified critical factors to achieve success in large-scale complex projects. Further empirical research is recommended to find out which success factors are associated with different types of complex projects or the benefit of using more project-type-specific success indicators in complex projects.

In relation to the second research question, we proposed an integrated list of failure factors impacting the successful delivery of complex projects. This systematic identification of failure factors in large-scale complex projects fills an existing gap in the project management literature and, from a practice perspective, assists in more effectively distributing limited resources, such as budget, time and manpower (Kardes et al., 2013; Toor and Ogunlana, 2010; Rezvani and Khosravi, 2018). As shown in Figure 16.3, poor project planning, redesign or changing project requirements and poor communications were identified as the most important factors that impede the chance of project success in large and complex projects. This indicates that technical and financial factors are not the only crucial factors that undermine the successful delivery of complex projects (Rezvani et al., 2012). To sum up, when it comes to complex project management, factors such as ineffective communication with internal and external stakeholders, project team instability and incompetent leaders can jeopardize the project's success. It would be worth considering these factors in more detail before the complex project is implemented in order to provide a useful guide to potential barriers that undermine high performance in complex projects. This could also provide additional insight into why achieving success in complex projects is so difficult for some organizations but not for others. In addition, the frequency used of critical success and failure factors must be interpreted carefully. The low frequency used of the remaining success and failure factors does not imply that they are not important. Clearly, more research is required to pay deserved attention to the remaining success and failure factors.

From the bibliometric analysis point of view, the number of academic references in the area of complex projects has increased in recent years, which is most likely due to the increase in infrastructure needs in developed and developing countries. Despite the significant cost overruns, revenue shortfalls and remarkably poor performance records in terms of economic and public domains, complex projects continue to be initiated in large numbers around the world (Flyvbjerg et al., 2003). As reported in Figure 16.2, most of the research on complex projects is based on data from developed countries. It may be worthwhile examining complex projects by specifically focusing on the context of developing countries to account for the nature and structure of the local industry; that is, how they differ from developed countries in terms of challenges, requirements or management styles, or what unique characteristics or specific challenges arise due to infrastructure, local cultural values or language barriers.

The research methods used in the project management literature on complex project topics appear to be more or less positivistic. Further research is needed that may focus on comprehensive qualitative and quantitative research to study project success indicators and barriers to success in complex projects.

16.6 Failure factors

Our review provides a comprehensive list of success and failure factors in large and complex projects. By identifying success factors in large and complex projects, project managers can determine improvement measures to raise the probability of success and reduce the chances of any setbacks in their own projects. There may also be practical benefits to policy development in improving the way project success is assessed in complex projects. This review may help organizations to effectively divert their resources to where maximum success lies while helping project leaders to accomplish their objectives.

There are also multiple benefits of using the comprehensive list of failure factors for practitioners. First of all, this study offers practitioners a more comprehensive understanding of the potential failure factors in managing complex projects so that they might proactively address those challenges prior to problems emerging, and effectively acquire and preserve the capabilities that are needed to perform well in a dynamic, uncertain and constantly changing environment. We suggest that, given the complexity and dynamics of complex projects, all stakeholders who are involved in complex projects should have an understanding of the different factors that impede the success of complex projects in order to implement proper strategies from the initial project stages (van Marrewijk et al., 2008). Second, an integrated list of failure factors in complex projects could help organizations to effectively distribute limited resources, such as budget, time and manpower (Toor and Ogunlana, 2010). Third, by increasing awareness of various failure factors, managers may be able to proactively respond to unexpected problems before they pose a significant threat. Proactive responses could significantly enhance project efficiency and increase the chance of success (Kardes et al., 2013).

Chapter 17

Performance and measurement

An interdisciplinary study of public sector projects

Maude Brunet, Jean-Sébastien Marchand and Mylaine Breton

17.1 Introduction

After more than six decades of project management research, interest in the notions of "performance" and "success" not only persists, but is actually growing (Padalkar & Gopinath, 2016). The number of projects, along with their scale, is increasing in many societies. Researchers have estimated that around one third of Western economies are now "projectified" (Schoper, Wald, Ingason, & Fridgeirsson, 2018), bringing increased reliance on temporary organizations (projects) to enhance action and strategic effort (Godenhjelm, Lundin, & Sjöblom, 2015).

Within this overall trend, it is important to look more specifically at public sector organizations. Interdisciplinary research that combines public administration, political science and project management to develop a more thorough understanding of public sector projects remains scarce. Godenhjelm et al. (2015) were concerned with identifying what is driving the projectification of the public sector, and in what ways the public context matters. They see a need for comparative research on the drivers and consequences of public sector projectification in supranational and national contexts. Schoper et al. (2018) responded to this call by comparatively analyzing three national economies: Germany, Norway and Iceland. Their extensive quantitative research programme produced estimates of the share of project work in different industries, including the public sector. They show that the public sector relies significantly less on project work than other sectors of the economy across two of the three countries: in Germany, 17.8% of public sector activity is undertaken through project work (versus 34.7% for the whole economy); in Norway the rate is 14.2% in the public sector (versus 32.6% for the economy as a whole); in Iceland, 33.3% of public sector activity is undertaken through project work (versus 27.7% for the economy as a whole). Among projects in the public sector, 12% are externally commissioned in Germany, 19% in Norway and 10% in Iceland. Clearly, though the public sector is not as highly "projectified" as other economic sectors, a significant portion of its activity takes the form of projects, and there is good reason to better understand project performance in public sector contexts.

This chapter aims to explore what is known about the performance of public sector projects. The first section looks at how project performance is defined. The second section discusses the development of performance measurement in the field of public administration and considers its application to projects. The third section considers how public sector project performance might be improved, and addresses management issues. The chapter makes two main contributions. It exposes project management scholars and practitioners to the public administration literature on performance. As well, it offers insights into public sector project performance that may contribute to enhancing the success of ever more common projects.

17.2 Project performance

This section presents a definition of project performance that is generally accepted in the project management literature. High and low-performing projects are presented to illustrate common causes of poor performance.

17.2.1 Defining project performance

The Oxford dictionary proposes the following two interpretations of "performance": (1) the action or process of performing a task or function; and (2) a task or operation seen in terms of how successfully it is performed. Applied to projects, these definitions cover two dimensions: the process of performing a project, and the performance of the project in terms of the outcomes it produces.

The project management literature includes a vast body of research around the criteria used to assess project success, and factors involved in success or failure. Söderlund (2011) described this trend as the "Factor School'" of thought in project management, which appeared in the 1960s and took off in the 1980s. The subjects of "success" and "performance management" remain alive and well in 21st-century project management literature, ranking respectively second and fifth most influential themes in a historiographic study by Padalkar and Gopinath (2016).

With regard to project performance, a fundamental distinction is made between project success – measured against the overall objectives of the project – and project management success – measured against traditional cost, time and quality indicators of performance (Cooke-Davies, 2002, p. 185). Though research has traditionally focused on project management success, applying an objectivist perspective and quantitative methodologies (Ika, 2009), there is a recent tendency to broaden the notion of success to include value creation, long-term perspectives and capacity building (Söderlund, 2011). Accordingly, theoretical perspectives and research methods have adapted to embrace this more multidimensional construct of performance. An illustrative example of project management success come from Serghei Floricel, Michela, and Piperca's (2016, p. 1369) quantitative study of complexity and project performance that presents four dependent variables in project performance:

1) Completion performance – whether the project met planned resource expenditures and deadlines, and accomplished the entire planned scope and all artefact functions;
2) Innovation performance – whether a project produced outstanding or pioneering achievements for artefact uses, functionality and performance;
3) Operation performance – the extent to which the project runs uniformly and reliably, with low maintenance and exploitation costs and few repairs; and
4) Value creation performance – the extent to which a project meets expected financial returns, satisfies user and stakeholder needs, and enhances promoter reputation.

Projects are complex and can assume many organizational forms: they may be temporary inter-organizational structures, or even networks of organizations from public, private, and civil society sectors. Projects involve numerous actors and, along with the specific objectives of different stakeholders, the contextual environment influences decision-making and power relations. While the notion of public organizations and what might be considered "public projects" is heterogeneous, Bozeman (2007) proposed that their common feature is that they are driven by the public interest and public values. For Bozeman (2007, pp. 12–13), the public interest is an ideal, referring to "the outcomes best serving the long-run survival and well-being of a social collective construed as a "public"; and a society's public values are those "providing normative consensus about (1) the rights, benefits, and prerogatives to which citizens should (and should not) be entitled; (2) the obligations of citizens to society, the state, and one another; and (3) the principles on which governments and policies should be based". While "public values" are contingent on the socio-political context and might evolve slowly, Flyvbjerg (2001) argues that researchers should take them into account in social science inquiries. He bases his phronetic approach to research on value rationality to study how values are applied in society, which contrasts with the classical epistemic model based on deterministic premises of rationality borrowed from the natural sciences.

The discussion above reveals that even the notion of "public project" is multifaceted and complex. Although it is tempting to clearly distinguish public from private projects, it seems more accurate to conceive of a continuum with one end being entirely public and the other entirely private, and a wide range of options in between. That said, the public sector has a number of distinct features, such as rigid bureaucratic and hierarchical structures, specific norms and regulations. Regarding the performance of public sector projects, the literature is quite scarce and inconclusive. A study by Besner and Hobbs (2013) suggests that the public context has a negative influence on project success. On the other hand, Flyvbjerg (2013) finds that inaccurate costing, forecasts and estimates for rail projects are more than twice as high in private than public sector projects. From a multilevel perspective, the interplay between project success and organizational success also presents interesting challenges (Too & Weaver, 2014). As projects are strategic drivers to implement an organizational strategy, there is a link to study between project and organizational performance. Rolstadås, Tommelein, Morten, and Ballard (2014) suggest using the Pentagon model to evaluate the performance of the project organization, based on two formal dimensions (structure and technology) and three informal ones (culture, social relations and networks, and interaction). Rolstadås et al. (2014) argue that the project management approach has an impact on project success, and needs to fit with the project's requirements and purposes. This notion of "fit" is important in project management, especially considering the uniqueness of projects, and has been extensively developed from a contingency-based perspective (Thomas & Mullaly, 2008). We will look, in the next section on high-performing projects, at how a project management approach "fits" with a specific context. We will then present characteristics of low-performing projects.

17.2.2 High-performing projects: Increasing the odds of success

In their study of megaprojects, Shenhar and Holzmann (2017) find that the most successful projects share three common points: (1) there is a clear strategic vision of the project's outcome which is communicated and understood; (2) there is total alignment of all parties with the goals, means and difficulties expected; and (3) project actors and structures adapt to complexity. We will briefly discuss each of these attributes.

Clear strategic vision

Project governance to coordinate information, work and communication is essential to establishing a clear strategic vision for a project. Project governance has been found to have a positive impact on project performance (Biesenthal & Wilden, 2014; Sirisomboonsuk, Gu, Cao, & Burns, 2018). Pitsis, Sankaran, Gudergan, and Clegg (2014, p. 1287) distinguish between governance mechanisms that are internal to the project (organizational structures, roles and responsibilities of boards and management, control systems, auditing and reporting mechanisms, lines of communication, and the complexity of contractual design and execution) and those that are external to the project (government policies, laws and regulations, financial markets and institutional frameworks, political environments, power in direct and indirect stakeholder relations, and the reporting of all these in various media).

Total alignment

The fit between project and organizational structure should be based on underlying values important to attaining explicit objectives and benefits. Thomas and Mullaly (2008) use the notion of "fit" to evaluate the relationship between business orientation, environment and organizational context, along with project management implementation and value generation. A study by Godenhjelm et al. (2015) suggests, on the other hand, that the project context should adapt to fit project work and needs. This might be difficult when organizational structures are static, as in the hierarchical and bureaucratic structures often still found in the public sector that limit horizontal relations and network formation (Kelman, 2011). Gil, Ludrigan, Pinto, and Puranam (2017) propose that for public sector projects, effectiveness should be measured in terms of economic performance, technical functionality, social fit, environmental fit, political legitimacy, and efficiency in terms of cost and time. The literature on project shaping, targeting the front-end phase, also emphasizes that justifying societal needs and clarifying underlying social values help to make sure that the best projects and best options are selected and implemented (Williams & Samset, 2010).

Adapting to complexity

Challenges in adapting to complexity relate to temporal dimensions – as the project life cycle is often much longer than the electoral cycle – to the politico-administrative drivers behind decision-making, and to the strong contextual embeddedness of project organizations (Godenhjelm et al., 2015). Investing effort at the front end to set up project governance structures and mechanisms has been found to improve project performance (Miller & Lessard, 2000; Pinto & Winch, 2016). Yet, those governance regimes need to be flexible so they can be adjusted throughout the project, as needs develop and practitioners reflect on them and adjust the systems in place (Miller & Hobbs, 2005). A governance regime must be dynamic, not static, to respond to the dynamic process of the project and its interaction with other organizational structures and actors

(S. Floricel, Piperca, & Banik, 2011). Risk management (Miller & Lessard, 2001), contract management (Benítez-Ávila, Hartmann, Dewulf, & Henseler, 2018), coordination (Pilbeam, 2013) and stakeholder inclusion (Eskerod, Huemann, & Ringhofer, 2015) are avenues for improving project performance that have been explored by researchers. For example, Mesa, Molenaar, and Alarcón (2016, p. 1089) found that the most influential drivers for project performance are communication, alignment of interests and objectives, team working, trust and gain/pain sharing. These provide interesting means of further exploring the performance of public projects, which remains very focused on financial performance in line with New Public Management (Andersen, Busi, & Onsøyen, 2014; Price, Schwartz, Cohen, Scott, & Manson, 2016).

17.2.3 Low-performing projects: Learning from failures

Many studies have been conducted to document and understand project failures (e.g. Flyvbjerg, 2014), notably in the context of megaprojects, which are often initiated/financed/owned by government (Winch & Leiringer, 2016). Gil et al. (2017) recognize several types of organizational pressure that might negatively impact project performance: legitimacy, commitment, evolving organizational structures, environmental uncertainty, and misalignment between product and organizational structure. Low-performing projects can be looked at from structural, network and evolutionary perspectives. The list below describes some of the causes of poor performance highlighted in the literature:

- The wrong projects are selected, costs and time are underestimated and benefits are overestimated (Flyvbjerg, 2014);
- The context and complexity of major government projects are poorly understood and systems are not adapted (Patanakul, Kwak, Zwikael, & Liu, 2016);
- The long duration of projects versus the short electoral cycle (Godenhjelm et al., 2015);
- Poorly adapted project governance (Miller & Lessard, 2000);
- Inadequate contractual agreements (Suprapto, Bakker, Mooi, & Hertogh, 2016);
- Conflicts between stakeholders (von Danwitz, 2018);
- The complexity of the project (Chapman, 2016; Kujala, Brady, & Putila, 2014);
- Inadequate or deficient risk management (Flyvbjerg, Bruzelius, & Rothengatter, 2003).

Moreover, the scale and complexity of projects continue to increase, posing additional challenges (Flyvbjerg, 2014). While project management researchers have long been interested in the question of project performance, there are still too few contributions from the field of public administration that have shed light on public sector project performance from that perspective. The next section looks at the public administration literature on measuring project performance to find additional insights on the question of performance.

17.3 Measuring performance

This section covers three themes. First, we discuss the use of a Performance Measurement System (PMS) in measuring project performance. Second, we explore PMS implementation and look at common challenges. Third, we explore pitfalls and unintended effects encountered with the use of PMS.

17.3.1 Measuring project performance

Measuring an organization's performance has never been simple (Kirby, 2005; Richard, Devinney, Yip, & Johnson, 2009). It requires some form of performance measurement system (PMS), which may be defined as "the regular collection and reporting of information about the efficiency, quality and effectiveness" of a programme or project (Agostino & Arnaboldi, 2015, p. 119; Nyhan & Martin, 1999, p. 348). The main use for performance measurement is to gather and display information on service quality, project costs and results, and inform managers on opportunities for improvement (Wholey & Hatry, 1992). Measuring performance also enables us to appreciate the success of project management.

There is no "one best measurement" system, especially for complex organizations, where a variety of indicators might be needed to adequately measure performance (Behn, 2003, p. 599). Over the last 50 years, cost, time and quality (the "Iron Triangle") have been the trio at the core of project performance measurement (Atkinson, 1999); a fourth musketeer is "meeting technical requirements". However, the effectiveness of PMS that rely exclusively on these four measures has gradually come into question (Bourne, Mills, Wilcox, Neely, & Platts, 2000; Walton & Dawson, 2001). Various additional indicators have been developed in the literature and applied in practice. Indicators may track inputs (e.g. costs), processes (e.g. activities), outputs (e.g. units produced) or outcomes (e.g. impact on a population) (Hatry, 2006; Melkers & Willoughby, 2005). Designing a performance measure requires an understanding of the purpose of the measurement, the entity measured, the dimension of quality being measured, the type of measurement, and the intended audience (Eddy, 1998). Indicators can be designed to control delivery, improve accountability and influence action (Micheli & Neely, 2010).

A set of three to seven indicators is usually privileged in a PMS; too many measures can be "difficult and costly" to collect (Center for Business Practices, 2005, p. 2). Frequently used indicators include:

- Return on investment (ROI – net benefit/cost);
- Productivity (output produced per unit of input);
- Cost of quality (cost of quality/actual cost);
- Cost performance (earned value/actual cost);
- Schedule performance (earned value/planned value);
- Customer satisfaction;
- Cycle time of a project;
- Performance regarding requirements;
- Employee satisfaction;
- Alignment with strategic business goals.

Models to measure performance have emerged in the literature. For example, the *Project management performance assessment* model proposes a set of six criteria: leadership, project management staff, policy and strategy, partnerships and resources, project life cycle management processes, and key performance indicators (Bryde, 2003). This sort of model, especially the use of "key performance indicators", has been supported by empirical evidence and linked to project success (Mir & Pinnington, 2014), knowledge acquisition and transfer in the project environment (Todorović, Petrović, Mihić,

Obradović, & Bushuyev, 2015), and performance of large-scale public sector development projects (Ogunlana, 2010).

Performance measurement is motivated in part by the assumption that performance data can inform the public about an organization's performance, increase managers' awareness of performance, and lead to more accountable behaviour (Radin, 2011). Using a PMS may render authorities more accountable and lead them to improve the use of resources and focus on achieving results (Van Der Knaap, 2006). However, while accountability is often conceptualized as a 2x2 matrix that varies according to the source of control (internal or external) and the degree of control (high or low) (Romzek & Dubnick, 1987, p. 229), performance measurement focuses on so-called bureaucratic accountability that corresponds to high internal control, instead of other forms of accountability, such as professional, legal or political accountability (Radin, 2011, p. 108). The evaluation process further depends on whether it is performed by external or internal auditors, or by academics (Siemiatycki, 2009). Other expectations of performance measurement might include control, ethical behaviour, performance, integrity, democracy or legitimacy, and justice or equity (Dubnick & Frederickson, 2009).

17.3.2 Implementing a Performance Measurement System (PMS)

The implementation of a PMS in a public organization is often associated with important complexity (Barrett, 2004). Measurement systems may be perceived negatively by employees and managers, for reasons ranging from not wanting their work to be monitored, to the burden associated with additional administrative tasks involved in measurement (Marchand & Brunet, In Press). Implementing performance measures in these organizations is influenced by political and cultural factors, such as the interests of different groups, openness to change, and attitudes toward innovation and risk taking (De Lancer Julnes & Holzer, 2001). Therefore, the decision to implement a PMS should be carefully considered.

In their classic introduction to the balanced scorecard, Kaplan and Norton (1993) identify four barriers to the implementation of PMS: (1) a vision and strategy that are not actionable, (2) discontinuity between the measurement strategy and individual or organizational goals, (3) a lack of resources and (4) feedback concentrated solely on short-term results. Similarly, Bourne et al. (2000) finds three barriers to the implementation of PMS: (1) resistance to measurement, (2) technical or information technology issues, and (3) unreliable top management commitment. Finally, in their literature review on the subject, Bourne et al. (2003) describe 10 barriers to PMS implementation: difficulties in evaluating the relative importance of different measurements; poorly defined metrics; negotiated goals rather than requirements adapted to the main stakeholders; inappropriate methods; time and cost; use of quantitative results in areas that are more qualitative in nature; a large number of measures; difficulty in breaking down goals for lower levels of the organization; the need for a highly developed information system; and striving for perfection. These barriers often cause or increase resistance among staff and management. PMS implementation "redistributes access to information which can be seen as threatening to senior managers whose power base is altered" (Bourne et al., 2000, p. 767).

Different ways of overcoming these barriers have been identified. Classic works point to the need for senior management support, incentives and information architecture (e.g. Eccles, 1991). More recently, Parmenter (2015, p. 110) stressed the importance of agreeing on "timing, resources and approach", but also of effective communication, empowerment of employees, training, adapted methodologies, support for employee learning, and the devolution of responsibility to teams for developing and implementing their own performance measures. Chances of success can be increased through "earlier involvement of IT specialists, application of data retrieval and manipulation tools and allocation of resources" (Bourne et al., 2000, p. 767).

Ultimately, there is no single "recipe" for measuring project performance or implementing a PMS. As the contingency-based perspective suggests, it is important to understand the contextual and institutional features of the project organization, and refer back to the underlying values and objectives of the project in order to adapt the PMS and provide the supports needed for its implementation (Flyvbjerg, 2001). If designed and implemented properly, performance measurement systems can bring about positive change and quality improvement (Levesque & Sutherland, 2017).

In the next section, we will look at some of the pitfalls and unintended effects encountered in implementing a PMS.

17.3.3 Performance measurement: Pitfalls and unintended effects

As we know, public projects and the context in which they are undertaken are particularly complex (Klakegg, Williams, Magnussen, & Glasspool, 2008), and this complexity may have a number of immediate and delayed consequences (Abdel-Hamid, 2010). At least three pitfalls have been reported in the literature related to the use of performance measurement:

1) *"Accountability dilemma"* refers to the situation where the effort required by managers to carry out performance measurement reduces effort in the actual work, and results in a decrease in performance (Bovens, Schillemans, & 't Hart, 2008, p. 228; Halachmi, 2002, p. 371).
2) *"Accountability trap"* results when managers who are measured frequently get better at meeting the formal "theoretical" requirements, without necessarily improving "real" organizational performance (Bovens et al., 2008, p. 228; Van Thiel & Leeuw, 2002, p. 271).
3) *"Innovation dissuasiveness"* is when innovative and entrepreneurial behaviour is not measured, and therefore goes unrewarded. Managers may then focus on measured activities and disengage from innovative pursuits (see Bovens et al., 2008, p. 228; Herzlinger, 2006, p. 62).

Strategies to avoid these pitfalls include the use of multiple and heterogeneous indicators (Behn, 2003). This approach may, however, create confusion among employees about what to prioritize from among a great number of indicators (Micheli & Neely, 2010). However, any attempt to select indicators will confront the dilemma of either choosing standard indicators that will enable comparison with other projects, or specific indicators that are better adapted to the particular project. The tension between these two approaches is referred to as the "one-size-fits-all" paradox (see Radin, 2006, p. 35).

The first approach usually leads to maladjustment between indicators and organization. The second may increase the difficulty of comparing the project to standards of practice, therefore complicating the assessment of performance.

The unintended effects of performance measurement on organizations are well recognized (see Ridgway, 1956). Foremost among them is the phenomenon known as "gaming", which refers to behaviours that satisfy the measure instead of the goal behind it (Bevan & Hood, 2006a, 2006b; Bird et al., 2005; Hood, 2006). At least three types of gaming have been identified in public organizations:

1) *"Threshold effect"* refers to the tendency for an organization to redistribute performance efforts, emphasizing domains that are below target, while tolerating deterioration on domains that perform above target (Bevan & Hood, 2006b, p. 521; Bird et al., 2005, p. 19).

2) *"Ratchet effect"* is defined as the tendency for managers to not exceed targets even when they can, so as not to set the bar too high for the next reporting period or next project (Bevan & Hood, 2006b, p. 521; Litwack, 1993, p. 272).

3) *"Output distortion"* describes the tendency to achieve targets at the expense of a significant decrease in performance on aspects of work that are not measured. In other words, "hitting the target, missing the point" (Bevan & Hood, 2006a, p. 421; 2006b, p. 521).

These gaming behaviours are difficult to anticipate and control. Efforts to counter one tendency may simply encourage the other. For instance, trying to limit the threshold effect by basing targets on prior performance may accentuate the ratchet effect (Bevan & Hood, 2006b). On the other hand, trying to limit the ratchet effect by applying system-wide targets may accentuate the threshold effect. Other unintended effects are also mentioned in the literature, such as seeking simplistic solutions to complex problems, or managers' use of measurement to serve their own agendas rather than organizational priorities (Adair et al., 2006). Hood (2006) also evokes the temptation to manipulate data and report false performance improvements.

Avoiding pitfalls and unintended effects of performance measurement is challenging. To reconcile performance measurement with accountability, the literature points to leadership, commitment to decisions made, and the use of participatory or collaborative approaches (Adair et al., 2006). A number of authors recognize the need for communication, cooperation and collaboration between the measured and the measurers (De Lancer Julnes, 2006; DeVore & Champion, 2011; Radin, 2006; Van Der Knaap, 2006). The use of multiple, diverse and heterogeneous sets of measures is considered helpful (Behn, 2003; Radin, 2006). Radin (2006) also recommends periodic revision of measures, the involvement of many actors in goal definition, and a constructive scepticism about PMS. It is also possible to prevent pitfalls during the implementation stage by, for example, performing an organizational readiness assessment, involving internal and external stakeholders, increasing implementation support, and promoting a "performance culture" (see De Lancer Julnes & Holzer, 2001, p. 703; Radin, 2006, p. 244).

This focus on pitfalls and unintended effects serves to heighten awareness of the limitations of PMS in public sector projects. For instance, it might be reasonable to consider that PMS information alone is inadequate for guiding decision-making and resources allocation (De Lancer Julnes, 2006). In summary, we find evidence supporting the importance of PMS for measuring public sector project performance, and the need to adapt PMS to the context of a project, and carefully consider implementation. Heightened awareness of common pitfalls and unintended effects might help to enhance both the design and implementation of a PMS and improve project performance. However, the human, relational dimensions of projects also need to be considered when seeking to improve the overall performance of public sector projects. These are addressed in the next section.

17.4 Improving the performance of public sector projects

Two themes are reviewed here. First, we discuss how to deal with a low-performing project, and address management concerns that arise in this context. Second, we look at some of the softer dimensions of performance in public sector projects.

17.4.1 Getting a low-performing project back on track

As stated by Ukko, Tenhunen, and Rantanen (2007, p. 39), "performance measurement can only support, not replace managers in leading people". On their own, PMS cannot guarantee high performance, nor are they able to get a low-performing project back on track. However, the literature offers some suggestions about how to improve ailing performance. For instance, Ukko et al. (2007) proposes increasing interaction between management and employees to explore reasons for poor performance. Other authors point to benefits of developing absorptive and adaptive capabilities within the project team (Biedenbach & Müller, 2012) and realigning the PMS with the organization's strategy (Bourne et al., 2000). However, the need to use these as salvage measures might be avoided by recognizing and dealing with these issues earlier on in project development (Thamhain, 2013).

In order to deal with the most common issues that arise in large-scale public sector projects, Patanakul et al. (2016), building on recommendations from 39 case studies, offer the following managerial considerations (see Table 17.1).

Even when conducted with due consideration for all these factors, complex projects may experience unexpected difficulties. Disruptions may be best managed with a combination of anticipation and resilience. Weick and Sutcliffe (2015) propose five "principles" to help organizations sustain performance through unexpected difficulties. First, a *preoccupation with failure* may help to anticipate small errors that could harm the project if they were to spread. Second, a *reluctance to oversimplify* reality by focusing on a small number of key issues or indicators can provide a more detailed view of what can go wrong in a project. Third, *sensitivity to operations* tends to increase capacity to detect anomalies and close calls, and therefore act to prevent them from worsening or being repeated. Fourth, an organization's *commitment to resilience*, by increasing flexibility, adds to its capacity to bounce back from inevitable errors and setbacks. Fifth, the ability of an organization to *defer to expertise*, by respecting domain-specific knowledge and increasing the decision-making authority of front-line staff, has been shown to reduce errors caused, for example, by delays in hierarchical decision-making or top management lack of on-the-ground expertise or experience. These principles, termed "mindful organizing", may help decrease vulnerability and increase learning capacity (Weick, 2015; Weick & Sutcliffe, 2015).

Table 17.1 Recommendations to improve public sector projects

Large-scale, public sector project characteristic	Management recommendations
Pursuing non-financial benefits	• Focus on benefit management throughout the life of the project • Define target benefit such that it is specific, attainable, and comprehensive in nature • Establish and agree upon a methodology for evaluating target benefit
Product service life:long-term utilization	• Focus on robust and flexible product design with consideration of future needs • Establish effective quality management process • Develop technology adoption strategy
Multiple stakeholders	• Engage stakeholders according to their influence on project performance • Establish cross-organization cooperation and agreement
Complexity	• Be aware of the size and complexity of the project • Break project down into subprojects • Use an integrated master schedule to coordinate project activities
Political environment	• Ensure alignment between project and current legislation • Ensure alignment between project and strategies of the government agency • Provide the project manager with the authority needed to properly respond to political stakeholders with various agendas
Formal processes	• Establish project management processes • Ensure proper utilization of these processes • Enhance project governance by assigning and empowering a senior project "owner"

Adapted from Patanakul et al., 2016, Table 2, p. 456.

As outlined above, investing in the front-end of a project is an effective way to achieve better project performance. However, as the project life cycle evolves, it is essential to consider feedback from the PMS and adjust in response. Monitoring project performance should be seen as a continuous process, to be undertaken carefully throughout the project, with adjustments made as needed to improve performance.

17.4.2 The performance of public sector projects: Softer considerations

Recent research shows that contingency theory still has considerable influence in project management (Aubry & Lavoie-Tremblay, 2018). In designing and implementing a PMS, there is a need to involve skilled people who understand the context and the project, and can establish diagnoses, reflexively evaluate results, and adapt the PMS accordingly.

Measuring the performance of public sector projects should foster rich discussion between the project team and organizational actors (decision-makers, promoters, coordinators) about why the PMS is needed and what it is meant to contribute. This highlights the importance of appropriation of the PMS tool by organizational actors. A tool needs to be viewed in relation to actors and context in order to be useful for the development of projects (Jarzabkowski & Kaplan, 2015). The appropriation process is an opportunity to reflect on the project and its objectives, to ask questions and commit to continuous improvement. A PMS can be implemented as a collective practice involving reflexive practitioners and experts (internal to the organization, or external such as academics and consultants) to bring about constructive discussion and positive outcomes. Experts from outside the organization and project might bring additional knowledge and reflexivity, as they provide an outside perspective and experience with other projects that are often useful (Flyvbjerg, Garbuio, & Lovallo, 2009). As building capacity and knowledge create important organizational assets, developing a culture of performance learning is critical for public sector organizations and project actors (Hall, 2003). Dynamic capabilities are required in public sector projects, at both operational and strategic levels (Davies & Brady, 2016; Davies, Dodgson, & Gann, 2016). Moreover, project governance structures enable greater performance when they allow for flexibility in the institutional setup at the organizational level, in transferring authority to the project level, and in developing the mindset of the project team as self-responsible and self-organizing (Müller, Pemsel, & Shao, 2015). However, cultural factors also have to be taken into account if an adapted PMS is to be implemented and adopted by project team members (Bredillet, Yatim, & Ruiz, 2010).

Culture, values and identities are pluralistic concepts, layered at national, organizational, project and individual levels. Understanding the range of cultures and implicit values is essential for improving performance (Dupuis, 2011). Efforts should be made to explicitly formulate underlying values, discuss them with all project stakeholders, and seek to address the competing values that are common in public sector projects (Koppenjan, Charles, & Ryan, 2008). For example, Brunet and Aubry (2016) identify efficiency, legitimacy and accountability as the three dimensions to be considered in the adoption of a governance framework for major public sector projects. This is in line with New Public Governance, which holds that the integration of multiple stakeholders, pluralistic perspectives, and a shared view of the public good encourage appropriation and improve performance (Osborne, 2010).

17.5 Conclusion: Beyond performance

The concept of performance is frequently associated with New Public Management, as it was conceived as a key instrument in results-based management (Godenhjelm et al., 2015). In highly complex public sector organizations, projects are not always easy to manage, as important temporal networks of public and private organizations are often assembled in order to reach project objectives. The performance of public sector projects is in itself a pluralistic concept, as stakeholders have different perspectives on the public good and public values. Adopting a PMS that is adapted to the project and organizational context is a first step to improving performance. However, leadership, collaboration and reflexivity are essential in this process, as the PMS is not only an instrument in evaluation, it also initiates the evaluation process. This chapter has built on theoretical pluralism in order to develop an interdisciplinary contribution to our understanding of performance measurement in public sector projects (Söderlund, 2011). The public administration and project management literature offer interesting insights into how to measure and improve the performance of public sector projects. The central message of this chapter is that judgement, skills and openness to learning are needed to fully understand the use of PMS in these projects, because the indicators measured most often represent underlying values. Another important message is that key stakeholders need to be involved in designing and adjusting the PMS used to evaluate performance. Research on public sector projects remains scarce, and we hope to see accelerated development of the theoretical and empirical knowledge base in this area. We believe that an interdisciplinary approach is the way forward.

Chapter 18

Creating value in infrastructure projects

The Public Value Chain[1]

Leonie Koops, Marian Bosch-Rekveldt, Hans Bakker and Marcel Hertogh

The Public Value Chain

Infrastructure projects are performed to add quality to society. However, the performance of the project's execution is far from optimal (Flyvbjerg et al., 2003; Merrow, 2011; Shenhar and Dvir, 2007). New contract forms between public organizations and private contractors are being introduced to increase the value for money (see for instance (Eversdijk and Korsten, 2015; Hayford, 2006; Van Ham and Koppenjan, 2002). These new contracts shift responsibilities and risks in earlier project stages from public to private parties and even more stress the importance of the cooperation between public and private parties. This might require different ways of working, or at least, more clarity about task distribution in order to be successful.

This chapter introduces the Public Value Chain concept to support the creation of value in projects. The concept is validated in an expert meeting. In reaction to the concept, a public project manager stated "this will increase the social benefits of the project". First, different perspectives on performance are explored, as different public parties involved might have different views. Understanding these perspectives is considered essential to create the best starting position for optimal performance in future projects.

Perspectives on performance

Four perspectives public project managers may have on project success were discovered in earlier research (Koops et al., 2016). By means of a Q-study, these perspectives were identified:

1. Traditional: a focus on controllability of the process up to project delivery and handover.
2. Delivering a fit for purpose project, meeting specific political or social factors within the given budget.

---

1 This chapter builds upon Chapter 8 of the dissertation of Koops, L.S.W., 2017. Creating public value: Optimizing cooperation between public and private partners in infrastructure projects. Delft University of Technology.

3. Meeting specific political or social factors within time.
4. Balancing between satisfying the needs of stakeholders, shareholders, users and specific political or social factors and the criteria of the iron triangle.

It seems that all perspectives except perspective 1 adopt the idea of the split between project management success and product success in defining the performance of projects (Al-Tmeemy et al., 2011; Baccarini, 1999; Munns and Bjeirmi, 1996), but specific elements of product success are highlighted in the different perspectives. Understanding these different focal points for the product success seems the main challenge (meeting specific political/social factors, fit for purpose and satisfy the needs of shareholders and stakeholders).

Also, the influence of external actors on the combined project organization of public and private partners was revealed in an earlier study (Koops et al., 2017). It was observed that after the procurement phase, the public project delivery organization and private project organization together form a combined project organization (CPO). The CPO executes the project. This CPO is acting in a network of stakeholders, needed in the process towards completion of the objectives, including stakeholders in the parent organizations. Deeper study of the interfaces between the CPO and respective parent organizations suggested improvement potential with the ultimate purpose of increasing efficiency and effectiveness of the CPO.

Given the existence of different perspectives on performance amongst the parties involved and the earlier identified improvement potential, it is investigated whether the improvement potential could be materialized using the concept of a value chain for the specific context of public infrastructure and construction projects.

Developing the Public Value Chain

First, it is sketched how the Public Value Chain is developed. Given the assumed importance of the support activities, these are further explained next. At this stage, activities and processes are distinguished on different levels and for different interfaces the CPO interacts with (see Figure 18.1).

The Value Chain of the Combined Project Organization (CPO)

The idea of a value chain is not new. Value Chain Analysis is a business strategy approach developed by Michael Porter to analyze specific activities or processes through which firms can create value and competitive advantage (Porter and Millar, 1985). A Value Chain is a chain of activities that a firm performs in order to deliver a valuable product

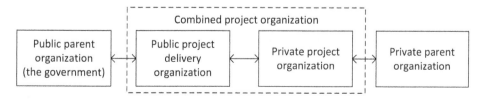

Figure 18.1 Different interfaces in project organizations.

to the market. In infrastructure projects, the deliverable is a physical product: a road, a railway, a bridge, et cetera. Value Chain Analysis distinguishes primary processes or activities and support processes or activities.

The chain of activities that the CPO performs in order to deliver a valuable product for society has similarities and differences with Porter's Value Chain. A key difference is that the project will cost money to the parent organization instead of generating money as in a commercial setting (see also literature on Project Oriented Organizations and Project Based Organizations, (Ajmal and Koskinen, 2008; Arvidsson, 2009; Hobday, 2000). The commercial operational activities that Porter distinguished are suitable in commercial settings where organizations produce goods. In these organizations the primary activities from production to market are Inbound Logistics, Operations, Outbound Logistics, Marketing and Sales and Service. These activities do not fit the combined project organization responsible for infrastructure projects. The primary processes constitute the "core business" of the organization. To translate the commercial Value Chain to a Value Chain that suits the combined project organization for infrastructure projects, those activities necessary to create the project result have to be taken into account, starting in the pre-construction phase (Cox et al., 2006). These activities are: Legalize, Prepare, Design and engineer, Construct and Hand-over, shown in Figure 18.2 on the right (Smyth and Pryke, 2008).

Porters Value Chain (left), Public Value Chain by this research (right)

These primary activities are explained as follows:

- Legalize is the activity that fulfills all legal preconditions required for the successful completion of all other stages, from the creation of a special legal basis for the project to obtaining building and opening permits.
- Preparing involves all activities necessary to create a suitable situation for constructing the project result. This includes mapping the quality of the current situation and removing possible obstacles in it, for example, assets of others.
- Design and engineer refers to activities aimed at developing the product of the CPO and construct refers to the actual building activities.
- The final handover activities consist of testing, delivering and transferring the assets to the owners.

Along with the primary activities, the value chain consists of support activities. The support activities Porter mentions are suitable for a permanent organization. The support activities of a CPO support the temporary CPO, and should be complementary to the support activities of the parent organizations. The equivalents for the support activities in the CPO are listed as follows: project management infrastructure, Human Resource and Knowledge management, Contract and procurement management, Stakeholder management and Decision process management. Why these are considered the support activities for the CPO is elaborated next.

Elaborating on the support activities

The purpose of the support activities is to enable efficient and effective primary activities. Project management infrastructure, Human Resource and Knowledge management, Contract and procurement management, Stakeholder management and Decision

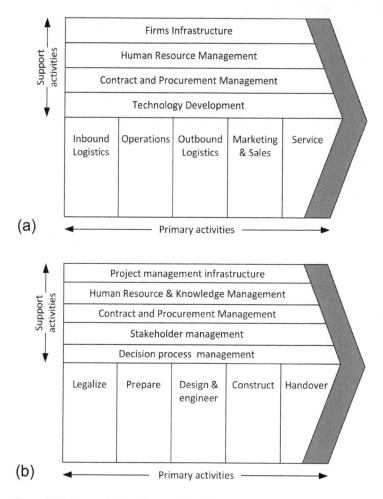

Figure 18.2 Porters Value Chain and the Public Value Chain.

process management all aim to support the controllability of the activities that create the project result.

Project management infrastructure

Porter mentions the management activities next to the primary and support activities. For the CPO, the project management practices are considered more dominant and thus part of the Value Chain. Porter's management comprises forecasting, planning, organizing, leading, directing, coordinating and controlling effort for the purpose of accomplishing the goal. These activities, also mentioned in the PMBOK Guide (PMBOK®, 2008), put much emphasis on tools and techniques that help to control the activities. Searching for efficiency, these control activities have a strong influence on the project activities in public infrastructure projects.

Human Resource and Knowledge Management

In the earlier study on identifying perspectives on project success, public project managers sorted the success criterion *personal growth and development* as not very important, but not unimportant either (Koops et al., 2016). Although technology is needed in the primary processes, the development of technological knowledge is not an activity for the CPO. However, the organization of the right knowledge in the team is important for effective processes. The response to too little knowledge typically is to add more people, resulting in new challenges. To avoid this, a position for HRM and Knowledge Management seems justified in support activities of the CPO. These activities refer to addressing the essential knowledge fields for the CPO and ensuring these in the project organization. The parent organization should provide the project with a (for the parent strategic) fulfillment of the knowledge question and provide the organization with proper Knowledge Management (Leendertse, 2015). Based on this it is proposed that the equivalent of Human Resource Management for the CPO is Human Resource and Knowledge Management.

Contract and procurement management

Prior to the composition of a CPO, procurement is an important process (Cox et al., 2006; Pryke and Smyth, 2006). A public–private partnership can only be started after a careful tendering procedure. Though procurement activities (tendering) are important in the construction industry, they are supporting the activities that construct infrastructure. After composition of the CPO, contract management supports the primary activities by monitoring the compliance with the contractual agreements made. Procurement is still relevant for the private project organization with respect to subcontracting.

Stakeholder management

The different perspectives on success (see also the section "Perspectives on Performance") revealed importance to satisfying stakeholders and/or the importance of satisfying shareholders. This seems of utmost importance for the CPO to carefully address. However, the CPO also has to deal with triangular relationships with parent organizations, unclear (informal) relationships and too many people involved in general (Koops et al., 2017). Stakeholder management as a supportive process is assumed to contribute to clear(er) involvement of people from outside the project organization, both in terms of role and responsibilities. Stakeholder management contributes to more effective processes without losing the support of partners. Therefore, the management of stakeholders is an important support activity in the CPO.

Decision process management

Also, decision process management is added to the support activities in the CPO. The purpose of the majority of the contacts of a CPO with the public parent and with other public organizations concerns decision-making (Koops et al., 2017). The complex decision-making in the public parent organization needs a carefully designed process. De Bruijn and Ten Heuvelhof (2010) point out that in a network, hierarchical management stands little chance. They state that the opposite of command and control is a process approach of *commit and prepare*. To reach decisions a process of consultation and negotiation with other parties is needed. As mentioned earlier, the product success was seen as important with criteria covering the satisfaction of (specific groups of) stakeholders. However, the lines with owner-operators and owner-clients often are unclear. Ambiguous relationships, decision-making in the public network and the long lines from private project organization to public parent bring up the need for a careful designed process of information flows leading to decisions. Therefore, the management of the decision-making process is proposed as part of the support activities of the CPO.

Defining activities at different levels

In an organization, different organizational levels can be recognized. In the combined project organization, the tactical and the operational level can be recognized. The purpose of the internal operations on the tactical level is to organize the assignment and to manage the execution of activities by the operational core. The actual work is done by the work floor, at the operational level, where production activities are undertaken. As the project organization is still seen as part of the parent organization, the strategic level in project organizations is formed by a representative or number of representatives of the strategic level of the parent organizations.

The effect of the characteristic *finite life* of a project is that the timeline seems less far away than it sometimes is and the assignment of the project manager seems a purely operational function: deliver the project. In forming the combined project organization modeled like a permanent production organization this feature is examined closer. The existence of a permanent organization is endless. These organizations form a strategic level that navigates the firms' activities in the constantly changing society (Mintzberg, 1980). The finite but still considerable long timeline of the CPO legitimizes a strategic level within the project organization to "navigate" the project into society. This strategic level must not be confused with the board or senior manager who supervises the proper implementation of the scope of the CPO (the project sponsor). The current involvement of a senior level from the parent organization functions in terms of *assist*, *monitor* and *support*. The strategic level introduced here is primarily part of the CPO and its task is to represent the interests of the CPO in the parent organization. Changes within the parent organizations that cause conflicts with the current scope of the CPO are to be addressed at this level.

The organizational levels in the CPO are supplemented with "navigate", as mentioned above. When the primary and support activities in the CPO are combined with processes for internal operations (produce, organize and navigate), the purpose per activity can be determined and formulated in terms of the project success criteria (see Table 18.1).

The Value Chain for the public–private partners

The activities of the Public Value Chain represent all activities of the combined project organization. The collaboration between the public and the private project organization ultimately yields the entire Value Chain. Primary and support activities are executed by public or private employees. They have to be performed for a commonly recognized

Table 18.1 Activities at different levels

Operational mechanisms	Primary activities: create purpose: add value	Support activities: control purpose: within given constraints	Result success criteria
Produce	Execute primary activities	Execute support activities	Product success (fit for purpose, value added)
Organize	Organize primary activities	Organize support activities	Project management success (within given constraints)
Navigate	Navigate the project through contextual changes (adapt)	Navigate the project along contextual changes (organize stability)	Stakeholders success (predictable and connected)

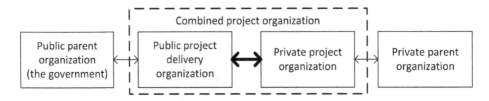

Figure 18.3 Public–private interface becomes an internal interface.

purpose and lead to an agreed result. In the analysis of relationships it was shown that activities and their purpose got separated, causing inefficiency. By positioning the partners together in the chain of activities towards the project result, this can be avoided. By doing so, the external interface between partners is changing into an internal interface within the CPO (Figure 18.3).

The chain of actions over the interfaces

When the combined project organization is positioned outside the parent organizations, internal interfaces change into external interfaces. In analyzing the external relationships, three roles of the public parent organization were distinguished: the client-owner, the future owner and operator, and the licensing authority. For decision-making, or to inform the parent organization in each role, activities in the CPO reach over the interface into the parent organizations. The activities that lead to the client-owner are first meant to show the client-owner that the CPO is in control and will deliver the project within given constraints – aiming at *project management success*. This information comes from the support activities, mostly from project management and contract management activities.

Besides these activities, there are activities that stem from the primary activities in the project and these are meant to show the client-owner that the project is *fit for purpose*. The client-owner will deliver the project to the owner-operator. Often different assets

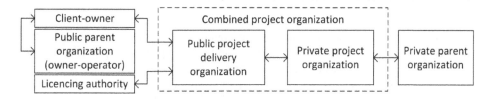

Figure 18.4 Interface public parent – public project delivery organization.

Table 18.2 Connecting CPO and public parent organization

Roles of public parent	Primary activities	Support activities
Client-owner and Owner-operator	Fit for purpose	Within time and budget
Licensing authority	According to requirements (product success)	Right process followed (project management success)

are delivered to several asset owner(s). Instead of via the client-owner, actor-project relationships are often directly to the operator-owner, in order to validate the developed solutions.

The public parent also acts as the licensing authority. The activities that connect the CPO with this role of the public parent organization are mostly prescribed to prove that the developed solutions are according to legal requirements. Hence, processes that connect the CPO with the parent organization must be separated in two different tracks (Figure 18.4).

So one of the tracks is to the licensing authority, proving that the project outcome is legitimate. The other track is to the client-owner presenting a fit for purpose result, within the constraints agreed beforehand (Table 18.2).

The private project organization is connected to the public project delivery organization on the one side, and its own parent organization on the other (see right part of Figure 18.4). Let's now look at the position of the private organization.

The activities performed in the combined project organization are also connected to the private parent organization, which is a commercial, project-based organization. The execution of the project is their link with the public parent organization. As the delivered assets will finally be owned by the public organization, this relation with the project organization ends with delivering the project. The primary activities in the CPO are partly activities of the private project organization. These activities link to, contribute to and even partially take over the activities in the public project delivery organization. However, the activities in the private project organization should never bypass the public project delivery organization. The merged activities together form the information needed in the processes that reach into the public parent organization. In the same line, it is argued that the support activities merge to one line of reasoning towards the public parent organization, though to a lesser extent.

Summarizing the proposed activities and processes

Bringing together the earlier pictures and figures, the Public Value Chain for the Combined Project Organization is composed. It contains all activities performed by the combined project organization without a distinction between private or public activities. Public and private activities *together* must range over the complete Public Value Chain.

The activities that are performed are either part of the primary activities that create the project result, or are part of the support activities that enable control of the primary activities. All activities extend beyond the CPO and intend to link to the parent organizations (Table 18.3).

The interaction with the parent organization can be on production (operational) level, managerial (tactical) level or navigation (strategic) level. The term navigate is introduced to put more emphasis on the need to keep the CPO on track during its perennial but finite existence. From the activities, their purpose and the organizational level they are performed on, the specific actions on the interface with the parent organization can be derived.

Validating the Public Value Chain

To validate this proposed approach for the CPO, the Public Value Chain and the corresponding activities were presented to experts. The specific activities in the CPO and at the interfaces were evaluated as part of the validation process. Based on the validation, the Public Value Chain was further simplified and its foreseen contribution to project performance was assessed.

The process of validation

The Public Value Chain was validated by means of three expert meetings. These expert meetings focused on collecting individual responses as well as facilitating discussions between the experts of the four groups involved:

- Public parents (five respondents).
- Public project managers (five respondents).
- Private project manager (seven respondents).
- Private parents (four respondents).

These experts were employed at different levels; the levels of national, regional and local governments. All experts had relevant experience in the field of infrastructure projects. The experts met each other in different settings divided over three back-to-back expert meetings (see Figure 18.5).

To prepare the expert meetings, individual data was gathered by means of an internet survey containing questions about the features of the CPO, the activities of the CPO, the interaction on the interfaces and some background information to help the data interpretation. During the expert meetings, the main focus was on the interactions at the interfaces of the CPO. This resulted in a number of recommendations for further operationalizing the Public Value Chain, which are elaborated next. After the expert meetings, another individual internet survey completed the data gathering cycle.

Table 18.3 Activities in CPO and processes linking activities to parent organizations

Value Chain process	Purpose	Level	Processes on the interface with		
			Public parent Client-owner	*Public parent Licensing authority*	*Private parent*
Primary activities CPO					
Licensing					
Prepare	create:	Operational	Harmonize trade-offs	Validating the results	Providing resources (people, materials, machines)
Design and engineer*		Tactical	Prioritize goals, align decisions	Explore possibilities	Alignment on needed resources, incl. knowledge
Build		Strategic	Ensure accountability (justify results)	Knowing the regulations	Introducing knowledge
Turn-over					
Support activities CPO					
Project management**					
Contract management	control:	Operational	Delivery on baseline	(Interim) approving products	Justify expenditures and gain
Knowledge & HR management		Tactical	Efficient use of resources, align processes	Ensure legitimacy	Informing on risks
Stakeholder management		Strategic	Keeping goals aligned	Check feasibility	Keeping goals aligned
Decision process management					

* including verification and validation.

** including scope management, risk management, planning management, quality management, information management, financial management.

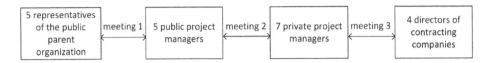

Figure 18.5 Overview of expert meeting setup.

Simplifying the Public Value Chain model

The Public Value Chain as presented to the experts in fact consisted of two parts: an overview of activities and processes that link to the public parent organization and an overview of processes that link to the private parent organization (Table 18.3).

The public experts in meeting 1 mentioned that they already organize a project team before contracting a private partner. During this discussion, one of the public project managers emphasized that in the pre–contract phase usually too little attention is given to the navigation of the project after tender. Several public project managers pointed to the dependence of the contractual arrangements and the division of responsibilities and tasks between public and private parties. They did not pay attention to the fact that the dividing line is set by them (not by the private partner).

In the second meeting, the private participants indicated that the distribution of tasks and responsibilities for these activities should be a discussion between partners in the CPO. The models introduced were considered helpful in the discussion about the purpose of activities and the most efficient division between public and private partner.

This resulted in the following recommendation regarding the use of the Public Value Chain: After contracting, jointly organize the combined project organization for effi-cient and effective production. Give explicit attention to the design of the Public Value Chain, especially to:

- The interaction and coherence in public and private activities and processes towards the same goal (and make it explicit).
- The differences in the contributions and responsibilities in the processes from pub-lic and private part of the project organization.
- The aligned, unambiguous action in the project area (network approach), each in his own strength.
- The formation of a shared view on decision-making processes, from project organi-zation into the parent organization.

These reflections lead to a simplified Public Value Chain, since the combined project organization (CPO) should be seen as the joint domain of the project partners. In all expert meetings, it was expressed that this shared domain must be of mutual interest and lead to the most satisfied stakeholders. The right distribution of tasks, responsibilities and risks has to be discussed to maximize the potential benefit of the model, and not be split beforehand. This was clearly expressed in the second meeting (between public and private project managers).

A private project manager compared the mindset of the CPO with his experience in an Alliance:

> Particularly in the team, the joint setup of activities was considered a success. There we created an imaginary fence around the joint organization. At some point the parent organizations experienced it (too) challenging. But it is in the people who take the experience with them to other projects and apply it again. Unfortunately it does not spread out so much yet.

The common interest is in satisfying the stakeholders of both public project partner as well as private project partner (meeting 2 and 3).

Both the adaptive capacity of the CPO and the quality of the project outcome are important to organize in the joint domain. The first aspect was expressed in meeting 1 (public experts), the second aspect mostly in meeting 2 and 3. In meeting 3 it was expressed that after tendering, contractual arrangements form restrictive barriers for a constructive discussion about the distribution of responsibilities. The private experts indicated that contractual frameworks to facilitate capturing the outcomes of the discussion have to be developed, accompanied by flexible and adaptive payment arrangements. The private experts in meeting 3 agreed that this can optimize the efficiency of the CPO.

The simplified Public Value Chain is shown in Table 18.4.

Table 18.4 Public Value Chain of a combined project organization

Value Chain process	Purpose	Division of tasks and responsibilities
Primary process CPO		
Licensing	create	Public lead, private contribution (formulation in the contract)
Prepare		Public lead, private contribution (formulation in the contract)
Design and engineering*		Formulation in the contract, task always include verification
Build		Private lead, always includes verification
Turn-over		Public lead in process to client-owner and owner-operator(s)
Support activities CPO		
Project management	control	Public control on general processes, with private contribution included. Contractual management as art of general management, as well as scope management to be adaptive to environmental changes.
Decision process management		With regard to project partners and asset-owners. Public lead, private contribution
Stakeholder management		Public lead, private contribution, always include validation
Knowledge and HRM*		Common subject, transparency needed for optimal effectiveness

* discussed later.

During the three expert meetings, various elements of the Public Value Chain were discussed. Experts agreed on the following remarks, accompanying the activities:

- Contracting is not part of the combined project organization. Contracting is important for the public part of the project organization to select a private partner. After tender, this process should be downgraded. A public project manager mentioned in meeting 1: "It is a supporting task which is made primary in current practice of the public part of the project organization". None of the participants mentioned the selection of subcontractors as an activity for the CPO.
- Preparation and legalization are primary processes of the Value Chain. However, nowadays they are hardly combined activities. The processes aiming for licenses are frustrating for both partners. Experts mentioned a continuous discussion on the responsibilities of the partner on this subject.
- Preparation includes several topics. Some of them, like land purchase, are legal responsibilities of the public organization. Interestingly, in all meetings the role of the parent organization is recognized as a possibility to achieve efficiency. Long-term agreements with stakeholders (owners of assets that are influenced by the project) can be made at the strategic or tactical level in the parent organization. A client-owner in meeting 1 noticed that at the program level if a start was already made, first results were very positive.
- An important improvement mentioned is joint validation as part of (joint) stakeholder management. Stakeholder management is a key task for the public part of the CPO, because the parent organization (the government) remains accountable for stakeholders after completion of the project. The private partner supports the public part with specific (operational) activities.
- Public and private project managers recognize the importance of active involvement in the decision-making process (expressed in meeting 2). In current practice this can be optimized.

The contribution of the Public Value Chain to project performance

In the second online questionnaire, which was sent after the expert meetings, the experts were asked if the final model of the Public Value Chain with primary and support activities would contribute to the improvement of the performance of the CPO. In other words, they were asked if this model would increase the probability of project success. Ten out of 11 experts agreed upon this.

A private project manager commented:

> With this Public Value Chain the focus of the project organization is more clearly on achieving the project goal. The management of the interface with the parent organization is more focused on whether or not the interests of the individual asset-owners are guaranteed.

And a public project manager indicated:

> In particular, the handover is the least well integrated phase in the production process. The positioning of the stakeholder management as supporting activity for both

partners, will increase the involvement of asset-owners during the execution. In my view, this will increase the social benefits of the project.

The expert that did not expect a positive contribution of applying this model (a private director) remarked that the role of the private partner in the support activities still was too small. Also, a public project manager commented in that direction: "The private partner can help us to control the scope, while they also benefit, maybe even more than the public partner." The public respondents of the final questionnaire noticed that the stakeholder management activities are related to scope management and preferably both are common activities. The position of these activities as support activities in the CPO puts more emphasis on the importance during all primary activities, up to the handover.

Implications of the Public Value Chain

The implications of the Public Value Chain are in the field of the development of people, the joint operation in the project's environment, the transparency in the purpose of joint processes and, last but not least, a change in the public parent organization.

The development of people

The management of knowledge and people was introduced as supporting activity in the combined project organization. In the meetings, both public and private project managers indicated "the management of people and knowledge" as a success factor in their projects. And thereby (for that reason) the management of people and knowledge already had their attention. However, the common interest for the project and the parent organization is insufficiently deployed as mutual interest. The experts in the three meetings acknowledged the value of a proactive interest from the parent in the development of people in the project. The representatives of (especially public) parent organizations recognized the active use of project roles in the development paths of staff from project to project. Pro-active interest from the parent organization in this subject is considered valuable. These observations lead to a specific recommendation for the public and private parent organizations when forming a new combined project organization: *Pay conscious attention to Human Resource and Knowledge Management in the project organization. Arrange a pro-active approach from the parent organization to the project organization for designing development programs for employees and monitoring of required and acquired knowledge.*
In the final survey one of the experts stated:

> This [recommendation, ed.] creates an interesting dynamic and reciprocity. It also requires two sided proactivity. (...). If we actively manage this reciprocity and development and open up to it, professionalism of both public and private parent organizations and project organizations, will probably develop quicker and more direct than has hitherto been the case.

Joint operation in the projects' environment

The next recommendation stems from the CPO model and the multiple decision lines to the public parent organization. Initially, this recommendation aimed to make a clear distinction between the role of the parent organization as licensing authority and the role of the parent company as client-owner. Interestingly, public and private experts had very different opinions on the necessity of this distinction. The public experts reflected in meeting 1 (only public representatives) that there is no need to express the subject of this recommendation so explicitly. In meeting 2, where public and private project managers interacted, a public project manager mentioned "it is evident that you must act from the project towards permitting authorities, if needed. Everyone must take responsibility and act in the project interest". In response to that, private project managers mentioned that they would like to use the knowledge and the network of their public partner in these processes for the benefit of project progress. However, the private project managers clearly expressed that they miss transparency and interaction with their public partner to understand the public network well enough for optimal use of relationships and influence to achieve project goals effectively and efficiently. Public project managers reacted surprised as the private project managers expressed that the processes are very unclear to them. The private project managers indicated that they at least want to understand the public decision-making, so that they can support their public partner more in this area, which contributes to more togetherness in the CPO.

In this discussion, the difference between the client-owner and the owner-operator was expressed. It showed a clear division between the role of owner–client and owner–operator. The discussion was triggered by the process verification and validation in the Public Value Chain. The handover process of the product (project success) connects the CPO to owner-operator, which makes them very important stakeholders for the CPO in achieving product success. The project closure process connects the CPO to the client-owner. On this connection, project management success (within time and budget) is most valued.

The public parent organization is therefore in the final model divided over three *roles* (Figure 18.6, adjusted from Figure 18.4). With this in mind, it is especially important for the public delivery organization and the public parent organization to be *transparent about the public roles and organizational context of functions towards the private partner*. It is recommended *to make a clear distinction in the roles played by the public parent organization (and public partner organizations), in particular about the role of the parent as licensing authority, the role of the parent as asset owner (owner-operator) and the role of the parent as a principal (client-owner)*.

For the CPO it is important to act jointly towards external stakeholders and validate the contractual design jointly to make sure the CPO is producing the right result. Furthermore, it is important for the partners in the CPO to create a workflow towards asset-owners jointly, including decision-making by the accountable stakeholder to ensure commitment from the stakeholders from the beginning.

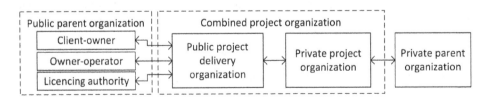

Figure 18.6 Interface public parent – public project delivery.

Experts were asked to note eventual bottlenecks. Several experts pointed at the responsibility struggle between public and private partners. Accepting the contractual design implies at least shared responsibility. Also, the openness and trust that is necessary between partners was expressed as a bottleneck for achieving the desired situation by some. A public project manager acknowledged the correctness of the recommendation but mentioned the lack of knowledge by the owner-operator as a serious bottleneck for an effective fulfillment in the desired process.

The recommendation presented in the expert meetings to put the public project organization at a clear distance from the licensing authority, so the public project partner can actively contribute in procedures without conflicts of interest, was least supported. The reasons to disagree varied from "this is already the case" to "we do not need a licensing authority if we do our jobs right".

Transparency in the purpose of joint processes

From the performed research a few recommendations that consider the internal activities of the CPO were formulated, with special interest in the position of each partner in these activities. For the public project partner in the CPO, who has the lead in the project management activities, the recommendation is to *make a clear distinction between project management success and product success and to provide balance between management of the primary – creating – and the support – controlling – activities*. It is recommended to communicate and report separately but simultaneously and equally on substantive technical process and risks, and procedural progress and risks. The public project managers expressed that this improves the positioning of their (project) responsibilities towards their parent organization and the contribution of the project result to the parent organization. For optimal efficient and effective processes, partners agreed on the fact that they should *share knowledge and information to support a joint approach to decision-making for a more successful outcome*. The difference between project success and project management success is not widely known, which makes it harder to act in line with this recommendation. An interesting remark was made by one of the experts who stated: "When procuring, the focus is (often), especially on the project management success (e.g. contract, planning, project plan). That probably sets a tone. An equal focus on the product's success therefore requires a lot of attention".

The recommendation to take care of transparency towards the partner about progress and risks in their own contribution to processes in the Public Value Chain to support the CPO in the management of risks is putting emphasis on the attitude of both partners. This cannot be considered without having the above line of reasoning in mind. It is to be considered for all primary and support activities to have one partner in the lead and the other partner supplying information in the process. In the expert meetings specific interactions were put forward:

- The public parent organization mentioned the difference in impact of failure in stakeholder management for the involved organization. The assessment of risk in this area is different as well as the level of acceptance of risks.
- A private project manager mentioned the importance of a joint validation process with stakeholders at the start of the joint organization. To control risks by the right partner, both partners should have a joint understanding of the risk.

- Especially in the project activity, *legalize* further horizontal integration of tasks if possible, as long as risks are allocated correctly. An expert from the private organization mentioned the absence of financial consequences of risk allocation. The common opinion of the experts on this is that the correct risk allocation and transparency in the management of risks leads to the most effective collaboration in the CPO. Or, to put it the other way around, to enlarge the effectiveness of the CPO at the start the issue of risk allocation and management has to be an integral part of the organization of controlling the activities in the CPO.

Finally, the navigation level is addressed as it is recommended for both partners *to appoint a representative Project pivot, visible and approachable for the partner.* Someone who has the respect of the decision-making level in the parent organization, and without direct responsibilities in the parent that might interfere with the project's interest. This Project pivot builds and maintains a project relationship on a strategic level, to be used for navigation rather than escalation. As one of the representatives of the private parent organization put it elegantly: "The coffee tastes better in relation than in escalation". Both public and private pivot should invest in involvement and comfort, and be able to explain and cover projects' actions in the parent organizations. This recommendation is fully supported in the final questionnaire. However, experts indicated the proper interpretation of the role of Project pivot as a potential issue for a successful implementation of this recommendation.

Contribution to the efficiency by the public parent

The Public Value Chain also offers opportunities for better involvement of the asset owners in the project; owners of assets that are affected by the project activities (without any improvement to the asset). As their assets are located in a public area, the assets are affected by several projects at different locations. There is no common interest for these asset-owners in the objectives of the projects. Common interest can be found on another level: the network level and the client level. The clients of both the parent organization and the asset-owner organizations are individual civilians. Arrangements for combining activities at least decrease the impact of the projects for their shared clients, which can be a driver to discuss arrangements on the network level. So instead of leaving arrangements with asset-owners of public networks to each project, providing alignment on the level of the parent organization ultimately benefits the civilians both financially and functionally. To put it in a more general way, public parent organizations should *organize a multiple project, multi-annual agenda with the owners of public assets.*

Several experts fear less flexibility and influence for the CPO or mention the actual organization of the Public Value Chain as a challenge. One enthusiastic public project manager noted, however: "Start with this tomorrow!"

Conclusion and discussion

In this chapter, the Public Value Chain and the activities of the Combined Project Organization on the mutual interfaces are presented. To develop the Public Value Chain, insights of previous research were used to build this model (Koops et al., 2017; Koops et al., 2016). To validate the outcome and the applicability of the model, three back-to-back expert meetings were organized, supported by a preliminary and final online questionnaire. The central question was "to what extent can the Public Value Chain approach be used to improve the efficiency and effectiveness of the public and private actions?" The answers in the meetings and the final questionnaire are affirmative and support the applicability and usability of the model for people working in infrastructure and construction projects. But there is more.

The Public Value Chain offers a framework in which several research perspectives on the subject of collaboration in projects can be positioned. It contributes to research at a strategic level, into the organizational fit (or the lack of it) for public–private partnerships. For instance, it addresses elements that Akintoye and Beck (2009) also labeled important for a private partner: before entering a partnership with a public organization, there should be a clear view on hierarchical organizational structure of the parent organization, the client's key activities and processes that have impact on the project, decision-making structures and the interfaces with the project organization.

The Public Value Chain offers the opportunity to address these important elements during the procurement phase and at the start of the collaboration in the project. It supplements Van Ham and Koppenjan (2002) by recognizing that explicit agreements between actors about activities and the specific contributions of partners are needed to facilitate trust. The Public Value Chain contributes to this, without falling back on contractual tools.

So in construction projects the Public Value Chain model can contribute to develop clear relationships, increase efficiency and keep the focus on added value and by doing so, it helps us to reach for high performance in both project management as well as product success.

Chapter 19

Evaluating project performance

A comprehensive approach studying EU structural programs

Göran Brulin and Lennart Svensson

19.1 A background and framework

Projects, especially in large and innovative ones, are difficult to assess. Evaluations often focus on activities, outcomes, and short-term results, while neglecting long-term effects and mechanisms or unanticipated results. It is, however, not easy to judge what works in an intervention. One could (in line with the terminology from Guba and Lincoln, 1989), ask for a fifth generation of evaluation based on joint learning, an ongoing approach, a partnership with different stakeholders, a focus on long-term and unexpected effects, and interactive research (see Svensson et al., 2009). The fifth generation aims toward a critical and constructive evaluation to make continuous changes in the project-organization. Often, evaluation is uncritical, comes too late, and is limited in interaction and analytical rigor. Due to such weaknesses, it has little impact on project performance (Brulin and Svensson, 2012).

This chapter is based on experiences of implementation of the EU's cohesion policy in Sweden during 2014–2020. EU regional and social funds have implemented more than 5,000 large innovation and competence projects. The conclusions could be generalized to any large-scale and innovative projects.

Learning through ongoing evaluation has become a strategic tool for the EU's structural funds, both for development and assessing strategic impacts. Learning from evaluating innovative projects cannot, primarily, be built on control and detailed follow-up of activities and short-term results. Rather, learning by project evaluations stands in sharp contrast to the traditional models that are based on "Control groups", "Cost-Benefit Analyses", and "Counterfactual Impact Evaluation" (Svensson et al., 2009; Brulin and Svensson, 2012).

Several objections can be made against the "three Cs" mentioned above (Brulin, 2013; Brulin and Svensson, 2013). The first is that they focus on measurement and control of goal attainment in the SMART-criteria sense (a commonly used formula that argues that interventions should be *Specific, Measurable, Attainable, Relevant, and Time-bound* if they are to be implemented and evaluated). Paradoxically, this focus appears to increase the risk of missing the projects' wider long-term effects. The SMART-criteria models tend to steer programs and projects toward what can be easily evaluated, although these factors often are not the main performance mechanisms. Another objection is the lack of insight into projects resulting from steering by means of "remote control" approaches and functions, features intrinsic to these models. Such evaluation approaches do not provide insight, especially not in innovative projects, and are not a basis for disseminating knowledge, quality assurance, and decision-making.

What is pivotal in carrying out innovative projects is the ability to manage complexity, contradictions, conflicts, and dilemmas. To assure learning from the performance of such projects, an evaluation model that captures both mechanisms and effects is needed. In this chapter, we try to develop a model for learning through ongoing evaluation, not least to capture what might cause long-term effects. The so-called *projectification* – a critical view of public innovation and competence policy (Fred, 2018) – calls for such models to capture mechanisms and long-term effects. We will discuss how such an evaluation model can be accomplished by combining different methods, both new and established.

19.2 Evaluation of project performance

Taxpayers have a right to know whether or not, and, if so, how, various development programs and projects make a difference, both in a circumscribed and wider meaning. However, it is even more important to develop well-functioning systems and procedures that can assure long-term impact. Control, monitoring, and traditional evaluation models are important prerequisites for legitimizing funded interventions. Thus, the demands on the implementers of programs and projects to use strictly formalized SMART-criteria-based methods and far-reaching standardization risk pushing the measures in a direction that is not expedient. To avoid these types of unwanted impacts, it is important to move away from one-dimensional evaluation and research. The idea behind this chapter is to provide a brief, clear, and concise picture of how evaluation of project performance can create knowledge about innovation and competence, taking into account that many of the effects might be hidden, surprising, or unintended.

EU cohesion policy, in addition to the internal market, is the main tool for growing the whole of Europe. Through the structural funds, the EU's 28 (27 when Britain has left) member states and regions gain access to EUR800 billion to fund innovative and regular policy actions that can contribute to smart and sustainable growth. Even if this might appear to be an astronomical sum, it constitutes only 1 percent of the member states' budgets, and cannot in itself make a difference to growth in Europe. Rather, learning is the key issue. The main focus of the structural funds is experiments that lead to innovation and competence development, which, by means of learning, can support smart, sustainable, and inclusive growth.

19.2.1 How to evaluate for long-term effects

Although large sums are invested in project-organized development, there are few evaluation models that capture mechanisms behind supposed long-term effects. The projects are supposed to be innovative, experimental, and additive in relation to regular activities in order to support structural transformation of Europe's regions. The projects should be preceded by analyses of what previously has been done in the targeted areas and continuously evaluated to support step-by-step changes. The overall objective is smart and innovative growth for all citizens. The goal is to implement projects that contribute to learning about innovation and competence development in the hundreds of regions in the 28 EU member states. "EU regulations not only improved managerial practices in European Regional Development Fund programs with the implementation of systematic monitoring and evaluation, but also induced spillovers on domestic management practices" (Riché, 2013: 64–65).

19.2.2 Evaluating for learning, change, and transformation

Traditional evaluation models are based on linear, mechanical, and list-checking approaches to development. In that context, it becomes natural to use evaluation as an instrument for measurement and control. Evaluation is not regarded as an instrument for creating knowledge about how programs and projects can create ripple effects, growth, innovation, new jobs, and entrepreneurship in the long run. Instead of contributing to an enlightened public debate on growth and development, evaluators communicate mainly with those responsible for programs and projects, almost invariably for reporting and administrative purposes.

19.2.3 Evaluation for structural change and development

The central problem with the implementation of structural change projects is the relationship with stability. In a functioning society, there are structures, institutions, and rules. This society is characterized by stability and predictability. At the same time, change and development are fundamental to a dynamic society and a growing economy. The challenge lies in the ability to understand and manage how interventions such as the EU's cohesion policy might transform structures and institutions. Structural change and development is pivotal for smart, sustainable, and inclusive growth to take place all over Europe.

The issue put forward by, e.g., Donaldsson et al. (2009) addresses what counts as credible evidence in applied research and evaluation practice. This is of major importance for evaluation, regarding both empirical findings and timing. One consequence is that *both* management *and* evaluation of projects must be able to respond quickly, flexibly, and innovatively to demands and changes. This is where the theory of *Agile project management* comes in. This means being able to respond to external change, and trying to exercise influence (Highsmith, 2010: 13). Therefore, we argue that evaluation should become an important part of the support system and highlight risks, as well as opportunities, in uncertain, prototypical situations. If we are to achieve results that can be used, the evaluations must be able to answer questions concerning which structures are transformed and which institutional conditions are changed. We have to demonstrate by evidence-based conclusions how these interventions work and could be improved.

19.3 An illustrative case – The implementation of regional venture capital fund projects

Findings from ongoing evaluation have to be generated so that interventions can be improved. Knowledge of what works has to be created and spread to make regions more innovative and to make the labor markets function better. Not least, unexpected and unintended effects are to be caught, analyzed, discussed, and communicated. Here, we will illustrate the form evaluation for project performance that we think is requested if we are to learn from innovative interventions.

Since 2005, Sweden has begun to use EU funds to finance interventions aiming to improve capital procurement for new, innovative, and growth-oriented enterprises. (Brulin, 2012: 24; Brulin and Svensson, 2012: 180). In 2009, 11 regional co-investment fund projects were initiated. They received over EUR60 million in the 2007–2013 programming period, which was to be matched with at least as much private financing. The regional co-investment fund projects have thus invested well over EUR120 million in small and medium sized enterprises (SMEs) in the early stages of their development along with a private sector party who contributes at least half of the investment. The intervention was motivated by an identified dearth of capital in Swedish SMEs with an ambition to grow as well as interest from the European Commission and national and regional stakeholders in working with revolving instruments instead of grants (Tillväxtverket, 2015). The goal of the fund projects is for more enterprises to be able to start up and grow in all of Sweden's 21 regions.

Very few regions, if any, in Sweden have well-developed venture capital markets. Could public investment fund projects throughout Sweden support the growth of SMEs, create new jobs, initiate structural change towards innovation and new businesses? When the fund projects started, there were no clear answers. The ongoing evaluation was to systematically follow the intervention logic in order to determine whether the desired effects would occur. The evaluation was based on quantitative data from monitoring and questionnaires and interviews with the fund projects and portfolio companies and private investors, as well as other venture capital investors in Sweden who have/have not co-invested with the funds, and eminent experts and researchers in the field. Seminars and workshops with both people in the regional development boards and the parliamentary committee on business development have been held.

Initially, it was revealed that the fund projects' specific expected results and overall goals were unclear. Consequently, the first year's evaluation led to changes in the intervention logic of the venture capital fund projects. They should not just focus on investing, but rather also support shaping regional structures of business angels and investors if they were to reach their goals. Furthermore, the key indicator "new jobs created" had to be abolished as it takes quite a lot of time before these SMEs really create new stable jobs. Furthermore, the ongoing evaluation highlighted the issue of an exit market if these fund projects were to revolve their capital. Also, the different possibilities to succeed in scarcely populated areas compared to city regions were problematized in the evaluation for fund project performance. Processes to channel venture capital to investments and breeding grounds for success were very much at hand in the latter type of regions.

Public debate, based on the ongoing evaluation, not least among politicians and regional development actors, has meant that the venture capital interventions were given a third try in the programming period 2014–2020. It was also decided that special venture capital fund projects for investments in enterprises aiming to develop technology to reduce climate change emissions were to be set up in 2017. Furthermore, at the end of the programming period, an experiment with four holding-fund projects will be started.

Which conclusions could, on a meta-level, be drawn from this ongoing evaluation of the capital fund projects? How has the evaluation managed to create knowledge from the evidences found in the implementation of these interventions? What are the implications for future evaluation of project performance? In the following sections, we will present the central elements in a general model for evaluation of project performance.

19.4 Three Ps in project performance

Evaluation for learning from innovative, additive, and experimental interventions must encompass a mix of methods, which could be summarized in three Ps: Program and project logic, Processes interacting with the environment, and Public debate/usability (see Brulin and Svensson, 2012: 78), as well as three Ks: Key activities, Key people, and Key figures/ratios. The main requirement is that evaluations of the projects should focus on impacts and be able to explain how projects contribute to innovation and competence development, that is, the mechanisms behind the effects. The evaluation should be based on a causal model that logically connects activities with results and long-term structural impacts, and takes into account the context and environment of the action. Long-term effects in the form of structural transformation towards innovative regions and the mechanisms behind the changes are to be captured. This means using a mixed methods approach, often termed triangulation (Bjurulf and Nilsson, 2013: 149).

These methods are based on many evaluations, interactive research and project evaluation reports, interviews with key persons, extensive questionnaires, group dialogues, review of existing material, etc. The empirical basis for our model is presented and thoroughly discussed in the book *Managing Sustainable Development Programmes* (Brulin and Svensson, 2012; Svensson et al., 2013), including a meta-study of the system for project and program evaluation.

19.4.1 Project logic reconstructed

Initially, an evaluation should critically examine *the project logic* and specify how it can be effective in line with its set of objectives and expected results. In innovation and competence development projects, the ongoing evaluation project logic must critically examine:

- how research activities can contribute to innovations, which should lead to results that can be commercialized;
- how education and training can be expected to lead to improved employability and operational development; and
- whether the project is based on an analysis of the conditions and prior experiences of measurements taken.

If there are deficiencies in the project logic in these respects, the likelihood is low that the project will lead to long-term effects. However, the project logic is not set in stone. Continuously, the project logic should be examined, adjusted, and reconstructed.

Projects that are innovative, additive, and experimental should be based on a reconstruction of the causal model that describes how an intervention is intended to be effective, what activities are to be carried out, and what impacts they should contribute to. Which mechanisms shape long-term effects? The starting point for the analysis is the reconstructed project logic, sometimes referred to as the intervention logic or theory of change.

The reconstruction of the project logic means that the evaluator establishes what the funders and manager "really" intend to do, and what objectives and results could conceivably arise from this. Because a certain amount of time passes, sometimes quite a long period of time from initialization and the setting of priorities, before a project is implemented, the reconstruction of the intervention logic can reveal significant differences in relation to what has been planned. Gradually revealing such differences, and learning more about how the intervention logic functions when it encounters "reality", means that the project can be reoriented.

19.4.2 Processes making the environment a breeding ground for the project

It is not enough to evaluate a project's objectives, plans, methodologies, and activities. Project logic can be very convincing in itself. However, if the logic does not clearly connect to processes in the receiving environment, the project will not have the impact it is aiming for. It is therefore important to evaluate whether the project management has a knowledge and understanding of the various processes in the local setting that can help a project "land on its feet" and function in its regional and local environment. Processes for receiving, managing, and nurturing a project, but also for getting it to give back to its environment, are of utmost importance for better innovation, more competitive regions, and more effective labor markets.

The project management plays an important role for the success of a project, but the task and the skills required will be different in a complex project with multiple cooperating actors in a dynamic environment. Being able to utilize the surrounding environment is one of the most important characteristics of project management (Shearmur and Bonnet, 2011). It has to be analyzed whether the project is capable of making use of the opportunities available in its surrounding environment. A project organization with active ownership and a professional steering group is a necessity to create mechanisms so project performance has long-term effects.

19.4.3 Public debate/usability – Dissemination and learning for multiplier effects

Feeding back results and knowledge gathered from the evaluation makes learning possible. Evaluations that are not communicated and spread are meaningless. Learning in various forms should be a central part of the overall evaluation system. This is the third P in the evaluation model. The task of the evaluation is to ensure that knowledge and instructive examples are communicated and become available in public debate, i.e., knowledge of how to achieve the objectives of innovation, commercialization, competence development, etc. The project evaluators have a great responsibility to ensure that results and knowledge are reported and communicated in various networks and arenas.

A critical and constructive evaluation of how projects work to further availability, dissemination, and effectiveness is an important task in an evaluation for the purposes of learning. This evaluation model aims to make a difference and lead to the overall Europe 2020 objectives. Far too much of the learning from the EU Structural Funds and programs is single-loop (Argyris, 1999); it is expected that good examples will be reproduced in regular activities. However, learning is a more complex process. It is, not least, important to learn from failures. Learning is not about reproducing what has been learned; rather, learning should be focused on development, that is, drawing conclusions from the failure and doing things differently. To do so, one must be willing to learn and learn again. An important part of learning is documentation, that is, whether it is a testimony of success or failure. The task of the evaluator is to see whether projects enable learning that can become a multiplier in the European dimension.

19.5 The three Ks in project performance evaluation

Project performance evaluation should take its point of departure in the two fundamental questions that evaluation is to answer: *what* works and *how* does it work. These two questions can be answered with various methods. How the theory of change is tested depends on what is feasible. The testing can be done through an experimental or a quasi-experimental design that uses a control or comparison group, or through a design without a comparison group that is based on various types of process tracing. This can be done using a combination of methods, with and without experimentation. Evaluations of complex programs will need several methods and multiple data sources to be credible. Thereby, the evaluation model for project performance looks like legal proceedings. The task of this is to see how an intervention has contributed to the achievement of different objectives. We will present three methods of doing this – the three Ks: identifying Key activities, interviewing Key people, and comparing Key ratios or figures.

19.5.1 Process tracing – Key events are identified

When key activities and events are identified, just as in a criminal case, we get to know how the crime might reasonably have unfolded. Vedung writes that this procedure can be compared to the court case's process tracing (2013: 59). In other words, in his opinion, project performance evaluation is about using a mix of methods, termed triangulation. Process tracing involves a thorough study of a project and its key activities. The entire process is traced in detail and made visible: from intervention to outcome. It involves understanding the intervention logic to see whether "beyond reasonable doubt" has led to the outcome.

Process tracing of key events and activities means that the evaluator first reconstructs and clarifies the actual intervention logic, which is more or less concealed. The reconstructed intervention logic virtually never corresponds to the project logic that was specified in the original project application. Things change all the time and concealed, or unintended purposes, become visible along the way. This reconstructed project logic is thus used as a tool to trace and understand how the project has actually unfolded. Process tracing means that the evaluator makes manifest the key activities in the implementation chain of events to try to find which mechanisms have produced impacts of various kinds.

19.5.2 Key people are interviewed – Shadow control

A second method for understanding the mechanisms in a project is *shadow* control. Shadow control means that insightful people estimate the significance of different activities. Shadow control gives rise to a counterfactual analysis. The value of opinions by external people obviously depends on their specific knowledge. The reliability of these opinions also depends on the people who have been selected for the shadow controls.

Practitioners involved in the project have an internal insight and knowledge of what might have occurred if the project had not been carried out, but their opinion can be biased because they may have profited themselves from the project. This bias must be highlighted and problematized in the evaluation analysis. All too often, evaluators have contented themselves with presenting answers to questionnaires and surveys without discussing the value of the answers.

Internal actors must therefore be complemented with external experts. Vedung (2013: 58) believes that when external experts are used, they should be well-versed in intervention and preferably have demonstrated their expertise in written publications. They should have good knowledge of the results of other evaluations in the field.

19.5.3 Key figures – A comparative analysis

It is hard (sometimes impossible) to evaluate innovative or novel interventions. Contra factual analysis means that the evaluator tries to compare the project with a zero situation, statistical data or a control group, which has not been exposed to the intervention. When dealing with interventions that are intended to be innovative, additive, and experimental, it is per definition impossible to find a reference object to compare the intervention with. If there is such a reference object, the intervention is not really innovative and original.

An evaluation based on randomized experiments does contain several weaknesses (Vedung, 2013: 48). They are wide open to the Hawthorne effect, which is based on their very participation in an experiment. This could partly be dealt with if a double-blind design is used; however, this is very difficult to organize and is also ethically problematic. There is a severe risk that a complicated reality will be simplified and the impact of contextual factors will be limited.

Nonetheless, when evaluating project performance, one should not avoid making comparisons with other types of similar interventions, statistical data, or changes in various indicators in order to highlight and find evidence for what works and does not work. It is important that the key figures in the counterfactual analysis/comparative analysis are embedded in firmly grounded theory-based project logic analyses. This is a necessity in order to generalize the results. Statistics and data regarding e.g., company turnover, profits, and competence give insights in the proceeding of a project's performance (Bjurulf and Nilsson, 2013: 155).

19.6 Serendipities and evaluation for project performance

Far too much effort has been put into the evaluation of implementation processes and structures. Questions concerning who the beneficiaries are, whether all prospective beneficiaries are aware of the programs, and whether the implementation is characterized by simplicity, clarity, and transparency are important, but have been afforded far too much space. Therefore, in the 2014–2020 programming period in the EU, evaluations should focus on the impacts of the cohesion policy for citizens, regional growth, and job creation. The focus is now on project performances, but with an openness for innovation and unexpected results.

In conclusion, an evaluation model for project performance must not work in such a way that it hinders learning from happy accidents (Taleb, 2010). On the contrary, our evaluation model is a methodological approach that clarifies surprises and tries to capture unexpected results. Major breakthroughs, such as penicillin and the World Wide Web, were based on unexpected outcomes. The Web was created because people needed a fast communication forum at CERN, and penicillin was discovered by Fleming by accident. An evaluation model for project performance should encompass such unforeseen events and serendipities, thereby clarifying what is innovative and useful in the intervention. To capture these, an evaluation model should focus on key events, witnesses from key actors, and comparing key figures.

The sociologist Robert K. Merton became known for his "middle range theories": theories which are based on the fact that neither in real life nor in science – especially in the social and human sciences – will we ever know everything (1957). We must content ourselves with provisional, dynamic theories in the mid-range. His ideas have had a wide impact and he has also developed the concept of serendipity (Merton and Barber, 2004). We can learn a lot from studying societal and social development processes, but we will never get definitive answers carved in stone and cast in concrete recommendations for action. The old fairy-tale of the Three Princes of Serendip, who wanted to get to know their country, illustrates this. Disguised as peasants, they traveled around their kingdom and spoke with its people. Their journey was full of setbacks and misunderstandings, and the princes never really got an answer to the question of how Sri Lanka (Serendip being its name in old Persia) actually functioned. On the other hand, the three princes learned a great deal about their kingdom, though seldom not what they had expected to learn. The moral of the story is that knowledge is not always found where you look for it and useful knowledge is not always the information you were looking for from the beginning. This tale is the origin of the word serendipity, that is, to come to an unexpected insight when you are looking for answers of something else.

Evaluation designed to ensure that activities internalize the results of projects and renew themselves are not enough. To find new approaches in working with innovation and competence development, concrete experimentation is required – for this, the project form is decisive. However, the opportunities it creates by trying out new approaches in practice are only meaningful if you have an evaluation model that captures the performance of the projects.

Sometimes the learning from the project is incorporated in regular activities; sometimes not. Even when the learning is not directly made use of, it makes it possible thinking in new ways. It is important to create an evaluation model of project performance that can capture the serendipities and which, in a pedagogical and interesting way, can communicate those. Critical and constructive analysis of the projects' logic and the processes that support their success warrants both better implementation and increased confidence in experimentation by means of projects.

19.6.1 Some practical implications

Project performances are difficult to assess, especially in large-scale and innovative programs. When the evaluation is made by a consultant, it is often uncritical and circumscribed to be of any strategic value. When the evaluation is made by a researcher, it is often abstract and distant. We argue that ongoing and interactive evaluation can be a way to improve project performance. We have introduced a model for evaluation of project performance, which is based on joint learning about mechanisms, an openness for unexpected outcomes, and with a focus on long-term effects and directed to different stakeholders. This model has now become an official guideline in the implementation of the Regional Structural Fund projects in Sweden. The idea is to catch both the *what* and the *how* in the project performance. To understand and analyze *what* has happened in a project, we use the three Ps: Project logic, Processes (in interaction with the context), and Public debate. To understand *how* the evaluation can be carried out, we use the three Ks: that is, getting information based on Key activities, from Key actors, and with the use of Key figures. We think this model can be a starting point in the improvement of the assessment of project performances. It shapes the basis for a continuous and critical learning process of how to make Europe's regions more innovative and competently managed.

Chapter 20

Project performance in the financial sector

Tiago Cardoso

Introduction

The market area that potentially offers one of the widest, broadest impacts in everyone's daily life. The sector that when business goes bad, millions of people's lives are changed (mostly, for worse) in a matter of days. The financial area, responsible of dictating how good or bad the world's economy is behaving, keeps pushing further on project management needs.

Such a critical market, definitely relies on state-of-the-art management techniques, right? Cannot be more wrong. As any other market, project management challenges in the financial market are popping up on a daily basis.

We'll be reviewing some of these challenges along this chapter, such as

- Are the challenges in the financial area the *same* as other markets?
- What are the *common key factors* that slows a project down in the financial area – and how to overcome them?
- How to assess if the project is slowing down? How to assess your project *performance* throughput in general?
- How to know if the project, even if not slowing down, is going in the *right direction*?
- How to continuously improve your project working model to deliver more and often?

Disclaimer

Besides being known for the skyrocket bonuses, the finance hubs are also known to have people moving around from bank to bank. The comments in this chapter contains experiences shared by people working on different finance institutions, not solely representing the experiences of the author.

Whenever the chapter refers to the "development" team, this team structure is based on the Agile concept of a development team, composed of versatile and seasoned professionals capable of doing not only actual code development, but all the other activities required to deliver a requirement.

So, why a chapter on the financial area? What's special about projects in the financial area, after all?

There are two aspects to consider when talking about projects for the financial area: the *methodology they're likely to use* and their *nature*.

Financial institutions and industry organizations generally consider the following as "valid" software development methodologies: the already well-known Waterfall and Agile methodologies, and also the less common Rapid Application Development (RAD) and End User Development (EUD) methodologies. What are they? RAD and EUD are methodologies usually used to automate relatively small manual processes, being created by IT people working closely to the end users in the RAD case or by the end users themselves in the case of EUD, usually with the assistance of macro-related tools (yes, if "Microsoft Excel" comes to your mind, you're completely right).

Along this chapter, we'll be mostly focused on the Waterfall and Agile methodologies, so why bother about RAD or EUD? Well, every time one reads in newspapers that there's a major financial project to replace "legacy" applications, there's a chance that these legacy projects were built on top of RAD or EUD. And one might ask – wouldn't it be better to have the automation done on a proper, structured project covering the broader problem rather than hundreds of small, less organized projects to address different tiny needs? Yes and no. *Yes*, everyone agrees that a "Strategic" solution to address the underlying problems faced by the end users is always the right option. *No*, because

1) There's usually a need for *immediate, short-term* results that can only be achieved through a "Tactical" solution that'll be replaced eventually by the proper Strategic solution (spoiler alert, it may or may not happen!)
2) The people involved in such automations started work on them to address *their own daily work and needs* (without considering whether there's more people doing the same tasks or not and their realities), but eventually such automations are handed over to other peers when the authors change roles or move to other companies
3) It's hard to standardize processes due to regional restrictions or needs, so a trader operating in London might not be eager to break his own tool just to have it working to his New Yorker peer

Thus, when talking about software development methodologies in the financial area, you may be surprised to face projects that are not *initially labelled* Waterfall or Agile at all. Initially labelled is an important concept to be explored further, as there's a lot "in between" Waterfall and Agile.

Now, when talking about project nature, there's a considerable amount of possibilities:

a) New business features: there are projects everywhere implementing new finance functionalities, improving and optimizing how the daily business is done.
b) New audit and policy constraints: banks in general must adhere to a plethora of new regulations and audit constraints on a constant basis. Every year, systems must be changed – while the system is still in use, so unless there's a major reason for starting a system from scratch, such implementations are done "patching up" the already existing platforms (and you might as well assume what happens to a platform being patched for years).
c) Standardization: most of the banks as we know nowadays are built on top of "merging" several different smaller financial institutions. One of the first items to be tackled when it happens is to standardize the tools used at the different branches and with a similar purpose. Besides, on today's world, the regional barriers are no longer as high as they once were, so the "globalization" also affects the financial area, enforcing banks and financial institutions operating across the globe to reduce the amount

of maintained applications and providing a standard platform that can be understood from Tokyo to New York. Also, when talking about standardization, the different teams need to speak a similar language and consider common data providers, and the definition of such standard data providers (a common chart of accounts, for instance) is one of the biggest challenges for major institutions. Everyone likes a standard, so long it's "their own" standard. Using someone else's defined standard to replace the standard one is already used to is uncomfortable, to say the least.

d) Decommission of legacy platforms: sometimes alongside the standardization, old "legacy" platforms are decommissioned. However, there are situations where hardware or operating systems, although "standard", are no longer supported. When it happens, companies must migrate or upgrade them accordingly, decommissioning the old systems. However, such projects are most of the times very challenging – the target platform must be very well tailored to be able to fit with the migration needs, and this usually (or at least, should) involve a considerable amount of regression testing, in order to ensure functionalities are not lost and no new problems are created. Besides, when considering the decommissioning of legacy hardware, the new platform must provide at least the same level of confidence and availability of the current platform, and that's not a trivial work. If the project considers a major platform migration, is vital to understand not only the "happy path" functionality but most specially understanding how the application behaves when going off-track: is there any resilience mechanism already in place to be mimicked? Is there any user need that's only used once a year but it's vital to business continuity? Or else, when dealing with a hardware migration, is the new hardware able to not only keep the platform up and running, but paving the way for future application demands? Are the non-functional requirements known and achieved? Is there a proper environment to test and ensure, with an acceptable level of confidence, such results? These are common questions one might need to ask at the early days of a decommission project.

e) Optimization of current platform: such projects are similar to the legacy ones and are addressing similar needs, however, the trigger is internal rather than external – before expecting the end of support knocking on the door, the management decides to proactively migrate the application to a new platform, taking advantage of a specific business need that requires a more powerful processing capacity, for instance.

So, there are four broadly accepted methodologies of development and five major groups of project natures being dealt on a daily basis inside an investment institution.

As a side note, it is worthy to also highlight that oftentimes a project is part of a broader *program* that comprises other projects for different layers, applications or users. This concept will be important for our next session on how to measure the performance of our projects.

With such a variety of projects, how to measure them in a consistent way?

The financial sector, as any other sector, is constantly evolving. Priorities are changing, new policies are created, current policies are lifted, hundreds of reports must be adjusted in a matter of weeks. While all this activity takes place, projects must keep up the pace to continuously deliver while improving working models to reduce or mitigate the historical pain points. One of these improvements is the rollout of projects based on Agile principles.

Thus, how to consistently measure a project regardless of the development model being utilized? In the financial sector, besides the common key performance indicators (KPIs) used everywhere such as the number of bugs detected, deviations from the original target dates and costs and others, there are a few finance-specific metrics that are usually considered – and could be applied in both Waterfall and Agile projects. Having such characteristics, such finance-specific metrics can be useful to assess whether development methodology changes are really improving such performance indicators. Common performance indicators are:

- **Time to market**: how long does a business demand take from request to delivery? This is potentially the most critical KPI measured. The complexity in the financial sector comes on major *programs*. The actual business value can only be added when *all the projects inside a program* are properly delivered. Such projects work as independent silos, up to a moment in time – usually late in the testing phase – when the complete workflow must be tested and validated. There's always margin for a successful project to be part of a failed program, so it's not a trivial activity to assess whether the delivery was a success or a failure. Like the failure of the NASA's Mars Climate Orbiter, if both teams have delivered the right project but their interfaces are not operational, the business value is not delivered at all.
- **Reduction of manual efforts**: banks are constantly investing efforts to reduce the amount of manual operations or End User Developed Applications (EUDAs). This KPI encloses several aspects of the problem (such as the operation costs and the risks due to manual failure), so the reduction of human intervention is always a very common KPI.
- **Service Level Agreement (SLA) improvements**: The regulations around the SLAs the banks should respond to are very restrictive, so new projects are constantly monitoring Non-Functional Requirements (NFRs) that could directly impact (negatively or positively) the application SLAs.
- **Amount of application functional failures or exception scenarios and the time taken to address them**: When changes applied have a considerable functional impact (i.e. they are not a platform migration), the elapsed time between the unexpected behaviour is detected up to the moment its fixed is also a fundamental KPI. Likewise, the number of occurrences of such behaviours also indicate whether the application is increasing or decreasing in quality.

As a rule of thumb, projects with high performance are the ones where the whole program have achieved its goals, sometimes disregarding the number of defects or extra efforts to obtain the results. Inspired in the Agile mind-set, some other potential double-edged perceptions of high-performance teams are linked to the amount of deliveries done to production. This could lead to a potential risk, since the relationship between business value and frequency of deliveries have no direct relationship between them beyond the *overall perception of achievement*. It may work in the short term but may also fail in the long term.

Because of it, projects should have their performance assessed against the business value they're adding on top of any other dimension. Interesting enough, by doing so projects will be following the first principle of the Agile manifesto: *to satisfy the customer through early and continuous delivery of valuable software.*

What does exist in between Waterfall and Agile in the financial sector?

Before answering this question, let's review a few concepts:

- Waterfall delivery considers the product completely delivered at the end of its cycle
- Waterfall does NOT consider rolling back to any previous step
- Agile comprises several methodologies, where Scrum and XP are only two examples
- Being Agile means fully embodying the Agile values

So, with the above said, what was the last time you worked on a fully Waterfall project, with clear interfaces and documentation delivered and signed off between each phase and without the need of going backwards to redo some of the work? What was the last time you worked on a fully Agile project, where the values and principles were known by all people involved and inspired most (if not all) project decisions?

If your answer is "I don't remember" for both questions, you might not be alone. Although there's a lot of documentation on both methodologies, to have a single project following strictly one or other may not be something as often as expected. Different projects have different levels of methodology maturity. There may be "Agile-labelled" projects working on "sprints" with teams built up of "analysts", "developers" and "testers", or where the user provides the requirement on a formal business definition document and checks the result when the project is completed; there are other "Waterfall-labelled" projects working with demonstrations every now and then and delivering incremental changes to users. All these projects are part of the bulk of projects which are either trying to evolve from Waterfall into Agile, or else working to deliver as fast as possible. At the end of the day, what each client wants is pretty clear, and that applies everywhere – more delivery and more quality, for less money. However, how the senior management – who is responsible for the strategy to make it happen – decides to reach this result is what lies in between Waterfall and Agile. It's important to highlight that, as in any other sector, there might be well functioning Waterfall and Agile projects in the finance area. However, this chapter is likely to be more useful for people who are more in the "everything in between" camp.

How to assess where my project stands?

The perspective of this chapter is that the projects you participate or manage is transitioning into a more Agile approach – or at the very least, looking for options to make stakeholders happier. With that in mind, we can use the four core Agile Values to assess where your project stands. Some of the below characteristics could be aligned to more than one Agile value, the below categorization of problems and solutions to specific Agile core values is just used for simplicity. Besides, the order they are presented is not considered for its criticality, as each project will have specific challenges.

Individuals and interactions over processes and tools

This is likely to be the most fundamental value for a long-term, sustainable team. Here, the communication is the cornerstone for a successful project.

Common trait of a low-performance project: Project members don't work as a single team, with a single purpose.

Steps to become a high-performance project: Projects moving from Waterfall towards an Agile environment have a major roadblock – the team structure. While Waterfall was focused on completely segregated silos, where each silo had a specific objective (analysis to provide as much accurate requirements as possible, development to build as strictly aligned to requirements as possible, testing to find as much gaps between requirements and actual results), this is no longer applicable on an Agile team. Every member on the project, and especially within the development team, must add its own views, skills and experiences to the project, so long they can consider the people besides them as doing exactly the same, with the same intensity.

In the financial sector, especially on projects transitioning from Waterfall to Agile, achieving a stable team structure is an arduous and effortful task for all people involved, not only for the development team.

The development team needs to switch mind-sets from their previous, rigid and restricted roles, and embrace a new, more fluid role. As allied a development team is, the better. Belonging to the same location, same time zone, with the same interests and sharing personal traces such as the same culture and interests definitely helps.

The management may have the demanding job of enabling the development team to switch mind-sets, laying the grounds for such teams to exist. Doing so might be complicated when there are conflicts of interests between parts. It could happen when there are external providers involved on each side, or different locations with the same skillset competing to become the more important for the project.

Common trait of a low-performance project: Team members are not confident enough to challenge current processes by the fear of not being heard or suffer retaliations from senior management.

Steps to become a high-performance project: Create an environment where people feel courageous to express themselves. It's not by chance that courage is one of the Scrum Core Values. Not all team members have the same responsibilities and, although it's evident some roles have the responsibility of taking more risks than others, every team member should feel minimally comfortable by expressing oneself. There are two key changes required to create this environment, one cultural and one organizational (in the sense of how the team organizes their tasks on a timely basis).

The cultural change is the buy-in from senior management, who should empower team members to express themselves. Good leaders ask for team opinions regardless of their ranks in the hierarchy.

The organizational change is to create opportunities or events where such ideas should be heard. And not only heard, but also tracked and followed up for proper answers. There's only a few things as frustrating as gathering the guts to raise a concern, raising it to senior management and then having it forgotten. Sometimes it is more important to let the team know the concerns are heard and not forgotten than actually addressing the problems.

Lastly, leaders must also consider the different cultures involved, and constantly empower and nurture their teams on how to work on such multi-cultural environments.

Each culture organizes and expresses ideas in a different manner, and to be open and master the art of understanding the messages being conveyed by each culture is a major factor for a project success (or failure).

Common trait of a low-performance project: Processes in place adding unknown or no real value to the value stream.

Steps to become a high-performance project: The value stream is the sequence of activities from design to delivery of a product or service. In case there's a process that's not helping to achieve the project objectives, this process should be either reviewed or removed. This is a constant process, and any project member must feel comfortable to challenge processes not adding value. Be glad if the team constantly asks the value of a given process and raise a concern in case people are simply following processes without question. On a project where most (if not all) of its members are knowledge workers, some challenge is expected and even healthy.

Common trait of a low-performance project: Processes not understood by everyone.

Steps to become a high-performance project: A process is usually created either to make a routine task simpler or to address problems faced in the past. How many processes adopted by your project are known and appreciated by the whole team? Are they still useful? As previously discussed, teams should feel confident enough to challenge the current processes in place. Be glad when someone asks why such processes exists. If no one knows the answer – or if the answer is not adding real business value to the value stream – then get rid of the process.

Common trait of a low-performance project: Tool usage considered as an objective in itself.

Steps to become a high-performance project: The purpose of any tool is to support the achievement of a given objective. However, sometimes the objective may be forgotten in the way and having the tool working for the sake of having the tool working becomes the objective, deviating from the actual value the tool should add. Sometimes, a good tool usage is implemented by people outside to reach some specific objectives, but during implementation of this tool usage the objectives are shadowed by the tool usage, which eventually lead to objectives being lost. How is your team handling the tools you use? The First Agile Value does not imply tools are not important; instead, it reinforces that the interactions between individuals and the results obtained by such interactions and individuals are more important than such tools.

Common trait of a low-performance project: Processes being implemented due to the success on other projects, without considering actual project realities.

Steps to become a high-performance project: Individuals working for a project for a fair amount of time have (or are expected to have) an acceptable vision on what the key problems are and why the project may not deliver as expected. People responsible for removing such problems and blockers are expected to be constantly following up with their project members on what are the fundamental problems and which ones, if addressed, could improve project delivery. Having such improvements being implemented to address actual problems might give project people the momentum required to buy in and be motivated to move them forward.

However, having a process implemented on your project because it worked somewhere else might be very risky, and could be a waste of efforts. This is noticed sometimes in the financial sector, as projects share several similarities, such as hardware and user mind-set. However, implementing a process should not be a target in itself. It should consider the current project realities and current project needs. There might be cases where implementing external successes work, there might not be. The project team can help on tailoring such implementations.

Working software over comprehensive documentation

This is value focus on delivering actual, usable software instead of months delivering very thorough documentation that never becomes reality. The amount of documentation a finance project needs to generate is from the start higher than usual due to the several controls it must adhere to. However, leaders must keep an eye to ensure the documentation being generated is as needed without over-complicating processes and slowing down – or even putting at risk – the actual deliverables. Besides, the lack of a sound development structure where the team can validate its changes and ensure such changes are not adding failures is a must regardless of the methodology used. As mature as the project is, as quickly such validations take place. Agile-based cultures like DevOps emerged to reduce the time between a change being added to the system and the change being placed into normal production environment, while ensuring quality.

Common trait of a low-performance project: Low testing automation.

Steps to become a high-performance project: Automate testing, prioritizing the activities that are adding more latency between development to production deployment. One great performance indicator your project can use is how many hours a team needs to ensure its newly developed functionality can be delivered to production. If the team has a dependency on external teams to test it or such testing cannot be executed on demand, the team must work on it the sooner the better. There are some development *techniques* such as Test Driven Development (TDD), Behaviour Driven Development (BDD) or Acceptance Test Driven Development (ATDD) intended to ensure changes are tested early on in the process as well as setting up some common ground on how a specific deliverable is expected to behave. Such techniques can theoretically be used in both Waterfall and Agile methodologies, however, it's more natural to perceive them on Agile environments. In Waterfall, there's a specific testing phase whereas in Agile the testing and development are more intertwined, so considering the usage of TDD in Waterfall, although possible, could lead to some confusion – what testing would be done if the "testing" is already done using TDD? One Waterfall possible approach could be having TDD applied during the development phase and the "testing" phase reserved for the User Acceptance Testing. This way, when the users are involved in the testing process, basic issues are not detected. When a project adopts this approach, it's natural to perceive as a project being "in between" Waterfall and Agile. Likewise, a "pure" Agile would not need the post-development User Acceptance Testing, as once the change is deemed completed, it's theoretically ready to go to production, which means that any eventual user validation has happened alongside functionality development.

Common trait of a low-performance project: Low release and deployment automation.

Steps to become a high-performance project: Like the testing automation, teams should be focused on delivering new functionalities instead of worrying about how and when a functionality will be delivered to production. Such steps should be natural and part of a common, controlled cycle. While Waterfall-oriented methodologies advocate the delivery of major and big deliverables containing months' worth of work, Agile methodologies focus on small, continuous deliveries. In Waterfall, due to the big nature of the deliverables, some level of complexity on a deployment is expected, and part of the steps towards a more Agile approach is to ensure such deployment is as smooth as possible.

Common trait of a low-performance project: Extensive documents not maintained or baselined (or maintained and baselined consuming a considerable amount of efforts).

Steps to become a high-performance project: In a Waterfall project, once all analysis is completed, an extensive documentation is handed over for development. Documents like the Business Requirement Document and Functional Design Document are common practice. Such documents are useful when the problem to be tackled is completely known and no further changes are expected to arise (such environment is where Waterfall is better applied). There are environments where requirements are gathered on such a format but expect an implementation on an Agile fashion. This creates a considerable amount of complexity for everyone involved. From the business side, once the first prototypes are delivered by the project, users understand the functionality was not either not covering all cases or not clearly written, requiring documentation maintenance. On the other side, the latency between flaw detection and requirement change creates massive gaps during development. Teams working in such fashion are clearly "in between" the Waterfall and Agile methodologies. To have a proper Agile working, users should be engaged during the whole process, and we'll be discussing this further in the third Agile value.

Thus, to become a high-performance project, the project needs to either engage users more often for a more open communication instead of extensive documentation or having clear lightweight processes to address such requirement changes.

Common trait of a low-performance project: Production deliveries not adding business value or dormant for a long time.

Steps to become a high-performance project: The usage of iterative deliveries to production with some features not completely enabled is something relatively common on mature projects. To do so, there are different techniques available, such as the usage of feature toggles or flags. Ideally, each and every production delivery should theoretically add business value, but such dormant deliveries are required for a short period of time for different reasons. The problem comes when such features are dormant for too long. Dormant features should be an exception, not a rule. The efforts to roll back a dormant feature might not pay off the efforts to deliver it in the first place. This usually happens when there are bureaucrats involved in the project, focused on delivering a piece of a program without concerned about the long-term project stability. We'll discuss the challenges bureaucrats add to project further on this chapter.

Such a problem is more a result of several poor practices prior to production rather than a problem in itself; it's a symptom. Addressing a symptom is not trivial, but clear and honest communication between project and stakeholders is a very important step.

Common trait of a low-performance project: Lack of structured, supportive documentation organization.

Steps to become a high-performance project: Working software is the key, but it doesn't mean that no documentation is required. The important part is to ensure the documentation available is useful and updated. Worse than no documentation is wrong documentation. An Agile project relies on different documentation tools. Small or co-located projects have the benefit of using physical boards, however, in the financial sector such projects are rare. Oftentimes projects have people from everywhere, and motivated by offering transparency at all levels, common online tools are a must.

To achieve this, project members should rely less on mails and have a better use of the available tools. The tool itself is not important, so long it offers key features such as versioning, indexation and reliable and accessible information. Project members should remember that the information being shared is not useful for today or tomorrow nor for the people involved in the current problem, but likely weeks or months from now for the people who need to have more background on the given piece of information.

Common trait of a low-performance project: Excessive manual efforts for a production delivery.

Steps to become a high-performance project: Automation and lightweight processes. In the financial sector, the complexity to deliver a change to production is heightened due to a series of validations and documentation required. One of the goals in an Agile approach is to have as frequent deliverables to users as possible, so as automated the processes are, the better. Having a taskforce with a specific goal to review the current processes and learn how similar projects are implementing their changes is also valuable, as the processes in the same institution are very similar across projects. In addition, there should be clear documentation available for such processes to explain why they are in place. Review and expand this documentation from time to time, especially when new institution constraints are created or new automation opportunities are made available. Lastly, a clear alignment with users about delivery dates is mandatory. Commitment to unrealistic dates tends to increase delivery complexity, increasing uncertainty and leading to unforeseen risks.

Common trait of a low-performance project: Several restrictions on when production can be incremented.

Steps to become a high-performance project: In the financial sector, there are several known constraints when applying a delivery to production. There are periods in time where restrictions are increased, such as the periods where business operations are closed. These are usually a few days at the end of the month and a few days after the end of the month (the month-end and year-end periods). This window changes from project to project. Sometimes, due to external factors (such as market volatility), some specific days may not allow platform changes as the operation volume may increase and any problems on business as usual process could lead to major problems.

There are projects covering several global time zones, and it could lead to complexity when having a specific downtime that could fit both eastern business hours, western business hours and different activity weekday periods (in Muslim-majority countries such as in the Middle East, weekends could cover Thursday and Friday or Friday and Saturday).

On top of the challenges from an application perspective, there are the enforced downtimes due to application and platform mandatory exercises, such as platform patching and the disaster recovery activities. Disaster recovery activities got even more attention past 9/11, and financial institutions must prove to different regulators the capability of recovery from a disaster.

Thus, stopping the platform to proceed with a production delivery when the application has a considerable amount of execution time with few potential downtime windows reserved for mandatory maintenance, every deployment must optimise the usage of its time.

Thus, to use wisely the available deployment windows, the project must focus on reducing technology complexity to reduce the overall deployment time and at the same time automate as much as possible deployment activities. There are development techniques that may help achieve this, such as the blue-green deployment. Such techniques are definitely worth exploring, although some may not be viable depending on the complexity of the platform.

Customer collaboration over contract negotiation

There are several projects in the finance sector where Agile related buzzwords are heard day in, day out. How to be Agile, let's have Scrum meetings, working in Sprints, let's implement DevOps. The challenge, however, is not to onboard the development team into Agile, as professionals with IT background in most cases are eager to do so. The challenge usually lies from the development team upwards, where the finance sector has created along the several decades of existence different layers between the developers and the end users. Because of it, this Agile value is likely to be one of the most challenging to be implemented. It not only implies a change on how the deliverables are built, but directly impacts the whole value stream for a deliverable.

It's not rare, however, to still see projects where requirements are gathered from users on colossal business requirement documents with hundreds of pages, handed over to project managers, who then hand them over to business analysts who then provide a high-level estimation in months by when such implementation will be ready. From this moment on, the "Agile in between" starts, where the development has to work on iterations and delivery results every couple of weeks.

Needless to say that such distance and the quantity of layers between development and end users is a great recipe for a mixture of different proportions of wasted money, disaster and extended hours working.

Common trait of a low-performance project: Politics.

Steps to become a high-performance project: Asking the financial sector professionals to define the single biggest challenge on big projects, it'll be no surprise hearing *politics* as the answer quite often. Politics are everywhere. For a big program composed of different projects to succeed, several factors are required: Buy in from a majority (if not all) end users; alignment between the different projects; alignment with the underlying bank-wide strategies from a functional strategy; alignment with the bank-wide platform strategies from an architectural perspective; and last, but not least, the aspirations of the professionals involved. Each of these factors must be assessed separately first, but then approaches like System Thinking must be applied. Missing any of these factors may lead a program to failure. Each area where politics are perceived as negatively impacting on collaboration needs to be assessed separately.

Customer politics: If the customers are not perceiving actual benefits on a given project, they won't be willing to be involved to help on it. People's brains are naturally wired to be averse to changes. Users may help because they *have* to, however, the subtle difference between *having* to help and *willing* to help may convert a program deemed to failure from a successful one.

To overcome this, when a project starts it is suggested to identify the users naturally willing to help (there may be only a bunch) and the naysayers (there may be lots of). If possible, pick as many people from the former, avoid as much as possible the latter.

Cross-project politics: If the different projects involved on a given program are not sharing the same clear objectives for a common goal, then there's room for extensive discussions on *who-should-fix-that* discussions, which in turn could drag the whole program into a loop of waste of time. This could happen when an interface is not clear, for instance. Let's say the producer project (also called upstream, using the oil industry business terms) is used to generate outputs in csv format and the consumer (or downstream) is supposed to receive an xml format. But there could be other problems, and who should fix that? Have you ever been in such a meeting, where senior management in both sides are involved and discussing (usually when there's already a problem in place) who should address a specific conflict? How productive was it? Usually it ends with one side feeling as losing a battle, and it shouldn't be like this, and it should be a zero-sum game – where no politics to win or lose are involved.

To avoid such a situation, ensure there's constant collaboration between the different projects since the project kick-off. This way, when the different projects have to tackle a problem, they won't be meeting each other for the first time in a conflicting situation. Having each project's subject matter experts (both functional and technical) knowing each other and openly discussing about the challenges early on is likely to reduce the amount of conflicts as the program evolves. If this collaboration can take place in person, even better: the personification of a mail or a voice is known to be a major factor to motivate people to deal with the problem in a more constructive and collaborative way.

Cross functionalities politics: If involved projects have overlapping functionalities, then the politics to discuss *who-should-perform-what* is also added. Continuing the example above, let's assume both projects are willing to expand the file formats each project deals with. In the mid to long term, the more versatile project (in this example, the one capable of dealing with different file formats) is likely to be more useful to be part of further programs, since the file format is no longer a problem. Now, apply a *finance functionality* to this example. See the plethora of opportunities each project may gain. Let's say a specific audit requirement requires a new report that no platform within the institution has readily available. The project implementing such report will then enable itself for future implementation opportunities for other areas or regions within the institution for a reduced effort, as the report core is already implemented. It implies more projects, which in turn could open room for bigger bonuses.

Handling this situation is far from trivial and potentially out of scope for the purpose of this chapter. However, having a senior management advising on what's the best strategy upfront might help avoiding such discussions during program evolution.

Architectural politics: On major institutions, the hardware and architectural solutions are oftentimes decided and agreed at very senior levels, since the platform to support applications running worldwide can have better deals if done in bulk. However, a *one-size-fits-all* solution is always challenging. Besides, contracts to be really profitable must be applied to the long run, which means that bad contracts could have negative impacts for a long time as well.

The downside comes further when such decisions are not fit for actual project needs, or maybe they were based on the past project realities. On top of it, finance institutions have to adhere to heightened controls, exposing such institutions to even more complex decisions. Consider big data. If an architectural contract was made without considering the boom of big data and the related technologies, it could take years for a financial institution to catch up to other institutions where big data contracts were properly set. Using third party Cloud services could be risky and needs to consider security and data privacy very wisely. Using in-house Cloud services could be either very expensive to provide a quality service similar to third party providers or simply suboptimal, as the expertise of a finance institution is finance, not IT.

Unless your role as manager is to help define such architectural strategy, a project does not have many options to tackle this problem besides identifying such constraints from a project perspective. The sooner such constraints are acknowledged, the better.

Contractual politics: Similar to what happened to architectural decisions, contractual decisions could hinder the capacity of a project to reach top performance. Let's consider a project that could benefit from a specific functionality that's offered by third parties tools, such as a tool which incorporates financial rules of a specific region which is a strategic area for the institution. In case the financial institution has no contracts with this specific provider, the project will have to work around such restriction. If the financial institution cannot use such a tool, the project will have to implement it in house, which may lead to several challenges that were not considered when the contract with other tools was taken.

Likewise, if a project could benefit from a specific vendor, but the actual bank strategy is not linked to such a provider, the project will have to adjust itself to suboptimal alternatives. Since early 2000, there's a constant flow of companies investing on in-house excellence centres in Asia. This could be an institution-wide strategy, but a problem if a specific project needs some specific knowledge in the South American financial system, for instance.

Personal politics: Every person has his personal and professional aspirations. Such aspirations are valuable for a project, as they're the fuel that moves the project forward, going above and beyond when challenges appear. A problem arises when people have hidden agendas not aligned to move the project forward, but to obtain other objectives like personal gains. A successful project is composed of people concerned about how to deliver the project, concerned about a single goal with a clear vision. Such professionals know that once the project is delivered, the acknowledgement of their work will take place. Not only this, but also understanding that the long-term project stability is a must, regardless of who's going to be dealing with this deliverable years from now. Every time someone takes a decision that's going to be beneficial only in the short term for the project and also professionally but bad for the project in the long run, then this decision is very likely to be taken by politics and self-interest rather than on project interest. Such behaviour is observed in people who change across institutions and projects relatively often – when the long-term problem materialises (likely to be years after the actual decision), and such decision maker is long gone. This is commonly observed when politicians make decisions and commitments. Often, the more complex the system, the harder it is to see the future impact of any decision. If a developer makes a bad decision on the assumption that a bug is not going to be perceived, the outcomes are likely to be detected in a few days. If a senior management decision is made based not on project or program benefits, the impacts of it are likely to be detected in months or years after such decisions.

Avoiding a personal agenda to influence on project decisions is an art, and the capacity to address such decisions is limited by the hierarchy position each person has in a project. One of the possibilities to mitigate such a problem is to centralise only strategic decisions and document the reasons why such strategies are decided. There are cases where such transparency may not be possible, and every time such situation arises, a step further from a real Agile world is taken. Every leader has the obligation to enforce transparency on the decision-making process, as there are only a few things more frustrating than not understanding the rationale for key strategic decisions.

Common trait of a low-performance project: Several layers between end user and developers adding low value.

Steps to become a high-performance project: Create and nurture long-term, versatile teams formed by knowledge workers, capable of understanding the business needs on business terms.

Usually, Agile teams are expected to be composed with seasoned team members, capable of covering a considerable spectrum of activities between analyses, development and testing. Such a team could deal directly with the end users to understand its needs.

On a less mature team, however, more layers in between are naturally required: to translate the specific business needs into application language, people to implement the already broke-down requirements, people to manage and constantly follow up the progress to ensure there are no deviations from planning or priorities, people focused to do a basic validation of the features – something like a quality assurance – and only then, have this deliverable handed for users again for testing.

Common trait of a low-performance project: Low to no communication between the end user and the development team.

Steps to become a high-performance project: Similar approach required to deal with the several layers between end user and development team. Sometimes the project structure has proxies between end users and development because one side is not readily available. However, when both sides are available, the project structure must promote the actual, constant communication between them. This requires maturity not only on the development side, but also on the end user side. In a sense, maturity only on the development side is not enough; maturity from the end user side, understanding how the application works and knowing what the project can provide is also key for a smooth deliverable.

Common trait of a low-performance project: Development team has its time deviated from actual development to other unplanned tasks.

Steps to become a high-performance project: High-performance projects have clear objectives, set on timeboxed meetings. Once such events take place, the development team is mostly focused on delivering the agreed functionalities. The problem arises when, due to different reasons, team attention is deviated from actual development to other tasks, such as extensive meetings, reprioritization discussions, "emergencies" or parallel, unprioritized needs.

Addressing this is hard and is an art that true Agile projects have mastered. If your project faces it, you're still "in between". It requires seniority from both the project leadership – to avoid creating interruptions and to push back external interruptions – and from the team itself, to have the comfort and be empowered to push back and deal in a constructive way with external interruptions. In case such interruptions come from the same external teams over and over, one strategy is to agree on a specific timeboxed window where the team can help on such external demands. It is suggested to have all specific questions raised in a written form prior to this session, as this way new joiners will be able to go through them and most especially, through the answers once they're clarified.

Responding to change over following a plan

Projects in the financial area are hardly isolated, but part of broader programs. If a project is successfully delivered but the program fails, the value added to business could be marginal to none. Such programs are usually covering different time zones, technologies and leadership strategies. On such environment, quickly responding to change is a must.

Common trait of a low-performance project: Bureaucrats and check boxers.

Steps to become a high-performance project: A true Agile project has no bureaucrats. People know that the objective is to deliver business value, not to tick boxes. Bureaucrats always add roadblocks on the way, without clearly explaining why. Processes must be fulfilled, and the financial sector is plenty of them, but a true Agile team must always challenge them and think of ways to overcome them in the future. A development team must be focused on development, instead of providing dozens of different reports. This needs to be done in an organized fashion, though. Agile does not mean *lack* of control. The control must exist, but it should not halt the flow of delivery. This mind-set change is especially challenging for people used to working on Waterfall, since there are hundreds of check boxes at each phase. In a project environment where there's trust between parts involved, such work becomes redundant.

Thus, to reduce bureaucracy, an environment of trust and partnership must exist. Such a stable environment is only possible when all people involved have the same level of knowledge and are willing to embrace responsibilities. Such teams should work as a single group and most importantly, feel as a single group. Management is responsible for structuring the projects in such a way that's possible, but it's up to the teams to embrace or not such responsibilities. It cannot be enforced. It should emerge from the team.

Common trait of a low-performance project: Lack of senior people in development and/or high technological complexity.

Steps to become a high-performance project: Small EUDA projects are regularly built on top of the technologies the (small number of) people involved know. However, when such applications grow or are merged with other applications and projects, if the technology landscape the new project covers are not simplified, it'll lead to a scenario where several technical skills will be required, especially from developers (but could also be more demanding from analysts and users, depending on how they'll obtain the information available). Expecting a project to become high performance demanding every single member to master four or five technologies is either too expensive or plain unrealistic. On top of it, there's not only the technical challenge a project offers; understand the application functional purpose is key to ensure the project can evolve in a sustainable way. The requirement could be crystal clear and, if a junior member is not aware of how the application works or is built, he'll be exposed to the risk of either re-implementing an already existing functionality or simply break the already existing one.

To address it, projects should considerably invest on platform simplification or invest in retaining as many seasoned members as possible. If both strategies can be applied, the better.

Common trait of a low-performance project: High costs to setup non-production testing environment.

Steps to become a high-performance project: To swiftly respond to changes, a development team must have the infrastructure required to work readily available. If a platform is composed of several different technologies and there isn't much virtualization available, the development team will struggle to respond to changes in a timely manner. As the previous suggestion to address the technology complexity, projects should consider platform simplification, automation and virtualization whenever possible as major enablers for faster deliverables.

Common trait of a low-performance project: Low automation level or high manual efforts in production.

Steps to become a high-performance project: Any application running in production should target zero manual maintenance cost. Interaction with the application should be minimal and happen only on an exceptional basis. However, if a project has a high production maintenance cost, then responding to change quickly may be impaired.

To address it, an assessment of the major requirements for manual intervention of the platform should be done and efforts dedicated to address them in a strategic way. Patching up production with layers of workaround is not going to be sustainable in the long run.

Common trait of a low-performance project: Overly restricted development access on development environment.

Steps to become a high-performance project: Developers are creative professionals, and as such, each one has specific habits or tastes for productivity tools. In the financial sector, there are several restrictions with regards to the usage of personal computing due to security constraints. Even further, when using institution provided infrastructure (personal computers, mobiles, etc.) they have several restrictions with regards to application installation and customizations. Such restrictions may eventually hinder the capacity the development team has to excel in their daily duties.

Overcoming such restrictions is not an easy duty. The project must help people to have the tools required for the daily work, and the manager should always support whatever follow-up the team needs, however, depending on the level of restrictions imposed the project can only raise the constraint and account this factor as hampering the overall project performance.

What are the steps to become a high-performance project?

As each challenge previously mentioned is addressed, a step towards a high-performance project structure is taken. It happens that each improvement might bring more or less benefit to the project at different costs.

A good first step towards becoming a high-performance project is asking oneself "why our project is not a high-performance project?" This single question might help decide how to pave the way for the next steps. Every team member might have a specific answer for "why" the project is not yet performing at peak, from different perspectives. Each answer is valuable. These reasons, the answer for these "whys", will be the fuel to make the change happen. This must be aligned to the finance institution strategy, which should also be known and as transparent as possible.

Notice that depending on the reasons why working model changes are implemented, actions may differ. Examples:

- **Scenario a:** Working model needs to change because there is communication latency between the development and operations team, which in turn leads to longer implementations
- **Scenario b:** Working model needs to change because development does not understand how operations work and operations does not have the same goals as development

In scenario a, one of the common solutions would be to merge both development and operations teams. However, it could lead to other problems. Managing a big team is more challenging than two small teams; besides, having a single team addressing operational problems and implementations could lead to confusion on how work is prioritized. Lastly, there may be cases where specific profiles are required for development and operations.

In scenario b, the problem is not in the latency between teams, but in the lack of knowledge in both areas. Training sessions could address this problem, without increasing project management complexity.

- **Scenario a:** Working model needs to improve because project is only delivering every quarter
- **Scenario b:** Working model needs to improve because the latency between the initial request and production delivery is around six months

In scenario a, having a more frequent delivery schedule is the answer. However, is there enough deliveries ready for production for a delivery every month instead of every quarter? Has this decision considered the costs of every production delivery? Has the project invested enough to ensure monthly releases are reliable or is there any risk costs implied on shorter delivery schedules?

In scenario b, however, the actual value stream is considered and latencies addressed by their root causes. This value stream mapping could show that one of the alternatives to addressing the problem could be shorter, more frequent releases, but could also be to improve the analysis process, improve communication between development and users, improve automation and so on. This analysis should be done in a transparent fashion and results made public.

Once the "why" answers provide the rationale for working model changes, such challenges should be discussed with the team to understand the reasons on why such challenge exists and what would be the possible alternatives to address them. A tracking of these actions should exist in a common forum, providing transparency to anyone interested. This should be a forum that new joiners could use to understand not only where the project is heading to, but also where the project was and why this change is being worked on.

Like any Agile project, at each major challenge addressed, a retrospective could be done at the project level to understand how it has been done and how this process could be improved in the past. This is important to ensure everyone is on the same page and questions are addressed before opening new questions.

Lastly, it is important to have a few considerations when thinking about changing the working model to move towards a high-performance project:

- Moving towards a high-performance team requires a change from top to bottom. Applying changes at the upper or lower levels will only mask problems. Having everyone buying in the change will avoid late conflicts or frustrations between people assuming to be improving from people not buying in the changes.
- Every person involved in this process should understand the benefits for him or herself when applying such change. If the team is not perceiving or understanding the benefits of the changes, they won't have the will to change.
- Identify where most of the time is wasted between the initial requests to the production delivery. Consider this information as fundamental when deciding which challenges to tackle first. For instance, if there is an early stage in the project where initial approvals are required and this process takes a few weeks to a month, improving the production delivery process at the end of the delivery cycle from one week to one day will not add as much value in comparison to optimizing the approval process.
- There are cases that, to do two steps forward, a step back may be required. Working model changes require dedication and increased communication to be effective. Consider the working model improvement as a project in itself. If you submit your team to work in a project on top of the current completely booked capacity they have, you are either forcing them to do all projects with less quality or simply ignoring the working model changes.
- As an Agile project in itself, do it in an incremental fashion. Avoid changing all at once. Celebrate each achievement to give momentum to the team to keep changing and improving.
- Involve the team on decisions that will directly affect the teamwork. Ask for the feedback. Even better, explain the problem to be addressed and ask for suggestions on how to address them. It will make the team accountable for the change.

How to have a smooth transition from the current Waterfall-like environment we live in into a more Agile environment?

There is not a single, unidimensional project model between Waterfall and Agile. Working models are better represented if considered in a two-dimensional triangle, where one end is Waterfall, other is Agile, and the third triangle end is "chaos".

Besides, it is important to highlight that being Agile does not mean doing Scrum. Scrum is an Agile methodology, as is Kanban or eXtreme Programming (XP). Being Agile is to adhere to the four core values already discussed.

Therefore, when a project starts, if no specific model is being implemented upfront since day zero, the working model might be located in the centre of this triangle – and that might not be a problem. It is a methodology-agnostic project. Work is simply done. There will be cases where this "model" works, usually very small projects. Once this methodology-agnostic project starts to grow, however, a specific methodology could be useful to avoid the problems and challenges faced by a project without a clear methodology. However, when such implementation is being discussed, it should be done in such a structured and reasonable way to avoid getting attracted to the "chaos" end. The "chaos" end is known by extended working hours, poor quality and increased frustration. This environment is not Waterfall, nor Agile, nor anything in between.

Likewise, a transition between Waterfall to Agile should not be painful. A transition between working models should be considered as any other project – with either a specific goal and incremental deliverables or a one-off massive goal to be delivered months from now.

It is interesting to notice that some projects transitioning into a more Agile culture still plans a big bang transition, instead of benefiting from the incremental deliverable benefits that actual Agile culture brings. If you hear about an Agile transition being implemented as a Waterfall project ("we have done all the analysis to transition, and we have to change A, B and C to be Agile") be careful, as it seems to be a suspicious implementation, to say the least.

In substantial projects, whenever possible, starts by automation. In a worst-case scenario, even if all methodology change work is lost for any reason, the automation will not be lost. After all, testing and deployment automation are a must-have regardless of the methodology (although Agilists usually tend to consider automation as a step towards an Agile working model). This automation might have a cost upfront, but rest assured that – so long as properly implemented – would definitely pay off in the short to mid-term.

Once there is enough automation and the development team is confident enough, then working on shorter iterations is the next step. The development team needs to be confident, since in a Waterfall approach the development team had months to work on several features, and now the deliverables, although smaller, are expected to arrive faster, which increases the pressure on the development team. In addition, the iterations should consider the reality of the requirements. If a requirement is estimated to take a month, then implementing two weeks' iterations "just because most Agile projects does so" is not a good practice. Forcing a two weeks' iteration because other projects does so will push the project towards the dark chaotic area and the development team will lose confidence on this implementation. An iteration (and at this stage, avoid calling this iteration a Sprint, explanation will follow) should be as big as the major requirement. The work must be done to break requirements further with users. Once it is possible to gather smaller requirements with users, iterations could be reduced.

At the reduced iteration work, there might still be silos and people specifically labelled as analysts, developers and testers inside the development team, however, everyone should have a single commitment for the whole group. Having specific iterations for analysts, development and testing is not moving towards an Agile model; instead, it is working on a faster Waterfall. It may even work. It may even be Agile, in some aspects. The project may decide if going further on Agile (such as implementing a specific Agile methodology, like Scrum or XP.

Usually, the Scrum path is the commonly chosen. At this stage, the boundaries should be gradually reduced between analysis, development and a testing team. As a single team, there must be trust and confidence between the whole team, as already discussed. There should be a continuous communication between a development team and users, and developers should understand the application and the business restrictions in the same way the users should minimally understand how the application works. The development team should not be strongly concerned about infrastructural issues, as most of the platform should be readily available. Once this stage is reached, this working model can be also scaled if required.

For large projects that are already working at limits with separated Scrum teams or large projects down on the chaotic end, there is scalable solutions. Needless to say, scalability will be faster when evolving from an already stable Scrum team that only has to deal with scalability challenges.

Scaled Agile Framework (SAFe) and Large Scale Scrum (LeSS) are the common names and methodologies used to scale Scrum projects in the financial sector. Several items advocated by SAFe are already referenced in this chapter, such as identifying the value stream mapping, reduction of management overhead and decentralization of non-strategical decisions. SAFe offers guidelines on how to implement each of them.

Regardless of methodology used, a few characteristics will always be common on high-performance projects:

- Coherent long-term vision
- Clear communication
- Transparency

Thus, obtaining a long-term sustainable working environment might be more productive and provide quicker results than focusing on specific methodology improvements.

Section IV

Responding to change

Chapter 21

Matching theory to practice in a complex world

A philosophical approach

Louis Klein

Introduction

Project management (PM) is a paradox. Project management is all about reducing complexity, and then the real world demands complexity and kills the project. Challenging project performance addresses the irony that it is the lack of complexity which comes into the way of further progress of the discipline as well as for the actual projects.

Improving project performance is a question of reintroducing complexity into PM theory and practice. While it is a major challenge for the theory, the practice has always been smarter. Projects get done despite the inherent complexity. With a grin, the experienced project manager speaks about muddling through, flexibility and improvisation. Ingenuity we may call it. The theory, however, has to catch up, not only to meet the real world but to enlighten what actually happens in practice, providing insights which allow further progress in theory and in practice.

The first part of this chapter, "Talking about Complex Project Management Performance", will address the phenomenological character of measurement. Project success is described, yet not explained. Moving from conventional project management to complex project management has opened a door for systems thinking and indicated a direction of further exploration, not only in the duality of Waterfall and Agile approaches in PM. We need to come from description to explanation.

Meeting social complexity in PM is what can and should be done already. The second part, "Meeting Social Complexity", looks into the character and balance of the dynamic interplay of technology, politics and culture. Mainstream management theory and praxis focuses almost exclusively on complexity reducing technology, the other two complex dimensions, politics and culture, i.e. social complexity, are rarely taken care of. Hence, management is almost blind.

Next, in the third part, "Venturing an Epistemological Turn" addresses the epistemological requirements not only for PM but for the entire venture of the Anthropocene beyond post-modernism necessary to meet the global challenges of the 21st century. This is not so much a revolution in thinking as it addresses an enrichment of the existing body of knowledge with systems sciences and integral theory. It allows moving from the notion of "getting things done" to "letting things grow" and back again.

Progress needs balance, argues the fourth part of this chapter, "Balancing Progress". Paradoxes, antagonisms and antinomies cannot be met with an idea that suggests one size fit all. It is neither Waterfall nor Agile, it is both. Finding and managing the balance is one of the crucial skills of the project manager of tomorrow.

In this respect, the final section, "Realising Good Project Governance", concludes that approaches to leadership and organisation need to be revaluated to realise good project governance. Captainship and organising organisations are two concrete aspects of complex project management excellence which credibly promise improvement in project management practice and project performance.

Talking about complex project management performance

Improving project performance is an imperative. On the one hand, it is a general imperative of modernity and industry culture; on the other hand, project management success statistics show that two thirds of all projects fail.[1] The bigger projects are the more likely is an unpleasant outcome. And projects in the public sector tend to fail spectacularly.

Project failure tends to lead to blame games. Listening to the discourse, the debates and the news, it is the people, the project managers and leaders, the stakeholder, the sponsors, and even the customers who are responsible for project failure. It is addressed to leadership deficits and people dynamics when projects fail. It is seemingly never the technology which lets projects down.

The other culprit for project failure is complexity. In 2008, the Defence Materiel Organisation (DMO) of the Department for Defence equipping the Australian Defence Force (ADF) encouraged together with prominent suppliers from the private sector the foundation of the International Centre for Complex Project Management (ICCPM). Faced with the failure of the large equipment projects for the military, like fighter planes and warships, the idea formed that it was the complexity of the project that led to failure, exceeding budgets, extended project realisation timelines and insufficient quality of the deliverables. The project management theory and practice, so the idea of the ICCPM, needed to be improved to cater for large projects in the public sector, where tax payers' money was at stake.

The investigation of the ICCPM into the subject led first of all to the distinction of complicatedness and complexity. Complicatedness addresses the sheer size and the technological nature of the project. However complicated technology may be, this is nothing the ingenuity of engineering could not cope with. Technical blueprints can be as large as they may as long as they are following the logic of cause and effect unfolding in one direction; creating a path of completion, things get done. Complexity is not a matter of size. It is the occurrence of feedback loops where activities create results or reactions which feed back into the very same activity. We do not see this in blueprints, however, the simplest of conversations is based on feedback creating complexity which we usually handle with great ease. Only, we cannot plan a conversation. Human interaction does rarely follow scripts and we are always in for a surprise. As long as people are involved things are complex. In complex projects, this matters. Here the norm of complicatedness meets the challenges of complexity. Planning meets real life.

All projects are complex projects. People are involved and as we learnt from the US military, we life in a VUCA world, which is volatile, uncertain, complex and ambiguous

---

1 The notion that two thirds of all projects fail is so widespread that even in *Harvard Business Review* articles authors are not bothered to quote any scientific evidence (*Harvard Business Review*, 2011). Nevertheless, based on a discourse analytical approach, the figure holds evidence and is not disputed.

(Hicks Stiehm, 2002; Bennett & Lemoine, 2014). The sheer existence of the VUCA concept reveals how far off modern ideas of *getting things done* went from the complexity of real life. It should not come as a surprise when people rebel against simplified standards not only in the military and in project management.

Back to those large projects in the public sphere, the trouble starts with what the ICCPM featured as the *conspiracy of optimism* (Chapman et al., 2006; Chapman & Ward, 2003; Hirt, 1996). If gatekeepers of tight budgets, e.g. parliaments, have to decide upon the realisation of projects, those who promote and offer the projects have a tendency to polish their project proposals along a best-case scenario. In the end, the lowest possible budget at the quickest possible schedule and the best possible quality of deliverables present an image of the project which is as attractive as it will fail. The best-case scenario remains statistically unlikely. Project performance measured against those project proposals will be at least disappointing, and count as another project failure.

Performance is perception. The *conspiracy of optimism* gives a taste of the nature of measuring project performance. Performance is always measured against expectation. The action-learning community seems to bring forward the most realistic and sober concept of performance, which they call *Return on Expectation* (RoE) (Kirkpatrick & Kirkpatrick, 2016; Anderso, 2007; Kirkpatrick, 1998). It bridges the gap between quantitative and qualitative measures and puts the stakeholder expectations into the focus. This does not mean that the iron triangle of time, cost and quality is outdated or obsolete. On the contrary, as long as we acknowledge that the iron triangle is an adequate tool to structure a specific set of expectations we shall keep enjoying it. And as long as we engage in the bigger picture we may as well enjoy concepts like cross-benefits or lifecycle cost. The *laws of observation* (Scott, 2009) brought forward by the British cybernetician Bernard Scott highlight the character of the field: for any given observation there is always a bigger picture, there is always more detail and always an alternative perspective. The making and texture of expectation depend on observations which lead to descriptions and eventually to performance evaluations. It is a question of *functional adequacy* which guides the selection of perspectives. However, if we forget that these perspectives are contingent and always a choice of a person, a group or a community, project performance measurement tends to become rigid and dysfunctional (Figure 21.1).

Project performance can be described and explained. Project performance description, however, tends to be a trap. It is a phenomenological approach which suggests ontological qualities. We believe our observation leads to a description which is true. However, it is only, as constructivists would say, a description which depends on the selection of a certain perspective out of plenty likewise functional adequate perspectives which would suggest other views and assessments.[2] Measurements are functionally adequate at its best. The pursuit of truth in this context is as tedious and futile as the search for culprits.

The explanation of project success leads to performative heuristics. Project performance explanation is a generic approach which leads to epistemology. In practice, we talk about excellence models and their underlying philosophy. Total Quality Management is such an approach and Kaizen, the according philosophy . Excellence models like the project excellence model of the International Project Management Association (IPMA) suggest a set of perspectives which explain how specific context conditions support desirable

2 On constructivism see Foerster (2002), Foerster & Pörksen (2001) and Watzlawick (1984).

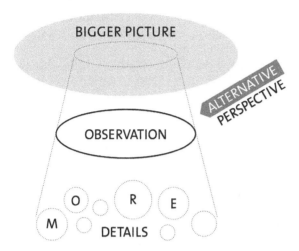

Figure 21.1 Scott's laws of observation.

action which leads to excellent performance (Szalajko et al., 2016). They explain how diverse activities come together to create progress towards specified ends. They distinguish between enablers which explain and results which describe project performance., Maturity models of project managers, projects and organisations build on the same foundation. They select perspectives which lead to descriptions and explanations suggesting development paths to improve the context settings which can foster successful projects.

As the investigation of the ICCPM already promoted, system thinking provides a theory which allows to encompass this phenomenological, generic, ontological and epistemological sensitivity to explain, assess and improve approaches to project performance and project management success. Especially the notions of emergence and contextuality allow for a better understanding of complexity at work. Emergence describes the phenomenon that the whole tends to be more and different than the sum of its part. Projects are more and different than the sum of its parts, more than blueprints, schedules, budgets and people. They are social systems in their own right, with their own politics and culture. Hence, we better account for this, as well as for contextuality. Context matters.[3] A penguin in the desert is a ridiculous creature, while at the South Pole it is best fit. And in social systems, as the frame of reference theory states (Neitzel & Welzer, 2011; Goffman & Berger, 1974; Goffman, 1972), we have to acknowledge that the logic of the context is always stronger than the logic of the intentions.

Meeting social complexity

Projects are social systems. They are more and different than the sum of its parts. They are sensitive to initial conditions and depend upon their context. They are more than technology, politics and culture, they are complex social systems.[4]

---

3 For the most charming illustration on the topic see Gladwell (2001).
4 On project as social systems see Linger and Owen (2012) and Klein (2016c; 2012a),

The US American management consultant, author and educator Noel Tichy suggested a model to cover the most relevant perspective on social systems like organisations and projects. He calls it TPC model (1983). The acronym deciphers as T for technology, P for politics and C for culture. The TPC model suggests equal weight for all three perspectives while we need to acknowledge that for the mainstream of management theory the technological perspective with its focus on methods and tools is more than dominant. There is a tendency to push the political and cultural perspective to the side, call them soft and refocus on technology. In the pursuit of becoming a hard science not only economics but also management theory tried to legitimise itself by formalising a mathematical calculus which produces "truth" beyond dispute. Yet, as soon as people are involved we are back to complexity beyond calculation. To the extent we find ways to account for social complexity we increase the likelihood for project success. Reducing our sight to one third of the relevant perspectives does match in a remarkable way with knowing that only one third of projects perform successfully (Figure 21.2).

Social complexity, following the TPC model, has a political and a cultural aspect (Klein, 2016c). The political perspective looks at politics on all levels; macro, meso and micro levels. It refers to the coexistence of various, diverse interests, in individual communication, in groups and entire social systems. Their coexistence can relate in any form of symbiosis reaching from mutualism to competition. We could speak of micro politics, however, the cardinal instrument of politics, the stakeholder analysis, reveals that we need to engage over all levels to compose a map that enables to navigate. To increase the systemic understanding of the political perspective of a stakeholder analysis, it has been supportive to engage on three levels of systemic inquiry: multicausality, interdependence and polycentricity.

Multicausality refers to the well-known form of the stakeholder analysis. We put ourselves, our project and our interests into the centre of attention and explore who has a stake in what happens. Multicausality then refers to the manifold of stakeholders and their interests in relation to the project in focus. Stakeholders and their interests can in the texture of the social system be seen as a source of complexity as the relating interests will create a dynamic interplay between stakeholder and project and vice versa. Illustrated, this creates the image of a star with the project in the centre of self-interest (Figure 21.3).

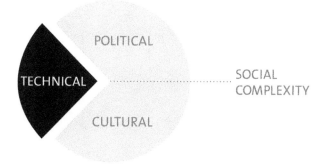

Figure 21.2 Social complexity.

Interdependence is from a cybernetician's perspective the next level of complexity. We need to assume that stakeholders do not only relate and bear interests towards the project but that they as well relate towards other stakeholders of the same project. Stakeholders can form alliances or be at war with another. Hence, knowing what relates the stakeholder to the project is only a fraction of the richer picture of interdependence. Illustrated, the star becomes a wheel with connections which do not necessarily run through the centre (Figure 21.4).

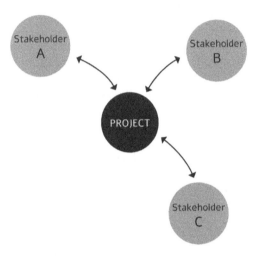

Figure 21.3 Stakeholder multicausality.

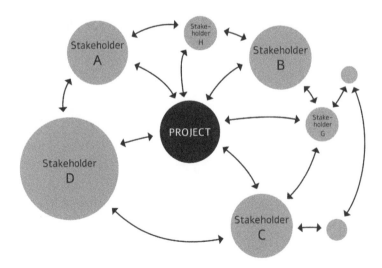

Figure 21.4 Stakeholder interdependence.

Polycentricity reveals a third dimension of complexity, an entire universe, and we may learn that our project is just a small project on the outer rim of the galaxy. Political decisions in a small office somewhere in the White House can out of the blue terminate the project in focus. Or a new law in China makes it more attractive for investors to seek for projects like the project in focus. Or the company's decision to build a kindergarten allows for female talent that had hitherto no perspective to engage in the company's projects. Or the project is sacrificed in an unrelated dispute between stakeholders far away. The most important lesson from polycentricity for project management, however, remains the insight that the project is not the centre of the universe. The earth is a sphere and revolves around the sun somewhere in a side galaxy of the Milky Way (Figure 21.5).

Culture is another game. Culture is the paradigmatic reference of a community of practice (Klein, 2016d; 2016a; 2013). It is not a placeholder for all the soft facts we cannot explain (Schein, 2004). At the very heart of culture, we find sensemaking (Weick, 1995) and meaning-creation (Luhmann, 1984). In the form of stories and narratives we organise the descriptions and explanations which constitute not only our worldview but in a philosophical and constructivist sense our world (Klein, 2005). This goes as far that we need to challenge the *discourse analysis* to become a *discourse praxis analysis* (Klein & Weiland, 2014). The paradigmatic reference given by a community of practice to describe and explain their world has sometimes very little to do with the espoused reference given. It is a bit like the French author, professor of literature and psychoanalyst Pierre Bayard illustrated the situation in his book *How to Talk about Books You Haven't Read* (2007). A lot of project management discourse practice is exactly this, talking about methods, models and instruments people only hear of. Culturally it does not make too much of a difference whether an assumption is true or not as long as it is accepted. There is no proof that Gandhi said be the change we want to see in the world. Nevertheless, we find it printed on t-shirts and brought in as a quote over and over again. This is not a debate about facts or alternative facts, it is not about truth but about worldviews which may be functionally adequate or bound to fail.

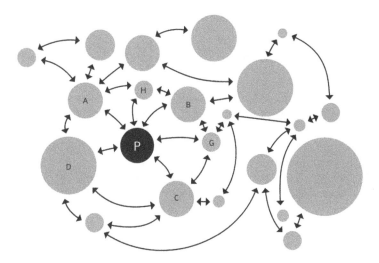

Figure 21.5 Stakeholder polycentricity.

Culture eats strategy for breakfast, Peter Drucker, the Austrian-born US-American management consultant, educator and author indeed said. It is not the espoused culture or its normative aspects, it is not about courtesy and conversations skills, it is not the eating habits or the dress code. What makes culture so dominant is sense and meaning. The German sociologist Niklas Luhmann defines meaning as the unity of the distinction between actuality and possibility (1984). Meaning refers not only to the empirical observation of actuality but its patterns and phenomenology. Meaning also refers to possibility. It describes and explains what could be possible, feasible and desirable. It describes the realms of possibilities for what could be next and consequently what could and shall not be. This is the power of culture.

Power is *sovereignty of interpretation* (Han, 2005). It is not coercive force which rules; it is the stories and narratives which create a world we choose to submit to, a world we believe in and according to our beliefs we will do what the is culture suggest doing by free will. Whenever coercive force is involved it is an indicator for a lack of power. A really powerful culture is a culture that does not apply force. The neoliberal paradigm with its focus on performance and merits can be seen as an example that shows to what extent performance-oriented managers submit to a performance culture until dying from a heart attack at their desks. There is no force involved but the compulsion of the individual's free will.

The more light the more shadow. Talking about culture in the context of project management, it is inevitable to touch the nature of project management as a management discipline which is created with the shining light of the body of knowledge; a *shadow* in the sense of the Swiss psychiatrist and psychoanalyst Carl Gustav Jung (Jung, 1912; Bertholo, 2018). The more we highlight what should be the more we push into the shadow what should not be. What is sought of being applicable for the psyche holds as well for social systems since both are autopoietic, i.e. self-generating and self-perpetuating systems which process meaning (Klein, 2012c; Luhmann, 1984). Project management is challenged by muddling through strategies, by improvisation, lust and love, to name but a few. As long as two thirds of projects fail it seems to be a good strategy to venture social complexity, pull it into the light, acknowledge it, talk about it and facilitate dialogue in order to find adequate and feasible ways to handle politics and culture.

Venturing an epistemological turn

"There is no right life in the wrong one", said the German philosopher and sociologist Theodor W. Adorno in his seminal book *Minima Moralia* (1951).[5] Especially looking at Nazi Germany, it conveys the insight that a ruling frame, ideology or doctrine of society may allow for pockets of decency and happiness. Those pockets, however, are the exceptions which prove the rule. The guiding frame will manifest in culture and always overrule and determine the further course of developments.[6]

We live in the Anthropocene. The challenges of the 21st century, be they climate change, ocean health, poverty, conflict, inequality to name but a few, testify for the

---

5 The wrong life Adorno initially referred to in the minima moralia was on a rather resigning and gloomy note of the life of immigrants in the US exile during WWII. The reference to Nazi Germany and the normative note it connotes today is a product of discursive iteration of its receptions, especially in Europe.

6 For an application of Adorno's philosophy to project management see Klein (2016c).

fact that humankind marshalled Genesis 1.28 and subdued the earth.[7] Humankind at the beginning of the 21st century is collectively so powerful that the future of our planet depends on its capabilities to cultivate, civilise and govern itself. Governing the Anthropocene is the vital challenge of the 21st century.

"We cannot solve our problems with the same thinking we used when we created them", is one of the quotes attributed to Albert Einstein. It calls for an epistemological turn. It questions the very propositions of our contemporary worldview, of what we believe in and hold true. It calls for a paradigm shift (Kuhn, 1962/1970) of our entire era, not only for change in specific discipline. And if we see a true paradigm shift it will change the foundation of all we know, our way to think about humanity, religion, politics and economics (Fleck, 1936). It will change our perspective on management, leadership and consequently projects.

Sociologically a paradigm shift is the challenge to navigate the distinctions between ontology and epistemology as well as the distinction between phenomenological description and generic explanation. This may trigger a search and inquiry process to determine what comes after post-modernism. However, a pragmatic approach especially with benefits for project management performance would suggest exploring what is already there that fulfils the criteria of providing a change of perspective, of worldview and in essence another epistemological turn.[8]

Systems thinking and integral theory seem to be the two most promising candidates for an epistemological turn we may label *Anthropocene Thinking*. Both approaches challenge the mainstream of rational modernity and reintroduce complexity based on epistemological insights. Ecologists, triggered not only but prominently by the report to the Club of Rome "Limits to growth" (Meadows et al., 1972), were first to venture the epistemological turn. Activists in civil society embarked to push a green agenda. Contemporary business and especially the human resources (HR) and organisational development (OD) community followed, since both HR and OD need to find access to the dynamics of collaboration and communication, culture and politics.

Integral theory is the more popular one. Its layout is more phenomenological, builds on descriptions and tends to slide into ontology. The US-American writer Kenneth E. Wilber brought integral theory forward as a theory of everything suggesting the synthesis of all human knowledge and experience (2000). Integral theory can accordingly be read as transpersonal psychology. Integral theory is strongest where it refers to the developmental psychology of Piaget (1950), Kohlberg (1981) and eventually Loevinger (1987, 1970) and Graves (1974; 1970). Stages of psychological development, be it cognition or morals, can be related to individuals as well as to groups and entire organisations. Frederic Laloux's book *Reinventing Organizations* (2014) had been the first widely received idea to use integral theory for the design of social systems as *holacracies* (Robertson, 2016) without hierarchy. While in industry, first attempts yield interesting results, the project management community has not been affected at large. Concerning an epistemological turn, integral theory

---

7 "And God blessed them, and God said unto them, be fruitful, and multiply, and replenish the earth, and subdue it: and have dominion over the fish of the sea, and over the fowl of the air, and over every living thing that moveth upon the earth".

8 The term epistemological turn was initially introduced to philosophy to describe the shift in philosophical attention from the classical and medieval focus on themes of metaphysics to human knowledge starting with Descartes and Kant. Today second order cybernetics suggest applying the term to describe a change in the epistemological foundations and implications of paradigms and their shifts.

allows for a more holistic view which integrates not only psychological and sociological perspectives, empirically as well as in terms of sense-making and meaning-creation, but also the relationship between psychological development stages and organisational implications. On a certain psychological development level, a person or an entire society will favour a specific epistemological proposition and according organisational implications. A law and order mind will favour a rule-based paradigm and a law and order organisation. A community-transcending mind will seek balance including perspectives off mainstream. The implications for HR and OD and eventually organisations and projects cannot be overestimated. It explains the importance of team and leadership dimensions beyond the current deficit orientation and provides interesting methods, models and instruments. Truth, however, as the universal criteria does not work in an integral world since different things are true for different people depending on their individual development stages. Ontology becomes relative. Truth is a construct which needs to be functionally adequate.

System thinking explains where integral theory can only describe. Decisive is the generic perspective of systems sciences and cybernetics. The questions of what generates and perpetuates the world, as well as the knowledge about it, drive systems thinking. It is a time component which leads from balance to *homeostasis*. In order to be, even a problem needs to be generated anew from moment to moment. It needs to be perpetuated actively, in the physical world and in the mind. The founding father of management cybernetics, the British theorist, consultant and professor Stafford Beer, may account as being the first to introduce system thinking to business in the 1970s (1979; 1972). It was not, however, before the turn of the century that another two system scientists, management educators and consultants, the US American Peter M. Senge (1990) and the British Michael C. Jackson (2002; 2000), brought systems thinking closer to mainstream management. Managing complexity ever since became the hallmark of systems thinking in business. In this line the strongest and most popular systemic concepts are the systemic perspective on context, culture and change.

The logic of the context is always stronger than the logic of the intentions. Systems are context dependent. Organisations as well as projects depend on their embedding context. Processes and structures will determine practice. Any team that espouses teamwork and organisationally rewards individual performance suffers the power of context. Any quality management system will yield due to the quality of its processes and benefit from a well-designed process landscape. And wherever the organisational emphasis is on individual leadership we can know that there is something wrong with the organisation's processes and structures. A context can be designed to support and foster a desirable practice. If this is neglected, we need management heroes to save every single day.

Culture is the paradigmatic reference of a community of practice (Klein, 2016d; 2016a; 2013). It rules the worldview, the interpretation of what is and what could be. It manifests in stories and narratives (Jorgensen & Largacha-Martinez, 2014; Boje, 2008; 2001). Knowing organisational culture is to know how an organisation thinks the world ticks, which perspectives are valid and which ones are heretic. Knowing its culture enlightens where we meet the organisation and what way forward is conceivable. Changing culture is as difficult as changing a religious belief. It starts with systemic inquiry and the open conversation about what is and what could be. Only what is surfaced can enter meaningful dialogue. Cultures are robust, yet, all cultures bear ideas about how they can be changed. It is worth exploring.

Figure 21.6 Rabbit-duck.

Change is unlikely but possible. Systems and consequently social systems like organisations or projects are robust (Klein, 2016c; 2016a). They are meant to be stable. They are conservative by nature. Their purpose is to maintain their existence based on historic success. However, systems are, as chaos theory states, sensitive to initial conditions. This indicates that a change of social systems is rather a question of finding and applying sweet spots and leverage points in order to trigger a *butterfly effect*. (Lorenz, 1963). So triggering change is rather a matter of small interventions than of large programmes. We can even assume relating to second order cybernetics that change in social systems can bear the quality of a picture puzzle, where the change occurs as a sudden change of perception without changes in the physical world, the same phenomena the Austrian-British philosopher Ludwig Wittgenstein describes in his Philosophical Investigations (1953/1958) as the puzzling nature of perception with the famous illustration of the so-called rabbit-duck (Figure 21.6).

Venturing an epistemological turn towards *Anthropocene Thinking* promises benefits of epic dimension. Nothing short of this would be suitable to meet the challenges of the 21st century. Nonetheless, for the future of complex project management a pragmatic approach should be sufficient to improve project performance in both the old and the new world. Adapting from integral and systems practice whatever works contributes to both the individual project's success as well as to the overall quest for models, methods and instruments fit for the Anthropocene. This is not abandoning all models, methods and instruments we already have. It calls for a new arrangement of the existing and enriching the toolbox with a few new items. In a more philosophical approach, we need to shift from a paradigm of *getting things done* to a paradigm of *letting things grow*. At its core we find more than rational linearity but ways to govern complexity.

Balancing progress

Know thyself is certainly the most prominent of the three inscriptions at the Apollo temple of Delphi. It is appraised as a guidance to wisdom. The two other lesser known maxims are: *Nothing in excess* and *be*. In a remarkable way, those three maxims foreclose what research in personal mastery reveals (Butler-Bowdon, 2003). Roughly half of the approaches of self-help classics start from the idea of self-knowing. *Know yourself* is regarded as a heuristic to understand what we really are to derive appropriate strategies of action from the essence of self-knowing. The other half of approaches to self-help follow the line of positive thinking. *Create yourself (be)* invites performative decision as the basis of further activities. If we combine those two with the third maxim, *balance (moderate/nothing in excess)*, it suggests that neither self-knowing nor self-creation alone will yield satisfactory lines of development. It is rather a sequence of mutual counter-balancing that promotes desirable results. Hence, personal mastery is seen as a process of oscillation between the two approaches. In the end it is a question of balancing progress.

Organisational mastery, and respectively any attempt of mastering developments of social systems, follows the same oscillating pattern of self-knowing and self-creation (Klein, 2018; 2005). In a more systemic way, it is the self-knowing in an environment and the self-creation in respect of culturally determined realms of possibilities. And if we move from organisational mastery to project mastery we can build on the same heuristic of balancing integrating reflection on the one hand and transformative creation on the other hand. And if we acknowledge that excellence describes an aspiration rather than a state we have found the key to move from mastery to excellence. Project excellence, hence, can be regarded as a process of balancing the self-knowing and self-creation of projects (Klein, 2018).

Philosophically, project excellence is an art of balancing antagonisms and antinomies. This is to say that project excellence in practice is far more challenging than reflection and decision making. An antagonism is a hostility which results in resistance and opposition. All the challenges that come with a systemic understanding of politics and conflicting interests are bound to face antagonisms. The mediation of interests lies on the surface of conflict resolution, however, most of the conflicts projects face are structural by nature and require more than a well-facilitated meeting. And changing the structural environment of a project has always been as difficult as desirable. An antinomy, in contrast to an antagonism, lies on a rather logical and epistemological level. It refers to incompatibilities and paradoxes. The German philosopher Immanuel Kant gives the example of the antinomy of a whole that consists of simple elements yet cannot be reduced to simple elements (1791). A statement of a project manager, all project managers were liars, resembles the logical paradox of the classic Crete liar. The statement cannot be true either way. For antinomies are not final, yet always workable solutions. However, those solutions are never true but functionally adequate.

For balancing both antagonisms and antinomies, there are little or no logically satisfactory solutions. For antinomies they do not exist and for antagonisms they are generally beyond reach. Successfully balancing antagonisms and antinomies usually follows the pragmatism of Daoism, which suggests the indifference of both and case by case a concrete balancing decision. Logically, antagonisms and antinomies lead to tetra-lemma solutions (Sparrer & Kibed, 2000): *either A or B, both A and B, neither A nor B,* and finally, the negation of the case as such, *nothing of all of that.* Balancing project management sounds theoretically highly complicated. In practice it is a pragmatic matter of self-reflection and self-creation. Two aspects, however, are vital to be considered, homeostasis and thrivability. *Homeostasis* is a cybernetic concept which acknowledges the generic idea of systems thinking that all what is needs to be generated and maintained constantly. Balance is delicate, and homeostasis depends on perpetuating activities. *Thrivability* shall be introduced as a systemic criterion beyond resilience, sustainability and health (Varey, 2008). Stafford Beer referred to viability beyond survival (1979; 1972).

Thrivability acknowledges a systemic perspective of the general interdependence of all what is and serves as the central criterion. Drawing on the Gaia hypothesis,[9] global multi-causality, inter-dependence and poly-centricity need to be regarded as an inevitability (Klein, 2012b). It creates a being in the world that the German philosopher Martin Heidegger characterised as *thrownness*.[10] Accordingly, all we can hope for are coping strategies of functional adequacy that promote thrivability.

In this light, there is no truth in the ongoing project management debate about Waterfall and Agile approaches. In the pursuit of thrivability we are looking for functional adequacy of the one or the other in regard of given contexts. A systemic perspective will always suggest avoiding extremes and find a homeostatic balance. The driver for the Waterfall approach, especially in a neo-liberal world, is the need for legitimising the disposition of funds. Especially in public projects and public–private partnerships the heat of the debate is about spending tax payers' money and in shareholder-owned public companies it is about safeguarding shareholder value. The linear structure of Waterfall approaches meets the communication needs of tax payers and shareholders. Waterfall approaches suggest compliance as a solution to social complexity. To the actual operations of projects Waterfall approaches are a source of constant frustration. The pragmatic solution for project operations are Agile approaches. However, in terms of compliance, Agile approaches are a major challenge. The legitimation requirements fight back in the form of overburdening bureaucracy. As suggested, the solution is homeostatic balance of both. The key lies in a more sophisticated management of social complexity which mitigates the stakeholders' interests and makes room of Agile performance.

Project management as a discipline is equally challenged. The shining *body of knowledge* suggests project management by the book based on project management certification levels. Yet, project management has always wrestled with its own shortcomings and failure to meet complexity. A lot of different schools of project management were conceived over the years and every attempt to come up with a unifying school did only add another school to the list (Turner et al., 2013; Bredillet, 2010). Project management veterans laugh about those attempts and refer to their own practice as successfully muddling through. They do not believe in project management schools but in project management heroes. However, the world is short of heroes and full of projects. So, the balancing solution combines formal project management education and improvisation (Klein et al., 2015). The more schools project managers are familiar with the richer is their repertoire and respectively the resilience of their performance in practice. And the better project managers' ability to improvise the better is their performance in practice. Yet, as the metaphor of musical improvisation shows, the better musicians master their instrument, the better is their improvisation. Accordingly, the more schools project managers are familiar with and the more they are prepared to improvise on this basis the better they master the challenges of complex project management. Again, it is balancing both that does the trick.

---

9 Although the Gaia hypothesis had invited a vast spiritual and esoteric resonance there is a lot of scientific evidence for the sober systemic insight of inescapable universal interdependence (Capra & Luisi, 2014; Volk, 2002; Margulis, 1998; Lovelock, 1972).

10 Heidegger's concept of *thrownness* as he brought it forward in his seminal book *Being and Time* (1927) bears more than a mere ontological reference to the present. It also reflects the dependency on the past, the inevitability of death to come and the irritating sense of freedom in between the two.

The world is short of management heroes. Organisation, however, has been the solution which allows ordinary people to fulfil extraordinary tasks. It is a systemic insight that the knowledge of an organisation lies in its processes and structures (Willke, 2007). Total Quality Management is certainly the discipline that took this insight furthest. If quality is not a property of the processes, no inspection will ever be able to cope. Standardisation allows for continuous improvement. However, the world is not a production line. The world is VUCA. And still it is not as VUCA as we lately tend to believe. In organisations, 20% of standardisation covers 80% of the volume; the remaining 20% require case-by-case approaches, in management as in project management (Klein, 2018). We can organise for performance. The organisation itself is built on this homeostasis.

Viability requires resilience. Vulnerability is a risk (Raue & Klein, 2016). Organising for efficiency comes at the price of reduced resilience. Organising for efficiency is a risk. Hence, project contingency could be handled wiser than setting aside a budget to throw at problems when they occur. Projects as well as organisations need what in the business process reengineering programmes in the 1990s and thereafter called "slag" and "non-value-adding activities". Especially "soft" activities suffer from those cuts. This increased the focus on the technical aspects of organisations and projects, exposing them even more to the challenges of social complexity. Communication allows for clarity. A project should plan for this, not only but as well to mitigate risk.

Change, to close the ray of examples, requires balance as well. It is the balance between continuous improvement and innovation. It is like in Tai Chi (Klein & Wong, 2012). One force, Yin is integrating. Continuous improvement integrates what is already there, realising learning curve effects. The other force, Yang, is transforming. Innovation realises what is new. Continuous improvement alone runs in marginalising effects. Innovation alone gets lost in dilettantism, not realising the benefits of the learning curve. In balance, in oscillation between the two, lies the real benefit of change. And finally, the balance between keeping things unchanged and change is equally delicate. The level of change needs to be sufficient. In an organism the constant renewal sustains life. Thrivability, however, requires viability beyond survival. In a project, likewise, a sufficient level of change is a prerequisite for survival and thrivability (Figure 21.7).

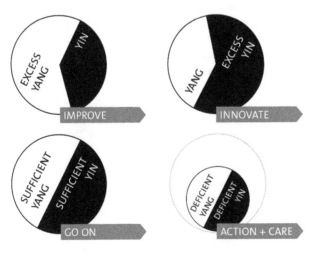

Figure 21.7 Tai Chi of change.

Grass does not grow faster if you pull it. However, *letting things grow* in contrast to *getting things done*, as proposed for an illustration for the required paradigm shift in *Anthropocene Thinking*, does not indicate an absolute preference. It remains a question of functional adequacy and thrivability in a specific context that needs to be answered embracing what is there already and being able to replace what is not functionally adequate with a promising alternative. Progress is a question of balance. Forget disruption and let us make time for our strongest ally.

Realising good project governance

Complex project management excellence is a question of good systemic governance. And based on the ides of *Anthropocene Thinking*, there are two sides to good systemic governance, providing and controlling a supportive framework as well as care for the individual case. It is a profoundly systemic understanding of *letting things grow* best illustrated with an agricultural example. The growth of any single vine cannot be determined. Vine grows into all directions. Cultivating vines, hence, is a question of providing supportive frames, a row by row setup of the field, poles to hold to, and in some cases even wire frames. This provides a corridor for the vines to flourish. Nonetheless, the wine farmer needs to pay attention and visit with a helping hand each vine at least 17 times a year. Without this attention vines will not yield properly and without a supportive frame wine farming is impossible. Good governance realises both organising organisations for performance and the attention of well-balanced captainship.

Organising projects for performance provides corridors and tram lines for desirable practice. This is realised best when in an integral way all parties involved co-create the desirable practice in constructive dialogue. Of course, this depends on the very individuals involved and can vary from project to project. However, it provides the possibility at an early stage to address all three perspectives of concern, technology, politics and culture, within the project and with regard to the relevant stakeholder universe, balancing Waterfall and Agile, schools and improvisation, efficiency and resilience. The other more systemic aspect is to know the distinction between a designable environment and the given environment. Sometimes it is a thin line, sometimes a robust wall. Changing the designable environment within the sphere of influence should be part of the co-creation process of a desirable practice. And on the same note it is necessary to acknowledge explicitly what is beyond the project's sphere of influence. Everything else, systemically spoken, is noise (Figure 21.8).

Once this desirable practice is settled it needs to be translated into process and structures leading and supporting this practice. And finally, personal implications need to be taken care of. Job descriptions, remuneration schemes, and career paths to name the most important ones ought to be in place to provide perspectives for the individual project team member. They need to know what they are in for.

Organising organisation is organising for homeostasis. It remains a delicate balance which needs attention over time and is not chiselled in stone. Organising is an activity which repeatedly adjusts based on external impacts and of course internal learning. Any practice bears the potential to learn and to improve. And the learning is best captured if it finds its way into the processes and structures of an organisation, respectively into the set-up of a project. Any individual lesson learnt is a case for reconsidering the processes and structures in a project set-up, to disseminate the learning and to improve performance.

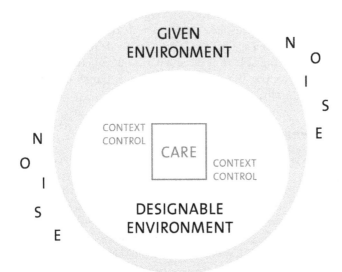

Figure 21.8 Systemic perspective on good governance.

Captainship builds on the insight that management does not equal leadership, and neither management nor leadership equal entrepreneurship (Klein & Popp, 2009). There has been a long debate throughout the 1990s and further on demanding that managers need to become inspiring leaders, intrapreneurs even (Oden, 1997). And in the start-up hype of the last decade the focus shifted on entrepreneurship. Only loosely linked in the public debate those three aspects had been systemically linked already in Stafford Beer's *viable system model* (1979;, 1972) in the 1970s and later in the 1980s in the *St. Gallen Management Model* (Bleicher, 1991). The latter divides management in operational management, strategic management and normative management. Leaning on Niklas Luhmann. this suggests leadership being the unity of the distinction of management and entrepreneurship. In Stafford Beer's terms it decomposes captainship functionally into operational management, strategic entrepreneurship and normative leadership (Figure 21.9).

Operational management builds on the notion of the popular MBA, the Master of Business Administration. This clearly sets the focus on the administration of operations, here and now. And the bulk of management activities are just this, administration. *Strategic entrepreneurship* is all about taking risk. This is what entrepreneurs do. In reference of the there and then they take and manage risks. Continued business as usual can be left to managers. *Normative leadership* provides orientation and gives directions. It mitigates between the here and now and the there and then. It is the unity of the distinction. Pure managers are bureaucrats, pure entrepreneurs are gamblers and pure leaders are dreamers. The manager/leader is the archetypical corporate man, the entrepreneur/leader is the venturous founder and the manager/entrepreneur who can be identified as the classic project manager.

Captainship comes with the responsibility for all three functions: management, entrepreneurship and leadership. For classic project managers this adds the dimension of leadership, of providing orientation and giving directions, not only within the realm of

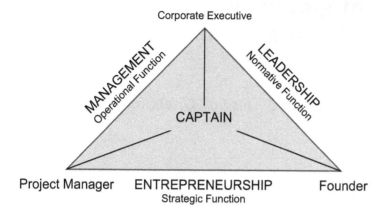

Figure 21.9 Captainship.

the project charter. And it readdresses the aspect of organising projects for performance, providing orientation not through charismatic performance but through context control and care.

Good project performance in the 21st century, in the volatile, uncertain, complex and ambiguous world of the Anthropocene, requires the innovation and continuous improvement of project management itself, embracing complexity and venturing new thinking. That's all! If we are successful, we save the planet.

Chapter 22

The future of global program leadership

A sci-fi narrative

Alejandro Arroyo Welbers and Thomas Grisham

A look back for context

It had been a comfortable ride to the site, but the AH (automated helicopter) was ten years old and did not have a plug-in for my VR (virtual reality) headset, so I could not order food at the site. Inconvenient, as I would have to eat the vegetable protein pack that my wife had stuck into my bag – she knows how unpredictable these trips to the frontier have become. As usual, we had met our customer in Kigali to review the CPE plan (Collaborative Program Enterprise) for their new facility, and to introduce the leaders of each organization involved. This Awakening Session was led by the CPE Executive, and began the Collaborative Sessions for the endeavor. Part of the success of each program that we have undertaken for the past 20 years springs from these initial sessions. When we started 30 years ago, it was difficult to convince people of the importance of these sessions, and even more difficult to persuade them to think about CPEs. Back then, the world was still locked into short-term thinking, with organizations only looking to their own self-interest. That all changed.

When we first started the Collaboration Sessions there was an immense push back from participants. Everyone was a trained Project Management Professional (PMP), and knew everything about how to run projects, thank you very much. They saw the Sessions as unnecessary and a waste of time. We had initially underestimated the arrogance and ignorance of organizations to the realities of leading complex programs from concept to operations. Each seemed interested in their own needs, and unwilling, or unable, to empathize with the other organizations. Despite all of the education, advice, lessons learned, and practical experience, the managers of the organizations could not accept that their fate was linked, inexorably, to the success of the other organizations. As Leonard Cohen once said: "they were starving in some deep mystery like a man who is sure what is true." And, there was a serious lack of leadership skills.

We were foremost in adopting technology to help managers to drop their preconceived notions, take a long-term view, and become leaders in thinking, and in actions. In the early days we used PowerPoint presentations, videos, and case studies. While they were perhaps 70% effective, we wanted and needed to get to 100%. As VR moved into the mainstream, and our app saw wider use, we were able to take the education, and the Collaborative Sessions, to a whole new level. It turns out that the Collaborative Sessions, coupled with our Shadowing Program, reduced global program failure rates from 60% to 10%, and we intend to reduce this to 1% in the next two years. Now, whether the program is in the Congo or Norway, extractive or IT, the CPE program prepares organizations to succeed. Each organization needs to field a leader, not a manager, and there of course must be a CPE executive to lead the overall effort .

For example, in the earlier part of the century, companies like Shell found themselves pursued for alleged bribery and corruption changes in places like Nigeria's OPL 245 parcel where the government expected to be lubricated. All this was driven by what was then known as the "Transboundary Litigation Concept," which originally meant that companies could be sued at home for offenses committed abroad. Back in the early 2000s, in Britain for example, the law stipulated that compensation claims by 3000 South African employees of a subsidiary of Cape Plc who were suffering from asbestosis could be heard in the UK given the lack of legal aid available in South Africa at that time. This opened the door for subsidiaries of UK companies to be held accountable for their operations abroad. While our Collaborative Sessions led by a trained CPE executive witnessed a gradual reduction of events like this one, we have noticed a marked increase in the risk of transboundary litigation, particularly for companies accused of human rights abuses or complicity in such abuses. This is just one of many areas where a solid CPE program has helped global companies, with activities in the emerging world to successfully avoid such mistakes. To this end, BP CEO Sir John Browne once said:

> Globalization has taken companies into a wider range of countries, some of which have fragile social structures and limited experience of the working of a market economy...that means working in some complex areas: in Southern Africa, in areas blighted by aids; in Angola, a country beset by civil war for 40 years; in Colombia, a country trying to escape the grip of organized crime and the impact of the drug trade; and in Russia, a country still coming to terms with transition to a market-based economy and lacking real enforcement mechanisms for their laws...if globalization marks the end of sovereignty for national governments it should also equally end any sense of splendid isolation which exists in the corporate world.

Although difficult to believe how slow we as a species were to learn, the values embedded in the CPE program have helped to almost eliminate disruptions that arise to endeavors around the world. Remember when it was not uncommon for government officials to route payments through opaque personal accounts, and use money for kickbacks, luxury homes in developed countries, Lear jets, offshore bank accounts, and worse. As the Global Unity took shape, extractive industries were the first to come under scrutiny, and the first to find themselves in the dock of the World Court. Most IT organizations took note, and adjusted their behavior toward big data, and privacy, before the Global Unity took them to task.

Speaking about the concept of Global Unity, incidents like those just mentioned brought about what was initially known as the United Nations Global Compact, or Sullivan Principles, which turned out to be concepts that served businesses and humanity well. Back then, they were regarded as good practices based on noble principles – all of which of course needed some time to evolve and adjust progressively. Despite the fact that some organizations adhered to these concepts, the reality was that many of them did it just to look politically correct for their global stakeholders. Nowadays virtual reality modeling and simulation, along with CPE site-applied practices, make it near impossible that an organization cannot embrace these values as they encompass the very essence of their sustainability and survival. There is simply no place to hide, yet some still try. This is not driven by altruism, it is driven by technology making actions transparent.

Globalization and the available technology at the turn of the century was incipient if compared with today's. Selfishness, carelessness, or ignorance used to lead an organization to prop up a corrupt foreign government, and perhaps unconsciously contributing to regional conflicts. Some of you may remember that it was well into this century before such things as Green Bonds took root. The idea of sustainable investing helped build the impetus for the Global Unity. Doing the right thing turned out to be good business as well, fortunately. It was a difficult time in our history, and has led to what we all hope will be a very promising future – more about that later.

Remember the Harvard Review case study back in the 2000s named "The Equator Principles: An Industry Approach to Managing Environmental and Social Risks." By looking back it is funny to see how primitive and naïve well reputed global financial institutions were, when the technology could have easily let them take a more local view of the programs they undertook. Their insouciance and inaction towards sustainability, and the power long-term thinking provides, is simply incredible in hindsight. It has been known for well over 25 years that a CPE provides a sort of shield against hidden agendas, inefficiences, risks, and the changes that are a normal part of any global endeavor.

A project in Kigali, Cameroon, Congo, or the Central African Republic requires infrastructure to enable extractive organizations to provide development and employment to citizens of these countries. It also increases the profitability of the developers, without compromising the long-term needs of the citizens. John Elkington suggested the importance of this years ago with the Triple Bottom Line (TBL). Looking back, organizations that adopted the TBL and connected long-term profitability to social and environmental stewardship have moved African countries into the place everyone wishes to be. The Chinese also played an important role in the awakening toward long-term thinking. Their hands-off philosophy, which looked the other way to the corruption and human rights abuses, proved the failure of short-term thinking. It turned out that once citizens were given respect, education, and a way to care for their families, everyone wanted it to continue. We may say that the Chinese were instrumentally, though not intentionally, the reason Africans began to put stipulations onto programs conducted on the continent – you must adopt the TBL if you are to do business with us. All this needed an adjustment and evolution.

On the environmental front, Ford Motor Company managed to find environmental solutions once they reached production capacity of fossil fuel passenger transport – environmentally friendly because there was no other choice. Unilever took a different approach, environmentally friendly by choice, leading the way by offering 100% organic production and distribution of food and consumer products. We might say they were one step ahead in the adjustment and evolution race.

You may remember that Dambisa Moyo and Ian Bremmer tried to make the trajectory of Africa clear back in 2018, but were only marginally successful. They emphasized the importance of long-term thinking as a foundation for improving the conditions for African citizens. As a species, it seems that we must have a major calamity to force us into action – first a forced adjustment that leads us eventually to evolve. Asia and the West aged, and Africa became the source of young labor that enabled everyone to improve their lives. Yes, it was like watching grass grow, but it eroded some of the more intransigent problems on the continent. And in Asia, once Dhaka was underwater due to climate change, and the migration flowed back toward Myanmar, India, and Pakistan, the world realized that attitudes toward migration needed to be overhauled. That change in perspective then paved the way for the easy movement of people in and out of Africa to supply the aging populations of the West.

Once maglev trains spread over Cameroon and its African neighbors, the increase in profits from cargo and passenger operations, and the use of robots and state-of-the-art logistics became a reality. The advent of infrastructures like maglev trains, roads, power, and the internet have transformed the face of the continent, and the perceptions of doing business there. The early introduction of robots, which could not be bribed (a major contribution to the Global Unity concept), helped encourage the political changes that 20th-century governments refused to make. Oddly, automation proved to be a key part of the solution, not only from a revenue standpoint but also, and most importantly, from a social sustainability perspective. As it turned out, technology brought financial equity, and with that peace and efficiency. The use of CPE endeavors helped as well as it enabled the local citizens and politicians to learn its use, and power, in getting every ounce of benefit from their resources.

Thinking about police in Cairo making US$50 per month seems like fiction. It is almost impossible to imagine the difference that a living wage made to the 1.5 billion young people in Africa. With no need to shake down travelers in order to feed one's family, corruption became too much trouble. It is ironic that corporate entities were the impetus for the increase in wages. The internet concentrated wealth in fewer hands, and fortunately with people like the Gates, Musk, and others, that wealth was redistributed more effectively than 100 years of donations on the continent. Past civil wars in places like Rwanda are unthinkable today and will hopefully be simply impossible in the future. They are supported by operations technology that continues to encourage integration, trade, social mobility, quality employment, specialization, productivity, and sustainable technology-related jobs. The global community has finally accepted that economic interdependence across regions and countries tends to substantially diminish the probability of armed conflicts – to which the advances in technology have clearly made its contribution. We may affirm today that it improves everyone's life on the planet.

Operational and surveillance technology and automation have made conflicts and inefficiencies almost a thing of the past. While these improvements are a necessary condition to continued improvement, they are insufficient. These things facilitate the non-tribal collaboration and cooperation that is required in a world that respects and celebrates diversity. We finally saw the connections about 18 years ago, when space and deep ocean programs helped us realize the scarcity of resources from conventional places. Space and deep-sea mining keep growing as resources on earth are depleted, and now must be acquired in places where human deployment on the program sites is not possible. CPE played a pivotal role in the way such endeavors are conducted now.

For example, the exploration of the world's seabed was impossible a few decades back. Today technology coupled with remote operations not only make exploration possible, but also its data becomes marketable to help corporations start planning on the physical deployment of remote-controlled technology. Extremely skilled human resources can now be mobilized to the job-sites much sooner. Even the Arctic and Antarctica's ocean floors are today fully scanned thanks to a double-loop sort of CPE-based crowdsourcing.

It was done by engaging global full-container shipping companies sailing across the North West Passage close to Canada and the Northern Sea Route along Russia. Global firms provided key ocean floor data while sailing commercially. As a result, they have gained a greener appreciation by customers and the general public.

In addition, global fishing fleets that depend on critical resource biomass and fish migration pattern data were part of the multi-disciplinary team that cooperated in the scanning of the ocean floor. Helping to alleviate world hunger, they did this while carrying out their usual fishing operations. World-class oil and gas operators with access to critical deep-sea geological data contributed with their off-shore facilities-based knowledge. Non-governmental organizations (NGOs) leading the global agenda on climate change focused their priorities on top technology-oriented universities around the world, where the data was used to design applied underwater technology and human deployment facilities.

Leading telecommunication firms interested in expanding their submarine cabling operations across the oceans to reach even the remotest spots within Africa, Indonesia, or the Philippines also cooperated actively. Both well-known and new global renewable energy operators have practiced a green approach since the Chinese demonstrated that it is a very profitable business – yes we are sometimes still motivated by money rather than by society's needs. Global hotel chains interested in predicting tsunamis and hurricanes in order to avoid exposure to climate incidents were talked into participating and proactively funded research. All this demanded international planning and detailed execution, geopolitics, and definition on who has access to the data. The Global Unity played a critical role in sorting this out. Remember back in 2018 when Facebook "pioneered" the way by stumbling around data ownership and privacy issues.

The use of technology, the deployment of automated and remote-control vehicles, and the lack of direct human intervention on-site make a CPE approach of vital importance. A CPE defines the roles and responsibilities of the stakeholders, and helps avoid costly disputes, misunderstandings, and unallocated risks. For example, surveillance in Botswana was carried out in the 20th century by engaging drones aimed at keeping a "close eye" on poachers supplying the black market for ivory. A blend of rangers patrolling huge areas with limited onshore resources and a bit of aerial surveillance was successful in controlling the supply side. However, little or nothing was done on the demand side. Buyers in India and China, and fashion-conscious customers in Europe, used to take advantage of the weak institutions and local rivalries. That changed when biometric tagging enabled law enforcement to police the demand side quickly and effectively. Technology again? Yes, though backed up by a CPE approach.

Politicians in the developing world became experts in the technology and effects, and this new transparency proved a powerful deterrent. Though drones are regarded today as a bow and arrow approach to keep stakeholders satisfied, aligning a program's mission and vision to what looks to be politically correct still requires attention. Today, little human intervention is required on the surveillance side with satellite imaging and effective communications. The technology enables the prompt onshore deployment of resources, make poaching too risky and simply unprofitable. Robots, planning, and transnational collaboration make the difference even in remote locations.

Technology did however have help. One significant contributor to change was China. As the American influence waned, China stepped into the vacuum to offer money with few strings attached. With roughly US$ four trillion of foreign reserves in 2010, China was undoubtedly a better bet for much needed foreign direct investment than its Western competitors. The West was pulling back politically, morally, and economically. Some say history runs in cycles, and here again as with China's Zheng He, who reached East Africa in 1400, China was an explorer. In Africa, culture and history matter, and it is a very complicated tapestry, just ask the Dutch, Portuguese, French, or Arabs! Western companies tended to believe that they compete with China by employing a youth-focused sort of approach. That proved to be nutty.

Now, China has become the owner for much of the natural resources in Africa thanks to their to their laissez faire approach. It continued the damage done by despots and corruption for too long, but finally ended as technology pulled back the veils and transparency became the norm. The Western approach made a difference, but as with the Chinese not in the way intended. A few statements on Western corporations and media are representative of the feelings of millions of young Africans:

- They only show my country as poor (15 years old)
- I am African and not all of us have HIV/AIDS (26 years old)
- China isn't perfect but at least they did not colonize us and rip us of our culture (17 years old)
- How come they do not show poor children from India or China on brochures? They only show Africans (22 years old)
- I do not believe western mining companies care about us, they care about themselves (24 years old)
- As Ghana's consular general in Canada once said, "A major challenge in Ghana and most of Africa is to help youth transform informal businesses into formal enterprises that will contribute to our economy."

Finding productive employment in the early 2000s for 200 million Africans between the ages of 15 and 24 was surely one of the continent's greatest challenges, per the World Bank Vice President for the African Region Mr. Obiageli Ezekwesilli. Understanding culture and history within a CPE structure today has brought about tremendous opportunities for companies that wish to succeed on a continent that has unlimited potential, but still needs understanding and skillful leadership. Today's technology no doubt helps, but respectful and empathetic leadership is more effective. Such leadership leads to outcomes through cooperating, listening, collaborating, exchanging views and impressions, rather than imposing developed world preconceived standards. Remember when the British or American Navy, Canadian, and Australian navies deployed battleships along the East African coast to combat piracy. For 40 years sea pirates have been growing, expanding, and acquiring technology to help them outsmart, not outgun, the Western navies. It was only when the underlying causes of piracy were addressed that suffering people did not need to risk their lives.

By comparison, Brazil's strategy was not deploying any frigates, not even a dinghy with a couple of frogmen on board. They kept inviting naval officers of Somalia, Ethiopia, and other countries in the region to Brazil in order to train them on antipiracy practices and marine intelligence. Most importantly, by far, they exchanged codes, norms, cultural habits, views and impressions about the world and their own cultural attitudes. They forged ties and became lifelong friends. They treated the Africans with respect, empathy, and trust. Who was more effective? Who opened doors for others to come and develop projects more effectively? The more interconnected the world became, driven by the technology, the greater the need to understand culture and history. The potential gains across Africa are still huge, yet the risks to company reputation are also great, if they ignore the lessons of the past 40 years.

As fate would have it, the world learn from Africa about the importance of security. The Global Unity, founded in 2030, was based in Timbuktu to underscore the developments in Africa, and to remind the world of the long intellectual, cultural, and economic history of the continent. It was designed to be a look backward, as a way to better see the way forward. And, perhaps most importantly, it made clear that the creative potential of the continent was untapped. Who better to see the importance of personal security and rights, than those who had struggled for so long? The Global Unity also made the TBL required of global organizations by treaty, ratified by all 250 countries. The United Nations grew to the higher number as many countries recognized the necessity to respect the cultural divisions ignored during colonization. They developed the LoF (失去面子-Shīqù miànzi, pérdida de prestigio, فقدان ماء الوجه-fiqdan ma' alwajh, loss of face) metric now used extensively to find organizations that put the environment and society on a level footing with profits. It puts to immediate shame those who ignored the treaty obligations, for there is nowhere to hide with the internet. The transparency provided by being on the list entitled organizations to be barred from participating in any endeavors for a period of one year.

As it turned out, having to teach robots ethics forced us all to re-examine our thinking. As the population peaked this year at nine billion, the Global Entity had to make adjustments to balance the necessity of robots against the need for employment. But we get ahead of ourselves. The purpose of this article is to look back on program management from our current knowledge base, and perhaps learn what we should be thinking about now, for our future.

CPE

Artificial Intelligence (AI), Virtual Reality (VR), and Augmented Reality (AR) changed the way we all live, forever. In CPEs, the adoption of the technology was slow, but finally became mainstream. Our Program Management Information Systems (IPMS) platform incorporated the technology as it became affordable and stable. IPMS provided a server-based collaboration platform that enabled all organizations to share information 24/7 globally. AI enabled us to tap into the World Bank database and use their subtask identification system.

You all know that new ID technology layers the information on scans and provides links to design, procurement, delivery, installation, testing, and operations data associated with any item. Coupled a few years back with video taken by the bots we now use on most programs. For an average global program, the level of data that has to be managed is simply too much for people, but easy for Bots. The construction industry has always been a slow adapter, and the IT business was changing too fast for people to keep up. But once Google demonstrated that they could do a better job of predicting cancer using Big Data than could the medical profession, the lesson was not lost on us. Although AR has been in wide use for over a decade, people are still wary about IT implants, but we see that becoming far more common within 10 years.

By the way, the use of the term project was always too narrow a view of how to think about global endeavors. Programs were considered a grouping of projects, a more macro view. While it is still true that each organization must plan their own work, stopping at the project level led to protectionism, excessive competition, secrecy, and a lack of communications. Yet, millions of people were trained to think that way. Individualism created the superhero, stoicism the method, and winning the goal. Is it any wonder that that led to failure rates north of 80% for global programs? Governments around the world exacerbated the problem by insisting upon competitive bidding, and in many cases no open communications between the government and prospective bidders. In the case of Puerto Rico and Haiti, multiple hurricanes caused huge suffering and hunger. Government processes, in the West no less, requiring competitive bidding on food services caused many people to starve. In developing countries, suffering from the so-called resource curse, this was maybe necessary, but they looked to the developed world as a model. And, that model was individualism, cut-throat competition, and no communication.

Today we call programs CPEs, where each organization looks at the endeavor from two perspectives: their contribution, and how it is connected to that of the other organizations. Think of it as a short-term Alliance, where multiple organizations are led as if an integrated organization, with a CEO. With our new technology and CPE structure, governments no longer need to fret about corruption and kick-backs. The old mindset required an organization to build a plan for their work. These plans required the integration of sub-plans for scope, time, cost, risk, quality, and communications. The failures arose because these individualized sub-plans of an individual organization then had to be integrated into an overall program plan that often had no designated leader or owner. With our ability to measure energy consumed (EC), the use of cost-reimbursable agreements, and CPE big data, customers now spend 30% less on endeavors globally. Figure 22.1 provides an overview of a typical CPE, and includes the CPE Executive. All of the agreements are directly with the CPE Executive organization.

So CPEs now employ cost reimbursable agreements that remove much of the fear and secretiveness. We invented war about 10,000 years ago, and peace about 10 years ago. The competitive bidding process was based on war, the CPE idea on peace. Yet, it is still a work in progress, and we continue to evolve. Some of you may remember the last version of the PMBOK Guide issued in 2038. One change was to declare that economic interdependence between nations, and organizations, fosters cooperation and avoids conflict. Now customers do not need to hire a specialized organization to write technical specifications and agreements for them, have other specialty organizations interpret those specifications, price the risk of uncertainty, compete with others who may underprice (knowingly or not) the work, and then try to estimate, measure, report and resolve the changes that they did not anticipate. As Dwight Eisenhower said: "plans are nothing; planning is everything." We will come back to this idea shortly.

We remember the early days of Big Data, and the way it changed commerce. As late as 2025, the documentation required for a cargo vessel could easily run into hundreds of thousands of documents, in multiple languages. Bills of Lading, packing lists, letters of credit, insurance policies, orders, invoices, sanitary certificates, certificates of origin were just some of these documents. The unnerving thing was that a Venetian merchant in 800 BCE would have used some of the same documents. The Phoenicians utilized Bills of Lading, and designed insurance policies, that became the basis of modern

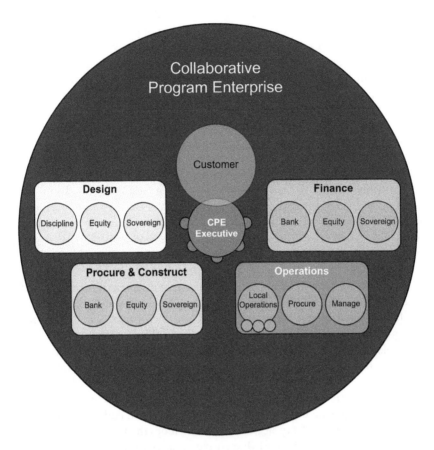

Figure 22.1 Collaborative program enterprise (CPE).

insurance, for trading between Byblos, Carthage, and Sidon. Their expertise in trading across the Mediterranean Sea was admirable and still works beautifully today.

Later, in the 16th century, Edward Lloyd's coffee house in London became recognized as the place for obtaining marine insurance. This is where the Lloyd's we know it today began, and now includes insurance for the outer space shipping business. The Phoenicians served as an inspiration, and template, for commercial law that deals with mining in outer space – literally, from ocean to outer space. It is funny to look back at the early years of this century, where even in the 20s, shipping was still conducted using fax machines where paper still ruled. Organizations like Maersk could take weeks to arrange paperwork for a shipment. Programs were still receiving bills of lading in multiple languages on paper well into this century. It was not until Amazon and Alibaba got involved in the business that technology crept in. Fortunately for consumers, they lowered the cost and time by orders of magnitude. That caused seismic shifts in the industry, and a spate of leveraged buyouts. In retrospect, it looks simply insane that it took us 1,000 years to fix this. In 2018, studies found that almost 25% of the costs were consumed by documentation. We really are a wasteful species.

The old 20th-century project approach and mindset proved too slow and costly in a distributed world driven by rapidly changing technology. Thus, in keeping with the project mindset, the fix in the early part of this century was to become more Agile. You may remember that Agile the noun, meaning the name of a process, was confused with Agile the adjective, meaning a more flexible organization. Those working in IT saw Agile as a way to reduce the cost of projects, and the time to market. Those not in IT saw Agile as a way to increase success on all types of endeavors. We all know how that ended, but we did learn, painfully, some ways to enhance our effectiveness. The IT version of Agile eliminated the writing of detailed scope documents, development of detailed estimates and schedules, geopolitical considerations, reporting, and the paperwork to record it all. It embodied short-term thinking. In hindsight, we went from medium-term individualist thinking with the PMBOK Guide, to short-term micro thinking with Agile. Agile reminded us of the importance of eliminating tasks that did not add value – to eliminate waste.

As these changes were occurring, organizations like the World Bank continued to face increasing exposure of their programs to a wide range of variables that they could not control, like environmental and social issues. As we said, we were all mired in short-term thinking about programs, until the World Bank required long-term planning. And, the private sector slowly began to realize that there was a lesson here; do the right thing and profits increase. The Chad–Cameroon pipeline project disaster was probably the inflection point that taught the World Bank that corruption should be taken seriously, and environmental management should be regarded as a competitive advantage. We seem to need such wrenching lessons to alter our perceptions and behaviors.

IPMS and CPE map

As we said earlier, the IPMS system was designed to provide a platform for CPEs. The apps associated enable teams to monitor, measure, and control all aspects of a program with a cell phone, connected to the server. Likewise, all of the data collected by Bots are integrated back onto the server, and available instantly to anyone with a cell phone and access to the server.

An IPMS system has been in use by all the organizations who contributed to the world's ocean floor scanning as well. AI, VR, and AR all contributed with the design and testing of remote operated vehicles, as well as psychological challenges like the level of stress on those at the surface in charge of monitoring the underwater robots. Technology not only helps to better deal with technical variables in a new frontier of exploration like the space or ocean floor, but also with the aspects affecting those who design and operate the technology. Data from these stressful situations was then used to improve the sensitivity of IPMS systems in less severe environments. Alibaba, Google, and others taught us the value of Big Data, and of the importance of looking across disciplines for knowledge.

Perhaps a brief review of the IPMS system will help clarify where we are today. Starting with scope, each requirement is broken down into energy modules (EMs), the most convenient size being 100 Joules. So with the World Bank database, and other private sector data, each level 1 requirement is broken down into tasks of about 4 hours each for labor. Most all of this is done using the AI software and the databases. As each task is identified it is assigned a unique ID, energy expenditure estimate, cost, duration, risk, the organization responsible, the quality requirements, the specifications or skill levels, and any inputs required, and any outputs that rely on this task. Countless global programs have been conducted with estimates and schedules at too high or low a level of detail. Then the use of such a foundation to measure progress made it all look poorly planned, and brought competence into question.

Keeping the data that was needed to build the databases was also a burden. On one program in India, there was a team of six people whose only job was to try and estimate progress and report on it. Then there is the issue of knowledge. BP struggled to build and keep current its worldwide knowledge base, and their inabilities became corporate frustrations leading to a sort of stop-and-go strategy globally. As we learned, their challenges were psychological not technological.

Many wanted to use Earned Value (EV) analysis on programs which were far too complex and diverse to measure, such as Public Relations. EV was expensive, and was not very accurate at the beginning and end of a program. Worse, the reports of progress caused disputes and arguments over the accuracy of the information, the basis for the evaluation, and the complaints about the changes which caused it to be lower than anticipated. It was costly, inaccurate, wasteful, and fomented disputes. Not useful data to inform future programs, nor to inculcate cooperation.

Then there were the risks. Fortunately the IPMS, and cost-reimbursable contract structures, eliminated the pricing risks. The Bots observed activity, be it design, procurement, construction or operations, and reported on any inefficiencies below the mean, and why. Given about 4-hour task duration, the measurements are quite accurate. The risks that always needed more attention are now emphasized, and better managed. With the use of cost-reimbursable contracts, issues of time extensions and reimbursement are automatic, so there is no necessity to build in contingencies to cover most risks. Now, contingencies are finally more oriented to operations rather than construction. With our VR and AI systems, contingencies are almost a thing of the past as the Global Database permits estimates of effort and risk at a 99.9% level. With the advent of the Global Unity and more economic equity, the majority of civil unrest, war, terrorism, and bigotry are a thing of the past. The most intransigent issues still remains the weather. Too little was done too late, and the results are that extremes are the new normal. Prediction is far better though, and access to the Global Weather model now enables projects to do a reasonable prediction for the geographical area where the program is being undertaken.

However, we are about to see an impressive step towards global weather prediction as we move forward with our CPE-based global deep-sea scanning and data management program. A better understanding on underwater geology, ocean temperature differences, marine currents, waves, winds, bathymetry, hydrology, and the potential oceans' carrying capacity to withstand negative impacts of CO_2-based global warming will put us in an advantageous position to predict what the weather will look like in a given location at a given period of time. Becoming more effective in weather forecasting is offsetting the impact of inadequate infrastructure on agriculture, energy, and mining projects across the developing world. This is especially true in remote locations where resource mobilization is still variable. As robotics progress, this will become less of an issue, and local people can be given training and education to enable them to share in the rewards of our technology. No more sweatshops or deaths.

The CPE map provides a broad overview of the program shown in Figure 22.2. The specific components of each step are not provided here, because of the limitations for this chapter. They are available in our older publications (Arroyo, 2017) (Grisham, 2016) (Grisham, 2009). With that as a brief overview of IPMS and CPE, now we will look at the major components of a CPE Map: Awakening Session, Norming and Planning Session, Collaboration and Reimagining Sessions, and Retrospective Session. Each was given a name to generally describe what the CPE is doing, but everyone knows that there are never clear boundaries for these Sessions – they are intended to bleed into one another. Twenty-five years ago, we partnered with the World Bank in pioneering a structure which put the CPE Executive as the primary contracting party, moving the customer into a secondary role, and eliminating expensive waits for decisions. Perhaps more important, assuring that decisions were in the best interest of the overall CPE. Best interest is defined in the Awakening Session, and is consensually agreed to by all participant organizations.

Figure 22.2 is a graphic timeline for planned CPE Sessions. We will look at each in more detail to provide a better view of what we have learned over the past 50 years, and what we hope to accomplish over the next 50 years. The Awakening Session is all about Eisenhower's earlier quote, it is about the act of planning, not the making of a plan.

Awakening session

Think of how an arranged marriage worked, say in Afghanistan. Forty years ago, the parents did their research, and planned their strategy for finding a suitable mate. A list of candidates was prepared, interviews and negotiations followed, and ultimately a marriage was arranged. The couple, often pre-teens, likely never saw each other, did not participate in the selection, and did not actually begin the marriage until much later. The process was similar to the competitive bidding approach, only difference was the highest bidder was often selected. Today in India the process relies on technology, and genetics, and is more like a negotiated contract approach. The Awakening Session is similar to a wedding, where the parties come together to celebrate, meet the relatives, and begin learning about each other.

Customers who are experts in their field should always seek out the services of a CPE Executive organization, certified by the World Bank. This lesson has been perhaps the most painful for many organizations. We took a page from the American Medical Association (AMA) that physicians should not self-prescribe medications. One reason is that they may be inclined to treat problems that are beyond their expertise or training. You may remember that the World Bank needed to develop a framework to improve the

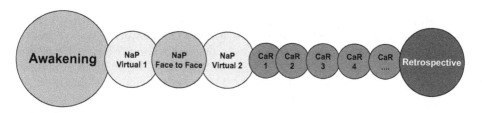

Figure 22.2 Time line for CPE sessions.

success of their loans around the world, and the private sector could not come together as quickly. So they developed the CPE Executive license requirement for their own efforts, and business quickly adopted it given the measured benefits.

Technology now provides both intelligent data and process-oriented devices that leads the project to take advantage of the environmental hazards and turn them into sustainable opportunities for the project and indirect stakeholders alike. Goals are far easier to bring together within a CPE structure where there is transparency, and sharing of detailed criteria and metrics using the cutting edge technology. The technology eliminates subjectivity.

The process has proven effective over the last 30 years, and begins with a meeting between the customer and the CPE Executive to establish the general scope of the work. This then enables the CPE Executive to solicit an order of magnitude prices from three or more participant organizations. Using this approach, organizations can drastically reduce their cost to provide proposals. Each organization maintains a registry of organizations who have done similar work in the past, and who have five star ratings. This was another World Bank idea to save costs by inviting any organization interested in participating on their endeavors to submit a proof of competence package in a standard format. The Bank only permits four and five star organizations to bid on their endeavors, where the private sector is sometimes more lenient depending upon the location of the endeavor. Thus, CPE Executive databases are more extensive as a result, and more dependable.

The next step is for the CPE Executive to interview the firms and select the primary organizations for the endeavor. So for example, an extractive industries mining project in a developing country would include organizations capable of design, procurement, construction, operations, public relations, politics, social services, and financing. Of course we all know about the emergence of global CPE Executive organizations that expanded to provide all of these services under one umbrella. This is a bit more expensive in practice, but generates higher levels of success (95% rather than 90%). Then the Awakening Session begins.

The purpose of this Session is to build a Level 1 plan. This is a summary level plan for the scope of the entire endeavor from design through obsolescence. We learned that industry specialists are more accurate in defining scope for the services required, and locals have a richer and fresher knowledge of local conditions. It was always inefficient to have a British firm in London writing the scope for an endeavor in Peru, two years in advance. Then there was the added cost of review, bidding, analysis, questions, different economic conditions, and different technology. And, the issue of pricing time and risk. When we learned from the Work Bank data that over 40% of a project budget was being consumed on average with determining scope, reporting upon it, changing it, and arguing about it was rather easy to convince organizations that an alternative was needed.

The functions of design, procurement, and construction need a local knowledge base component. This helps to avoid big variances that lead to endless discussions, disputes, and bias from those who do not understand local practices. Those who view the program and people from Canary Wharf in London will be decidedly different from those who view the program from the jungles of Peru. This sounds obvious now, but there are still organizations that believe that they can afford to plan programs without first considering the history, culture, and local knowledge. As we all know now, understanding location, local culture, and the environment are crucial to success.

The benefits from this Awakening Session are in the building of relationships, empathizing, communications, and the process of planning. The focus is not on creating a plan, though that results. The level 1 plan is for the Bots, so that they can use it to build the mass of data required for a level 4 plan (down to 100 joules). Even with this level of detail, plans should never be considered fixed, just a guide. More important than the detail are the relationships. When Jeff Sutherland first described Agile, the primary notion was of having experts that self-aggregated into teams. The idea of picking who you work with was a game changer, though in his context it was confined to individual organizations, in a common location. It took a few years to move the idea to the virtual environment across organizations in a CPE. And it required an intimacy that could only happen with transparency.

This session is where organizations can see if the chemistry is right, as can the CPE Lead and the Customer. The database does a good job of initial parings, with a success rate of around 98%. But, because of young companies sometimes there is simply inadequate data to make a solid prediction, so a personal meeting is required. At the completion of this session, organizations function more like what used to be called an alliance, intimate like a husband and wife, complete transparency, and a common bank account for the endeavor. It produces almost no competition, eliminates fear, and establishes common goals. We knew back in 2018 that the brain changes with different environments and functions. It was only about five years ago, however, that neurological research was able to predict the effects of different experiences accurately and dependably. It showed that the Awakening Sessions do indeed change the brains of those involved, and the sessions were in turn adjusted to maximize the synchrony of the participants with neurological guidance.

Awakening Sessions usually last for 10 days, and are in person, not virtual. The first five days are interaction intensive. Then there is a two-day break for non-thinking joint activities, and time for the Bots to do their magic. The CPE then comes back together to review the CPE map. The map comes on a tablet provided to each participant. The tablet links, via the Global Web micro satellite system, anywhere on the planet, to the CPE server. All of the data on energy, time, risk, design, procurement, operations, quality, communications, video, and photos is available 24/7. The Bots keep continual observations on all aspects of the program, regardless of location or organization. So, the CPE Lead may be in Buenos Aires, but can see the actual work (birds eye, worms eyes, design, or actual installation) at any time, for any component. If the work is consuming more resources than anticipated, the Bots issue an alert with the expected overrun and three options to remedy the problem. The Alerts are sent to all participants of the CPE, so that everyone knows the issue, who is responsible for it, and can then offer ideas or assistance. The alert system begins here.

The work of people like Lara Boyd led to the new integrative sciences, and we will talk more about that in the last section of this report. While the biotech industry designs fixes, we now know that repetition is essential for freezing in the brain changes and building autonomic habit. Sutherland bumped into the idea, and saw it worked, beginning with the morning scrum meetings. In the late 20s we moved the idea into what we call Norming and Planning Sessions.

Looking back, there are endless examples where a CPE map, and its global micro satellite link, would have enabled programs that failed to successfully overcome, or at least minimize, obstacles and challenges that even the most daring and skilled engineers could not solve. The blend of nonexistent or inadequate infrastructure, along with the power of nature, used to make rich-resource regions the ideal place for programs to fail. A Canada-based oil exploration project that took place in the Loreto department on the northern strip of Peru, near the border with Ecuador, is one such example. Base camps were located in extremely remote spots on the Marañon River, where access could only be gained by helicopter or a 14-hour fast boat trip. Supplies and personnel mobilization up to the drilling station, which lay even farther away from the base camp, could only be done by helicopter, provided that the ever-present wind and rains allowed a safe flight. With our new hovercrafts, and 90% micro-weather accuracy, it sure is hard to imagine why we had such troubles in the past.

Ocean shipping, river barging, fast boats, inland depots by the river, helicopters, small aircrafts, and truckloads across the Andes and in the rainforest seemed an impossible curse. The Amazon rainforest and the skills and assets needed to carry out construction logistics could well be compared to programs in the Philippines, Indonesia, Vietnam, Papua New Guinea, or in Colombia. Human decision-making far away from a headquarters in Canada, for example, was made in a complex socio-economic environment where biases and lack of control led to corruption and failure. Today's remote-controlled barging and self-sustainable air-fish type of crafts for personnel transportation are not only utilized worldwide in extreme locations such as these, but are also available for other programs. Efficient and safe contracting and operations are in comparison easy today with a CPE map and global data. Had such organizations heeded our warnings and recommendations at the time, fewer programs might have failed. Of course, the improvements in technology reduced some of the risks, but the leadership and people issues were not helped with the technology improvements.

In 2014, an organization specializing in barge and air operations across the Canadian Arctic, supplying operational backup to oil and gas programs, listened to our advice, took the longer view, and leveraged their assets. They had a successful program, and then used the lessons globally. They identified areas of the world, like the southern hemisphere, where they could use their assets to work during the off-season. The goal was to conduct 12-month operations worldwide, by using mobile assets and traditional local knowledge. They formed alliances with organizations in South America, South Africa, and Oceania willing to share and transfer their Arctic-focused operational knowledge, while making good use of expensive floating stock and valuable personnel. All under the umbrella of a strategic alliance or partnership that enabled them to offset the lack of activities during the northern winter.

Search and rescue operations were an offshoot provided by exploration activities on ocean sea beds. Global market penetration is always a competitive advantage if offered by a truly global technology-driven operator with field experience around the world. In the early 2000s, the search for a suitable partner entailed months if not years of negotiations and permitting. Today, it is much easier to join efforts and leverage organizational assets and knowledge to exploit bigger goals as global opportunities can be more easily identified, and partners vetted quickly. Had these organizations used a CPE map, and had access to World Bank data and information, it is very likely they would have expanded more rapidly not only on off-season ice operations, but also across warmer areas of the world with comparable logistic challenges.

The goal of the Awakening Session is to build trust, build long-term relationships, craft common goals and objectives, build effective communications, and to make transparency more comfortable. Neurologically it rewires circuitry to make these things habits.

Norming and Planning session (NaP)

Using our wedding metaphor, this is the honeymoon, and moving in together part of the relationship. Are the partners morning people or evening people; do they like coffee or tea; do they spend lots of time on social media? Everyone gets to know everyone, and their quirks and habits. The bio and story form a foundation for getting to know the members of the CPE as quickly as possible.

Bruce Tuckman developed a model in the early 60s of forming, storming, norming, performing, and regretting to describe the phases teams went through. The idea was accepted but not tested until decades later. What the research then found was that the phases did indeed occur, but not sequentially as he imagined. They happened more simultaneously. Most who have worked on a team would likely recognize these phases, as did we, because they were built on common sense human interactions that everyone saw. Last century, the pace was significantly different Teams were co-located, meetings face-to-face, and the roles of organizations far more conventional and distinct. Remember fax machines?

As the technological revolution gained momentum, teams became more virtual and diverse, organizations more specialized, efficiency more critical, and time shrank. Of course this was the epitome of a boiled frog problem as technology progressed – a frog cannot feel the gradually increasing heat until it is too late. Remember on global endeavors when we had to DHL documents? Later came faxes, then email, then PDFs, then the cloud, then VR, and next AvR, augmented virtual reality. Despite the unrelenting push of technology, by most accounts it takes about 10,000 years for an evolutionary change to occur in our species. So even with AI and AR, we continue to struggle with the speed and complexity of our world. Like the frog we could not see it coming.

Our original CPE efforts began decades ago, and have evolved over time with the technology. The foundation principles are however unchanged. People need to interact, empathize, communicate, learn, and go through the Tuckman phases even if simultaneously. This reduces fear and uncertainty, enables people to be happy, productive, and seek collaboration with others. This collectivism norming is the foundation for building a CPE. This is where the CPE Executive earns her keep. She must instill the vision, goals, and collaboration that are required to build a cross-cultural, cross-disciplinary, and multi-organizational enterprise. Remember the quote we provided from Eisenhower earlier, the act of planning is essential. Not because it produces a durable plan, but because it brings the CPE team together to work through a puzzle or mystery, as a team. It establishes the way the CPE works, by example. It creates a norm for the way people are treated, respected, and valued.

We recommend that the Norming and Planning Sessions include three interactions. The first is virtual, the second face-to-face, and the third virtual again – as shown in Figure 22.2. The duration of the second one is determined by the CPE Executive on the fly. Face-to-face meetings were first introduced by Nonaka and Takeuchi, who promoted transverse efficiencies and communities of practice (COP) across global organizations in order to identify untapped efficiencies and promote best practices. This began with conventional face-to-face meetings, and in the early 2000s evolved by making use of technology in order to leverage its role as a knowledge facilitator in a virtual world. Culture still plays a critical role, whether it be individual, societal, organizational, micro (CPE), or global. AR is now regarded as a critical tool to gain empathy and understanding of other cultures.

Naturally, the more we move towards 2070 the more comfortable people feel with VR tools and remote technological devices. Culture still exerts its influence on all programs, now more than in 2000. In any case, it is becoming a VR-based culture we live in, and impression needs to be managed and optimized. Culture and technology complement each other whereas it needs to be used in concert with face-to-face interaction, wisely. Programs are mostly virtual, as you all know, and the first virtual session offers a practice interaction before the virtual completion of the program. The face-to-face interaction can sometimes be virtual, if the teams have accepted the norms, and have demonstrated the ability to collaborate effectively in a virtual environment, and have done this successfully before. Our experience is that this happens in only about 4% of the cases. We expect AvR will increase this to 20% within five years. We still need human interaction to exercise our abilities fully. By the end of the century we expect this will be a thing of the past as evolutionary genetics comes into wide use.

These three sessions are intended to create the habit of communicating effectively, often, and using any format. They also buttress, by repetition, the relationships built during the Awakening Session. In the first virtual sessions we have found that not all of the lessons from the Awakening Session have been fully adopted. This Session provides another chance to get the bugs out and to re-emphasize the importance of relationships and communications.

Collaboration and Reimagining sessions (CaR)

This is the living together phase of the relationship. The actions of each party have an effect upon the other. The children, sub-sub-contractors, sometimes do things the parents correct. Parties don't always keep their promises, calamities arise which show up the strengths and weaknesses of the parties, and people leave the CPE. When new people arrive, the wedding needs to occur again, and the CPE Executive needs to explain the culture, and repeat the process of Awakening.

The Collaboration and Reimagining sessions are for working with the friction, challenges, opinions, goals, aspirations, and needs of the various participants. It is like a marriage in that the parties must come to know one another intimately, not just how I hold my teacup, but what I feel about myself and others, and how I empathize with my partner. It is also a celebration and leveraging of the diversity of the CPE. In some ways CPEs are easier than marriages since there are numerous parties, numerous ideas, and alternative communication channels. The key is to have the parties recognize the gift of diversity. After the honeymoon, the work of crafting and adjusting needs to take center stage, and this is a continuing priority for the entire endeavor – and beyond. It frequently changes as new participants arrive and cherished colleagues depart. This is the center of the universe for a CPE Executive.

As with a marriage, the parties find that their plans for careers, family, children, retirement, and friends must be adjusted, or reimagined. Back in 2018, it became clear that far too much time and effort were being spent on getting a perfect plan. Better to accept the fact that we as Homo sapiens live in a fast-changing world, and that we have difficulty seeing a year in advance, let alone two or three. Remember the shuffling around about global warming? Again the focus of the CPE Executive is on the relationships. Though we have come to understand that we must try to think in a trans-generational way, we still are constrained by evolution. This led us, and others, to the idea that it was better to embrace the idea that performing global programs is a constantly changing journey, like marriage. For some cultures, according to Hofstede's work, uncertainty avoidance was cooked in. It has really only been in recent years that a sort of global normalization became the norm – the speed of technology required a rethink on the part of humanity.

Though it is 2050, and we think of ourselves as far evolved from the last century, we still need repetition, and failure to learn. Frequent interactions are essential in working through our human issues. In a marriage, frequent interaction leads to a more intimate understanding of one's partner, both the things that we admire, and don't – likewise for the Collaboration and Reimagining sessions. Some friction in the first one is expected, and measured, but diminishes over time. The rate of change is mapped to the database which then provides the CPE with a metric to assess progress in relationships, and reinforces the importance. It took some time to experiment with different social and psychological tools to find those that inspire people to change. The biggest gains were back in the 20s, and fortunately now the techniques are widely practiced. We still grin to ourselves when we train CPE Executives to encourage failure. It is how we learn.

As with a marriage, there will be disagreements. Despite all of the enhanced mindfulness knowledge we have today, we still must deal with our evolutionary limitations. One of the keys to healthy CPEs is the celebration of diversity, and the acceptance of other views. The continuing discussion of alternatives, needs, and transparency is the norm. Frequent sharing of emotions, ideas, fears, needs, and even wants builds strong relationships. It reduces the fear of uncertainty and change, and revels in conflict. Think back on the days when organizations like Odebrecht and operação lava jato (operation car wash) represented a way to do business that brought quick returns, but required that they be done quietly. Everyone knew they were wrong, but offered a short-term advantage. It took some time before people were brave enough to step forward and stick up for their principles. We all remember whistleblowers in the USA being pilloried for whistleblowing. The Global Unity, led by the EU and Canada, helped change this around where whistleblowers were rewarded as heroes, rather than reviled as villains.

As is always the case, the technology has been a blessing and a curse. The curse being the speed of change, the blessing that it gave us more time to deal with people, and less with data. Knowing each day what happened the previous day, and the impact it had on productivity, time, and costs, enabled conversations over adjustments rather than arguments over facts. With our software, the CPE knows everything, all the time. Including where we were yesterday, where we should be today, and where we think we need to be tomorrow. Thus, the adjustments are small, not wrenching. The CPE can see the future a little more clearly, because all of the adjustments, and alternatives, can be assessed in real time. Then, the leaders of the various CPE organizations and the CPE Executive can discuss the top issues for today, and decide upon a plan for the next eight hours.

For example, if the steel for a building has been delayed for two days by a storm in the Indian Ocean, the planning algorithms project that the delay will cause a four day delay in the work, and offer three options – buy from a local supplier close to the project site; rearrange the erection sequence; expedite the following work. Each requires other members of the CPE to make adjustments, and possibly suffer higher costs. Thanks to the refinements in satellite imagery, accurate weather forecasting allows projects to anticipate such problems, and make decisions that increase productivity, rather than cause losses.

Contingency planning can optimize operations, decrease worry, and thus increase productivity. It may ease human interactions, virtual or face-to-face, to the benefit of the overall program. Amapá is Brazil's poorest and most isolated State, it is close to the Caribbean Sea. Most of its territory is covered with rainforest, with the remaining areas covered with savannah and plains. This makes floods a recurrent problem that impact on its two most important activities: logging and agriculture. Nature hit its shores with unusual violence in the early 2000s, to the extent that it hindered this resource-rich region of the country from receiving investment and creating quality employment. Even metal-made piers at Santana port on the great Amazon River did not withstand the power of tropical storms and tides, further to sedimentation which caused limited and low scale operations on the part of global renowned mining companies. As a matter of fact, the majority of the area's population of 760,000 lived in poverty because of the limited access of the port and its exposure to climate change.

Iron ore mining saw itself pretty much limited to an uncertain operational window, which condemned those who invested there to forget about achieving economies of scale. Combined operations with ores coming from more productive and operationally sheltered States across Brazil was not an option either given the draft restrictions on Santana port and the entrance channel. This exacerbated the little protection that the port offered in bad weather. VR and lately AR along with the world ocean-floor project's partial deliverables proved to be instrumental to cope with bad weather conditions. VR and AR became key tools that allowed project operators to simulate scenarios and plan adequate responses to the many forms the weather might impact the operations.

Sea-bed global scanning, even though still in progress, has already made available a number of deliverables that ease weather prediction with an admirable accuracy, all this leading to optimize the operations window and plan for a more resilient and adequate infrastructure. Who is to benefit from all this? Naturally, both primary and secondary stakeholders, by providing a vehicle to gain a competitive advantage, rather than a cost center subject to be hidden or ignored. A suitable combination of technology, virtual interaction, and face-to-face approaches contributed significantly in the pursuit of such goals that were unimaginable a couple of decades back.

Another example we may refer to is Guyana, a country that not only lies next to Amapá but also presents a comparable topography and demography in terms of people living in poverty and available resources. There, the weather was even more unpredictable, the rains being its major obstacle for planning and executing operations in gold mining by the border with Venezuela. VR and AR turned out to be instrumental in an efficient operations planning by considering not only a number of contingencies to better cope with the weather, but also to foresee the potential attitude loggers and farmers would adopt to prevent miners from controlling trucking, utilization of roads, and barge operators. Normally, the local pricing would be set exclusively by the loggers and farmers. Consequently, technology provided innovative social strategies as well as technical data to overcome the climate impact. It enabled endeavors to consider alternatives based in data and fact, and to build contingencies accordingly.

With over 15 years of data using this system for CPEs, we find that very strong relationships are built across the globe. The levels of trust at the beginning of endeavors has increased over 40% in the last ten years, and looks to be headed higher, faster. With English being the lingua franca globally, communications are easier today. The drive to keep linguistic diversity has also paid big dividends, especially in empathy and emotional intelligence development. Learning to read some Russian, Spanish, Arabic, and Chinese poetry can help to more quickly bond people. Having Xi show Angela how to read a poem, and them switch chairs, provides a rich and more intimate way to understand one another. But, perhaps the biggest change came in the inter-cultural marriages that exploded in 2030. Households that are quadrilingual became more common, and children who grew up speaking multiple languages are now prevalent in the workforce.

Mastering various languages and becoming, not just tolerant, but interested in knowing other cultures has become a successful strategy that both people and corporations could have ever adopted, in the pursuit of becoming more efficient and competitive. In 2017, Japan adopted an educational plan for their children named "brave change" or "futoji no henko." Its master goal was to transform their children into world citizens by focusing the education on business mathematics, reading, IT, governance, and culture. In culture they encompass languages, alphabets, and religions along with compulsory living abroad experiences for a while in family houses across the USA, China, the Arabic world, Latin America, etc. Today, they became experts in computers; they read 52 books a year; respect the law, the ecology, and others' opinions; and hold an enviable understanding on the way business is conducted worldwide.

It requires a lot of time to do what we all still need in human interaction. The technology continues to help us with making more time available. As the remaining parts of the world adopt a 30 hour work week, and a living wage, AI and AR will play an even more important and critical role. Technology offers more people a life that is rewarding, comfortable, and safe, which results in less fear and inequality. That, in turn, has fueled a willingness to listen to others, and that has pushed empathy to center stage. Conflict and disagreements are essential for a healthy CPE. The difference is in the way they are harmonized. Where it used to be guns, it is now a playful joke. This is akin to holding up a mirror without recrimination, but with respect and humor.

The CaR Sessions are simply intended to build a habit of frequent communications and sharing of knowledge in an atmosphere of trust, empathy, respect, and transparency.

Retrospective session

This has proven to be one of the most important sessions long-term. The lessons learned from the program are reviewed, internalized, captured in the World Bank database and in the individual organization's metrics and databases. The details are collected and analyzed by the Bots as the program proceeds, so there is not much to do in that regard. Lessons learned, assessment, revisions to the plans and map, changes, impacts, disputes, and contingency are all addressed in the CaR sessions immediately. In the law, justice delayed is justice denied. For global programs, the habit of dealing with challenges of any kind is a habit that must be practiced. Our heuristic is a simple one, in today out today.

It is always useful to review the retrospective summaries and the comparisons to other programs – mostly for the connections to the human issues, and leadership. AI is based on machine learning, and certainly the Bots put on an engaging self-assessment as part of this session. With recent enhancements, it presents more like standup comedy, and keeps the session healthy and humorous. The lessons have been already been learned, and the challenges defeated. Now is a time to put it all into the long-term context, and build the relationships.

CPE in 2100

As Marshall McLuhan said, we march backward into the future, we look at the future through our rearview mirror. Thus far we have looked into the history of programs, and how we have progressed, failed, learned, and grown. Now let us look into the future, where the milestones events are more predictable than the time frames in which they may occur.

The speed of change in technology is increasing, with perhaps the largest changes occurring in genetics and life expectance. With current trends it appears that we will have solved the issue of cellular degeneration. People will live hundreds of years without debilitating diseases and suffering. Drugs will be a thing of the past, pain eliminated, surgery no longer necessary, and we will look back on the 20th century as a dark age in medicine. No matter where one lives, no more disease and suffering. Super bugs are gone, as are pandemics that wreaked havoc in the early part of this century. We are able to reprint organs and limbs, and to reduce the subsequent healing time for injuries to a night's sleep. No more children and mothers dying in childbirth, and no more deformed children. No more suffering because of a person's income, race, or place of residence. No more hunger or lack of work.

People need to feed themselves, educate themselves, and feel productive, and to do this requires resources or an income. Through the middle of the century, economic inequity was still a problem for many. As the Global Unity grew into a solid and pervasive organization, its impact on income inequality was obvious, and the trend is toward almost total equity by the end of the century. As became apparent, many global issues, including the sharing of resources, were rooted in our evolutionary predispositions. People like Bill and Melinda Gates crafted a vision that all people should be productive, as a way of building dignity and respect for themselves. Income was the vehicle that translated this human need into tangible necessities.

The Global Unity grew out of the United Nations, with the idea of moving from tribalism to unification. Keep the cultural diversity, lose the nationalism. All 200 countries have signed up so far, and are in varying stages of adoption. Each citizen of the planet has a subcutaneous biogenic identification chip readable in all languages – machine and human. It contains all of a person's information, including medical and genetic data, and is impossible to hack. With it one can travel between any countries without permits, visas, or passports. It entitles each person to medical help, food, shelter, and employment, anywhere. It also entitles people to vote in the Global Entity elections directly by individual name. Parties ceased to be useful in 2045 as the technology had condemned the practice to the waste bin of history.

The Global Unity sees to the equality of all citizens. It matters not if you live in a megacity like Lagos (now at 50 million people), or in a rural area like Pala in Kerala India. Once the pursuit of money to take care of health, education, housing, food, clothing, and such was no longer necessary, people could devote themselves to becoming all they could be through their individual gifts and passions. Winning became less important than growing and fulfillment. The Global Unity saved Homo sapiens from extinction, by helping us all see the long term picture, and how closely our fates were actually intertwined – which, of course, made the Global Unity a no-brainer. Those of you who are older will remember the killing and destruction that still plagued our planet in the early part of the century. Remember the conundrum of Bashir Assad.

Everyone knew humans were suffering unlawfully, yet the global community was frozen in inaction. We needed the Global Unity to enforce decency and humanity across national boundaries.

One last touch point before we look at CPEs specifically – AR and Augmented Biology (AB). In 2045, the first humans were given bio implants that connected their brains directly to technology. Now we can see that by the end of the century, the AB along with genetic modification will enable us to accomplish unimaginable things, and to take, as some estimate, a 10,000-year leap in evolution. The Bots will still be around, but they will be doing the menial jobs that are unrewarding and possibly dangerous.

So, CPEs in 2100 will be different. First, the need for a CPE lead Executive will no longer be necessary. Organizations existed to collect expertise, and exploit it by outcompeting other organizations, with leaders to create a coherence. As with political parties, there will be no need for economic organizations. Expertise is available online globally on a pay for use basis – simply an extension of the "gig" economy. The cost of running an organization is simply wasteful. So, everyone has leadership skills, and will be connected via neural nets for seamless and instant communications.

As with the Global Unity, there is no need for setting up contracts and walls between organizations to imbue competition – unity will be the key. If there is a need for more copper, experts in extraction from around the globe may be consulted immediately – everyone is in the database. After a data analysis it shows that the deposits in Chile are most advantageous, so local expertise is enlisted individually. If the technology from Uganda is best for the situation, it will be sourced from there. Language and time zones are unimportant with the technology, scale does not matter, and there is no need for currency conversion. We use virtual currency, a technological version of the wampum beads used by the Iroquois a millennium ago.

In 2100, many will work on continuing development of Bots. They will conduct the manual work, and the data acquisition and analysis. With human biogenic evolution, the speed of development for Bots seems to be a constriction. In 2070, the Bot Hub in Kandahar is due to come online as the center of global knowledge. When it does, everyone will be able to link with the global database through their embedded biogenic implants. And then there is the global center for spiritual development in Australia at the Aboriginal Center for Learning near Alice Springs. Here the work on religion is changing everyone's life for the better. They helped us quit killing one another over beliefs in 2048.

Looking back to 2018, it is hard to believe we were stuck doing such silly things for so long. Undertaking global endeavors was not a problem of technology. It was a problem of fear, greed, selfishness, immaturity, poor communications, and nationalism. As we can see clearly now, no amount of process could help achieve success. It was then, and always will be, people. Remember when CRISPR began to be used on people in 2025? No one was prepared for the massive changes, and ethical issues, that it would provoke. Humankind finally took a global view of a global issue, and it proved to be a blessing in disguise. Just like our Awakening Sessions, the global community came together and saw that our similarities were stronger than our differences.

The medical community now projects that CRISPR gene editing will permit us to completely eliminate disease, and prolong our lives even further. The Japanese say *Pen Pen Kori*, or long sprightly life and a quick painless death. By 2100, the Global Unity expects to see 99.2% of the world's population living long, healthy, rewarding, peaceful, and happy lives. No more war, no more disease, no more birth defects, no more hunger, full employment, and the opportunity to be a productive engaged member of our global society.

The year 2100 will find us all immersed in carrying out operations both across the globe's ocean floor, the poles, further to colonizing and exploiting outer space resources. Remote-controlled outer space mining and manufacturing, along with experimental migratory contingents, are compared to those early colonizers of the Americas. The use of technology in any of its varied forms along with global undertakings characterized by international cooperation, and the disappearance of corruption-driven nationalistic or populist governments, will make crystal clear a conceptual contrast with the way programs tried to move forward during the 21st century.

Rich-resource countries around the globe used to manage their programs by having technology transferred and deployed in the field when owners deemed it necessary to move forward and make some progress. The process used to take too long and was mired in distrust, suspicions, greed, and too often a voracious fiscal appetite on the part of the host governments. Foreign Direct Investment growth used to be a critical target for most emerging and less developed economies whereas capital markets, technology, R&D capability, and trading channel dominance remained in the hands of a few developed economies. However, the most significant difference between the early decades of the 21st century and what looks to become the final stretch of it, is the way cross-cultural and operational management has been mutating towards a much more collaborative approach. All based on technological developments, and the free unfettered access to it.

Mining, infrastructure, and transportation as well as hydrocarbon projects in Africa, Latin America, or SE Asia experienced almost impossible obstacles that led to either substantial CAPEX increases if performed as planned. The other option at the time was simply to give up and turn the page. Cultural biases amongst global teams; superiority feelings of a few over too many; underestimation of what were phenomenal operational restrictions such as lack of infrastructure and complex socio-economic contexts; the conviction or false belief on the part of management that their technical expertise could overcome whatever obstacle they would come across; the almost blind reliance on expats deployed in the field to report genuinely to their headquarters on contracting practices and operational expenses. These things are rarely seen today and will most likely vanish by the turn of this century. A certain level of technology was available in the early part of the century, but Bots capable of operating in outer space, in the depth of the Arctic Ocean, or on the highest peaks along the Andes were not possible. Nor was a fully IT-driven CPE-based approach to global programs.

In the early 21st century, programs were based on capital funding access and technical expertise. Further advances in technology for things like terrain-applied capital goods made great changes to the way resources were sourced, and societies were supported. The technology advances were necessary, but the changes were more steps taken by the wealthy north, to focus their efforts on the resource-rich south, than a global effort based on knowledge sharing and transfer of best practices. It was also the magnitude of the effort towards exploring new geographical frontiers, either in space or on the ocean floors that made a significant number of countries unite, and dispose of their rivalries and hidden agendas. Other changes like expanding the New Agricultural Frontier across northern Brazil to feed billions of people, enlarging the operational window of the Great Canadian Prairie, and combining its productivity with today's fully operational North West Passage, feeding 100% of the world, shortening the sailing time between Asia and Europe by taking advantage of today's fully operational Northern Sea Route, building self-sustainable underwater cities in the South Atlantic and Indian Ocean to alleviate onshore demographic pressure, and of course colonizing Mars are just a few examples where the magnitude and importance of the endeavor was such that technology and global cooperation finally converged.

Shale gas deposits were regarded to be the upcoming energy jewel in 2020 by countries such as the USA, Canada, Mexico, and Argentina, to name a few. The conventional crude oil-producing countries, mostly around the Arabic world, used to keep their output at a level to prohibit the shale gas deposits to develop and flourish. All this changed with the appearance of global leadership to undertake world-class projects aimed at conquering new spaces and mastering the exploitation of resources. The battle looks childish now that fossil fuel is completely banned.

We are still a short-sighted species, but are evolving rapidly with the help of technology. By 2100, we envision programs will be prioritized globally on a ten-year time scale. Resources will be compared to the needs of the programs, and allocated by these priorities. With virtual currency residing with the World Bank, all 200 countries contribute to the improvement fund, and share these resources. The greatest global good determines the priorities for all global programs. Our grandchildren will no doubt learn from our mistakes, and design better ways to utilize precious resources, in more equitable and humane ways.

Chapter 23

Mindfulness

Achieving performance in an accelerating technology landscape

Anthony Phillips

The pace of life in the early twenty-first century is one of acceleration. Regardless of the industry, technological advances are coming at us faster than ever. Couple these changes with the ability to share information across the world with the swipe of a finger, and we can feel like the future is approaching more quickly than we can keep up. We hardly have time to digest the latest innovations before new ones are introduced. The moment of the Present, the right now, passes us by before we are even fully aware.

As project managers (PMs), we are accustomed to a rapid pace that rarely allows us to be in the Present. There is always a future milestone for which we are planning or a past event that we are assessing. Days, weeks, and months are spent creating project plans, identifying tasks, and assigning resources for upcoming work. Once the work is underway, an equal number of days, weeks, and months can be spent understanding what went well, what did not, and diagnosing why.

The day-to-day life of this profession, focusing on future needs while equally trying to understand and learn from the past, can be a restless one. However, due to the incredible progress of digital and web-based tools, we are starting to see a shift in the way work is done. The integration of Artificial Intelligence (AI) in our lives is coming and will most definitely have a strong impact on how project managers do their jobs or, really, what those jobs entail moving forward.

In this chapter, we will review what it means to be a project manager in this context. The profession is moving toward a heavier reliance on technology to do much of the Tetris (™) type of project management work. Given this momentum toward automation, how does the PM role evolve with the technology? What are the best skills sets and approaches, methodologies and best practices that will allow the profession to keep pace with advances in tools and systems?

This chapter proposes that we balance the massive technological push forward, the need to accelerate in order to just keep up, and the integration of AI into project management by incorporating mindfulness. There are already various forms of AI already in use; however, as it proliferates and becomes more commonplace, we have a unique opportunity to guide the profession.

Many Fortune 100, multibillion-dollar companies are already putting serious time and resources behind mindfulness training, and with good reason. Research has shown that a corporate culture based in this practice reaps significant benefits, including the bottom line. As the project management discipline integrates more with AI, a PM's true value will be in their ability to represent the human factor. The role will have to evolve because the tasks in which we spend our time now may soon be done by a machine. This evolution will be greatly helped through a methodology that has mindfulness at its core.

Our minute-to-minute moments are filled with never-ending streams, posts, Tweets, updates, notifications. These are constantly flowing into our brains, with rings and bells letting us know there is something new to look at. This creates an odd sense of time. There is always a new Now, a new piece of information. Just as we try to absorb that first bit of data, along comes another, erasing the previous one from our screens and from our minds, with the ease of a swipe. This is what I refer to as an age of immediacy.

In contrast, as quickly as a post becomes old news, the content of that post never goes away. A momentary expression of love or hate or outrage will forever be linked to the author—searchable across the entire internet for all to see.

In fact, there is so much information flooding our senses that much of it ends up becoming noise through which it is hard to filter. Relevant information gets diluted, distorted, distracted away. Our focus is pulled in almost all directions except the intended one. This is clearly not conducive to keeping a project team on track when every beep is a potential interruption from our work.

We must be careful to pay close attention amidst this bombardment of information. The emails are coming fast and furious at times and our reactions may be just as quick. This age of immediacy, in addition to bringing us incredible amounts of information at every instant, brings significant risk.

Immediate consequences can come from immediate actions. With the push of a button, millions of dollars can be moved, millions of private records can be exposed. The specter of these immediate consequences looms even larger in digital environments. A construction project manager helping build a highway faces consequences of their actions, but those consequences may not be live for the world to see with only the click of a mouse.

Pausing for a moment before taking another step sounds like it could really help.

Project Managers are always trying to squeeze more into a single day. As the first point of contact for anything project related, we must know what is going on in all aspects of our project at any given moment.

You have 5 hours' worth of meetings, including 2 pitches to new clients, a 1:1 with your supervisor, an internal review with the copywriters, and a mid-project budget review with a current client. The site update is going live at midnight, so you'll monitor the launch and have already coordinated the plan should anything go awry. A PM's job is never done.

We are also constantly jumping timeframes—from the future to the present to the past and back again. You are always planning ahead, reviewing past performance against the baseline, trying to execute an immediate deliverable so you can move onto the next one—all at the same time.

Consider how the Project Management Institute (PMI) views the role of the PM in its definition of Integration Management as "the practice of making certain that every part of the project is coordinated."[1] Yes, that is fairly straightforward—make certain every single part of a project is planned and executed.

While I do not disagree with that, I prefer to look at our role in a slightly different way. The American designer Charles Eames has a quote about life and work. In a way, it describes an approach akin to how I like to view project management:

> "Eventually everything connects—people, ideas, objects.
> The quality of the connections is the key to quality per se."

Every interaction is important to the overall whole. Every conversation with a colleague or client, every prototype created, even every thought we have can strengthen or weaken the connection. Each action will contribute to the final outcome. This approach is not that different from the PMI's stance, but it's coming from a more fluid place, less mechanical. It also assists in breaking down the project process into smaller bits so we can see each moment and individual action as important to the greater whole.

Sometimes (most of the time actually) my colleagues are going from fire drill to fire drill, only spending their energy and brain power on situations that are going terribly wrong—which is fine. Things do go wrong and must be addressed ASAP. However, there seems to be only minimal time spent on truly value-adding work. There is always another milestone coming up.

Looking to the Eames's quote for guidance, we can give our thought and attention to the goal of creating higher quality connections. Even though we may be talking about designing and building a marketing website for a startup company selling organic dog food, those connections are relevant. Some insight may be gleaned from a single conversation, contributing to a greater experience for the user than we ever imagined.

As a project manager, our function is to deliver concrete results in an ever-changing landscape. Budgets are reduced, resources leave, strategic directives from CEO's alter the entire scope of the project, but we still have to deliver. A discussion around Human Connections may be received less kindly if the project is considerably over budget.

We know that it will not be an easy path since work is messy by nature. Unpredictable and usually out of one's control, we go into our offices every day with the goal and hope of clearing it up, making headway on our project, and minimizing setbacks. We strive for those smooth days where schedule remains on track and scope is unchanged. While we know that is not a realistic expectation, we must ensure that the quality of our connections stays strong throughout all of these changes.

After managing digital projects for close to 20 years, I can safely say that navigating this terrain takes patience and perspective. Actually, I have learned to enjoy the constant change. To be able to bob and weave, and make mid-project adjustments is part of the rush of the discipline.

Yet as invigorating as that can be, there is a tendency to get lost in the details of the unpredictability. There are too many opportunities for a disconnect. Especially in the

---

1 The PMP Exam. 4th edition Andy Crowe, PMP

digital space, there are increasingly more aspects of work that pull apart those bonds. Technology allows us to work from anywhere with anyone at any time of day or night. Similarly, it enables us to work from anywhere and not come in contact with another single living soul for days on end. All these factors have an impact on making quality connections.

There are so many separate tools, across clients, partners, vendors, that all must fully integrate with parent systems. Physical distance from team members working remotely, different time zones, and language barriers can all contribute to a disconnection in your project. Your team may need to contend with these time/space barriers in addition to the standard differences in human beings. We must maintain the connections and the project health, while not letting our personal health decline severely.

I have spent countless nights lying awake in bed replaying the Past day—what went well, what did not, and what I was unable to get finished. At the same time, I am in the Future: The next day, month, the rest of the project—what milestones are coming up and what can I do to help move the work forward. Eventually my body takes over and I get some sleep. However, my eyes don't stay closed long as I awake before my alarm goes off, picking up the mental checklist right where I left it the night before. I can speak from experience that this is not only exhausting, but it's unhealthy. Anxiety levels spike thinking of the Future, and thoughts of what was missed run rampant dwelling in the Past. This cycle can lead to decreased productivity.

According to the Anxiety Disorders Association of America (ADAA) 2006 Stress & Anxiety Disorders Survey in 2006, this kind of stress and anxiety impacts performance, relationships with coworkers, and the quality of the work, not to mention its effects on home life and relationships.

- 72 percent of people who have daily stress and anxiety say it interferes with their lives at least moderately
- 40 percent experience persistent stress or excessive anxiety in their daily lives
- On the job: Employees say stress and anxiety most often impact their ...
  - Workplace performance (56 percent)
  - Relationship with coworkers and peers (51 percent)
  - Quality of work (50 percent)
  - Relationships with superiors (43 percent)

Add this stress to our growing, interwoven relationship with computer systems and you can see how the human factor needs additional support. Project Management is no exception to the never-ending waves of innovation, and we are currently learning how to surf with Artificial Intelligence. For the time being, the end user is (most likely) going to be a human, so we must keep that link.

Perhaps by slowing down and changing the patterns of their own behavior, a project manager can raise the level of performance in their project for all team members. In the current landscape of increasing automation, the true value of a project manager will be in bringing a human perspective to a project. This is where incorporating mindfulness practices into your project planning and delivery will assist—keeping the human element.

AI is already being used by retailers such as Amazon and Netflix to market their products specifically to you. Google utilizes AI in its email filters, maps, and translator, at the very least. Consider an imminent future with caravans of driverless semi-trucks cruising coast to coast 24 hours a day and retail stores with absolutely zero onsite human employees. AI is a multi-layered technology with the potential to fundamentally alter our lives, both for the positive and the negative.

While we don't know exactly what an AI future will look like, it's also not a complete unknown as its proliferation into our products and patterns is already happening. Each of us will decide to some extent how much AI enters our personal lives. For example, I was generously gifted an Alexa (™) but was not ready for that level of interaction with my machines. In our work lives, however, employers could deliberately choose to incorporate AI enabled systems, processes, and interfaces. We will have to build a comfort level to some extent.

This is not an in–depth dive into the various forms that AI can take, so for the purpose of this discussion, let's define how AI is being used. It is a fairly general term at this point for a machine/program that learns and continually gains its own intelligence. It doesn't need to be constantly programmed for new tasks, it initiates them, taking clues from previous situations, interactions with other systems, and the surrounding environment.

AI not only automates tasks, it can also notice trends over millions of data points, offer recommendations for efficiencies, and make decisions on how best to proceed with an issue. It can imitate human behaviors and thinking patterns and translate them into several life-like actions such as speech, motion, action. However, AI is not some single set of behaviors or finite state. It's constantly moving.

So how is Artificial Intelligence going to affect the project management role? We will be working differently in the near future, but what can we expect?

There are numerous tasks that I know from experience would be better suited for a machine. That suggestion may invoke fears of robots taking over all jobs, but we must learn to work *with* the machines, otherwise we'll be working *for* the machines. Part joke, part warning I suppose.

Working with AI would allow one to use the strengths of human understanding and collaboration to enhance the quality of connections that Eames speaks of. Although we are in highly automated times, an individual human is still the single greatest asset to the project, as well as its largest danger and liability. We will all have to learn what tasks are appropriate for a human vs. robot.

Technology writer Mary Branscombe wrote on CIO.com about how AI may first start altering the world of the PM.

> Estimation, resource management and KPIs are just a few of the key areas where machine learning and predictive analytics can have a positive impact on project outcomes. AI could identify slowly ramping trends in that stream of data that are significant but hard to see — or easy for humans to ignore even if they see them.[2]

---

2 CIO | JAN 12, 2018 3:00 AM PT https://www.cio.com/article/3245773/project-management/how-ai-could-revolutionize-project-management.html

In the same article, Lance Olsen, director in Microsoft's Cloud AI team, echoes the same sentiments, "'Reducing monotonous and time-consuming tasks that aren't necessarily high value but show up in every project' doesn't just free up time, Olsen points out; it also reduces errors."[3]

He goes on to point out that

> AI will be most helpful by removing risk in projects, 'whether that's prediction for the project up front or removing risk in the execution.' That's going to make projects more efficient: 'There's so much uncertainty and how we deal with it now is that we create giant buffers,' he says.[4]

What are some of the specific tasks that an AI-PM could take on? When first thinking about this topic, a quick list comes to mind. As a Resource and Demand Manager, I spent a significant part of my days doing these very activities. It's with excitement and fear that I think that a machine could be doing all of this soon:

- Resource alignment across availability, need, and skillset
- Utilization monitoring and notification of trends
- Time tracking accuracy comparing Actuals against Forecasted
- Balancing team demand and team capacity
- Create estimates based on type of work and historical performance
- Keep all relevant stakeholders informed of various metrics

In a blog post, Rachel Burger provides a list that is not completely Project Management-centric but brought up a few additional important items applicable to PMs: Knowledge Management, Safety, and Fatigue.

Match the right resource to the right role. Piggybacking off the success of applicant tracking systems, HR managers are investing in more technology to further improve their hiring processes. Ideal, an AI-based recruitment software company, finds that "Companies that have adopted AI for recruiting software have seen their performance increase by 20%, their revenue per employee improve by 4%, and their turnover decrease by 35%." Now, imagine if that kind of accuracy could be used for *project* team selection.

Automatically reduce individual idle time. No need to worry about level of effort (LOE); project management AI can learn the cadence of each team member's output and assign regular work based on that individual's ability to comply. Tools that can do this are covered later in this article.

Create an ecosystem for knowledge management. When an employee leaves a company, she takes a discrete amount of nontransferable understanding of her role. Use your project management AI to aggregate patterns of workplace behavior and to centralize worker knowledge to improve consistency, quality, and to prevent "reinventing the wheel" when change arises. While this function is largely still theoretical, it will likely become available and affordable to enterprise-level businesses in the next year or two, and popularize quickly after that.

---

3 Ibid
4 Ibid

Foster a safe environment. For companies that have varying working conditions, artificial intelligence can detect invisible-to-the-human-eye warning signs that influence the likelihood of a workplace accident. For example, a construction project management AI could observe equipment performance, air quality, and employee facial expressions to predict unsafe behavior or an unsafe work environment, and alert the proper parties to prevent an accident.

Deliver untiring objectivity and vigilance. While humans can grow fatigued when checking their deliverable for accuracy and quality, an AI system doesn't tire, nor does it make compromises or excuses because it's burned out on the project.[5]

Nadya Duke Boone is the director of product management for platform at New Relic—a performance monitoring and management company that offers a digital intelligence platform that "lets developers, ops, and tech teams measure and monitor the performance of their applications and infrastructure."[6] She makes a distinction in the type of work that suits a machine vs. a human:

> A large part of AI in any industry right now is removing the work that's tedious and letting the humans focus on the part machines don't do well. So much work in project management is not number crunching; it's about do we have clear goals, is everyone moving in the same direction and is their work coordinated.[7]

One of today's top business leaders, Elon Musk, is a massive proponent of robotic industrialization, aiming for a fully automated production process. Even he has openly wrestled with this topic, promoting it while simultaneously warning against it. In a statement from 2017 to the National Governors Association, Musk states, "On the artificial intelligence front, I have access to the very most cutting edge AI, and I think people should be really concerned about it."[8]

He goes on to say, "AI is a fundamental existential risk for human civilization, and I don't think people fully appreciate that." In that same speech, he acknowledged that "there certainly will be job disruption. Because what's going to happen is robots will be able to do everything better than us. … I mean all of us."[9]

Yet, when Tesla production in his state-of-the-art robot-driven factory failed to meet the goal of 5,000 cars per week, Musk tweeted: "Yes, excessive automation at Tesla was a mistake. To be precise, my mistake. Humans are underrated." 12:54 PM—13 Apr 2018[10]

This is clearly a complicated issue that will continue to be debated while the inevitable integration with our lives moves forward. Almost every part of our lives will involve some sort of AI-like functionality, but it is not without its dangers. We will all adapt in some way—some will deeply embrace the technology while others may reject or barely dip their toe in to test the waters.

---

5 https://blog.capterra.com/i-project-manager-the-rise-of-artificial-intelligence-in-the-workplace
6 https://newrelic.com/
7 https://www.cio.com/article/3245773/project-management/how-ai-could-revolutionize-project-manag
   ement.html
8 http://fortune.com/2017/07/15/elon-musk-artificial-intelligence-2/
9 https://www.cnbc.com/2017/07/17/elon-musk-robots-will-be-able-to-do-everything-better-than-us.html
10 https://twitter.com/elonmusk/status/984882630947753984

Let's allow all of this to frame our general idea of the near-term future involving Artificial Intelligence. Based on this understanding, what comfort level should the Project Management discipline establish—is it a full, deep embrace or a tentative courting? In order to answer this, it's important to ground ourselves in the definition of Project Management. Not a technical dictionary definition of the word but more of its essence. At its core, what is the role about? Once we frame the job, we can better place it in the right space within the AI context.

Whether one sees it this way or not, project management is about awareness. We spend a huge percentage of our time creating the right formats to disseminate information and then review them at various intervals. We have daily stand-ups, weekly client calls, monthly capacity reviews, and quarterly forecast updates. Much of our responsibility is to report out on progress and ensure the project as a whole stays on track.

There is always much more going on than you realize in any given situation. The hope is to open our focus to see the greater whole while filtering out any irrelevant noise. But first, the desire to open must be cultivated.

A good project manager can anticipate potential risks and identify opportunities on which to capitalize. They are viewing the project in a way to increase their self-awareness of these factors. I hesitate to use a sports analogy, but it's incredibly appropriate. The PM is the Point Guard of the team. The ability to see the full court and have the vision for how the play will unfold. You're four steps ahead—hopefully. This vision, almost a constant wide-eyed scanning of the field of play, makes project managers a natural vehicle for deeper-level awareness.

> Awareness is always the first step
> because if you are not aware,
> there is nothing you can **change**.[11]

This quote is from Don Miguel Ruiz's self-help book called *The Four Agreements* (1997). It is purportedly based on Toltec wisdom and could fall into the category of New Age Philosophy. The goal is to assist in self-transformation. Through a few simple guidelines, the philosophy allows you to free yourself to be yourself. Although this may seem a great leap away from the tactical framework of Project Management, I find that it actually captures the same essence with its emphasis on awareness.

Another way of putting this can be found in the eloquent and wise words of Thich Nhat Hanh, a Vietnamese Buddhist Monk who has written over 100 books on the subject of mindfulness in our daily lives. His approach is based on various forms of Buddhism. There is an elegant simplicity and a caring spirit in his words.

> Awareness is like the sun.
> When it shines on things, they are **transformed**.[12]

---

11 The Four Agreements, Don Miguel Ruiz. Amber-Allen Publishing, Inc. 1997
12 http://www.mysticalearthadventures.com/thich-nhat-hanh-quotes.html

The two quotes above are very closely aligned in their messages and also in their grand perspective. Awareness brings growth, brings life, brings change. Without making too big of a stretch, these two statements make a direct link in my mind to another particular saying. This is one that you may have heard numerous times as a project manager:

That which is measured, **improves**.

I have found the above words attributed to more than one person. The most commonly cited are either Karl Pearson, a mathematical statistician, or Peter Drucker, a business and management consultant.

Whether placed in the context of scientific experimentation and observation, or in the light of business management, this quote makes a lot of sense and is beautiful in its simplicity, almost poetic. It almost has the feeling of a haiku poem, capturing an entire manner of behavior in five words. The phrase reinforces a rational train of thought in which one must understand the goal and the factors that affect the path. Without measurement, one is unable to track performance.

All of these quotes are saying the exact same thing: Pay the !@$#% attention, and good things will happen. Change, transformation, improvement—the road to delivering innovative results is paved with awareness.

We've touched on how much access to receive and transmit information there is right now. The speed at which these transmissions are made is staggering. So are we necessarily gaining any awareness by getting more information at a faster rate? No. The increasing advances in AI technology will not slow this down. I expect the acceleration to continue, the cacophony of data to grow. Consider that the data only builds.

Remember the interesting paradox in the non-stop flow of information and the of-the-moment post is that none of the data actually goes away. It may be gone from our immediate consciousness, yet, as it slides off the bottom of your phone screen, it is stored forever. Just ask any number of politicians, athletes, or entertainers that have stuck their virtual foot in their digital mouth recently. The content can check out, but it can never really leave.

Every click and mouse movement is logged so you really cannot hide from any online actions. Insert into this equation machines that can think and act on their own and this becomes a highly volatile place to work and play. It is exactly this volatility that makes the environment primed for mindfulness.

Just as we defined our term of AI, the same will be done for mindfulness. Here is a good general, yet clinical explanation:

Mindfulness has its roots in Eastern spiritual, especially Buddhist traditions. It has been defined as a state of being in which individuals bring their "attention to the experiences occurring in the present moment, in a nonjudgemental or accepting way."
(See also Brown & Ryan, 2003)

Mindfulness has several key characteristics (Brown, Ryan, & Creswell, 2007): First, mindfulness involves a receptive awareness and registration of inner experiences (emotions, thoughts, behavioral intentions) and external events. Second, mindful information processing is pre-conceptual. In a mindful state, individuals are purely noticing what is happening without evaluating, analyzing, or reflecting upon it. Third, mindfulness is characterized by a present-oriented consciousness in which individuals focus on moment-to-moment experiences rather than thinking about the past or fantasizing about the future. Fourth, mindfulness is an inherent human capacity that varies in strength, both across situations and persons.[13]

Mindfulness has been a buzz word as of late. There is a lot of attention and promotion of how to incorporate it into our daily lives somehow. Books, seminars, apps, there is no shortage of tools at our disposal. I want to explore how this applies to Project Management, especially in a time where our integration with and reliance on technology is growing almost faster than we can keep apace.

When you take the time to stop, assess, bring your attention to a single task, filter out the noise, what happens? As project managers, we are masters of the multitask. With so much to do, we try to get many of our tasks done concurrently. Does it work?

There have been a number of studies multitasking, such as this one from Stanford researcher Clifford Nass in 2009:

Nass challenged 262 college students to complete experiments that involved switching among tasks, filtering irrelevant information, and using working memory. Nass and his colleagues expected that frequent multitaskers would outperform nonmultitaskers on at least some of these activities.

They found the opposite: Chronic multitaskers were abysmal at all three tasks. The scariest part: Only one of the experiments actually involved multitasking, signaling to Nass that even when they focus on a single activity, frequent multitaskers use their brains less effectively.[14]

Perhaps by trying to multitask less, trying to get fewer things done at a single time, you actually get more accomplished.

Inserting mindfulness into the corporate world is not an entirely new concept, but has some incredibly strong momentum right now. In fact, some of the largest companies in the world are putting significant time and money towards establishing a culture centered on mindfulness. These are massive Fortune 50 (Yes, 50, not 500) organizations that impact our lives every single day. We will explore a few companies that you may have heard of that are using a formal mindfulness protocol right now to improve team performance, individual health, and happiness.

Google impacts most of our lives every day—search, email, phones. Their technology has become woven into the fabric of our modern lives, much as General Electric had previously.

13 https://pdfs.semanticscholar.org/05c1/4273f0d3d4acdac20ee49c76ba3aa3afe7a5.pdf
14 http://business.time.com/2013/04/17/dont-multitask-your-brain-will-thank-you/

More than just the proliferation of their products, their focus and reach have extended beyond.

In 2007, a Senior Engineer at Google named Chade-Meng Tan—who was Google Employee Number 107—started a program within the company called Search Inside Yourself. The goal was to help employees approach their work with greater focus and perspective. It was so successful that it spun off into an independent nonprofit venture working to help individuals, companies, and organizations cultivate mindfulness. The name of this public program is called Unlock Your Full Potential.

Clearly Chade-Meng Tan, and the leadership within Google that supported this program internally, feel there is real, measurable benefits to a Mindful Life. It goes over steps to achieving mindfulness, to creating moments of clarity and awareness that are the equivalent of looking up from your screen, but mentally.

In a *Harvard Business Review* article from December 30, 2015, written by Chade-Meng Tan, he states the following:

> These skills did not take long to learn. In every example above, the benefits were realized with fewer than 50 hours of training. But getting the training's earliest benefits doesn't even require 50 hours.
>
> My colleague Karen May, vice president at Google, developed the ability to mentally recharge by taking one 'mindful breath' before walking into every meeting. It takes her roughly six seconds, and in that time she brings her full attention to one breath, resetting her body and mind.[15]

Similarly, UnitedHealth Group, which is the parent company of UnitedHealth Care and Optum, and Number 6 on the Fortune 500 with 2017 revenues over $200 billion, has instituted a Culture Training rooted in mindfulness. This is a company whose work touches over 115 million people.

One of the main tenets of the training is to Be Here Now. You may have heard that phrase before, but in a different context. The spiritual teacher named Ram Dass published a book of the same name in 1971 centering on the topics of yoga, meditation, and mindfulness.

Spirituality might not be one to expect from the sixth largest company in the world. But this is a training that all employees over a specific pay and responsibility grade *must* attend. The company spends tens of thousands of dollars per year in travel, lodging, food, and lost productivity in doing this culture training. However, there is clearly enough evidence in the benefits to continue this. They are actively creating a culture centered on mindfulness for the good of their employees as well as all those they serve.

Another healthcare giant in Aetna has also instituted a mindfulness-based program led by Mark T. Bertolini, Chairman and Chief Executive Officer of Aetna. Bertolini has had a personal interest in yoga and the practice of mindfulness. When he found the incredible benefits for his body and mind after a 2004 ski accident, he began to promote the incorporation of mindful practice into his company's various health and wellness

---

15 https://hbr.org/2015/12/just-6-seconds-of-mindfulness-can-make-you-more-effective

plans. In an essay titled 'The Journey of Personal and Organizational Wellness' from the company's website, Bertolini explains his views on mindfulness and personal wellness:

> Personal wellness is a journey, one that can last a lifetime. My journey has led to a yoga routine where I perform asana, pranayama, meditation, and Vedic chanting before work. A skiing accident in 2004 resulted in a spinal cord injury and constant pain from neuropathy. This daily practice helps alleviate my discomfort without the use of medication. It also helps me to be more centered and fully present in the moment.
>
> My personal wellness journey has also influenced Aetna's organizational wellness. Based on my personal experience, I fully supported the development of yoga and mindfulness-based programs at Aetna. I know that some of my colleagues were rolling their eyes when they heard about it. Just because our CEO practices mindfulness and does yoga, does that mean that we have to learn? Can this really help?
>
> The results since launching these programs in 2011 show that they do actually help. Employees participating in our initial mind-body stress reduction pilot programs (mindfulness and Viniyoga) showed significant improvements in perceived stress with *36 and 33 percent decreases in stress levels respectively.*
>
> Helping employees build resilience and reduce stress isn't just the right thing to do—it can also help the bottom line. The International Labour Organization estimated that 30 percent of all work-related illness is due to stress, accounting for $6.6 billion of losses in the U.S. alone. Our research supported these facts, as the participants reporting the highest stress level in Aetna's pilot programs had medical costs nearly $2,000 higher for the preceding year than those reporting the lowest stress levels.
>
> In addition to improving health, these programs can improve employee productivity and decision-making. With the success of the pilot, the program was expanded to all Aetna employees. More than 13,000 employees have participated in one of these programs over the past three years. Participants are regaining 62 minutes per week of productivity with an approximate dollar return, in terms of productivity alone, of more than $3,000.[16]

Even though we are now more accustomed to yoga and meditation in the Western world, this is still progressive to hear from the CEO of a $60 billion American company.

Another study from researchers at Case Western Reserve University in March 2016 back up Bertolini's own experiences.

> A new comprehensive analysis of mindfulness research, co-directed by a management scientist at Case Western Reserve University, suggests...that injecting a corporate culture of mindfulness not only improves focus, but the ability to manage stress and how employees work together.
>
> Christopher Lyddy, an organizational behavior doctoral candidate at Case Western Reserve's Weatherhead School of Management, said:

16 https://news.aetna.com/2014/09/journey-personal-organizational-wellness/

"When you are mindful, you can have a greater consciousness in the present," Lyddy said. "That's vital for any executive or manager, who, at any given moment, may be barraged with various problems that call for decisions under stress."

The researchers considered 4,000 scientific papers on various aspects of mindfulness, distilling the information into an accessible guide documenting the impact mindfulness has on how people think, feel, act, relate and perform at work.

- Mindfulness appears to positively impact human functioning overall. Research in such disciplines as psychology, neuroscience, and medicine provide a wealth of evidence that mindfulness improves attention, cognition, emotions, behavior, and physiology.
- Mindfulness has been shown to improve three qualities of attention—stability, control, and efficiency. Mindfulness can stabilize attention in the present. Individuals who completed mindfulness training were shown to remain vigilant longer on both visual and listening tasks.
- Mindfulness affects interpersonal behavior and workgroup relationships.
- Mindfulness may improve relationships through greater empathy and compassion.

Lyddy said the research indicating significant and diverse benefits of mindfulness coincides with growing practical interest in mindfulness training nationally and worldwide. For example, British Parliament has recently launched a mindfulness initiative called "Mindful Nation UK" that leverages mindfulness to benefit diverse sectors and improve national health, productivity, and flourishing.[17]

If the potential benefits are increased productivity, increased enjoyment, and increased health, it is understandable why some of the top companies in the world are using mindfulness to drive their corporate culture—infuse it with awareness.

Looking at this situation from a certain perspective, Artificial Intelligence and Mindfulness are both progressing at a rapid rate. AI moving to enhance (maybe supplant?) human thought, intelligence, and action with that mimicked by machines. The Mindfulness Movement is striving to create and maintain connections within yourself and with others in every action we take. It could almost seem like they're moving in complete opposite directions. However, it doesn't have to be so divergent.

In project management, we do try to bring awareness and attention to items with daily standups, weekly progress reports, project trackers, and the like. However, it's not enough to be grinding away on dashboards, as this is not where the quality connections will occur. There is a place still for the heads down cranking out of documents, but that is not the singular approach. We must consider ways to incorporate mindfulness and present-moment being into our days.

You will have to consciously practice it. Just as one builds their knowledge and skills over time, this is another skill that must be cultivated in order to achieve full benefits. It's going to be up to you, as the business is not paying for you to achieve inner balance. Unless you work for Google, or UHG, or Aetna.

17 https://www.sciencedaily.com/releases/2016/03/160310141455.htm

It's Urgent and Important. If the research continues to reflect, this will actually help you deliver more value. The quality of your connections will be higher and you will be happier making those connections.

While I am not saying to incorporate this as yet another item on a To-Do List, I do think that a number of tools that we already use as project managers will aid in the practice of mindfulness. Use Outlook (^{TM}) to schedule your mindfulness. You can block ten minutes. The productivity and time management tools that are available these days are many, so pick one that works for you and put a reminder in your app to Breathe.

Put in basic Project Management terms: We need to plan for it. If it's not on the list, it won't get done.

By first understanding that there is a different way to "see" the situation, to observe your own behavior, and make a consistent effort to have that larger scale awareness, one can cultivate a mindful approach. When the pace gets hectic, when you're feeling the tasks pile up and the deadlines rapidly approaching, that is the right time to take a breath. Don't send that email you just typed reactively at break-neck speed. If we can learn to insert a Pause before Action, we greatly increase our chances of avoiding a serious mistake.

Athletes talk about being in The Zone. That special state of body and mind where you rise above the Earth-bound constraints, the muck, and can truly float above—seeing not just the forest for the trees, but seeing them as part of a full landscape of the world. Take a break in the beat and pause the rhythm so you can soak in the song. How great would it be for your first reaction to be …. nothing. A computer does not get tired, it does not need to pause—which plays to a human advantage.

Make sure you fully understand what has happened, assessing different options, thinking of the present first and paying attention to what has happened. Taking no direct action right away, so when you do, you are Acting and not Reacting.

Given the radical workplace changes underway, the way in which we learn has to grow and adapt as well in order to succeed in the workplace of the future. My elementary school-aged children are educated with a different emphasis than they used to be, and certainly than how I was educated. It is much less focused on *what* to do learn—X event happened on X date—and concentrated on teaching *how* to learn. There is a conscious intention to use Project Based Learning methods, emphasizing a multidisciplinary approach, centralized on collaboration with others to achieve the specified goals. This sounds like a future generation of project management professionals.

So are you now going to breathe through every challenging time on every project? Will you stop going to bed reviewing your To Do list in your mind? Probably not. But perhaps you can approach each challenge with a different perspective.

We have a huge opportunity right now to truly add the very best of the Human Factor. If you want to be an agent of change and provide the most value in our role as it shifts in the machine/human balance, you have the incredible gift of being flesh and blood. Put Mindful Focus as a method to approach our tasks and we can learn to ride the overload of acceleration, immediacy, and information. The quality of our individual connections will improve, and therefore, the quality of our results.

Chapter 24

Continuous Digital and #NoProjects

Allan Kelly

Today growth businesses are digital businesses. Microsoft, Adobe and Oracle were the prototypes. Amazon, Salesforce, Google and Facebook showed the way but today it is not just Uber, Monzo, Just Eat, Lime or Airbnb who depend on digital technology for growth. It is Walmart, Rentokil, John Deere, Domino's Pizza and more. Only today I talked with an office moves company which is reinventing itself as a digital business.

Digital businesses differ from traditional business because their success depends on creating new technology and exploiting that technology. The business is technology and the technology is the business. Many but not all digital businesses create software, but all digital businesses are dependent on software.

Traditional businesses used technology – specifically computers and software – to supplement their central functions to reduce costs, accelerate transactions, improve efficiency and manage at scale. Banks and airlines existed before computers and could exist again without the internet. Digital technologies have changed the way these companies operate but the essential business model is the same.

Without copious cheap CPU power, Uber would be little more than a San Francisco taxi company. Ubiquitous CPU power, in our smartphones, in internet routers, in massive server farms and in cars, makes it possible for one taxi company to operate worldwide.

For such companies, creating new technology, new systems and applications is not an occasional special event. Writing and enhancing software is business as usual. Enhancing software systems is in the lifeblood of digital-first companies.

The project model is a model for managing temporary work. Look at the Project Management Institute (PMI) or Association of Project Management (APM) definitions. Projects are created to deliver a defined thing, they start and they stop.

Projects make sense when they deliver a complete thing. Decades of experience shows that successful software is never done. Software which is used demands change, the software itself lives as users ask new things of it and as the world around it changes.

Faced with this inconvenient truth, organisations the world over fudged. As one project closes and is declared a success another one starts. Often the same people work in the same team, on the same software product for decades, each project begets another project.

Despite driving a coach and horses through the fundamentals of the project model, this approach kind of works. It isn't perfect – and I'll go in the reasons for that in a moment – but it kind of works. As long as each project maintained the illusion that there was an "end" it kind of worked.

While this works it isn't optimal. The world has moved on. Agile is the obvious change but the proliferation in cheap CPU cycles is a more significant change.

It is not 1970 any more

The IBM 360/195 launched in 1970 offering 10MIPs of CPU with 4Mb of RAM. Programs were typically written in COBOL using the hierarchal IMS database and communicated with users via green screens or teletypes. Most customers rented these machines for $250,000 per month. That is about $1.6m per month in 2018 prices.

1970 was the year Winston Royce published "Managing the development of large software systems," which is generally regarded as the first description of Waterfall software development. This came the year after the founding of the Project Management Institute.

In 1970, CPU cycles and memory were very expensive. Consequently it made sense to do lots of up-front planning. Machine time was expensive so it made sense to do lots of analysis, planning and desk-checks before going anywhere near a machine.

Compare that with the Raspberry Pi 3B for sale on Amazon.com at $39 in July 2018. This offers between 3,000 and 6,500 MIPS and 1 GB of RAM. The Pi runs an Open Source Linux operating system (nobody wrote open source in 1970) and can be programmed in Scala, Ruby, Python or many other advanced languages. Figure 24.1

In 2018, CPU cycles are infinitesimally cheap, ubiquitous and omnipresent. Why would one expect processes from 50 years ago to be the optimal way of working?

Technology adoption follows a predictable pattern. First new technologies are used to speed up existing processes. It takes time for the limitations imposed by the previous technology to be replaced by new processes which make the most of new technology.

Think of the way electricity changed the operations of factories. Or the way containerisation first changed the shipping industry and then world trade.

Figure 24.1 Raspberry Pi 3B+ computer.

Today's digital technologies have a passing resemblance to yesterdays but they are an order of magnitude more powerful at a fraction of the cost. Management thinking needs to change to leverage such technology changes.

The Agile menace

The rise of Agile software development created additional problems for the project model because Agile dropped the pretence that the final state could be known. While traditional projects considered "scope," sacred Agile played fast and loose with the "what are we building" question.

Traditional project managers were trained to vary everything except scope. The project mission was to deliver the defined thing. Traditional project managers looked at their iron triangle and varied the schedule. In doing so they varied the cost. Changing the resources employed would also vary the cost and occasionally they tried to dial quality down. Figure 24.2

Agile came along and changed the game. An Agile team regards date and resources as fixed in the short term and varied the scope while keeping quality as high as possible.

Still the project model responded and somehow these fudges were incorporated too.

In openly flexing the scope, Agile made a massive theoretical change to the project model but a trivial implementation change. In truth, every project flexed – and cut – scope once there was no more money, time or people available. Once a deadline was immutable scope was cut. All Agile really did was bring the moment of flex to the front rather than the end of the project.

It is hardly surprising that Agile approaches can be married with traditional project approaches because if you look at the underlying values and principles the two aren't far apart. Both aim to deliver valuable working products.

Just because traditional project management and Agile can be married doesn't mean they should. The question to be asked is: "What is the benefit of using both?"

Arguably, marrying traditional project management with Agile brings the costs of both and the benefits of neither. The required compromises, and the odd conflict. If Agile is great why not embrace it entirely? If project management is great why not embrace it entirely?

As Agile has become more and more prevalent more and more people have noticed the problems. But it is the rise of digital-first businesses that are forging a new, project-less, model.

Figure 24.2 Classic project manager's iron triangle.

Before I describe my own Continuous Digital model, let me discuss some of the problems with the project model.

The problem with projects

The term "project" is somewhat elastic and means different things to different people, typically people in different roles. These different definitions cause problems as programmers and managers talk at cross purposes. It also makes it important to be clear what I mean when I say "project" and "the project model." I take my definition directly from the American PMI and British APM:

"What is a project? It's a temporary endeavor undertaken to create a unique product, service or result." Project Management Institute, https://www.pmi.org, April 2018

"A project is a unique, transient endeavour, undertaken to achieve planned objectives, which could be defined in terms of outputs, outcomes or benefits." Association of Project Managers, https://www.apm.org.uk, April 2018

The defining feature of the project model is that the work is transient. It has a start date and an end date. Indeed, the project ideal is that both start and end can be determined in advance and honoured. It is this temporary nature of projects which create a number of problems.

The fundamental assumption that the project will end is in conflict with the nature of business. Most businesses strive to continue. With only a few exceptions, businesses cease to exist, which is not considered good. The English language has many words to describe businesses which cease to exist: insolvent, liquidation, receivership and bankruptcy to name a few. It has few words to describe the closure of a business in a positive sense. In fact, I struggle to think of one.

Projects plan to close and end. Businesses plan to continue. If you walk into your local supermarket and find the shelves empty, something is probably wrong. The supermarket manager is unlikely to welcome you saying "Good news! We are done, we sold everything!"

Maybe it made sense to close a project when the project was an optional extra to the business. But when the business is inherently based on technology then does it ever make sense to end? Stopping digital advances suggest stopping business change and growth.

When a digital business wants to expand it most likely requires software changes. Indeed, every change requires a technology change. Changing technology is a permanent state of affairs.

End dates create goal displacement

Imposing an end date and tying success to that end date induces a number of damaging behaviours.

Managers expend copious amounts of time and energy arguing over which work requests will fit in the time available. Work becomes based on estimates which are notoriously unreliable. Obstacles are erected to prevent further requests. But little or no attention is paid to the value of the work being requested.

The project model induces goal displacement. "Success" is measured against scope, time and costs so these measures become the goal rather than the creation of business benefit and value.

For a digital business delivering on schedule, to budget and scope is failure. They need to do better.

Quality

In the process, quality suffers. By quality, I mean internal structural quality and the defect count. (Programmers frequently describe this as "technical debt," which while capturing the emotions is a somewhat confused metaphor.)

Many managers believe that quality can be traded against time and cost. In their minds, *higher quality costs more time and money, reducing quality reduces both time and cost.* Experience and research shows this trade-off is the reverse.

Software engineering is not the only discipline which exhibits this trait. In fact, industry after industry seems destined to learn the same lesson. Philip Crosby saw this in the rocket industry in the 1950s and 60s and went on to write the best seller *Quality is Free* (1980). The silicon chip manufacturing industry learnt that higher quality is cheaper from Richard W. Anderson in 1980 (*The Chip*, T.R. Reid, 1984). The car industry learnt it from Toyota in the 1990s (*The machine that changed the world*, Womack, Jones & Roos, 1991). Every generation of managers seem to need to learn the same message for themselves.

Keeping software quality high keeps software *soft*. Thus work proceeds faster and in a more predictable fashion. There are fewer external costs – customer calls to the support line or lost monies from errors. Less management time is spent agonising over fixes or apologising to customers.

Reducing software quality quickly results in code which is difficult to work with and a breeding ground for bugs. Perhaps more importantly, the common management request to programmers "don't make it perfect, we only need good enough" saps motivation and commitment from front line staff.

Such exhortations directed at programmers leads to programmers who care less and less about the product under development. It leads to programmers who are unwilling to "go the extra mile" or help in a crisis.

There is no such thing as a "quick and dirty fix" only "slow and dirty." Even if the reduced quality does not immediately slow work – which is itself quite likely – the cost will be felt soon.

Trading quality for rapid results is less like taking a mortgage and more like a payday loan. Eye-watering interest rates mean only desperate, or ignorant, borrowers ever consider such loans.

This is not to argue for "gold plating" or the creating of unnecessary functionality. There can be a fine line diving gold plating from good quality and it requires experience to know the difference.

Nor is it only programmers who "gold plate" work. Formal requirements documents are little more than an adult version of a child's Christmas. Indeed, the whole requirements processes seem designed to encourage unnecessary requests. The day before a requirements document is agreed, the barrier for adding additional requests is low. The day after, the barriers are high. The phase "change request board" induces fear and loathing. Thus there is an incentive to ask for more than is needed just in case something is needed later.

There is no penalty for asking for something which is later cancelled but there is a significant penalty for not asking for something which is later wanted. Added to the real requests are requests cut from previous projects, not to mention bargaining chips to be used later as leverage.

Knowledge loss

Inevitably the closer the nominal end date gets the greater the management time and energy expended arguing over features. Once a project is closed, getting any work done to a software product can require a new project, which itself is uncertain. The longer the gap between the last project closing and a new one commencing, the greater the knowledge lost.

Closure of a project leads to the dissolution of the temporary organisation, the team, which delivered the project. People leave the company or are redeployed. Yet every time a team dissolves knowledge is lost; more is lost every day those people are away from the work.

Documentation is typically offered as a solution to the loss of knowledge but documentation is a poor way of storing knowledge. Yet documents seldom capture important tacit knowledge essential to understanding how a system works.

Documents cost to create, cost to read, are imperfect and date very quickly. Software metrics expert Capers Jones says that on large projects documentation is often more expensive than the code itself (*Applied Software Measurement*, Capers Jones, 2008).

Of course, documentation only pays back if more work is undertaken on the same product. If the product fails in the market then documentation is pure cost.

In the worst cases the time spent on documentation increases the chances of failure, while the costs of documentation increase the cost of that failure.

Teams

When work is restarted a new team is required. With luck, some of the previous team members may be available but this is far from certain. Every new team will go through the storming-forming-norming and performing stages. In other words: a lot of the initial time is lost.

It takes time to recruit and form a team. It costs time for them to read documentation. It costs for the team members to learn the application. And all of that happens before they become productive. Finally, having created a performing team, the organisation finishes the project and dissolves the team.

The overheads of team formation and dissolution alone are astonishing. For a company which needs to be reactive – Agile – and compete with digital competitors, it can be crippling.

Pre-project

Of course, team formation is not the only overhead a new project creates. It takes time to decide what the outcome of a proposed project is, more time to decide the resources to be deployed, more time to plan out the work in advance, time to get the work approved and then action it.

Indeed, the "pre-project" phase of a project is really a project in its own right. Yet such pre-project phases are often overlooked in accounting because the project does not exist yet.

The poor track record of project success – over 70% are failures according to some sources – means organisations often engage in more detail pre-project work. More analysis of requirements, more rigorous examination of work request, more detail in project planning and so on. By increasing the pre-project phase, such additional planning delays the start of the work. Delays to the start of work increase the chances of failure. Greater detail in the plans reduces the scope for workers on the project to make real decisions, thereby reducing motivation and flexibility in the face of change.

It is easy to understand how a failed project leads managers to demand greater planning and analysis before the next project. However, such behaviours can have exactly the opposite effect of that intended.

Cost of delay

Delaying the start has two consequences. Most obviously it reduces the amount of time available to deliver the project. If one wants to deliver a project sooner then it is best to start sooner.

Less well understood are the effects of cost of delay. Reinertsen described cost of delay in detail in *The principles of product development flow* (Donald G. Reinertsen, 2009). Suffice to say, value is not a binary event. Different delivery dates result in different amounts of value being released. Figure 24.3, for example, is a time-value profile showing total revenue over four months and marginal revenue, at two-week intervals.

Usually, but not always, an earlier delivery releases more value if only because the product is in the market for longer. But sometimes early delivery dates make little difference, in some cases deliveries may be deferred and still generate similar value. That means, when prioritising work, one must consider the value elasticity with respect to date as well as the absolute value.

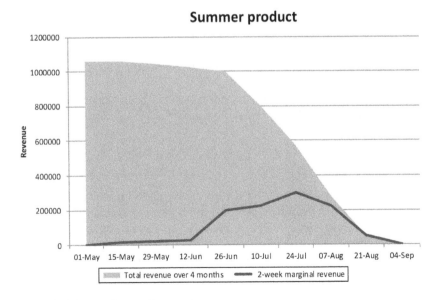

Figure 24.3 Time-value profile over time.

Even minimal products can unlock value. Managers frequently underestimate the benefits of releasing an "incomplete" product into the market. Such products generate revenue (or cost savings) far earlier. Early revenue has an amazing effect on return on investment (ROI) calculations. Minimal products allow for market testing, customer feedback and test the quality of the delivery team itself.

With continuous delivery approaches, minimal products can be released and quickly enhanced at little cost. This approach can also be used to de-risk endeavours by testing product and hypothesis before more costs are incurred.

Risk and sunk costs

The project model encourages an all or nothing mindset. By shifting decisions from the build and deliver phase to the pre-project planning phase, projects miss opportunities to do smaller, cheaper and less risky initial versions.

This approach increases sunk costs because analysis, planning and decisions are made early on. They are paid for at the start. However, when decisions are deferred the costs are deferred too.

The traditional project approach brings decisions up front in the belief that this will de-risk the project and allow for economies of scale. But deferring decisions means decisions can be made closer to the time they are needed. This increases the information available to the decision makers. It also means decisions are only researched and decided (and therefore paid for) if they are needed. Consequently, sunk-costs are reduced.

This decision strategy also means that teams have more difficulty forecasting an end date because less is known and decided in advance. While an end date forecast is frequently sought by managers, such forecasts are notoriously wrong.

One common answer to poor forecasting is to allow for contingency time. This too tends to make things worse because humans tend to use the time available. Think back to your own days at school or college when you were set "course work" or "project work" – work which needed to be completed in your own time and handed in several weeks. *When did you do this work?*

When I ask this question to software professionals, people overwhelmingly answer "The day before." Humans are very good at working to deadlines but hopeless at forecasting end dates.

For these reasons, and others, projects have a natural tendency to grow. Grow in time, budget, people and work to be done. This happens before work begins and during work. Consequently, some projects become *too big to fail.*

This is especially true of high profile projects which hit problems. Take for example the BBC Digital production project which was cancelled in 2013 after £98 million was spent, or the FBI Virtual Case File project which was cancelled in 2005 when $200 million had been spent.

It boggles my imagination that such projects can spend so much money and have nothing to show. Why weren't such endeavours cancelled sooner? The only explanation I can imagine is that when such projects encounter problems *good money is thrown after bad.* More money is spent on them in an attempt to rectify the problems. Once an executive has signed-off a $10 million spend it may well be easier to spend another $10 million than explain where $10 million has gone.

Implementation failures

Some would argue that failures such as these represent a failure to use project management techniques correctly. Yet, in an industry obsessed with projects, which seemingly employs millions of project managers who go on millions of courses each year, it is not uncommon to hear that 50% or even 70% of all projects fail.

In all honesty, I don't know the real rate of project failure. While I have seen many figures quoted it is hard to find a really definitive figure. That most people believe project failure runs at over 50% probably indicates that many projects fail.

Time and time again, inquiries into project failure report inadequate requirements, poor planning, failure to consider some eventuality or other or perhaps a lack of risk management. In an attempt to rectify such failing, subsequent projects devote more time and energy to these issues.

As project plans become more detailed they offer up more opportunities where the plan can be mistaken. And as the precursors to actual work become greater so too does the control exercised on those executing the plan. A plan that is not executed correctly is of little use.

Plans are as much a means of control as they are a guide to activity. By making decisions early on plans close down options for those who will undertake the work. This itself is disempowering and demotivating for the workers who must execute the plan. The planning processes assume that a small cadre of planners – in the pre-project phase – can make all important decisions and the larger delivery workforce merely execute.

Such an approach is at odds both with the Agile approach and the preferences of the millennial workforce. Both Agile and millennials seek individual authority and responsibility.

In digital work, the worker is often the best place person to make decisions because they have the most knowledge about the decision that must be made. They are also in the right place at the right time. Delaying decisions makes sense because it allows the maximum amount of learning to occur before the decision is made. Therefore, the worker requiring the decision is also in the most timely position to make the decision.

Modern digital tools enhance this position. Modern tools are an order of magnitude more powerful than previous instruments. Such tools allow for more rapid prototyping and development. Today it can be far faster and cheaper to build something than to analyse it. Building a minimal product, pushing it into the market and watching customer reaction can be faster, cheaper and more accurate than conducting extensive research and analysis into what is wanted.

When the failure rate is so consistently high, is it right to blame implementation details? Perhaps there could be something wrong with the model? Or the success criteria?

Requirements for an alternative

An alternative to the project model needs to avoid these problems but it also needs to satisfy some additional requirements.

In over 25 years in the software industry, I have never seen any development method applied perfectly. The closest I ever saw was a major ISO 9001 certified railway system for Railtrack PLC. This was effectively underwritten by the Government and while managers were cost conscious the project was extremely wasteful. While that project was able, on dubious criteria, to claim "success," every rail traveller in the UK experienced the failure of rail privatisation and Railtrack.

What software development needs is an approach that, when it fails – through over-ambition or incorrect implementation – minimises the damage and cost. One way of achieving this objective is to create a method with plenty of safe places. When problems occurred, work could fail to a safe place where some value could be realised.

Think of a rock climber. Climbers secure positions before attempting to advance. If an advance is problematic they can return to their secure position.

Such an approach will minimise sunk costs. By ensuring that software is developed and delivered in small pieces any failure can be minimised. Organisations can bank the early work and still walk away from a failing endeavour.

This approach matches the way Agile and, more recently, continuous delivery, operate. Plan a little, build a little, deliver, review and repeat until the goal is met or the effort becomes too troublesome.

Such an approach is logical given that software development exhibits diseconomies of scale. Rather than software getting cheaper per unit (line of code, function, object, module or other unit of delivery), the creation of software gets more expensive per unit as the size grows.

Compare this to milk. Milk exhibits economies of scale. A four-pint carton of milk is cheaper per unit than four one-pint cartons. But if one bought software by the pint, one would find the total costs of four one-pint cartons of software to be less than one four-pint carton of software.

Delivering large cartons of software increases risk. A single defect in a software deliverable renders the whole deliverable problematic. But a single defect in one of four deliverables leaves three usable deliverables.

To be clear, once a piece of software has been delivered there are extraordinary economies of scale to be had. The marginal cost of producing a second identical copy is so low as to be effectively zero. Such economies of scale only apply to deliverable software. Creating the first releasable product is extremely expensive; in economic terms, the marginal costs are very high.

More importantly, the development activity itself has diseconomies of scale. A slightly bigger piece of software is a lot more expensive to build.

The application of economies of scale thinking to the development process has escalated marginal costs. Take reusable program code for example. Reusing existing code is very efficient, but writing software to be reused is very inefficient. Salvaging code to use again is efficient but second guessing what is reusable is expensive.

When code is written for reuse, the work increases while worker focus is diluted. First use is delayed on the promise of accelerated second use. However, all too often the second, third and subsequent uses fail to materialise.

Together these factors mean software needs to be developed in the small. Companies, managers and teams need to find ways to be efficient working in the small. The continuous delivery movement has provided the technology tools for this, and what managers need is an efficient management model.

Such a management model would still set goals but defer decisions how those goals are met to the teams. The teams could then postpone decision making – and therefore cost of decision making – until late in the day. One way of doing this is to make the teams the centre of production and devolve authority to the team to decide on the right thing to do.

Management needs a way of governing those teams. While teams can, and should, be measured against progress to goal, that alone is not enough. Using one measure alone could mean the team slip back into a project-like model.

Measuring the teams against the value-add would help governance and encourage teams to work in the small by delivering small increments. Together with devolved authority, one can expect to see value-seeking teams which are able to determine how to progress towards their goal while adding value at regular intervals.

Continuous digital

Businesses need a management model which promotes continued software enhancements and change, not a model which aims to finish. Projects are, by definition, temporary endeavours. It is doubtful if successful software ever was temporary but in the age of digital businesses software is a key part of growth and continuity.

What is needed is a management model for continuous work. A model that supports software development and the digital businesses built on that software over the longer term.

The *Continuous Digital* model does just this. In this model the team exists to create, grow and maintain software which supports businesses. The software team is as much part of the business as the accounts or marketing department.

Team centric

Teams are stable and exist for the lifetime of the software. This does not mean the teams are static. People will naturally leave the team and new people will join. Team success is inherently tied to the success of the product and the business.

Teams may expand at times and shrink later. Teams may split – amoeba style – when products become large. The important thing for every team is to have a clear understanding of how their work, and their product, creates value.

A team may service just one product or several depending on the nature of the business and technical solution. When a business line is shrinking, teams may merge together and support multiple products.

Throughout the whole process, the team is delivering new versions of the software product(s) at regular intervals. Each update aims to add value and move the team towards their objective.

To do so each team needs to be fully staffed with all the skills it needs to do the work: programmers, testers, analysts, security experts and others. Obviously, this is easier to do where individuals have multiple skills and are happy to wear multiple hats.

Teams need to be as independent as possible. As with software, coupling needs to be reduced and cohesion increased. Dependencies on others outside the team lead to delays and complicates priority setting.

As well as technical skills to build the product, teams need skills of analysis and product management. They need to work with business partners to identify opportunities to add value. Not all opportunities will add value, some experiments will fail, but the team makes those decisions for itself.

Importantly, the team also has a strategic goal, a mission, a massively transitive purpose, a Big Hairy Audacious Goal (BHAG) or some other statement of higher purpose. Such a higher purpose positions the team within the business strategy and gives meaning to individuals on the team.

MVT

Teams are expected to find most of their own work. Unlike traditional projects, scope creep is the lifeblood of Continuous Digital. New ideas for improvement are what add value.

Still, some work will be required which teams do not identify themselves – perhaps opportunities identified by another team. In general, such work flows to the team.

On occasions there will be work which does not fit with any team – perhaps because the company wants so investigate a new opportunity. In these cases, a new *Minimally Viable Team* will be formed. Figure 24.4

The Minimally Viable Team (MVT) contains only the essential skills and people needed to investigate an opportunity. This probably means two people: one with technical skills and one with business skills. Perhaps a third can be justified on some occasions to make the MVT a real team. It might be reasonable to appoint a second analyst or a second technical expert to accelerate work.

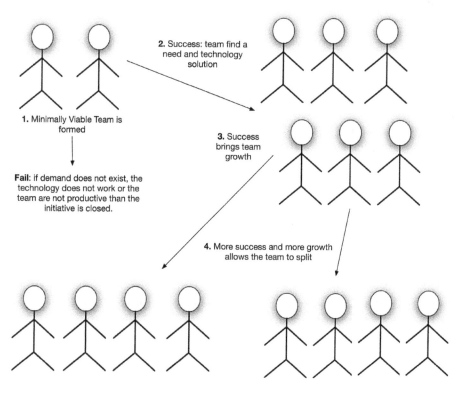

Figure 24.4 Minimally viable team model of organic growth.

Many readers will be surprised to hear such low staffing numbers. In truth, nobody is suggesting that two or three people can deliver the whole endeavour. If the initial team validates the mission and finds a workable technology solution, then they are expected to pull in more team members as and when required.

Teams are minimally staffed in the beginning for two reasons. First, the best composition of team members is unknown. Should the team contain a database specialist? A user experience designer? A tester? A security expert?

Second, adding more people to the team increases the costs of the team. Larger teams incur a higher burn-rate and become more difficult to justify.

For both technical and financial, the desire to staff the team "correctly" should be avoided. Experience with *Conway's Law*[1] shows that team staffing affects architecture; teams make work for all team members. Put a DBA on a team and the team will use a complex database whether they need one or not.

Financially, the larger the team the greater the call to do some pre-work in order to justify the extra cost. Larger, and longer, pre-work phases costs more, delay the start of construction and add more demands to the team, which eventually build the product.

In project terms, an MVT absorbs the "pre-project" phase. The "project" is back-dated to the start of the MVT. The first task for an MVT is to undertake the "pre-project" work – validating the mission, understanding the market, testing the technology, prototyping a solution, etc.

Critically, the MVT is tasked with actually building something. An MVT is not a paper-based planning group. While some upfront planning is valuable, continued planning has rapidly diminishing returns. Therefore, the MVT aims to both analyse what is needed and build potentially releasable solutions in parallel. Modern development tools make this approach entirely possible.

Of course, most MVTs will fail. Their mission will fail to validate, the market will not exist, technology will not be up to the problem or the solution may escape the team. This is to be expected when an organisation is trying risky – but potentially profitable – ideas.

Consequently, it is vital that the team costs be kept low. Traditional projects frequently become too-big-to-fail. They continue to receive funding because closing the work would be too embarrassing to someone.

Portfolio

Teams sometimes need to be dissolved – perhaps because their mission was completed but more equally because the product has been replaced or something has gone wrong. While one would like to think that a team might voluntarily offer to disband once it is no longer delivering value, it is probably too optimistic to assume all such teams will.

Therefore, while authority is devolved to the teams, there still needs to be a portfolio and governance mechanism on top. Critically though, governance needs to be fit for purpose. Reverting to the on-schedule, on-budget, on-scope criteria would be contradictory for a team which was being measured against value created.

---

1 *How do committees invent?*, Melvin Conway, Datamation, April 1968

Senior management needs to set up an active portfolio review process which regularly considers team progress and value-add. Teams which are not adding-value, or not meeting the hurdle rate, can expect closure. Of course there will need to be some remediation – "special measures" – for failing teams which cannot be closed. During portfolio review, resources may be increased or reduced depending on team performance and business strategy.

At first sight the portfolio review process differs little from traditional processes. However, as authority is devolved to the team, it becomes more important. Reviews are no longer simply a checkpoint where teams report percentage done. Teams need to demonstrate value delivered and suggest how they will add more. The days of troubled projects reporting amber in the face to failure need to end.

Equally, "extend or lose everything" ultimatum no longer works.

When teams are making regular deliveries, value cancellation becomes a real option. When teams go extended periods without any deliveries, managers are faced with unpalatable choice: give a failing team more money and time or explain why they gave them so much in the first place.

Software as an asset

Underlying Continuous Digital is the belief that software products are an asset. Digital businesses use software in the same way bricks-and-mortar businesses use shops, warehouses, delivery trucks, ships, cars and more. These are assets that need to be maintained.

A delivery business which fails to maintain and renew its fleet of trucks may save money in the short term. In the long term, costs will increase, but more importantly, reliability will suffer: trucks break down, deliveries are late, promises get broken and customers leave.

Only businesses which see their software as an asset will value the software and invest in quality. Too often companies destroy value by a million small cuts.

Venture capital parallels

While the Continuous Digital model may seem new and strange to readers in corporate IT, those familiar with the Silicon Valley venture capital (VC) process should recognise the approach. (This is not to say everything about venture capital is good, only that it has been successful at creating many software firms.)

In the beginning, work starts on a restricted budget. A small team of founders who race to both build a product and validate the market they plan to enter. Success brings more resources, either via successive funding rounds or via cash flow. Investors monitor progress and revenue at regular intervals.

Success follows a well-trodden path. But failure can strike at any time. The market may not exist, competitors may enter first, or it may be smaller than expected. Equally, the technical team may be unable to create a suitable product – perhaps because of their own dysfunctions or because of bad technology choices.

VC investors operate a portfolio themselves and may invest in competing companies. In time some of these may fail but investors are still exposed to technology advances. Or, if multiple investments succeed, the VC might engineer a merger, or just float them off and pocket the money.

There is little or no attempt to exploit synergies across the portfolio. Each entity must succeed, or fail, on its own.

How long will it take?

One obvious problem with the Continuous Digital model is that of forecasting an end-date. It is not alone here, end-date forecasting has bedeviled software developers since the early days. The "how long will it take" question is poorly addressed by the traditional project model. While the project model promises a done-date, the model has a poor record of achieving this date.

There is no silver-bullet for producing end-dates and meeting deadlines. Instead, multiple bullets are needed. Stable teams, historical data, deadline focus and question reframing all have a part to play.

The Continuous model turns the problem around. In the first instance, important dates are prioritised. Rather than ask "How long will it take to produce X?" the question becomes "How much of X can be produced in the time available?" Instead of aiming for a complete solution, the team aims for a partial solution which will deliver some value. The team know they will be able to continue working and update the product and unlock more value with more time.

Flexing work allows something to be available on the target date. In truth, traditional projects always flexed the work to be done once there was no more time or money to be had.

Stable teams in control of their own processes stand a much better chance of meeting deadlines. Statistical data of past performance can be used to produce forecasts when needed. The more data available the more reliable the forecast.

Traditional teams usually find factors outside their control, changing priorities and resourcing. Value-seeking teams with devolved authority are better positioned to reduce such problems and manage changes when they occur.

In time the question "When will it be done?" needs to be replaced by "When will the next valuable delivery occur?"

Reframing the questions changes the entire approach to engineering. Teams can accept such dates as a constraint to be worked within. The aim is not to produce the *best ever piece of software* but to produce a *pretty good piece of software by the given date*. Faced with such a constraint, teams can evaluate different potential solutions against the deadline and select the optimal one.

Working to a deadline has another advantage: faced with a meaningful deadline they are motivated to meet people change their behaviour and focus their minds on meeting the deadline. Humans are poor at estimating time – even retrospectively after the fact. Adding contingency to time estimates actually makes the problem worse because the "deadline" is postponed.

Business deadlines

Too often programmers are asked for an estimate of how long work will take only to find the estimate is returned as a deadline. This approach not only incentivises programmers to give larger estimates, it is an abdication of business responsibility.

New and enhanced products should be introduced by reference to the revenue-making opportunities and business needs. Business representatives should set the parameters within which a team will create a solution. The desired delivery date is a constraint to be met rather than the product of an effort estimate.

As demonstrated by the time-value profile above, deadlines are rarely binary. Rather they are analogue. Different delivery dates result in different returns. Commonly an earlier date will generate more revenue and a later one less. But that also means that delivering *less, sooner,* can generate more revenue than *more, later.*

For too long, business representatives abdicated responsibility for analysing the cost-of-delay and the difference in delivery dates. They have been content to let programmers set dates and then bemoan late delivery.

Budgeting

Some readers may be troubled that little has been said about budgeting so far. The fact is that under the Continuous Digital model with stable teams, budgeting becomes almost trivial. However, budgeting does become more strategic.

Forecasting the spending on a team is easy, for any given period:

$$\text{Cost} = \text{Team size} \times \text{Average wage costs} \times \text{Duration}$$

Consider a team of six: four programmers, one tester and one analyst. If the average annual salary is $100,000 the cost for the year is:

$$\text{Annual cost} = 6 \times 100,000 = \$600,000$$

One might add 20% for benefits, office rental and other sundries:

$$\text{Annual cost} = \big(6 \times 100,000\big) \times 120\% = \$720,000$$

Equally one might add a cost for computers, and/or cloud processing time and storage.

Rather than allocate budget based on projects, companies allocate money based on teams. Teams are attached to business line and strategic objectives. If an objective does not justify such a spend, then the money and resources are reduced strategically.

$$\text{Budget} = \$500,000$$

$$\text{Team size} = \$500,000 \,/\, \big(100,000 \times 120\%\big) = 4 \text{ team members}$$

Again, the size of the team is considered a constraint for the team to work within rather than a variable.

Contracts

One of the most regular questions asked both of Agile projects and continuous teams is *how does one agree on a contract?* – After all, clients and suppliers expect to agree on a set of deliverables, a schedule and a fixed price.

In truth, this approach has not always worked well. Schedules are often extended, costs rise and deliverables change. Within a traditional contract framework, there is often much negotiation and even disappointment.

Consequently, there are plenty of clients who are looking for alternatives to the traditional contract model. Indeed, the few supplies I know who offer alternative models find work is booming. Undoubtedly, many clients want to sign a fix-fix-fix contract but there are also plenty who are looking for an alternative.

In the Continuous Digital model, a contract is goal focused without any requirements. The team – which is staffed from both client and supplier – are tasked with deciding what is needed to meet the goal and building it. The work is bounded by time and budget. The job of the team is not to build the best possible solution but to build the best solution possible within the constraints of time and money.

Naturally, the team can go back and ask for more time and money. The portfolio process described above can be used just as well with outsourced teams as in-house. That requires the supplier to take on slightly more risk but here again the continuous model has the advantage: only suppliers confident of their ability to work this way will bid on such contracts.

In other words: the model itself acts as a filter. Suppliers who cannot work within time and budget will not bid for such work.

Main points

- Software development exhibits diseconomies of scale, therefore optimise processes and practices to work in the small.
- Get good at working in the small.
- Start new work with a minimally viable team.
- Plan less, release more. Learn from planning and doing.
- Teams should conduct analysis in parallel with development from the very start.
- Teams should be stable but not static.
- Teams need a higher purpose and are value-seeking.
- Teams have the responsibility for deciding what gets built.
- Teams should be staffed with all the necessary skill.
- Teams can pull additional resources and grow in time, they may split and they may shrink.
- Active portfolio management is vital.
- Software is an asset so treat it as such.
- Keeping quality high pays back in faster development and reduced costs in production.
- Each team is considered a stand-alone business unit; synergies may emerge over time but the emphasis is on reducing dependencies not extracting economies.
- The time available is determined by the business.
- Spending is determined strategically and team size determined by burn-rate of available money.

Work run on a Continuous Digital model may, in retrospect, resemble a project. An MVT team may come into being, grow, deliver a product, shrink and eventually disband. But attempting to manage work as such creates more problems than it solves.

Businesses work this way

By now I'm sure some readers will be saying "this could never possibly work?" Others will be asking: "do companies actually work this way?" The short answer is *No*. Neither do families have 2.4 or 3.14 children.

Nobody follows the Continuous Digital model exactly as described here because it is a model. Models by definition are abstractions. But there are companies that come close.

Every practice and process described here exists somewhere or other. Some organisations follow more, some less, some are on a journey and many are far closer than they realise.

Take for example the MVT model. Many companies create mini-teams to investigate innovative ideas but few name and formalise the process.

Or consider projects themselves. While many organisations claim to follow the project model – and may even feel guilty where they deviate – often the project model is observed in language only.

Many organisations have products, products which require continued changes. However, the company packages sets of changes into a *project*. While the project has a nominal start-date and end-date the project really starts before the start-date when the package is assembled. End-dates may be extended or work may be reassigned the project which comes after this one.

Where companies deliver project after project, the delivery team is unlikely to be a temporary organisation. At which point one has to ask: if dates are flexible, teams are semi-permanent and requirements variable, is the organisation really following the project model? Or are they using the language of projects to complicate a much simpler actual process?

Let me suggest, applying the project model – even just the language – where it is not applicable adds to costs and increases risk. The model is being used where it is not applicable and thus creates tensions.

Conclusion

I have no doubt that in some contexts the project model is the right solution. In some contexts, it makes complete sense and provides a great management model.

When it comes to creating software applications and digital businesses, the project model performs poorly. The model delays work, reduces value, causes quality to be reduced in ways which increase costs and further delay work. At its worst, goal displacement causes delivery teams to lose site of the real objectives.

I suspect that it is not just software development and digital business that see these problems. But I make no claims for other domains.

Projects are not a natural phenomenon. They do not exist by divine providence. Projects are a management model. As such, one can choose to use the project model or adopt another model such as Continuous Digital.

In the twenty-first century, technology has changed the way growth businesses work. At the moment, what passes for digital business is merely a faster way of working. Only by changing management models and processes can the true power of digital business be realised.

Afterword

What the heck are we studying? Projects, performance, and laws

Mark Phillips

We've come to the end of our journey together. As practitioners, it's clear we have many tools at our disposal to help manage and improve project performance. Some of these tools feel very engineering based. They are reductionist, atomistic methods focused on quantifying and managing elements impacting project performance. These elements are encased in causal chains explaining and predicting behavior. Practitioners can use these tools to help plan, set expectations, take measurements on project status, communicate and potentially act to change status.

Other approaches in the volume feel less engineering based. They are the fuzzy side of our emotional well-being, our mental states. They highlight the value of mentoring, communication based in listening, mindfulness. They discuss the role of positive inter-personal interactions and community. Practitioners can use these approaches for the people side of projects. And projects are all about people [Phillips 2014]. People decide on projects. People work on projects. People overcome challenges on projects. People innovate. People look back and talk about the performance of projects.

Project performance is an interplay between and across this spectrum because people, in all their roles on a project, are different. Different tools speak to different audiences and help practitioners communicate and manage those audiences.

Yet somehow, the breadth of the spectrum of tools, while useful for practitioners, makes the field feel imprecise. Is it a science, with scientific laws? Can people and human actions be understood through the lens of science, be engineered? Before we take our final leave of each other for this volume, we'll dive into these waters in this Afterword. We'll use some well-formed ideas on criteria for a science or separate field of study [Popper 2002, Vada 2015]. We'll look at three potentially relevant domains: physics, economics and neuroscience. All the while, we'll keep circling back to reflect on project performance.

- What is it that we are studying?
- Is there a fundamental set of elements or interactions we are observing or learning about?
- How do we determine valid explanations of project performance?
- If our predictions are wrong, does that invalidate our theories?

These seem foundational questions. Can we or should we study project performance without clear answers?

Let's start with physics. Physics often comes to mind as the Gold Standard for a field which is unquestionably a science. Physics is succinctly defined as the study of force [Dienes 2017]. This clarity can be encoded into mathematical models. These models can be wildly precise in making predictions. We can bounce the predictions against empirical observation and make claims on the accuracy of the models. We can ask if the theory encoded into a model pencils out. Does observed reality conform to the model? Have we uncovered some way of consistently describing the world around us?

For the most part, the answer seems to be yes. The dialogue in physics among scholars, practitioners, engineers and others is, I'm sure, as messy as any other field. But the output is wonderous. Witness the everyday marvels of producing millions of cars a year at specific levels of safety, quality and performance. Or, look at the power of the internet-connected devices in billions of pocketbooks and pockets around the globe. Or, gaze at the moon and know we've walked there. Or gaze beyond and be reminded that one person [Einstein 1918, 2005], deep in the dialogue, used mathematical models and imagination to predict gravitational waves. This phenomenon was confirmed a hundred years after the prediction by observing an event which happened a billion years ago, using instruments which themselves are a testament to the wondrous output of the field.

How well does project performance fit as a field of study compared with physics? Does it matter that we are studying people?

Let's now move to economics. In the realm of studying people, economics has an aura of precision. Economics is defined as the study of human decision making under conditions of scarcity [Schwalberg 1987]. Economic theories have been encoded into mathematical models yielding specific predictions. The jury is out on the accuracy of economic predictions of single point events or outcomes occurring in a relatively short period of time. We have yet to predict asset prices at all points in time. Doing so would generate a fortune. We haven't yet figured out how to keep all businesses in business all the time or keep people happy at work.

Observed reality may not conform to economic models. Economics may not have uncovered some way of consistently describing the world around us. However, dialogue in the field generates artifacts, a language, a taxonomy that works well with the way we make policy decisions. Economic outcomes on a macro-scale have been breathtaking. Over the last 25 years, more than a billion people have moved beyond subsistence poverty [World Bank 2018]. Many more have seen their material standard of living improve. It is hard to pin this exclusively on the accuracy of economic predictions. It is even harder, though, to say modern economics has nothing to do with it.

The dialogue around economics seems to straddle a wider audience than that of physics. The line between scholars and practitioners blurs when academics are appointed to government decision making roles or are hired by financial firms to calculate large bets. Like the children's game of telephone, economic arguments lose fidelity the wider the audience grows. People farther out from the original authors forget the operating assumptions or simplifications which make most economic models possible. This forgetting gives economics an illusion of exactness. This is particularly acute when it forgets the assumptions made on human decision making. It then takes people outside the field, like the psychologists Tversky and Kahneman [Tversky and Kahneman 1974, Lewis 2016], to remind us of the existence and frailty of these assumptions, and shake up the conversation.

How wide is the audience for the dialogue taking place in project performance? What assumptions do we make about human behavior?

In terms of understanding human behavior, the field of neuroscience seems to be providing breakthroughs in mapping how people work. I am not very familiar with the details of the field. But philosophers like Daniel Dennett [Dennett 1991] convincingly use findings from the field decades ago, along with the work of Darwin [Darwin 1871] and Dawkins [Dawkins 1976], to demystify metaphysical concepts such as consciousness. He paves the way for a scientific understanding of seemingly inscrutable elements of human behavior like our sense of self or the continuity of a consistent, singular self, making decisions and feelings things, over time. It is gleefully rational and skeptical in the most positive sense of the words.

The social psychologist Erich Fromm once defined character, the unique elements of each person, as "the relatively permanent system of all noninstinctual strivings through which man relates himself to the human and natural world" [Fromm 1973] We may one day find there aren't "noninstinctual strivings" and that science can identify and explain all our choices and actions. It may take years to see the direct instrumentalist success of the field. Neuroscience, though, has begun making its way into project performance [Osterweil 2019] and the impact is being felt. The field is shaking foundations of meaning and morality [Caruso and Flanagan 2018]. Its promise is both exciting and terrifying.

Are we shaking foundations? What is the promise of project performance?

Project performance holds incredible promise. Imagine if we were able to discover repeatable and consistent methods to create and foster world–changing innovation. Imagine the types of medical or agricultural improvements we could produce, with savings in cost and resources. Or, imagine if we discovered repeatable and consistent methods to have happy people and happy communities. Yes, it sounds dangerously like social engineering, and comes with the caveats and warnings of history (as well as that of The Mule in Asimov's Foundation series). But project performance could paint the path to understand dialogue around specific topics, prescribing ways to parse and mold together the right elements in the right way to deliver tremendous results. These could underlie outcomes we've described above such as revolutions in physics, effective dialogues around economic policy and advances in understanding human behavior. It holds great promise.

The question around shaking foundations is harder to answer. Sometimes it feels we are not shaking foundations. We see practitioners making a significant impact in their particular environment, in their companies, organizations, on their projects. We see academics having rigorous dialogue in journals and conferences. It sometimes seems the dialogues aren't talking to each other.

Zooming out further, though, the world is deeply touched by performance management approaches. Agile has permeated the daily business vocabulary and changed the way people work. Lean, a concept that is decades old, is now applied to start-ups and innovation. Together they have spawned the field of DevOps which has gone hand-in-hand with the rise of cloud computing, creating a revolution in innovation across fields and reducing costs across industries.

Looking back further, the pioneering work of W. Edwards Deming set the foundation for high volume, high quality, repeatable processes. The fruits of his work are seen in manufacturing in industries including cars, cell phones, chips and candy.

The volume, quality and relatively low cost of so many products and services across the globe can be connected to Deming's work. His work in statistical sampling is also used in conducting the census in the United States, influencing how the very government is constituted. Henry Gantt created an everyday tool so common and practical for talking about projects that people even forget it had an inventor – the Gantt chart.

Do ideas like Agile and Lean Innovation, or inventors like Deming and Gantt, belong to the field of project performance? Or, rather, are they part of industrial engineering, statistics? Many fields draw ideas from other domains. For example, the psychologists Kahneman and Twersky impacting economics. But what are the boundaries of what's in and out of the field? Does it matter that the area of impact is now being seen as how people work and discuss projects? Do we encompass Agile, Lean, Deming and Gantt in a new narrative of a new field? It feels like we should. It feels like there's value, instrumentalist and in advancing our problem-solving capabilities, to define the field with a few constants to clarify and answer the questions posed at the beginning of this Afterword. To help answer, truly, what the heck are we studying?

To get started, I would suggest the following constants for the field, based on observation, practice and research.

- It is always instrumentalist. We are concerned with outcomes. We are a rich arena to which the scientific method can be applied to study social sciences, human behavior and philosophical concepts.
- Communication in and about the field spans a wide audience and often requires multiple artifacts and varied communication objects to effectively communicate with the audiences involved.
- There is always a dialogue between the holistic and the specific. We may sometimes run the risk of seeing a unified whole or totality in which to fit our observations [Benjamin 2016]. But uncertainty and unknowableness will always bring us back to the specific.
- Project participants and outcomes are always impacted by their orientation towards uncertainty and unknowableness [Phillips 2014].

Let's also consider project performance as a performative field [Austin 1975]. The words and methods used, the communication artifacts created and theories proposed are there to serve a performative purpose, within a project environment. They are different than logical statements or statements about the world. They are meant to direct or change the world or environment in which they occur. Law and legal argumentation are an example. The performative nature of project performance adds credence to using instrumentalism to determine valid explanations. It could also help explain why leadership is a go-to answer and successful area of management studies.

These determinations, and the projects themselves, are made in a social and human reality. (It is an interesting and elucidating thought experiment to think how the field would be different if we were talking about optimizing the performance of machines). These realities are full of traditions and rituals, in the anthropological sense. There is a burgeoning literature using performative authenticity as a tool for understanding traditions [Phillips 2019]. Many legal systems have enshrined the role of tradition in the principle of precedent, where previous outcomes impact current or future outcomes.

And it is here that we may find a solid perch to rest our questioning. Project performance, for all the potential trappings of engineering and science, may be best understood as a field unto itself, most similar to law. Every case is unique, every project is unique. Yet we try to find sufficient similarities across projects to inform the outcome of current or future projects. This could explain the basis of the case study method used in many business schools. There is an ongoing dialogue between the holistic and the specific. Threads in one direction or the other are pulled to serve the needs of the project and the practitioner. Sometimes practitioners follow strict interpretations of previous outcomes. Other times, practitioners lean in on more novel interpretations. The practitioner, and the field itself, is concerned with outcomes. Current outcomes, future outcomes, reinterpretation of past outcomes.

Both law and project performance have heavy performative elements. Words are used to impact outcomes rather than to make statements about reality. Both have a wide variety of audiences and require different artifacts and communication objects to speak to those audiences. They can incorporate methods and artifacts of hard sciences and mathematical models, such as forensic evidence or risk-adjusted schedules. Or, they can rely on the arts of persuasion, listening and communicating, leveraging interpersonal relationships or power dynamics in an environment and an understanding of the social landscape in which the case, or project, is taking place. Thinking about legal cases which may be discussed in the general public, for example, how much of the outcome depends on accurate statements about physical reality compared to the attorney's ability to read and manipulate the social aspects of a case?

Prediction is very difficult in both law and project performance. Much of the outcome depends on the specific people involved. The role of uncertainty and unknowableness may be greater in project performance. Though uncertainty, and orientation towards uncertainty, seem to play a role in how often cases are settled out of court or on the deals parties come to before going to court or before an official verdict is rendered. This may be a fruitful area of research to find cognates applicable to project performance.

Neuroscience or shifting of more and more project work to artificial intelligence may one day make both fields mute. Neuroscience by providing laws of human behavior. Artificial intelligence by reducing the problem space away from human behavior. Until then, there is promise in studying how to create and manage high performing and effective projects. It can help us achieve all sorts of desirable outcomes.

The content of this volume goes a long way in providing tools and approaches for creating and managing high-performing projects. The promise of the field will be even further accelerated through greater clarity and a shared understanding of what we are studying and how we determine valid explanations. I would argue we are studying social, human phenomena where valid explanations are determined within the context of the project, with particular emphasis on the people in and around the project. Universal concepts or Laws of Nature in project performance exist only to the extent they influence communication in and around the project, increasing or decreasing the probability of delivering the desired outcome. As we've seen throughout this volume, there are many ways to get things done. It is up to the skilled practitioner, much like a skilled attorney, to use the many approaches at our disposal to deliver high-performing projects.

References and further reading

Chapter I

Anari, N.N. (2012). Teachers: Emotional intelligence, job satisfaction and organizational commitment. *Journal of Workplace Learning, 24*(4), 256–269.

Bar-On, R. (1997). *The Emotional Quotient Inventory (EQ-i): Technical Manual.* Toronto, Canada: Multi-Health Systems.

Beech, N. (2011). Liminality and the practices of identity reconstruction. *Human Relations, 64*(2), 285–302.

Bono, J.E., Foldes, H.J., Vinson, G., & Muros, J.P. (2007). Workplace emotions: The role of supervision and leadership. *Journal of Applied Psychology, 92*(5), 1357–1367.

Côté, S., Lopes, P.N., Salovey, P., & Miners, C.T. (2010). Emotional intelligence and leadership emergence in small groups. *The Leadership Quarterly, 21*, 496–508.

Darwin, C. (1965). *The Expression of Emotions in Man and Animals.* Chicago, IL: University of Chicago Press (Original work published 1872).

Druskat, V., & Druskat, D. (2006). Applying emotional intelligence in project working. In: Pryke, S., & Smyth, H. (Eds.), *The Management of Complex Projects: A Relational Approach.* Oxford: Blackwell, 78–96.

Gardner, H. (1983). *Frames of Mind: The Theory of Multiple Intelligences.* New York: Basic Books.

Goleman, D. (1995). *Emotional Intelligence.* New York: Bantam Books.

Kafetsios, K., & Zampetakis, L.A. (2008). Emotional intelligence and job satisfaction: Testing the mediatory role of positive and negative affect at work. *Personality and Individual Differences, 44*(3), 712–722.

Kellett, J.B., Humphrey, R.H., & Sleeth, R.G. (2002). Empathy and complex task performance: Two routes to leadership. *The Leadership Quarterly, 13*(5), 523–544.

Kerr, R., Garvin, J., Heaton, N., & Boyle, E. (2006). Emotional intelligence and leadership effectiveness. *Leadership & Organization Development Journal, 27*(4), 265–279.

Maurer, I. (2010). How to build trust in inter-organizational projects: The impact of project staffing and project rewards on the formation of trust, knowledge acquisition and product innovation. *International Journal of Project Management, 28*(7), 629–637.

Müller, R., & Turner, R. (2010). Leadership competency profiles of successful project managers. *International Journal of Project Management, 28*, 437–448.

O'Boyle, E.H. Jr., Humphrey, R.H., Pollack, J.M., Hawver, T.H., & Story, P.A. (2011). The relation between emotional intelligence and job performance: A meta-analysis. *Journal of Organizational Behavior, 32*(5), 788–818.

Pheng, L.S., & Chuan, Q.T. (2006). Environmental factors and work performance of project managers in the construction industry. *International Journal of Project Management, 24*(1), 24–37.

Reevy, G.M., & Deason, G. (2014). Predictors of depression, stress, and anxiety among non-tenure track faculty. *Frontiers in Psychology, 5*, 701.

Rezvani, A., Chang, A., Wiewiora, A., Ashkanasy, N.M., Jordan, P.J., & Zolin, R. (2016). Manager emotional intelligence and project success: The mediating role of job satisfaction and trust. *International Journal of Project Management, 34*, 1112–1122.

Sy, T., Tram, S., & O'Hara, L.A. (2006). Relation of employee and manager emotional intelligence to job satisfaction and performance. *Journal of Vocational Behavior, 68*(3), 461–473.

Thorndike, E.L. (1920). Intelligence and its uses. *Harper's Magazine, 140*, 227–235.

Troth, A.C., Jordan, P.J., Lawrence, S.A., & Tse, H.H.M. (2012). A multilevel model of emotional skills, communication performance and task performance in teams. *Journal of Organizational Behavior, 33*, 700–722.

Vecchi, G.M., Van Hasselt, V.B., & Romano, S.J. (2005). Crisis (hostage) negotiation: Current strategies and issues in high-risk conflict resolution. *Aggression and Violent Behavior, 10*, 533–551.

Chapter 2

Snowden, David J., & Boone, Mary E. (November 2007). A leader's framework for decision making. *Harvard Business Review*, 69–76.

Chapter 3

Madsen, S. (2019a). *The Power of Project Leadership: 7 Keys to Help You Transform from Project Manager to Project Leader*, 2nd edition. Kogan Page.

Madsen, S. (June 2019b). *Developing Project Leaders* [Web blog]. Retrieved from https://www.susannemadsen.co.uk/blog (accessed May 2019).

Chapter 4

Argyris, C., & Schön, D.A. (1978). *Organizational Learning: A Theory of Action Perspective*. Reading, MA: Addisson-Wesley.

Atkinson, R., Crawford, L., & Ward, S. (2006). Fundamental uncertainties in projects and the scope of project management. *International Journal of Project Management, 24*(8), 687–698.

Bandura, A. (1998). Personal and collective efficacy in human adaptation and change. In: Adair, J.G., Belanger, D., & Dion, K.L. (Eds.), *Advances in Psychological Science: Vol. 1. Personal, Social and Cultural Aspects*. Hove: Psychology Press, 51–71.

Barton, M.A., & Sutcliffe, K.M. (2009). Overcoming dysfunctional momentum. Organizational safety as a social achievement. *Human Relations, 62*(9), 1327–1356.

Barton, M.A., & Sutcliffe, K.M. (2010). Learning when to stop momentum. *MIT Sloan Management Review, 51*(3), 69.

Barton, M.A., & Sutcliffe, K.M. (2017). Contextual engagement as resilience-in-action: A study of expedition racing. *Paper presented at the 33rd EGOS Colloquium*. Copenhagen, Denmark.

Barton, M.A., Sutcliffe, K.M., Vogus, T., & DeWitt, T. (2015). Performing under uncertainty: Contextualized engagement in wildland firefighting. *Journal of Contingencies and Crisis Management, 23*(2), 74–83.

Beck, K., et al. (2001). *Manifesto for Agile Software Development*. Retrieved from http://agilemanifesto.org/ (accessed 01 November 2017).

Bertolini, L., & Salet, W. (2007). *Coping with Complexity and Uncertainty in Mega Projects: Linking Strategic Choices and Operational Decision Making, Working Paper Series 2.7*. London: Bartlett School of Planning.

Bigley, G.A., & Roberts, K.H. (2001). The incident command system: High-reliability organizing for complex and volatile task environments. *The Academy of Management Journal, 44*(6), 1281–1299.

Blomquist, T., Hällgren, M., Nilsson, A., & Söderholm, A. (2010). Project-as-Practice: In search of project management research that matters. *Project Management Journal, 41*(1), 5–16.

Bodin, P., & Wiman, B.L.B. (2004). Resilience and other stability concepts in ecology: Notes on their origin, validity and usefulness. The ESS Bulletin, *2*(2), 33–43.

Böhle, F., & Porschen-Hueck, S. (2014). Improvisation in Musik und Arbeit. *praeview, 5*(1), 26–27.

Bonanno, G.A. (2004). Loss, trauma, and human resilience: Have we underestimated the human capacity to thrive after extremely aversive events? *American Psychologist, 59*(1), 20–28.

Borgert, S. (2013). *Resilienz im Projektmanagement. Bitte anschnallen Turbulenzen! Erfolgskonzepte adaptiver Projekte.* Wiesbaden: Springler Gabler.

Borgert, S. (2015). *Die Irrtümer der Komplexität. Warum wir ein neues Management brauchen.* Offenbach: Gabal.

Bouquet, C., & Birkinshaw, J.M. (2008). Managing power in the multinational corporation: How low-power actors gain influence. *Journal of Management, 34*(3), 477–508.

Brookes, N., Locatelli, G., & Mikic, M. (2015). *Learning Across Megaprojects: The INNOMET Working Group Report.* Leeds: University of Leeds.

Checkland, P. (1999). *Systems Thinking, Systems Practice.* Chichester: Wiley.

Christianson, M.K., Farkas, M.T., Sutcliffe, K.M., & Weick, K.E. (2009). Learning through rare events: Significant interruptions at the Baltimore & Ohio Railroad Museum. *Organization Science, 20*(5), 846–860.

Cléden, D. (2009). *Managing Project Uncertainty.* Farnham: Gower.

Cooper, C., Flint-Taylor, J., & Pearn, M. (2013). *Building Resilience for Success: A Resource for Managers and Organizations.* Basingstoke: Palgrave Macmillan.

Darkow, P., & Geiger, D. (2017). Managing for resilience: The emergence of coordinating practices in disaster relief operations. *Paper presented at the 33rd EGOS Colloquium.* Copenhagen, Denmark.

De Meyer, A., Loch, Ch.H., & Pich, M.T. (2002). Managing project uncertainty: From variation to chaos. *MIT Sloan Management Review, 43*(2), 60–67.

Dorniok, D., & Mohe, M. (2011). Nichtwissen als vernachlässigte Variable im Verhältnis von Organisation und Umwelt. In: Conrad, P., & Sydow, J. (Eds.), *Managementforschung 21.* Wiesbaden: Springer, 91–132.

Drury, M., Conboy, K., & Power, K. (2012). Obstacles to decision making in Agile software development teams. *Journal of Systems and Software, 85*(6), 1239–1254.

Endsley, M.R. (2003). *Designing for Situation Awareness.* London/New York: Taylor & Francis.

Farjoun, M., & Starbuck, W.H. (2007). Organizing at and beyond the limits. *Organization Studies, 28,* 541–566.

Fletcher, D., & Sarkar, M. (2013). Psychological resilience: A review and critique of definitions, concepts, and theory. *European Psychologist, 18*(1), 12–23.

Geraldi, J.G., Lee-Kelley, L., & Kutsch, E. (2010). The Titanic sunk, so what? Project manager response to unexpected events. *International Journal of Project Management, 28*(6), 547–558.

Giezen, M. (2013). Adaptive and strategic capacity: Navigating megaprojects through uncertainty and complexity. *Environment and Planning B Planning and Design, 40*(4), 723–741.

Gigerenzer, G., Hertwig, R., & Pachur, T. (2011). *Heuristics: The Foundations of Adaptive Behavior.* New York: Oxford University Press.

Hamel, G., & Valikangas, L. (2003). The quest for resilience. *Harvard Business Review, 81*(9), 52–65.

Heidling, E. (2015). Erscheinungsformen und Typen von Ungewissheit in Projekten. In: Böhle, F., et al. (Eds.), *Umgang mit Ungewissheit in Projekten.* München: GPM, 13–57.

Hobbs, B., & Petit, Y. (2017). Agile methods on large projects in large organizations. *Project Management Journal, 48*(3), 3–19.

Kamoche, K.N., Cunha, M.P., & Cunha, J.V. (Eds.) (2002). *Organisational Improvisation.* London/New York: Psychology Press.

Laufer, A., Hoffman, E.J., Russel, J.S., & Cameron W.S. (2015). What successful project managers do. *MIT Sloan Management Review, 56*(3), 43.

Littau, P., Burcar Dunović, I., Pau, L. Mancini, M., Irimia Dieguez, A., Medina-Lopez, C., Spang, K., Travaglini, A., Colombo, R., Nahod, M., & Lukasiewicz, A. (2015). *Managing Stakeholders in Megaprojects. The MS Working Group Report.* Leeds: University of Leeds.

Luhmann, N. (2000). *Organisation und Entscheidung.* Opladen: Westdeutscher Verlag.

Masten, A.S. (2007). Resilience in developing systems: Progress and promise as the fourth wave rises. *Development and Psychopathology, 19*(3), 921–930.

Nachbagauer, A.G.M. (2018). When risk management is not enough: Project managers' experiences when confronted with the unexpected. In: Conference Proceedings: *Challenging the Status Quo in Management and Economics.* Bucharest: Tritonic, 1131.

Neuberger, O. (1995). *Mikropolitik.* Stuttgart: Enke.

Neumer, J. (2009). *Neue Forschungsansätze im Umgang mit Unsicherheit und Ungewissheit in Arbeit und Organisation. Zwischen Beherrschung und Ohnmacht.* Aachen: RWTH Aachen.

Norris, F.H., Stevens, S.P., Pfefferbaum, B., Wyche, K.F., & Pfefferbaum, R.L. (2008). Community resilience as a metaphor, theory, set of capacities, and strategy for disaster readiness. *American Journal of Community Psychology, 41*(1–2), 127–150.

Ong, A.D., Bergemann, C.S., & Boker, S.M. (2009). Resilience comes of age: Defining features in later adulthood. *Journal of Personality, 77*(6), 1777–1804.

Ortiz-de-Mandojana, N., & Bansal, P. (2016). The long-term benefits of organizational resilience through sustainable business practices. *Strategic Management Journal, 37*(8), 1615–1631.

Pellerin, C.J. (2009). *How Nasa Builds Teams: Mission Critical Soft Skills for Scientists, Engineers, and Project Teams.* Hoboken, NJ: John Wiley & Sons.

Perminova, O., Gustafsson, M., & Wikström, K. (2008). Defining uncertainty in projects – A new perspective. *International Journal of Project Management, 26*(1), 73–79.

Pitsis, T.S. Clegg, S., Marosszeky, M., & Rura-Polley, T. (2003). Constructing the Olympic dream: A future perfect strategy of project management. *Organization Science, 14*(5), 574–590.

Rees, C.S., Breen, L.J., Cusack, L., & Hegney, D. (2015). Understanding individual resilience in the workplace: The international collaboration of workforce resilience model. *Frontiers in Psychology, 6*, 1–7.

Robertson, B.J. (2015). *Holacracy.* New York: Henry Holt.

Sanderson, J. (2012). Risk, uncertainty and governance in megaprojects: A critical discussion of alternative explanations. *International Journal of Project Management, 30*(4), 432–443.

Saunders, F.C. (2015). Toward high reliability project organizing in safety-critical projects. *Project Management Journal, 46*(3), 25–35.

Saunders, F.C., Gale, A.W., & Sherry, A.H. (2016). Responding to project uncertainty: Evidence for high reliability practices in large-scale safety-critical projects. *International Journal of Project Management, 34*, 1252–1265.

Schaub, H. (2012). Wahrnehmung, Aufmerksamkeit und 'Situation Awareness' (SA). In: Badke-Schaub, P., Hofinger, G., & Lauche, K. (Eds.), *Human Factors.* Berlin: Springer, 63–82.

Senge, P.M. (2006). *The Fifth Discipline.* New York: Doubleday.

Snowden, D.J., & Boone, M.E. (2007). A leader's framework for decision making. *Harvard Business Review, 85*(11), 68–76.

Söderholm, A. (2008). Project management of unexpected events. *International Journal of Project Management, 26*(1), 80–86.

Stacey, R. (2011). *Strategic Management and Organizational Dynamics.* Harlow: Prentice Hall.

Stingl, V., & Geraldi, J. (2017a). Errors, lies and misunderstandings: Systematic review on behavioural decision making in projects. *International Journal of Project Management, 35*(2), 121–135.

Stingl, V., & Geraldi, J. (2017b). Toolbox for uncertainty: Introduction of adaptive heuristics as strategies for project decision making. In: *Conference Proceedings of International Research Network on Organizing by Projects.* Boston, MA: INROP.

Sull, D., & Eisenhardt, K.M. (2015). *Simple Rules: How to Thrive in a Complex World.* Boston, MA: Houghton Mifflin Harcourt.

Sutcliffe, K.M., & Vogus, T.J. (2003). Organizing for resilience. In: Cameron, K., Dutton, J.E., & Quinn, R.E. (Eds.), *Positive Organizational Scholarship*. San Francisco, CA: Berrett-Koehler, 94–110.

Sutcliffe, K.M., Vogus, T.J., & Dane, E. (2016). Mindfulness in organizations: A cross-level review. *Annual Review of Organizational Psychology and Organizational Behavior, 3*, 55–81.

Välikangas, L. (2010). *The Resilient Organization*. New York: McGraw-Hill.

van Marrewijk, A. (2005). Strategies of cooperation: Control and commitment in mega-projects. *M@n@gement, 4*(8), 89–104.

Wearne, S., & White-Hunt, K. (2014). *Managing the Urgent and Unexpected: Twelve Project Cases and a Commentary*. Farnham: Gower.

Weick, K.E. (1993). The collapse of sensemaking in organizations: The Mann Gulch disaster. *Administrative Science Quarterly, 38*(4), 628–652.

Weick, K.E. (1995). *Sensemaking in Organizations*. Thousand Oaks, CA: Sage.

Weick, K.E., & Sutcliffe, K.M. (2007). *Managing the Unexpected: Resilient Performance in an Age of Uncertainty*, 2nd edition. San Francisco, CA: Jossey-Bass.

Weick, K.E., Sutcliffe, K.M., & Obstfeld, D. (1999). Organizing for high reliability: Processes of collective mindfulness. In: Sutton, R.S., & Staw, B.M. (Eds.), *Research in Organizational Behavior*, Vol. 1. Stanford, CA: Jai Press, 81–123.

Wilson, S.M., & Ferch, S.R. (2005). Enhancing resilience in the workplace through the practice of caring relationships. *Organization Development Journal, 23*(4), 45–60.

Winch, G.M. (2010). *Managing Construction Projects: An Information Processing Approach*, 2nd edition. Oxford: Wiley-Blackwell.

Winch, G.M., & Maytorena, E. (2012). Managing risk and uncertainty on projects. In: Morris, P.W.G., Pinto, J.K., &. Söderlund, J. (Eds.), *The Oxford Handbook of Project Management*. Oxford: Oxford University Press, 345–364.

Wright, M.O.D., Masten, A.S., & Narayan, A.J. (2013). Resilience processes in development: Four waves of research on positive adaptation in the context of adversity. In: Goldstein, S., & Brooks, R.B. (Eds.), *Handbook of Resilience in Children*, 2nd edition. New York: Springer, 15–37.

Chapter 5

Kallman, T., & Kallman, A. (2018). *Flow: Get Everyone Moving in the Right Direction…And Loving It*. New York: Morgan James.

Chapter 6

Flyvbjerg, B. (2003). *Megaprojects and Risk: An Anatomy of Ambition*. Cambridge: Cambridge University Press.

Kerzner, H. (2014). *Project Recovery: Case Studies and Techniques for Overcoming Project Failure*. Hoboken, NJ: Wiley.

Moustafaev, J. (2016). *Project Portfolio Management in Theory and Practice: Thirty Case Studies from around the World (Best Practices and Advances in Program Management)*. Boca Raton, FL: Auerbach Publications.

Prinzo, R. (2014). *Collaborative Intervention: How to Identify, Assess and Intervene in Troubled Technology & Transformation Projects*. Alpharetta, GA: The Prinzo Group.

Smith, J. (2001). *Troubled IT Projects: Prevention and Turnaround*. Hertfordshire: Institution of Engineering and Technology.

Standish Group. (2011). *CHAOS Report 2011*. Boston, MA: Standish Group International.

Standish Group. (2012). *CHAOS Report 2012*. Boston, MA: Standish Group International.

Standish Group. (2013). *CHAOS Report 2013*. Boston, MA: Standish Group International.

Standish Group. (2014). *CHAOS Report 2014.* Boston, MA: Standish Group International.

Standish Group. (2015). *CHAOS Report 2015.* Boston, MA: Standish Group International.

Standish Group. (2016). *CHAOS Report 2016.* Boston, MA: Standish Group International.

Williams, T. (2011). *Rescue the Problem Project: A Complete Guide to Identifying, Preventing, and Recovering from Project Failure.* New York: AMACOM.

Chapter 7

Carroll, L., Tenniel, J., & Newell, P. (2010). *Alice's Adventures in Wonderland (1865).* Engage Books/ AD Classic.

Cialdini, Robert B. (2007). *Influence: The Psychology of Persuasion: Robert B. Cialdini.* New York: Collins. Retrieved from https://www.influenceatwork.com/principles-of-persuasion/ (accessed July 2018).

Denning, Stephen. (2006). *Eight Narrative Patterns.* Retrieved from http://www.stevedenning.com/ Documents/Leader-Ch-1.pdf.

Denning, Stephen. (2011). *Forbes.* Retrieved from https://www.forbes.com/sites/stevedenning/201 1/06/08/why-leadership-storytelling-is-important/#764eb73a780f (accessed July 2018).

Denning, Stephen. (2015). In: Pilkington, Ann (2018) *Guide to Storytelling for PR and Internal Communication Published by PR Place.* https://pracademy.co.uk/insights/do-tell-stories/. Accessed August 2019.

Gregory, Anne. (2010). *Planning and Managing Public Relations Campaigns: A Strategic Approach.* Kogan Page.

Harrison, Kate. (2015). *A Good Presentation is About Data and Story.* Forbes. Retrieved from https:// www.forbes.com/sites/kateharrison/2015/01/20/a-good-presentation-is-about-data-and-stor y/#6e60c6fa450f.

Harrison, Paul. (2015). In: Pilkington, Ann (2018) *Guide to storytelling for PR and internal communication published by PR Place.* https://pracademy.co.uk/insights/do-tell-stories/. Accessed August 2019.

Horton, Louise, & Pilkington, Ann. (May 2014). Rolling back from the power/interest matrix. *PM World Journal, III*(V), 3–4.

Parsons, Patricia. (2008). *Ethics in Public Relations: A Guide to Best Practice.* London: Kogan Page.

Perloff, Richard M. (2017). *The Dynamics of Persuasion: Communication and Attitudes in the Twenty-First Century.* New York: Routledge Taylor & Francis Group.

Pilkington, Ann. (2013). *Communicating Projects: An End to End Guide to Planning, Implementing and Evaluating Effective Communication.* London: Routledge.

Pilkington, Ann. (2015). In Ruck, Kevin. (Ed.) *Exploring Internal Communication.* Routledge.

Pilkington, Ann. (April 2016). Getting the most from your project communicator. *PM World Journal,* V(IV), Series Article 3.

Pilkington, Ann. (2018a). *PR Place Guide to Story Telling.* Retrieved from https://www.prplace.com/ resources/guides-toolkits/guide-to-storytelling-for-pr-and-internal-comms/.

Pilkington, Ann. (2018b). *Guide to Storytelling for PR and Internal Communication Published by PR Place.* https://pracademy.co.uk/insights/do-tell-stories/. Accessed August 2019.

Pilkington & Horton. (2014). https://pmworldlibrary.net/article/rolling-back-from-the-powerint erest-matrix-a-new-approach-for-role-based-stakeholder-engagement-in-projects-advances-in- pm-series/. Accessed August 2019.

Ruck, Kevin. (2015). *Exploring Internal Communication.* London: Ashgate Publishing, Ltd.

Smith, Paul. (2012). *Lead with a Story: A Guide to Crafting Business Narratives That Captivate, Convince, and Inspire.* New York: AMACOM.

The Guardian. (2013). Does a government nudge make us budge? *The Guardian.* Retrieved from http://www.theguardian.com/politics/2013/nov/12/government-nudge-theory-budge (accessed July 2018).

Government Communication Service UK. (2015). UK Government OASIS Model for Communication Planning. Retrieved from https://gcs.civilservice.gov.uk/wp-content/uploads/2015/09/OASIS-Campaigns-Guide-.pdf (accessed July 2018).

Theaker, Alison & Yaxley, Heather. (2017). *The Public Relations Strategic Toolkit. An Essential Guide to Successful Public Relations Practice.* Second Edition. New York: Routledge. (Revised edition of the authors' The public relations strategic toolkit, 2012: Routledge.)

Chapter 8

Anbari, F.T., Carayannis, E.G., & Voetsch, R.J. (2008). Post-project reviews as a key project management competence. *Technovation, 28,* 633–643.

APM. (2006). *APM Body of Knowledge,* Buckinghamshire: Association for Project Management.

Argyris, C. (1999). *On Organizational Learning.* Oxford; Malden, MA: Blackwell Business.

Bakker, R.M., Cambré, B., Korlaar, L., & Raab, J. (2010). Managing the project learning paradox: A set-theoretic approach toward project knowledge transfer. *International Journal of Project Management, 29,* 494–503.

Basili, V., Mcgarry, F., Pajerski, R., & Zelkowitz, M. Lessons learned from 25 years of process improvement: The rise and fall of the NASA software engineering laboratory. In: Proceedings of the 24th International Conference on Software Engineering, ICSE 2002, Orlando, Florida, Published by the IEEE Computer Society.

Boh, W.F. (2007). Mechanisms for sharing knowledge in project-based organizations. *Information and Organization, 17,* 27–58.

Boje, D.M. (1991). The storytelling organization: A study of story performance in an office-supply firm. *Administrative Science Quarterly, 36,* 106–126.

Boyce, M.E. (1996). Organizational story and storytelling: A critical review. *Journal of Organizational Change Management, 9,* 5–26.

Bresnen, M., Edelman, L., Newell, S., Scarbrough, H., & Swan, J. (2003). Social practices and the management of knowledge in project environments. *International Journal of Project Management, 21,* 157–166.

Bresnen, M., Goussevskaia, A., & Swan, J. (2004). Embedding new management knowledge in project-based organizations. *Organization Studies, 25,* 1535.

Busby, J.S. (1999). An assessment of post-project reviews. *Project Management Journal, 30,* 23.

Coan, H. (2002). Risk, error and blame in organizations: A communication approach. *Corporate Communications: An International Journal, 7,* 232–240.

Cowles, T. (2004). Criteria for lessons learned (LL). In: Raytheon (Ed.), *4th Annual CMMI Technology Conference and User Group.* Denver, CO: Raytheon.

Dalkir, K. (2005). *Knowledge Management in Theory and Practice.* Oxford: Elsevier Butterworth-Heinemann.

Davenport, T.H., & Prusak, L. (1998). *Working Knowledge: How Organizations Manage What They Know.* Boston, MA: Harvard Business School Press.

Desouza, K., Dingsoyr, T., & Awazu, Y. (2005). Experiences with conducting project postmortems: Reports vs. stories and practitioner perspective. In: HICSS '05. *Proceedings of the 38th Annual Hawaii International Conference on System Sciences,* 3–6 January 2005, Big Island, HI, 233c.

Dixon, N. (2000). *Common Knowledge – How Companies Thrive by Sharing What They Know.* Boston, MA: Harvard Business School Press.

Duffield, S. (2015). Application of a systemic lessons learned knowledge model for organisational learning through projects. In: Australian Institute of Project Management National 2015 *Conference,* Hobart, AIPM, 978-0-646-93699-4, 56–69.

Duffield, S. (2016). Application of the Syllk model wiring an organisation for the capability of an online community of practice. *VINE Journal of Information and Knowledge Management Systems, 46,* 267–294.

Duffield, S., & Whitty, S.J. (2012). A systemic lessons learned and captured knowledge (SLLCK) model for project organizations. In: Global, P. (Ed.), 9th Project Management Australia Conference (PMOz 2012). Melbourne, VIC: Eventcorp Pty Ltd.

Duffield, S., & Whitty, S.J. (2015). Developing a systemic lessons learned knowledge model for organisational learning through projects. *International Journal of Project Management, 33*, 311–324.

Duffield, S., & Whitty, S.J. (2016a). Application of the systemic Lessons Learned Knowledge model for organisational learning through projects. *International Journal of Project Management, 34*, 1280–1293.

Duffield, S., & Whitty, S.J. (2016b). How to apply the Systemic Lessons Learned Knowledge model to wire an organisation for the capability of storytelling. *International Journal of Project Management, 34*, 429–443.

Duhon, H., & Elias, J. (2008). Why it is difficult to learn lessons: Insights from decision theory and cognitive science. *SPE Projects, Facilities & Construction, 3*, 1–7.

Dvir, D., & Shenhar, A. (March 2011). What great projects have in common. *MIT Sloan Management Review, 52*(3), 19.

Fernie, S., Green, S.D., Weller, S.J., & Newcombe, R. (2003). Knowledge sharing: Context, confusion and controversy. *International Journal of Project Management, 21*, 177–187.

Firestone, J., & Mcelroy, M. (2003). *Key Issues in New Knowledge Management*. Burlington, MA: Elsevier Science.

Garvin, D.A. (1993). Building a learning organization. *Harvard Business Review, 71*, 78–91.

Goffin, K., & Koners, U. (2011). Tacit knowledge, lessons learnt, and new product development. *Journal of Product Innovation Management, 28*, 300–318.

Halse, L.L., Kjersem, K., & Emblemsvåg, J. (2014). Implementation of lean project planning: A knowledge transfer perspective. In: IFIP International Conference on Advances in Production Management Systems, Springer, 248–255.

Harris, J., & Barnes, B.K. (2006). Leadership storytelling. *Industrial and Commercial Training, 38*, 350–353.

Hayes, J., & Maslen, S. (2014). Knowing stories that matter: Learning for effective safety decision-making. *Journal of Risk Research, 18*, 714–726.

Hedman, S., Påhlman, L., & Törnby, A. (2015). *The Production of Comfort – How Financial Auditors Experience that they Become Comfortable with IT-Auditors*. Master's thesis, Uppsala University.

Hoegl, M., Parboteeah, K.P., & Munson, C.L. (2003). Team level antecedents of individuals' knowledge networks*. *Decision Sciences, 34*, 741–770.

Huang, J.C., & Newell, S. (2003). Knowledge integration processes and dynamics within the context of cross-functional projects. *International journal of Project Management, 21*, 167–176.

Keegan, A., & Turner, J.R. (2001). Quantity versus quality in project-based learning practices. *Management Learning, 32*, 77–98.

Koners, U. (2005). *Learning from Research and Development Projects/The Role of Post-Project Reviews*. Cranfield University.

Leal-Rodríguez, A.L., Roldán, J.L., Ariza-Montes, J.A., & Leal-Millán, A. (2014). From potential absorptive capacity to innovation outcomes in project teams: The conditional mediating role of the realized absorptive capacity in a relational learning context. *International Journal of Project Management, 32*, 894–907.

Li, A. (2001). GAO-01-1015R Survey of NASA's Lessons Learned Process. In: Office, U.S.G.A., Washington DC.

Li, A. (2002). GAO-02-195 NASA Better Mechanisms Needed for Sharing Lessons Learned. In: Office, U.S.G.A., Washington, DC.

Liebowitz, J., & Megbolugbe, I. (2003). A set of frameworks to aid the project manager in conceptualizing and implementing knowledge management initiatives. *International Journal of Project Management, 21*, 189–198.

Linde, C. (2001). Narrative and social tacit knowledge. *Journal of knowledge management, 5*, 160–171.

Macrae, C. (2014). *Close Calls: Managing Risk and Resilience in Airline Flight Safety*. Palgrave Macmillan.

Madden, J., &Stewart, R. (1996). *One Hundred Rules for NASA Project Managers*.

Maqsood, T. (2006). *The Role of Knowledge Management in Supporting Innovation and Learning in Construction*. RMIT University.

Maqsood, T., Walker, D., & Finegan, A. (2004). Project histories and project learning–a knowledge management challenge. In: *20th Annual ARCOM Conference, 2004 Heriot Watt University*, Association of Researchers in Construction Management, 561–70.

Midha, A. (2005). How to incorporate "Lessons Learned" for sustained process improvements. In: *NDIA CMMI Technology Conference*, BAE Systems.

Milton, N. (2010). *The Lessons Learned Handbook: Practical Approaches to Learning From Experience*. Oxford: Chandos Publishing.

NASA. (2011). *LPR 7120.6 Lessons Learned Process for Sustained Process Improvements*. Langley Research Center. Revised: 8 March 2011.

Neef, D. (2005). Managing corporate risk through better knowledge management. *The Learning Organization, 12*, 112–124.

O'Dell, C., & Grayson, C.J. (1997). *Identifying and Transferring Internal Best Practices*. Houston, TX: APQC.

O'Dell, C., Grayson, C.J., & Essaides, N. (1998). *If Only We Knew What We Know: The Transfer of Internal Knowledge and Best Practice*. New York: Free Press.

O'Dell, C., & Hubert, C. (2011). *The New Edge in Knowledge: How Knowledge Management is Changing the Way We Do Business*. Hoboken, NJ: John Wiley & Sons.

Parry, K.W., & Hansen, H. (2007). The organizational story as leadership. *Leadership, 3*, 281–300.

Pässilä, A., Oikarinen, T., & Kallio, A. (2013). Creating dialogue by storytelling. *Journal of Workplace Learning, 25*, 159–177.

Peet, M. (2012). Leadership transitions, tacit knowledge sharing and organizational generativity. *Journal of Knowledge Management, 16*, 45–60.

Project Management Institute. (2016). *Exposure Draft – PMBOK® Guide-Sixth Edition (Standard Section) Exposure Draft*. Newtown Square, PA: PMI Inc.

Project Management Institute. (2017). *A Guide to the Project Management Body of Knowledge (PMBOK® Guide)*, Sixth Edition. Newtown Square, PA: PMI Inc.

Prusak, L. (2005). Storytelling in organizations. In: Denning, S. (Ed.), *Storytelling in Organizations: Why Storytelling is Transforming 21st Century Organizations and Management*. Elsevier-Butterworth-Heinemann.

Raelin, J. (2001). Public Reflection as the Basis of Learning. *Management Learning, 32*, 11–30.

Reason, J. (1997). *Managing the Risks of Organizational Accidents*. Aldershot; Brookfield, VT: Ashgate.

Reich, B.H., Gemino, A., & Sauer, C. (2008). Modelling the knowledge perspective of IT projects. *Project Management Journal, 39*, S4–S14.

Sanne, J.M. (2008). Incident reporting or storytelling? Competing schemes in a safety-critical and hazardous work setting. *Safety Science, 46*, 1205–1222.

Schindler, M., & Eppler, M.J. (2003). Harvesting project knowledge: A review of project learning methods and success factors. *International Journal of Project Management, 21*, 219–228.

Shergold, P. (2015). *Learning from Failure: Why Large Government Policy Initiatives Have Gone So Badly Wrong in the Past and How the Chances of Success in the Future Can Be Improved*. Australian Public Service Commission.

Simon, H.A. (1991). Bounded rationality and organizational learning. *Organization Science, 2*, 125–134.

Sims, D., Huxham, C., & Beech, N. (2009). On telling stories but hearing snippets: Sense-taking from presentations of practice. *Organization, 16*, 371–388.

Snowden, D. (2000). Storytelling and other organic tools for chief knowledge officers and chief learning officers. In: Phillips, J.J., & Bonner, D. (Eds.), *Leading Knowledge Management and Learning*. ASTD, 237–252.

Sole, D., & Wilson, D.G. (2002). *Storytelling in Organizations: The Power and Traps of Using Stories to Share Knowledge in Organizations.* LILA, Harvard Graduate School of Education, 1–12.

Swap, W., Leonard, D., Shields, M., & Abrams, L. (2001). Using mentoring and storytelling to transfer knowledge in the workplace. *Journal of Management Information Systems, 18,* 95–114.

Taylor, S., Fisher, D., & Dufresne, R. (2002). The aesthetics of management storytelling: A key to organizational learning. *Management Learning, 33,* 313–330.

Virolainen, T. (2014). *Learning from Projects: A Qualitative Metasummary.* Master's Degree in Knowledge Management and Information Networks, Lappeenranta University of Technology.

Von Zedtwitz, M. (2002). Organizational learning through post–project reviews in R&D. *R&D Management, 32,* 255–268.

Williams, T. (2007). *Post-Project Reviews to Gain Effective Lessons Learned.* Newtown Square, PA: Project Management Institute.

Williams, T. (2008). How do organisations learn lessons from projects–and do they? *IEEE Transactions in Engineering Management, 55,* 248–266.

Chapter 9

> Knowledge is of two kinds. We know a subject ourselves, or we know where we can find information upon it. When we enquire into any subject, the first thing we must do is to know what books have treated of it. This leads us to look at catalogues, and at the backs of books in libraries.
> – Samuel Johnson, 1709–1784

These sources were referenced and consulted while writing this chapter. This list is a sample of the approaches to technical and programmatic risk management and is meant to motivate more research and collection of resources to improve the understanding of the complexity of risk and its management and impact on the probability of project success.

We apologize in advance for any missed sources or books. When these are found, please send them for inclusion.

Acker, D.D. (Summer 1979). Management disciplines: Harbingers of successful programs. *Defense Systems Management Review, 2*(3), 7–20.

Alberts, C.J., et al. (1996). *Continuous Risk Management Handbook.* Software Engineering Institute, Carnegie Mellon University.

Ali, T., Boruah, H., & Dutta, P. (April 2012). Modeling uncertainty in risk assessment using double monte carlo method. *International Journal of Engineering and Innovation Technology (IJEIT), 1*(4), 114–118.

Alleman, G.B. (2014) *Performance–Based Project Management: Increasing the Probability of Project Success.* American Management Association.

Alleman, G.B., Coonce, T.J., & Price, R.A. (2014). Building a credible performance measurement baseline. *The Measurable News,* Issue 4.

ALTESS. (22 August 2007). *Probability of Program Success Operations Guide.* Acquisition, Logistics, & Technology Enterprise Systems & Services.

Alzaharna, I.T., Seering, W.P., & Yang, M.C. (2012). Exploration of the use of design methods with the design structure matrix for integrating new technologies into large complex systems. In: *Proceedings of the ASME 2012 International Design Engineering Technology Conferences & Computers and Information Engineering Conference,* August 12–15.

Apeland, S., Aven, T., & Nilsen, T. (2002). Quantifying uncertainty under a predictive, epistemic approach to risk analysis. *Reliability Engineering & System Safety, 75*(1), 93–102.

Arena, M.V., et al. (2013). *Managing Perspectives Pertaining to Root Cause Analyses of Nunn-McCrudy Breaches, Volume 4: Program Manager Tenure, Oversight of Acquisition Category II Programs, and Framing Assumptions.* RAND MG1171/4, Rand Corporation.

Atin, A. (2016). Project Risk Propagation Modeling of Engineering, Procurement and Construction. PhD thesis, Wayne State University.

Bartolomei, J.E., et al. (2012). Engineering systems matrix: An organizing framework for modeling large-scape complex systems. *Systems Engineering, 15*(1), 41–61.

Becerril, L., Sauer, M., & Lindemann, U. (2016). Estimating the effects of engineering changes in early stage product development. In: *18th International Dependency and Structural Modeling Conference*, August 29–30.

Beer, M. (2016). *Alternative Approaches to the Treatment of Epistemic Uncertainties in Risk Assessment.* Institute for Risk and Reliability, Leibniz Universität Hannover.

Blickstein, I., et al. (2012). *Root Cause Analyses of Nunn–McCurdy Breaches: Volume 2.* Rand Corporation, MG1171z2.

Bilardo, V.J., et al. (April 2008). *Seven Key Principles of Program and Project Success: Best Practices Survey,* NASA/TM-2008-214692.

Bolten, J.G., Leonard, R.S., Arena, M.V., Younossi, O., & Sollinger, J. (2008). *Sources of Weapon System Cost Growth: Analysis of 35 Major Defense Acquisition Programs*, MG-670-AF. Rand Corporation.

Bordley, R.F. (2014). Reference class forecasting: Resolving its challenge to statistical modeling. *The American Statistician, 68*(4), 221–229.

Browning, T.R. (November 2002). Adding value in product development by creating information and reducing risk. *IEEE Transactions on Engineering Management, 49*(4), 443–458.

Charette, R., Dwinnell, L., & McGarry, J. (August 2004). Understanding the roots of process performance failure. *CROSSTALK: The Journal of Defense Software Engineering*, 18–24.

Clemen, R.T. (1996). *Making Hard Decisions: An Introduction to Decision Analysis*, 2nd edition. Duxbury Press.

Conrow, E. (2003). *Effective Risk Management*, 2nd edition. AIAA.

Cooke-Davies, T. (2011). *Aspects of Complexity: Managing Projects in a Complex World.* Project Management Institute.

Cox, L.A.T. (2008). What's wrong with risk matrices? *Risk Analysis, 28*(2), 497–512.

Davis, D., & Philip, A.S. (21 March 2016). *Annual Growth of Contract Costs for Major Programs in Development and Early Production.* Acquisition Policy Analysis Center, Performance Assessments and Root–Cause Analyses, OUSD AT&L.

Davis, G.A., Giles, M.L., & Tate, D.M. (December 2017). *Complexity in an Unexpected Place: Quantities in Selected Acquisition Reports.* Institute for Defense Analyses, IDA P-8490.

Davis, P.K. (2002). *Analytic Architecture for Capabilities-Based Planning, Mission-System Analysis, and Transformation*, RAND MR-1513-OSD.

Davis, P.K. (2012). *Lessons from RAND's Work on Planning Under Uncertainty for National Security.* RAND Corporation, TR-1249.

Dezfuli, H. (21–22 September 2010). *NASA's Risk Management Approach, Workshop on Risk Assessment and Safety Decision Making Under Uncertainty.* Bethesda, MD: NASA.

Dezfuli, H., et al. (April 2010). *NASA Risk–Informed Decision-Making Handbook.* NASA/SP-2010-576, Version 1.0.

DOD. (20 June 2012). *Integrated Program Management Report (IPMR)*, DI-MGMT-81861.

van Dorp, J.R., & Duffey, M.R. (1999). Statistical dependence in risk analysis for project networks using Monte Carlo methods. *International Journal of Production Economics, 58*, 17–29.

Dwyer, M., Cameron, B., & Sazajnfarber, Z. (November 2015). A framework for studying cost growth on complex acquisition programs. *Systems Engineering, 18*(6), 568–583.

Erikson, J. (6 July 2016). *Analysis of Alternatives (AoA) Handbook: A Practical Guide to the Analysis of Alternatives: Office of Aerospace Studies.* Headquarter Air Force HAF/A5R-OAS.

Fang, C., Marle, F., & Xio, M. (2016). Applying importance measures to risk analysis in engineering project using a risk network model. *IEEE Systems Journal, 11*(3), 1548–1556.

Fleishman-Mayer, L., Arena, M., & McMahon, M.E. (2013). *A Risk Assessment Methodology and Excel Tool for Acquisition Programs.* RAND Corporation, RR 262.

Frazier, B., McBride, J., Hsu, A., & Weir, A. (8 May 2014). *Technical Risk Identification at Program Inception Product Overview. U.S. Space Program Mission Assurance Improvement Workshop (MAIW)*. Aerospace Corporation, Dulles, VA.

Galway, L.A. (February 2004). *Quantitative Risk Analysis for Project Management: A Critical Review*. RAND Corporation, WR-112-RC.

Gano, D. (2008). *Apollo Root Cause Analysis: Effective Solutions to Everyday Problems Every Time*, 3rd edition. Atlas Books.

GAO. (2015). *Defense Acquisitions: Assessments of Selected Weapon Programs*, GAO-15-342SP.

Garner, W.J. (1962). *Uncertainty and Structure as Psychological Concepts*. John Wiley & Sons.

Gerstein, D.M., et al. (2015). *Developing a Risk Assessment Methodology for the National Aeronautics and Space Administration*. RAND Corporation, RR 1537.

Grady, J.O. (2006). *Systems Requirements Analysis*. Academic Press.

Hahn, D.E. (27–29 May 2015). *Recognizing and Mitigating Risk in Acquisition Programs*. DAU Professional Development Institute.

Hamaker, J.W. (1994). But what will it cost? The history of NASA cost estimating. *Readings in Program Control*, 25–37.

H.A.S.C. (29 October 2013). *Twenty-Five Years of Acquisition Reform: Where Do We Go from Here?* Committee on Armed Services, House of Representatives.

Helton, J.C., & Burmaster, D.E. (1996). Treatment of aleatory and epistemic uncertainty in performance assessments for complex systems. *Reliability Engineering and System Safety, 54*(2–3), 91–94.

Hillson, D., & Simon, P. (2007). *Practical Risk Management: The ATOM Method*. Management Concepts.

Ho, V. (16 November 2010). *The Risk of Using Risk Matrix in the Assessing of Safety*. HAKRMS, Safety Engineering Lecture Series 2.2.

Hofbauer, J., et al. (2011). *Cost and Time Overruns for Major Defense Acquisition Programs: An Annotated Brief*. Washington, DC: Center for Strategic and International Studies.

Hubbard, D. (2009). *The Failure of Risk Management: Why It's Broken and How to Fix It*. John Wiley & Sons.

Hulett, D.T., & Hillson, D. (May 2006). Branching out: Decision trees offer a realistic approach to risk analysis. *PM Network*, 43.

Husband, M. (2013). Information on framing assumptions. PARCA in *Identifying Acquisition Framing Assumptions Through Structured Deliberation*, RAND, TL 153.

INCOSE, "Technical Measurements," prepared by Garry J. Roedler, Lockheed Martin and Cheryl Jones, US Army, INCOSE-TP-2003-020-01.

Jaber, H. (2016). *Modeling and Analysis of Propagation Risk in Complex Projects: Application to the Development of New Vehicles*. Chemical and Process Engineering, Université Paris-Saclay.

Jolly, S. (1 June 2009). Is software broken? IEEE Fourth International Conference of System of Systems Engineering, Albuquerque, New Mexico.

Karim, A.B.A., "The Development of an Empirical-Based Framework for Project Risk Management," PhD thesis, University of Manchester, 2014.

Kerzner, H. (1998). *Project Management: A Systems Approach to Planning, Scheduling and Controlling*. John Wiley & Sons.

Kim, Y., et al. (2015). *Acquisition of Space Systems, Past Performance and Future Challenges*, RAND MG1171z7. Rand Corporation.

der Kiureghian, A. (26–27 March 2007). Aleatory or epistemic? Does it matter? In: *Special Workshop on Risk Acceptance and Risk Communication*, Stanford University.

Kwak, Y.H., & Smith, B.M. (2009). Managing risks in mega defense acquisition projects: Performance, policy, and opportunities. *International Journal of Project Management, 27*, 812–820.

Laitonen, J. (Project manager), Losoi, H., Losoi, M., & Ylilammi, K. (24 May 2013). Tools for analyzing epistemic uncertainties in probabilistic risk analysis. Final report, Mat-2.4177 Seminar on Case Studies in Operations Research.

Lehman, D., Groenendaal, H., & Nolder, G. (2012). *Practical Spreadsheet Risk Modeling for Management*. CRC Press.

Lempert, R., & Collins, M. (27 August 2007). Managing the risk on uncertain threshold responses: Comparison of robust, optimum, and precautionary responses, *Risk Analysis*. Rand Corporation, 1009–1026.

Leveson, N., et al. (June 2005). *Risk Analysis of NASA Independent Technical Authority*. Massachusetts Institute of Technology.

Lorell, M.A., Leonard, R.S., & Doll, A. (2015). *Extreme Cost Growth: Themes from Six U. S. Air Force Major Defense Acquisition Programs*, RR-630-AF, RAND Corporation.

Lorell, M.A., Lowell, J.F., & Younossi, O. (2006). *Implementation Challenges for Defense Space Programs*, MG-431-AF. Rand Corporation.

Lorell, M.A., Payne, L.A., & Mehta, K.R. (2017). *Program Characteristics That Contribute to Cost Growth: A Comparison of Air Force Major Defense Acquisition Programs*. Rand Corporation, RR1761.

Maier, M., & Rechtin, E. (2009). *The Art of Systems Architecting*, 3rd edition. CRC Press.

Marle, F., & Vidal, L-A. (2011). Project risk management processes: Improving coordination using a clustering approach. *Research in Engineering Design*, 22, 189–206.

McManus, H., & Hastings, D. (2005). "A framework for understanding uncertainty and its mitigation and exploitation in complex systems. In: *Fifteenth* Annual *International Symposium of the International Council on Systems Engineering (INCOSE)*, 10–15 July 2005.

De Meyer, A., Loch, C.H., & Pich, M.T. (Winter 2002). Managing project uncertainty. *MIT Sloan Management Review*, 43(2), 60–67.

NASA. (December 2011a). *Probabilistic Risk Assessment Procedure Guide for NASA Managers and Practitioners*, NASA/SP-2011-3421, 2nd edition. NASA.

NASA. (2011b). *NASA Risk Management Handbook*, NASA/SP-2011-3422. NASA.

NASA. (July 2011c). *Joint Confidence Level Requirement: Policy and Issues*, NASA/TM-2011-216154. NASA.

NASA. (29 August 2013). Probabilistic schedule reserve allocation. NASA 2013 Cost Symposium.

NASA. (September 2014). *NPR 7120.5E, NASA Space Flight Program and Project Management Handbook*, NASA/SP-2014-3705. NASA.

NASA. (February 2015). *Appendix G: Cost Risk and Uncertainty Methodologies, NASA Cost Estimating Handbook*, Version 4.0. NASA.

Navy (September 2008). *Naval PoPS Guidebook, Guidance for the Implementation of Naval PoPS, A Program Health Assessment Methodology for Navy and Marine Corps Acquisition Programs*, Version 1.0. Department of the Navy.

Nilchiani, R.R., Mostashari, A., Rifkin, S., Bryzik, W., & Witus, G. (29 May 2013). *Quantitative risk—Phase 1*. Systems Engineering Research Center–University Affiliated Research Center, Stevens Institute of Technology.

Nilchiani, R.R., & Puglises, A. (30 April 2016). *A Complex Systems Perspective of Risk Mitigation and Modeling in Development and Acquisition Programs*. Naval Postgraduate School.

DePasquale, D., & Charania, A.C. (2008). *I-RaCM: A Fully Integrated Risk and Life Cycle Cost Model*. American Institute of Aeronautics and Astronautics.

Pawlikowski, E., Loverro, D., & Cristler, T. (Spring 2012). Disruptive challenges, new opportunities, and new strategies. *Strategic Studies Quarterly*, 6, 27–54.

Perez, E.J. (September 2016). *Air Force Project Risk Management – The Impact of Inconsistent Processes*. Thesis, Air Force Institute of Technology, AFIT-ENV-MS-16-S-047.

Petković, I. (2–8 September 2012). *Risk Management using Dependency Structure Matrix*. Workshop in Opatija, German Academic Exchange Service.

Price, R.A., & Alleman, G.B. (2016). *Critical Thinking on Critical Path Analysis*. College of Performance Management, EVM World.

Public Works and Government Services Canada. (May 2015). *Project Complexity and Risk Assessment Manual*, Version 5.

Raiffa, H. (1968). *Decision Analysis: Introductory Lectures on Choice Under Uncertainty*. Addison Wesley.

Razaque, A., Bach, C., Salama, N., & Alotaibi, A. (July 2012). Fostering project scheduling and controlling risk management. *International Journal of Business and Social Science, 3*(14), Special Issue.

Reeves, J.D. (19 May 2013). *The Impact of Risk Identification and Trend on Space Systems Project Performance.* PhD thesis, Schools of Engineering and Applied Science, The George Washington University.

Rendleman, J.D., & Faulconer, J.W. (August 2011). Escaping the space acquisition death spiral: A three-part series. *High Frontier Journal, 7*(4), 51–57.

Riesch, Hauke. (2011). Levels of uncertainty. In: Rosener, S., & Hillebrand, R. (Eds.), *Handbook of Risk Theory: Epistemology, Decision Theory, Ethics, and Social Implications of Risk.* Springer.

Roedler, G.J., & Jones, C. (27 December 2005). *Technical Measurement: A Collaborative Project of PSM, INCOSE, and Industry,* INCOSE-TP-2003-202-01.

Roedler, G.J., Rhodes, D.H., Schimmoller, H., & Jones, C. (29 January 2010). *Systems Engineering Leading Indicators Guide,* Version 2.0, MIT, INCOSE, and PSM.

Rogers, J.L., Korte, J.J., & Bilardo, V.J. (February 2006). *Development of a Genetic Algorithm to Automate Clustering of a Dependency Structure Matrix,* NASA/TM-2006-212279.

Salado, A., & Nilchiani, R.R. (2014). The concept of problem complexity. In: *Conference on Systems Engineering Research (CSER 2014), Procedia Computer Science,* 28

Scheinin, W. (27–29 February 2008). Start early and often: The need for persistent risk management in the early acquisition phases. *Paper to the Aerospace Corporation/Air Force SMC/NASA Seventh Symposium on Space Systems Engineering & Risk Management Conference.*

Schwartz, M. (30 April 2014). *Reform of the Defense Acquisition System.* United States Senate Committee on Armed Services, Congressional Research Service.

SMC. (5 September 2014). *Space and Missile Systems Center Risk Management Process Guide,* Version 2.0.

Timson, F.S. (December 1968). *Measurement of Technical Performance in Weapon System Development Programs: A Subjective Probability Approach,* RAND RM-5207-ARPA.

TOGAF. (21 July 2011). *Open Group Standard. TOGAF Version 9.1,* Document G116.

Tzeng, S. (2007). *Management Towards Success – Defense Business Systems Acquisition Probability of Success Model.* George Mason University.

USAF. (July 2008). *Probability of Program Success (PoPS) Model, SMART Integration, Operations Guide,* Version 1.0., U.S. Air Force.

USAF. (2013). *Air Force Instruction 90–802, Risk Management.*

Virine, L., & Trumper, M. (2003). *Project Think – Why Good Managers Make Poor Project Choices.* Gower Publishing Limited.

Vrouwenvelder, A.C.W.M. (2003). Uncertainty analysis for flood defense systems in the Netherland. In: *Proceedings, ESREL. European Safety and Reliability Conference 2003,* Maastricht, the Netherlands

Walker, W.E., Harremoës, P., Rotmans, J., van der Sluijs, J.P., van Asselt, M.B.A., Janssen, P., & Krayer von Krauss, M.P. (2003). Defining uncertainty: A conceptual basis for uncertainty management in model–based decision support. *Integrated Assessment, 4*(1), 5–17.

Williams, T. (2017). The nature of risk in complex projects. *Project Management Journal, 48*(4), 55–66.

Wood, H.L., & Ashton, P. (10 May 2010). The factors of project complexity. In: 18th CIB World Building Congress, Salford, United Kingdom.

Younossi, Obaid, et al. (2008). *Improving the Cost Estimation of Space Systems: Past Lessons and Future Recommendations,* RAND Project Air Force, MG-690.

Zack, M.H. (Summer 1999). Managing organizational ignorance. *Knowledge Directions, 1,* 36–49.

Zarikas, V., & Kitsos, C.P. (June 2015). Chapter: 18. Risk analysis with reference class forecasting adopting tolerance regions. In: *Theory and Practice of Risk Assessment.* Springer International.

Zhang, Y., Bai, S., & Guo, Y. (2010). The application of design structure matrix in project schedule management. In: *2010 International Conference on E-Business and E-Government,* 2813–2816.

Zio, E. (January 2007). From complexity science to reliability efficiency: A new way of looking at complex network systems and critical infrastructures. *International Journal of Critical Infrastructures, 3*(3/4), 488–508.

Chapter 10

> Knowledge is of two kinds. We know a subject ourselves, or we know where we can find information upon it. When we enquire into any subject, the first thing we must do is to know what books have treated of it. This leads us to look at catalogues, and at the backs of books in libraries.
> – Samuel Johnson, 1709–1784

These sources were referenced and consulted while writing this chapter. This list is a sample of the approaches to technical and programmatic risk management and is meant to motivate more research and collection of resources to improve the understanding of the complexity of risk and its management and impact on the probability of project success. These are separate from the References used to directly support contents of the chapter.

We apologize in advance for any missed sources or books. When these are found, please send them for inclusion.

Acker, D.D. (Summer 1979). Management disciplines: Harbingers of successful projects. *Defense Systems Management Review, 2*(3), 7–20.

Alleman, G.B. (2014). *Performance–Based Project Management: Increasing the Probability of Project Success.* American Management Association.

Aroonvatanaporn, P., Sinthop, C., & Boehm, B. (2010). *Reducing Estimation Uncertainty with Continuous Assessment: Tracking the 'Cone of Uncertainty'.* Center for Systems and Software Engineering, University of Southern California, Los Angeles, CA 90089, ASE'10, September 20–24, 2010, Antwerp, Belgium.

Atin, A. (2016). *Project Risk Propagation Modeling of Engineering, Procurement and Construction.* PhD thesis, Wayne State University.

Banazadeh, A., & Haji Jafari, M. (3 October 2012). A heuristic complexity-based method for cost estimation of aerospace systems. In: *Proceedings of the Institute of Mechanical Engineers, Part G: Journal of Aerospace Engineering, 227,* 1685–1700.

Bellos, V., Leopoulos, V., & Sfantsikopoulos, M. (13–15 February 2004). Cost uncertainty assessment and management: The integrated cost–risk analysis model. In: *Proceedings of the WSEAS International Conference, Information Systems, Decision Support Systems, Internet Computing,* Salzburg, Austria.

Bickel, P.J., Chen, A., & Levina, E. (2011). The method of moments and degree distributions for network models. *Annals of Statistics, 39*(5), 2280–2301.

Biedermann, W., & Lindemann, U. (November 2008). Cycles in the multiple–Domain matrix–Interpretation and applications. In: 10th International DSM Conference, Stockholm, Sweden.

Bronson, P. *Correlating Earned Value Management to Technical Performance.* Institute for Defense Analyses, Cost Analysis and Research Division. Unpublished internal paper.

Carroll, T.N., Burton, R.M. (March–June 2012). A contingency approach to designing project organizations: Theory and tools. *The Engineering Project Organization Journal, 2,* 5–14.

Chapman, C., & Ward, S. (2003). *Project Risk Management: Process, Techniques, and Insights,* 2nd edition. John Wiley & Sons.

Davis, G.A., Giles, M.L., & Tate, D.M. (December 2017). *Complexity in an Unexpected Place: Quantities in Selected Acquisition Reports.* Institute for Defense Analyses, IDA P-8490.

DOD. (20 June 2012). *Integrated Program Management Report (IPMR),* DI-MGMT-81861.

van Dorp, J.R., & Duffey, M.R. (1999). Statistical dependence in risk analysis for project networks using Monte Carlo methods. *International Journal of Production Economics, 58,* 17–29.

Eppinger, S.D., & Browning, T.R. (2012). *Design Structure Matrix Methods and Applications.* The MIT Press.

Filippazzo, G. (6–13 March 2004). Complexity based cost estimating relationships for space systems. In: *IEEE Aerospace Conference Proceedings,* Big Sky, MT.

Gano, D. (2008). *Apollo Root Cause Analysis: Effective Solutions to Everyday Problems Every Time*, 3rd edition. Atlas Books.

Grady, J.O. (2006). *Systems Requirements Analysis*. Academic Press.

Helton, J.C. (2009). *Conceptual and Computational Basis for the Quantification of Margins and Uncertainty*. Sandia National Laboratories, SAND2009-3055.

Helton, J.C., & Burmaster, D.E. (1996). Treatment of aleatory and epistemic uncertainty in performance assessments for complex systems. *Reliability Engineering and System Safety, 54*(2–3), 91–94.

Ho, V. (16 November 2010). *The Risk of Using Risk Matrix in the Assessing of Safety*. HAKRMS, Safety Engineering Lecture Series 2.2.

Holley, V., Janovic, M., & Yannou, B. (June 2014). Physical interface ontology for management of conflicts and risks in complex systems. *Concurrent Engineering – Research and Applications, 22*, 148–161.

Innal, F., Mourad, C., Bourareche, M., & Mohamed, A.S. (October 2013). Treatment of uncertainty in probabilistic risk assessment using Monte Carlo analysis. *3rd International Conference on Systems and Control (ICSC)*.

Jaber, H. (2016). *Modeling and Analysis of Propagation Risk in Complex Projects: Application to the Development of New Vehicles*. Chemical and Process Engineering, Université Paris-Saclay.

Kelton, W.D., Sadowski, R.P., & Zupick, N.B. (2014). *Simulation with Arena*. McGraw-Hill.

Kennedy, M.C., & O'Hagan, Anthony. (2001). Bayesian calibration of computer models. *Journal of the Royal Statistical Society, Series B, 63*(3), 425–464.

Latouche, G., & Ramaswami, V. (1 January 1987). *Introduction to Matrix Analytic Methods in Stochastic Modeling*. Society for Industrial and Applied Mathematics.

Lin, G., Engle, D.W., & Eslinger, P.W. (February 2012). *Survey and Evaluate Uncertainty Quantification Methodologies*. Pacific Northwest National Laboratory.

Litvinenko, A., & Matthies, H.G. (2014). *Inverse Problems and Uncertainty Quantification*. Center for Uncertainty Quantification, King Abdullah University of Science and Technology.

MacKenzie, C.A. (9 February 2014). *Summarizing Risk Using Risk Measures and Risk Indices*. Defense Resources Management Institute, Naval Postgraduate School, published in Risk Analysis.

Marle, F. (2008). Analysis of Current Project Risk Management Methodologies and Required Improvements (Working). École Centrale Paris.

Marle, F. (2010) Interactions–Based risk network simulation for project risk prioritization. PMI Research Conference: Defining the Future of Project Management, Washington, DC.

Marle, F., & Vidal, L.-A. (11–12 November 2008). Potential applications of DSM principles in project risk management. In: *10th International Design Structure Matrix Conference*.

Marle, F., & Vidal, L-A. (2011). Project risk management processes: Improving coordination using a clustering approach. *Research in Engineering Design, 22*, 189–206.

Mohan, S.N. (2002). Managing unmanned flight projects using methods in complex product development. *IEEE Aerospace Conference Proceedings, (7)*, 3478–3488.

Nilchiani, R.R., Mostashari, A., Rifkin, S., Bryzik, W., & Witus, G. (29 May 2013). *Quantitative risk—Phase 1*. Systems Engineering Research Center–University Affiliated Research Center, Stevens Institute of Technology.

Oduncuoglu, A., & Thomson, V. (15–18 August 2011). Evaluating the risk of change propagation. In: *International Conference on Engineering Design*.

Petković, I. (2–8 September 2012). *Risk Management using Dependency Structure Matrix*. Workshop in Opatija, German Academic Exchange Service.

Pilch, M., Trucano, T.G., & Helton, J.C. (September 2006). *Ideas Underlying Quantification of Margins and Uncertainties (QMU): A White*. Sandia National Laboratories Report SAND2006-5001.

Price, R.A., & Alleman, G.B. (2016). *Critical Thinking on Critical Path Analysis*. College of Performance Management, EVM World.

Rogers, J.L., Korte, J.J., & Bilardo, V.J. (February 2006). *Development of a Genetic Algorithm to Automate Clustering of a Dependency Structure Matrix*, NASA/TM-2006-212279.

Salado, A., & Nilchiani, R.R. (June 2013). Assessing the impact of uncertainty propagation to system requirements by evaluating requirement connectivity. In: *Annual INCOSE International Symposium*.

Scheinin, W. (27–29 February 2008). Start early and often: The need for persistent risk management in the early acquisition phases. *Paper to the Aerospace Corporation/Air Force SMC/NASA Seventh Symposium on Space Systems Engineering & Risk Management Conference*.

Schwabe, O., Sheha, E., & Erkoyuncu, J. (2015a). Geometric quantification of cost uncertainty propagation: A case study. *Procedia CIRP, 37*, 158–163.

Schwabe, O., Shehab, E., & Erkoyuncu, J. (2015b). Uncertainty quantification metrics for whole product life cycle cost estimates in aerospace innovation. *Progress in Aerospace Sciences, 77*, 1–24.

Stewart, D.V. (1981). The design structure system: A method for managing the design of complex systems. *IEEE Transactions on Engineering Management, 28*(3), 71–74.

Veland, H., & Aven, T. (2015). Improving the risk assessment of critical operations to better reflect uncertainties and the unforeseen. *Safety Science, 79*, 206–212.

Virine, L., & Trumper, M. (2013). *Project Think – Why Good Managers Make Poor Project Choices*. Gower Publishing Limited.

Walker, E., Hemsch, M., & West, T. (5–9 January 2015). Integrated uncertainty quantification for risk and resource management: Building confidence in design. In: *Frontiers of Uncertainty Management for Complex Aerospace Systems, 17th AIAA Non-Deterministic Approaches Conference*.

Walker, W.E., Harremoës, P., Rotmans, J., van der Sluijs, J.P., van Asselt, M.B.A., Janssen, P., & Krayer von Krauss, M.P. (2003). Defining uncertainty: A conceptual basis for uncertainty management in model-based decision support. *Integrated Assessment, 4*(1), 5–17.

Whitley, S. (13 August 2014). *Schedule Uncertainty Quantification for JCL Analysis*. Applied Physics Laboratory, Johns Hopkins University.

Wierman, M.J. (20 August 2010). *An Introduction to the Mathematics of Uncertainty: Including Set Theory, Logic, Probability, Fuzzy Sets, Rough Sets, and Evidence Theory*. Center for the Mathematics of Uncertainty, Creighton University.

Williams, T. (2017). The nature of risk in complex projects. *Project Management Journal, 48*(4), 55–66.

Yao, W., Guo, J., Chen, X., & van Tooren, M. (17–19 March 2010). Utilizing uncertainty multidisciplinary design optimization for conceptual design of space systems. In: *8th Conference on Systems Engineering Research*.

Yassine, A.A. (January 2004). *An Introduction to Modeling and Analyzing Complex Product Development Processes Using the Design Structure Matrix (DSM) Method*. Urbana, IL: University of Illinois at Urbana.

Chapter 11

Aaronaught. (29 September 2013a). *Do We Need a Weekly Project Status Meeting in Agile?* [Blog comment]. Retrieved from http://softwareengineering.stackexchange.com/questions/212835/do-we-need-a-weekly-project-status-meeting-in-agile.

Aaronaught. (29 September 2013b). *Do We Need a Weekly Project Status Meeting in Agile?* [Blog comment]. Retrieved from http://softwareengineering.stackexchange.com/questions/212835/do-we-need-a-weekly-project-status-meeting-in-agile.

Alleman, G. (19 August 2009). *Percent Complete?* Retrieved from http://herdingcats.typepad.com/my_weblog/2009/08/percent_complet.html.

Alleman, G. (7 July 2010). *Physical Percent of Planned Progress*. Retrieved from http://herdingcats.typepad.com/my_weblog/2010/07/physical-percent-of-planned-progress.html.

Alleman, G. (9 April 2014). *We Can Know the Business Value of What We Build?* Retrieved from http://herdingcats.typepad.com/my_weblog/2014/04/we-can-know-the-business-value-of-what-we-build.html.

Alleman, G. (30 November 2017). *Aleatory and Epistemic Uncertainty in Software Development Projects.* Retrieved from http://herdingcats.typepad.com/my_weblog/2017/11/aleatory-and-epistemic-uncertainty-in-software-development-projects.html.

Alleman, G. (21 June 2018). *The Fallacy of #NoEstimates.* Retrieved from http://herdingcats.typepad.com/my_weblog/2018/06/the-fallacy-of-noestimate.html. [Glen's blog]. Retrieved from http://herdingcats.typepad.com/my_weblog/, click on the #NoEstimates Category for many related posts.

Beck, K., Beedle, M., van Bennekum, A., Cockburn, A., Cunningham, W., Fowler, M., Grenning, J., Highsmith, J., Hunt, A., Jeffries, R., Kern, J., Marick, B., Martin, R.C., Mellor, S., Schwaber, K., Sutherland, J., & Thomas, D. (2001a). *Agile Manifesto.* Retrieved from http://agilemanifesto.org/.

Beck, K., Beedle, M., van Bennekum, A., Cockburn, A., Cunningham, W., Fowler, M., Grenning, J., Highsmith, J., Hunt, A., Jeffries, R., Kern, J., Marick, B., Martin, R.C., Mellor, S., Schwaber, K., Sutherland, J., & Thomas, D. (2001b). *Principles Behind the Agile Manifesto.* Retrieved from http://agilemanifesto.org/principles.html.

Brodinski, P. (n.d.). *Estimation and Forecasting.* Retrieved from https://www.agilealliance.org/estimation-and-forecasting/.

Flvbjerg, B. (2008). Curbing optimism bias and strategic misrepresentation in planning: Reference Class Forecasting in practice. *European Planning Studies, 16*(1), 3–21.

Goodrich, B. (7 November 2014). *Analogous vs Parametric Estimating.* Retrieved from https://www.linkedin.com/pulse/20141107215651-36477877-analogous-vs-parametric-estimating/.

Hamel, G., & Zanini, M. (October 2014). *Build a Change Platform, not a Change Program.* Retrieved from https://www.mckinsey.com/business-functions/organization/our-insights/build-a-change-platform-not-a-change-program.

Henderson, Kym. (Spring 2004). Further developments in Earned Schedule. *The Measurable News.*

International Society of Parametric Analysts. (2008). *Parametric Estimating Handbook,* 4th edition. Vienna, VA: International Society of Parametric Analysts.

Issacs, M. (n.d.). *The #NoEstimates Debate: An Unbiased Look at the Origins, Arguments, and Thought Leaders Behind the Movement.* Retrieved from https://techbeacon.com/noestimates-debate-unbiased-look-origins-arguments-thought-leaders-behind-movement.

JFG. (2013). The personal communication was a response from a colleague of mine to an article on Earned Schedule for Agile projects. The article was returned with a note, the text of which is in the quote. Taking the comment seriously, I spent time researching and developing a response. You see the results in this chapter.

Kahneman, D. (2011). *Thinking, Fast and Slow.* New York: Farrar, Straus and Giroux.

Kahneman, D., Slovic, P., & Tversky, A. (Eds.) (1982). *Judgment under Uncertainty: Heuristics and Biases.* Cambridge: Cambridge University Press.

Kahneman, D., & Tversky, A. (1984). Choices, values, and frames. *American Psychologist, 39*(4), 341–350. (See Tversky for more.)

Kotter, J.P. (1996). *Leading Change.* Boston, MA: Harvard Business School Press.

Lipke, W. (Summer 2003). Schedule is different. *The Measurable News.*

Lipke, W. (2006). Statistical methods applied to EVM…the next frontier. *CrossTalk, 19*(6), 20–23.

Lipke, W. (2009a). The to complete performance index…an expanded view. *The Measurable News, Issue 2,* 18–22.

Lipke, W. (2009b). *Earned Schedule.* Raleigh, NC: Lulu Publishing.

Lipke, W. (2013). Is something missing from project management? *CrossTalk, 26*(4), 16–20.

Lipke, W. (2016). Examination of the threshold for the to complete indexes. *The Measurable News, Issue 1,* 9–14.

Lipke, W. (2019). *Earned Schedule Forecasting Method Selection1.* Manuscript in preparation.

Little, J. (2014). *Lean Change Management: Innovative Practices for Managing Organizational Change.* Happy Melly Express.

Sprint Planning. (24 September 2014). *See Scrum Events/Sprint Planning.* Retrieved from https://www.scrumalliance.org/learn-about-scrum/the-scrum-guide.

Sulaiman, T., Barton, B., & Blackburn, T. (2006). AgileEVM—Earned value management in scrum projects. In: *Agile '06: Proceedings of the Conference on AGILE 2006*, IEEE Computer Society, 7–16.

Tversky, A., & Kahneman, D. (1974). Judgment under uncertainty: Heuristics and biases. *Science*, *185*(4157), 1124–1131.

Van De Velde, R. (2014). Earned schedule for Agile projects. *The Measurable News*, 1, 29–35.

Van De Velde, R. (2017a). Agile's earned schedule baseline. *The Measurable News*, 4, 37–43. See pp. 37–38 in particular.

Van De Velde, R. (17 January 2017b). *ES for Agile Projects…Relative Estimates Hit a Speed Bump* [Blog post]. Retrieved from http://www.projectflightdeck.com/cESExchange000.php?blog_archive=2017-01.

Van De Velde, R. (17 November 2017c). *ES for Agile Projects…Relative Estimates Hit More Speed Bumps* [Blog post]. Retrieved from http://www.projectflightdeck.com/cESExchange000.php?blog_archive=2017-11.

Van De Velde, R. (2018). *Schedule Adherence: Calculating the P-Factor* [Blog post]. Retrieved from http://www.projectflightdeck.com/cESExchange000.php?blog_archive=2018-04.

Velocity. (n.d.). Retrieved from https://www.agilealliance.org/glossary/velocity/.

Wake, B. (17 August 2003). *INVEST in Good Stories, and SMART Tasks* [Blog post]. Retrieved from http://xp123.com/articles/invest-in-good-stories-and-smart-tasks/.

Chapter 12

Chabris, C., & Simons, D. (2010). *The invisible gorilla: And Other Ways Our Institutions Deceive Us.* New York: Crown.

Deming, W.E. (1994). *The New Economics for Industry, Government, Education.* Cambridge, MA: The MIT Press.

Fleming, Q.W., & Koppelman, J.M. (2010). *Earned Value Project Management—Fourth Edition.* Newtown Square, PA: Project Management Institute, Inc.

Frei, F., & Morris, A. (2012). *Uncommon Service.* Boston, MA: Harvard Business School Publishing.

Frohnhoefer, R. (2018). *Accidental Project Manager: From Zero to Hero in 7 Days.* Escondido, CA: PPC Group, LLC.

Greiman, V.A. (2013). *Megaproject Management: Lessons on Risk and Project Management from the Big Dig.* Hoboken, NJ: John Wiley & Sons, Inc.

Haji-Kazemi, S., Andersen, B., & Krane, H.P. (2013). A review on possible approaches for detecting early warning signs in projects. *Project Management Journal*, *44*(5), 55–69.

Hayes Munson, K.A. (2012). How do you know the status of your project?: Project monitoring and controlling. Paper presented at PMI® Global Congress 2012—North America, Vancouver, British Columbia, Canada. Newtown Square, PA: Project Management Institute.

Johnson, J. (2006). *My Life is Failure: 100 Things You Should Know to Be a Successful Project Leader.* West Yarmouth, MA: The Standish Group International, Inc.

Klakegg, O.J., Williams, T., Walker, D.H.T., Andersen, B., & Magnussen, O.M. (2011). Identifying and acting on early warning signs in complex projects. Paper presented at PMI® Global Congress 2011—EMEA, Dublin, Leinster, Ireland. Newtown Square, PA: Project Management Institute.

Meadows, D. (2008). In: Wright, D. (Ed.) *Thinking in Systems: A Primer.* White River Junction, VT: Chelsea Green Publishing.

Moriux, Y. (2013). As work gets more complex, 6 rules to simplify. Paper presented at TED@BCG San Francisco. https://www.ted.com/talks/yves_morieux_as_work_gets_more_complex_6_rules_to_simplify/transcript. Accessed 7/31/2018.

Moriux, Y., & Tollman, P. (2014). *Six Simple Rules: How to Manage Complexity without Getting Complicated.* Boston, MA: Harvard Business School Publishing.

Project Management Institute. (2017). *A Guide to the Project Management Body of Knowledge (PMBOK® Guide)*, Sixth edition. Newtown Square, PA: Project Management Institute.

Senge, P.M., et al. (1994). *The Fifth Discipline Fieldbook: Strategies and Tools for Building a Learning Organization*. New York, NY: Doubleday.

Stackpole, C.S. (2010). *A User's Manual to the PMBOK® Guide*. Hoboken, NJ: John Wiley & Sons, Inc.

Williams, T., Klakegg, O.J., Walker, D.H.T., Andersen, B., & Magnussen, O.M. (2012). Identifying and acting on early warning signs in complex projects. *Project Management Journal*, *43*(2), 37–53.

Chapter 15

Aubry, M., Hobbs, B., & Thuillier, D. (2007). A new framework for understanding organisational project management through the PMO. *International Journal of Project Management*, *25*(4), 328–336.

Blomquist, T., & Packendorff, J. (1998). Learning from renewal projects: Content, context and embeddedness. In: Lundin, R.A., & Midler, C. (Eds.), *Projects as Arenas for Renewal and Learning Processes*. Boston, MA: Springer, 37–46.

Brown, J.S., & Duguid, P. (1998). Organizing knowledge. *California Management Review*, *40*(3), 90–111.

Ciborra, C.U. (1992). Innovation, networks and organizational learning. In: Antonelli, C. (Ed.), *The Economics of Information Networks*. North-Holland, 91–102.

Cicmil, S., & Hodgson, D. (2006). New possibilities for project management theory: A critical engagement. *Project Management Journal*, *37*(3), 111–122.

Cooke-Davies, T. (2002). The "real" success factors on projects. *International Journal of Project Management*, *20*(3), 185–190.

De Hertogh, S., Janssens, M.A.R.K., & Viaene, S. (2011). *Consolidating customer analytics at Mobistar Pragmatic Project Management in Business Intelligence (No. 2011-08)*. Vlerick Leuven Gent Management School.

Engwall, M. (2003) No project is an island: Linking project history and context. *Research Management*, *32*(5), 789–808.

Flyvbjerg, B., Garbuio, M., & Lovallo, D. (2009). Delusion and deception in large infrastructure projects: Two models for explaining and preventing executive disaster. *California Management Review*, *51*(2), 170–194.

Gann, D.M., & Salter, A.J. (2000). Innovation in project-based, service-enhanced firms: The construction of complex products and systems. *Research Policy*, *29*(7–8), 955–972.

Gourlay, S. (2003). The SECI model of knowledge creation: Some empirical shortcomings, 377–385.

Grabher, G. (2002). Cool projects, boring institutions: Temporary collaboration in social context. *Regional Studies*, *36*(3), 205–214.

Haimes, G. (2001). Project culture: A paradigm shift in project management. In: *Proceedings of the Project Management Institute Annual Seminars & Symposium*, Nashville, TN.

Hastie, S., & Wojewoda, S. (2015). Standish group 2015 chaos report-q&a with jennifer lynch. *Retrieved*, *1*(15), 2016.

Hobbs, B., & Aubry, M. (2007). A multi-phase research program investigating project management offices (PMOs): The results of phase 1. *Project Management Journal*, *38*(1), 74–86.

Hodgson, I. (2002). *Keeping Your Head Above Water*. Retrieved from http://www/conspectus.com/2002/november/article19.asp.

Jensen, R., & Szulanski, G. (2004). Stickiness and the adaptation of organizational practices in cross-border knowledge transfers. *Journal of International Business Studies*, *35*(6), 508–523.

Koskela, L., & Howell, G. (August 2002). The theory of project management: Explanation to novel methods. *Proceedings IGLC*, *10*(1), 1–11.

Miller, R., & Lessard, D.R. (2000). Public goods and private strategies: Making sense of project performance. In: Miller, R., & Lessard, D.R. (Eds.), *The Strategic Management of Large Engineering Projects: Shaping Institutions, Risks and Governance*. Cambridge, MA: MIT Press, 19–49.

Milosevic, D., & Patanakul, P. (2005). Standardized project management may increase development projects success. *International Journal of Project Management, 23*(3), 181–192.

Morris, P.W. (2013). *Reconstructing Project Management*. John Wiley & Sons.

Morris, P.W., & Geraldi, J. (2011). Managing the institutional context for projects. *Project Management Journal, 42*(6), 20–32.

Morris, P.W.G. (1994). *The Management of Projects*. London: Thomas Telford.

Nonaka, I., & Takeuchi, H. (1995). *The Knowledge Creation Company: How Japanese Companies Create the Dynamics of Innovation*. Oxford University Press.

Othman, R., & Hashim, N. (2004). Typologizing organizational amnesia. *The Learning Organization, 11*(3), 273–284.

Packendorff, J. (1995). Inquiring into the temporary organization: New directions for project management research. *Scandinavian Journal of Management, 11*(4), 319–333.

Polanyi, M. (1967). *The Tacit Dimension*. Garden City, NY: Anchor.

Project Management Institute. (2013a). *Pulse of the Profession: PMO Frameworks*. Project Management Institute.

Project Management Institute. (2013b). *Pulse of the Profession In-Depth Report: The Impact of PMOs on Strategy Implementation*. Project Management Institute.

Project Management Institute. (2015). *Pulse of the Profession: Capturing the Value of Project Management*. Project Management Institute.

Project Management Institute. (2017a). *Pulse of the Profession: 9th Global Project Management Survey*. Project Management Institute.

Project Management Institute. (2017b). *A Guide to the Project Management Body of Knowledge (PMBOK Guide)*, 6th edition. Project Management Institute.

Schon, D. (1938). The reflective practitioner. *New York*, 1083.

Shenhar, A.J., & Dvir, D. (2007). *Reinventing Project Management: The Diamond Approach to Successful Growth and Innovation*. Harvard Business Review Press.

Silva, M. (2017). *Managing Projects for Legacy: The Role of Institutional Barriers in Rio 2016 Olympic Games*. MSc Dissertation in Strategic Management of Projects (unpublished). UCL, London.

Silva, M., & Jeronimo, C. (2013). From Taylor to Tailoring – In pursuit of the organizational fit. In: *Second International Scientific Conference on Project Management in the Baltic Countries*.

Suda, L.V. (2007). The meaning and importance of culture for project success. Paper presented at PMI® Global Congress 2007—EMEA, Budapest, Hungary, Newtown Square, PA: Project Management Institute.

Szulanski, G. (1996). Exploring internal stickiness: Impediments to the transfer of best practice within the firm. *Strategic Management Journal, 17*(S2), 27–43.

Winter, M., Smith, C., Morris, P., & Cicmil, S. (2006). Directions for future research in project management: The main findings of a UK government-funded research network. *International Journal of Project Management, 24*(8), 638–649.

Yazici, H.J. (2009). The role of project management maturity and organizational culture in perceived performance. *Project Management Journal, 40*(3), 14–33.

Chapter 16

Adoko, M.T., Mazzuchi, T.A., & Sarkani, S. (2015). Developing a cost overrun predictive model for complex systems development projects. *Project Management Journal, 46*(6), 111–125.

Ahern, T., Leavy, B., & Byrne, P.J. (2014). Complex project management as complex problem solving: A distributed knowledge management perspective. *International Journal of Project Management, 32*(8), 1371–1381.

Akkermans, H., & van Oorschot, K.E. (2016). Pilot error? Managerial decision biases as an explanation for disruptions in aircraft development. *Project Management Journal, 47*(2), 79–102.

Alshawi, M., Goulding, J., Al Nahyan, M.T., Sohal, A.S., Fildes, B.N., & Hawas, Y.E. (2012). Transportation infrastructure development in the UAE: Stakeholder perspectives on management practice. *Construction Innovation, 12*(4), 492–514.

Anthopoulos, L., Reddick, C.G., Giannakidou, I., & Mavridis, N. (2016). Why e-government projects fail? An analysis of the Healthcare.gov website. *Government Information Quarterly, 33*(1), 161–173.

Art Gowan, J. Jr., & Mathieu, R.G. (2005). The importance of management practices in IS project performance: An empirical study. *Journal of Enterprise Information Management, 18*(2), 235–255.

Bing, L., Akintoye, A., Edwards, P.J., & Hardcastle, C. (2005). The allocation of risk in PPP/PFI construction projects in the UK. *International Journal of Project Management, 23*(1), 25–35.

Brady, T., & Davies, A. (2014). Managing structural and dynamic complexity: A tale of two projects. *Project Management Journal, 45*(4), 21–38.

Braun, V., & Clarke, V. (2006). Using thematic analysis in psychology. *Qualitative Research in Psychology, 3*(2), 77–101.

Brookes, N.J., & Locatelli, G. (2015). Power plants as megaprojects: Using empirics to shape policy, planning, and construction management. *Utilities Policy, 36*, 57–66.

Chang, C.Y. (2013). Understanding the hold-up problem in the management of megaprojects: The case of the Channel Tunnel Rail Link project. *International Journal of Project Management, 31*, 628–637.

Chua, C.E.H., Lim, W.-K., Soh, C., & Sia, S.K. (2012). Enacting clan control in complex IT projects: A social capital perspective. *MIS Quarterly-Management Information Systems, 36*(2), 577.

Clarke, N. (2010). Emotional intelligence and its relationship to transformational leadership and key project manager competences. *Project Management Journal, 41*(2), 5–20.

Cooke-Davies, T. (2002). The "real" success factors in projects. *International Journal of Project Management, 20*(3), 185–190.

Davies, A., & Mackenzie, I. (2014). Project complexity and systems integration: Constructing the London 2012 Olympics and Paralympics Games. *International Journal of Project Management, 32*(5), 773–790.

Davis, K. (2014). Different stakeholder groups and their perceptions of project success. *International Journal of Project Management, 32*(2), 189–201.

Dey, I. (2003). *Qualitative Data Analysis: A User Friendly Guide for Social Scientists*. Routledge.

Dimitriou, H.T., Ward, E.J., & Wright, P.G. (2013). Mega transport projects—Beyond the 'iron triangle': Findings from the OMEGA research programme. *Progress in Planning, 86*, 1–43.

Dvir, D., Ben-David, A., Sadeh, A., & Shenhar, A.J. (2006). Critical managerial factors affecting defence projects success: A comparison between neural network and regression analysis. *Engineering Applications of Artificial Intelligence, 19*(5), 535–543.

Ferratt, T.W., Ahire, S., & De, P. (2006). Achieving success in large projects: Implications from a study of ERP implementations. *Interfaces, 36*(5), 458–469.

Flyvbjerg, B. (2008). Curbing optimism bias and strategic misrepresentation in planning: Reference class forecasting in practice. *European Planning Studies, 16*(1), 3–21.

Flyvbjerg, B. (2014). What you should know about megaprojects and why: An overview. *Project Management Journal, 45*(2), 6–19.

Flyvbjerg, B., Bruzelius, N., & Rothengatter, W. (2003). *Megaprojects and Risk: An Anatomy of Ambition*. Cambridge University Press.

Flyvbjerg, B., Stewart, A., & Budzier, A. (2016). The Oxford Olympics Study 2016: Cost and cost overrun at the games. *Said Business School WP 2016–20*. SSRN. Retrieved from https://ssrn.com/abstract=2804554 or doi: 10.2139/ssrn.2804554.

GAPPS. (2007). *A Framework for Performance Based Competency Standards for Global Level 1 and 2 Project Managers*. Global Alliance for Project Performance Standards.

Giezen, M. (2012). Keeping it simple? A case study into the advantages and disadvantages of reducing complexity in mega project planning. *International Journal of Project Management, 30*(7), 781–790.

Guest, G., MacQueen, K.M., & Namey, E.E. (2011). *Applied Thematic Analysis.* Sage.

Hall, M., Kutsch, E., & Partington, D. (2012). Removing the cultural and managerial barriers in project to project learning: A case from the UK public sector. *Public Administration, 90*(3), 664–684. doi: 10.1111/j.1467-9299.2011.01980.x.

Han, S.H., Yun, S., Kim, H., Kwak, Y.H., Park, H.K., & Lee, S.H. (2009). Analyzing schedule delay of mega project: Lessons learned from Korea train express. *IEEE Transactions on Engineering Management, 56*(2), 243–256.

Hartmann, A., Ling, F.Y.Y., & Tan, J.S. (2009). Relative importance of subcontractor selection criteria: Evidence from Singapore. *Journal of Construction Engineering and Management, 135*(9), 826–832.

Hogg, M.A., Van Knippenberg, D., & Rast, D.E. (2012). Intergroup leadership in organizations: Leading across group and organizational boundaries. *Academy of Management Review, 37*(2), 232–255.

Hui, P.P., Davis–Blake, A., & Broschak, J.P. (2008). Managing interdependence: The effects of outsourcing structure on the performance of complex projects*. *Decision Sciences, 39*(1), 5–31.

Hyväri, I. (2006). Success of projects in different organizational conditions. *Project Management Journal, 37*(4), 31–42.

Ika, L. (2009). Project success as a topic in project management journals. *Project Management Journal, 40*(4), 6–19.

Janssen, M., Van Der Voort, H., & van Veenstra, A.F. (2015). Failure of large transformation project from the viewpoint of complex adaptive systems: Management principles for dealing with project dynamics. *Information Systems Frontiers, 17*(1), 15–29.

Jugdev, K., & Müller, R. (2005). A retrospective look at our evolving understanding of project success. *Project Management Journal, 36*(4), 19–31.

Kardes, I., Ozturk, A., Cavusgil, S.T., & Cavusgil, E. (2013). Managing global megaprojects: Complexity and risk management. *International Business Review, 22*(6), 905–917.

Karlsen, J.T., Andersen, J., Birkely, L.S., & Ødegård, E. (2005). What characterizes successful IT projects. *International Journal of Information Technology & Decision Making, 4*(04), 525–540.

Kent, D.C., & Becerik-Gerber, B. (2010). Understanding construction industry experience and attitudes toward integrated project delivery. *Journal of Construction Engineering and Management, 136*(8), 815–825.

Khosravi, P., Rezvani, A., Subasinghage, M., & Perera, M. (January 2012). Individuals' absorptive capacity in enterprise system assimilation. In: *ACIS 2012: Location, location, location: Proceedings of the 23rd Australasian Conference on Information Systems,* ACIS, 1–7.

Koppenjan, J., Veeneman, W., Van der Voort, H., Ten Heuvelhof, E., & Leijten, M. (2011). Competing management approaches in large engineering projects: The Dutch RandstadRail project. *International Journal of Project Management, 29*(6), 740–750.

Kwak, Y.H., & Smith, B.M. (2009). Managing risks in mega defence acquisition projects: Performance, policy, and opportunities. *International Journal of Project Management, 27*(8), 812–820.

Lech, P. (2013). Time, budget, and functionality?—IT project success criteria revised. *Information Systems Management, 30*(3), 263–275.

Levy, Y., & Ellis, T.J. (2006). A systems approach to conduct an effective literature review in support of information systems research. *Informing Science: International Journal of an Emerging Transdiscipline, 9*(1), 181–212.

Ling, Y., & Lau, B. (2002). A case study on the management of the development of a large-scale power plant project in East Asia based on design-build arrangement. *International Journal of Project Management, 20*(6), 413–423.

Liu, L., & Leitner, D. (2012). Simultaneous pursuit of innovation and efficiency in complex engineering projects—A study of the antecedents and impacts of ambidexterity in project teams. *Project Management Journal, 43*(6), 97–110.

Liu, S., & Wang, L. (2016). Influence of managerial control on performance in medical information system projects: The moderating role of organizational environment and team risks. *International Journal of Project Management*, *34*(1), 102–116.

Liu, Z.-Z., Zhu, Z.-W., Wang, H.-J., & Huang, J. (2016). Handling social risks in government-driven mega project: An empirical case study from West China. *International Journal of Project Management*, *34*(2), 202–218.

Locatelli, G., & Mancini, M. (2012). Looking back to see the future: Building nuclear power plants in Europe. *Construction Management and Economics*, *30*(8), 623–637.

Locatelli, G., Mancini, M., & Romano, E. (2014). Systems Engineering to improve the governance in complex project environments. *International Journal of Project Management*, *32*(8), 1395–1410.

Long, N.D., Ogunlana, S., Quang, T., & Lam, K.C. (2004). Large construction projects in developing countries: A case study from Vietnam. *International Journal of Project Management*, *22*(7), 553–561.

Lyneis, J.M., Cooper, K.G., & Els, S.A. (2001). Strategic management of complex projects: A case study using system dynamics. *System Dynamics Review*, *17*(3), 237–260. doi: 10.1002/sdr.213.

Mazur, A., Pisarski, A., Chang, A., & Ashkanasy, N.M. (2014). Rating defence major project success: The role of personal attributes and stakeholder relationships. *International Journal of Project Management*, *32*(6), 944–957. doi: 10.1016/j.ijproman.2013.10.018.

McGillivray, S., Greenberg, A., Fraser, L., & Cheung, O. (2009). Key factors for consortial success: Realizing a shared vision for interlibrary loan in a consortium of Canadian libraries. *Interlending & Document Supply*, *37*(1), 11–19.

Mok, K.Y., Shen, G.Q., & Yang, J. (2015). Stakeholder management studies in mega construction projects: A review and future directions. *International Journal of Project Management*, *33*(2), 446–457.

Molloy, E., & Chetty, T. (2015). The rocky road to legacy: Lessons from the 2010 FIFA World Cup South Africa stadium program. *Project Management Journal*, *46*(3), 88–107.

Morgan, G., & Smircich, L. (1980). The case for qualitative research. *Academy of Management Review*, *5*(4), 491–500.

Müller, R., & Jugdev, K. (2012). Critical success factors in projects: Pinto, Slevin, and Prescott-The elucidation of project success. *International Journal of Managing Projects in Business*, *5*(4), 757–775.

Müller, R., & Turner, R. (2007). The influence of project managers on project success criteria and project success by type of project. *European Management Journal*, *25*(4), 298–309.

Neuendorf, K.A. (2002). *The Content Analysis Guidebook*. Sage.

Ogunlana, S.O. (2008). Critical COMs of success in large-scale construction projects: Evidence from Thailand construction industry. *International Journal of Project Management*, *26*(4), 420–430.

Patanakul, P. (2014). Managing large-scale IS/IT projects in the public sector: Problems and causes leading to poor performance. *The Journal of High Technology Management Research*, *25*(1), 21–35.

Pemsel, S., & Wiewiora, A. (2013). Project management office a knowledge broker in project-based organisations. *International Journal of Project Management*, *31*(1), 31.

Pinto, J.K., & Slevin, D.P. (1987). Critical factors in successful project implementation. *IEEE Transactions on Engineering Management*, *1*, 22–27.

Remington, K., & Pollack, J. (2007). *Tools for Complex Projects*. Gower Publishing, Ltd.

Rezvani, A., Barrett, R., & Khosravi, P. (2018). Investigating the relationships among team emotional intelligence, trust, conflict and team performance. *Team Performance Management: An International Journal*, *25*, 120–137.

Rezvani, A., Chang, A., Wiewiora, A., Ashkanasy, N.M., Jordan, P.J., & Zolin, R. (2016). Manager emotional intelligence and project success: The mediating role of job satisfaction and trust. *International Journal of Project Management*, *34*(7), 1112–1122.

Rezvani, A., & Khosravi, P. (2018). A comprehensive assessment of project success within various large projects. *The Journal of Modern Project Management*, *6*(1), 114–122.

Rezvani, A., Khosravi, P., & Ashkanasy, N.M. (2018). Examining the interdependencies among emotional intelligence, trust, and performance in infrastructure projects: A multilevel study. *International Journal of Project Management, 36*(8), 1034–1046.

Rezvani, A., Khosravi, P., & Dong, L. (2017). Motivating users toward continued usage of information systems: Self-determination theory perspective. *Computers in Human Behavior, 76*, 263–275.

Rezvani, A., Khosravi, P., Subasinghage, M., & Perera, M. (January 2012). How does contingent reward affect enterprise resource planning continuance intention? The role of contingent reward transactional leadership. In: *ACIS 2012: Location, location, location: Proceedings of the 23rd Australasian Conference on Information Systems*, ACIS, 1–9.

Ritchie, J., Lewis, J., Nicholls, C.M., & Ormston, R. (Eds.) (2013). *Qualitative Research Practice: A Guide for Social Science Students and Researchers*. Sage.

Robinson, C. (2002). *Real World Research: A Resource for Social Scientists and Practitioner-Researchers*, 2nd edition. Oxford: Blackwell Publishers Ltd.

Robinson Fayek, A., Revay, S.O., Rowan, D., & Mousseau, D. (2006). Assessing performance trends on industrial construction mega projects. *Cost Engineering, 48*(10), 16–21.

Rose, J., & Schlichter, B.R. (2013). Decoupling, re-engaging: Managing trust relationships in implementation projects. *Information Systems Journal, 23*(1), 5–33. doi: 10.1111/j.1365-2575.2011.00392.x.

Sauer, C., Gemino, A., & Reich, B.H. (2007). The impact of size and volatility on IT project performance. *Communications of the ACM, 50*(11), 79–84.

Savolainen, P., Ahonen, J.J., & Richardson, I. (2012). Software development project success and failure from the supplier's perspective: A systematic literature review. *International Journal of Project Management, 30*(4), 458–469.

Shenhar, A.J., Holzmann, V., Melamed, B., & Zhao, Y. (2016). The challenge of innovation in highly complex projects: What can we learn from boeing's dreamliner experience? *Project Management Journal, 47*(2), 62–78.

Slywotzky, A., & Wise, R. (2003). The dangers of product-driven success: What's the next growth act? *Journal of Business Strategy, 24*(2), 16–25.

Söderlund, J., & Lenfle, S. (2013). Making project history: Revisiting the past, creating the future. *International Journal of Project Management, 31*(5), 653–662.

Somech, A., Desivilya, H.S., & Lidogoster, H. (2009). Team conflict management and team effectiveness: The effects of task interdependence and team identification. *Journal of Organizational Behavior, 30*(3), 359–378.

Tai, S., Wang, Y., & Anumba, C. (2009). A survey on communications in large-scale construction projects in China. *Engineering, Construction and Architectural Management, 16*(2), 136–149.

Thamhain, H. (2013). Managing risks in complex projects. *Project Management Journal, 44*(2), 20–35. doi: 10.1002/pmj.21325.

Toor, S.-u.-R., & Ogunlana, S.O. (2009a). Construction professionals' perception of critical success factors for large-scale construction projects. *Construction Innovation, 9*(2), 149–167.

Toor, S.-u.-R., & Ogunlana, S.O. (2009b). Ineffective leadership: Investigating the negative attributes of leaders and organizational neutralizers. *Engineering, Construction and Architectural Management, 16*(3), 254–272.

Toor, S.-u.-R., & Ogunlana, S.O. (2010). Beyond the 'iron triangle': Stakeholder perception of key performance indicators (KPIs) for large-scale public sector development projects. *International Journal of Project Management, 28*(3), 228–236. doi: 10.1016/j.ijproman.2009.05.005.

Tranfield, D., Denyer, D., & Smart, P. (2003). Towards a methodology for developing evidence-informed management knowledge by means of systematic review. *British Journal of Management, 14*(3), 207–222.

Turner, R., & Zolin, R. (2012). Forecasting success on large projects: Developing reliable scales to predict multiple perspectives by multiple stakeholders over multiple time frames. *Project Management Journal, 43*(5), 87–99.

Van Marrewijk, A., Clegg, S.R., Pitsis, T.S., & Veenswijk, M. (2008). Managing public–private megaprojects: Paradoxes, complexity, and project design. *International Journal of Project Management, 26*(6), 591–600.

Venkatesh, V., Morris, M.G., Davis, G.B., & Davis, F.D. (2003). User acceptance of information technology: Toward a unified view. *MIS Quarterly, 27*, 425–478.

Williams, T. (2016). Identifying success factors in construction projects: A case study. *Project Management Journal, 47*(1), 97–112

Whitty, S.J., & Maylor, H. (2009). And then came complex project management (revised). *International Journal of Project Management, 27*(3), 304–310.

Yang, J., Shen, G.Q., Ho, M., Drew, D.S., & Xue, X. (2011). Stakeholder management in construction: An empirical study to address research gaps in previous studies. *International Journal of Project Management, 29*(7), 900–910.

Yau, N.-J., & Yang, J.-B. (2012). Factors causing design schedule delays in turnkey projects in Taiwan: An empirical study of power distribution substation projects. *Project Management Journal, 43*(3), 50–61. doi: 10.1002/pmj.21265.

Yetton, P., Martin, A., Sharma, R., & Johnston, K. (2000). A model of information systems development project performance. *Information Systems Journal, 10*(4), 263–289.

Zhang, L., & Fan, W. (2013). Improving performance of construction projects: A project manager's emotional intelligence approach. *Engineering, Construction and Architectural Management, 20*(2), 195–207.

Chapter 17

Abdel-Hamid, T.K. (2010). Single-loop project controls: Reigning paradigms or straitjackets? *Project Management Journal, 42*(1), 17–30.

Adair, C.E., Simpson, E., Casebeer, A.L., Birdsell, J.M., Hayden, K.A., & Lewis, S. (2006). Performance measurement in healthcare: Part II—State of the science findings by stage of the performance measurement process. *Healthcare Policy, 2*(1), 56–78.

Agostino, D., & Arnaboldi, M. (2015). How performance measurement systems support managerial actions in networks: Evidence from an Italian case study. *Public Organization Review, 15*(1), 117–137. doi: 10.1007/s11115-013-0264-5.

Andersen, B., Busi, M., & Onsøyen, L.E. (2014). Performance management practice and discipline: Moving forward or standing still? *International Journal of Business Performance Management, 15*(2), 117–126. doi: 10.1504/ijbpm.2014.060149.

Atkinson, R. (1999). Project management: Cost, time and quality, two best guesses and a phenomenon, its time to accept other success criteria. *International Journal of Project Management, 17*(6), 337–342. doi: 10.1016/S0263-7863(98)00069-6.

Aubry, M., & Lavoie-Tremblay, M. (2018). Rethinking organizational design for managing multiple projects. *International Journal of Project Management, 36*(1), 12–26. doi: 10.1016/j.ijproman.2017.05.012.

Barrett, S.M. (2004). Implementation studies: Time for a revival? Personal reflections on 20 years of implementation studies. *Public Administration, 82*(2), 249–262.

Behn, R.D. (2003). Why measure performance? Different purposes require different measures. *Public Administration Review, 63*(5), 586–606.

Benítez-Ávila, C., Hartmann, A., Dewulf, G., & Henseler, J. (2018). Interplay of relational and contractual governance in public-private partnerships: The mediating role of relational norms, trust and partners' contribution. *International Journal of Project Management, 36*(3), 429–443. doi: 10.1016/j.ijproman.2017.12.005.

Besner, C., & Hobbs, B. (2013). Contextualized project management practice: A cluster analysis of practices and best practices. *Project Management Journal, 44*(1), 17–34.

Bevan, G., & Hood, C. (2006a). Health policy: Have targets improved performance in the English NHS? *BMJ: British Medical Journal, 332*(7538), 419–422.

Bevan, G., & Hood, C. (2006b). What's measured is what matters: Targets and gaming in the English public health care system. *Public Administration, 84*(3), 517–538.

Biedenbach, T., & Müller, R. (2012). Absorptive, innovative and adaptive capabilities and their impact on project and project portfolio performance. *International Journal of Project Management, 30*(5), 621–635. doi: 10.1016/j.ijproman.2012.01.016.

Biesenthal, C., & Wilden, R. (2014). Multi-level project governance: Trends and opportunities. *International Journal of Project Management, 32*(8), 1291–1308. doi: 10.1016/j.ijproman.2014.06.005.

Bird, S.M., David, C., Farewell, V.T., Harvey, G., Tim, H., & Peter, C. (2005). Performance indicators: Good, bad, and ugly. *Journal of the Royal Statistical Society: Series A (Statistics in Society), 168*(1), 1–27.

Bourne, M., Mills, J., Wilcox, M., Neely, A., & Platts, K. (2000). Designing, implementing and updating performance measurement systems. *International Journal of Operations & Production Management, 20*(7), 754–771.

Bourne, M., Neely, A., Mills, J., & Platts, K. (2003). Implementing performance measurement systems: A literature review. *International Journal Business Performance Management, 5*(1), 1–24.

Bovens, M., Schillemans, T., & 't Hart, P. (2008). Does public accountability work? An assessment tool. *Public Administration, 86*(1), 225–242.

Bozeman, Barry. (2007). *Public Values and Public Interest: Counterbalancing Economic Individualism.* Washington, D.C.: Georgetown University Press.

Bredillet, C., Yatim, F., & Ruiz, P. (2010). Project management deployment: The role of cultural factors. *International Journal of Project Management, 28*(2), 183–193. doi: 10.1016/j.ijproman.2009.10.007.

Brunet, M., & Aubry, M. (2016). The three dimensions of a governance framework for major public projects. *International Journal of Project Management, 34*(8), 1596–1607. doi: 10.1016/j.ijproman.2016.09.004.

Bryde, D.J. (2003). Modelling project management performance. *International Journal of Quality & Reliability Management, 20*(2), 229–254.

Center for Business Practices. (2005). *Measures of Project Management Performance and Value: A Benchmark of Current Business Practices.* Center for Business Practices.

Chapman, R.J. (2016). A framework for examining the dimensions and characteristics of complexity inherent within rail megaprojects. *International Journal of Project Management, 34*(6), 937–956. doi: 10.1016/j.ijproman.2016.05.001.

Cooke-Davies, T. (2002). The "real" success factors on projects. *International Journal of Project Management, 20*, 185–190.

Davies, A., & Brady, T. (2016). Explicating the dynamics of project capabilities. *International Journal of Project Management, 34*(2), 314–327. doi: 10.1016/j.ijproman.2015.04.006.

Davies, A., Dodgson, M., & Gann, D. (2016). Dynamic capabilities in complex projects: The case of London Heathrow terminal 5. *Project Management Journal, 47*(2), 26–46. doi: 10.1002/pmj.21574.

De Lancer Julnes, P. (2006). Performance measurement : An effective tool for government accountability? The debate goes on. *Evaluation, 12*(2), 219–235.

De Lancer Julnes, P., & Holzer, M. (2001). Promoting the utilization of performance measures in public organizations: An empirical study of factors affecting adoption and implementation. *Public Administration Review, 61*(6), 693–708.

DeVore, S., & Champion, R.W. (2011). Driving population health through accountable care organizations. *Health Affairs, 30*(1), 41–50.

Dubnick, M.J., & Frederickson, H.G. (2009). Accountable agents: Federal performance measurement and third-party government. *Journal of Public Administration Research and Theory, 20*(suppl. 1), i143–i159.

Dupuis, J.-P. (2011). Performance et organisation multiculturelle: le cas d'entreprises montréalaises. *Les Cahiers du Cedimes, 5*(2), 9–28.

Eccles, R. (1991). The performance measurennent manifesto. *Harvard Business Review, 69*(1), 131–137.

Eddy, D.M. (1998). Performance measurement: Problems and solutions. *Health Affairs, 17*(4), 7–25.

Eskerod, P., Huemann, M., & Ringhofer, C. (2015). Stakeholder inclusiveness: Enriching project management with general stakeholder theory. *Project Management Journal, 46*(6), 42–53. doi: 10.1002/pmj.21546.

Floricel, S., Michela, J.L., & Piperca, S. (2016). Complexity, uncertainty-reduction strategies, and project performance. *International Journal of Project Management, 34*(7), 1360–1383. doi: 10.1016/j.ijproman.2015.11.007.

Floricel, S., Piperca, S., & Banik, M. (2011). *Increasing Project Flexibility: The Response Capacity of Complex Projects*. Project Management Institute.

Flyvbjerg, B. (2001). *Making Social Science Matter: Why Social Inquiry Fails and How It Can Succeed Again*. Cambridge University Press.

Flyvbjerg, B. (2013). Quality control and due diligence in project management: Getting decisions right by taking the outside view. *International Journal of Project Management, 31*(5), 760–774. doi: 10.1016/j.ijproman.2012.10.007.

Flyvbjerg, B. (2014). What you should know about Megaprojects and why: An overview. *Project Management Journal, 45*(2), 6–19.

Flyvbjerg, B., Bruzelius, N., & Rothengatter, W. (2003). *Megaprojects and Risk: An Anatomy of Ambition*. Cambridge: Cambridge University Press.

Flyvbjerg, B., Garbuio, M., & Lovallo, D. (2009). Delusion and deception in large infrastructure projects: Two models for explaining and preventing executive disaster. *California Management Review, 51*(2), 170–193.

Gil, N., Ludrigan, C., Pinto, J., & Puranam, P. (2017). *Megaproject Organization and Performance: The Myth and Political Reality*. Project Management Institute.

Godenhjelm, S., Lundin, R.A., & Sjöblom, S. (2015). Projectification in the public sector – The case of the European Union. *International Journal of Managing Projects in Business, 8*(2), 324–348. doi: 10.1108/IJMPB-05-2014-0049.

Halachmi, A. (2002). Performance measurement, accountability, and improved performance. *Public Performance & Management Review, 25*(4), 370–374.

Hall, M., & Robin, H. (2003). Developing a culture of performance learning in U.K. public sector project management. *Public Performance & Management Review, 26*(3), 263–275.

Hatry, H.P. (2006). *Performance measurement: Getting Results*: The Urban Insitute.

Herzlinger, R.E. (2006). Why innovation in health care is so hard. *Harvard Business Review, 84*(5), 58–66.

Hood, C. (2006). Gaming in targetworld: The targets approach to managing British public services. *Public Administration Review, 66*(4), 515–521.

Ika, L.A. (2009). Project success as a topic in project management journals. *Project Management Journal, 40*(4), 6–19.

Jarzabkowski, P., & Kaplan, S. (2015). Strategy tools-in-use: A framework for understanding "technologies of rationality" in practice. *Strategic Management Journal, 36*(4), 537–558. doi: 10.1002/smj.2270.

Kaplan, R.S., & Norton, D.P. (October 1993). Putting the balanced scorecard to work. *Harvard Business Review*, 134–147.

Kelman, S. (2011). 2010 John Gaus Lecture: If you want to be a good fill-in-the-blank manager, be a good plain-vanilla manager. *PS: Political Science & Politics, 44*(2), 241–246.

Kirby, J. (2005). Toward a theory of high performance. *Harvard Business Review, 83*(7), 30–39.

Klakegg, O.J., Williams, T., Magnussen, O.M., & Glasspool, H. (2008). Governance frameworks for public project development and estimation. *Project Management Journal, 39*, S27–S42.

Koppenjan, J., Charles, M.B., & Ryan, N. (2008). Editorial: Managing competing public values in public infrastructure projects. *Public Money & Management, 28*(3), 131–134.

Kujala, J., Brady, T., & Putila, J. (2014). Challenges of cost management in complex projects. *International Journal of Business and Management, 9*(11), 48–58.

Levesque, J.-F., & Sutherland, K. (2017). What role does performance information play in securing improvement in healthcare? A conceptual framework for levers of change. *BMJ Open, 7*(8), e014825.

Litwack, J.M. (1993). Coordination, incentives, and the ratchet effect. *The RAND Journal of Economics, 24*(2), 271–285.

Marchand, J.-S., & Brunet, M. (2017). The emergence of post-NPM initiatives: Integrated impact assessment as a hybrid decision-making tool. *International Review of Administrative Sciences*, 0020852317694947.

Melkers, J., & Willoughby, K. (2005). Models of performance-measurement use in local governments: Understanding budgeting, communication, and lasting effects. *Public Administration Review, 65*(2), 180–190.

Mesa, H.A., Molenaar, K.R., & Alarcón, L.F. (2016). Exploring performance of the integrated project delivery process on complex building projects. *International Journal of Project Management, 34*(7), 1089–1101. doi: 10.1016/j.ijproman.2016.05.007.

Micheli, P., & Neely, A. (2010). Performance measurement in the public sector in England: Searching for the golden thread. *Public Administration Review, 70*(4), 591–600.

Miller, R., & Hobbs, B. (2005). Governance regimes for large complex projects. *Project Management Journal, 36*(3), 42–50.

Miller, R., & Lessard, D. (2000). *The Strategic Management of Large Engineering Projects: Shaping Institutions, Risks, and Governance*. Cambridge: MA: Massachusetts Institute of Technology.

Miller, R., & Lessard, D. (2001). Understanding and managing risks in large engineering projects. *International Journal of Project Management, 19*, 437–443.

Mir, F.A., & Pinnington, A.H. (2014). Exploring the value of project management: Linking project management performance and project success. *International Journal of Project Management, 32*(2), 202–217. doi: 10.1016/j.ijproman.2013.05.012.

Müller, R., Pemsel, S., & Shao, J. (2015). Organizational enablers for project governance and governmentality in project-based organizations. *International Journal of Project Management, 33*(4), 839–851. doi: 10.1016/j.ijproman.2014.07.008.

Nyhan, R.C., & Martin, L.L. (1999). Comparative performance measurement: A primer on data envelopment analysis. *Public Productivity & Management Review, 22*(3), 348–364.

Ogunlana, S.O. (2010). Beyond the 'iron triangle': Stakeholder perception of key performance indicators (KPIs) for large-scale public sector development projects. *International Journal of Project Management, 28*(3), 228–236.

Osborne, S.P. (2010). *The New Public Governance?: Emerging Perspectives on the Theory and Practice of Public Governance*. New York: Routledge.

Padalkar, M., & Gopinath, S. (2016). Six decades of project management research: Thematic trends and future opportunities. *International Journal of Project Management, 34*(7), 1305–1321. doi: 10.1016/j.ijproman.2016.06.006

Parmenter, D. (2015). *Key Performance Indicators: Developing, Implementing, and Using Winning KPIs*. New York: John Wiley & Sons.

Patanakul, P., Kwak, Y.H., Zwikael, O., & Liu, M. (2016). What impacts the performance of large-scale government projects? *International Journal of Project Management, 34*(3), 452–466. doi: 10.1016/j.ijproman.2015.12.001.

Pilbeam, C. (2013). Coordinating temporary organizations in international development through social and temporal embeddedness. *International Journal of Project Management, 31*(2), 190–199.

Pinto, J.K., & Winch, G. (2016). The unsettling of "settled science:" The past and future of the management of projects. *International Journal of Project Management, 34*(2), 237–245. doi: 10.1016/j.ijproman.2015.07.011.

Pitsis, T.S., Sankaran, S., Gudergan, S., & Clegg, S.R. (2014). Governing projects under complexity: Theory and practice in project management. *International Journal of Project Management, 32*(8), 1285–1290. doi: 10.1016/j.ijproman.2014.09.001.

Price, A., Schwartz, R., Cohen, J., Scott, F., & Manson, H. (2016). Pursuing performance and maintaining compliance: Balancing performance improvement and accountability in Ontario's public health system. *Canadian Public Administration, 59*(2), 245–266. doi: 10.1111/capa.12151.

Radin, B.A. (2006). *Challenging the Performance Movement: Accountability, Complexity, and Democratic Values.* Washington, DC: Georgetown University Press.

Radin, B.A. (2011). Does performance measurement actually improve accountability? In: Dubnick, M.J., & Frederickson, H.G. (Eds.), *Accountable Governance: Problems and Promises.* Armonk, NY: M.E. Sharpe, 98–110.

Richard, P.J., Devinney, T.M., Yip, G.S., & Johnson, G. (2009). Measuring organizational performance: Towards methodological best practice. *Journal of Management, 35*(3), 718–804.

Ridgway, V.F. (1956). Dysfunctional consequences of performance measurements. *Administrative Science Quarterly, 1*(2), 240–247.

Rolstadås, A., Tommelein, I., Morten, S.P., & Ballard, G. (2014). Understanding project success through analysis of project management approach. *International Journal of Managing Projects in Business, 7*(4), 638–660. doi: 10.1108/IJMPB-09-2013-0048.

Romzek, B.S., & Dubnick, M.J. (1987). Accountability in the public sector: Lessons from the challenger tragedy. *Public Administration Review, 47*(3), 227–238.

Schoper, Y.-G., Wald, A., Ingason, H.T., & Fridgeirsson, T.V. (2018). Projectification in Western economies: A comparative study of Germany, Norway and Iceland. *International Journal of Project Management, 36*(1), 71–82. doi: 10.1016/j.ijproman.2017.07.008.

Shenhar, A., & Holzmann, V. (2017). The three secrets of megaproject success: Clear strategic vision, total alignment, and adapting to complexity. *Project Management Journal, 48*(6), 29–46.

Siemiatycki, M. (2009). Academics and auditors: Comparing perspectives on transportation project cost overruns. *Journal of Planning Education and Research, 29*(2), 142–156. doi: 10.1177/0739456X09348798.

Sirisomboonsuk, P., Gu, V.C., Cao, R.Q., & Burns, J.R. (2018). Relationships between project governance and information technology governance and their impact on project performance. *International Journal of Project Management, 36*(2), 287–300. doi: 10.1016/j.ijproman.2017.10.003.

Söderlund, J. (2011). Pluralism in project management: Navigating the crossroads of specialization and fragmentation. *International Journal of Management Reviews, 13*(2), 153–176.

Suprapto, M., Bakker, H.L.M., Mooi, H.G., & Hertogh, M.J.C.M. (2016). How do contract types and incentives matter to project performance? *International Journal of Project Management, 34*(6), 1071–1087. doi: 10.1016/j.ijproman.2015.08.003.

Thamhain, H. (2013). Managing risks in complex projects. *Project Management Journal, 44*(2), 20–35.

Thomas, J., & Mullaly, M. (2008). *Researching the Value of Project Management.* Newtown Square, PA: Project Management Institute.

Todorović, M.L., Petrović, D.Č., Mihić, M.M., Obradović, V.L., & Bushuyev, S.D. (2015). Project success analysis framework: A knowledge-based approach in project management. *International Journal of Project Management, 33*(4), 772–783.

Too, E.G., & Weaver, P. (2014). The management of project management: A conceptual framework for project governance. *International Journal of Project Management, 32*(8), 1382–1394. doi: 10.1016/j.ijproman.2013.07.006.

Ukko, J., Tenhunen, J., & Rantanen, H. (2007). Performance measurement impacts on management and leadership: Perspectives of management and employees. *International Journal of Production Economics, 110*, 39–51.

Van Der Knaap, P. (2006). Responsive evaluation and performance management: Overcoming the downsides of policy objectives and performance indicators. *Evaluation, 12*(3), 278–293.

Van Thiel, S., & Leeuw, F.L. (2002). The performance paradox in the public sector. *Public Performance & Management Review, 25*(3), 267–281.

von Danwitz, S. (2018). Managing inter-firm projects: A systematic review and directions for future research. *International Journal of Project Management, 36*(3), 525–541. doi: 10.1016/j.ijproman.2017.11.004.

Walton, E.J., & Dawson, S. (2001). Managers' perceptions of criteria of organizational effectiveness. *Journal of Management Studies, 38*(2), 173–200.

Weick, K.E. (2015). Ambiguity as grasp: The reworking of sense. *Journal of Contingencies and Crisis Management, 23*(2), 117–123.

Weick, K.E., & Sutcliffe, K.M. (2015). *Managing the Unexpected: Sustained Performance in a Complex World*, 3rd edition. Hoboken, NJ: Wiley.

Wholey, J.S., & Hatry, H.P. (1992). The case for performance monitoring. *Public Administration Review, 52*(6), 604–610.

Williams, T., & Samset, K. (2010). Issues in front/end decision-making on projects. *Project Management Journal, 41*(2), 38–49.

Winch, G., & Leiringer, R. (2016). Owner project capabilities for infrastructure development: A review and development of the "strong owner" concept. *International Journal of Project Management, 34*(2), 271–281. doi: 10.1016/j.ijproman.2015.02.002.

Chapter 18

Ajmal, M.M., & Koskinen, K.U. (2008). Knowledge transfer in project-based organizations: An organizational culture perspective. *Project Management Journal, 39*, 7–15.

Akintoye, A., & Beck, M. (2009). *Policy, Finance & Management for Public-Private Partnerships.* Wiley-Blackwell.

Al-Tmeemy, S.M.H.M., Abdul-Rahman, H., & Harun, Z. (2011). Future criteria for success of building projects in Malaysia. *International Journal of Project Management, 29*, 337–348.

Arvidsson, N. (2009). Exploring tensions in projectified matrix organisations. *Scandinavian Journal of Management, 25*, 97–107.

Baccarini, D. (1999). *The Logical Framework Method for Defining Project Success.* Project Management Institute.

Cox, A.W., Ireland, P., & Townsend, M. (2006). *Managing in Construction Supply Chains and Markets: Reactive and Proactive Options for Improving Performance and Relationship Menagement.* London: Thomas Telford.

De Bruijn, H., & Ten Heuvelhof, E. (2010). *Process Management: Why Project Management Fails in Complex Decision Making Processes.* Springer Science & Business Media.

Eversdijk, A., & Korsten, A.F. (Februari 2015). Motieven en overwegingen achter publiek-private samenwerking. *Beleidsonderzoek Online.*

Flyvbjerg, B., Skamris Holm, M.K., & Buhl, S.L., (2003). How common and how large are cost overruns in transport infrastructure projects. *Transport Reviews, 23*, 71–88.

Hayford, O., (2006). Successfully allocating risk and negotiating a PPP contract. In: *6th* Annual National Public Private Partnerships *Summit*: Which Way *Now for* Australia's *PPP* Market?, Rydges Jamison, Sydne.

Hobday, M. (2000). The project-based organisation: An ideal form for managing complex products and systems? *Research Policy, 29*, 871–893.

Koops, L., Bosch-Rekveldt, M., Bakker, H., & Hertogh, M. (2017). Exploring the influence of external actors on the cooperation in public–private project organizations for constructing infrastructure. *International Journal of Project Management, 35*, 618–632.

Koops, L., Bosch-Rekveldt, M., Coman, L., Hertogh, M., & Bakker, H. (2016). Identifying perspectives of public project managers on project success: Comparing viewpoints of managers from five countries in North-West Europe. *International Journal of Project Management, 34*, 874–889.

Koops, L.S.W. (2017). *Creating Public Value: Optimizing Cooperation Between Public and Private Partners in Infrastructure Projects.* Delft University of Technology.

Leendertse, W. (2015). Publiek-Private Interactie in Infrastructuur Netwerken: Een zoektocht naar waardevolle marktbetrokkenheid in het beheer en de ontwikkeling van publieke infrastructuurnetwerken, University of Groningen, Groningen, p. 294.

Merrow, E. (2011). Oil industry megaprojects: Our recent track record. In: Offshore Technology Conference, Houston, TX.

Mintzberg, H. (1980). Structure in 5's: A synthesis of the research on organization design. *Management Science, 26*, 322–341.

Munns, A.K., & Bjeirmi, B.F. (1996). The role of project management in achieving project success. *International Journal of Project Management, 14*, 81–87.

PMBOK®. (2008). *A Guide to the Project Management Body of Knowledge, PMBOK Guide,* Fourth Edition. Newton Square, Pennsylvania: The Project Management Institute.

Porter, M.E., & Millar, V.E. (1985). How information gives you competitive advantage. *Harvard Business Review, 63*, 149–160.

Pryke, S., & Smyth, H.J. (2006). *The Management of Complex Projects. A Relationship Approach.* Oxford: Blackwell Publishing Ltd.

Shenhar, A.J., & Dvir, D. (2007). Project management research-the challenge and opportunity. *Project Management Journal, 38*, 93.

Smyth, H., & Pryke, S. (2008). *Collaborative Relationships in Construction: Developing Frameworks and Networks.* West Sussex: Blackwell Publishing Ltd.

Van Ham, H., & Koppenjan, J. (2002). *Publiek-private samenwerking bij transportinfrastructuur: Wenkend of wijkend perspectief?* Utrecht: Uitgeverij LEMMA BV.

Chapter 19

Argyris, C. (1999). *Organizational Learning.* Oxford: Blackwell.

Bjurulf, S., & Nilsson, A. (2013). Measuring the effects of regional development. In: Svensson, L., Brulin, G., Jansson, S., & Sjöberg, K. (Eds.), *Capturing Effects of Projects and Programmes.* Lund: Studentlitteratur, 149–162.

Bjurulf, Staffan, Vedung, Evert, & Larsson, Carl-Göran. (2013). A triangulation approach to impact evaluation. *The International Journal of Theory, Research and Practice, 19*(1), 54–71.

Brulin, G. (2012). *A Synthesis of the Ongoing Evaluation in the Regional Structural Programmes. 23 Conclusion.* Stockholm: Tillväxtverket Rapport 0136.

Brulin, G. (2013). Effects in the regional fund. In: Svensson, L., Brulin, G., Jansson, S., & Sjöberg, K. (Eds.), *Capturing Effects of Projects and Programmes.* Lund: Studentlitteratur, 81–98.

Brulin, G., & Svensson, L. (2012). *Managing Sustainable Development Programmes: A Learning Approach to Change.* London: Gower Publishing Company, 189–192.

Brulin, G., & Svensson, L. (2013). Knowledge for long-term, surprising and unexpected effects: Summary of conclusions. In: Svensson, L., Brulin, G., Jansson, S., & Sjöberg, K. (Eds.), *Capturing Effects of Projects and Programmes.* Lund: Studentlitteratur, 239–254.

Donaldson, S.I., Christina, A.C., & Mark, M.M. (2009). *What Should Count as Credible Evidence in Applied Research and Evaluation Practice.* London: SAGE Publication.

Elg, M., Ellström, P.-E., Kloftsten, M., & Tillmar, M. (2015). *Sustainable Development in Organizations. Studies on Innovative Practices.* Cheltenham: Edward Elgar Publishing Limited.

Fred, M. (2018). *Projectification: The Trojan Horse of Local Government.* Öresund: Lund University and Malmö University.

Gaffey, V., & Riché, M. (November 2015). Theory based evaluation: A range of approaches to assess impact. *Monograph Chapter,* 299–312.

Guba, E., & Lincoln, Y. (1989). *Fourth Evaluation Generation.* Newbury Park, CA: Sage.

Highsmith, J. (2010). *Agile Project Management: Creating Innovative Products,* 2nd edition. Upper Saddle River, NJ: Addison-Wesley.

Merton, R.K. (1957). *Social Theory and Social Structure.* London: Collier-Macmillian.

Merton, R.K., & Barber, E. (2004). *The Travels and Adventures of Serendipity*. Princeton, NJ: Princeton University Press.

Riché, M. (2013). Theory based evaluation: A wealth of approaches and an untapped potential. In: Svensson, L., Brulin, G., Jansson, S., & Sjöberg, K. (Eds.), *Capturing Effects of Projects and Programmes*. Lund: Studentlitteratur, 63–80.

Sandberg, B., & Faugert, S. (2016). *Perspektiv på utvärdering*. Lund. Studentlitteratur.

Shearmur, R., & Bonnet, N. (August 2011). Does local technological innovation lead to local development? A policy perspective. *Regional Science Policy & Practice, 3*(3).

Svensson, L., Brulin, G., Jansson, S., & Sjöberg, K. (Eds.) (2009). *Learning Through Ongoing Evaluation*. Lund: Studentlitteratur.

Svensson, L., Brulin, G., Jansson, S., & Sjöberg, K. (Eds.) (2013). *Capturing Effects of Projects and Programmes*. Lund: Studentlitteratur.

Taleb, N. (2010). *The Black Swan*. London: Penguin Books.

Tillväxtverket. (2015). *Regionala riskkapitalfonder. Slututvärdering*. Rapport 0195.

Vedung, E. (2013). Side effects, perverse effects and other strange effects of public interventions. In: Svensson, L., Brulin, G., Jansson, S., & Sjöberg, K. (Eds.), *Capturing Effects of Projects and Programmes*. Lund: Studentlitteratur, 35–62.

Chapter 21

Adorno, T. (1951). *Minima Moralia: Reflections on a Damaged Life* (trans. E.F.N. Jephcott, Übers.) (Ed. 2006). London; New York: Verso.

Anderso, V. (2007). *Value of Learning: From Return on Investment to Return on Expectation*. London: Chartered Institute of Personnel & Development.

Bayard, P. (2007). *How to Talk About Books You Haven't Read*. New York: Bloomsbury.

Beer, S. (1972). *Brain of the Firm* (2nd edition, 1981). Chichester: Wiley.

Beer, S. (1979). *The Heart of Enterprise* (reprint with corrections, 1988). Chichester: Wiley.

Bennett, N., & Lemoine, J. (2014). What VUCA Really Means for You. *Harvard Business Review, 92*(1/2), 27.

Bertholo, J. (2018). *Shadow Working in Project Management: Understanding and Addressing the Irrational and Unconscious in Groups*. Abingdon; New York: Routledge.

Bleicher, K. (1991). *Das Konzept Integriertes Management*. Frankfurt am Main: Campus Verlag.

Boje, D.M. (2001). *Narrative Methods for Organizational & Communication Research*. Thousand Oaks, CA: Sage Publications.

Boje, D.M. (2008). *Storytelling Organizations*. Thousand Oaks, CA: Sage Publications.

Bredillet, C.N. (2010). Blowing hot and cold on project management. *Project Management Journal, 41*(3), 4–20.

Butler-Bowdon, T. (2003). *50 Self-Help Classics* (Ed. 2017). London: Nicholas Brealey Publishing.

Capra, P.F., & Luisi, P.L. (2014). *The Systems View of Life: A Unifying Vision*. Cambridge: Cambridge University Press.

Chapman, C., & Ward, S. (2003). Constructively simple estimating: A project management example. *Journal of the Operational Research Society, 54*(10), 1050–1058.

Chapman, C., Ward, S., & Harwood, I. (2006). Minimising the effects of dysfunctional corporate culture in estimation and evaluation processes: A constructively simple approach. *International Journal of Project Management, 24*(2), 106–115.

Fleck, L. (1986). The problem of epistemology [1936]. In: *Cognition and Fact* (reprint 1986, pp. 79–112). Dordrecht: Springer Netherlands.

Foerster, H. von. (2002). *Understanding Understanding: Essays on Cybernetics and Cognition*. New York: Springer.

Foerster, H. von, & Pörksen, B. (2001). *Understanding Systems, Conversations on Epistemology and Ethics* (trans. K. Leube, Übers.) (Ed. 2002). Heidelberg: Carl-Auer-Systeme-Verlag.

Gladwell, M. (2001). *The Tipping Point: How Little Things Can Make a Big Difference*. New York: Little, Brown and Company.

Goffman, E. (1972). *Relations in Public*. Harmondsworth: Penguin Books.

Goffman, E., & Berger, B. (1974). *Frame Analysis: Propaganda Plays of the Woman Suffrage Movement: An Essay on the Organization of Experience* (1986. Aufl.). Boston, MA: Northeastern University Press.

Graves, C.W. (1970). Levels of existence: An open system theory of values. *Journal of Humanistic Psychology, 10*(2), 131–155.

Graves, C.W. (April 1974). Human Nature Prepares for a momentous leap. *The Futurist*, 72–78.

Han, B.-C. (2005). *What Is Power?* (Ed. 2018). Medford, MA: Polity.

Harvard Business Review (Ed.). (2011). *HBR's 10 Must Reads on Change Management*. Boston, MA: Harvard Business Review Press.

Heidegger, M. (1927). *Being and Time* (trans. J. Stambaugh, Übers.) (Revised edition 2010). Albany, NY: State University of New York Press.

Hicks Stiehm, J. (2002). *U.S. Army War College: Military Education in a Democracy* (Ed. 2010). Philadelphia, PA: Temple University Press.

Hirt, P.W. (1996). *A Conspiracy of Optimism: Management of the National Forests Since World War Two*. Lincoln, NE: University of Nebraska Press.

Jackson, M.C. (2000). *Systems Approaches to Management*. Boston, MA/Dordrecht/London: Kluwer Academic Publishers.

Jackson, M.C. (2002). *Systems Thinking: Creative Holism for Managers*. Chichester: Wiley.

Jorgensen, K.M., & Largacha-Martinez, C. (2014). *Critical Narrative Inquiry: Storytelling, Sustainability and Power*. New York: Nova Science Publishers.

Jung, C.G. (1912). *Psychology of the Unconscious* (Ed. 2002). Mineola, NY: Dover Publication.

Kant, I. (1781). *Critique of Pure Reason* (eds. P. Guyer & A.W. Wood, Übers.) (Ed. 1999). Cambridge: Cambridge University Press.

Kirkpatrick, D.L. (1998). *Evaluating Training Programs: The Four Levels*, (2nd edition, San Francisco, CA: Berrett-Koehler Publishers.

Kirkpatrick, J.D., & Kirkpatrick, W.K. (2016). *Kirkpatrick S Four Levels of Training Evaluation*. Alexandria, VA: Association for Talent Development.

Klein, L. (2005). Systemic inquiry – Exploring organisations. *Kybernetes: Heinz von Förster - in Memoriam. Part II, 34*(3/4), 439–447.

Klein, L. (2012a). Cross-cultural complex project management: Balancing social and cultural complexity. In: Linger, H., & Owen, J. (Eds.), *The Project as a Social System: Asia-Pacific Perspectives on Project Management*. Clayton, VIC: Monash University Press, S. 21–35.

Klein, L. (2012b). The three inevitabilities of human being: A conceptual hierarchy model approaching social complexity. *Kybernetes, 41*(7/8), 977–984.

Klein, L. (2013). Notes on an ecology of paradigms. *Systems Research and Behavioral Science, 30*(6), 773–779.

Klein, L. (2016a). Exploring the organisational collage of memetic paradigms for (a) change – A research note. *Journal of Organisational Transformation & Social Change, 13*(1), 54–63.

Klein, L. (2016b). Minima Moralia in project management: There is no right life in the wrong one. *Project Management Journal, 47*(3), 12–20.

Klein, L. (2016c). Towards a practice of systemic change – Acknowledging social complexity in project management. *Systems Research and Behavioral Science, 33*(5), 651–661.

Klein, L. (2016d). Understanding social systems research. In: Nemiche, M., & Essaaidi, M. (Eds.), *Advances in Complex Societal, Environmental and Engineered Systems*. Cham: Springer International Publishing.

Klein, L. (2017). *Business Excellence: Die Vielfalt erfolgreich managen*. Wiesbaden: Springer Gabler.

Klein, L., Biesenthal, C., & Dehlin, E. (2015). Improvisation in project management: A praxeology. *International Journal of Project Management, 33*(2), 267–277.

Klein, L., & Popp, F. (2009). Leadership 21: Unleashing the full potential of leadership. *Zeitschrift Für Politikberatung – ZPB Policy Advice and Political Consulting, 2*(2), 323–334.

Klein, L., & Weiland, C.A.P. (2014). Critical systemic inquiry: Ethics, sustanability and action. In: Jorgensen, K.M., & Largacha-martinez, C. (Eds.), *Critical Narrative Inquiry: Storytelling, Sustainability and Power*. New York: Nova Science Publishers, S. 145–158.

Klein, L., & Wong, T.S.L. (2012). The Yin and Yang of change: Systemic efficacy in change management. In: Prastacos, G.P., Wang, F., & Soderquist, K.E. (Eds.), *Leadership through the Classics*. Berlin/Heidelberg: Springer, S. 475–486.

Kohlberg, L. (1981). *The Philosophy of Moral Development: Moral Stages and the Idea of Justice*. San Francisco, CA: Harpercollins.

Kuhn, T.S. (1962). *The Structure of Scientific Revolutions*. Chicago, IL: The University of Chicago Press.

Laloux, F. (2014). *Reinventing Organizations: A Guide to Creating Organizations Inspired by the Next Stage in Human Consciousness*. Brussels: Nelson Parker.

Linger, H., & Owen, J. (Eds.) (2012). *The Project as a Social System: Asia Pacific Perspectives on Project Management*. Clayton, VIC: Monash University Publishing.

Loevinger, Jand. (1970). *Measuring Ego Development* (Latest Second Edition!!!!!!). San Francisco, CA: Jossey-Bass Inc Pub.

Loevinger, Jane. (1987). *Paradigms of Personality*. New York: W.H.Freeman & Co Ltd.

Lorenz, E.N. (1963). *The Essence of Chaos* (Reprint, 1996). Seattle, WA: University of Washington Press.

Lovelock, J.E. (1972). Gaia as seen through the atmosphere. *Atmospheric Environment (1967), 6*(8), 579–580.

Luhmann, N. (1984). *Social Systems* (trans. J. Bednarz & D. Baecker, Übers.) (Ed. 1996). Stanford, CA: Stanford University Press.

Margulis, L. (1998). *Symbiotic Planet: A New Look at Evolution*. New York: Basic Books.

Meadows, D.H., Meadows, D.L., Randers, J., & Behrens, William W. III. (1972). *The Limits to Growth: A Report for the Club of Rome's Project on the Predicament of Mankind*. New York: New American Library.

Neitzel, S., & Welzer, H. (2011). *Soldiers: German POWs on Fighting, Killing, and Dying* (Reprint 2013). New York: Vintage.

Oden, H.W. (1997). *Managing Corporate Culture, Innovation, and Intrapreneurship*. Westport, CT: Quorum Books.

Piaget, J. (1950). *The Psychology of Intelligence* (Ed. 2001). London; New York: Routledge.

Raue, S., & Klein, L. (2016). Systemic risk management: A practice approach to the systemic management of project risk. In: Bodea, C.-N., Purnus, A., Huemann, M., & Hajdu, M. (Eds.), *Managing Project Risks for Competitive Advantage in Changing Business Environments*. Hershey, PA: IGI Global, S. 70–85.

Robertson, B.J. (2016). *Holacracy: The Revolutionary Management System that Abolishes Hierarchy*. London: Portfolio Penguin.

Schein, E.H. (2004). *Organizational Culture and Leadership*, 3rd edition. San Francisco, CA: Jossey-Bass.

Scott, B. (2009). The role of sociocybernetics in understanding world futures. *Kybernetes, 38*(6), 863–878.

Senge, P.M. (1990). *The Fifth Discipline: The Art and Practice of the Learning Organization*. New York: Doubleday/Currency.

Sparrer, I., & Kibed, M.V. von. (2000). *Ganz im Gegenteil. Tetralemmaarbeit und andere Grundformen Systemischer Strukturaufstellungen – für Querdenker und solche, die es werden wollen* (5., übearb. Aufl., 2005). Heidelberg: Carl Auer Verlag.

Szalajko, G., Boxheimer, M., Ellmann, S., Koutintcheva, M., Mansson, E., Polkovnikov, A., … Ros, J. (2016). *Project Excellence Baseline: For Achieving Excellence in Projects and Programmes*. Zürich: International Project Management Association.

Tichy, N.M. (1983). *Managing Strategic Change: Technical, Political, and Cultural Dynamics.* New York: John Wiley & Sons.

Turner, J.R., Anbari, F., & Bredillet, C. (2013). Perspectives on research in project management: The nine schools. *Global Business Perspectives, 1*(1), 3–28.

Varey, W. (2008). Apithology: An emergent continuum. *Aspects of Apithology: Journal of Apithological Practice, 1*(1), 1–7.

Volk, T. (2002). Toward a future for Gaia theory. *Climatic Change, 52*(4), 423–430.

Watzlawick, P. (1984). *Invented Reality: How Do We Know What We Believe We Know?* New York: W.W. Norton and Company.

Weick, K. (1995). *Sensemaking in Organizations.* Thousand Oaks, CA: Sage Publications.

Wilber, K. (2000). *A Theory of Everything: An Integral Vision for Business, Politics, Science and Spirituality* (Ed. 2001). Boston, MA: Shambhala.

Willke, H. (2007). *Smart Governance: Governing the Global Knowledge Society.* Frankfurt/Main: Campus Verlag.

Wittgenstein, L. (1953). *Philosophical Investigations* (trans. G.E.M. Anscombe, P.M.S. Hacker, & J. Schulte, Übers.) (4th edition, 2009). Chichester; Malden, MA: Wiley-Blackwell.

Chapter 22

Arroyo, A., & Grisham, T. (2017). *Leading Extreme Projects – Sategy, Risk and Resilience in Practice.* London: Gower.

Grisham, T. (2009). *International Project Management – Leadership in Complex Environments.* Hoboken, NJ: Wiley.

Grisham, T. (2016). *Leading Agile Projects.* Amazon Digital Services LLC.

Chapter 23

Brown, K.W., & Ryan, R.M. (2003). The benefits of being present: Mindfulness and its role in psychological well-being. *Journal of Personality and Social Psychology, 84*(4), 822.

Brown, K.W., Ryan, R.M., & Creswell, J.D. (2007). Mindfulness: Theoretical foundations and evidence for its salutary effects. *Psychological Inquiry, 18*(4), 211–237.

Carroll, Michael. (2004). *Awake at Work.* Shambhala Publications.

Crowe, Andy. (2009). *The PMP Exam – How to Pass on Your First Try.* PMP, Velociteach.

Delaney, Senn. (2011). *The Human Operating System: An Owner's Manual.* Senn Delaney Leadership Consulting.

Hanh, Thich Nhat. (1998). *The Heart of the Buddha's Teaching.* Broadway Books.

Hanh, Thich Nhat. (2007). *The Art of Power.* HarperOne.

Kabat-Zinn, J. (1994). *Wherever You Go There You Are.* Hyperion.

Kemps, Robert R. (1992/2011). *Fundamentals of Project Performance Measurement.* Humphreys & Associates.

MacKenzie, Gordon. (1996). *Orbiting the Giant Hairball.* Viking Penguin.

Quoted book is "Emotional Intelligence: Why it can matter more than IQ" Daniel Goleman.

Levit, A. (2017). *Why Automation Won't Take Your Job.* Retrieved from https://www.quickbase.com/blog/why-automation-wont-take-your-job.

Staughton, J. (2016). *Can Humans Actually Multitask?* Retrieved from https://www.scienceabc.com/humans/can-humans-actually-multitask.html.

Lapowsky, I. (2013). *Don't Multitask: Your Brain Will Thank You.* Retrieved from http://business.time.com/2013/04/17/dont-multitask-your-brain-will-thank-you/.

Ruiz, Don Miguel. (1997). *The Four Agreements.* Amber-Allen Publishing, Inc.

Chapter 24

Conway, Melvin (April 1968). *How Do Committees Invent?* Datamation.

Crosby, Philip B. (1980). *Quality is Free: The Art of Making Quality Certain.* New York: Mentor.

Inamori, Kazuo. (2013). *Amoeba Management.* CRC Press.

Jones, Capers. (2008). *Applied Software Measurement: Global Analysis of Productivity and Quality.* New York: McGraw-Hill.

Kelly, Allan. (2018a). *Project Myopia.* LeanPub.com.

Kelly, Allan. (2018b). *Continuous Digital.* LeanPub.com.

Reid, T.R. (1984). *The Chip: The Microelectronics Revolution and the Men Who Made It.* New York: Simon and Schuster.

Reinertsen, Donald G. (2009). *The Principles of Product Development Flow.* Celeritas Publishing.

Womack, James P., Daniel T. Jones, & Daniel Roos. (1991). *The Machine that Changed the World: The Story of Lean Production.* New York: HarperPerennial.

Afterward

Austin, J.L. (1975). *How to Do Things with Words.* Oxford University Press.

Benjamin, W., Jennings, M.W., & Jephcott, E. (2016). *One-Way Street.* Cambridge: The Belknap Press of Harvard University Press.

Caruso, G., & Flanagan, O. (Eds.) (2017). *Neuroexistentialism: Meaning, Morals, and Purpose in the Age of Neuroscience.* Oxford University Press.

Caruso, Gregg D., & Flanagan, Owen J. (2018). *Neuroexistentialism: Meaning, Morals, and Purpose in the Age of Neuroscience.* New York: Oxford University Press.

Darwin, C. (1871). *The Descent of Man, and Selection in Relation to Sex,* 2 Vols. London: Murray.

Dawkins, R. (1976). *The Selfish Gene.* Oxford: Oxford University Press.

Dennett, D.C. (1991). *Consciousness Explained.* Boston, MA: Little, Brown and Co.

Dienes, K.R. (2 February 2017). *Rethinking the Rules of Reality, Lecture 1 of the University of Arizona Science Lecture Series Rethinking Reality* [Podcast]. Retrieved from https://podcasts.apple.com/us/podcast/rethinking-the-rules-of-reality/id1201353127?i=1000380720013 (accessed 1 July 2019).

Einstein, A. (1918). On gravitational waves Sitzungsber. preuss. *Academy Wiss, 1,* 154.

Einstein, A. (2005). Näherungsweise integration der feldgleichungen der gravitation. *Albert Einstein: Akademie-Vorträge: Sitzungsberichte der Preußischen Akademie der Wissenschaften 1914–1932,* 99–108.

Fromm, E. (1973). *The Anatomy of Human Destructiveness: Erich Fromm.* New York: Fawcett.

Lewis, Michael. (2016). *The Undoing Project: A Friendship That Changed Our Minds.* New York: W.W. Norton & Company.

Osterweil, C. (2019). *Project Delivery, Uncertainty and Neuroscience.* Leighton Buzzard: Visible Dynamics.

Phillips, A. (2019). *Heirs to the Underground: Performing Tradition in Chicago's Contemporary Dance Music Community.* Master of Arts Program in the Social Sciences, The University of Chicago, MAPSS/CIR Thesis Database.

Phillips, M. (2014). *Reinventing Communication: How to Design, Lead and Manage High Performing Projects.* Routledge.

Popper, Karl. (2002). *Conjectures and Refutations.* Routledge Classics.

Schwalberg, B. (1987). *Introduction to Economics,* Lecture Notes, Brandeis University, delivered Fall 1987.

Tversky, Amos, & Kahneman, Daniel. (1974). Judgment under uncertainty: Heuristics and biases. *Science, 185*(4157), 1124–1131.

Vada, Ø. (2015). What happened to Memetics. *Emergence: Complexity & Organization, 17*(2).

World Bank. (2018). *Decline of Global Extreme Poverty Continues But Has Slowed,* viewed 30 June 2019. Retrieved from https://www.worldbank.org/en/news/press-release/2018/09/19/decline-of-global-extreme-poverty-continues-but-has-slowed-world-bank.

Author profiles and resources

Introduction and Afterword

Mark Phillips is a business executive, author, speaker and adjunct professor. His business experiences range from software start-ups to senior leadership in the automotive sector. He is the editor of this volume, author of *Reinventing Communication: How to Design, Manage and Lead High Performing Projects* and numerous articles and blog posts. He has spoken around the world to thousands of people. He can be most readily reached through his personal website http://reinventingcommunication.com.

Chapter 1

A. Geoffrey Crane is a Canadian public speaker, researcher and entrepreneur. As a pioneer in the field of motivational intelligence, he has written numerous articles on the importance of emotional and social skills in the workforce. Well-versed in the changing demands of today's project-based work environments, Geoff spends his days helping leaders design and build a balanced repertoire of soft skills to help them achieve what matters most. He can be reached via his professional website http://adaptimist.com.

Chapter 2

Steve Berczuk is a software developer and expert in Agile software development. A Certified Scrum Master, he has over 25 years' experience helping teams work together effectively. Steve is co-author of the book *Software Configuration Management Patterns: Effective Teamwork, Practical Integration* and a frequent contributor to Techwell (https://www.techwell.com). Steve's articles and his blog can be found at https://www.berczuk.com.

Chapter 3

Susanne Madsen is an internationally recognized project leadership coach, trainer and consultant. Working with organizations globally, she helps project managers step up and become better leaders.

Prior to setting up her own business, Susanne worked for almost 20 years in the corporate sector leading high-profile programs of up to $30 million for organizations such as Standard Bank, Citigroup and JPMorgan Chase. She is a fully qualified Corporate and Executive coach, accredited by DISC and a regular contributor to the Association for Project Management (APM).

Susanne is also the co-founder of The Project Leadership Institute, a world-class learning organization dedicated to building authentic project leaders by engaging the heart, the soul and the mind. Susanne can be found online at https://www.susanne-madsen.co.uk.

Chapter 4

Andreas G.M. Nachbagauer is Deputy Head of studies of the study programs in Project Management at the University of Applied Sciences BFI Vienna, Austria. After completion of his degrees in Business Administration and Sociology, he became assistant professor at the Institute of Human Resource Management, Vienna University of Economics and Business. Before joining the UAS BFI Vienna, he worked as free-lance market and opinion researcher and as lecturer at several Universities and Universities of Applied Sciences. His current work focuses on: Organization studies, esp. micro–politics in organization, constraint decision making and systems theory; Strategizing, change management and HRM; New world of work and social change.

Iris Schirl-Boeck is Director of the master's program "Project Management and Organization" at the University of Applied Sciences BFI Vienna, Austria. After she had completed her master's studies in Sociology and European Studies, she became project manager in sociological research. Since 2008, she has worked in Higher Education, i.e. managing EU-Projects. Her current work and research focuses on: Management of project-oriented organizations and Higher Education research.

Chapter 5

Andrew Kallman has over 30 years of experience leading, transforming, training, coaching, mentoring and consulting with start-ups to executive-level assignments in Europe, the US and Asia. He trains, coaches and mentors teams, leaders and organizations on how to attain a sustainable pace that Flows. He coaches, trains and leads Agile transformations, transitions and governance from Waterfall to Agile/Scrum/Flow. He also is skilled in Enterprise Agile (including Agile Portfolios and Programs), SAFe (Scaled Agile Framework), Large-Scale Scrum, Scrum at Scale and Scaling Agile.

Ted Kallman has worked directly or in a consulting role as CEO, COO, CMO and PMO for various companies both in Europe and in the US. As an Enterprise Agile Coach, he has facilitated the common-sense adoption of Lean-Agile methods and practices to increase project and organizational effectiveness. Ted is currently the CEO of Tiba USA, a division of TIBA Management Consulting in Munich, Germany, which is one of the world's leaders in training and consulting in the project management space and has been for almost 30 years.

Jeff Kissinger is a senior project manager in the IT Department at Grand Rapids Community College. He has 19 years of experience managing information technology projects in academic and commercial organizations. He also has over 25 years of experience as a volunteer managing strategic and event-driven projects for several non-profit organizations. He presents regularly on a variety of project management topics and works diligently to advance the project management profession. In addition to being a PMP® certified project manager, he is a Flow certified trainer and professional, and a Certified Scrum Master. Jeff has a B.A. in communication studies from the University of Nevada, Las Vegas, a master's certificate in IS/IT project management from Villanova University and is a 2017 graduate of the Project Management Institute's Leadership Master Class.

Chapter 6

Jamal Moustafaev, MBA, PMP, a president and founder of Thinktank Consulting, is an internationally acclaimed expert and speaker in the areas of project management, project portfolio management, project scope management and corporate training. Jamal has done work for more than 60 private-sector companies and government organizations in more than 30 countries in North America, Asia, Europe and the Middle East.

He is an author of three books including *Project Portfolio Management in Theory and Practice*. More information can be found at www.thinktankconsulting.ca.

Chapter 7

Ann Pilkington is the author of the book *Communicating Projects*. She is a communication consultant specializing in change and also the founder and director of PR Academy, the largest centre for PR and communication qualifications accredited by the UK Chartered Institute of Public Relations. She holds a master's in PR and communication from the University of Stirling and is qualified in project management through the Association for Project Management, the chartered body for the project profession for which she also volunteers. She writes regularly for PR Academy's communication community PR Place and has authored guides on topics such as stakeholder engagement, developing communication strategies and use of communication theory. She can be reached at the websites PRAcademy.co.uk and PRPlace.com.

Chapter 8

Stephen Duffield, PhD, is currently a person with Parkinson's. He is interested in researching and fundraising for finding a cure for Parkinson's Disease. He has more than 25 years' experience working in Aerospace, Transportation, Health and Information Technology in Australia with projects ranging up to $150 million. He is an adjunct professor at the School of Business and Tourism at Southern Cross University and subject to his Parkinson's reviews and researches topics including Lessons Learned, Knowledge Management, Risk Management, Safety Performance, Project Management and Systems Engineering. He is a Certified Practising Project

Director from the Australian Institute of Project Management, a Fellow of the Australian Institute of Project Management and an Associate Fellow of Action Learning Action Research Association.

Chapters 9 and 10

Glen B. Alleman leads the Program Planning and Controls practice for Niwot Ridge, LLC. In this position, Glen brings his 30 years' experience in program and project management, systems engineering, software development and general management to bear on the problems of performance-based management. Glen's experience ranges from real time control systems, enterprise IT systems, business and program performance improvement, IT strategy and new business development in a variety of technical domains to product development management. From this background, Glen has experienced a wide variety of project domains in which mission critical applications have fixed completion dates, constrained budgets and emerging requirements.

Tom Coonce is an adjunct research staff member at the Institute for Defense Analyses.

Rick Price had a distinguished 36+ year career in Project/Program Management for Lockheed Martin Space Systems, and is currently the principal for Waypoint Consulting and works with both ClearPlan Consulting and Cornell Technical Systems (CTS). He has specialized in program planning and control including critical path analysis, schedule risk management and schedule performance management (Including Earned Value Management). He has been an industry leader in defining and applying schedule margin as a schedule risk management tool and applying and interpreting schedule risk assessments to enable on-time performance on schedule constrained programs.

Chapter 11

Robert Van De Velde, PhD, PMP, CSM owns and operates ProjectFlightDeck.com, a company focused on Earned Schedule products and services. Rob has extended Earned Schedule to the Agile framework, packaging practices, tools and theory as AgileESM© (Agile Earned Schedule Management). For more information, visit: http://www.projectflightdeck.com/AgileESM.php.

As a project manager, Rob has a 35-year track record of delivering large, complex programs and projects in a variety of domains, including financial services, natural resources, telecommunications and health care. His project management accomplishments have been recognized by several awards.

Rob is an experienced speaker, who also writes about Earned Schedule, including a blog www.EarnedScheduleExchange.com and numerous articles in project management publications.

Chapter 12

Kristine A. Hayes Munson, MBA, PMP, CIA, CISM, is an IT leader with a proven track record of successfully completing high-profile, cross-discipline projects in the financial services industry. She oversees a risk and compliance program balancing internal controls, regulatory requirements, information security best practices and entrepreneurialism.

Ms Hayes Munson is a member of the University of California Irvine Continuing Education Division's project management certificate faculty. She volunteers for the PMI Global Accreditation Center (GAC) and her local PMI chapter.

Ms Hayes Munson earned a BA from Brigham Young University and an MBA from California State University San Marcos.

Chapter 12 Sidebar

Emma-Ruth Arnaz-Pemberton, a Fellow of the Association for Project Management, is a PMO, Project, Programme and Portfolio specialist with extensive experience in the change management industry and a particular focus on collaboration, PMO conception and strategy, method and capability development. Emma-Ruth is accredited in PRINCE2 Agile, PRINCE2, MSP, MoR and as a coach. She is involved extensively with a number of organizations; notably the Association for Project Management where she supports the organization as a judge for the annual awards, a full membership application reviewer and she is currently chair of their PMO Specific Interest Group. An APM Accredited Trainer, Emma-Ruth is a prolific speaker and writer on PMOs and is involved in various project management charitable organizations such as Project Management Without Borders, Project Managers Against Poverty and PM4Change.

Chaptes 13 and 14

Dr Jim Young, PMP, is a retired New Zealand Army officer who for the last 30 years has been a project management practitioner, mentor and lecturer. Jim has managed projects in New Zealand and overseas and given this experience has developed practical project management courseware and training materials for managers at all levels. He is currently the director of SkillPower, a project management consultancy. His webpage is skillpower.co.nz.

Chapter 15

Marisa Silva, the Lucky PM, is a senior PPM consultant, trainer and speaker in PPM. Marisa is undertaking a PhD in Project Management at Alma Mater Europaea University, holds an MSc (with distinction) in Strategic Management of Projects from University College London (UCL), a BSc in Management, a specialization in Competitive Intelligence and a PgDip in Foresight, Strategy and Innovation by ISEG (Portugal). Her research on the importance of managing for project legacy made her a finalist in 2017 for the prestigious IPMA Young Researcher Award. Marisa's main research interests focus on the topic of PMOs, future-oriented project management, sustainable project management and project anti-fragility.

Chapter 16

Azadeh Rezvani is a lecturer and research fellow in the Business School at The University of Queensland, Australia. Her research interests include project management, emotional intelligence and innovation adoption. Her work appears in various top tier journals and conferences including *International Journal of Project Management*, *International Journal of Information Management*, Team Performance Management, Computers in Human Behaviors and *International Journal of Project Organisation and Management*.

Pouria Khosravi is a researcher in the School of Management at the Queensland University of Technology, Australia. His research focuses on project management, innovation adoption, leadership and IS implementation. His work appears in journals including *International Journal of Project Management*, *International Journal of Information Management*, *Computers in Human Behaviors* and *International Journal of Medical Informatics*.

Chapter 17

Maude Brunet, PhD, PMP, is Assistant Professor at HEC Montréal. Her research interests focus on the governance of major public infrastructure projects, and on the use of new information and communication technologies in construction projects. In 2017, Maude won the "Young Researcher Award" presented by the *International Project Management Association*. She has done postdoctoral research in the Department of Construction Engineering at École de technologie supérieure, and completed her PhD in management – with a specialization in project management – at the Management School of Université du Québec à Montréal (UQAM). Maude has published in several project management and administrative science journals. She has more than 10 years of experience in project management, including working as a consultant, a research assistant and a lecturer at UQAM for the master's program in project management.

Jean-Sébastien Marchand, PhD, MPA, is a postdoctoral researcher at University of Sherbrooke and at Centre de recherche Charles-Le Moyne – Saguenay-Lac-Saint-Jean sur les innovations en santé (CR-CSIS). He completed his PhD in 2018 at École nationale d'administration publique (ENAP) in Montréal. His main research interests are the implementation of performance management systems, the governance of healthcare organizations and hybrid networks in public administration. He recently published in *International Review of Administrative Sciences* and *Journal of Clinical Oncology*. Jean-Sebastien is also Senior Vice-President and associate at DNH Consultants.

Mylaine Breton, PhD, MBA, is Associate Professor in the Department of social science and medicine at the University of Sherbrooke at campus Longueuil. She is also a researcher scientist at Hospital Charles-Le Moyne Research Center. She holds a Canadian Research Chair in clinical governance on primary healthcare. She has basic training as an occupational therapist. She did a MBA, a doctorate in Health Service Management from University of Montréal in 2009 followed by a Postdoctoral research at Université de Sherbrooke/McGill University. Her current research focuses on primary health care to better understand promising organizational innovations to improve accessibility and continuity such as the implementation of centralized waiting list for patients without primary healthcare providers and advanced access. She is also leading a research project on the implementation of mandated comprehensive performance management systems in Quebec healthcare organizations.

Chapter 18

Leonie Koops is Project Manager, business unit manager and holds a PhD in Managing Engineering Projects. She studied Civil Engineering at the Delft University of Technology in The Netherlands. In 1999 she started working at Witteveen+Bos Engineering Consultant. in the area of urban development. In this position she worked with public and private partners in projects initiated by local and regional governments. From 2005 to 2011 she held the position of head of the branch office in the city of Breda (NL). Next to this she kept working in infrastructure, city development and water management projects. From 2011 she has been a project manager for large Infrastructure projects and she worked on a PhD study at Delft University of Technology. In 2017 she successfully defended her dissertation entitled *"Creating Public Value, optimizing cooperation between public and private partners in infrastructure projects"*. From January 2017 she was leading the business unit Construction Management at Witteveen+Bos.

Marian Bosch-Rekveldt studied mechanical engineering at Twente University in Enschede, The Netherlands (1999). She worked seven years at TNO as a project engineer and project manager till 2006 and then returned to university to do a PhD study in project management at Delft University of Technology. In 2011, she finished her PhD research titled "Managing project complexity: a study into adapting early project phases to improve project performance in large engineering projects". As an assistant professor in the group Infrastructure Design and Management at the faculty Civil Engineering & Geoscience of Delft University of Technology, she is involved in teaching (BSc, MSc, DE graduate school and professional education, both on campus and online) and research in the field of project management of large (infrastructure) projects. Her research focusses on the development of fit-for-purpose project management to create value by projects. List of publications available on: www.tudelft.nl.

Hans Bakker is a full professor at TU Delft and holds the chair Management of Engineering Projects sponsored by the NAP Netwerk, the knowledge network within Dutch process industry. He received his PhD in Solid State Physics at Vrije Universiteit Amsterdam (1985). In the same year he joined Shell Research as a research physicist. After a few years in research he further developed into a general manager. He held positions as refinery maintenance manager, refinery operations manager, consultant for Shell's maintenance and inspection methodologies, project services manager, global discipline head for project management and Vice President contracting and procurement for projects. He is the founding father of the Shell Project Academy. In 2007 he was appointed to the chair Management of Engineering Projects at TU Delft, initially part time and since 2015 full time. The chair is governed by a Foundation from the Process Industry and sponsored by 22 companies. List of publications available on: www.tudelft.nl.

Professor Marcel Hertogh is a full professor and head of the research group Infrastructure Design and Management of civil infrastructures at the faculty of Civil Engineering and Geosciences at the Delft University of Technology. The research group focusses on project management of mega projects engineering asset management and building information modeling. He is the chairman of the Delft Research Initiative "Infrastructures and Mobility", that facilitates and coordinates research and education on infrastructures and mobility for the eight faculties of the TU Delft. Professor Hertogh studied civil engineering at TU Delft and economics at Erasmus University Rotterdam, obtaining master's degrees in both. He did his PhD at Erasmus University (social sciences) and ETH Zurich (project management) on "Playing with Complexity, Management and Organization of Large Infrastructure Projects". He is (co)author of eight books on design, management and organization of large projects: infrastructure and urban development. He wrote numerous articles and essays on design and management of infrastructure programs, corridors and projects. List of publications available on: www.tudelft.nl.

Chapter 19

Göran Brulin, PhD, is a senior analyst at the Swedish Agency for Economic and Regional Growth (goran.brulin@tillvaxtverket.se). He has been responsible for the on-going evaluation of the European Regional Development Programs. He is also adjunct professor in local and regional innovations at Linköping University and he has been associated with HELIX VINN, Centre of Excellence (see www.liu.se/helix). His research interests include local and regional development, organization of work, business administration and management and economic sociology. His research field has for the last decade covered local and regional innovation, collaboration between academia and the business society, interactive research, networks, learning evaluation, partnerships and program-based development. The research of large projects and programs has focused on results and long-term effects, the steering processes and developmental evaluations.

Lennart Svensson is Senior Professor of Sociology at Linköping University, and one of the research leaders at HELIX VINN Excellence Centre (see www.liu.se/helix). His research field covers local and regional development, interactive research, networks, learning evaluation, partnerships and projects. The research of large projects and programmes has focused on long-term effects, the steering processes and learning approaches. He has developed and practiced an interactive research approach. The ambition is to make research *with* – not *on* – the participants. He has worked closely with the Social and Regional Funds in EU in order to make the project outcomes more sustainable. He has also worked as a coordinator of large-scale regional developmental programs. He has developed university courses in learning evaluation, project leadership and steering of projects.

Chapter 20

Tiago Cardoso, BSc (Computer Science), MBA (IT Management), was born in Brazil and currently lives in Valencia, Spain. He has worked with global financial institutions and Forbes 500 companies for over 17 years specializing in IT management (as a qualified Scrum Master) and Project Management for large IT implementations. Tiago has extensive business knowledge and IT delivery skills. He has led strategic delivery work-streams in complex onshore and offshore environments working with local and international teams in the UK, US, Brazil and Spain. Tiago has extensive experience on multi-year programs and has worked to develop and embed new Agile methodologies across functions and teams. Tiago is a certified ITIL, ScrumMaster and SAFe agilist professional.

Chapter 21: Author Profile

Louis Klein, PhD, is a thought and practice leader in the field of systemic change and governance. Currently he serves as dean of the European School of Governance and senior director of its Systemic Change Lab. Being an internationally renowned change management and organizational development consultant, Louis re-entered the PM research field when joining the International Centre for Complex Project Management in 2008 as research director for cross-cultural complex project management. He was assigned IPMA project excellence assessor and serves on the editorial board of the *Project Management Journal*. After several years as VP of the International Society for the System Sciences and board member of the World Organisation of Systems and Cybernetics, he was elected VP of the executive board of the International Federation of Systems Research. In 2018 he co-founded the *Systemic Change Journal*. His website is www.louisklein.de.

Chapter 22

Thomas Grisham, PhD, has over 44 years of global experience across a variety of business sectors including medical, infrastructure and utilities, finance, and manufacturing. His last full-time job was running a Japanese trading company in Tokyo.

Thomas has gained this experience in 81 countries, and has lived in Turkey, Saudi Arabia, Thailand, Japan, Korea, China, Hong Kong, Germany, Brazil, and part time in the UK, Singapore, India and Spain. His experience spans over 400 global organizations such as the UN, Nestle, the NSA and ZTE. He currently does global corporate training, mentors Doctoral students for a University in Switzerland, is a visiting professor at University in Germany, Mexico and Brazil, and provides public and cruise ship speaking. He has authored four books, chapters in three others, and with Dr Arroyo, a new book about working in extreme locations like the Amazon. His webpage is www.thomasgrisham.com.

Alejandro Arroyo Welbers, Doctor of Project Management (RMIT University, Melbourne, Australia), MBA (Marine Resource Management, AMC, Launceston, Australia), MSc (Maritime Economics and Operations, WMU, Malmoe, Sweden), has more than 30 years of experience as operator and consultant in global project logistics, stakeholder management, and strategic contextual assessment with respect to mining, oil and gas, hydropower, nuclear power and alternative energy projects. Alejandro has worked for and cooperated with a long list of well-known companies both in the natural resources and global transportation industry such as Pan American Silver, Silver Standard, Aura Minerals, Talisman Energy, Talon Metals, AECL-CANDU, and others.

He is at present heading two graduate programs on project operations at ITBA in Buenos Aires as well as lecturing on global operations and project-related topics at various universities across Latin America, in addition to running his own company SOUTHMARK LOGISTICS with branches across South America and worldwide operations.

Further information:

https://www.routledge.com/Leading-Extreme-Projects-	Strategy-Risk-and-Resilience-in-Practice/Arroyo-Grisham/p/book/9781472463128

https://www.itba.edu.ar/postgrado/maestrias-y-especializaciones/maestria-en-logistica-de-proyectos-de-integracion-regional/

http://www.austral.edu.ar/cienciasempresariales/sobre-la-facultad/docentes/docentes-buenos-aires/

https://ucema.edu.ar/posgrado/maestria-en-evaluacion-de-proyectos/los-profesores

Chapter 23

Anthony Phillips, BA, PMP is currently Senior Demand Manager for a major healthcare insurance corporation. After acquiring a degree in Art History from the University of Michigan, he pursued studies in Industrial Design, working with two international leading design firms in New York and San Francisco. As the work environment shifted into more digital/internet based systems, he was drawn into the developing discipline of project management, initially focusing on software development. This experience led him to PM positions over the past 20 years in a variety of industries including healthcare, furniture design, print/broadcast/digital advertising and agriculture. He practices integrating mindfulness into his daily workflow and long-range goals.

Chapter 24

Allan Kelly is a recognised expert in software development processes and management. He uses Agile approaches to help teams and companies enhance their processes and improve their digital products. Past clients include: Virgin Atlantic, Qualcomm, The Bank of England, Reed Elsevier and many small innovative companies, especially in Cornwall. He invented Value Poker, Time-Value Profiles and Retrospective Dialogue Sheets. His blog is at https://www.allankellyassociates.co.uk/blog/.

Index

#noprojects 374–375, 377, 379, 381

accountability dilemma 262
accountability trap 262
adaptability 4–5, 9, 16, 20, 23, 29, 50, 122, 126
adaptation xiv, 23, 26–28, 53
Adorno, Theodor W. 326
Agile Manifesto xv, 68, 184, 300
aleatory risk 148–150
alignment 91, 121, 172, 235, 257, 284, 305–306, 365
amount of schedule earned 173, 177–178, 188
anarchy 52, 61, 69–70
anecdotes 123
anthropocene 319, 326–327, 329, 333, 335
anti-flow 63
anxiety 14–15, 69–70, 212, 363
anxiety disorders 363
artificial intelligence 248, 342, 360, 397
Asimov, Isaac 395
asking questions 46, 203
assurance 61, 132, 150, 207–208, 219, 239, 286, 309
authenticity 396
authority 5, 15, 29, 52, 63–71, 95, 165, 185, 235, 261, 274–275
autonomy 24, 26, 28, 30, 58, 61–63, 66, 75, 77–78, 234
awareness 4–5, 39, 50, 105, 138, 192, 210, 254, 261, 367–368

backlog 22, 172
backsliding 29
balance 54, 84–85, 128, 208, 212, 238, 283, 319, 342, 360, 372–373
balanced scorecard 173, 261
balancing 106, 269, 319, 329–331, 333, 365
Bayesian 151, 166
behaviour change 15–16, 105–107
benefits from earned schedule 171, 186
benefits map 225

benefits realisation, benefits realization 208, 221–222, 239
big data 49, 308, 337
blaming 55
breathe 3, 373
Bricolage 209, 237–238
burndown 176, 195

candy game 73–74
captainship 320, 333–335
CERN 294
Challenges to Earned Schedule 171, 176, 181, 183
change control 110, 132, 194–196, 199, 203, 210
change management 209–213, 215, 219–221, 239, 252
chaos 18, 20, 69, 71, 313–314, 329
chaotic 49, 72, 314–315
coach 33–34, 66, 110, 209, 374
collaborate 18, 39, 352
Collaborative Program Enterprise, CPE 336, 344
Combined Project Organization, CPO 269–270
common cause 133, 200
communication xv, 7, 18, 36, 54, 75, 83, 100, 116, 132, 137, 158, 170, 193, 213, 239, 248, 258, 294, 301, 323, 393
communication planning 101–102
communication preferences 111–112
communication strategy 100–102, 104–105, 107, 109, 112
communities of practice, cop 52, 122, 208, 237, 351
comparative performance 174
competency 9–10, 84, 238
completion performance 256
concern for others 76
conspiracy of optimism 321
Continuous Digital 374
continuous risk management, CRM 125, 144, 168

control chart 200
Conway, Melvin 386
coping 4–5, 8, 47, 217–218, 331
corrective action 191, 193, 199, 213–214
counterfactual impact evaluation 286
critical management studies 233
critical success factor 126, 236
cybernetic 327–330
Cynefin 18

Darwin, Charles 4, 395
Dawkins, Richard 395
deadlines 33, 61, 74, 172, 225, 256, 373, 381
decision making 133, 194, 207, 330
decision matrix 95–96
decreased productivity 363
Deming, W. Edwards 192, 200–203, 395
democracy 81, 261
Dennett, Daniel 395
disbenefits 222–224, 229, 231
disengagement 8, 16
disrupt 58, 62, 201, 217
disruption 9, 47, 72, 150, 218, 234, 264, 333, 337, 366
diverse teams 117
diversity xiv, 52, 55, 59, 61, 247, 339, 352–354, 356
Drucker, Peter 235, 326, 368

Eames, Charles 362, 364
early warning 197–198, 203
Earned Schedule metric 177–178
Earned Value, Earned Value Analysis, Earned Value Management, EVM 117, 171, 191, 233, 260, 346
economics 8, 106, 128, 184, 229, 248, 323, 394
economies of scale 354, 381
Einstein, Albert xvi, 327
emotional intelligence, EI, EQ 3–4, 36, 44, 46, 55, 212, 355
emotional skills 13–14
employee satisfaction 260
empower 33–34, 37–38, 54, 62, 301
empowerment 262
end user 144, 297, 299, 309, 363
end user development, EUD 297
engagement 14, 21, 54–56, 78, 100, 194, 209, 212
epistemic risk 148–150
epistemological 157, 319
estimate at completion for time, EACt 174
ethics 30, 107, 233, 342
Extreme Programming, XP 23, 313

failed projects 70, 86, 89–90, 130
failure factor 250

fear 15, 20, 33, 72–73, 105, 212, 284, 301, 343, 364–365, 378
feedback loop 106, 198–199
flexibility 8, 29, 51, 126, 250, 264, 284, 319, 380
framing assumptions 128–130

gaming 263
Gandhi, Mahatma 325
Gantt, Henry 396
goal displacement 377
governance 89, 207, 239, 258–259, 320, 333–334
GROW model 42–45

high reliability 52
holacracies 327
holacracy 58
human element 363
Human Resources, Human Resources Management, HRM 61, 83, 92, 193, 327, 339

identity 8, 266
impact of change 218
improving performance 53, 175, 180–181, 266
innovation dissuasiveness 262
innovation performance 256
institutional context 234–235
instrumentalist 395
integration points 71
International Centre for Complex Project Management, ICCPM 320
Invisible Gorilla 196
iron triangle 233, 260, 269, 321, 376

Kaizen 321
Kanban 66, 238, 313
Key Performance Parameters, KPP 128–129, 144, 159, 169
knowledge dissemination 116
knowledge transfer 240

Large Scale Scrum, LeSS Framework 315
latency 303–304, 312
law 7, 143, 258, 321–322, 337, 393, 396
leadership 3, 33, 54, 64, 119, 198, 206, 215, 235, 244, 260, 309, 320, 336, 370
learning 12, 37, 47, 66, 108, 113, 157, 191, 208, 214, 221, 235, 259, 286, 321, 347, 363
Legacy hardware, Legacy platforms 298
lessons learned xiv, 53, 72, 99, 113, 202, 231, 237, 336
linkage of value to time 173
listening 15, 39, 57, 66, 122, 212, 320, 341, 372, 397

long-term effects 286
low performance 21, 92, 175, 180

McLuhan, Marshall 356
measurement 4, 21, 104, 120, 134, 145, 174,
    228, 233, 255, 286, 319, 346, 368, 379
Measures of Effectiveness, MoE 125, 159
Measures of Performance, MoP 125, 144, 170
measuring project success 133, 221
mentoring 37–39, 116, 214, 237
methods and standards 207
mindful life 370
mindfulness 51, 353, 360
minimally viable team, MVT 385
Monte Carlo 141, 155
morale 30, 75, 97, 213, 223
multiplier 36, 291
Myers-Briggs Type Indicator, MBTI 111

neuro-linguistic programming, NLP 107
neuroscience 372, 397
New Public Management 259, 266
Nhat Hanh, Thich 367
non-blaming 55
non-monetary benefits 223
nudge 106–107

ontological 137, 149, 321
operation performance 256
optimal performance 63, 232, 268
organisational development 327
organizational amnesia 237
organizational culture 52, 235
organizational learning 52, 117, 235
organizational project management, OPM 235
orientation towards uncertainty 396

paradox 52, 262, 319, 368
PDCA cycle, Plan-Do-Check-Act 117, 203
Pearson, Karl 368
performance efficiency 174
performance-improvement ladder 175
performance indicators 20, 53, 222, 260, 299
Performance Measurement System, PMS 259
performative 321, 396
performative purpose 396
personality 4, 50, 111
phenomenological 319
phone screen 368
pitfalls 29, 45, 60, 259
planned value baseline 198
poetry 355
points must be costed 177
politics xiv, 68, 92, 229, 306, 319, 348
Porter's Value Chain 270
portfolio registers 206

power - interest matrix 103
predicting 3, 21, 134, 171, 340
prediction 48, 74, 139, 223, 346, 365, 397
principle of independence 172
product adoption 210, 220
product lifecycle 228
project environment xvi, 8, 34, 52, 68,
    117, 260, 310
project failure 68, 85, 100, 244, 320
projectification 255, 287
project lifecycle 206, 253
Project Management Office, PMO 142,
    205, 238
project performance over the years 86
project portfolio scoring model 84
project recovery plan 92, 96
project types 48–49
psychological safety 36–37
psychology 36, 50, 105, 327, 372
public projects 257, 331
Public Relations, PR 100, 346
public value chain 268

RADAR model 101
Rapid Application Development, RAD 297
recovery 53, 92, 161, 305
recovery decision matrix 96
red bead experiment 201
release points 173
resilience 8, 30, 47, 240, 264, 298, 330
retrospective 25, 71, 312, 347
return on expectation, ROE 321
return on investment, ROI 84, 260, 381
risk areas 132
risk interactions 151
risk models 137, 148
risk relationships 147
ritual xiv, 115, 396
roadblocks 25, 63, 310
root cause 70, 91, 125, 144, 194
root causes of poor project performance,
    of project failure 91

safe environment 37, 366
saving troubled projects 92
Scaled Agile Framework, SAFe 315
schedule efficiency 172
schedule performance 117, 161, 170, 260
Schedule Performance Index for Time,
    SPIt 174, 179
scientific management 237
scoring 84, 98–99
Scott's laws of observation 322
Scrum artifacts 25–26
Scrum events 24–25, 30
Scrum pillars 25

Scrum roles 24
Scrum Values 23–24, 26
Search Inside Yourself 370
SECI model 236–237
Senge, Peter 49, 192, 203, 328
sequence of delivery 171–172
serendipities 293–294
Service Level Agreement, SLA 299
situational awareness 192
SMART: Specific, Measurable, Achievable,
    Relevant, Timed 104, 221, 286
social benefits 268, 281
social complexity 319, 322–323, 326, 331–332
social intelligence 4
special cause variation 200
spokesperson 11
stakeholder communication 185–186
stakeholder interdependence, stakeholder
    polycentricity 324–325
status report 191, 198
steps to become a high-performance
    project 301–306, 309–311
stories 10–11, 21, 214, 325
storyboards 119
story interpreters 119
story points 22, 173
storytelling 108, 113, 117–119, 121–124
stress xv, 4, 50, 217, 268, 345, 363
stress management 4–5, 7, 10, 16
stress reduction 7, 371
structural change 61, 288–289
structural programs 286
success factors 244, 248–249, 253–254
successful projects 9–10, 18, 20–21, 86,
    144, 244, 257, 322
systematic review 244–245
Systemic Lessons Learned Knowledge
    model, Syllk 113, 120, 124
systems thinking 192, 199, 319, 327–328, 330

Tai Chi of Change 332
team building 20, 55
teamwork 74, 126, 145, 224, 252, 313, 328
Technical Performance Measures, TPM
    128–129, 131–132, 134, 144, 159, 166, 169
Test Driven Development, TDD 23, 303

The Zone 373
threatened 29, 216
Three C's 286
Three K's 290
Three P's 290
timeframes 361
timeline is critical 172
time to market 299, 345
tips on how to estimate 184
To-Complete Schedule Performance
    Index, TSPI 188
Total Quality Management, TQM 321, 332
tradition 396
triple constraints 34, 191, 232
triple fallacy 232–233
troubled projects 89, 92
trust 11, 20, 36, 54, 63, 198, 251, 259, 283,
    310, 342

uncertainty 10, 18, 47, 125, 144, 171, 198, 211,
    223, 238, 243, 259, 305, 343, 365, 397
uncertainty, orientation towards 396
unexpected 47, 77, 143, 196, 206, 216, 221,
    254, 264, 286
Unified Vision Framework, UVF 64–65
unintended consequences 200, 203
unintended effects 259, 262–264, 288
unpredictable environment 237

Valley of Despair 218
value creation performance 256
value delivery 171–173, 179, 183, 190
Vedic 371
velocity 22, 175–176, 183, 188, 190
virtual reality, VR 336–337, 342, 351
vision 9, 19, 45, 64, 91, 103, 126, 144, 173,
    213, 235, 257, 302, 340, 367
volume of delivery 171–172
VUCA, Volatile, Uncertain, Complex,
    Ambiguous 209, 320–321, 332

warning signs 21, 92, 366
What's In It For Me, WIFFM 217
working remotely 363

Yin Yang 332